Liberty, Equality, and the Market
Essays by B. N. Chicherin

Russian Literature and Thought
Gary Saul Morson, Series Editor

Liberty, Equality, and the Market

Essays by B. N. Chicherin

Edited and Translated by G. M. Hamburg

Yale University Press

New Haven and London

Published with assistance from Institute for Scholarship in the Liberal Arts at the University of Notre Dame.

Printed in the United States of America

Library of Congress Cataloging-in-Publication Data

Chicherin, B. N. (Boris Nikolaevich), 1828–1904.
[Selections. English. 1998]
Liberty, equality, and the market : essays / by B. N. Chicherin ; edited and translated by G. M. Hamburg.
p. cm.
Includes bibliographical references and index.
ISBN 0-300-07232-5 (cloth : alk. paper)
1. Political science—Russia. 2. Russia—Politics and government—1801–1917. 3. Liberalism—Russia. 4. Philosophy, Russian—19th century. 5. Political science. I. Title.
JA84.R9C49213 1998
320'.01'1—dc21 98-13867

A catalogue record for this book is available from the British Library.

The paper in this book meets the guidelines for permanence and durability of the Committee on Production Guidelines for Book Longevity of the Council on Library Resources.

10 9 8 7 6 5 4 3 2 1

To my teachers,
Terence Emmons and Andrzej Walicki,
and to the memory of my friend
Natal'ia Pirumova

Contents

Foreword: Why Read Chicherin?

Gary Saul Morson

It may seem odd that the writings of Boris Chicherin, who was probably the most accomplished nineteenth-century Russian liberal thinker, should never before have been translated into English. Apparently, he was dispensable. An American graduate student who read Russian intellectual history before 1991 would have to have been very dedicated indeed to have much of an idea of Chicherin's beliefs. Even in Russia, Chicherin was until recently almost unknown.

That date, 1991, explains a great deal. The Russian liberal tradition was largely ignored during the Soviet period. Official historical mythology presented the tsarist period as a struggle between the regime and the revolutionaries. Such a view necessitated dismissing the philosophical alternative to socialism as naive, ill-intentioned, and insignificant. If Bolshevism were the only viable alternative to the regime, then its triumph would appear all the more desirable and historically necessary.

In the West, a different form of "backshadowing" (foreshadowing after the fact) appeared. Scholars asked why the regime weakened and fell, and, however unfortunately, why the revolutionaries triumphed.

Alternative paths were overlooked, as if what had not happened could not have happened. In this light, Russian liberalism appeared to have been a rather pathetic enterprise. To be sure, Slavophilism, which received a good deal of attention, also lost out, but it was easy to show that, transformed into Pan-Slavism and Russian nationalism, Slavophilism had exercised a decisive effect on the thinking of the radicals and the Soviets. Like the Slavophiles, Herzen idealized the Russian village commune, which he interpreted as proof that the Russian people were innately socialist, much as the Slavophiles believed in the people's intuitive Christianity. The Slavophiles praised Russians for never having developed the concept of legality, which they regarded as rationalistic, dead, cold, bourgeois, and almost reptilian. Populists typically held similar views, and Marxists, of course, regarded law before the Revolution as mere oppression and, after, as a noxious way to restrain the working class from its historical tasks. Only the liberals, and Chicherin in particular, insisted on the importance of the rule of law, valued processes apart from their particular results, and saw that Russians could never be free so long as power was conceived as something necessarily arbitrary.

The rapid transition from tsarism to Bolshevism, then, cast Russian liberalism into obscurity. Undoubtedly, the ethos of the Cold War had something to do with this neglect. If one studied Russian history to understand how Russia had arrived at its present state, then why bother considering more than cursorily roads not taken? We have here a variety of what Herbert Butterfield called "the Whig interpretation of history," only this time it was the "Whigs" themselves who were overlooked.

In both Russia and the United States, the fall of the Soviet Union has changed all that. Now Russia is trying to build a liberal society, like those of the West, and it has naturally tried to find elements in its own tradition that could further that objective. We may say: time is a field of possibilities, and to understand events involves grasping not only what did happen but also what might have happened. Sometimes what does happen at last provokes us to consider those unactualized but real possibilities—such as Russian liberalism.

We also have reasons of our own to consider Russian liberal ideas. American liberals—to use the term in its current American sense—have found themselves on the defensive, in part because they do not seem to have any new and compelling ideas to solve long-standing problems. Liberal politicians often seem to adopt traditionally conservative policies. At such a time, it may be worthwhile to examine other alternatives within the liberal tradition itself. Traditions are usually much broader and richer in possibilities than their current formulation, but "presentism" usually conceals most of the wealth until there is a reason to seek for it.

In part, the Russian liberal tradition has something to teach us because it often proceeded from premises different from Western counterparts. That is especially true of Russian liberals at the turn of the century, like the group around the celebrated (or notorious) anthologies *Problems of Idealism* and *Landmarks*. These figures were unable to derive liberal ideas from Mill, Bentham, and other such thinkers because those ideas had already been appropriated and given an extremist reading by the socialists and terrorists. Materialism in particular had been appropriated by the radicals, who often drew conclusions from Western thinkers that those thinkers would have found surprising, to say the least. Dostoevskii observed that a Russian *intelligent* (a member of the radical intelligentsia) was someone who could read Darwin and promptly decide to become a pickpocket—for the good of humanity, of course. Western skepticism became Russian nihilism, and Western agnosticism Russian antinomianism. From the Western liberals the radicals drew conclusions that rejected any moral norms, or any ideals, except (for some reason) those already held by the radicals themselves. And these were presented as necessary consequences of materialism. As the philosopher Vladimir Solov'ev's well-known *mot* has it, there is an "intelligentsia syllogism": man is descended from the apes; therefore, love thy neighbor as thyself.

When a liberal movement began to gather real support in the late nineteenth and early twentieth centuries, then, it turned to versions of idealism. Liberalism was also derived from a revival of religion, which provided a basis, as materialism apparently could not, for the doctrine of the infinite worth of each individual soul and person. It is worth recalling that to justify the Bolsheviks' killing of existing and potential enemies, Leon Trotsky's *Terrorism and Communism* refers with contempt to the "bourgeois" notion of the sanctity of human life. This position was a commonplace, long held by the Russian Jacobins and terrorists, from Nechaev and Tkachev on. It was just the sort of thinking that liberalism sought to oppose with another vision of life and politics. For liberals of this sort, the market was a secondary consideration. The whole cast of mind of these liberals differed considerably from what we usually associate with the term *liberal*.

Chicherin became prominent much earlier than the *Landmarks* group, and unlike them, he was not an ex-socialist or ex-Marxist. Trained by Granovskii, whom Dostoevskii satirized in *The Possessed* as the dreamy, impotent, and criminally negligent Stepan Trofimovich Verkhovenskii, Chicherin took over his mentor's role and developed a set of ideas remarkable in their range, erudition, and argumentative force. Neither the groupthink of the intelligentsia nor the obscurantism of the regime (which had him dismissed from his professorship) intimidated him. He took intelligentsia leaders like Herzen head on, and advanced against them arguments that speak to us today. His predictions of what dictatorial socialism would mean in practice have been largely vindicated in the twentieth century: that civil liberties would disappear along with independent trade unions, that initiative and innovation would be stifled, and that the elites who governed in the name of the people would be corrupted into a new privileged class. His warnings that the tsarist regime's policies would lead to disaster were of course vindicated long ago.

Closer to Western liberals—despite his severe critique of some of them, such as Mill and Spencer—than the turn-of-the-century idealists, Chicherin did believe strongly in a market economy. But like later Russian liberals, he derived fundamental premises from German idealism, especially from his hero Hegel. Chicherin is often considered a "conservative liberal," but that term obscures, or rather labels prematurely, the considerations that led him to his specific judgments. Chicherin repeated that one cannot arrive at wise recommendations for particular societies by deducing them from universal abstractions. His essay on Montesquieu makes clear that he regards proper forms of government as dependent on particular historical circumstances, as well as on the customs and manners of a given people at a given time of its development, so that no absolutes can be offered. The mad quest for universally applicable solutions was, indeed, a characteristic of the radicals that particularly repelled him, and his liberalism shied away from such thinking. Liberalism must differ from place to place.

In spite of his adoration of Hegel, then, Chicherin avoids the sort of categorical formulations so often associated with people who try to think axiomatically. He criticizes Hegel for his habit of abstract deduction, for assuming too great a uniformity in the historical process, and for treating national character as static. Like everything else in the social world, national character must be treated historically. Contingencies shape it, and it develops in unforeseen ways, changing perceptibly over time. Therefore, even if we keep broadly liberal ideals in mind, we will arrive at different judgments for the same people as time elapses. Characteristically, Chicherin, though he strongly opposed both serfdom and absolute monarchy, states at several points that there were probably times when these now-repellent institutions played a constructive role, or were at least unavoidable.

This approach shapes the recommendations Chicherin makes for Russia, recommendations that contrast markedly with liberalism today as well as with reformers then. Indeed, it may well be said that the often poor advice Russians have received from Western experts may be traced to the advisers' failure to grasp points that Chicherin stressed. Those who offer prescriptions to Russia, or other countries emerging from authoritarianism, typically have in mind a blueprint for what a liberal society should look like and then tell Russians (or whomever) to do *a,* and *b* and *c.* A model is lowered onto local material, which may be recalcitrant. Those who resist are too readily classed as benighted or reactionary. Disagreements among the experts often focus on which step to take first: must a competent legal system precede privatization, or the reverse? Prioritization of goals may or may not be specified, but if they are, they are done not with respect to local history and conditions but in terms of the sequence given by an abstract model. Chicherin does not think this way.

Chicherin has a keen sense of local conditions and the need to ground reforms in them. To take just one example, he draws a distinction between civil and political liberties. By civil liberties, Chicherin means his "seven principles": freedom of conscience, of speech, and of the press; openness of court proceedings and government business; academic freedom and freedom from servile status. These are to be distinguished from actual power to select a government or its policies. Chicherin believes strongly in both civil and political liberties but maintains that in the Russia of his day political liberties would lead to chaos or self-destruction. How can people govern themselves who have not been educated to think of the common good or to avoid regarding power as a way to despoil others? Will a people who do not comprehend civil liberties respect them?

One needs a certain *culture* for political liberties to work, and that culture does not come automatically, by government decree. It didn't then and doesn't now. Thus, in the 1850s and later, Chicherin proposes that Russians first be granted civil liberties as a way of educating them into the culture needed for political liberties at a later point. He foresees the danger of parliamentary rule in a Russia unprepared for it. These fears, we may reflect, proved justified when the Duma was set up after the 1905 revolution and when too many legislators looked at representative government as nothing more than a preliminary step to socialism or as something to undermine in order to move further. Chicherin proposed as an intermediate step an expanded State Council, which could eventually become an upper house of the legislature. For much the same reason, he saw a constitutional monarchy as the next step. In fact, Chicherin set great store on the fact that for decades the Russian tsar was a constitutional monarch in Finland, which was not fully integrated into the Russian empire. He was therefore particularly distressed when the government, under Nicholas II, in effect abrogated this status for Finland, a move that Chicherin attributes to the very success of Finnish constitutional monarchy. It was apparently a living reproach to the absolutists within Russia itself.

Chicherin's respect for contingency, the particularities of circumstance, and the diversity of situations places him in a tradition of thinkers who wanted to reason up from experience, with all its messiness, rather than down from neat theoretical abstractions. This tradition (or countertradition) was resolutely antiutopian. The essays in which Chicherin considers socialist utopianism make clear his opposition not only to specific socialist recommendations but also to the very style by which they were conceived and advanced.

One might usefully compare Chicherin's approach to that of Konstantin Levin in Tolstoi's *Anna Karenina.* Levin, who is writing a book about agriculture, endeavors to discover why all the progressive methods instituted by forward-looking Russian proprietors fail. Whenever Levin introduces an imported piece of British machinery, it soon breaks, and his English seed oats somehow always mildew. He knows that sabotage is not the explanation; the peasants like him and try their best, but the experiments always fail, for him as for everyone else. Yet they clearly work in England. Whenever Levin proposes a new plan, every steward he has ever employed replies with an expression that says: that's all very well, but as God wills. Levin ponders long and hard on that frustrating "as God wills."

Tolstoi indicates that the problem confronting Levin has broader significance. Reading the novel's many discussions of diverse political questions, from Poland to the peasants, we recognize that Tolstoi examines reform per se. But he goes much further than that. When Kitty, still unmarried to Levin, travels abroad, she decides to copy Madame Stahl and Mademoiselle Varenka by throwing herself into a life of "charitable" work. She unconsciously "imitates" everything Varenka does, down to her gait. To her horror, Kitty winds up doing more harm than good and concludes correctly that she failed because her actions were "fake." Her work did not grow out of who she was but rather resulted from mere mechanical reproduction. The problem lay not in her desire to help others, because Varenka's efforts manifestly do succeed, but in the inauthenticity of her endeavors. Kitty realizes that she must find a way to help others that grows out of who she is. If she is to change herself, she must do so not all at once by imitating a model, but bit by tiny bit, changing one habit at a time.

In like manner, we learn that Vronskii will never be a successful painter because he proceeds by first considering what school of painting he admires and then imitating it. "He had no conception of the possibility of knowing nothing at all of any school of painting, and of being inspired directly by what is within the soul, without caring whether what is painted will belong to any recognized school. Since he knew nothing of this . . . his inspiration came very quickly and easily, and as quickly and easily came his success in painting something very similar to the sort of painting he was trying to imitate."[1] By contrast, the true artist Mikhailov never imitates, and as a result he knows of his picture "that no one had ever painted a picture like it. He did not believe that his picture was better than all the pictures of Raphael, but he knew that what he had tried to convey in that picture no one had ever conveyed" (494). He can be sure of this uniqueness because the picture derives from the sensitively observed particulars of his own inimitable experience. Genuine art, like authentic actions and thoughts, comes from the bottom up, from the minutiae of finely perceived particulars.

Tolstoi wants to emphasize the process by which conclusions are reached, rather than, as the novel's intellectuals usually do, the results. Thus Levin comes to appreciate the views of a certain "reactionary landowner" with whom he disagrees because of the way the landowner arrives at his opinions. "The landowner unmistakably spoke his own thought—a thing that rarely happens—and a thought to which he had been brought not by a desire of finding some exercise for an idle brain, but a thought which had grown up out of the conditions of his life, which he had brooded over in the solitude of his village, and considered in its every aspect" (AK). Levin comes to appreciate *opinions,* so long as they are authentic, because he can learn something from them. They testify to a particular sense of experiences he has not had, and if he can come to grasp what those experiences have been, he can consider them from his own point of view. There is no question that, in valuing opinion, Tolstoi is rejecting intelligentsial conformity (which he hated) while calling attention to the value of diverse points of view.[2] Although the author of *Anna Karenina* was no liberal, he provides a strong defense of this key prerequisite of liberal polity—namely, the sense that different opinions are not just something to be tolerated but also a real asset to society.

When Levin returns to his book, he realizes that he must reject the very kind of thinking behind European economics, which works with such abstractions as capital, labor, and land, all presumed to be measurable and uniform quantities. He insists on taking into account the contingent "culture of the laborer." English machines break in Russia because they derive from English experience, where laborers have particular work habits. Because everyone's mind wanders when working, and different work habits create different dynamics of attention, a machine that operates in one society may not function in another, because the first lapse of attention may lead it to break. The same consideration applies to reforms more generally: they must grow out of local culture and circumstances or they will fail.

Railroads make sense in England because they grew out of English needs. But for the Russian government to sacrifice investment in agriculture to imitate the West and build railroads would be to think like Vronskii or the novel's inauthentic intellectuals. Tolstoi is often misinterpreted here as a Slavophile—as if what he opposes is railroads and reforms per se—but he means nothing of the sort, any more than he is opposed to charitable work. How and when that work is done and those railroads built: that is his concern. One must think from the bottom up.

If one does not think this way, one will, with overconfidence, offer universal solutions, based on laws of economics or politics, to very different cultures. Perhaps we can trace to such universalist thinking the failure of so many postwar development programs, whether capitalist or socialist, in the Third World. And perhaps, in the initial enthusiasm over building democracy in Russia, too many of such solutions, ill-adapted to the culture and the people, were advanced and tried.

Thinkers of the bottom-up, "prosaic" sort are by no means unique to Russia. Chicherin picks out such elements in many thinkers, like Machiavelli, who was able to support or oppose republican government according to circumstances. But the fanatic dogmatism of the Russian intelligentsia, which took top-down reasoning to an extreme, made some Russians particularly polemical, insightful, and articulate in their defense of the alternative. Both Tolstoi and Chicherin wound up in immoderate polemics advocating moderation and opposing polemics. The contributors to *Landmarks* shared the same contradiction.[3]

Chekhov and Bakhtin were almost alone in their consistently prosaic prosaics and moderate moderation.

We may identify a number of tenets shared, to some degree, by members of this "prosaic" tradition. They distrust what Bakhtin called theoretism, which regards specific experience as something that conforms, or must be made to conform, to a model. For Bakhtin, such an approach led both to misunderstanding (of language and literature) and to ethical lapses, because ethics must be approached *casuistically*—as a matter of sensitive reasoning from particular cases, a view shared by Tolstoi. For Chicherin, theoretism applied to politics would lead to solutions bound to produce tyranny. Such thinkers consequently tend to value practical wisdom—what Aristotle (whom Chicherin greatly admired) called *phronesis.*

Prosaic thinkers are therefore suspicious of universalistic solutions, as if truths, like mathematical propositions, must apply at all times and places. They value a multiplicity of "truths," as Isaiah Berlin would say, and distrust the reduction of several distinct realms of thought and practice to each other. Chicherin insisted that law and ethics, though they have much to do with each other, must not be identified, or the autonomy of the private realm, and thus all liberty, would be destroyed. Although the ethical also impinges on the economic, it would be disastrous to arrive at economic decisions on the basis of ethics alone. As Hamburg mentions in his introduction, Chicherin stressed that the moral "does not supplant all other elements of human life." Like science and art, economics "is an autonomous sphere of human activity. It has its own special laws and imperatives." The reference to science and art recalls that the Russian intelligentsia did apply uniform ethical principles to those activities, too. The result was bad propaganda novels in the nineteenth century and socialist realism in the twentieth; and in science, the rejection of ideas because of their (alleged) political implications and the adoption of pseudosciences, like Lysenkoism or Marr's linguistics. Bakhtin was to observe in the early days after the Revolution that unless ethics was regarded as distinct from politics, it could never be a check on it; and indeed the party did insist that whatever was in its interest was necessarily ethical.

Closely connected with this prosaic style of thought is an appreciation of contingency, which limits predictability and the effectiveness of theory. Instead of seeing the world as potentially in a state of perfection, which the appropriate theory can define and the appropriate policies implement, prosaic thought regards mess, inconsistency, and unforeseen events—in short, imperfection—as essential to life. Good policies must not overlook these elements. Chicherin also links freedom to imperfection. He argues that only a perfect being would never deviate from law, because only the perfect being would never make use of "the freedom to deviate from the law." Though a believer in liberty, Chicherin also understands, as Hamburg puts it, that "the scope of liberty, therefore, cannot be defined by abstract reasoning; it can be determined only by life's contingencies."

Chicherin wrote well, manifesting a clear commitment to clarity of exposition, fidelity to facts, and care not to sacrifice truth to polemical urgencies. In this respect he differs markedly from Herzen, who (as most readers will attest) is captivated by the dramatic phrase or allusion, the poetic turn of speech, and the bombastic or emotional declaration. In his public dispute with Herzen, Chicherin faults him precisely for this weakness, which, Chicherin believes, leads Herzen and his followers to irresponsible political recommendations—like the plea that peasants "sharpen the axes."

Herzen had written in an open letter to Chicherin that "your secular, civic, and legal religion is the more terrible for being deprived of all that is poetical, fantastic, of all that is child-like in character."[4] Chicherin's "Indictment" of Herzen points out that aestheticizing (not to say infantalizing) politics is supremely dangerous. The most poetic solution is often politically and socially disastrous; it tends to grand symmetries, and in politics that means what we have come to call totalitarianism. Poetry and emotionality lead people to embrace extreme solutions, Chicherin observes, and in practice such extremism will produce needless violence or even "the most cruel despotism." Almost every revolution, in fact, "is an example of a like process." The intelligentsia is especially drawn to such solutions, which is why *Landmarks* called for transforming the intelligentsia into reasonable, sober, educated people. In our time, the appeal of fascism and communism to so many twentieth-century intellectuals might lead us, as Tzvetan Todorov observes, to wonder whether bourgeois democracy simply did not seem poetic enough.[5]

In such a milieu, mere cleverness often substitutes for considered thought. "We have no surer way to win ourselves a universal tribute of gratitude and approbation than to resolve all national and philosophical questions by clever remarks. This saves the reader from work, from intellectual exertion."

The grand theatrical gesture, in which Herzen excelled, encouraged him to minimize means and focus on ends, as if the denouement were all that mattered. Chicherin indicts him: "You wish to reach a goal no matter what the cost, and by what means it is reached—insane and bloody or peaceful and nonviolent—this for you is a secondary question." Blood just adds red to the canvas. "In your eyes, such an outcome is the poetic caprice of history! Tell me, please, when you wrote these words, how did you look upon yourself: as a statesman directing society along a rational path, or as an artiste, observing the accidental play of events?"

True statesmen keep in mind the means, because means may become an end in themselves. They also know that goals require negotiating the contingencies of "time, people, circumstances." Poets, and rhetoricians like Herzen, gravitate to personified abstractions like "the people," history, nature, the age. "That which you call the poetic caprice of history, the movement of nature itself, is in fact the product of human volition. 'Nature' in this case is you, I, a third person, everyone who contributes his mite to the common cause." As so often in this collection, Chicherin, in criticizing a particular target, goes beyond it; he specifies potential dangers in the thought of intellectuals generally.

Above all, the rhetorical gesture, and Herzen's specific appeals, encourage hurry and impatience where everything worthwhile depends on deliberation. Here one is reminded of Solzhenitsyn's comment that the mid-nineteenth-century intelligentsia's rush to eliminate injustice made it impossible to eliminate it, so that, as Solzhentisyn writes a century later, the injustice has not only remained but has grown worse.

Reading Chicherin, we sense a mind with commitments, but that most of all wants to get things right and express them clearly. He appeals to reason, even when he knows that in the current Russian atmosphere, and indeed in the West (which he does not idealize at all), reasoned argument is often ineffective. If Chicherin's style has a fault, it is a tendency to prolixity. But sentence by sentence, paragraph by paragraph, it reads very well, as it does in Hamburg's translation.

This volume's essays extend over decades and cover a variety of topics, from specific reforms and current issues—such as the abolition of serfdom and Russian education—to broad philosophical or social problems, such as the nature of liberty and equality, styles of political discourse, and the nature of the market. Of particular merit are the essays on individual thinkers, which can be read today as outstanding commentaries in their own right.

A few highlights from the present collection may help us to understand the character of Chicherin's thought. The opening essay, "On Serfdom," outlines the moral, economic, and political case for emancipation, then surveys the various methods for doing so. It also shows Chicherin thinking about real

Russian peasants, not an abstract people. "It would be hard to find someone less capable of democratic government than the Russian peasant. Democracy requires constant initiative, activity, and commitment from each member, and all these qualities the Russian peasant lacks." Hence the need, if democracy is to come to Russia, not only to liberate the peasant but also to create conditions that will encourage initiative.

In "Contemporary Tasks of Russian Life" Chicherin speculates, in a way reminiscent of Montesquieu, on the role of geography in shaping the Russian character: "There is therefore no people in whom the civic spirit is so little developed as among the Russians." Wisely, he notes the dangers of authoritarian government to its own stability: "The government's great power is also the source of its vulnerability. There is no surer axiom in politics than that the state must never act with too much persistence. Statecraft is nothing but a series of uninterrupted compromises." For Chicherin, unlike most of his critics, *compromise* was not a pejorative word. "Everything in Russia is improbably placid and calm," he observes. The government's distance from the people and the people's silence breed a culture of the lie: "From this issues one of Russia's greatest problems—the omnipresent official lie. One can say without exaggeration that every official statement is nothing other than a lie. . . . All statistical data are lies." All this reads eerily like a statement about Russia a century later.

In Russia, Chicherin observes, corruption is almost a prerequisite for government service and so the incompetence of government officials is not an accident. Freedom of speech must counteract such tendencies. In the meantime, "officially everyone is improbably happy"—as was true in the late twentieth century, when the government of improbably happy people collapsed overnight. Chicherin also discusses the seven kinds of civil liberty that Russia lacks and requires, but he refuses to indulge in the tone of a victim. "Civic courage is a virtue that has almost disappeared among us," he observes. "We ourselves are to blame for much in the current state of affairs in Russia." Liberals today sometimes say about the Soviet period that we should stop talking about what was done to us and start talking about what we did. True civic courage would also exclude the sort of rhetoric faulted in "Indictment."

Part Two of this collection consists of four excerpts from Chicherin's *On Popular Representation.* "Representation and Sovereignty" explores the concept of representation—how it comes to replace direct assembly and what is wrong with Mill's view that all opinions should be represented, even if they cannot win a seat in a given district (an argument that obviously has relevance to parliamentary rule in several countries today). "Political Liberty and Its Development" considers the extent of the franchise and the dangers to property of complete democracy. Dealing with the relation of local self-government to national representative government, Chicherin explains how the former can exist without the latter.

"The Doctrine of Popular Sovereignty" considers different concepts of the people (as the nation or the collectivity of individuals) and then proceeds to a host of key themes: the problems with checks on government power; difficulties in the logic of the French constitution; shortcomings in the doctrine that the only proper limitations on an individual's freedom is restraint from abridging another's freedom; and the weaknesses of natural law theory. Most interesting, the essay treats at length the inner contradictions of Rousseau's theory and explains why it leads to tyranny, the forbidding of parties, and the doctrine of "religious deception." Characteristically for Chicherin, the fundamental problem he discovers in Rousseau is a fondness for purely theoretical starting points. Rousseau would have done better to begin with people as they really are, situated in a given place at a given time.

To Rousseau's famous statement "Man is born free, but is everywhere in chains," Chicherin replies: "In practice, man is never born free; on the contrary, he is always dependent. From the cradle he is a member of a certain family, society, political community. . . . The original state of nature . . . never existed and could not have existed; it violates human nature." Also, Rousseau's contradictions derive from taking liberty as the only social norm, whereas in fact there are several, and liberty must be balanced against others. "For this reason the greater or lesser degree of liberty extant in a particular polity depends on the other elements of political life: on the government's needs, on order, on the law, on various material interests over which the government presides, and on the conditions under which the government operates. . . . It follows that the degree to which liberty develops, its role in the polity, its primary or secondary importance, are determined not by the abstract dictates of reason but by the contingencies of life."

"Properties of Popular Representation" considers the general advantages of popular representative government while insisting that these advantages do not apply equally in all conditions. They outweigh the disadvantages in certain circumstances, as when citizens are well educated. Chicherin also inserts a lengthy attack on the culture of Russian journalism. Where journalism rather than representative government takes on the main role of expressing popular opinion, there will be a tendency to extremism and closed-mindedness. "The rare reader undertakes the effort to read journals of different ideological perspectives: the overwhelming majority holds to one journal and therefore has no possibility of seeing questions from various angles. . . . The journals confirm their readers in a single ideology." Respect for different opinions does not develop. The journalist does not have to compromise, as parliamentarians do, and so, "because his ideas do not have to be applied in practice, they necessarily assume a theoretical character."

Part Three contains some of Chicherin's accounts of European political thinkers. We are not surprised that in "Plato and Aristotle" Chicherin stresses the dangers of Plato's approach, grounded as it is in distant and airy abstractions. Plato sees one and only one standard of the good: "Taking as his point of departure the ultimate aim of any political association—namely the common good—he lost sight of all other legitimate public aspirations. . . . In the name of these ideals he constructed a uniformity that contradicts human nature." We are no less surprised at Chicherin's enthusiasm for the philosopher of *phronesis.* Chicherin sees Aristotle's *Politics* as "the most remarkable of all the political treatises ever published" because of its combination of philosophy and practical understanding. If one reads the *Politics* in the context of its time, Chicherin writes defensively, the more objectionable parts become understandable. Aristotle's better ideas today would lead to "constitutional monarchy." Admirably, Aristotle does not wish to "remake people after his own fashion and to impose upon them laws conforming to the pure dictates of reason"—an observation that contrasts him not only with Plato but also, we may presume, with the Russian intelligentsia.

Chicherin's discussion of Thomas More's *Utopia* (in "More and Machiavelli") misses the irony of the work and takes it to be a straightforward political program. Chicherin finds the book still more objectionable than Plato's *Republic.* Plato, at least, did not extend communism beyond the guardians, but More extends it to all workers. In Chicherin's view, the renunciation of all selfish goals denies the very nature of human beings understood as unique personalities, each with "peculiar inclinations and affections, passions and vices. Utopia presupposes only virtuous citizens; it is based entirely on the false idea that the individual's ambitions and passions are [ultimately] rooted not in the individual psyche but in social circumstances," a view that, of course, was fashionable in Chicherin's own time. Today, we sometimes hear of a tradeoff between liberty and material equality, or between individual freedom and social justice, but Chicherin forcefully argues that, the question of liberty aside, to give everyone the same is in itself unjust, because it is just for people to own what they have earned. "Therefore, private property, not communism, is the basic requirement of justice."

In Chicherin's view, Machiavelli, for all his deplorable cynicism, understood "that not every form of government is applicable everywhere. . . . One government is necessary to create a state, another to preserve institutions; one for a strong and moral people, another for a weak and dissolute people." Chicherin also grapples with the role of morality in politics, arguing that morality must be observed wherever possible, if circumstances allow. But the present reader may wonder, who is to decide which circumstance is which?

In his discussion of Montesquieu, Chicherin points to the weakness of that thinker's beginning with "first principles": "We see here, as with Locke, a system constructed from pure theory, in which particular cases and the relationships among them serve as a justification [for the theory]." Chicherin also contrasts Montesquieu with Locke and discusses the relativity of laws to the particular society, an idea close to Chicherin's heart. "Liberty itself, says Montesquieu, sometimes seems insupportable to peoples who are unaccustomed to it, just as fresh air is harmful to inhabitants of marshy countries. In general, a legislator should follow the spirit of the people, for people do better that which they do voluntarily." Here Chicherin sounds very much like Dostoevskii's Grand Inquisitor and Tolstoi's Konstantin Levin. Chicherin also contends that "the fundamental rule of political life should be to observe moderation, which flows from mutual respect among autonomous political elements. These profound views on politics should make Montesquieu's work the standard reference book of all rulers, whether they be autocrats or democrats."

Chicherin also states his own views on law:

> The relative good of laws consists in their relation to the condition of the people, for whose sake they are promulgated. One epoch does not resemble another, nor does one people resemble another. Legislation must take account of these differences. The very best laws may be harmful if applied under inappropriate circumstances. In general, the receptivity of a people to law is the first precondition of its conscientious observance. It is therefore very important that new laws be introduced only when the need for them is felt and when people's minds are properly prepared for them.

He specifies the basic problem with eighteenth-century political thinkers:

> On the one hand, they began with particular principles and tried to analyze the interactions of these principles; on the other hand, because their initial assumptions were theoretical rather than empirical, they ultimately subordinated reality to the

> imperatives of abstract reason. This tendency manifested itself in all the reform programs of the eighteenth century, and ultimately, and most graphically, in the history of the French revolution.

Again, Chicherin is evidently thinking of the theory-mad Russian intelligentsia as well.

The essay on Hegel shows a particular liberal reading of that philosopher, then offers some telling criticisms. One idea Chicherin found congenial was Hegel's notion that "just as every other term reveals its true essence only at the end [of the dialectical process], so, too, will becomes fully free only when it reaches its highest stage of development." Even if the Russian people are not ready for liberty yet, they have the potential for freedom. The idea that the essence of things is revealed at the end is used frequently by Chicherin to refute those who look *too* closely or exclusively at current conditions.

Chicherin observes that real freedom consists not in doing what one wills, but in willing what to will—a freedom of the second order:

> Content does not correspond here to form, because content is for will something external and accidental; consequently, arbitrary choice involves an inner contradiction. This contradiction appears in the guise of struggle between various appetites. . . . Choosing between them, arbitrary choice posits for itself a general goal—happiness. . . . [But] happiness, defined as the satisfaction of the appetites, is something unattainable. . . . We must [therefore] distinguish between will's essential appetites and its inessential ones. . . . Self-determining will is free will in the true sense. Its purpose is to actualize its own freedom in the external world. This is free will which desires to be free will.

Interestingly enough, Chicherin praises Hegel for beliefs we usually seek elsewhere: "At the basis Hegel places the true source, freedom of the will, which he described with such profundity as to leave nothing to be desired." Decidedly, this is Hegel in a liberal interpretation.

Chicherin next enunciates Hegel's significance. Are there patterns and a direction to history, as Hegel says? Yes, Chicherin answers: "The real issue is this: should history be seen as a product of arbitrary human choice and of accidents, or as a process governed by general laws? . . . Accidents remain accidents; an accident has meaningful consequences only when it coincides with the general tendencies of a historical period. . . . From this remark one cannot draw a justification for successful crimes, nor can one find legitimation for every political order that establishes itself." Herzen famously had accused

Hegel and the Russian Hegelians of falling into such spurious legitimations. Apparently, Chicherin clung to a Hegel-inspired promise of the triumph of his ideals, but when he later saw Marxists' use similar arguments, he came to question historical necessity, as Hamburg observes.

Chicherin faults Hegel for "formulations derived not from historical experience but from speculative reasoning," and so Hegel was weak on the empirical. Chicherin also objects that "there is absolutely no reason that a given historical epoch should be associated with a single dominant nationality. . . . At one and the same time, various aspects of the Spirit find their expression in different nationalities." Chicherin's is a typical Russian reaction to Hegel, whose theory seems to exclude Russia from making a real historical contribution.

The essay on Marx considers the labor theory of value, to which Chicherin offers a principled critique. He teases out the contradictions in Marx's formulations and the ways in which he keeps shifting definitions to yield the desired result. Chicherin also analyzes the style or argumentation of a thinker who claims to be deriving conclusions from analysis of empirical data but who has in fact derived them from axioms and then forced the data to fit. He treats as well Marx's idea (which he quotes from *Capital*) that the transformation of capitalist property to socialist property is comparatively easy because, in this case, comparatively few people would have to be eliminated. Chicherin replies: "This very same prescription was offered by Marat in hopes of making humanity happy. Marat thought that it was worthwhile to cut off a few thousand heads so that humanity might flourish. But the most immediate result of the practical application of this ideology was that those who cut off others' heads soon lost their own heads as well"—a prescient comment in the context of Russian history.

"Liberty," the first essay of Part Four (excerpts from *Property and State*) begins strongly, in a Russian spirit: "We are social beings: this is the first, incontestable and universally recognized premise from which any investigation of social relationships must proceed." Human societies are different from animal societies because our sociality includes liberty; and so "unlike animal societies [bees], human societies are by their very nature subject to change. . . . One and the same society over time will pass through quite different forms of community organization. The reason is that we create our own laws and change these laws at our discretion."

Chicherin distinguishes different kinds of liberty—external and internal, of action and of will—and observes that too often thinkers proceed as if a favored one were the only one. Locke, for instance, recognizes only external liberty, but external liberty loses all meaning except as a manifestation of internal liberty. "The law of necessity that reigns supreme in the physical world does not extend to us. The analogies drawn from this view do not stand up to criticism."

Chicherin then offers a critique of the tradition of thought that equates liberty with obedience to the dictates of moral law or reason and that equates any other use of the will with servitude. On this ground, Spinoza "explicitly rejected the freedom of the will," for anyone not guided by reason was subject to external causes, which is slavery. Fichte held that "without mercy or quarter, and whether it understands it or not, humankind must be compelled to submit to the rightful authority of sublime reason. This compulsory submission constitutes not only the right but also the most sacred obligation of anyone who possesses such understanding." Chicherin replies that in the system Fichte devised, "we become mere tools for the realization of universal objectives." Fichte defines liberty metaphysically, and "from this definition, with mathematical precision, flow consequences which lead to the complete destruction of liberty." Any Russian reader would have understood the Russian targets of this analysis. Chicherin contends that freedom has no meaning unless it includes the freedom to do evil. It involves, as we have seen, imperfection.

In contrast to the socialists who saw the private realm as thoroughly political, Chicherin insists that the separation of the two is essential to liberty:

> The entire sphere of private interests and relations must be left to liberty [even if] . . . by its very nature the boundary between private and general community interests is a shifting one. . . . We should therefore unequivocally reject the opinion of those who strive for the complete subordination of the individual to society and consequently to sacrifice individual liberty to that of the community. Such was the doctrine of Rousseau. He demanded that the individual surrender all liberty into the hands of the community in order to receive this liberty back in the form of participation in common decisions.

The socialists go even further: "they simply obliterate human freedom for the sake of the community as a whole."

Chicherin is not afraid to say that "liberty, by its very nature, is bound up with the individual, for in it is expressed the autonomy of the individual. Therefore, the struggle against individualism is a struggle against liberty." This struggle is legitimate when people attempt to treat the public realm as if it were only a larger private realm. "In the state, private liberty should take second place to public prerogatives. But this struggle loses all justification when it leads to the entire private sphere being engulfed by the public sphere and to the sacrifice of individual liberty to the community's needs. . . . And that is the very essence of socialism, which for this reason must be considered the great evil of our time."

"Equality" begins strongly by citing Aristotle on two types of justice, commutative (where all are equal) and distributive (where rewards are properly proportional—say, to one's efforts). To apply numerical equality in the second case actually violates justice. Criticizing Babeuf, Chicherin paraphrases the idea that in order for equality not to remain "an empty word, simple equality of rights was not enough. . . . Not only should everyone have the same material resources . . . but everyone should have the same intellectual level as well." Everything beyond minimal education would be a "luxury, which leads to the development of artificial appetites and to the perversion of the natural qualities of the individual. Freedom of thought, of course, is not permitted; all useless pursuits are banished from the state. Human needs are reduced to the bare minimum." Education becomes pure molding. One suspects an allusion to Dostoevskii's *Possessed,* where the chief revolutionary, Petr Stepanovich, endorses Shigalev's concept of equality: "All are slaves and equal in their slavery. . . . To begin with, the level of education, science, and talents is lowered. A high level of education and science is only possible for great intellects, and they are not wanted. . . . They will be banished or put to death. Cicero will have his tongue cut out, Copernicus will have his eyes put out, Shakespeare will be stoned. . . . Down with culture. We've had enough science. . . . Complete equality! . . . Only the necessary is necessary."[6]

For Chicherin, "in the final analysis, it is nevertheless clear that material equality is tantamount to slavery; material equality is possible only with the complete suppression of human liberty and all personal peculiarities." Legal equality favors liberty, but material equality is incompatible with it, for "to eliminate material inequality one must . . . transform individuals into tools of the government, a government which . . . may establish inequality, but an equality not of liberty but of slavery."

To extend this logic, justice "would be violated if we should maim the healthy because others are crippled, if we should deform the beautiful because others are hideous, if we should deprive the intelligent of an education because the stupid are unable to learn. . . . If we are free to confiscate the legacy of the rich, we shall also be free to cut off the legs of the healthy, to pour acid on the faces of the beautiful, or to bind the crania of the newborn so as to reduce them to the same degree of intellectual stupefaction." Behind this thinking lies Chicherin's belief in "the infinite variety of life."

The analogy of economics with creative work is developed in "Capitalism and Socialism":

> If someone proposed a plan according to which all initiative in scholarship or in art would be removed from private individuals, and all scholars and artists would become agents and tools of the state, which would take upon itself the direction of all scholarly investigations and of all artistic works, then without doubt such a proposal would be taken for the fantasy of a madman. But this is precisely what socialists are demanding in the sphere of economic activity.

The irony, of course, is that the Soviets in fact did what Chicherin regards as inconceivable.

In Chicherin's view, socialism is bound to produce corruption. "If individual self-interest, having been suppressed in the private sphere, has no other channel in which to operate except in the government, and if the government has open access to the pockets of every citizen, then there will be no end to official corruption. One can scarcely imagine anything more terrible than the exploitation of the entire material wealth of a nation and of the resources of private individuals for the sake of the ruling party. But that is precisely where socialism leads."

In an especially interesting passage, Chicherin suggests that the experience of time would change under socialism: "The individual will cease to be future-oriented, to turn his or her gaze afar, to take care to guarantee his or her children's future; that individual will be concerned with the present alone." Innovation will cease, because inventors will have to submit inventions to bureaucrats, who "have no personal stake in whether a new product is introduced and quite often are self-interested in seeing that a new product will not be introduced, for that would violate the prevailing routine and would entail new arrangements." Again and again we are struck with how accurate were these predictions.

Under socialism, government would have an interest in population size, for it must feed the people. Individuals would no longer be restraining family size, because they would rely on the state for support. Therefore the state would wind up having to control reproduction and the relations of the sexes—an argument that looks forward to Chinese society of recent years. Because each person's wealth depends on what others do, work would become compulsory.

Everyone would have an interest in making every one else work. Here we detect the reasoning that was to produce Soviet laws on "parasitism."

Chicherin's boldness and willingness to stand alone strike one forcefully. When he criticized Herzen, many liberals were aghast, much as, after *Landmarks* was published, many Kadets attacked it. They adopted a policy of "no enemies to the left." Chicherin understood that such a view was fatal to liberalism itself, as it indeed proved. For him, liberalism was not a way-station but the expression of cultural and political maturity. It was rich in ideas and it fostered creativity much more than its opponents on both sides. For liberalism to flourish, it must believe in itself.

Translator's Preface

This edition of B. N. Chicherin's essays on "Liberty, Equality, and the Market" consists of texts written between 1856 and 1882. Of these texts only three have been reprinted in Russian since the author's death in 1904. The same three texts were originally published anonymously, so that contemporaries sometimes did not associate them with Chicherin's name.[1] Several essays are bibliographic rarities in Russia, and most of them are hard to obtain in the United States except at the very largest research libraries. So far as I know, none of the essays has appeared previously in translation.

A first draft of the translation was prepared in 1989–1990 under a translation fellowship from the National Endowment for the Humanities. I wish to thank the NEH, particularly Martha Bohachevsky-Chomiak, for extending financial and moral support at this most crucial stage in the project's gestation. The introductory essay and editorial annotations were written subsequently, with research partially funded by a summer grant from the Institute for Scholarship in the Liberal Arts at the University of Notre Dame in 1992. The Institute also underwrote a portion of the cost for publication of the volume. Permit me to express to Robert Burke and Jennifer Warlick at ISLA my deep gratitude for their timely support. Thanks also to the history department at the University of Notre Dame for approving leaves of absence.

My greatest intellectual debts are to my teacher Terence Emmons, who introduced me to the history of Russian thought; to my colleague Andrzej Walicki, who has graciously shared his insights into Russian intellectual history with me for the past decade; to Samuel C. Ramer of Tulane University for his commentary on an early version of the translation and for his uncommon friendship over the past twenty years; to Gary Saul Morson of Northwestern University for his interest in Russian liberalism and his energetic promotion of scholarship on modern Russian culture; and to Jonathan Brent of Yale University Press for enthusiastically agreeing to consider this unusual project. As this book reaches print, I am mindful of my intellectual and personal debts to the late Natal'ia Pirumova, whose wise advice and profound kindness contributed so much to my understanding of Chicherin and of Russia.

Rendering Chicherin's prose into readable English has presented a series of challenges. In the early political writings Chicherin's prose is informal, pointed, and often acerbic; in his book *On Popular Representation* and the various studies in European thought translated in Part Three, Chicherin's style shifts between the detachedly philosophical and the pungently polemical. I have tried to capture these nuances rather than to present the reader with an artificially concocted but stylistically consistent version. I have taken the liberty of dividing Chicherin's compound-complex sentences into shorter English sentences in those cases where reproducing the Russian syntax would be virtually impossible and where any single-sentence English equivalent would be convoluted. In most instances, however, I have sought an English version that exhibits Chicherin's thoughts as well as his idiosyncratic style without altering the length of the Russian.

Where, for clarity's sake, I have found it expedient to interpolate a word or phrase, the interpolation is marked by brackets [ ]. Parentheses and italicized words are found in the original Russian unless otherwise noted.

Because Chicherin is not well known to readers of English, I have provided an extended introductory essay. The first quarter of the introduction summarizes biographical data and interpretive arguments that I have presented elsewhere; the remainder of the introductory essay is based on heretofore unpublished research.[2] The conclusions rest on unpublished archival sources as well as documents already in the public domain. The introductory essay should therefore be of use to specialists as well as to readers unfamiliar with nineteenth-century Russia.

At the beginning of each translated essay the reader will find a reference to the Russian source and, where necessary, a brief account of the publication history. I have taken care not to repeat material already presented in the introductory essay. Several of the translated essays include Chicherin's annotations, which are most often short bibliographic references. These annotations are presented without emendation. In a few instances, where Chicherin's quotations do not match his original sources, I have provided corrected citations in the notes. In cases where confusion concerning the source of an annotation is possible, Chicherin's annotations are marked as [BNCh] and editorial annotations as [ed.].

Abbreviations

IPU	B. N. Chicherin, *Istoriia politicheskikh uchenii,* 5 vols. (Moscow, 1869–1902)
MSG	*Vospominaniia Borisa Nikolaevicha Chicherina: Moskva sorokovykh godov* (Moscow, 1929)
MU	*Vospominaniia Borisa Nikolaevicha Chicherina: Moskovskii universitet* (Moscow, 1929)
ONP	B. N. Chicherin, *O narodnom predstavitel'stve* (Moscow, 1866)
PZG	*Vospominaniia Borisa Nikolaevicha Chicherina: Puteshestvie za granitsu* (Moscow, 1932)
ROBL/RO RGB	Rukopis'nyi otdel biblioteki imeni Lenina/ Rukopis'nyi otdel Rossiiskoi gosudarstvennoi biblioteki (Moscow)
SIG	B. N. Chicherin, *Sobstvennost' i gosudarstvo,* 2 vols. (Moscow, 1882–1883)
TSGAOR/GARF	Tsentral'nyi gosudarstvennyi arkhiv oktiabr'skoi revoliutsii/Gosudarstvennyi arkhiv Rossiiskoi Federatsii (Moscow)

TSGIA/RGIA	Tsentral'nyi gosudarstvennyi istoricheskii arkhiv/Rossiiskii gosudarstvennyi istoricheskii arkhiv (St. Petersburg)
ZMD	*Vospominaniia Borisa Nikolaevicha Chicherina: Zemstvo i Moskovskaia Duma* (Moscow, 1934)

Introduction An Eccentric Vision: The Political Philosophy of B. N. Chicherin

The most sophisticated, consistent, and passionate defender of individual liberty in late imperial Russia was Boris Nikolaevich Chicherin. A tireless advocate of civil rights, he sought for a half-century to persuade his countrymen to recognize legally those guarantees of private freedom that English, French, and German citizens took for granted. He helped end serfdom in Russia. He called for freedoms of conscience, of association, of speech, and of the press. He demanded public access to Russian courtrooms and favored an independent judiciary and jury trials. He vigorously condemned administrative infringements upon academic freedom. Almost alone among intellectuals of his generation he considered entrepreneurial liberty a civil right and a precondition of wider political liberty—a conviction that earned him the contempt of Russian socialists, whether of the Populist or Marxist camps. Chicherin's ideas about constitutional government were controversial and widely misunderstood even by those who shared his commitment to the rule of law. Not surprisingly, the progressive intelligentsia branded him a hopeless conservative, whereas certain imperial officials considered him a "red." In fact, he was neither a reactionary nor a revolutionary. He was a Rechtsstaat liberal, the most prolific, subtle, inventive, and original theoretician of constitutional government that Russia has produced.

Until recently, Boris Chicherin was virtually unknown in his native land. Well-educated Russians owing their formation largely to the Soviet regime almost invariably associated the name Chicherin with the early Bolshevik commissar of foreign affairs, Georgii Vasil'evich Chicherin, Boris Nikolaevich's nephew.[1] Specialists in early Russian history remembered *diadia* [uncle] Chicherin for his first major publication, a monograph on seventeenth-century Muscovy that shed considerable light on the origins of Peter the Great's governmental reforms.[2] Scholars of the nineteenth century read his voluminous memoirs, works of penetrating genius that trace the stormy confrontations between left and right from the 1840s to the 1890s.[3] Still, his political essays, some published anonymously, remained obscure and inaccessible, obtainable only in the central research libraries. His general reputation was that of a brilliant, sardonic, lonely reactionary, a fanatical and blind worshiper of the tsarist state and the established imperial order, a tragically misguided intellectual from a background of privileged nobility who resisted Russia's inevitable evolution from feudalism through capitalism to socialism.[4]

Until recently, scholars outside Russia did not evince much interest in Chicherin. Western historiography focused on a range of topics suggested by the Bolshevik Revolution: the instability of the old regime, the genesis of the Russian revolutionary movement, the appearance of class antagonisms in cities and countryside, the development of working-class consciousness, the rise of ethnic nationalisms in the empire, and the bankruptcy of political alternatives to Bolshevism, including especially the liberal constitutionalist parties. A few distinguished scholars wrote about Chicherin's political outlook. Victor Leontowitsch, Leonard Schapiro and Sumner Benson treated him as a champion of progressive Hegelian *étatisme,* a sensible partisan of liberal reforms and the rule of law.[5] Aileen Kelly excoriated him as a fanatical Right Hegelian statist who was an enemy of liberty. Andrzej Walicki described him as a "classical liberal" in Friedrich Hayek's sense of the term.[6] Neither Soviet nor Western scholars agreed on fundamental questions: whether Chicherin was a statist or libertarian, a conservative or a liberal. Consequently, his place in Russian political and intellectual history was murky at best.

The collapse of Soviet power in the late 1980s and early 1990s has led inevitably to a revision of Russia's imperial past and to a reassessment of Chicherin's politics. The post-Soviet attempt to build a new political system combining a powerful executive branch with guarantees of political liberty has directed attention toward Chicherin's program of "conservative-liberalism" and his motto, "a strong state and liberal measures." The post-Soviet liberal reformists' equation of command economy with socialism, of market economy with liberty uncannily recalls a position Chicherin staked out in the 1870s and 1880s. The post-Soviet attempt to recover and revitalize lost elements of Russia's "national tradition" has led to intensive scholarly study of previously neglected non-Marxist thinkers, including Chicherin.[7] Meanwhile, in the West, the sudden disappearance of the Soviet state has prompted a renewed interest in Russia's submerged free-market, constitutional, and liberal traditions. In such circumstances, a systematic attempt to examine the problems of liberty, equality, and the market in Russian thought and politics is certainly justified.

This book is the first collection of Chicherin's selected essays to appear in English. The essays span the middle of the nineteenth century—the decades between Alexander II's accession to the throne in 1855 and the aftermath of his assassination in 1881. Three themes dominate the collection: the problem of liberty in its civil and political dimensions; the nature of social equality and the impact of social egalitarianism upon liberty; and the free market as economic engine and political force. The essays embody the main tenets of Chicherin's so-called conservative-liberalism, but they also throw light on Russia's political destiny. They suggest that, decades before the Bolshevik Revolution and civil war, Chicherin had recognized some of the fundamental dangers posed by extremism from left and right. They demonstrate that not every close observer of imperial politics saw the domestic arena as a forum for a winner-take-all contest between the regime and the radical left; that certain Russians considered it theoretically possible and attractive to imagine a political order combining dynastic prerogatives with legal norms. These essays also indicate why Chicherin's conservative-liberalism remained a minority movement in Russia, for, by Chicherin's own accounting, the objective preconditions for constitutional government did not exist in the mid-nineteenth century and perhaps existed only in embryonic form at century's end.

From a philosophical perspective Chicherin's essays are of interest because they raise questions about the intellectual origins of liberalism. In Anglo-Saxon countries, historians trace liberalism's gradual emergence from the seventeenth century to the nineteenth century. Its genealogy is said to begin with the Parliamentary struggle to vindicate the legislature's rights against the English crown.[8] John Locke's *Second Treatise on Government* was perhaps the best summary of early liberal principles: the rejection of the divine right of kings, along with the assertions that individual freedom and property rights exist in the state of nature and that the political compact comes into being in order to protect these freedoms and property. In the late eighteenth century Mary Wollstonecraft demanded that civil and political freedom be extended to women. Finally, between the late 1850s and late 1860s, John Stuart Mill, building on Locke, Wollstonecraft and others, provided a multilayered defense of the private sphere against governmental and societal interference. In France, the genealogy of liberalism looks rather different. Here the defining moment did not come until the eighteenth century, when the philosophes elaborated their critiques of religious intolerance and princely despotism. The crucial figure in liberalism's crystallization was Montesquieu, who tried to link religious toleration, nobiliary rights, and monarchical government subordinate to public law. The greatest nineteenth-century French liberal in Montesquieu's tradition was Alexis de Tocqueville, whose fear of the "tyranny of the majority" was echoed by Mill but whose emphasis on religion and communitarian values sharply contrasted with Mill's individualism.[9] In Germany, the two most formidable sources of modern liberalism were Immanuel Kant and G. F. W. Hegel, both of whom explicitly identified individual rights in the private sphere but entangled the free individual in a web of duties to state and society.[10] In Russia, liberalism in the programmatic sense did not appear until the mid-nineteenth century.[11] Would-be Russian liberals thus had the opportunity to borrow from already-articulated Western models. As we shall see, Chicherin's conservative-liberalism was a hybrid, drawing from sources as diverse as Aristotle, Montesquieu, and contemporary German Idealists. Chicherin argued for individual liberty in the private sphere, but he subordinated the realization of individual political rights to larger societal, state, and national interests.

Boris Chicherin was born in 1828 in Tambov province, part of the relatively fertile region in central Russia that constituted the backbone of the nation's agrarian economy. Chicherin's parents, both descended from nobility, were unusually shrewd businesspeople. Although they had inherited enough land and serfs to live prosperously, they built upon their legacy by investing heavily in Tambov's risky vodka trade. Within twenty years the Chicherin family was among the wealthiest in Tambov: by 1861, they owned one of the most beautiful manors in the entire region, several thousand acres of land, and more than 1,300 peasant souls.[12]

Wealth in preemancipation Russia did not determine a family's political outlook. Like many of their peers, the Chicherins were fervent monarchists, but unlike others, they thought of themselves as citizens able to assume political positions regardless of the prevailing wisdom in St. Petersburg. On the walls of the family study hung pictures of the republicans George Washington and Benjamin Franklin, as well as the "liberator of nations" Simón Bolívar.[13] The family employed the nephew of the Decembrist rebel Bestuzhev-Riumin as a tutor in history—a possible indication of sympathy for the failed palace-military conspiracy of 1825.[14] The Chicherins' best friend, the writer N. F. Pavlov, was a critic of serf owners' cruelty. We know from Boris Nikolaevich's memoirs that his father prided himself on treating the family's serfs fairly and without violence. One of the Chicherins' neighbors, the former diplomat N. I. Krivtsov, circulated an abolitionist tract that the family read and kept in its archive.[15] Circumstantial evidence from the mid-1840s suggests that Nikolai Vasil'evich Chicherin spoke guardedly with neighboring landowners about the consequences of abolishing serfdom.[16] Although the Chicherins' political comportment was studiedly correct, their independence of judgment was such as to encourage their children to think for themselves, as free citizens. No doubt, therefore, it was in the family nest that Boris Chicherin first learned about the autonomy of the individual.

The Chicherins were quite literate for provincials and spared no expense in educating their children. They secured tutors in European languages, history, mathematics, and the fine arts. They subscribed to the "thick journals" that were modish in Moscow. They built a library of those German, French, English, Greek, Latin, and Russian classics then considered indispensable by the learned elite. When their three eldest sons were of age, the family moved temporarily to Moscow, hired the best faculty members to train them for university entrance examinations, and located quarters for the children in the choicest area of the city. As the eldest son, Boris Nikolaevich was perhaps the chief beneficiary of his parents' desire to provide the finest education available in Russia.

In 1844 Boris Chicherin enrolled in Moscow University's school of jurisprudence, then thought to offer the university's finest program. Chicherin studied Russian law with the engaging and brilliant K. D. Kavelin, a man who a decade later was to emerge as a principal intellectual architect of the serf emancipation. Kavelin taught that early Russian jurisprudence had begun from premises different from those held in medieval western Europe, yet he believed that in the modern period western European law and Russian law were converging on the same goal—the full development of the free individual.[17] From a young German-trained jurist, P. G. Redkin, Chicherin learned Hegel's approach to the philosophy of law. Redkin's courses stressed the significance of the modern state as a mechanism for protecting individual rights and for balancing the conflicting claims of free individuals. Chicherin also took preparatory courses in national history from the young S. M. Solov'ev, who taught that contemporary Russia was the result of centuries of successful state building and enlightenment. Solov'ev cited Peter the Great's reforms as evidence of Russia's historical progress, and he hinted that in the near future Peter's successors might complete the construction of a dynamic, free society in Russia.[18] These men encouraged Chicherin to interpret the past as a struggle for freedom, a struggle connected intimately with the evolution of human self-consciousness guided by the Hegelian *Geist,* or spirit.

The most charismatic of Chicherin's teachers was the historian of classical and medieval Europe T. N. Granovskii. In his celebrated lectures Granovskii alerted students to the enormous political and social progress that Europe had made since antiquity. Slavery and serfdom had been abolished; religious intolerance and political arbitrariness had vastly diminished; freedom and citizenship, once the domain of a tiny minority, had been extended significantly. Granovskii emphasized that in many cases these positive developments owed to the will of visionary kings; in other cases they were consequences of persistent social engineering by modern states or the fruit of free thought itself. Although Granovskii did not draw any parallels between the Russian present and the western European past, he invited students to make the comparison for themselves.[19] After hearing Granovskii, Chicherin concluded that if Russia were to attain genuine parity with the leading European states, it would have to abolish serfdom, introduce freedom of conscience and other guarantees of individual rights, and construct a progressive Rechtsstaat. The liberal values that were implicit in Granovskii's university lectures thus later became the explicit tenets of Chicherin's early liberal program.

By subscribing to progressive Hegelianism and Granovskii's view of history, Chicherin aligned himself with the moderate Westernizer faction in the Slavophile-Westernizer debate of the 1840s. At one extreme in the debate were the Slavophiles, retrospective utopians who upheld the unsullied character, the pristine Orthodoxy, and community spirit they believed typical of pre-Petrine Russia. The Slavophiles decried the pernicious effects upon contemporary Russia of Western individualism, rationalism, and science. They sharply criticized Granovskii's lectures on history for suggesting that Russia should attempt to imitate Western political models. Since Russia was an exceptional country with a unique identity based on Eastern Christianity, the Slavophiles thought that imitating the West would be suicidal apostasy.[20]

At the other extreme in the debate were the radical Westernizers, the progenitors of Russia's socialist movement. They considered freedom a vital political goal, but they generally preferred collective liberation to mere individual freedom. Hence, as a group they gravitated not toward a moderate liberal Rechtsstaat but toward what Alexander Herzen called a "social republic" designed to advance the common interest of the laboring classes. The radical Westernizers regarded Western philosophical analysis and the exact sciences as important means for liberating Russia's human potential. The most extreme among them rejected religion as superstition and a sign of cultural backwardness; consequently, they considered Eastern Christianity a rotten foundation for Russia's national identity.[21]

Granovskii was a moderate Westernizer. As a historian, he saw that Russia was at a different stage in its historical evolution than was western Europe, but he resisted the Slavophile idea of Russian exceptionalism. As a Christian, he understood the Slavophiles' commitment to Orthodoxy even if he did not share their messianism. His own religious belief, of course, differentiated him from the radical Westernizers, who no longer accepted God or the institutional church. Furthermore, his sympathy for victims of religious discrimination disposed him to consider freedom of conscience as the most fundamental civil right—a position that the scientifically oriented radical Westernizers found antipathetic. Granovskii opposed political reaction and governmental arbitrariness because such forces historically put individual liberties in jeopardy, and it was individual liberty above all that he wished to safeguard. Granovskii looked warily upon the mass politics of contemporary France, and he was far less certain than were the radical Westernizers about the virtues of a "social republic."

Chicherin himself was too young to play a major role in the Slavophile-Westernizer debate. Thus his allegiance to Granovskii's cautious Westernism was, at least at first, little more than a personal tribute to a beloved mentor. Yet Chicherin's alliance with moderate Westernism was a fateful step in his life, for after Granovskii's premature death in 1855, Chicherin took up his teacher's fallen banner.[22] Lacking Granovskii's charisma and personal connections with the leading Slavophiles and radical Westernizers, Chicherin soon found himself embroiled in bitter controversies with these adversaries. The stakes in these disputes were high, for by the mid 1850s Russians could openly debate their political future. The long-awaited moment for "great reforms" had arrived at last.

Between 1848 and 1855, the "dark seven years" of Nicholas I's reign, the Russian government pursued a conservative, even reactionary domestic policy. Official consideration of abolishing serfdom was suspended. The regime imposed rigorous censorship on the press. Educational authorities tightened ideological controls over university instruction; even the teaching of philosophy was banned for its allegedly seditious impact.[23] Leading politicians and ideologues repeatedly underscored the government's alliance with the Orthodox Church, and official intolerance toward non-Orthodox confessions became increasingly apparent. The regime signaled its hostility toward the Jews by a series of measures, including the burning of Hebrew-language books, the forced registration of Jewish citizens, and the announcement of punishments for alleged Jewish "parasites."[24] Meanwhile, the government extended its control into many areas previously beyond its reach, thereby gradually bureaucratizing and militarizing Russian life. To his friends, Nicholas I seemed a great and benign, if awesome, paternal figure. To his enemies, he was a despot, an emperor whose obsession with petty regulations and military discipline recalled Rome's emperors of the Praetorian guard.[25]

Nicholas's death in 1855 occasioned shock among his supporters, elation among his adversaries, and universal uncertainty over the government's future course. During this brief moment of uncertainty reformist bureaucrats and intellectuals began to urge the new tsar, Alexander II, to depart from Nicholas's policies. The forms taken by this still timid progressive political movement included the hand-to-hand circulation of reformist tracts and the opportunistic publication abroad of critical essays that could not be printed in Russia because of the residual censorship. Chicherin's earliest political essays were contributions to this reformist "manuscript literature" campaign. Like other contributions to the genre, his writings sprang from outrage over Nikolaevan despotism and from opposition to serfdom. Unlike most other works of that time, however, Chicherin's reformist tracts were systematic statements of principle around which the author hoped to rally the educated public's support. Retrospectively, we may think of these essays as the first efforts to define the programmatic content of Russian liberalism.

In Chicherin's opinion, the key problem facing post-Nikolaevan Russia was not a political issue in the strict sense: it was the social question of serfdom. In his essay "On Serfdom" he argued that continuation of the system could not be warranted. Like slavery, it was cruel and immoral. It violated norms of good government because its maintenance required the state to alienate coercive authority into private hands. It was economically deleterious because it destroyed the entrepreneurial spirit among both lords and peasants. If at one time, in the sixteenth and seventeenth centuries, serfdom had constituted a necessary evil in Russia, that historical justification had long ago disappeared. After 1762 the nobility had lived free of compulsory service obligations to the state and virtually free of taxation, yet the enserfed peasantry continued to shoulder public burdens of military service and taxation, plus the innumerable private duties imposed by the serf-owning class. Chicherin felt that the inequity inherent in serfdom was "a crying injustice." Worse yet, serfdom's existence had corrupted Russia's national character. Nobles had become "lazy, careless, extravagant, incapable of serious work, proud and vain, servile toward [their] betters and vulgar toward [their] inferiors." Peasants had turned "lazy and careless as the lord, secretive, crafty, and empty of any appreciation for [their] own moral worth."[26] In general, serfdom contributed to the "disappearance in Russia of the sense of . . . moral dignity" and to disrespect for the rule of law. Finally, serfdom's continuation increased the danger of a peasant revolution, of a bloody uprising like the the one led by Emelian Pugachev in 1773–1774. So long as serfdom existed, Chicherin thought, "the resolution of [Russia's] other problems—political, administrative, and social—will be impossible."[27]

Since serfdom barred the path to progress in Russia, it would have to be abolished. What would replace it? Recent experience in Russia and western Europe suggested three different approaches to peasant emancipation: landless emancipation; legal emancipation plus cotenancy of lords and peasants on existing estates; and landed emancipation providing full compensation to lords for land allotments granted the peasants and eventual full peasant ownership of the land allotments. In Chicherin's view, it would be a mockery to emancipate the serfs without providing them the land necessary to sustain them. Alexander I's experiment with landless emancipation in the Baltic region had resulted in the mass impoverishment of Baltic peasants, many of whom wound up homeless and itinerant.[28] Chicherin regarded as more promising a legal emancipation of peasants and the creation of a landed cotenancy arrangement between former serfs and their ex-masters. Still, this approach, tried in Russia's western provinces in the 1840s, carried significant disadvantages, for it placed peasants and nobles in a competitive situation that could not be stable in the long term without the government's intervention. Worse, cotenancy limited the peasants' ability to seek more rewarding labor; as tenants on land owned by their former masters, peasants lacked the legal status to sell their lands.[29] Although he was willing to endorse cotenancy as a transitional measure, Chicherin advocated landed emancipation as the best approach to abolish serfdom. His goal was to transform serfs into independent small property owners after the fashion of the small-holding French peasantry.

Chicherin's desire for landed emancipation rested on prudential and theoretical grounds. He thought that the state should not allow landless emancipation, because doing so would risk a terrible revolution. "Laborers are the main supporters of all rebellions. As a mobile mass, which has neither stable connections nor associations and which has nothing to lose, the propertyless comprise the most democratic element [in society]. On the contrary, a property holder, always anxious about his property, fears disturbances most of all."[30] Chicherin's practical concern for social stability was coupled with his theoretical conviction that property rights are key components of civil liberty. He argued that the liberty to choose one's occupation and the right to sell property—in other words, the fundamental economic freedoms—are necessary elements of "freedom in the private sphere." He insisted that such "personal freedom is the fundamental precondition of any life deserving the title of human."[31]

Why did Russia lack freedom in the private sphere? In "Contemporary Tasks of Russian Life," Chicherin answered this question by alluding to two peculiarities of Russia's past. First, in the medieval period the nation proved incapable of constructing a viable legal culture. Political chaos led to insecurity in property relations. The people themselves were too immature and passive to build the stable communities that might have compensated for the absence of deeply rooted legal culture or for the paucity of effective government.[32] Second, in the modern period, the Russian state came to dwarf society. Although the state manufactured an artificial stability in the economic and political spheres, this ersatz order came at a high price: confronted by an all-powerful state, the Russian people virtually lost hope of influencing events. The nineteenth-century state assumed hypertrophied form. As it became "all-encompassing," "the people grew ever weaker and finally shrank before it."[33] The baneful consequences of the state's expansion included bureaucratism, militarism, official lying, widespread official corruption, inconsistency in legislation, unnecessarily burdensome taxation, false patriotism and increasing indignation directed against the government.

Chicherin contended that in any well-functioning modern polity the relative power of the people and the government should be balanced. The people should articulate their demands and interests; the government should establish harmony between interest groups by mediating conflicts and reconciling private demands with the common good. In order to perform this task, of course, the government must possess material power and moral authority, but it must not use its strength to infringe on the people's autonomy. For the state's raison d'être derives from the people: "For their sake . . . government itself is established, having no other purpose than to promote the common welfare."[34]

In order to balance government and society, Chicherin demanded that the imperial law recognize seven principles: freedom of conscience, freedom from servile status, freedom of speech, freedom of the press, academic freedom, the open conduct of governmental business, and public access to court proceedings.[35] He defined these principles as the essence of liberalism, and he expected their implementation to "heal our profoundest wounds, . . . heal our inner corruption, [and] give us the opportunity to stand next to other peoples and, with renewed strength, to set off on a great course a harbinger of which lies in the great achievements of the Russian nation."[36] Chicherin's seven-point program, then, represented a sharp departure from the spirit of Nicholas I's thirty-year reign.

Perhaps because "On Serfdom" and "Contemporary Tasks of Russian Life" were the clearest expositions of liberal ideas to appear in the pivotal first years of Alexander II's reign, critics attacked what they regarded as their shortcomings. The Slavophiles, for example, were unhappy about Chicherin's approach to peasant emancipation. They did not want to transform Russian peasants into individual property holders on the French model.[37] They prized the cooperative ethos of the peasant commune over economic liberty. The Slavophiles also disagreed with Chicherin's program of civil liberties because the seven-point program reminded them of formal, European-style legal guarantees. In the Slavophile worldview, European law codes were cold, dead, soulless mechanisms that sundered the vital, organic ties that ideally bind people together into a community.[38] Part of the Russian genius was to have escaped legal formalism for the sake of living community.[39]

When Konstantin Kavelin arranged for liberal manuscript literature, including Chicherin's essays, to be published in London by Herzen's Free Russian Press, he discovered that Herzen, too, had many criticisms of the liberal platform. First, Herzen would not accept a peasant emancipation aimed at the creation of small, independent property owners. The peasants had recently shown themselves the most conservative class in France: their votes had led directly to Napoléon III's election as president of the Second Republic. Later, the peasants had supported Napoléon's coup d'état and the inauguration of the

Second Empire. More broadly, peasant small owners and petty shopkeepers epitomized what Herzen regarded as the bourgeois mentality—grasping, selfish, superficial, hypocritical, and aesthetically vulgar. In his opinion, such a mentality produced mass conformism and mediocrity.[40] Like the Slavophiles, Herzen sought to avert the creation of a propertied, independent peasantry in Russia. Like the Slavophiles, he hoped to maintain the peasant land commune as the foundation of rural life. Unlike the Slavophiles, however, Herzen did not picture the mir as a conservative, religiously oriented community. Instead, he viewed the communal assembly as a protosocialist agency whose ethos was democratic and egalitarian.

Second, Herzen argued that the Russian liberals, operating on the government's sufferance, were not inclined to hurry along the peasant emancipation. They were apparently content to produced gradualist plans of the sort Chicherin had written.[41]

Third, Herzen objected in principle to Rechtsstaat liberalism and the philosophy of history upon which it was based. He rejected the doctrinaire assumption that the state is an engine of social progress. He disputed Hegel's contention that existing states are logical moments in the forward march of the World Spirit. He thought it repellent to clad the educated individual in a straitjacket of laws and regulations, however "rational" or "necessary" such formal rules might appear.[42]

Fourth, Herzen suspected Russian liberals of subservience to the crown. The essay "Contemporary Tasks of Russian Life" had rejected Nicholas I's despotic rule, but not autocracy as such. The essay was conspicuously silent about the prospects for constitutional government in Russia. Nowhere did the author raise the possibilities of electoral democracy or a political republic, much less a "social republic" in Russia. From Herzen's perspective, "Contemporary Tasks of Russian Life" was a sign of liberal timidity in the presence of an autocratic government that still imagined itself master of the political scene.

But Chicherin's decision not to raise the problem of representative government was not the result of timidity. Rather, that decision, which was carefully considered, had both a tactical and a strategic justification. According to Chicherin's memoirs, the original draft of "Contemporary Tasks of Russian Life" had contained an appeal for the future establishment of a constitutional monarchy, but he had dropped the appeal on the advice of Kavelin.[43] A man with wide connections among reformist bureaucrats, Kavelin had reasons to think that a liberal endorsement of constitutional government might prove counterproductive: by alarming Alexander and mobilizing court conservatives, he feared, the liberals would decrease the chances of attaining official sanction for the seven-point program. Kavelin calculated quite sensibly that the quickest way, indeed, perhaps the only way to engineer the peasant emancipation and the desired guarantees of personal freedom would be to dissociate these already sweeping programs from the further demand for constitutional representation.

The decision not to broach the subject of the regime's future also rested on a weighty strategic consideration. Chicherin thought that civil rights must take priority over political rights. He felt that the educated public desperately needed civil rights and that it was mature enough to use these rights wisely. He believed that Russians as a people, however, were far from prepared for representative government. In "On Serfdom" he had observed that "it would be hard to find someone less capable of democratic government than the Russian peasant." He was convinced that the nation would profit from a more or less extended period of experience with civil rights. Once the habit of respect for civil rights had rooted itself in the people and the regime, then the time would become ripe for introducing constitutional government. The distinction between civil and political rights was a central tenet of Chicherin's conservative-liberalism, yet it was a distinction easily misunderstood or parodied by more radical thinkers like Herzen.

Herzen met the liberals halfway when he agreed to publish their manuscript literature in an anthology, entitled *Voices from Russia.* Yet he pressed his own solutions to Russia's social and political problems. The tension between the liberals and Herzen persisted until 1858, when Chicherin tried to find a resolution. In late summer, he visited Herzen in London. He hoped to convert Herzen to rights-oriented liberalism, a move that Herzen countered by calling Chicherin a state worshiper. This unsuccessful personal meeting led to a polemic in print.[44] Taking the initiative, Herzen sarcastically impugned Chicherin's "doctrinaire" cast of mind, remarking that Chicherin had made obedience to the state an "article of civic and legal religion." "You want man set free from the church only to linger for a couple of centuries in the hall of a government office, while the caste of high-priest officials and monks of dogma decide in what way and to what degree he is to be free, like our committees for the emancipation of the peasants. All that repels us," Herzen concluded.[45]

Chicherin responded to Herzen's accusations by pointing out that Tsar Alexander II had recently given a speech insisting that the peasant emancipation go forward. Chicherin added that Herzen himself had earlier praised the tsar for endorsing serfdom's abolition. Chicherin suggested that Herzen had made the charge of doctrinairism in bad faith.[46] Furious over this riposte,

Herzen printed an article in his journal *The Bell* containing a call for peasants to "sharpen the axes" for use against the nobility.[47] Herzen answered Chicherin's other criticism in an article, "They Reproach Us," that sarcastically observed that "people with passionate temperaments [like Herzen himself] respond to daily impressions, exhaust themselves in anger and indignation, fall and die in battles [for freedom]," while doctrinaires like Chicherin "are never carried away by passion and never carry away others either."[48]

These articles provoked Chicherin's open letter to Herzen, printed in the December 1858 issue of *The Bell* under the title "Indictment."[49] It is hard for us to imagine, in our century of ideological hatred, the furor Chicherin's letter stirred among Russian intellectuals. At the time of its writing, however, the educated public was not yet divided into hostile political parties. Disagreements, as between Westernizers and Slavophiles, existed to be sure, but it was thought that disparate opinions might be overlooked or minimized in view of the cardinal objective shared by all honest people: the abolition of serfdom. Yet Chicherin said plainly that broader issues were at stake in the emancipation debate. To him, the emancipation's form, the celerity of its implementation, the degree of public cooperation with the government in its enactment mattered as much as the end of serfdom itself. He could not be happy if serfdom were to be abolished from below, by bloody revolution. To him, *The Bell*'s intemperance, flippancy, and cynicism about the government's motives were indicators of Herzen's personal political irresponsibility. Although Chicherin demanded nothing of Herzen apart from greater sobriety, he expressed the fear that Herzen would shrink from no measure, however unworthy, to achieve revolutionary objectives. "Let [civic spirit] be lost in a fatal battle, let the habit of relying on the ax be introduced instead of respect for rights and the law—you are little concerned about that," Chicherin wrote. "You wish to reach a goal no matter what the cost, and by what means it is reached—insane and bloody or peaceful and nonviolent—this for you is a secondary question."[50]

Chicherin's "Indictment" of Herzen won praise from a handful of his close associates, but many intellectuals rushed to Herzen's side. Chicherin's erstwhile ally, Kavelin, angrily observed that Chicherin had "no right" to accuse Herzen of sympathizing with bloodshed, for Herzen's entire career had shown an aversion to violence. In Kavelin's opinion, Chicherin had misunderstood Herzen's role as publisher: to print an appeal to "take up the ax" was not the same as to write the appeal oneself. In any case, Kavelin believed, Herzen was only pointing to a fact recognized by Chicherin himself: namely, if serfdom were not abolished from above, it would certainly be ended from below, by revolution. Kavelin circulated his rebuke to Chicherin among prominent abolitionists.[51] It was quickly signed by several men whom Chicherin admired, including the literary critic P. V. Annenkov and the novelist I. S. Turgenev. Meanwhile, Herzen and other radicals repudiated Chicherin.

In retrospect, some historians have claimed that the Herzen-Chicherin polemic of 1858 represented the definitive break between Russian socialism and Russian liberalism.[52] This assertion is too categorical in view of the liberal Kavelin's defense of Herzen. Moreover, the line of demarcation between socialism and left liberalism was to remain indistinct even two generations later, as the politics of the Right Mensheviks and Left Kadets in 1917 surely illustrates. Still, the Herzen-Chicherin dispute was an important moment in the ideological differentiation of Russian progressives. In attacking Herzen, Chicherin signaled that a conservative-liberal could not collaborate with Russia's leading socialist. Of course, Chicherin realized that hereafter his own name would be anathema to radicals. He accepted this consequence out of the conviction that civil rights are worthy ends in themselves, not mere way stations on the road to a stateless future society.

The peasant emancipation, promulgated on 19 February 1861, resolved the largest question facing Russia in the nineteenth century. The government put an end to peasants' personal subordination to their seigneurs; it mandated that peasant communes receive land allotments from former seigneurial lands. The government required the peasants to redeem the value of these allotments over a period of forty-nine years. Meanwhile, the government issued bonds to noble landowners to compensate them for the land allotted to the peasants. In the future, peasant communities, like other juridical persons, would have the right to buy and sell property.

This extraordinary legislation affecting the economic and legal status of twenty-two million serfs opened the way for a panoply of other changes. In 1862 the government published its budget for the first time. In 1863 it inaugurated a new university charter that broadened academic liberty and gave greater autonomy to university faculties. In 1864 the government announced judicial reforms incorporating trial by jury and creating a judiciary independent of administrative authority. That year the government announced the formation of rural councils, the so-called zemstvos, that made elective local self-government possible for the first time in modern Russian history. In 1870 the government extended elective principles to city administration. Meanwhile, the government lifted the most onerous censorship restrictions on the periodical press and broadened the scope of religious practice permissible under Russian law.

This burst of reform activity, so unexpected just a few years earlier, enacted into law many of the ideas Chicherin had been advocating. Freedom of religion was now closer to realization; serfdom had been abolished; freedoms of speech and the press and academic liberty were more secure than earlier; government business was more openly conducted and legal proceedings were publicly accessible. Chicherin was aware that legislative guarantees of civil rights were still imperfect, and he deplored the government's high-handed and still arbitrary ways of enforcing the new laws. On balance, however, he thought that the St. Petersburg government had brought Russia into a new era. He was one of the first Russians to name this epoch the era of "great reforms."[53]

Inevitably, the government's success in promoting reforms led to pressure for a constitutional order, to be accompanied by the franchise and an elective parliament. The pressure came from various sources: from wealthy landowners who sought political power as additional compensation for the economic leverage they had lost in 1861; from left liberals genuinely committed to representative government; from radicals who considered a political republic a way station to a social republic; from cynical intellectuals who anticipated that the tsarist government would quash talk about a constitution, thereby destroying society's illusion that the crown had embraced the cause of social progress.[54] The early 1860s witnessed repeated disagreements between the St. Petersburg administration and these assorted partisans of representative government. In 1865 the exasperated Alexander II issued a ukase forbidding public agitation for a constitution.[55] Yet this decree, which temporarily quieted public discussion, did nothing to remove the underlying pressure for a constitutional regime.

By 1865 Chicherin felt that he could no longer skirt the problem of Russia's possible adoption of a constitutional order. He feverishly wrote a long treatise, *On Popular Representation,* which examined the preconditions of successful constitutional government. The treatise consisted of four books, the first of which I have translated here.

Chicherin began by distinguishing direct democracy from representative government. In ancient city-states, in small medieval cities, in Swiss cantons and New England towns, citizens, the source of sovereign authority, could meet to decide matters of common concern. In larger polities, however, the assembly of the citizenry in a single place became a practical impossibility; many communities therefore came to rely on the device of representation. In representative systems, citizens delegate their will to their representatives, who then set policy independent of the electorate. This autonomy vis-à-vis the electorate is never absolute, for at the next election citizens may remove from office a representative who has departed too far from their will. Moreover, there exists the moral expectation that, in a legislative assembly, a representative will enunciate the citizenry's desires.[56]

In any society, of course, the range of desires may be very extensive, and not all opinions will be heard in the legislature. To some commentators, such as John Stuart Mill, narrowness of political debate in the legislature seemed to indicate a defect in the electoral formula—a defect that could be remedied only by changing the law to guarantee the representation in Parliament of every numerically significant minority. In Chicherin's opinion, however, the purpose of representative government is not to guarantee the expression of every opinion but to provide a forum where public opinion as a whole might contribute to legislation in the common interest. Inevitably, he thought, well-functioning representative institutions will cater to the opinion of the majority of citizens, or at least to those opinions widely disseminated among the public. "Representation," he declared, "is both a manifestation of liberty and an instrument of government."[57]

By the mid-nineteenth century, thinkers of the "democratic school" considered the franchise an inherent right of adult citizens, regardless of social status or gender. True democrats would exclude from the vote only the mentally ill and convicted felons: the former because they were presumed incompetent to cast a ballot, and the latter because they had forfeited their rights by committing crimes. Chicherin, though, defended a far more restrictive theory of suffrage. He defined voting as a duty and a right. As duty, the vote carries the responsibility of weighing the common good over one's private interest. As right, the vote originates in membership in a community upon whose operation one's survival and welfare may well depend; the right to vote derives also from the practical need to safeguard one's liberty against incursions by the state and by other citizens.

Any practical understanding of the electoral right must take into account both historical and actual circumstances affecting the political community. Historically, Chicherin wrote, "political liberty is . . . the culmination of individual liberty."[58] By his lights, the right to vote is the logical extension of such civil rights as the freedoms of speech and assembly. Chicherin assumed that citizens, before enjoying the right to vote, must first have enjoyed civil liberty for a substantial period of time, for without acculturation to civil rights, political rights will prove empty or even pernicious. In Chicherin's opinion, the right to vote should be confined to that group of persons possessing the competence to identify the common interest. He thought property ownership the most reliable index of political competence because property "provides . . . the chance for an education, the leisure to consider political questions, a high stake in public administration, an attachment to order, and, finally, independence of position."[59] Because the laboring classes had historically lacked property sufficient to guarantee political competence, and because in many societies the laboring classes still lacked access to property and to education, Chicherin approved the exclusion of these classes from voting until such time as the requisite indexes of competence came within their possession. He also called for the exclusion of children and women from the ballot: children because of their social dependence and immaturity of judgment, and women because of a purported "difference between the two sexes" recognized by "the common sense of the human race" and by every previously constituted representative government.[60]

In practice, Chicherin believed, political communities may sometimes properly choose to avoid electoral government altogether, to institute a very restrictive franchise, or to broaden suffrage, depending on prevailing circumstances. This view, which elevated prudential considerations above the abstract principle of inherent rights, ran headlong against the theory of popular sovereignty endorsed by democrats and radicals. In order to defend his own theory of contingent rights, Chicherin had to demonstrate the inadequacy of popular sovereignty as an underpinning for representative government.

In Chicherin's opinion, the doctrine of popular sovereignty rested on the assumption of innate human freedom: everywhere human beings are born free; government is the result of a compact between individuals seeking to safeguard their liberty from violation by others; once constituted, government uses coercive authority to deter or punish infringement of citizens' liberty; government remains dependent on free citizens, however, and may be dismissed at their initiative. The difficulty with this theory manifests itself when the will of one free individual collides with another's, for who will arbitrate such disputes? If a dispute has to do with objects made by or possessed by one individual but desired by another, who will adjudicate between their conflicting claims to the property? If the resolution of disputes over conflicting individual freedoms or property interests is left to the majority, then individual liberty will certainly perish, because the majority will not resist the temptation to despoil property owners. Rather than protect freedom the government actively destroys it. If, in such circumstances, the individual retains the right to secede from the social compact, then anarchy will ensue, because individuals will withdraw their sanction from government whenever public policy violates their private interests.[61]

Rousseau had answered these objections with a more rigorous theory of popular sovereignty. Its elements—freedom in the state of nature, the surrender of individual liberty to the collective through the social compact, its return to the individual in "socially useful" form, government by the "general will," the banning of political parties, the approval of a fundamental law drafted by a wise legislator and popularized through a campaign of "religious deception"—struck Chicherin as seriously flawed. Rousseau's conception of the state of nature was a fiction, Chicherin contended, because the individual is born into a family, a society, a state, not into abstract freedom.[62] Rousseau's social compact was ahistorical; real states derive from conquest, from alliances between governments, or from organically evolving polities whose legitimacy may be traced to changing customs, accumulated experience, and the like.[63] Rousseau's notion of the general will amounted in practice to despotism, for the Rousseauian assembly was an undivided authority: no obstacles prevented it from exercising power arbitrarily over an individual's freedom or property. The banning of political parties itself was a blatant limitation of the rights to free speech and association. The image of a legislator winning assent for sagacious fundamental laws through a religious deception shocked Chicherin, who pointed out the contradiction between Rousseau's abstract appeals to reason and actual reliance on subterfuge.[64]

At root, Chicherin charged, popular sovereignty erred in its initial premise of unfettered human freedom. In Chicherin's view, liberty is but one aspect of human nature and but one element in public life. Individual liberty can be understood only in a concrete social context wherein duties to others, responsibility for the common welfare, material needs, the imperatives of law, custom, and public authority also operate. The scope of liberty, therefore, cannot be defined by abstract reasoning: it can be determined only by life's contingencies. Political liberty is neither an inalienable nor an unlimited right.[65]

If each polity is to fix the limits of liberty on prudential grounds, then it must weigh the concrete advantages of representative government against its disadvantages. Chicherin enumerated many of the positive contributions representative government could make to a community: restraint of administrative arbitrariness; broadening the scope of popular activity; increasing the community's material prosperity; providing a vehicle for the expression of public opinion; placing issues on the governmental agenda; offering advice to resolve difficulties in existing legislation; controlling finances; training statesmen; and inculcating in the people a greater respect for the established order.[66]

Such contributions, however, are dependent on the political maturity of a given nation—that is, on a people's ability to harmonize freedom with authority, and order with the common good. Absent this maturity, representative institutions can be extremely destructive. In some countries, the public is incapable of self-sacrifice for the sake of the common interest; representative government thus operates only as a vehicle for securing selfish ends. If a majority of the public does not grasp the common interests of the entire community, then the result may be a political disaster that will haunt subsequent generations.[67] Parliamentary government may give rise to internal dissension leading to inconstancy in policy or to social instability. Representative assemblies may waste vast amounts of precious time on trifles; they may avoid important business; they may draft laws incompetently; they may prove unable to pass innovative reforms on the order of Russia's peasant emancipation. Parliamentary bodies may not exercise effective control over the executive, or, alternately, they may interfere so persistently with the executive that public administration may become paralyzed. Representative bodies are prone to domination by unscrupulous political parties, which may ruthlessly undermine the opposition, sabotage elections, and appeal to the public's basest instincts. Greater political liberty may mean a larger arena for one-sided ideology, mean-spirited journalism, and revolutionary agitation. To counteract the effect of constant criticism, statesmen may have to switch their attention from administrative business to defending themselves against the drumbeat of criticism. In extreme cases, the premature adoption of representative institutions may lead to a revolution, the disappearance of public order or the installation of a dictatorship.[68]

The trick for statesmen is to decide when a given nation is ready for a representative system. In book four of *On Popular Representation* Chicherin discussed the preconditions for representative rule. Following Montesquieu, he argued that geographical circumstances must be favorable, because smaller countries with homogeneous populations have the unity appropriate to representative government, whereas larger countries with heterogeneous populations may be too disunited for such a legislative system to work.[69] National character may prove more or less conducive to free institutions. Those peoples who respect the rule of law, who are conscious of legal rights, who are tolerant of open debate and willing to seek compromises, who are morally disciplined—

such peoples are more likely to find representative institutions congenial.[70] Those peoples who have little respect for law, whose legal consciousness is poorly developed or nonexistent, who shy from taking initiative in setting public policy, who have no traditions of compromise or of concerted action, who are morally degenerate—such peoples are not appropriate candidates for free institutions.

Chicherin argued that the deeper class antagonisms run in a society, the less hospitable that society may be to free institutions. He felt that a prosperous middle class, bridging the social gap between common laborers and the landed elites, might be crucial to the survival of constitutional government.[71]

Representative institutions also require the presence of a responsible journalistic tradition and of stable, responsible political parties. As we have already seen, effective constitutional government presumes the prior existence of civil liberties: the freedom from arbitrary arrest and from unreasonable searches and seizures of property; the right to own property; freedom of the press and academic freedom; freedom of assembly; and the right to trial before an independent court. Of these civil liberties, Chicherin now rated trial before an independent tribunal as most important.[72] Following Tocqueville, Chicherin added that a tradition of strong local self-government might contribute to the success of representative institutions at the national level, provided that local authority did not intrude into the proper jurisdiction of the central government.[73] Unlike Tocqueville, however, Chicherin admired energetic centralized governments where those governments mingled authority with freedom.

On Popular Representation was meant to inform the educated public that Russia was not prepared for constitutional government. The nation was ethnically heterogeneous; the national character had been corrupted by serfdom; there was no significant middle class, and the social chasm between peasants and nobles was too wide easily to bridge; Russian journalism was irresponsible; political parties had not yet taken shape; civil liberties had only begun to germinate in the national soil; the Russian experiment with local self-government was only starting as Chicherin wrote; the central government had never trusted Russian society as a political partner. Consequently, of all European peoples Russians were the least suited to representative government.[74]

This message was of little comfort to the imperial government because in theory Chicherin still held representative government to be "an enormous step forward" in political life. He obviously hoped that one day in the future Russia might adopt constitutional institutions. For Russian democrats Chicherin's book was infuriating, for it suggested that the nation was so distant from political freedom as to make the goal practically unattainable.[75] How long would Russia have to wait for the "true day" to come?

By the time *On Popular Representation* had appeared in print, Russia's political atmosphere had changed drastically. In April 1866 a young former student from Moscow University, Dmitrii Karakozov, attempted to assassinate the emperor. Responding to this attack, Alexander II dismissed his old security chief, sacked his liberal minister of education, and signaled other officials that the government must now show its teeth to a rebellious society. Under such circumstances, government officials misinterpreted Chicherin's recent book as a symptom of the pernicious freethinking that had derailed Karakozov from a healthy course. When, in late 1866 and early 1867, a series of tawdry abuses of power by the academic council at Moscow University and by the ministry of education prompted several professors to protest against the illegality, the new, archconservative minister of education, D. A. Tolstoi, used the protest to force Chicherin into resigning the professoriate. Chicherin now saw himself as a victim of an unholy conservative cabal, and he read the conservative mood in St. Petersburg as unmistakable evidence of the government's retreat from the reformist path.[76]

Shaken by violence from the left and by arbitrariness on the right, Chicherin left Moscow for his country estate in Tambov to consider his options. He had long felt that political extremism in Russia was partly a function of society's ignorance of the history of political thought. To an educated public unaware of Europe's greatest political thinkers, the most vulgar and unoriginal revolutionary doctrines seemed promising and fresh. To bureaucrats habituated to ministerial arbitrariness, any political alternative to the existing system seemed frightening. Given their unfamiliarity with the rich European literature about politics, then, Russians would likely perpetuate the current unsatisfactory situation wherein the discredited utopian ideas circulating among the untutored young justified cruel oppression from the unlearned authorities. Chicherin's remedy for escaping this vicious circle was to write a *History of Political Doctrines.*

He initially planned a two-volume study, the first devoted to ancient and medieval political philosophy, and the second to modern theory.[77] Chicherin wrote the first volume according to this prospectus, but soon decided that he could not compress the history of modern political thinking into a single book. In the decade after volume one of the history appeared in 1869, Chicherin published three more volumes on modern politics, plus several essays intended for volume five. In the event, volume five of the *History of Political Doctrines* was printed only in 1902. Even then, Chicherin hoped to finish a sixth book but did not live to complete it.[78] The project had outgrown the author's control.

Even by nineteenth-century standards of prolixity, the *History of Political Doctrines* is mind-numbingly long—more than two thousand printed pages, roughly twice the length of Lev Tolstoi's *War and Peace.* The book's sweep is astonishing: Chicherin gives a close reading of more than one hundred thinkers by recapitulating their main works, criticizing their shortcomings and commenting on their interrelationships. Although *History of Political Doctrines* sometimes reads like a university handbook for students of political philosophy, the discussions of individual thinkers are connected by an intricate underlying logic.

Chicherin argued that political philosophy has developed in an invariant pattern, in a cycle of teachings about the state. At a cycle's beginning, one school of thinkers emphasizes that the state is a public authority, the external representation of society's unity, a unity to which individuals owe fealty. Other thinkers may soon realize, however, that too much public authority may generate unwanted pressure on individuals who are constituent members of the polity; thus the second group of thinkers insists on the rights of free individuals vis-à-vis the state. Of course, individual rights must be accompanied by duties, by imperatives for action grounded in ethical principles and regulated by law. Those who treat law and ethics as the central concerns of political theory constitute the third school of political thinkers. Given the tensions between society and free individuals, given the troublesome nexus between individuals and the law, a properly functioning community will attempt to harmonize all elements of the polity by promoting the common good, which is an abstract ideal toward which the entire community ought to strive. Those thinkers who value the abstract purpose of communal life above other ends form a fourth school of political thought. To these four schools Chicherin assigned the names *social, individual, ethical,* and *Idealist,* respectively. He claimed that in each cycle of political philosophy each of these schools makes an appearance.[79]

The cycles of political thought, Chicherin contended, were embedded in a larger pattern of development. Humanity's point of departure was primitive unity; this unity dissolved amid contradictions; the contradictions eventually generated a new order, a unity arising from the synthesis of dialectical opposites as "moments" within itself. Chicherin described the ancient polis as primitive unity, for here the state engulfed all aspects of citizens' lives and activity. Yet the polis rested on slavery and could not accommodate the individual interests of its few free citizens. Forward-looking political philosophy defended the personal ambitions of free citizens against the polis and voiced abstract moral criticisms of the civic order, to the extent that that order was founded on slavery. Eventually, the ancient world dissolved into the medieval world, in which society was divided into two separate alliances, based on two opposing elements of the community. The church represented the ethical and religious element of the community, whereas civil society was built on the principles of private law and individual rights. The tension between these contradictory elements, between theocratic and secular authority, marked virtually all medieval political theory. The dialectical contradiction within medieval society generated a new order, in which the modern state came to subsume the church and civil society. Modern political theory took as its point of departure the need for an authority powerful enough to force an end to medieval disunity. The triumph of the new nation-states led to a search for forms of government that would guarantee unity to a society less by coercion from above than by popular consent. Modern governments would ideally permit the church and civil society to exercise freedom under the law; they would end slavery; they would liberate entrepreneurs from unreasonable regulation; they would protect citizens' privacy against outside encroachment. Thus the ancient world's history was the dissolution of the all-encompassing polis, while the modern world's history involved the construction of a new, pluralistic, harmonious polity.[80]

Chicherin's combination of cyclical and dialectic logic lent his *History of Political Doctrines* both static and dynamic qualities. By referring to the repetitive nature of political theory, he could dismiss certain elements of modern thought as old, long-discredited impulses. He warned modern readers not to forget Goethe's aperçu:

> Die Wahrheit war schon längst gefunden,
> Hat edle Geisterschaft verbunden,
> Das alte Wahre fass es an![81]

Yet by pointing to the progressive logic of historical development, he could also rebut reactionaries who wanted to return to a "golden age." The "eternal" truth of ancient political theory should not blind the historian to the Spirit's self-revelation in historical time.

This book includes five of Chicherin's essays on leading political thinkers. Each piece illuminates some facet of Chicherin's own political theory. In his treatment of Plato and Aristotle, Chicherin underlines the central limitation of classical political thought: the absorption of the individual by the polis. In *The Republic* Plato subordinated citizens to an ideal political order. Private property was rigorously banned among the elites. The educational enterprise was designed to regulate the passions and inculcate those virtues appropriate to the maintenance of the polis. Chicherin found this arrangement "inherently unworkable" and "unattainable."[82] In *The Laws*, a treatise meant to describe not the political ideal but real practice, Plato prescribed "the entire life of citizens from cradle to grave."[83] Here as well, Plato had "sacrificed liberty to public utility." Chicherin approved Aristotle's objection that the Platonic system imposed upon citizens a straitjacket of uniformity: "To build a political community on a model of indivisibility is to pervert its nature, to destroy the distinction and variety within it, a distinction and variety that are vital in a genuine community."[84]

In Chicherin's opinion, Aristotle's realism and moderation offered tremendous advantages over Plato's single-mindedness. Aristotle's *Politics* was "the most remarkable of all the political treatises ever published," the "only treatise that is simultaneously philosophical, juridical, and political."[85] Yet Aristotle also erred by exaggerating the significance of the state. For him, the state was an all-encompassing community preexisting the individual, a community outside which human life is inconceivable, a community that orders and determines the individual's life. Aristotle's famous defense of slavery was connected logically to his definition of the polis. He distinguished between a master class, predestined by nature to rule within the polis, and slaves, predestined by nature to do manual labor and obey the masters. Both masters and slaves were, in different ways, utterly absorbed by the polis. Chicherin pointed out that modern political thinkers no long defended slavery and that the best among them no longer imagined the individual citizen being completely dominated by the state.[86]

In spite of their flaws, Plato and Aristotle remained model political thinkers. In his commitment to the Good, Plato was an exemplar for every future theorist seeking to elevate the human lot. Aristotle's argument in the *Nicomachaean Ethics* that no stratum of society can properly equate its superiority in virtue with the imperatives of justice opened the door to those thinkers who saw mixed government, including constitutional monarchy, as the most appropriate regime for a pluralistic society.[87] Aristotle's high regard for the middle classes as the underpinning of political stability and his sober assessment of the causes and consequences of political revolutions opened fruitful paths for future speculation.[88] Aristotle's insistence on moderation in political practice and his theory of justice impressed Chicherin. The ancient roots of Chicherin's *juste-milieu* liberalism can be found in Aristotle's *Politics.*

In the essay on More and Machiavelli, Chicherin explored political theory at the dawn of the modern age. Like Plato, More was a utopian who subordinated citizens to an all-powerful state. Like Plato, More was an enemy of private property. The difference between them was that Plato, as a son of the ancient world, limited communism to the political elite, whereas More extended it to all members of society, including manual laborers. More's communism reflected two Christian principles unknown to the ancient world: the equality of all people and the sacred nature of work.[89]

Chicherin argued that More's communism rested on a misunderstanding of human nature. Human beings en masse cannot be expected to renounce selfish gain in the name of virtue. Chicherin believed that we work for ourselves, for the sake of personal material prosperity. As More himself admits, in the absence of coercion or large monetary rewards we tend to shirk heavy or unpleasant labor. To make our labor really productive we may wish to make a heavy capital investment, but no accumulation of capital is possible under utopian conditions. We think we deserve to own what we have earned by the sweat of our brows, and we think that ownership entails the right to pass our property and earnings to our children. If these propositions generally describe the human attitude toward labor and property, then Chicherin was right to declare that "private property, not communism, is the basic requirement of justice."[90]

Chicherin admired Machiavelli for the same reasons he respected Aristotle: Machiavelli was a supreme realist, a master observer of political manipulation with a deep, if jaundiced, understanding of human nature. Like Aristotle, Machiavelli grasped that not every form of government is applicable everywhere, that the state's structure "depends both on the social milieu in which it is established and on the purpose for which it is intended."[91] For strong and moral peoples, Machiavelli prescribed republican institutions; for the weak and dissolute, he prescribed a principate. Because Machiavelli based his political advice on historical contingencies, Chicherin disagreed with those critics who found a contradiction between the ardent republicanism of *The Discourses* and the "shameless despotism" of *The Prince.* Above all, Machiavelli, like Aristotle before him, regarded politics as a science.

The truly modern element in Machiavelli's worldview was his assertion that the state's survival sometimes justifies the commission of crimes. Chicherin's response to this ignoble doctrine was an equivocation. On the one hand, he admitted that "one cannot defend [Machiavelli] from this reproach" of brazenly discarding moral precepts. Chicherin piously declared that moral principle must be observed in politics "where possible."[92] He took comfort in civilization's advance, because he believed that nineteenth-century politics afforded to moral precepts greater scope than they had in Machiavelli's time. As proof that modern patriotism might be compatible with morality, Chicherin cited Cavour's achievement in unifying Italy "without resorting to crimes and without losing the respect of his contemporaries." Yet Chicherin's condemnation of Machiavelli was far from categorical. Sixteenth-century Italy was riddled by violence, deception, and crimes of every sort. Machiavelli, as a creature of this corrupt milieu, naturally "wished . . . to employ [such tactics] to good end." Chicherin agreed with Machiavelli that, in a vulgar, corrupt, or unstable society, "unscrupulous methods are not infrequently a precondition of success."[93] Chicherin's moralism sat in tension with his historicism and political realism.

Chicherin's ambiguous attitude toward Machiavellianism was shared by many other thinkers and politicians of his day. It is worth remembering, though, how startling was this attitude in the context of nineteenth-century Russian thought. Democrats and Populists saw in Machiavelli an archenemy of the just civilization. Anarchists like Bakunin denounced any justification of state coercion. As Orthodox Christians, the Slavophiles rejected Machiavellian doctrines root and branch. Fyodor Dostoevskii parodied the assertion that civilization's forward march entails moral progress; indeed, Dostoevskii's Underground Man had said "from [the advance of] civilization humanity has become no less bloodthirsty, rather it has become more culpable, more debased in bloodthirstiness than before."[94] Reasoning from the Christian tenet of nonresistance to evil, Tolstoi concluded that a genuinely civilized person must condemn violence without equivocation. Chicherin's conditional acceptance of Machiavelli struck most of his intellectual peers as the worst kind of state worship.

Chicherin ranked Montesquieu along with Aristotle and Machiavelli among the greatest of political thinkers.[95] The essence of Montesquieu's capital work, *The Spirit of the Laws,* was the contrast between government based on law and lawless government. Like Aristotle and Machiavelli, Montesquieu refused to recommend a single form of government as perfect under all conditions, for government must adapt to widely varying climates, territories, customs, and economic circumstances. So long as sovereign authority operates through the appropriate legal channels, Montesquieu thought, liberty and stability may be safeguarded. In republics and monarchies alike, liberty and stability depend mainly upon the division of powers among governmental agencies—that is, among legislative, executive, and judicial branches. In republics and monarchies it was crucial that the law respect the moral force or principle animating the particular state in question. In democratic republics the law should encourage love of the commonweal; in oligarchic republics it should foster moderation in all things; in monarchies it should take into account the honor of the noble Estate. According to Montesquieu, when the division of powers is inappropriate or the principle upholding a particular government is violated, then that form of government may become corrupt and may degenerate into despotism. By Montesquieu's lights, despotism is a lawless form of government, for here everything depends on the despot's will. Under despotism, no one and nothing is safe from the potentate; the principle that animates a despotism is fear. Yet if fear can level all obstacles for a time, it is nevertheless a principle so antipathetic to the majority of human beings that they will seek means to escape its grip. Despotisms are consequently inherently unstable and generally short-lived.

Chicherin's liberalism owed much to Montesquieu's *Spirit of the Laws.* Montesquieu's distinction between government under laws and lawless government was of capital importance to Chicherin, whose objective was the construction of a rule-of-law state in Russia. Chicherin accepted Montesquieu's argument that no form of government is perfect under all conditions—an argument also found in Aristotle and Machiavelli but made with incomparable erudition in *The Spirit of the Laws.* As we have already seen, Chicherin had incorporated Montesquieu's theory on the division of powers into *On Popular Representation.* Chicherin also endorsed Montesquieu's contested theory concerning the principles underlying different forms of government; indeed, he asserted that "nowhere perhaps is [Montesquieu's] genius so profound as in these propositions."[96] Montesquieu's attempt to classify despotism as a form of government without resemblance to monarchy struck Chicherin as wrong-headed, perhaps because Chicherin had just lived through the despotic reign of Tsar Nicholas I. Chicherin agreed with Voltaire that a monarch and a despot are "two brothers" who so closely resemble one another that they are often confused.[97] This caveat aside, Chicherin felt Montesquieu was right to emphasize the absence of checks—legal and moral—in despotic government. Chicherin himself noted the tendency of despots to rely on military force, to misappropriate citizens' property, and to corrupt their subjects' morals. Like Montesquieu, he found despotism repugnant to human dignity, but he warily observed that despotism can easily occur when governments lack restraint. Perhaps he was more suspicious of human nature than Montesquieu had been and therefore more alert to the dangers posed by corrupt government.

Chicherin's most serious disagreement with Montesquieu had to do with the concentration of power in the state. Montesquieu had tried to identify elements of the body politic that should remain autonomous from the state, and he had treated these elements as counterweights to the executive. Chicherin was convinced that Montesquieu had exaggerated the significance of autonomous elements as counterweights to the state and had therefore minimized the importance of "their cooperation in pursuit of a common objective."[98] Chicherin's belief in the political necessity of concentrated power distinguished him from Montesquieu and from Montesquieu's latter-day follower Tocqueville. It placed Chicherin squarely in the tradition of Hegel.

In the second half of the nineteenth century Chicherin was Russia's foremost interpreter of Hegel. In his essay on Hegel, Chicherin focused on three elements of Hegel's system: 1. the dialectic as outlined in the *Logic;* 2. the link between will and right in *Philosophy of Right;* and 3. Hegel's idea of the state.

Since Plato had "invented" the dialectic, it had played such a crucial role in Western thought that without it no one could understand the first principles of philosophical inquiry. Hegel's service was to transform the dialectic into an "entire science," thereby earning a "leading place in the history of human thought."[99] In spite of its prominent position in modern philosophical thought, however, Hegel's dialectic was structurally flawed. It incorporated only three terms (thesis, antithesis, synthesis) instead of the four terms Chicherin identified as necessary. This structural flaw led Hegel to "lacunae" in various arguments, to "artificial transitions" between stages of dialectical development, and even to "confusion" of those stages.[100] It led Hegel mistakenly to treat pure thought as the basis of his system and to regard philosophy as its highest manifestation. Chicherin's own version of the dialectic placed greater emphasis than did Hegel's on particular being, history, and empirical reality.

In Chicherin's opinion, Hegel offered a splendid proof of individual free will and a satisfying account of the way that will constitutes the foundation of justice or right. In Hegel's opinion, formal rights are self-definitions of will in the external world—that is, they are abstract manifestations of individual liberty. The capacity to "bear" or enjoy rights is what imparts to an individual the status of person or citizen enjoying protection under the law. By virtue of free will, a person lays hands on nature and acquires property. Free individuals may enter into contractual relationships with one another. Because the unilateral violation of a contract negates the bilateral or multilateral action of those free individuals signing the contract, such a violation is an infringement of collective will and an attack on freedom: in short, a crime. The restoration of freedom requires that the abrogated contract be restored, that restitution be made to injured parties, and that the violator be punished. Thus, for Hegel, property rights and their protection were inextricably related to the free will of the legally protected person or citizen. Hegel also connected free will to moral and ethical duties. As free individuals we may act to secure personal gain, but we may also strive to achieve a common purpose, that is, secure the Good. Attaining the Good is a moral imperative, a duty, but Hegel thought morality itself a poor guide in defining the Good. To discover the Good, to bring together our abstract rights and concrete duties, we need objective laws and institutions: the family, civil society, and the state. These free associations are what Hegel called "ethical" agencies. For him, the state was the realization of the ethical imperative.

In Chicherin's opinion, Hegel's doctrine of will contained the "most remarkable and profound reflections ever uttered about the freedom of the will."[101] Chicherin accepted free will as the basis of legally protected personhood or citizenship, and he endorsed Hegel's conclusions linking freedom and property, rights and duties. But Chicherin expressed several reservations about Hegel's discussion of will. He argued that human will usually manifests itself in the context of a community. Indeed, only in this context can a will assert itself in concert with or against others; hence, only in this context does the category of right make sense. Because Hegel had made right a manifestation of individual freedom outside the community context, Chicherin accused him of exaggerating the importance of right and of underestimating the significance of law and authority. Like other commentators, Chicherin pointed to Hegel's idiosyncratic and confused distinction between morality and ethics. This confusion was crucial because it prevented Hegel from developing satisfactory notions of virtue, or of accounting for the relationship between free will and morality. In Chicherin's view, Hegel's teaching about morality was the "weakest aspect of his philosophy of right."[102] Chicherin found Hegel's discussion of ethics better, but still flawed, for Hegel omitted the church from the list of "ethical" agencies. Chicherin himself defined the basic human associations as family, civil society, church, and state.

Hegel's doctrine of the state was the most interesting and controversial aspect of his teaching. He regarded the state as the supreme ethical agency, as the institution responsible for creatively synthesizing individual rights and morality. As such, the state necessarily stood above the individual, family, and civil society. The state also stood above the church (in this context, Hegel did address the church's significance) at least in the institutional sense. The church represented only the inner authority of conscience and the "subjective" knowledge of the Spirit, whereas the state represented external authority and an "objective" knowledge of the Spirit. Hegel went so far as to say that, in exercising its legitimate power, the state might even require citizens to belong to the religious confession of their choice, although he quickly added that the state could not dictate which church or prescribe citizens' religious beliefs. In practical terms, Hegel preferred constitutional monarchy over other forms of government. To him, the monarch embodied the principle of authority, the "pure will" needed to arbitrate internal disputes and to defend the polity's interests against other states.

To this sketch of the state, Hegel added two elements. First, he claimed that each stage of history's advance had been associated with a dominant nationality. Modern history, he asserted, was a product of the Germanic spirit. Second, he argued that the modern state was the fruit of the Spirit's self-revelation throughout time; in other words, the modern state was no accident, but rather the culmination of history's dialectical logic. In this sense, Hegel said, "everything real is rational and everything rational is real." Some of Hegel's followers and many of his critics took this doctrine of the state as an apology for the Prussian model of administration, for authoritarian government and for the established order generally. Chicherin disagreed with this interpretation of Hegel but also quarreled with Hegel himself.

Chicherin rejected Hegel's teaching about German nationality as the inspiration for modern history. In Chicherin's opinion, because various nationalities had contributed to modern development, Hegel was wrong to claim preeminence for the German spirit. Moreover, in Chicherin's view, nationality was not a static category. "One and the same people passes through different stages of development," he wrote. "The national spirit can change its content." By Chicherin's reckoning, Hegel's claim about the German spirit rested on a static rather than dynamic understanding of the German nation. Such an error was typical of Hegel, "whose formulations derived not from historical experience but from speculative reasoning."[103] Hegel was an ingenious philosopher but a terrible historian.

Chicherin read Hegel as an advocate of freedom under law. If the state stood above the individual, the family, and civil society, it did so as an agency designated to protect their autonomy, to promote their freedom, and to seek the common good. These tasks required the state to possess external authority—that is, the power to make and enforce law. So long as the state confined legislation to these tasks, however, Chicherin saw no reason to treat state authority as a threat. Like Hegel, Chicherin believed that the state must stand institutionally above the church, but Chicherin drew an analogy between the state's superiority to the church and its superiority to civil society. The state's responsibility, he thought, was to protect the church's autonomy along with the believer's freedom of conscience. As a Russian who had grown up in the shadow of an established church, Chicherin was perhaps more nervous than Hegel had been about the dangers of state intrusion into religious life. Maybe that was why Chicherin obliquely noted that "in certain passages [Hegel] confused private [religious] ends with public ones."[104]

Chicherin defended Hegel against the charge of being an apologist for authoritarian government and the established order. After all, Hegel had advocated constitutional monarchy at a time when that form of government did not exist in Prussia or almost anywhere else east of the Rhine. Hegel wanted the ideal monarchy to represent external authority and pure will, but, Chicherin emphasized, Hegel's monarch would be operating in the context of a representative system under a binding legal charter. Hegel's remark that "the prince must only say *yes* and dot the *i*" expressed a desire for limited, not unlimited, government. Chicherin compared Hegel's ideal state to that of the modern French liberals who, after 1830, argued that the French "king should reign but not govern."[105]

Chicherin did not interpret the dictum "everything real is rational" as an assertion that the individual must ethically support the political status quo, for Hegel himself had not supported absolute monarchy in central Europe. Nor did Chicherin accuse Hegel of making individuals into blind tools of the World Spirit. For Hegel and for Chicherin, the individual was a free actor, able to do what he or she wished. The real question was this: "Should history be seen as a product of arbitrary human choice and of accidents, or as a process governed by general laws?" Both Hegel and Chicherin understood history as process governed by dialectical logic. Just as the individual was not free to violate the laws of nature, so the individual was "not empowered to violate the laws of the Spirit."[106] Put another way, rational freedom consisted in cooperating with the laws of nature and of history.

Chicherin's Hegelian conception of liberty combined negative liberty (the individual's freedom from the state) with positive liberty (the individual's freedom to cooperate with the state in facilitating the lawful unfolding of the

Spirit). According to this conception, the individual simultaneously inhabited the private and the public sphere. In the private sphere the individual ought to remain autonomous from the state; in the public sphere the individual should accept the state's limited authority and cooperate with it. If the state intruded on the private sphere or exceeded its proper authority, then the individual might criticize it, refuse to cooperate with it, or even attempt to change it. If the individual's exercise of rights interfered with the rights of another citizen, or if the individual violated statutory restraints, then the state might rectify the situation by arbitration or by use of its legitimate coercive authority. According to Chicherin, negative and positive liberty should complement one another in practice.

Chicherin took up the problem of modern socialism in the context of his researches on German Idealism. His correspondence with A. V. Stankevich demonstrates that he started to think about the German socialists Rodbertus, Lassalle, and Marx sometime in 1876. He was very impressed by Lassalle, about whom he remarked to Stankevich that "this is an extremely interesting man. In history one scarcely encounters another instance of this combination of scholar and agitator. Only a German Jew is capable of it."[107] Later, in another letter to Stankevich, Chicherin added: "In spite of his fanaticism and his petty Jewish [zhidevskuiu] nature, he [Lassalle] nevertheless was an exceptionally bright [nediuzhinnyi] man." Chicherin's high regard for Lassalle did not extend to Marx, about whom he wrote: "Karl Marx is unbearable and repellent. Up to this point I have not been compelled to read such a trite and vulgar thinker [takogo poshliaka]."[108] In November 1876 Chicherin was still fuming about the painful task of reading *Das Kapital:* "Karl Marx's works are one of the most repellent phenomena in scholarly literature. In Russia they even translate him and praise him in journals! What journals!!"[109]

Chicherin planned his critique of German socialism for the end of volume four of *History of Political Doctrines,* which was to be published in late 1877. This plan was thwarted, however, perhaps by the censor but more likely by the publisher. Chicherin had to look for another outlet for his studies of the German radicals. He asked his associate, Prince V. P. Bezobrazov, to include it in a new academic miscellany, *Sbornik gosudarstvennykh znanii.* About this decision Chicherin lamented to Stankevich: "I promised Bezobrazov the article on German socialists. I chose to publish in his anthology because I had no other option [ia inache negde], yet in Russia exposing the socialists is crucially important."[110] Thus the most severe critique of German socialism written in nineteenth-century Russia, a critique meant to place socialism in the context of European thought, to indicate its many debts to ancient and medieval thought, and to demonstrate its manifest weaknesses, was first published out of that context, in a narrow academic journal with few general readers. Chicherin's essays on German socialists did not appear in book form until twenty-five years later, when the last volume of *History of Political Doctrines* was printed.

Chicherin began his analysis of *Das Kapital* by alerting readers to Marx's philosophical inconsistency. On one hand, Marx depicted himself as a materialist who insisted that truth reposes in the material world and that consciousness itself derives from material life. On the other hand, Marx demanded that existing reality be altered to correspond to an ideal of justice invented by Marx himself—just the sort of demand that one might expect from a philosophical Idealist. In Chicherin's opinion, "extreme materialism and extreme Idealism" combined in Marx's dialectic. "Karl Marx evidently does not suspect that he is serving two different gods [dvum raznym bozhestvam]."[111] Marx accompanied his inconsistency with a methodological sleight of hand. He claimed that all his results derived from empirical research, but he presented his argument as a set of abstract deductions from a single premise. To this procedure Chicherin responded that "a basic proposition must be proven, and [in the process of proof] it becomes apparent whether the proof is grounded in abstract speculation or empirical observation. An author may assure us a thousand times that he, in ways not known to the reader, has derived his principle from the most detailed factual research; the reader who has some familiarity with scholarly standards nevertheless will not believe him: the reader knows that scholarly proof precisely depends upon elucidating the process by which a principle is derived."[112] In fact, Chicherin contended, *Das Kapital* rested on unproved premises, and its argument moved arbitrarily so as to arrive at predetermined conclusions.

To show the inconsistency and methodological legerdemain in *Das Kapital,* Chicherin carefully studied Marx's recondite language, particularly his use of such technical terms as *use value, exchange value, labor power, socially necessary labor power, intensified labor, multiplied labor,* and *surplus value.* Marx asserted, for example, that the value of one commodity being exchanged for another has nothing to do with the commodity's utility [*use value*] and everything to do with the *labor power* that had been required to produce the commodity, for only labor creates value. The monetary value of the commodity is a function of the amount of *socially necessary labor* invested in the commodity's manufacture. Chicherin criticized each part of this assertion. He suggested that commodities would not be exchanged at all if they had no utility; that the comparative value of commodities derives not only from labor but also from relations of supply and demand; that labor contributes to the value of commodities, but so do raw materials obtained from nature and inanimate machines involved in the manufacturing process; that labor itself is not a generic process, for sloppily done labor may diminish the value of a commodity significantly, even to nothing; that the quality of labor cannot be reduced, as Marx tried to do, to some numerical ratio of undifferentiated labor power; and that labor does not serve as the real measure of commodity value, which is in fact measured by money. To speak of a commodity containing "not a single iota of use value," as Marx had done, and then to claim that for labor to generate value, "that abstract labor must necessarily be useful," as Marx had also done, was, from Chicherin's perspective, to "admit through the back door what we have driven out of the front door."[113]

If Marx's description of commodity exchange was wrong, his analysis of capitalism was deliberately misleading. To make the case that labor is the sole source of value in a commodity, Marx, like other socialists, had to deny the positive economic contributions of capitalists. He therefore refused to credit the merchant capitalists for obtaining goods from distant markets; he refused to reward capitalists for risking capital in new enterprises; he denied the time value of money. Worse yet, Marx regarded capitalists as parasites, extracting *surplus value* from commodities workers had created. This the capitalists allegedly did by deceiving employees into working a portion of the day without compensation. Chicherin contended that the "deception" identified by Marx was played not by capitalists but by Marx's own pen. Laborers freely agree, under contract, to perform a given task in a given time, in return for a given wage. Contractual wages compensate laborers for all work they perform. Wages are not payment for abstract *labor power* but for real toil. Moreover, corporate incomes cover not only labor costs but legitimate business expenses, among which owners' profits and management salaries are key items. Under circumstances where corporate survival depends on efficient machine production, constant technological innovation, and clever marketing, the capitalist rather than the laborer is the more crucial economic player. Without the hope of profit a capitalist will not invest in new machinery, the corporation will collapse, and the worker will suffer. Finally, by Marx's logic, an industry relying more on workers than on machines should be more profitable than one relying heavily on advanced machinery, because a labor intensive manufacturing process ought to produce more *surplus value*. Such logic, Chicherin noted, goes against everything we know about how modern industry makes money.[114] Thus Marx's premise leads to an absurd conclusion.

Marx had linked his moral condemnation of capitalism with the familiar socialist claim that capitalism represented a transient stage in European history. According to Marx, with the enclosure of landed estates in sixteenth-century England, the proletariat was born. Factory production exploited landless laborers ever more mercilessly. As the proletariat increased, the capitalist class, beset by internal competition for markets, diminished in size. Capitalism sowed the seeds of its own destruction at the proletariat's hands. Marx predicted that capitalism would disappear in a revolutionary explosion, in which workers would seize control of the means of production and install themselves in state power. Chicherin found this vision of history wrong. At best, Marx's account could explain the appearance of industrial capitalism in England. It said virtually nothing about the origins of those forms of capitalism that had existed long before enclosure. Furthermore, enclosure had occurred only in England, so the English case could not constitute a classical model for the Continent. The modern capitalist class was not diminishing in size but increasing.[115] The notion of capitalism's imminent self destruction had no factual foundation.

Incidentally, in the expanded 1902 version of his critique of Marx, Chicherin confronted Marx's prognosis of a violent socialist revolution. Chicherin denied that such a revolution was likely: "One cannot place much faith in revolutions that [promise to] undermine what has sustained humanity since its inception and that [promise to] suddenly elevate [to power] what for centuries has constituted an underclass: those deprived of everything as of yesterday are to become, by the wave of a magic wand, today's possessors of all wealth. Such teachings may beguile only those persons completely ignorant of history and the social sciences." He added that, even if a socialist revolution should occur, it would provoke a reaction that would "reestablish society's links to the past." Marx's idea of history, Chicherin concluded, was "nothing but an errant fantasy."[116]

In the same expanded version of his essay on Marx, Chicherin analyzed Marx's vision of a dictatorial worker-state. Marx wanted the worker-state to place all individuals "under general control"; the proletariat's collective "freedom" in the economic sphere would be achieved by "obedience to the laws of necessity."[117] Marx's particular equation of freedom with necessity, Chicherin thought, entailed the inevitable enslavement of individual workers. Under the banner of Marxian liberty, "an eternal element of the human spirit" would be sacrificed. A Marxian revolution would be a double tragedy because history, properly understood, was "a process not of the individual's enslavement, but of the individual's gradual liberation." "What Marx imagined as a perverted and accursed world is a vibrant reality, and what he will put in the place of this reality is only the fruit of cloudy fantasies, at the basis of which is pure nonsense."[118]

Chicherin's 1902 rejection of Marx's equation between freedom and necessity was the culmination of an extremely important shift of emphasis in Chicherin's theory of liberty. Whereas in 1877, in the essay on Hegel, Chicherin had still insisted that the individual was not free to violate the laws of historical necessity, by 1902 he decried the dangers posed by notions of historical necessity to individual liberty. The key historical element in this shift of emphasis was Chicherin's realization that revolutionary socialism sought to combine, in the name of historical necessity, absolutely egalitarian social order with absolutely undivided government. He predicted that the resulting regime could only be fatal to individual liberty, for it would license enforcement of majoritarian tyranny through a despotic state.

Chicherin's essay on Marx did not fail to generate controversy. When Prince Bezobrazov published the volume of *Sbornik gosudarstvennykh znanii* containing Chicherin's views on Marx, the bibliographic section of N. K. Mikhailovskii's *Otechestvennye zapiski* (Notes of the Fatherland) prepared an attack on Chicherin. According to the censor's report, the anonymous critic from *Otechestvennye zapiski*—Mikhailovskii himself—"summarized Marx's *Das Kapital* in a socialist fashion, and the journal's reviewer took this work under his protection, trying to prove the inadequacy of Chicherin in the struggle with the German scholar, [to prove] the narrowness and backwardness of the professor's [Chicherin's] political economy, and leaving Karl Marx on an untouched pedestal." The censor also complained that the journal "recommends to the readers that they acquaint themselves with the socialist compositions of Lassalle, whose works are banned in Russian language and foreign language versions [in Russia]." Motivated by these considerations, the censor asked that the July number of *Otechestvennye zapiski* be held up. The government ordered the offending article removed from the issue before publication.[119]

In response to this censorship, Mikhailovskii smuggled a rebuttal of Chicherin into a later number of *Otechestvennye zapiski.* Mikhailovskii's critique was incorporated into an open letter he wrote concerning a book on the Russian landed commune—a book cowritten by V. L. Guerrier [Ger'e] and Chicherin.[120] In the letter Mikhailovskii claimed that "Russian literature has not seen in a long time more blatant and self-satisfied ignorance" than in

Chicherin's Marx article. He mocked Chicherin's scheme of historical laws, pointing out that, by Chicherin's own logic, socialism's appearance was an inevitable development. "You do not like the socialists. But they are a historically determined product of European civilization, and how could they have come into existence against history's laws?" If Chicherin wished to import European civilization into Russia, one result would be the introduction of socialism, Mikhailovskii observed.[121]

For purposes of the letter, Mikhailovskii read Marx as a defender of common laborers against the gospel of liberal economists like Chicherin, who demanded ever higher production regardless of the social costs:

> [Marx] had sufficient erudition and intelligence to discover, among the most diversified representatives of economic literature, a whole arsenal of opinions, aphorisms and assertions declaring that "national wealth is identical with the poverty of the people." This at-first-glance paradoxical proposition can be attributed to a certain old and well-intentioned scholar—a French Physiocrat, if I am not mistaken, but the notion has earned almost universal recognition. Even at the dawn of economic science perceptive people saw clearly that the growth of wealth as an abstract category, unconnected to the fate of the human personality and to the living condition of the masses, leads to the impoverishment (absolute or relative) of those same masses. . . . Later, this fundamental economic axiom was deliberately muddled by pseudo-scholarly arguments launched cavalierly by French economists, especially Bastiat. They tried in a thousand ways to prove that the only requirement is for production and exchange, that the more is produced and the more exchanged, the happier is the country, and one need worry about nothing else. It is at this stage [of economic thought] that you [Chicherin] are arrested.[122]

Such beliefs, Mikhailovskii charged, ignored the great contribution to economic thought made by modern socialists, especially the German *Katheder-sozialisten,* who stood for the egalitarian distribution of social wealth.[123]

A second criticism of Chicherin's article appeared in the February 1879 issue of the Populist journal *Slovo,* under the title "B. Chicherin *contra* K. Marks (Kritika kritiki)."[124] The author of this rebuttal was N. I. Ziber, a radical political economist who, in the 1870s, had been Russia's most enthusiastic propagator of Marxian economic ideas.[125] Against Chicherin, Ziber made four objections. First, he denied that Marx was philosophically inconsistent. For Ziber, Marx was a materialist who criticized existing material reality because of the glaring contradictions inherent in that reality. Marx had not invented an abstract ideal of social justice in order to have a perspective from which to attack capitalism; rather, his recognition of capitalism's faults led him to wish for its dissolution.[126] This sort of objectively oriented criticism, grounded in assessments of material reality, had nothing in common with philosophical Idealism. Indeed, Ziber suggested that Chicherin himself misunderstood the term *Idealism.* Second, Ziber found Marx's use of terminology perfectly self-consistent and appropriate to the task of analyzing capitalist production. Ziber refused to accept Chicherin's idea that commodities are exchanged solely because of their utility. "When and where have you encountered, for example, a society wherein . . . an individual 'compares in every exchange the use which he gives with that which he receives.' Can a Sheffield pinmaker fasten his own clothes with the billions of pins which he manufactures for sale? Can a Lyons silk maker wear on himself the millions of yards of cloth . . . he sells?"[127] In Ziber's opinion, Marx's analysis of commodity exchange, which distinguished *use-value, exchange-value* and all the rest, was correct beyond doubt.

Third, Ziber rejected Chicherin's notion of the utility of capital and of the capitalist. He found machines useful only because of the labor expended in their manufacture and because of the labor devoted in applying them during production.[128] For him the laborer was the key agent in the productive process. Ziber expressed skepticism concerning the capitalist's importance in financing production, because he considered capital investment only a means for the extracting of *surplus value*—in other words, a means of bringing about an undesirable consequence. He believed that industrial production could be underwritten in a different manner: by societies of consumers and producers that would collectively support enterprises and buy their products, thus rendering the capitalist superfluous.[129]

Fourth, for Ziber *Das Kapital*'s significance lay chiefly in Marx's exposé of capitalism's moral bankruptcy. Marxism was "a way of understanding the mutual relations between people, relations obscured by the social division of labor. In fact, *exchange-value,* its implications and significance are nothing but myths, and what exists today is only socially divided labor which, due to the human desire for connectedness, seeks to establish a link [between laborers] and finds this connection in the strange form of commodities and money." According to Ziber, the perverse link through commodities and money had blinded workers to the truth of their condition: they were not free agents but slaves of the capitalist class. Everywhere laborers were paid only subsistence wages, as an 1870 English study of industrial wages around the world had allegedly demonstrated.[130] Chicherin's adherence to outmoded French models of political economy, his distortion of Marx's message, his inability or unwillingness to recognize capitalism's immorality proved to Ziber that Chicherin was dishonest as well as ignorant.

Ziber's article provoked another discussion in the Main Press Administration, during which council members charged:

> The journal *Slovo,* declaring itself an unconditional adherent of Marx's socialistic utopias and borrowing much of his phraseology, fell upon Chicherin with a whole stream of accusations, following in this case the rule long ago learned by the revolutionary portion of our press—to persecute and slander anyone who dares to hinder its propaganda's success. Thus this article attracts attention not by its substance [ne podrobnostiami svoego soderzhaniia]—it mostly consists of empty phrases in defense of Marx's utopias—but by its method of terrorizing public opinion and by its merciless treatment of all moderate persons, for it is in this way that journals like *Slovo* always attain their objective: to win over to themselves the unformed and inexperienced youth in our schools.[131]

The committee voted to warn *Slovo* for Ziber's article—an action that entailed the threat of future closure.[132]

The articles by Mikhailovskii and Ziber demonstrated that by the late 1870s the hold of Marxism over the progressive intelligentsia was already strong. Andrzej Walicki has argued in *The Controversy over Capitalism* that "classical Russian Populism was, first of all, a reaction to Marxism. . . . It is by no means an accident that the beginning of the full-fledged classical Populism coincided in time with the first wave of the diffusion of Marxist ideas in Russia."[133] In Mikhailovskii's case, Marx's influence was especially evident. Mikhailovskii's basic assumptions about the division of labor's deleterious psychological consequences for the worker, his conviction that "national wealth is identical with the poverty of the people," his hostility toward liberal individualism were all drawn from or reinforced by reading of *Das Kapital.*[134] For this reason Mikhailovskii could not pardon Chicherin's liberal individualist exegesis of Marx's classic work.

It is perfectly true, of course, that Mikhailovskii's sarcastic remarks concerning Chicherin's belief in historical laws could have been directed with equal justice at the author of *Das Kapital.* Indeed, already in the 1870s Mikhailovskii had rejected Marxian historical determinism. In his 1877 article entitled, "Karl Marx Before the Tribunal of Mr. Zhukovskii," Mikhailovskii pointed out that Marx's scientific explanations of history placed Russian socialists in a moral dilemma: adherence to Marx's idea of historical laws would compel his Russian adherents to accept the inevitability of capitalist development in Russia, yet, in bowing to the inevitability of capitalism, Russian socialists would also be consenting to the deleterious moral consequences of capitalism for the Russian people.[135] What is fascinating is that Mikhailovskii, whatever his reservations about Marxian determinism, still felt closer to Marx than to Chicherin.[136]

Unlike Mikhailovskii, Ziber was no Populist. Walicki considers Ziber a forerunner of legal Marxism and a liberal interpreter of Marxian economics in the sense that Ziber saw *Das Kapital* as a "continuation and development of the same principles upon which the doctrine of Smith and Ricardo has been built."[137] Ziber was also a determinist who regarded capitalism as a historical inevitability in Russia and who thought the land commune doomed to disappear. Retrospectively, it is surpassingly odd that Mikhailovskii and Ziber were not enemies. What united them in 1878–1879 was, above all, their faith in the masses and collectivism, both notions condemned by Chicherin as dangerous shibboleths.

During the last three years of Alexander II's reign the political situation in Russia quickly deteriorated. In January 1878 the young Vera Zasulich attempted to kill the St. Petersburg police chief F. F. Trepov in revenge for Trepov's part in the beating death of a political prisoner earlier that winter. When Zasulich was tried for this deed, the jury, indignant over Trepov's complicity in police violence and over the regime's high-handedness, voted to acquit her. This verdict, flying in the face of the uncontroverted evidence that Zasulich had deliberately shot a policeman, shocked the central government because it seemed to suggest that the public now sided with the revolutionary cause. The Zasulich acquittal also emboldened the revolutionary underground to consider launching a campaign of political terrorism. In August 1878 the anarchist S. M. Stepniak-Kravchinskii killed Chief of Gendarmes N. V. Mezentsov. In April 1879 A. K. Solov'ev tried to kill the tsar. By October 1879 a new revolutionary organization, the People's Will, devoted itself to regicide. In February 1880 this group planted a bomb inside Alexander's main St. Petersburg residence, the Winter Palace; the emperor barely escaped death when the charge destroyed the state dining room. Finally, on 1 March 1881 the People's Will achieved its objective when two bomb-throwing assassins murdered Alexander in broad daylight on the streets of the capital.

Following the Zasulich affair, the imperial government tried to eliminate the terrorist threat by adopting various expedients. It proclaimed martial law in key cities; it appealed to the public for support against the revolutionaries; it promulgated minor reforms aimed at the amelioration of public grievances. The government even debated whether the public role in policy making should be expanded by adding zemstvo representatives to the advisory State Council. As the historian P. A. Zaionchkovskii has shown, none of these expedients had the desired impact. Repressive measures were of limited utility against dedicated conspirators. Reform measures rallied opinion temporarily to the government's side, but the public remained a fickle god. Progressive writers continued to be critical of government actions, and many young people continued to be attracted to the socialist cause.[138]

Chicherin closely watched the mounting struggle between the government and the revolutionary left. He attended the Zasulich trial in 1878 and reported his outrage over her acquittal.[139] In 1879–1880 he visited St. Petersburg on several occasions and discussed high politics with influential officials, including Ober-Procurator of the Synod K. P. Pobedonostsev. Chicherin expressed alarm at the revolutionaries' brazen defiance of the law and shock at the regime's inconsistent response to terrorism.[140] He shared Pobedonostsev's pessimism over the government's long-term prospects.[141]

In summer 1880 Chicherin decided to write a new critique of socialist thought. He saw that his earlier work in *History of Political Doctrines* had not had the hoped-for resonance among Russian youth, partly because that longer study had treated so many questions extraneous to socialism. He now promised to concentrate exclusively on demolishing the socialists' logic, which he described as a modern variant of sophistry.[142] By helping young people to see the logical untenability and political impracticality of socialism, he expected to contributed to terrorism's defeat in Russia. "Police measures preserve order on the street," he wrote; "order in our minds can be introduced only by the light of reason."[143]

Property and State, written between summer 1880 and September 1881, contrasted Chicherin's views of liberty, equality, and the market with those held by contemporary socialists. In the chapter called "Liberty" Chicherin sketched his philosophical conception of freedom. He argued that human freedom may be understood in two senses: inner liberty, or the will's capacity to determine itself free of external coercion; and external liberty, or the individual's capacity to act independently of another's will and in conformity to his or her own will. According to this conception, inner liberty is unique to human beings, for self-determination requires self-consciousness of a sort that animals lack. Self-determination involves moral choices whereby human beings, guided by reason, evaluate whether particular actions are right or wrong and opt to define their wills by conforming or not conforming to moral standards. Because moral choices must be freely made, neither government nor society may interfere with them. In Chicherin's view, therefore, morality must be sharply distinguished from legality. Governmental regulation of inner liberty constitutes an improper intrusion of law into the moral sphere. When the law imposes constraints upon the individual's conscience, when it controls or determines moral choices, then it coerces or even enslaves the individual's will, thus destroying liberty at its source.[144]

Whereas inner liberty pertains to individual self-determination, external liberty has to do with the scope of action permitted to an individual in society. In one society the individual may be tightly constrained, while in another society the individual may enjoy wide latitude for action. In either case, Chicherin argued, the degree of external liberty will be established by law. If inner liberty is the sphere of morality, external liberty is the sphere of legality. Indeed, Chicherin maintained, external liberty cannot be understood apart from the law. In Chicherin's words, external liberty is "juridical liberty, governed by the coercive law of right."[145]

We have already seen that, according to Chicherin, external liberty is of two types: civil liberty and political liberty. Whereas inner liberty, as a property inherent to the individual, remains constant across time, the writ of external liberty is historically contingent. Over time, the degree of external liberty in European society had dramatically increased: civil liberty had been extended from a tiny minority to the vast majority of the population; in the most advanced countries on the continent, political liberty had also been attained. Although many factors contributed to this development, the main reason for the growth of external liberty was the innate preference for liberty over slavery. To be sure, external liberty was not an aboriginal condition of human life, not a property granted us in the state of nature; rather, it was an imperative of the human psyche, a longing to be free that is realized gradually in the external world. In short, external liberty was a *telos* of human social development.[146]

What was the relation between inner liberty and external liberty? As we saw above, at some points Chicherin emphasized the distinctiveness and incommensurability of these two types of liberty. At other points, however, he seemed to imply that they are complementary or even interrelated. He claimed that inner liberty provides a metaphysical grounding for external liberty. Because it posits that the human will is shaped by moral choices instead of blind necessity, inner liberty lends to external acts a moral weight they otherwise would lack. "Without inner liberty, external liberty loses its foundation and its significance.

Taken in isolation, the right to choose [a particular action] has no claim to respect; it is respected and preserved by coercive law, solely because it is a manifestation of inner liberty." On the other hand, Chicherin admitted, without the freedom to act in the world, an individual cannot achieve the fullness of human dignity. A Christian may be spiritually free even in slavery, but as a bondsman that Christian will be nothing more than the master's tool, unable to follow his or her true vocation. Without external liberty, Chicherin said, inner liberty lacks "actuality."[147]

To this analysis of liberty, Chicherin added one more element. Inner liberty and external liberty belong to individuals, either in isolation or in society. Yet every well-functioning society possesses a state standing above individuals. The state may never violate the sanctum sanctorum of inner liberty, for the moral sphere is off-limits to the law. In regulating external liberty, the state may prohibit one individual from violating the rights of other individuals. Indeed, the state's main reason for existence is the defense of the individual and the arbitration of conflicts between individuals. Understood in this fashion, the state's main purpose is the "negative" function of serving as as the night watchman of liberty. Yet the state also has "positive" tasks to perform. When necessary, it may legitimately require the individual to act in a prescribed fashion—for instance, to pay taxes or to do military service. In defining its positive role, the state itself possesses a kind of freedom vis-à-vis the individual, and this liberty of the state inevitably limits the individual's external liberty. Chicherin recognized that the proper boundary between the individual's external liberty and the state's positive liberty was a historically "changeable notion not given to precise definition." His test for this boundary was that "the legal constraint of [individual external] liberty ought to be permitted only to the extent that it is required to satisfy these common interests [of society]." In principle, "the entire sphere of private interests and relations must be left to [external] liberty." State interference in this sphere might be justified "only in emergencies, and then only as an exception, never as a rule."[148]

Chicherin's conception of inner liberty owed a great deal to Kant's doctrine of individual moral autonomy, although he explicitly warned against Kant's tendency to confuse ethical imperatives with legal mandates. Chicherin's definition of external liberty incorporated Humboldt's notion that the liberty of one individual should be limited only by the freedom of another, but added to Humboldtian "negative" liberty the Hegelian idea of the state's "positive" tasks in promoting the common welfare.[149] It is possible, as Andrzej Walicki has suggested, that Chicherin was influenced by Benjamin Constant's distinction between "ancient freedom" (freedom in the public sphere) and "modern freedom" (freedom in the private sphere).[150] This influence is not explicitly acknowledged by Chicherin, however, in the first part of *Property and State.* Moreover, as our discussion of *History of Political Doctrines* suggests, it is a misreading of Chicherin to suppose that he wanted the modern state to combine "ancient" and "modern" liberty.

Chicherin tried hard to distinguish his idea of liberty from that of Spinoza, who equated freedom with obedience to rational necessity. Chicherin also contrasted his idea of liberty with that of Locke, for Locke's sensationalist psychology stood in the way of recognizing the self-determination of the human will.[151] Indeed, in Chicherin's opinion, neither Spinoza nor Locke was a forerunner of liberalism at all: both were progenitors of the eighteenth-century materialists who supposed that human life is shaped by blind forces of nature rather than by free will. Chicherin sharply attacked the younger Fichte, who wished to employ state power to enforce the moral law. According to Chicherin, Fichte's desire to compel human beings to embrace the Good would lead in practice "to the complete destruction of liberty," because it would deny the very possibility of moral choice. "If I must unfailingly observe a [moral] law, if I cannot deviate from it," Chicherin wrote, "then my freedom disappears, and along with it my moral dignity."[152] Fichte's error was not unique to him but was, Chicherin argued, commonly made by modern socialists.

A no less dangerous error lay in the socialists' confusion of liberty with material welfare. "Many thinkers," Chicherin said, "see the emancipation of the lower classes as a task for the future. Socialists constantly assert that the working class is still in bondage, just as before: for the sake of bread the impoverished working class is forced to work for a miserly wage and is completely under the control of the owners. Socialists claim that only the form of slavery has changed, not its substance."[153] To Chicherin, this argument was specious because in all European countries slavery had been abolished and, in most countries, the working classes enjoyed fundamental civil rights. Juridical liberty was a universal phenomenon. True, the workers' standard of living was often low, but Chicherin believed that it would improve only if the market were allowed to operate freely. The key to material prosperity was the expansion of liberty, not its destruction in the name of social equality.

In his essay on "Equality," Chicherin discussed the relation between liberty and different types of equality. He argued that in the civic sphere numerical equality should predominate, that is, with respect to civil rights all individuals should be considered equal under the law. In the political sphere, however, the basic principle should be proportional equality, that is, political rights should be distributed to those with virtues and talents but not to others lacking the requisite political skills. Meanwhile, in the material sphere inequality must be the rule. This was so because external liberty entails the possibility to control the disposition of one's own talents and resources. "A strong person will acquire more than a weak one, an intelligent person more than a stupid one, an industrious person more than a lazy one; and if they have children, and if we do not wish to violate natural human sentiments, then they will pass the unequal material wealth to their children."[154]

Chicherin opposed Rousseau's assumption that material equality makes possible civic equality. Chicherin also rejected Mably's contention that equality is a more basic characteristic of human nature than is liberty. In Chicherin's view, "[civic] equality issues from liberty, not vice-versa." Material equality, he thought, did not issue from liberty at all but contradicted it.[155] "To demand that the [material] result of liberty be the same for everyone means to destroy liberty at its root and to subordinate the individual to a universal, externally imposed norm."[156]

Many nineteenth-century socialists insisted that material equality is a human right. The Saint-Simonians and Fourierists wanted material goods to be distributed by formulas of proportionate equality, whereas Cabet's communists wanted distribution based on a numerical formula. Proudhon demanded neither proportionate nor numerical equality in distribution of goods; rather, he desired numerical equality in the resources allotted to individuals for acquiring these goods. In each case the equality being recommended was justified by the ethical duty to assist others in need. Chicherin argued, however, that the ethical imperative must not be institutionalized in the form of state control over the distribution either of goods or of economic opportunity. For him altruism was, at root, a religious impulse. In Christian societies, this impulse was understood to spring from Christ's command to "love thy neighbor." Yet this religious commandment posited an individual at liberty either to obey or not to obey it, according to the individual's own predisposition. True, Christianity as a religion had always upheld human equality and brotherhood as spiritual ideals. In Chicherin's recollection, however, "no Christian state had ever dreamt of transforming love into a right and of making it the basis of the civic order. Compulsory love is a monstrous notion, an infringement upon the most sacred elements of human nature."[157] In Chicherin's view, therefore, material equality should not be thought a human right at all; it should be regarded as an aspiration worthy of pursuit to the degree that its pursuit is consonant with the exercise of individual philanthropy. In those societies where charity proves ineffective in remedying gross material inequalities, then the "state can provide assistance [to the poor] through its bureaucracy." Still, in such cases, the state should never "take it into its head to alter legal rights in the name of philanthropy," for "to despoil the rich for the sake of the poor . . . would be not only a violation of justice but a perversion of the basic laws of the human community."[158]

Chicherin believed that "the inequality inherent in human nature reflects a general law of the physical universe." Some human beings will be born into more favorable material environments than will others. Some individuals will be members of "apparently privileged" races. Some individuals will be born stronger, more healthy, more intelligent, or more beautiful than will others. In addition to their dependence on these so-called "innate" sources of inequality, human material circumstances also depend on behavioral factors. Some individuals will pass on to their progeny the material advantages they have accrued. If individuals may transmit material resources to their heirs, then so may historically favored generations and historically advantaged societies transmit their wealth to their successors. Indeed, Chicherin asserted, civilization itself, being a treasure accumulated over centuries, depends precisely on the intellectual legacy originating in human inequality.[159]

In 1869 the Russian socialist Petr Lavrov had published an essay on progress in which he had lamented: "Humanity has paid dearly so that a few thinkers sitting in their studies could discuss its progress." Lavrov contended that the appearance of "critically thinking individuals" had been "bought by the blood, sufferings, or toil of millions." He concluded that the educated minority must never forget this debt to the masses. He urged the minority to discharge its debt to the masses by helping institute socialism.[160]

Like Lavrov, Chicherin recognized that progress and inequality have been historically linked. But Chicherin saw the linkage in a different light and drew radically different conclusions from it. He argued that "as soon as historical progress begins, social inequality inevitably is introduced. The upper classes are set apart from the general mass." It was precisely the educated minority that had introduced intellectual fermentation into the largely homogeneous mass of society. As this fermentation proceeded, social homogeneity diminished: "The different elements contained within the mass separate themselves from it and stand apart; some rise to the top, others sink below."[161] In early stages of historical development, the differentiation of society led to the subjugation of the weak by the strong—that is, to slavery, to serfdom and Estate privileges. In modern societies, however, the spread of education had led to the development of intermediate strata in society, to the diminution of extreme material inequality, and to the recognition of equality in the legal sphere. In other words, human progress had depended on gross material inequality in the early stages of development; later, during the more advanced stages of history, progress had transformed material conditions by generating the heterogeneity of the modern social order. In the future, Chicherin predicted, this heterogeneity would be accompanied by numerical equality in the civic sphere and by proportionate equality in the material sphere; if so, then a just society in the Aristotelian sense would come about. Chicherin thought that any attempt to introduce numerical equality in the material sphere would destroy social heterogeneity and would restore the homogeneity of primitive, undifferentiated society. In his view, socialism was "nothing other than an irrational attempt to destroy the fruits of humanity's entire preceding history, and, under the pretext of equality, to return us to a condition of primitive homogeneity—that is, to a condition of savagery."[162]

Chicherin's discussion of material inequality made him vulnerable to the accusation that his economic doctrine sanctified selfishness. He considered this objection in a chapter of *Property and State* entitled "Liberty as an Economic Principle." According to Chicherin, the most powerful stimulus to economic activity is personal interest. This was so because the prospect of individual gain mobilizes the laborer's energy and creativity in ways that involuntary servitude does not. This is also the case because individuals strive to satisfy needs that they have freely defined as economic goals, whereas the same individuals resist the satisfaction of economic "imperatives" identified by someone else. It follows, of course, that economies resting on individual choice are more productive than ones relying on unfree labor. It also follows that economies resting on personal choice are more in harmony with human nature than those based on coercion. To the extent that socialists had tried to limit individual freedom of economic choice, they had rejected human nature itself. What was worse, they had attempted to refashion human nature in the name of ethical and social postulates. "Rejecting universal [human] experience, they [the socialists] juxtapose to that which is that which ought to be."[163]

At root, socialists equated personal economic interest with egoism. They envisioned a market economy as an arena of pitiless struggle in which the few "winners" regard the many "losers" with cold, unpitying eyes. They juxtaposed to the free market a legally regulated economy based on the ethical principle of the common welfare. They tried to shift economics from the individualistic orientation of the laissez-faire model to a new set of collectivist and egalitarian assumptions. In short, they constructed what Chicherin called the "moral school" of economic science.

In Chicherin's opinion, the moral school committed two errors. First, it failed to distinguish between egoism and legitimate personal interest. Chicherin claimed that "egoism and personal interest are not identical at all. Egoism is a corrupted form of personal interest. It is personal interest that negates all ethical sensibilities in the individual and recognizes nothing except itself."[164] Personal interest properly understood, however, is "not only an economic but an ethical principle." Labor freely directed toward material improvement can be understood as the most efficient means of providing an adequate material foundation for intellectual advancement and spiritual growth in society. The accumulation of capital can be a virtuous activity to the extent that it provides a hedge against future misfortunes that might affect the individual and to the degree that it guarantees the future security of the individual's family. Accumulated capital can be consumed by the capitalists, of course, but it can also be freely given to those less fortunate. Thus the pursuit of personal interest can "serve concomitantly as a source of charity."[165] Understood in these senses, then, personal interest is compatible with deeply ethical impulses.

Second, Chicherin thought, the moral school of economists erred by subordinating economic activity to ethics. Although Chicherin recognized that ethical norms must exercise powerful claims on the human conscience, he insisted that the moral law "does not supplant all other elements of human life." Economics, like science and art, "is an autonomous sphere of human activity. It has its own special laws and imperatives, from which arise a whole series of unique relationships rooted in the very bases of human nature and having a completely legitimate right to exist."[166] A firm based not on profit and loss but on charity will not survive. An economy based entirely on altruism will not be productive. To pretend otherwise, Chicherin said, was to close one's eyes to reality.

Between Chicherin's idea that personal interest is compatible with ethical impulses and his idea that economics must be distinguished from ethics as an autonomous field of activity, there is some tension, to be sure, but no necessary contradiction. For him, the crucial point is that a successful laborer or a businessperson who has accumulated capital should be free to dispose of earned wages or capital savings as he or she chooses. One may criticize the capitalist for not engaging in philanthropy, but one may not punish the capitalist by confiscating legitimate profits. The decision to help others by disposing of profits in charitable activity is an ethical choice, and hence it must be freely made. Ethical norms may well limit individual economic gains, but the limits must spring from individual self-restraint, from the capitalist's conscience, rather than from legal impediments on savings. When socialists demanded that charity be institutionalized through laws governing the distribution of wealth, they transformed charity from a "free impulse of the heart" into a matter of coercion. In so doing, the socialists sanctioned what Chicherin called "tyranny."[167]

Chicherin's vindication of the autonomy of economics drew on at least three sources, two of them not identified in *Property and State.* Aristotle contributed the notion that each field of human endeavor has its own "principle" or "motive force." Adam Smith's *Wealth of Nations,* a book Chicherin had read in his first year at Moscow University, portrayed economic activity as the attempt to satisfy needs and desires of the individual, not those shaped by religion, nation, government, or legal Estate. The third source was the French liberal Adolphe Thiers, whose defense of private property asserted that "for each type of endeavor, a different incentive is necessary."[168] All three thinkers represented the empirically oriented, antiutopian tendency in Western thought that Chicherin most admired.

Those like Chicherin who regarded personal interest as the motive force of economic life were open to another socialist criticism: namely, that the study of economic relations must focus not on the individual entrepreneur but on the collectivity, on economic society as a whole. This criticism was generally predicated on the assumption that economic society is an organism whose needs govern individual economic strategy and whose survival takes precedence over individual success. In the books of Rodbertus, for example, the life of the economic organism was said to inhere in the division of labor. In the work of the German *Kathedersozialist* Adolph Wagner, the sustaining principle of the economy was said to be the nation, identified either as a political or as an ethnic unit. According to the elaborate, multivolume treatise of the economist Schäffle, the economy can be compared to the human body and the individual to a small portion of a cell within the body: the cell may perish so that the body can survive.

In a chapter of *Property and State* called "Economic Community," Chicherin traced the biological analogy to early nineteenth-century Idealist philosophers who spoke of society and state as organisms because they wished to distance themselves from the misguided individualism of the Enlightenment. He pointed out that the organic analogy had a certain plausibility in that it emphasized the connectedness of individuals, but he accused of one-sidedness those

Idealists who forgot about individual freedom or neglected the relative autonomy of small social units (the family, church, and civil society). As a metaphor for describing economic activity, Chicherin found the organic analogy completely unconvincing.[169]

At the end of the chapter Chicherin took up Herbert Spencer's *Principles of Sociology*. Spencer had argued that in industrial countries social evolution had been a process of gradual heterogenization and individuation—that is, a process in which the social organism had become internally differentiated. If one agreed with Spencer in accepting the organic metaphor as a valid description of classical or medieval societies, one might also agree with him in finding the biological metaphor imprecise as a description of modern industrial society. Spencer's logic showed that organicist premises did not necessarily yield socialist conclusions.

Underlying the discursus on Spencer was a hidden polemic with Russian Populists, especially Mikhailovskii. According to Mikhailovskii, Spencer had correctly defined the terms in which one should think about progress. Spencer's error was to misanalyze the nature of progress itself and therefore to make wrong deductions about the location and direction of social differentiation. In Mikhailovskii's opinion, progress was "the gradual approach to the integral individual and the most diversified division of labor among man's organs and the least possible division of labor among men." In other words, Mikhailovskii rejected the ever more specialized division of labor characteristic of modern industrial economies. He idealized the Russian peasant commune where the number of economic tasks was rather limited but where the personalities of the peasant householders were supposedly well rounded and multifaceted. For Mikhailovskii, village life was perfectly organic, for the peasant community comprised strikingly similar but internally differentiated and interdependent individuals.[170] From Chicherin's critique of Spencer it is clear just how fundamental was the disagreement with Mikhailovskii. The only Spencerian ideas that Chicherin endorsed were the notions that modern industrial economies rest on a complex division of labor, voluntary cooperation, and individual freedom.

The essay "Capitalism and Socialism" was the capstone of Chicherin's argument against socialism. He invited readers to picture two ideal types of society in their daily operations. Capitalism, of course, he depicted as a system of production rooted in the liberty of individuals. He specified that any capitalist order functioning in the real world must base itself on private property, voluntary contracts, occupational choice, free labor, freedom to dispose of capital in a wide variety of ways (that is, to save it, consume it, give it to charity, or transmit it by legacy to one's children), and legal guarantees of the above. Because natural forces and historical circumstances vary so widely and because liberty necessarily entails the competitive and therefore unpredictable interaction of economic agents, Chicherin thought the number of actual shapes that capitalism might assume must be infinite.[171] In his opinion, capitalism is essentially a protean system, a dynamic order that continually adapts itself to life's contingencies.

Chicherin portrayed socialism as an essentially stagnant, unitary system in which ownership and control of productive capacity repose in the public domain—that is, in the state's hands.[172] Under socialism, the central bureaucracy monopolizes all economic activity: it determines what is produced, by whom it is produced, and to whom economic rewards are distributed. In theory, the objectives of central planning are the elimination of market "anarchy," the realization of social justice through an egalitarian distribution of goods, and thus the enhancement of individual dignity. In practice, Chicherin predicted, logically consistent socialism would leave planning decisions to the whim of irresponsible bureaucrats guided only by the whims of the socialist ruling party.[173] Because real power over daily life would rest with the government, bureaucrats would come to constitute a privileged stratum in socialist society. Anyone ambitious would therefore seek to join the bureaucratic elite. The asymmetry in authority between government and private citizens would lead to corruption because citizens seeking private advantage would bribe bureaucrats to secure it. Because entrepreneurial risk taking would be discouraged and inventions would fall under the control of the state, socialism would mean the virtual elimination of economic innovation. Under socialism workers would become public employees and would therefore lose the right to strike to win wage increases. Without the right to strike, workers would lose the leverage necessary for effective collective bargaining over working conditions. Socialism would naturally involve government fixing of prices and wages, but it would also lead the government to limit or even dictate occupational choice, because only by controlling labor inputs can a socialist regime control production. Because socialism must concern itself with the equal distribution of goods to the population, a socialist government must inevitably interest itself in the size of the population as such; hence, socialism logically leads to population control and restrictions on individual reproductive freedom. In place of the promised planned society, egalitarian order, and enhanced individual dignity, socialism would deliver arbitrary economic planning, social inequality, and the virtual elimination of individual liberty. In a revealing moment Rodbertus had likened socialism to the ancient Persian state where kings had absolute control over their subjects, with the difference that under socialism the absolute control would be exercised by the nation itself. Rodbertus had meant this comparison as a recommendation in behalf of socialism, but Chicherin saw it as an admission of the devastating truth: socialism had nothing to offer but the "unendurable tyranny" of Oriental despotism.[174]

Chicherin's impassioned advocacy of individual liberty in *Property and State* did not constitute a new departure in his political thought. As we have seen, his early writings identified civil liberties as the core of liberalism. Nor should we imagine that *Property and State* represented a turn against strong government, for Chicherin continued to believe that the state is ideally the best defender of liberty. Still, Chicherin himself regarded *Property and State* as a shift in emphasis. Whereas in his earlier works he had stressed the legitimate uses of state authority and, in particular, the state's role in promulgating progressive reform, he now devoted the lion's share of his attention to the defense of the individual. Why was this so? In some small measure Chicherin felt concern over the central government's conduct. The declarations of martial law in major cities, ministerial intrusiveness in university politics, and St. Petersburg's tendency to interfere with the functioning of local self-government were certainly not happy developments from the perspective of civil liberty. Yet if Chicherin eyed these policies warily, he did not entirely reject them, because he believed that in revolutionary situations, when the normal sanctions of the law prove ineffective, a government may temporarily violate civil liberties to restore order. No, the main source of his anxiety was not the government's threat to civil liberty but the threat emanating from society itself.

Modern socialists spoke in the name of the people, in the name of society as a whole. The exploitation by the few of the many was to be ended as an injustice to the people, as an affront to the nation. If rule by wealthy elites—nay, the mere existence of such elites—was tantamount to enslavement of an entire society, then it was society's responsibility to eradicate these elites. This vision of justice struck Chicherin as nightmarish, for it would unleash Tocqueville's tyrannous majority, with its millions of prying eyes, upon the educated, propertied minority. Driven by envy, society would try to dispossess the wealthy of "surplus" material goods, compensate for biological and natural inequalities by redistributing monetary resources, end inequality of opportunity, and forcibly equalize economic outcomes. In the name of democracy, society would seize control of the state and would hover above it, an omnipresent superego waiting to smite the unsuspecting individual. It was this threat to individual freedom, the threat of society as superstate, that so alarmed Chicherin:

> Now, above the state a new monster has risen, society, which heretofore was thought to be the totality of free forces but now is a kind of mysterious entity swallowing up not only the state but the private sphere as well, an entity directing all to its own ends and prohibiting any autonomous activity. In essence, society is also a state, only under another title and with a much more extensive jurisdiction. From this Moloch, to whom the so-called progressive thinkers are prepared to sacrifice everything, one must guard humanity's most precious achievement—liberty and all connected with liberty.[175]

After nearly fifteen years of terrorism, Alexander II's assassination on 1 March 1881 appeared to some Russians as a long-expected and therefore quite normal event. The conservative journalist E. M. Feoktistov received news of the murder at home: "A strange spectacle unfolded before me: it was as if nothing unusual had occurred; the greater part of my guests sat around card tables absorbed in their games; I chatted with one, now another, they answered quickly with a few words and then again: 'Two no trump,' 'Three spades,' and so on. The next day the same numbness."[176] As details of the conspiracy against the tsar came to light, however, public numbness turned into fear. The discovery of the assassins' apartment, the uncovering of a tunnel armed with mines under Alexander's parade route, the receipt of threats from the People's Will against the life of the new emperor Alexander III, the circulation of wild rumors about the extent of the conspiracy—all these events made St. Petersburghers tremble for the future.

In government circles the assassination generated two kinds of activity. Police frenetically mobilized themselves to forestall new terrorist deeds. Alexander III entrusted his security to the newly appointed municipal governor N. M. Baranov, a man whose paranoia exceeded all bounds. Baranov covered St. Petersburg with plainclothes agents, ordered police workers to dig a trench in front of the Winter Palace to search for hidden mines, demanded rigorous surveillance of train passengers coming into the capital, and suggested that these passengers be forced to call cabs through a police intermediary so that the passengers' addresses would be known to the authorities. On Baranov's advice Alexander III left the capital for the suburban palace in Gatchina. There the atmosphere resembled that of a military camp, or rather a prison. Every entrance to the palace was surrounded by uniformed horsemen and armed sentries.[177]

Meanwhile, the new tsar's advisers fought a pitched battle over the policies of the new reign. One faction, led by Minister of Internal Affairs M. T. Loris-Melikov, tried to persuade Alexander III to sanction the addition to the State Council of elected delegates from the provinces. Although the State Council was an advisory body, it played a vital role in the drafting of most important imperial legislation. Many contemporaries thought Loris-Melikov's proposal a step toward representative government, and some even considered it a de facto constitution. Another faction, led by Pobedonostsev, urged the tsar to restore unlimited government. Pobedonostsev interpreted Loris-Melikov's plan as a Western-style constitution that would open the door to political democracy and eventual chaos. He told the tsar the plan would bring about the "end of Russia." Still another group, led by N. P. Ignatiev, lobbied for the convocation of a *zemskii sobor,* an assembly of the land, on the pattern of old Muscovy.[178]

Many insiders anticipated a victory by Loris-Melikov and his "liberal" bureaucratic allies. In the royal family itself only Grand Duke Sergei and Tsar Alexander III expressed misgivings about the State Council proposal. Grand Duke Alexei probably spoke for most of the royals when he told lady-in-waiting A. F. Tiutcheva: "In the end, Russia will have to come to a constitution."[179] In spite of these expectations, however, Pobedonostsev's ultraconservatism won the day. On 29 April 1881, Alexander III issued a manifesto, promising to uphold "the truth of autocratic power." Within days, Loris-Melikov and his allies were forced to resign from the government. After another year Count Ignatiev was also pushed from power. The triumphant Pobedonostsev now spread his "owl's wings" over the Russian land.[180]

From April 1881 to the revolution of 1905 Russia's domestic policy was conservative, even reactionary in spirit. Although the government never attempted to restore serfdom, it retreated from other legal monuments of the great reform era. The central government substantially diminished the autonomy of the zemstvos by increasing the authority of provincial governors over them and by issuing from St. Petersburg a stream of regulations that the zemstvos had to enforce. The central government reduced the number of the those eligible to vote in zemstvo elections by imposing high property qualifications on electors and instituting ethnic and religious discriminations against non-Russian, non-Orthodox electors. It infringed on the independence of the judiciary by pressuring trial judges to reach "appropriate" conclusions in high-profile cases. It abolished the rural justices of the peace, replacing them with new office holders called land captains, who, like "mini-pashas," combined judicial with police authority. It all but destroyed academic freedom in the universities. Preliminary censorship was not reinstituted, but the government became more aggressive in prosecuting those editors whose journals were critical of government policy. Thus, in many respects, arbitrary bureaucratic rule was restored. As if this were not bad enough already, persecution of minority religious communities quickly became a general phenomenon. In 1891 the government caused an international scandal by expelling Jewish artisans en masse from Moscow. In the Baltic provinces it arrested Lutheran pastors for propagating their faith. On the western periphery it took steps to bring Uniates forcibly under Orthodox control. The central government tried to russify the non-Russian peoples of the empire by requiring the use of the Russian language in educational institutions. Poland and Finland were fastened more tightly into the imperial orb.

How did Chicherin react to these dispiriting events?

Immediately after Alexander II's assassination Chicherin pressed St. Petersburg officials to embark on a dual strategy: while vigorously suppressing the revolutionary movement, the government should cautiously broaden the role of the educated public in political decision making. In early March 1881 he drafted a short programmatic essay, "Tasks of the New Reign," justifying that strategy.[181] He circulated manuscript copies to his friends in Tambov. On 11 March he sent two copies to the capital, one directly to Pobedonostsev and the other, through Pobedonostsev, to Tsar Alexander III.[182] Later that same month, Chicherin visited St. Petersburg himself, bringing more copies of the essay to various ministers, including Loris-Melikov and War Minister D. A. Miliutin.[183]

"Tasks of the New Reign" made three main arguments. First, it located the cause of Russia's political instability in the swift pace and sweeping nature of Alexander II's great reforms. These reforms, Chicherin said, were a "revolution from above," comparable to the French Revolution of 1789.[184] The reforms had undermined traditional social relationships in the countryside and had thoroughly transformed the serfdom-based legal order. In the process, the reforms had also shattered extant worldviews held by the educated public. In the wake of the reforms, when educated Russians began to search for alternative worldviews to adopt, they gravitated toward materialism and especially socialism; this radicalism led directly to political terrorism and the current instability. Second, the essay ridiculed the notion that solutions to Russia's instability might be found in what was commonly known as the St. Petersburg "liberal" program: greater freedom for the press, concessions to university students, greater latitude for the zemstvos than that provided in 1864, economic subsidies for the peasantry, equalization of the tax burden imposed on peasant and noble landowners. Least of all could a solution be found in granting a constitutional charter. All these "liberal" recommendations, Chicherin thought, would diminish the authority of the central government just at the juncture when it needed maximum power. The order of the day, Chicherin argued, must be the struggle against socialism. In this struggle, he said, "any attempt to adhere to legalistic solutions would be a sign of weakness."[185] In other words, over the short term Chicherin endorsed martial law. Third, the essay called on the government to collaborate with "healthy forces" from the educated public. Concretely, Chicherin suggested that this collaboration take the form of adding elected provincial delegates to the State Council.

"Tasks of the New Reign" offered something to Loris-Melikov as well as to Pobedonostsev. Loris-Melikov read Chicherin's essay as "conservative" support for his own State Council project.[186] Meanwhile, Chicherin's advocacy of martial law heartened Pobedonostsev, who read it as "liberal" support for a strong autocracy.[187] Chicherin's position was obviously somewhere in between the so-called "liberal" and "conservative" camps, but shaded toward the latter. On 24 March, Chicherin discussed high politics with the procurator of the Synod; he noted that Pobedonostsev "had adopted an outlook not much different from my own."[188] On 26 March Chicherin wrote his wife: "Only one thing is desirable: if Loris and company remain in power, that they should forget about their liberal tricks, for playing such tricks is bound to be disastrous [in the current climate]. In this respect, Pobedonostsev is very useful. Although he himself is incapable of governing and he has absolutely nothing positive to offer, at least he can call a halt to many stupidities."[189]

Chicherin's plan had no chance of being adopted, because it tried to reconcile two political platforms that, in March 1881, were irreconcilable. If the government were to rely on martial law, why should it experiment with representative elements in the State Council? If it were to move toward a constitution and a rule-of-law state, why should it enforce emergency procedures that would surely undercut civil rights? P. A. Zaionchkovskii was right to observe that "Chicherin's project was contradictory in content": it fell between two stools.[190]

Twenty years later, Chicherin drafted another programmatic political essay, the third and last such essay of his career. *Russia on the Eve of the Twentieth Century* dropped Chicherin's previous support for martial law. It repeated the 1881 proposal to add elected provincial delegates to the State Council, but now Chicherin said explicitly that this plan would be a step toward representative government: "If, in addition, one were to transform the State Council into an upper legislative house and to purge from it those members who are currently there only because of their bureaucratic office, then one would have a ready-made constitutional structure. One does not have to rack one's brains much about it."[191] He also told his readers that "the civil liberty established by [Alexander II] must be fortified and stabilized by political liberty. Sooner or later, by one means or another, this will occur, but it will inevitably happen, for it is something rooted in necessity. The force of events will lead irresistibly to this conclusion."[192] Within five years of Chicherin's prediction, the Russian government sanctioned a constitutional arrangement, whereby the State Council became the upper chamber of the newly inaugurated legislative branch. As Chicherin had prophesied, the "force of events" did lead, if only temporarily, to a representative assembly in Russia.

How do we account for Chicherin's tactical shift between 1881 and the turn of the century? Why had his support for emergency rule waned and his enthusiasm for representative institutions and constitutional government increased?

Behind Chicherin's disappointment with the autocracy was a series of very specific, sometimes personal, grievances. From late 1881 to May 1883 he had served as the elected mayor of Moscow's city council. He had been compelled to resign from this position after telling an assembly of mayors from other Russian cities that "we [must] carry away a consciousness of our common purpose and of the need for collaborative activity"—an assertion interpreted by the St. Petersburg authorities as a demand for a constitution.[193] Chicherin also felt the hand of the St. Petersburg government in 1889, when the justices of the peace were abolished. One of his younger brothers had served several terms in Tambov province as a justice of the peace. The Chicherin family bitterly resented the elimination of this very important and worthy office.[194]

In 1891, when the Moscow authorities expelled the Jews from Moscow, Chicherin joined Lev Tolstoi, the philosopher V. S. Solov'ev, and the activist V. G. Korolenko in condemning the government's violation of Jewish rights. Solov'ev asked each critic of anti-Semitism to write a letter expressing his views on the subject. The letters of protest were then published in the preface to a short book called "Slovo podsudimomu!" [Word to the Accused!].[195] Chicherin wrote Solov'ev in part:

> In my conviction there is no people [narod] in the world to whom humanity ought to show greater gratitude than to the Jews. It is enough to say that from them issued

> Christianity, which transformed world history. Whatever opinions we may have on religious questions, there is no doubt that that the book that has served as spiritual nourishment for millions and millions of individuals, the Bible, is of Jewish origin. From the Greeks we received secular education, but the Greeks disappeared [as a civilization], while the Jews, despite unprecedented persecutions and their dispersion all over the globe, have preserved their national identity and their faith. In this I see a testimony to their great calling. I also think that the state is obligated to defend and protect all the subjects that Providence places under its care. . . . On this issue, I observe with profound sadness that many of my compatriots take not the Christian perspective of love toward their neighbors, but an absolutely pagan and even barbarian perspective. *The anti-Semitic movement is the scandal of our time.* I would give much to cleanse from my fatherland this stain.[196]

The publisher printed more than two thousand copies of "Slovo podsudimomu!" only to discover that the Main Press Administration had issued a temporary injunction on its distribution. Between March and May 1891 the censors deliberated over the book's fate; on 28 May the Main Press Administration ordered the St. Petersburg Censorship Committee to prohibit distribution of the volume and to confiscate the publisher's copies and destroy them, saving one archival copy for each relevant government agency. The responsible censor defended the decision on the grounds that "this harmful defense of the Jewish people at the expense of Christianity and the Russian nationality . . . cannot appear in the Russian press, since it will arouse emotions, fortify the Jews in their struggle, and undermine the Russian nationality."[197] By 1899, Chicherin had become so incensed over Russian anti-Semitism and anti-Polonism that he published abroad an open letter to the anti-Semite A. N. Rennenkampf in which he indicted the Russian government policy concerning the Jews and Poland.[198]

Finally, in late 1898 and early 1899, Chicherin involved himself in the defense of a peasant, accused of belonging to a small sectarian community of flagellants, the so-called *khlysty.* After the sectarian was arrested as a member of an "especially harmful" religious society, Chicherin offered to testify in his defense. The local prosecutor denied Chicherin the possibility of appearing in court.[199] In the subsequent trial, the sectarian was convicted, partly on the testimony of a thirteen-year-old girl and on that of a seminary professor who contended that the khlysty must be destroyed at all costs.[200] Chicherin decided to publicize this injustice in an article he sent to *Russkie vedomosti* [Russian News], but the editor rejected publication out of fear of punishment by the censors. In response, Chicherin appealed unsuccessfully to Pobedonostsev and to the head of the Main Press Administration to overturn the editor's decision.[201] He also pressed the government to overturn the erroneous guilty verdict. Eventually, the Imperial Senate ordered the sectarian pardoned and released, but even this decision did not satisfy local authorities, who threatened a new trial.

Chicherin felt that the government's conduct in the case against the sectarian demonstrated the complete impossibility of guaranteeing civil rights in the absence of formal political representation. In July 1899, the same month in which the sectarian's case was "resolved," Chicherin drafted *Russia on the Eve of the Twentieth Century* and read it to friends. Thus there was a direct correlation between his personal frustration over civil rights' violations and his new enthusiasm for instituting political liberty in Russia.

At a more general level, the political reasons for Chicherin's shift in emphasis are easy to specify. In March 1881 Chicherin thought Russia faced a political emergency. Accordingly, he advocated martial law, but only for a short period and only if combined with "liberal" changes in the State Council. By 1900 the immediate political crisis had passed. Meanwhile, the government had unwisely continued to enforce martial law in the main cities of the empire. In a variety of fields the government's reactionary policies had unnecessarily violated civil rights and had contravened the spirit of the great reforms. The official pretext for the political reaction had been the need for a strong autocracy. Pobedonostsev and others had claimed that, without autocracy, Russia would disintegrate. Yet the autocracy was, in the last analysis, an anachronism in an age belonging to civil and political liberty. Consequently, Chicherin's constitutional project fit the historical climate of fin-de-siècle Russia better than did his more conservative "Tasks of the New Reign."

To analyze the shift in Chicherin's political program exclusively against the background of events, however, is to miss the more interesting connection between his political platform and the deep structure of his "conservative-liberal" ideology. Chicherin was a committed defender of individual freedom, but he was never a libertarian. He agreed that the individual must have the right to be morally self-determining regardless of political circumstances, but he always held that "external" liberty must vary according to circumstances. Neither civil rights nor political rights, therefore, could be conceived as absolute. Because civil and political rights can never theoretically assume the status of prelegal or supralegal guarantees, external liberty can be defined only by law, and this law cannot be concretized outside the framework of existing states. In a real sense, therefore, the actual existence and contours of civil and political rights must depend upon the will of the state. That was why Chicherin could speak of the state's "freedom" relative to the individual. That was also why he admired Aristotle, Machiavelli, and Hegel, who made the case for the state as a positive and free historical force.

Because external liberty is historically contingent, the individual and the state must constantly renegotiate their relationship. Either explicitly or implicitly, the negotiation must entail mutual recognition of legitimacy: the individual must recognize the historical legitimacy of the state, while the state must acknowledge individuals as its reason for existence. To succeed, the negotiation between individual and state must take account of the slow historical movement of societies toward greater liberty, but it must also react to specific events. What happened in late imperial Russia was a double failure: much of the educated public rejected not only particular policies of the imperial government but also the legitimacy of the imperial state; meanwhile, the state failed to grant to educated Russians historically appropriate recognition in the form of legal rights. As a result, late imperial history was dominated by political terrorism on the one hand and by arbitrary rule on the other. The "healthy forces" in Russian society were caught between the radical left and radical right, were essentially powerless, and would remain so until the educated elite and the state mended their errant ways. Only when educated individuals acknowledged the utility of a rule-of-law state and when the state acted to guarantee to the educated public both civil and political rights, only then would Russia find political harmony.

By nature, liberals tend to be optimists. They believe that the desire to live in freedom is a deeply rooted human need. They hope that the future will bring humanity closer to the hour when liberty will be universally shared. They generally trust that, when this hour has arrived, individuals will be capable of enjoying freedom responsibly. At bottom, their optimism rests on zealous faith in human nature, in its essential goodness, rationality, and imaginative creativity. For liberals, the overabundant historical evidences of human frailty, cruelty, irrationality, and stupidity demonstrate not the maleficence of human nature but its historically contingent, therefore transitory and remediable, imperfection. To liberals, such phenomena as the masses' incomprehension or fear of liberty, the ruling elites' visceral fear of representative government, the contempt for law that is so widespread even in so-called "advanced" societies—

these phenomena are mere symptoms of ignorance, cases of wrongly calculated self-interest, or evidence of self-delusion. On the assumptions of human goodness and rationality, these phenomena, in fact, can be nothing more than temporary aberrations that will be corrected in due course by enlightenment, the genie of progress, the "laws" of historical development, the march of the World Spirit. Liberals cannot abide J. G. Hamann's argument that human nature is inherently irrational; or Joseph de Maistre's claim that not the philosophe but the executioner is the figure upon which the future of civilization hinges; or Dostoevskii's assertion that most human beings prefer "miracle, mystery, and authority" over genuine freedom. To liberals such propositions seem unwarranted and repellent, for they seem to deny the reality of human goodness and the possibility of moral improvement.

Like other liberals, Chicherin believed in human goodness, rationality, and creativity. He accepted the reality of social progress. He saw history as a logical, law-governed, providentially ordained process in which human beings have gradually increased their self-consciousness and have erratically but inexorably responded to the deepest call of their own hearts, the call to freedom. As we have seen, this credo ran like a thread through all Chicherin's political thought from the 1850s to 1900. It proved his political outlook was essentially forward-looking and optimistic.

Yet Chicherin's optimism was balanced by a very realistic assessment of Russia's past and future prospects. He wrote repeatedly that, after centuries under serfdom and absolute government, Russia constituted a sociopolitical environment that was uncongenial to free institutions. He understood that, if the reforms of the 1860s had done much to advance the cause of civil rights, the task of cementing these rights into popular consciousness remained daunting. He described in detail how the struggle between would-be revolutionaries and the still-influential absolutist faction in government had prevented the reformers from succeeding in this task and how, in fundamental ways, political polarization had seriously compromised the reformers' achievements on the legal front. He lamented that western European nations no longer offered Russia a healthy example, for the western European governing classes had lost their way and the academic elites had been seduced by socialism.

As early as 1886 Chicherin had began to warn about the apparently insurmountable difficulties facing his country. In one passage of his memoirs Chicherin compared the fate of his generation to a well-known painting depicting the people of Israel crossing the Red Sea. "The canvas is empty because the artist has picked the moment when the people of Israel have still not yet crossed, the Egyptians have still not arrived, but the sea has already parted. In Russia, unfortunately, the canvas has not remained empty; in the artist's absence, the framework prepared for an elegant picture has been covered by God knows what. Poor Russia! Was it this for which her most noble sons hoped when they labored for the future?"[202]

Chicherin's pessimism increased with age. In an Easter letter in 1899 he wrote his old friend A. V. Stankevich: "In spite of my seventy years, I do what I can, even though I am sure that it will not really change anything [chto eto ne k chemu]. Here again the only hope is a future springtime or a social resurrection; but you and I will not live to see it. Subsequent generations will see it, although who knows what good will come of it, since with the new spring will arrive a new filth worse than that which, in the form of nihilism, accompanied the epoch of reforms. It is difficult to live on the earth under such conditions, when you see no reason to rejoice anywhere."[203] As we have seen, in *Russia on the Eve of the Twentieth Century* Chicherin said flatly that Russia's immediate future would more likely bring some sort of "catastrophe" than any kind of political harmony.

Between Chicherin's irrepressible confidence in the distant future and his genuine despair over what tomorrow might bring there is an emotional gulf that we may find difficult to navigate. We may decide that the dissonance between Chicherin's optimism and pessimism is the result of unavoidable tension between his comprehension of what should be and what is. We may argue that, like any intellectual with a unitary vision, Chicherin was doomed to disillusionment when he realized that he would never experience in reality the glorious future he had dreamt. Or again, we may interpret Chicherin's psychological discomfort as the consequence of an unnerving and tragic pattern in Russian history. Blessed by enormous material and human resources, Russia has too often wasted its potential. Chicherin the optimist saw the almost limitless possibilities within Russia's grasp; Chicherin the pessimist underlined the laboring classes' historical passivity, their lack of formal education and of developed political culture; and he, the pessimist again, realized that the nation's political class, by its exceptional cruelty, irrationality, and stupidity, would almost surely squander the national potential.

This peculiar mixture of optimism and pessimism, liberalism and conservatism, nationalism and cultural despair, moralism and Realpolitik was virtually unique to Chicherin in the nineteenth century. It helps explains why, despite their energetic elaboration and brilliance, his ideas attracted few followers and also why among Russian thinkers he has been so little read and understood. In a country famous for its political extremism, he was one of a tiny number of intrepid souls who chose to occupy what Isaiah Berlin has rightly called the "notoriously exposed, dangerous and ungrateful position" of the middle ground.[204] Unlike other occupants of this territory who had the gift of empathizing with their adversaries even while disagreeing with them, Chicherin felt no moral sympathy with his political opponents. To him, socialists were irresponsible, deluded utopians; Slavophiles were mystics and madmen masquerading as patriots; St. Petersburg officials were, by and large, reactionaries ignorant or fearful of modern realities; all his opponents were cursed by the "one-sidedness" of their outlook. His lack of magnanimity further isolated him and reduced his historical influence.

Yet in the end, Chicherin made very significant contributions to the advancement of Russian social thought. At a moment when the imperial government reacted suspiciously to any talk about individual rights and when it tended to equate rights with constitutional demands, Chicherin introduced into Russian political discourse a saving distinction between civil rights and political rights. This distinction made it possible to defend the introduction of civil rights without simultaneously inaugurating constitutional guarantees, and thereby freed a portion of the educated public to collaborate with reforming officials. In a country that was generally uncongenial to Western-style legal codes and where many leading intellectuals censured the law as a cause of Russia's social ills or as a barrier to their cure, Chicherin defended a Rechtsstaat as his country's best hope for the future. He did so without pretending that existing statutory law was inerrant and without dismissing the empirical evidence that certain decrees had done great damage to the social order. At a moment when Russia's budding market economy was attacked by socialists and undercut by governmental policies, Chicherin defended entrepreneurial freedom, the validity of free contracts and the vital significance of capitalism. At a moment when the established church and conservative politicians found it convenient to blur the difference between or to conflate legal and religious duties, Chicherin insisted on making a categorical distinction between legality and morality. He claimed that the content of the law is determined not by moral principles but by social imperatives. He suggested, nonetheless, that upholding the law is the best way to protect morality, for the law, properly interpreted, guarantees individuals the requisite latitude to make free moral choices. Finally, at a juncture when the imperial state dwarfed Russian citizens and when the social collective began to threaten individual freedom, Chicherin defended the sanctity of personhood. Indeed, as the philosopher Nikolai Berdiaev observed in 1907, three years after Chicherin's death, "respect for the individual personality, for rights and liberty, constituted the guiding spirit of Chicherin's life. It was his religion."[205] In imperial Russia, to live and die by such a "religion" was an eccentric but good thing, good enough, perhaps, to merit remembering.

Part One **Early Political Writings**

On Serfdom

The crucial questions that preoccupy statesmen and affect the vital interests of contemporary societies are of two kinds—political and social.[1] Political questions perhaps arouse more controversy and enmity, for they visibly split a people into parties each of which stubbornly pursues its own objective. Defenders of the old order and adherents of the new enter into competition, and if the government by wise concessions fails to introduce peace between the parties, then not infrequently internal strife will result and reforms will eventually have to be inaugurated by force of arms. Nevertheless, it is relatively easy to resolve most political disputes, for only partisan prejudice inhibits their resolution. Each side clearly understands its own objectives, knows how to achieve its ends, and, as soon as it becomes the dominant party in the government, immediately implements its political program. The prerogative of the legislature is to grant more or less liberty, to increase or decrease the rights of social Estates, to alter in this way or that the administrative structure. Such legislative business can be expeditiously discussed, and, given reasonable clarity of vision and a certain practical sense on the part of legislators, it can also be expeditiously transacted.

Social questions are quite different. Their impact extends beyond the narrowly political to the nation's material welfare as a whole; they surely influence the public sphere, but also profoundly affect private life, for they are bound up with the interests of every individual, and they leave their mark on popular mores and customs. In a word, they encompass the entire life of a people, and there is no sphere, no corner in which their impact is not felt, in which they fail to constitute a subject of the most lively concern.

This characteristic makes their resolution extremely difficult. It is impossible to transform all private and public life by a single stroke of the pen, as for example one might publish a new press law or establish a new type of court system. Many years are required to bring about the thoroughgoing transformation of an entire society. To effect such a transformation requires a detailed knowledge of material life, a clear understanding of existing social relationships, careful consideration of entrenched habits, a deliberate and incremental pace of change, and a firm, undeviating determination to reach the proposed objective.

Yet if it is admittedly quite difficult to resolve social questions, neither is it wise to tarry in their resolution, for these questions are too intimately bound up with the common welfare. As soon as a people has become mature enough for a certain type of civic development, as soon as old forms have ceased to be compatible with new ideas, aspirations, and needs, then the time has arrived to set about changing them. Otherwise, discord will be felt in every part of society, and the longer the government delays the resolution of a question hanging over a people, the more sharply this discord will make itself felt. Dissatisfaction will become stronger and stronger, the collision of opposed interests will be more and more violent, demands will become more intransigent and inflexible, and it will be fortunate if matters end with only minor troubles and uprisings. And it may easily transpire that certain individuals will seek to address their unacknowledged grievances by using force, and then a frightful struggle may ensue: one class will rise up against another and the new order will be baptized in a fountain of blood.

Among social questions urgently requiring immediate resolution in Russia is the problem of serfdom. Twenty-two million persons of both sexes, more than a third of the entire population of Russia, now are the property of private individuals. An appalling phenomenon! In the nineteenth century, when the inner reserves of nations are mobilized to meet external threats, when industry and education move so swiftly forward, when political might itself depends not only on governments' military resources but on citizens' intellectual and economic activity, in the nineteenth century, across enormous areas of Russia, there exists an institution which inhibits every positive development and which reduces Russia to a semibarbarian power. This fact alone should suffice to persuade us that, at present, we cannot expect to compete with Western states on equal terms. A man bound hand and foot cannot hope to best a rival who enjoys free use of his appendages. Serfdom is a ball and chain which we drag behind ourselves and which confines us to virtual immobility while other nations forge irresistibly ahead. Without the abolition of serfdom the resolution of [our society's] other problems—political, administrative, and social—will be impossible. Wherever one looks, serfdom looms as an insurmountable obstacle, a stigma upon all civic and political relations.

In fact, regardless of the angle from which we view the question, serfdom cannot be justified. At the outset we are confronted by an ethical consideration—one person's belonging to another, who arbitrarily can make him happy or unhappy, who can deprive him of his property, his family and his home, who can subject him to innumerable torments outside the scope of the law, who finally can sell him as chattel, as a thing valued only for profit, though, as if in mockery, this thing is called a human soul. We have become so accustomed to this spectacle that we consider it something quite normal. And yet upon the slightest reflection we will see that it is one of the most disgraceful and inhuman institutions in our realm. True, mores have recently become less cruel: one no longer encounters private prisons where once serfs sat like convicts in chains confined for petty offenses; today it is difficult for lords to escape prosecution for capriciously beating serfs to death; yet abuses have not been rooted out and can never be rooted out. Always and everywhere there will be many cruel, choleric, wayward individuals, and always they will be tormentors to those under their power. The law cannot end these abuses unless it abolishes their source, for the problem is inherent in serfdom as a social arrangement. Today it is pointless even to speak about [closing] loopholes in the few existing statutes by which the law tries to protect serfs from their masters' arbitrary will. Malefactors who torture their serfs not infrequently escape the legal retribution they deserve; moreover, the authorities are now afraid to touch these questions, they are afraid to punish the lords out of fear of disturbing the already shaky deference of serfs [to their masters]. Unfortunately, cruel treatment of serfs cannot be classified as the exception; on the contrary, too often it is the rule. And this says nothing about the fact that in Russia the most disgraceful acts are not even considered cruel treatment. We are not surprised when an irascible master scolds his innocent lackey or beats him about the neck for some false step or clumsiness. It does not occur to anyone that the lackey should have exactly the same right to scold and beat his master. Yet even if cruel treatment were the exception, even then the exception would suffice to lay a stigma of shame upon the entire institution of serfdom. No matter how few the victims, their sufferings cry out against the lawlessness now sanctioned by the law.

There is just as little justification for serfdom from the political perspective. A polity is society taken as an integral whole, as a community encompassing all its members. If individuals band together in order to live in a community, they must mutually agree to limit the freedom of their actions and must agree to prohibit one individual from harming another. For this purpose they need an authority, an agency to exert the power of the community as a whole over its parts. This authority is entrusted to the government, the head of society, the embodiment of its integrity, and no private individual may be invested with this authority, for a private individual is a part of society, not the whole of it. Therefore there is a general rule that in a well-ordered polity, sovereign power must be vested in the government (absolutist, constitutional, or republican—it makes no difference), which then divides this authority among its agents, whatever may be the method of their appointment. An official wields authority not as a private individual but as an agent of the state; he is powerful in the sphere in which he represents the government, to the degree to which he represents it, and only insofar as he serves the government's interests rather than his own selfish ends.

A noble landowner does not fulfill any of these criteria. He is a private individual who lacks the status of a public official; while he has been entrusted with the exercise of vast authority over other individuals, he nevertheless uses this authority for his own private advantage, giving no accounts to anyone. Seigneurial power is the alienation into private hands of political authority over a third of the populace, an alienation that is so contradictory to the ideal definition of political authority that no enlightened government can tolerate it. In Russia the emancipation of the peasants is generally thought to be a liberal measure. This is certainly true, for emancipation does entail liberty for the serfs; but emancipation is also a matter of good government, a step that must eventually be undertaken by any government having political sense. Only in the Middle Ages or at the dawn of the modern era, when private law was intertwined with every aspect of public administration, could such an institution as serfdom have arisen. But the more the state apparatus developed and came to understand its ultimate purpose and task, the more clearly incompatible serfdom became with the imperatives of good government.

Serfdom is also harmful to the economic life of the nation. There is no need to explain that only free labor, only activity driven by the mainspring of personal gain, only these things can significantly advance industry, while serfdom can only diminish the productivity of labor and industry. This is an axiom requiring no proofs. An individual works hard only for his personal profit, and no one will work if the results of his labors are not guaranteed by law. Of course, there are circumstances when serf labor will be more profitable for a state than free labor: in a semisavage country, where it is necessary to till vast expanses of land, where the lower classes have neither the enterprise nor the energy nor sufficient education to accomplish this feat, and where the upper classes do possess the significant advantage of education—there, perhaps, serf labor can achieve greater results than private initiative. But Russia at present does not belong in this category. What was accomplished by serf labor in past centuries cannot be measured accurately, for there are no data to assess. Formerly, given endless internal migrations of the sort that occurred before the enserfment of the peasantry, only the most primitive kind of agriculture was possible; therefore serfdom, which fixed the agricultural Estate to the land, significantly advanced the cultivation of fields. None of these conditions exists today, though. Today peasants can no longer migrate freely from place to place. The population has become more dense and settled, political institutions have become more developed, and fields will not remain uncultivated if they are dependent on free labor. Today land itself has value independent of the number of hands bound to it—a situation that did not obtain earlier. Finally, there exist today certain circumstances that are absolutely incompatible with serfdom's continuation. Russia is not divided from Europe by an impenetrable border but maintains long-standing and vigorous trade relations with Europe, borrows from it new inventions, and implants on native soil numerous branches of manufacturing industry. By necessity Russia must strive for economic parity with Europe, but parity cannot be achieved so long as serfdom exists. Maintenance of Russia's political position demands intensified industrial activity. In order successfully to compete with other great powers, Russia must possess the requisite economic resources. A state's finances are based on its wealth, and wealth, in turn, is produced by the labor and enterprise of a nation. But the labor of a serf can exceed in productivity only the labor of a semisavage Asian barbarian; it cannot compare with the labor of a free individual in a modern economy, where that individual finds endless incentives to act and develop.

It is said that the Russian peasant is by nature lazy, that without compulsion he will not diligently work, and that [if serfdom is abolished] the fields will be in a much worse condition than they are in today. Let us grant that this is partly true; yet the very character of the Russian peasant was formed by serfdom. A man may well become lazy and apathetic when for centuries he has lived under continual oppression, when he has no property, when, by the arbitrary will of another individual, he may suddenly be deprived of the fruits of many years' labor, and when he becomes accustomed to thinking that, however hard he works, he will always have what is necessary to live, whereas he will always be uncertain of obtaining anything superfluous. If you desire the Russian peasant to become more industrious, then it is necessary first to remove his fetters; then as industry develops, as material conditions improve, as transportation is perfected, he will understand his own interests and, using his mind and wit, will not lag behind others in improving agriculture. Of course, the lands of free peasants are now cultivated less efficiently than lands belonging to landlords, but the cause is not serf labor but the greater capital and education of the landlords, and also—and this is very important—the fact that landlords' property is separate and permanent, a condition that does not even obtain [on the land cultivated by] state peasants. With the abolition of serfdom, the level of agriculture will not deteriorate. Peasant lands will be cultivated no worse than before, and landlords' land will probably be better cultivated than formerly. Today a landlord cannot even determine how much cultivation of the fields costs; when using serf labor, one cannot even estimate expenses or begin to keep accurate accounts, and this is an elementary precondition for any industrial enterprise. Is it possible to make any improvements on an estate when it is impossible to compare income with expenditures? For this reason agriculture stagnates, and even a majority of conscientious lords, being in no position to keep proper accounts, content themselves by conforming to long-established routines; or, on the contrary, having in hand a certain labor force whose value they are in no position to calculate, they throw themselves into enterprises that lose money. If one considers all the resources that the landlord provides the peasant for working, one can surely conclude that free labor will be much cheaper than serf labor. The annual salary of workers cannot equal the income of half an estate, yet in most cases the land given to peasants [for their communal use] comprises half a seigneurial estate. All this capital is wasted—without advantage to the landlord or to the peasant; it is wasted on unproductive peasant labor. If the landlord sold peasants half his estate in exchange for cultivating the other half, he would benefit and so would they. But no one has dared do that, because it is impossible to estimate income precisely. Besides we lack the entrepreneurial spirit. Everyone prefers to travel the beaten path, to avoid undertaking risky new ventures.

The absence of the entrepreneurial spirit is also a consequence of serfdom. Every viable enterprise must be based on accounting, accounting breeds the entrepreneurial spirit, and without the latter what kind of success can one expect from agriculture? For this reason alone, agriculture in Russia is underdeveloped. When [the British politician Richard] Cobden was in Russia, he was surprised at the success of factory production and at the sorry condition of agriculture. The reason is clear: in the one case, labor is free labor, in the other it is serf labor; in the one case, the enterprise is based on mathematical accounting, in the other it follows ancient routine. It is not surprising that the landlords' own standard of living suffers for the same reasons. Most landlords are insolvent or live under the burden of debts which they service with greatest difficulty despite the fact that state credit institutions have set very moderate interest rates. Delving into the causes of this phenomenon, we see that it is also mostly a consequence of serfdom.

But does the present order somehow work to the benefit of peasants? Guaranteed the necessities of life, receiving from the landlord a parcel of land sufficient for subsistence and alms in case of unforeseen misfortune, the peasant cannot fall into the kind of poverty which we see among the lower classes in western Europe. Indeed, many people consider serfdom a means of avoiding pauperism, but this view is quite unjustifiable. Among our state peasants there is also no pauperism, despite the fact that they must deal with notoriously corrupt official overseers. In general, in Russia the cupidity of officials is quite astounding. Landlords even cite this official cupidity as a favorite argument in defense of their own prerogatives: they brazenly claim that their peasants live better than state peasants and that any reform will do more harm to the peasants than good. There is not a single state peasant, however, who would agree to be a privately owned serf, while serfs grasp at any opportunity to become free. The fact is that although state officials squeeze out of the state peasants everything that they can, the state peasants nevertheless have what is necessary to live, and they do not suffer from pauperism. The reason has to do partly with the communal organization of village life and especially with the enormous expanses of virgin land in Russia. In western Europe a dense populace mingles in a relatively small area, so more than half the people are deprived of landed property; in such countries as England, where the aristocracy dominates, all land is concentrated in a few hands. In Russia, on the contrary, the population is comparatively sparse while the land is vast and fertile, abundantly rewarding even the modest exertions of the ploughman. In this respect, one cannot fruitfully compare us with the peoples of western Europe, who live under different physical conditions, but rather with the North American States, where there are also large expanses of rich and virgin soil. But there, at least in the northern states, which constitute the original and main core of the union, labor is free and industry is developed to an astounding degree; there the population grows as it does nowhere else, enormous territories are settled as if by miracle, railroads reach from one ocean to another, flourishing cities rise up where a few years earlier there were only deserts, state capitals grow with stunning rapidity and prosperity flows to every class of the populace. In Russia . . . but it seems there is no point in continuing the comparison [ellipsis Chicherin's]. True, in North America there is a motive force that accounts for the miracles, a motive force which we lack—namely, education. But it should not be forgotten that the first prerequisite of education is liberty, that the first precondition of social activity is also liberty and the legal protection of the individual against governmental arbitrariness. Therefore if we want education in Russia to move forward, if we want our territories to be settled, if we want vast cities to arise and for agriculture to flourish, then our first step must be emancipation of the peasants.

Speaking of America, however, we cannot fail to mention that in that country there also exists an institution similar to our serfdom. The enslavement of the Negroes in the southern states even involves cruelty which is unexampled in Russia. Yet it should be noted that, despite the harshness of laws and mores, [American] slavery does not generate economic consequences comparable to those fostered by our serfdom: 1.) slavery is limited to southern plantations on which a European cannot work since he cannot bear the sun's intense heat, a heat to which the Negroes have adapted by virtue of their physical makeup; 2.) Slaves in North America constitute a population that, [by comparison to the European population], is utterly alien not only in origin, but also in physical and intellectual qualities, whereas in Russia the serf population consists of the indigenous Russian populace, a populace that perhaps still harbors some of the best native characteristics and promises to display even more in the future. In North America, the European population is entirely free, and it is responsible for the miracles in the development of industry and general prosperity. Yet even in North America slavery is a most painful social wound, for ethically speaking, it is no less disgraceful than is our serfdom. Today the issue of slavery is leading to very great difficulties [in North America]; antagonism has reached the point that the union is threatened with dissolution, and who knows what may occur in the future. Comparable phenomena always produce similar consequences, regardless of differences in external circumstances.

Thus no matter what perspective we adopt, serfdom cannot be justified. We see that it is not only immoral and inimical to the established system of government, but it is harmful to the material welfare of the nation. How did such an outrageous institution come into existence in the first place?

We have already hinted at the answer. At the end of the sixteenth century, when ukases on the enserfment of the peasants were promulgated, the condition of Russia was such that enserfment was indeed necessary. Whereas in western Europe during the Middle Ages, tillers of the soil subordinated themselves to powerful feudal lords from whom they sought protection against rampant violence and thus became fixed to the land, in Russia the agrarian Estate, as a result of various circumstances, favored the wanderer's life to such an extent that the peasantry resembled more a nomadic tribe than it did an estate engaged in cultivating the soil. The peasants moved in droves from place to place; villages and country settlements arose, then were suddenly abandoned by their inhabitants; cultivated fields were transformed into deserts, and social instability reached its apogee.

Of course, the nascent government could not tolerate such a system. Among the prerequisites for state building are a settled populace, stability of social relations, and fixed responsibilities. The government needed material resources, and in the midst of general disorder its resources could only be meager. The government could not rely on the voluntary service of social Estates, for these Estates were too little cognizant of their civic responsibilities; it was necessary to compel the Estates to serve the state, and so the government imposed civic burdens upon them.

First, the government turned to the nobility and placed upon it the duty of continual service both in the military and civilian bureaucracy. Yet the state was in no position to compensate noble servitors by monetary payments. Instead, the state resorted to granting servitors landed estates [*pomestiia*], the income from which would support the service nobility. Of course, in order to obtain income from his landed estate, a noble had to have access to a labor force—something that was very difficult to obtain, given the sparseness of the populace and continual peasant migrations. Thus the government had to secure for the nobility the possibility of concentrating on state service; meanwhile, the nobility needed to secure peasant laborers. The first objective could not be achieved without the second, and so the government willy-nilly was compelled to prohibit peasant migrations. Furthermore, the government needed money, which it could gather only from the peasants and from those engaged in commerce. Given the land's lack of market value, the only source for tax revenue was labor; land was cultivated for a year, then was turned back to fallow, so it could not be a basis for collection of taxes. The government wanted to calculate tax burdens on a per capita basis, but how could it locate an individual taxpayer who moved constantly across the land, who lived God knows where, who fled from the arms of the law? To secure its financial base, the government had to fix taxbearers to the land: and the people so enserfed were peasants and traders. Finally, internal migration was an obstacle to state security; the eradication of brigandage, the establishment of order in the realm also required the enserfment of the lower classes.

It must be admitted that, at the time, this measure was useful and not at all unjust, for all social Estates bore civic burdens; each Estate had its own onerous duties, which it had to discharge in accordance with its prescribed role in society. Of course, a more developed legal code might have established more appropriate juridical relations between landlords and peasants, but one cannot make the same demands in a less enlightened society that one can make in a more enlightened one. Old Russia knew no juridical distinctions; it understood citizenship as total subjection, without any limitation whatsoever. A citizen was a slave of the sovereign, an enserfed peasant could only be the slave of his lord. And such he became; two quite different legal concepts—enserfment to the land and personal slavery—were gradually conflated, and little by little the social Estate of peasants merged with the Estate of slaves.

Thus passed a century and a half. During this period the state achieved conspicuous successes. Under Peter the Great's potent leadership a rationally designed state apparatus took shape, a state possessing significant financial resources and yielding nothing in its might to the other European powers. The education implanted by the government began to yield fruits, the budget grew, a standing army was established, the government was properly organized and extended its jurisdiction to the most distant spheres of public life. The state no longer needed to require continual compulsory service from social Estates; a more liberal system of government appeared. In the middle of the eighteenth century Peter III and later Catherine II granted the nobility a charter freeing it from compulsory service. Catherine also granted a charter to the merchantry, whom she relieved of service burdens. Logically the same should have been done for the peasantry: if the nobles were liberated from their service to the tsar, then by rights the peasants should have been emancipated from service to their lords. In fact, we have reason to think that under Catherine a charter to the peasant Estate was actually drafted; at any rate, in several passages of the *Complete Code of Laws* there are references to such a charter, as already existent. The prohibition against entering the enserfed Estate shows that the government considered serfdom to be harmful to the state. Yet nothing came from this. The reason is unknown. Modern Russian history is shrouded in such darkness, because the most important sources are inaccessible, and because it is prohibited to write the truth. Not only did the peasantry not receive a charter like those granted to other Estates, but the Ukrainian peasants, who heretofore had been free, were also enserfed, while in Russia itself a great number of state peasants were given as serfs to imperial favorites who had risen to high government posts by unworthy means.

This was a crying injustice, one which deprived serfdom of its legitimacy. In Old Russia the burden of service fell equally on all Estates; all carried duties, however onerous, that were necessary for the grandeur of the Russian state. Modern Russia lifted this burden from the upper Estates but placed a double yoke on the lower Estate. "On the shoulders of poor people lay all the burdens of the realm," said one of our most noted legislators. In fact, in Russia the poor answer for everyone else. They bear the ultimate responsibility for paying the head tax, since pomestiia are immune from taxation; they also shoulder the burden of the liquor taxation system, the second-most important source of treasury funds; they are torn away from their homes and families in order to serve the state in the difficult and unrewarding capacity of soldiers; finally, they satisfy all the demands of the nobility. In addition to the serfs' obligation to cultivate the nobility's land and to serve the nobility in person without compensation, the expenditures made by the nobility for the sake of the state or for their own needs usually fall upon the serfs and are collected from them along with the head tax. In truth, peasants in Russia today are what French peasants were in the eighteenth century: *la gent taillable et corvéable à merci*—that is, a class of men created in order that money might be squeezed out of them. Nobles serve when it is most advantageous and convenient for them, and if they do not wish to serve, then they relax on their estates, they amuse themselves in the district capitals or go abroad, heedlessly spending money earned by the sweat and blood of the peasants. But when someone mentions the abolition of serfdom or even a certain limitation on the lord's power, immediately cries are heard that this will mean a popular rebellion, that this is the inspiration of the liberals, that this means the confiscation of property and the ruin of the nobility, the primary support of the throne. "Support" apparently connotes not those who stand beneath the throne, who bear its burden and grow exhausted under its weight, but the elites who enjoy the fruits of others' labor.

But injustice never occurs without consequence. The entire civic life of Russia has come to reflect the profound injustice done the peasants, who are bound to the lord in a dependent status from which they should have been liberated long ago, and who bear the entire burden of state services and taxes—a burden that should have been equally divided among all Estates. Having permitted injustice to permeate its own institutional structure, the government has become inured to it. Respect for rights, respect for the rule of law, which even in the absence of serfdom was not really native to the Russian character, has now become quite foreign to it. Justice in social relationships and in the law is out of the question. Governmental arbitrariness surprises no one and is considered a virtually normal aspect of public life. We look with indifference upon the most disgraceful official acts, and everyone hopes only to circumvent somehow the burdens that the law imposes upon him. The nobility, which controls a class of people without rights, is in turn without rights and without voice before the government. Being the most educated Estate in the realm, the nobility might play a vital role in public issues and strive to defend justice and the law throughout the state, but what noble can raise his voice in behalf of justice when he himself is a defender of the greatest injustice, a defender who takes advantage of a false civic position?

In many arenas of action, the improvement of public institutions is impossible because serfdom stands as an insuperable obstacle. Shall we speak about the establishment of a proper financial system? We immediately run into serfdom. As long as serfdom exists, it will not be possible properly to organize recruitment of soldiers or to support retired soldiers; neither will it be possible to shorten the term of military service or to advance common soldiers to officer rank; for how can a former serf be a true comrade-in-arms to his master when the serf's closest relatives remain completely under the master's power? Shall we ask for freedom of the press, something that is essential for the spread of enlightenment? But uncensored journals and books will discuss serfdom, and who knows what kind of troubles and turmoil they may provoke? Shall we mention our judicial institutions, our civil and criminal codes, or measures to promote industrial development and popular education? Everywhere serfdom stands as the central obstacle to the realization of justice and good, as an eternal reproach to our conscience.

Serfdom's harm to the realm does not end here, however. It has also left its impression on private life, and it is reflected in our national character. Heretofore the seigneurial mentality [*barstvo*] has been a distinguishing feature of Russian life. A landlord lives surrounded by numerous servants who do nothing and are absolutely superfluous. That which in other countries requires the efforts of one man to accomplish requires the efforts of ten men in Russia. Idleness and negligence are the fundamental traits of the household serf. The masters themselves understand this, but what can they do to remedy the situation? To turn over a sponger to the army or to send him back to the village is cruel, and not everyone is fit for the army anyway; to free the sponger is out of the question, for freedom is a reward and one cannot reward the negligent while punishing the diligent. Willy-nilly the lords find themselves forced to maintain many superfluous people and, in order to make some use of them, the lords try to manufacture all items of necessity on their estates. Of course, home production is both qualitatively and quantitatively inferior to goods bought at market; in effect, if you take into account the cost of supporting the workers, domestic production cannot cover its cost. Meanwhile, it is an obstacle to the development of free industry. Noble landowners are the only well-to-do class in the provinces, and insufficient demand on their part can mean failure for a properly organized free industry. For this reason, the number of conveniences in the provinces is absolutely negligible and the whole tenor of life is semibarbarian. In order to get something out of his serfs, a landlord must constantly resort to compulsion. Everyone knows that without the birchrod you can accomplish nothing on your estate, and yet the birchrod leads to the harshness of morals that prevails all around us. A man who is accustomed to using the rod in dealing with his own serfs is difficult to restrain from treating free peasants in the same fashion. To whip someone is considered a sign of boldness, such that this is praised even by people belonging to the so-called educated class. In general, nobles treat people from the lower classes like animals of an entirely different species from their own. Nobiliary conceit, which is so irrational and deleterious to public life, has its roots in serfdom. A noble knows that he is a noble—that is, a man who by birth is destined to live off the labor of others—and therefore he considers doing his own work to be a dishonor to himself. How indeed can a petty landowner condescend to undertake any commercial endeavor or work that would put him in personal dependence on another person, when he has two or three souls who are obligated to serve him their entire lives and whom he can whip with impunity, as much as he may desire?

It is not surprising that a lord, finding himself in such circumstances, should become lazy, careless, extravagant, incapable of serious work, proud and vain, servile toward his betters, and vulgar toward his inferiors. All these traits are a direct consequence of serfdom. For his part the peasant, who even under the ancient yoke of oppression has not lost all his good qualities, has also become as lazy and careless as the lord, secretive, crafty, and empty of any appreciation for his own moral worth. Without doubt, serfdom has contributed much toward the utter disappearance in Russia of the sense of the moral dignity of man and citizen, and without this sense of dignity men lack noble aspirations, are incapable of energetic activity, and lack respect for the rule of law and for justice. The servants' quarters are schools of falsehood and corruption for the children of the nobility. In a word, one may say that the subordination of one Estate to another corrupts both public and private life, prevents any improvement in them, perverts the national character and paralyzes all forces in the realm, both material and moral.

In light of serfdom's tangible impact on the state and the people, what is the government doing? The government apparently understands that the situation is deteriorating, unjust, and deleterious, but its actions unfortunately manifest neither a clear understanding of the problem nor sufficient energy to resolve it. The government adopts half-measures that irritate by turns both noble landowners and peasants and increase the antagonism between them. At first the government thought it could achieve its objective simply by persuasion alone: a law concerning obligated peasants was promulgated, and landlords were invited voluntarily to introduce a new set of legal relations between themselves and their serfs. But to the eternal shame of the Russian nobility, everyone was indifferent to this invitation save for a few magnates who wanted to win the sovereign's favor. The main objection to the voluntary manumission of serfs was that, as a result of poor organization of the rural police, the punctual performance of contractual obligations [by freed peasants] could not be guaranteed to the landlords. Yet according to the law, the person chiefly responsible for sorting out disputes between landlords and peasants is the district noble marshal; moreover, the head of the rural police, the district police superintendent, is selected by nobles of that district. Obviously, the objection was simply a pretext covering up selfish calculations. The real problem is that the Russian nobleman, like Russians in general, will do nothing for the public good unless forced to do so. In him the sense of public duty and justice has died out, so that the government's measure had no impact whatsoever.

Then the government changed its tactics: it began to publish new legislation intended to limit the landlords' authority in certain circumstances and to grant certain rights to peasants. Unfortunately, these measures were so ill-conceived and ineffective that neither goal was attained and everything remained as before.

It is well known that existing legislation is so poorly drafted that, under its cloak, a landlord may commit all sorts of abuses. Peasants are ostensibly permitted to have property, but there is no legal protection of this property, for a peasant cannot bring suit against his master. In addition, the latter is permitted to force the peasants to pay every conceivable variety of obligation, monetary or in-kind, without limit. Consequently, it is obvious that if a peasant has property, this property does not reside with him as a right, and that the peasant's entire stock of possessions belongs to the master, who may dispose of them at will. Therefore even government agencies recognize, in accordance with the spirit of the existing laws, that the peasant's property is the lord's. After this, what is the point of other regulations intended to protect the peasants from oppression—as, for example, the law limiting labor obligations to three days per week? What is the point of limiting labor obligations to three days when the landlord can demand four days' work or can simply require performance of some other service? Every landlord has the authority to transform a field serf into a household serf, and the landlord can force household serfs to cultivate the fields, to work seven days a week. There are small settlements where all the peasants work in the fields in return for monthly allowances of food, clothing, and cash. True, the imposition of extra labor has its risks, but intrepid masters sometimes resort to maneuvers of this sort. Finally, even when a seigneur openly flouts the law by forcing a peasant to work four or five days a week, the latter cannot rectify the situation. The peasant's complaint has no legal force: the authorities have the discretion whether to follow up on it or not, and the authorities are always on the side of the powerful. The authorities' chief concern is to maintain discipline in all social relations; they are afraid that deciding in the peasant's favor will inculcate in the peasants a spirit of willfulness and disrespect for authority, so the landlords are always in the right. Furthermore, the law makes proof of violations extremely difficult: peasants' testimony against the landlord is not accepted as valid, and to find outside witnesses is hard—so in most cases a proper investigation is impossible to conduct.

Thus neither property nor the labor power of the peasant is guaranteed by law against the landlord's arbitrary will. By the same token, the peasant's person is also unprotected. If a landlord is found guilty of cruel treatment, then the law permits his estate to be placed under trusteeship. But cruel treatment is a very imprecise term, and how can it be proven? Moreover, the decision to place an estate under the administration of a trustee is made by the assembly of noble marshals and deputies, and they will always protect a member of their own Estate. Appeals courts and agencies of the central government exceed even the nobility in their determination to uphold seigneurial authority, which in their eyes is a crucial element in the existing political system. Therefore even the most flagrant evidence of cruelty, such as bodily wounds, is rarely taken into consideration, and those peasants who make complaints are handed back to the master, who sometimes receives only a warning to be more careful the next time. Naturally, the fate of these peasants is most unenviable.

This system could not help but attract the government's attention. In order to place some limit upon the limitless arbitrariness of the landlord, the government promulgated a law that a seigneur may not inflict more than fifteen blows on the peasant at one time. But to whom will a serf turn for justice if this law is violated? And who investigates how many blows were in fact received? Clearly the only result of a complaint will be that the dissatisfied peasant will receive even more blows than before. Besides, the law does not prohibit the seigneur from beating the peasant in intervals—for however long it may please him and for whatever reason. What is the point of such statutes? It would be better not to publish them at all.

The same can be said about the law permitting peasants to acquire immovable property with the master's permission. The peasants' rights are still not defensible under the law, and their property depends as before upon the favorable disposition of the lord.

Finally, in order to provide the peasants a chance to free themselves, they received the right to purchase their freedom when an estate is sold at auction. But here, too, the right is a complete fiction. The purchase period is so brief that peasants have no possibility of paying any kind of significant sum. This statute only deepened the serfs' desire for emancipation, so the government, which became frightened at its own act, hastened quietly to repeal the law. Nothing significant could have come from this law anyway. Apparently, however, in 1848 more substantive measures were being prepared by the government. There were rumors that a decree on emancipation of the peasants had already been signed; people grew anxious at the news. But at this very moment revolutionary troubles broke out in western Europe, and although in Russia these events could not have had any impact, the government thought it necessary to put aside the business [of emancipation]. Under the influence of irrational fear, the government sought in the nobility a support against democratic movements, and for the nobility's benefit it repealed even the law on [voluntary] redemption of peasants. However, the alarm was temporary. When everything calmed down, the idea of eliminating serfdom reappeared, and there were efforts to implement it, but on a piecemeal basis. At first, [landed cotenancies or] inventories were introduced in the southwestern provinces, then in Belorussia and Lithuania. Yet here again the government acted precipitately. The issue was not thoroughly discussed; interested parties were not invited to offer their views, and the last inventories were so restrictive to seigneurs, who were deprived of a third of their labor force, that the government, yielding to the seigneurs' complaints, finally abrogated the arrangements. Yet discontent among the peasants intensified; it was a mistake to deprive the peasants of rights so recently granted to them, and today inventories introduced in these provinces are tailored to respect all the interests of the landlords, who were finally invited to offer their views on the matter. For this reason the interests of the peasants did not receive proper attention. Below, when we examine different means of emancipating the peasants, the shortcomings of the inventory system will be indicated; here we shall note that, in general, the inventories were drafted without a clear understanding of the existing situation and without any thought of their long-term implications. They lack principles upon which long-term legal relations between lords and peasants can be based. They are limited to piecemeal regulations, often ill-defined, confused, and self-contradictory. The inventories doubtless were a step forward, and we must be grateful to the government for this step, but this was a timid and far-from-satisfying step.

Meanwhile, the result of all these measures was to inculcate more and more into the peasantry the idea of freedom. The peasants' former patriarchal relations with the seigneurs disappeared long ago, with the exception of a few out-of-the-way places that still observe ancient mores and customs. At present the [seigneurial] father and his [peasant] children are no more; instead, there is a violent master and unfree laborers. The number of peasant protests increases annually; to suppress them in recent years the government has had to resort on several occasions to military force. Last winter the whole of Petersburg was horrified to learn of the murder of a certain member of high society by two household servant boys, who voluntarily sacrificed themselves for the sake of their fellows. Several years ago a titled seigneur was whipped by his serfs, an example repeated subsequently more than once. Every convenient pretext, every false rumor is used by the peasants as an excuse to disobey the master and to run away even from those lords with whom they are content. In the reign of the Emperor Paul the government already abolished the peasants' loyalty oath because peasants interpreted this oath of allegiance to the sovereign as a liberation from seigneurial authority. At the beginning of the Crimean War, during the levy of personnel for the navy, the peasants flocked to enlist, even though they were not forced to do so. This year, during the general levy of military personnel, the government distributed a circular to churches intended to raise popular enthusiasm for the defense of the faith and the fatherland. State peasants, among whom the patriotic spirit was not so high, remained calm; but privately owned serfs again rushed in crowds to volunteer. They did not accept the notion that if they served, they would remain serfs—so the government was forced to cancel its circular. Thus the most critical measures taken for the defense of the fatherland remained without effect because the government feared that such measures would disturb the peasants. What if—perish the thought—the enemy managed to penetrate into the very interior of Russia and the entire people had to rise up as one in order to defend the fatherland? Since 1812 relations between landlords and peasants have significantly changed, for today the peasants will not so eagerly rush into the field of battle behind their masters. Finally, it should not be forgotten that Pugachev found his main source of support among privately owned serfs, even though serfs were then much more tightly bound with the lord than they are today. And as long as the preconditions for an uprising exist, who knows whether Pugachev's times might not return? This is a terrifying thought that should force each one of us to reflect.

It should be apparent that this question has reached the stage where its resolution is essential. The longer we delay a resolution, the worse will become relations between these two Estates, and who can foresee how things will end? It is also clear that half-measures will not do, that, while [the government must approach] with care and attention rights, customs, and interests implanted centuries ago, it must nevertheless act firmly and energetically. Otherwise, instead of establishing more appropriate relationships, there will ensue disorder that will shake the very foundations of the realm.

But how can such contradictory interests be reconciled so as not to offend either side? Many people are convinced that the emancipation of the peasants is a necessary step, but they consider it so difficult that it probably cannot be taken without compulsion, or indeed without a bloody outcome. We shall attempt to indicate the basic principles that should guide the resolution of this problem, and to draw from them legislative regulations that are best suited to facilitating the achievement of the desired goal.

Serfs may be divided into two categories—peasants and household serfs. Originally, they constituted two separate Estates, but subsequently they were amalgamated so that a seigneur might arbitrarily shift persons from one category to the other. Nevertheless, heretofore they have preserved their defining characteristics, which are based not on their legal statuses but on the very nature of their Estates. Peasants occupy and till the land, while household serfs perform personal service for the lord. An intermediate category between them is occupied by peasants working in industry who do not cultivate the land and who use proceeds from their industrial work to pay money dues [obrok] to the master. For our purpose industrial peasants can be assigned to the category of household peasants, because the fundamental criterion in the matter of the emancipation is control of land, and nothing else. Let us analyze each category individually.

Peasants occupying the land must be considered in terms of their original status as individuals bound to the land, rather than as the lord's personal servants. True, since they were originally bound to the land, they have been transformed into personal servants, but, aside from arbitrary actions and exactions by the lord, this status of personal servant, which can be legally abolished without any compensation to the lord, means only that peasants can be transferred to another piece of land or into household service. For those on the land, relationships with the lord remain as before and consist essentially of the following: the lord concedes to the peasants a part of his land in return for their cultivation of another part and in return for their execution of certain duties connected with the land's cultivation. If one adds that these relations are maintained by coercion, then one will have defined the central fact of the position of those peasants who perform mandatory labor. Peasants who owe money dues to the lord differ only insofar as they cultivate the land for themselves and must pay their dues out of the proceeds. History leads us to look at the question from this perspective, and this perspective in no way works to the disadvantage of the lord, for we leave out of account only those arbitrary rights [usurped by the lord], and disregarding such rights does not affect the essence of present relations.

Peasant agriculturalists may be emancipated in three ways: 1.) one can legally abolish serfdom without any compensation to the landlord. One can return to him full possession of that part of his land now tilled by peasants, and the peasants can be turned into free laborers. 2.) One can juridically define relations between lord and peasants and make them cotenants of peasant land. This is the approach of our inventories. 3.) One can give to the peasants the right to purchase from the lord the land that they now occupy, and thereby turn them into free tillers of the soil, full owners of their own parcels of land. Let us examine each of these proposals in turn.

If we recall our point of departure and return to the original relationship between peasants and seigneur, then the peasants' personal emancipation without compensation to the seigneur will strike us as entirely justified. The lord permitted peasants to use part of his land in exchange for their cultivation of the remainder, or he gave them the use of all his land in exchange for a certain annual payment. But these arrangements were imposed by force. As soon as coercion is eliminated, everything reverts to the original situation: the peasants will return the land to the seigneur and will become free. The lord will lose nothing, for the land formerly in the peasants' use will now revert to him, as compensation for the loss of their work or the dues they formerly paid to him. The lord receives something equivalent to that which he surrenders. If in certain cases peasant labor may be worth more than the value of the land returned to the lord, then this is an exceptional circumstance to which the law cannot pay attention. The main thing is that justice be done in fundamentals. The landlords themselves recognize this principle; many would agree to liberate peasants without land and not to demand compensation, for this would be a measure applied uniformly across the nation and they would have no reason to fear a shortage of laborers. Only unexampled greed can make a seigneur demand that the peasants pay for land being returned to him. The law cannot do so, for if it demanded compensation, it would be treating field serfs as household servants, even though those Estates are functionally distinct, each having its peculiar origin and peculiar relationship to the lord.

If this method of emancipation seems superficially just, it nevertheless presents insuperable difficulties that compel us to reject it. We know several examples of peasant liberation without land: in England it was accomplished long ago; in the Baltic provinces it occurred recently. The results were identical: terrible impoverishment of the lower stratum of the populace. In England this impoverishment led to the Poor Laws, which devoured countless millions, millions which only England was able to afford; in the Baltic provinces the authorities tried to ameliorate poverty by setting long-term leases of land and by creating peasant banks. In either case, the problem of impoverishment is a real one and its cause is clear. The stratum of the population that otherwise would have settled on the land and tilled the soil was made homeless and itinerant.

A defining trait of the industrial Estate—of commercial and factory workers—is mobility. This Estate depends on labor and capital, and, in response to changes in commerce and the market, its members move wherever they can find the most advantageous situation. These market fluctuations, these contingencies, offer a resourceful person many opportunities to improve his material circumstances, saying nothing of the broad prospects that industry offers to those with skill and inventiveness. But the industrial Estate resides mostly in cities where industrial enterprises are concentrated, where means and resources are greater, where it is easier to find work and to sell goods and where it is relatively easy to shift from one occupation to another should the former prove disadvantageous.

The position of the agrarian Estate is quite different. Here economic opportunity exists to a much smaller degree, there are almost no advantageous situations that suddenly present themselves, the occupation itself is much more monotonous and demands much less skill, competition is not developed to such an extent as in the city because landowners are dispersed over vast distances, and the worker does not have at hand the possibility of choosing more advantageous work. In addition, all agricultural work revolves around the land. From land the farmer receives sustenance and his every means of livelihood; to it he is bound with his entire being, and with sadness he is separated from his native soil. The land is something immovable, unchanging, and this character it stamps upon the agrarian Estate, just as capital, being essentially mobile, communicates its essence to the workers who seek in it the basis of their labor.

It follows that the agrarian Estate should be settled, while the industrial Estate should be mobile. The entire well-being of the agrarian Estate is connected with hearth and home, with a parcel of land, and, once deprived of these things, the peasant falls into destitution. This is a general rule that applies particularly well to Russia, where expanses are vaster than elsewhere, where agriculture is the chief, if not the exclusive basis of the national economy, and where the agrarian Estate comprises three-quarters of the population. Among the members of this Estate are twenty-two million serfs. To release such a quantity of people to wander the earth, to sunder their connection with the land that has fed them, to deprive them of their homes and to entrust their fates to the accidents of the labor market and to the whims of wealthy landowners would be sheer madness. To act in such a fashion would be to return Russia to its medieval way of life, to erase from its history two and a half centuries of serfdom, the real significance of which was to create a settled populace. Such a step would undermine all the bases of national welfare and national power, which depend primarily on the agrarian class, and would cause unparalleled turmoil in national life. For twenty-two million people, forcibly uprooted from the land to which they are so intimately connected, would certainly not remain pacific.

Peasant renting of seigneurial land would not ameliorate the problem, for the seigneur could always drive the peasants from his land and transform them into workers. Moreover, long-term and stable ownership of the land is a precondition not only for the peasants' welfare but also for the success of agriculture. Only a landowner or a long-term tenant can treat the land as it should be treated, can make economic improvements that will bear fruit over time. A short-term tenant, trying quickly to extract everything possible from the land, will exhaust the soil and will avoid improvements that might bear fruit only for someone else. For this reason, in those countries where the land is in flourishing condition, such as in England, land leases to farmers generally run for terms of ninety-nine years, and often on a hereditary basis. But such arrangements should not be adopted in Russia if we want free labor to cultivate our land. English lords do not involve themselves in farming, but receive an income from it. They see landownership not so much as a source of wealth but mainly as a means to support their political position. Our landlords, being themselves mostly active farmers, care only to receive from the land the largest possible income, and therefore they will not wish to transfer their land into alien hands. If we mention in addition the primitive and insecure state of Russian agriculture, whose methods can still be significantly improved and which in several years may yield even greater incomes than today; if we add the continual growth of purchase and lease prices of land, then it will become clear to us that no landlord will agree to rent his land for a century, much less transfer it to a peasant on a hereditary basis. In order to facilitate agricultural successes, in order to guarantee the peasants' welfare, we must abandon this first plan of emancipation and consider a second plan, according to which peasants will become cotenants of the land in their use.

As noted earlier, this approach served as the foundation for the earlier laws on obligated peasants and on inventories. The land remains the eternal and inalienable property of the seigneur, the peasant becomes its eternal tenant, and, in exchange for use rights, the peasant either performs for the landlord various labor duties established by law or defined by voluntary agreement, or he pays a certain annual fee. Such a system involves two innovations vis-à-vis serfdom: the seigneur is prohibited from forcing peasants off the land, and arbitrary relationships are replaced by legally defined ones. It would seem that this is the very least that can be done. No one has ever objected that such regulations are unjust; instead the problem is how to enforce them. Seigneurs assert that once they have surrendered land to the peasants, they will have fulfilled once and for all their obligations in relation to the peasants, yet the peasants' demands will have no end. Seigneurs complain that under the rules imposed by the government there is no reciprocity, for the seigneur is deprived of the right to turn the peasants off the land when the peasants fail to perform their duties. Having no real authority, the seigneur is unable to make sure that the law is carried out, especially given the sorry state of our rural police. According to the seigneurs, these complexities can only work to the peasants' advantage, for the peasants have nothing to lose and much to gain, whereas the lords' position will be insecure and defenseless.

It must be admitted that though these objections contain a kernel of truth, they also are exaggerated. If the chief judges and mediators of disputes between lords and peasants are marshals of the nobility and local police superintendents, then the question is not how the lords will compel the peasants to perform their legal obligations, but rather how to defend the peasants against seigneurial oppression. Selecting judges and arbitrators from their own midst, being wealthy, having more resources than the peasants, the lords will always hold the advantage; therefore, from this perspective their objections are groundless. It is true, however, that, given the set of rules imposed by the government, peasants and lords will become embroiled in endless difficulties and misunderstandings, which doubtless will lead to more inimical relations between them and cannot help but harm agricultural production. This may be a necessary evil, from which there can be no escape. Rectification of a completely abnormal situation such as the one created by serfdom cannot occur without difficulties of some sort, and so a seigneur whose land is in long-term use by peasants must experience a certain discomfort. Perhaps the lord would prefer to have absolute authority over the peasant, but how would this strike the peasants? Today the whole burden of mandatory obligations falls on them, while after the introduction of a set of legally mandated duties, this burden will be divided between the peasants and the lords—which is only right. Unless we begin by limiting seigneurial authority and replacing existing seigneurial-serf arrangements with governmentally regulated relations, we shall not succeed in ending serfdom.

But a statutory definition of the relationship between lords and peasants cannot itself foster a normal relationship between them, and from this perspective the objections against the establishment of a common right of land use are completely justified. Normal relations between an employer and worker, between a property owner and a tenant should be completely free and should be defined by voluntary agreement. This is the basic precondition for the contraction of any obligation, the precondition of success of every variety of industrial enterprise. After voluntary agreements are concluded, all difficulties and misunderstandings that arise subsequently can be resolved in a simple fashion:

namely, by annulling the original agreement—something that cannot be done when obligations are externally imposed by law. Imposed statutory obligations will generate endless discontent, leading to the most petty litigation and ultimately to continual government interference in the private sector—a prospect that is intolerable. And what kind of government wants to preside over two Estates constantly antagonizing each other? Such a solution is acceptable only temporarily, as the necessary cost for overcoming a still greater evil, as a step leading to the natural development of mutually free relations. But to make of it a fixed, unchanging norm can only be classified as the height of absurdity.

It must be added that this measure falls far short of satisfying the peasants' needs. An inventory system is a step toward emancipation, but not emancipation itself. Peasants will remain subordinated to the lord and will be compelled to work, although arbitrariness in work assignments will be eliminated. Under this system a peasant cannot change his social Estate and seek more advantageous work, he cannot alienate his land; yet he must be able to do both if the entrepreneurial and civic spirit is to develop and if equity is to be introduced in the realm. As long as the lord can coerce the peasant, the latter will be a victim of social inequity; for justice requires that Estates equally bear the burden of taxation and equally share in civil liberties. The particular prerogatives of Estates may differ, depending on their importance and status in the realm, but why should a peasant sitting on seigneurial land not enjoy the same personal liberty enjoyed by a state peasant, a small trader, a noble, and a merchant? The law should never permit considerations of equity to slip from view; otherwise, it will undermine its own foundation.

For industry and civic life the harmful consequences of coercion are obvious. The success of industry and civic life depend on the freedom of the individual to take up that occupation that is most advantageous to him and in which he can best make use of his talents. The free transfer of land to the owner who can extract the most use from it is also essential. In general, freedom in the private sphere is the first and most essential foundation of developed industry and of civic life. One may even claim that personal freedom is the fundamental precondition of any life deserving the title of human. In the light of the past, coercion in the private sphere appears to be an inevitable historical misfortune which nations temporarily endure for the sake of attaining higher ends; such coercion can never remain the norm for any enlightened state. A government dedicated to the common good must recognize this and must strive to eliminate those institutions which cannot be reconciled with equity, enlightened standards, and the common good. For this reason we argue that the statutory definition of relations between lord and peasants falls short of the government's ultimate objective, that it marks a step toward real emancipation, not the completion of the emancipatory process.

While we recognize the limitations of imposed statutory norms, we nevertheless consider their introduction to be beneficial. We must therefore analyze the premises that should inform a law limiting the lord's authority, so that the law may be as equitable as possible to each party.

Earlier we asserted that a proper perspective on this question suggests that peasants should receive from the lord a parcel of land in return for the cultivation of another portion of land for the lord's benefit or in exchange for a fixed monetary payment. This is the basic relationship between lord and peasant, a relationship not debasing to either party; all the other elements of the relationship are arbitrary. For this reason everything extraneous to this basic relationship must be strictly prohibited. Among the prohibited actions are the following: 1.) transfer of peasants to another piece of land; 2.) transformation of field peasants into household serfs; 3.) assignment of peasants to nonfield work; 4.) compulsory assignment of peasants to factory work, which is outside the normal sphere of peasant activity and is therefore just as arbitrary as transformation of peasants into household serfs. The law can permit only such nonfield work as does not escape the sphere of normal estate and field occupations, such as cutting firewood, digging the earth, transporting various items for the lord's domestic use. Peasants may do agricultural labor on the lord's behalf, not extraneous industrial activity, for which the lord may hire them as free laborers. 5.) All arbitrarily assigned exactions, monetary or in-kind, which are nothing but mechanisms for the arbitrary exploitation of the peasants, must be abolished. 6.) The rights to exile peasants and to assign them as recruits to the army must be eliminated. The basis for military recruitment should be either one's place on the government recruitment list or in a lottery; the lord must not be able to interfere in the recruitment process. The same should be said concerning payment of treasury obligations, a matter that does not concern the lord. Government warrants to collect arrears or to confiscate goods should be issued only with the lord's knowledge or consent, for in this case the government's demands may conflict with the peasants' proprietary obligations to the lord. 7.) The lord's right to settle civil disputes between peasants must be abolished. This is a matter falling under the jurisdiction of elected communal officials and does not concern the lord. 8.) The same should be said of the right to impose punishment in any case where there is no injury to the lord. If a peasant fails to discharge his duties toward the lord, then the lord should have the right to punish the peasant within certain limits, but only in the presence of elected village elders and only when the offense and punishment are duly recorded in a manual of discipline, which the peasant may use as a basis of complaint to higher authorities if he is unjustly punished.

All these limitations on seigneurial authority logically flow from the substitution of subordination to the land for subordination to the person of the lord. Meanwhile, our inventories are far from satisfying these requirements. In certain circumstances they permit the transfer of peasants to another piece of land, the transformation of field serfs into household serfs, and the assignment of serfs to factories. They give the lord the right to oversee collection of taxes, a right that can lead to no good, for the lord himself does not bear tax obligations and cannot bear responsibility for tax arrears. Finally, as far as the lord's rights to judge peasants and impose punishments are concerned, these are not limited at all under the inventory system. Even the rare restrictions found in earlier inventories have been eliminated in the newest ones. All this reveals the lack of a clear perspective. The absence of a guiding principle is obvious everywhere, and leads to the oddest contradictions. The law aims to regulate by statute the relations between peasants and the lord, yet it simultaneously says that the former must remain in complete subordination to the latter. What does this suggest? It is virtually a mockery. Once a set of statutory norms is established, then the peasant must be considered a free person in everything bearing no relationship to the legal duties imposed upon him. There can be no question of complete subordination [to the lord], for the law is replacing this with subordination in certain well-defined circumstances. Otherwise, there is no point to the new law.

Thus only those measures we have enumerated, taken together, can eliminate all vestiges of the lord's arbitrary authority. The elimination of this arbitrary authority will be most useful, for, given its current scope, this authority exceeds the limits of equity and brings no advantage to the lord. The next step is to determine the quantity of land under the peasants' control and the extent of their duties to the lord. Here the legislator should be guided by the existing situation, for a significant change cannot be made without detriment to one party or the other; in approaching this problem, the government must bear in mind that in transforming property arrangements it assumes a very grave risk. When the issue under consideration is arbitrary rights, then there can be no question of compensation to the seigneurs; any right unfairly enjoyed by the lord is canceled by the abolition of serfdom itself. But the lord's legitimate property rights must remain inviolable and cannot be taken away from him without proper compensation. For this reason the law must take as its point of departure the status quo: the quantity of land in the peasants' use before the introduction of the inventory should remain at their disposal afterward. Only in exceptional cases, where as a result of an abuse of seigneurial authority there is a marked discrepancy between the amount of land tilled by the peasants and that tilled by the seigneur, may the government resort to corrective land redistribution. To deal with such cases, the government should determine the normal ratio of peasant to seigneurial land in each province and district, and may correct any egregious deviation from the norm. Otherwise, the current ratio of property use should remain unchanged.

For the same reason, the quantity of labor done by the peasants ought not to change. The law defines three days per week as the normal quantity of working days which the peasant is obliged to devote to the landlord. Thus it should remain. But scheduling of the days should not be left to the lord's arbitrary choice, for that would be too disadvantageous to the peasant. For this reason the law itself should determine the order of peasant days and seigneurial ones, while leaving to the parties the right to make changes by voluntary agreement. That is how the earlier inventories worked, but the latest ones do not contain this provision—a serious shortcoming. Other useful provisions eliminated in the latest inventories are regulations according to which working days are defined by certain set tasks. This is advantageous both for the peasant, who can more quickly perform the assigned task, and for the lord, who is also guaranteed against peasant laziness and negligence. This perfected means of assigning labor has recently been introduced on some privately owned estates, and so it cannot be ignored. It would be even more useful to substitute monetary payments for personal labor duties, or to substitute an in-kind payment of grain for a certain number of working days. Such a system would benefit both lords and peasants. The former would possess a sure income in place of working days, on which, especially in winter, they do not know what work to assign. The peasants would be completely emancipated from seigneurial authority and would be able freely to allocate their own time. Moreover, both parties would be spared the inconveniences arising from coercion in their mutual relations. Of course, a peasant may sometimes be unable to pay [the lords], and the lords may fear that in certain localities they may not have enough free laborers. Therefore, deviations from the norm should be permitted by voluntary agreement of the two parties.

But that is not enough. A law based on the status quo will give the lord everything that is his due. Once serfdom is replaced by land relations based on statutory regulations, it would be unjust to permit the lord to take advantage of an increase in the size of the labor force. As a result of this measure, the peasant will become personally free from seigneurial authority; he will be responsible for discharging only certain legally specified duties, and he will discharge them from income generated on the land he cultivates. The number of land parcels given to the peasants will be determined by the quantity of laborers at the lord's disposal. Both quantities must remain fixed. If a new household forms and no parcel of land is available on communal land due to a reduction in the number of old households, then members of the newly formed household should naturally receive the right to seek alternative employment. A lord may settle the new household unit on his own land, but not without concluding a voluntary agreement defining the responsibilities of the new tenant to the landowner.

Finally, it goes without saying that if under the new inventory system the peasant should be treated not as a serf but as a legally recognized individual having certain responsibilities—that is, as an individual having certain obligations vis-à-vis the lord but who is otherwise free—then certain rights should be returned to the peasants which, as serfs, they could not enjoy. Among these rights are: 1.) the right to marry without the consent of the lord; 2.) the right to bring suit in a court of law and to give testimony in person; 3.) the right to sue the lord himself when a complaint, brought by the peasant to the district noble marshal, remains without satisfactory resolution; 4.) the right to leave the land at will, so long as the departing peasant supplies a substitute laborer to take his place during the period of absence. These rights are enjoyed by all the other Estates and must be returned to the peasant as soon as his complete subordination to the lord is terminated.

These are the chief measures that should be taken with a view to emancipating the peasants. But the law should not regard the inventory system as fixed and unchanging. It is only the first step toward the establishment of normal relations, and normal relations can take shape only following the adoption of the third proposal mentioned above as a means for emancipating the serfs.

The third proposal consists of the redemption by the peasants of those land parcels which they now occupy. Against this proposal none of the objections made against the first two proposals applies. The peasants' well-being will be guaranteed by landed property; they will be completely emancipated from seigneurial authority; neither common tenancy on the same piece of land nor the element of coercion in the private sphere will engender the endless difficulties, arguments, and hostilities of the kind that today provoke continual governmental interference in private affairs. The condition of the agrarian enterprise will be quite normal: the lords will constitute a class of more or less well-to-do landowners; they will be surrounded by small property owners, who, having much free time, will hire themselves out to the lords to cultivate fields or who will themselves rent seigneurial land. A portion of these small property holders, especially in provinces where land is densely populated and parcels are small, may not be able to subsist by cultivating their own parcels or may have no land at all; in these places they will settle on seigneurial land or will live on estates as hired laborers. Free relations, voluntary conditions of work will become everywhere the norm, while agriculture and the peasants' prosperity doubtless will significantly advance.

Prosperity of the people and of the agricultural industry is a very desirable end. One may only ask if it can be reconciled with the demands of equity. Will the mandatory confiscation of land from its present owners not constitute a violation of the right of property ownership and the destruction of the seigneurial class? On the other hand, will the peasants, given their current poverty, be able to redeem their lands?

Concerning violation of the proprietary right there is nothing that can be said. If we apply natural notions of equity, then no one can deny the peasants the right to that land to which they were bound by force, which for two and a half centuries they have cultivated with their own hands, and which comprises for them the sole reward for enduring all the burdens of serfdom. Today they sit on this land, but they may be driven from it at any point. An inventory statute making of them hereditary tenants on their land parcels also gives them a certain right to these parcels, although the parcels formally remain the lord's property. But this joint tenancy should be eliminated for it leads to endless disputes and difficulties. In whose possession will the land remain? Natural equity suggests that it cannot be granted to the lords who possessed it by virtue of legal writ alone, but to the peasants who, as a result of centuries-long tenancy, have invested in it a part of their being. The peasants have cultivated it, and to them it must belong. It has been irrigated with their own blood and by that of their fathers; here lie the bones of many generations of their ancestors, and to deprive them of this good, acquired by centuries of labor and suffering, would be the height of injustice.

On the other hand, if we attempt to base a solution of this question on strict reading of the existing law, we shall discover that the right of property always yields to the needs of the realm. If the government needs to build a road or street through private property, then it does not need to acquire the consent of the property owner. According to the letter of the law, it may confiscate this land for its own purposes and is obliged only to pay fair-market value to the owner. Can a highway or railroad be more important to the realm than the welfare of twenty-two million citizens? It may be objected that, in the first case only a small amount of land is confiscated for the road, whereas in the second case the property of an entire class of people is being taken away. But if this objection is valid, then how can the government even begin to think about emancipating those peasants who are the chattel of noble landlords? Shall the government wait for the lords' consent? The state cannot afford to admit such an objection. The point is that, from a legal perspective, the scale on which a principle is applied is irrelevant; if something is equitable on a small scale, it is also equitable on a large scale. The greatness or smallness of scale is not a matter of equity but only of the relative impact of the change. Therefore it will not do to claim that a certain act is justified on a small scale but unjustifiable on a large scale; one can only argue that in the one case the harm done is insignificant, whereas in the other case the harm may be very considerable—that is, in the one case the landowner hardly feels the loss, whereas in the second case he may be ruined.

But even this last objection has no force. One might well point out that the economic might of several hundred thousand individuals must not take precedence over the welfare of twenty-two million citizens who bear the greatest part of the national tax burden and who are unjustly subordinated to the higher Estate. Moreover, having granted the nobility freedom from compulsory service obligations, the government may rightfully demand that the nobility grant a corresponding reward to the peasantry; therefore, if the government finds that the emancipation of the peasants with land is advantageous to the state, then it may implement this measure even if it causes significant losses to the seigneurs. In reality, however, significant losses will not occur. When the government introduces transitional measures establishing joint land tenancy and imposing appropriate rules to regulate relations between lords and peasants, the equity and necessity of which no one can doubt, then the lord's right to land that he neither cultivates nor controls will appear as simple fiction. This "right" will be seen to rest on the letter of the law alone; depriving the lord of this right cannot cause him significant economic injury, for he will receive compensation based on fair value. In fact, the alienation of this land will be very beneficial to the lord, not only in comparison with the inventory, but even in comparison with the current operation of his estate. Today the lord gives the peasants a portion of his land in exchange for their cultivation of the remainder and their help in running the estate. But it is apparent that when serf labor is utilized, there is always a significant loss due to laziness, negligence, and the peasants' lack of skill; moreover, unlike hired laborers, serfs must be supported the year around and therefore must be fed even during periods when it is useless to do fieldwork. Furthermore, as we noted above, today the lord is in no position to keep proper accounts, and, in the absence of such, significant economic losses will accrue to any enterprise. Finally, the lord bears all the responsibility for governing the peasants, who are not always obedient; he must guarantee their well-being, provide alms in case of need and food in famine years. All these factors must be considered in drawing up a balance sheet of the advantages of serf labor. It must be admitted that the enumerated disadvantages lend considerable weight to the case against serfdom. It should be added that today seigneurs do not have in hand sufficient capital to apply to estate improvement. Like it or not, the lords must compensate peasant laborers by giving them land, for there is no money, and there is an abundance of land. Moreover, capital is a necessary element of any rational farming operation; it is something without which agriculture cannot advance a single step. The shortage of capital is mostly attributable to the primitive condition of agriculture on seigneurial lands.

To ameliorate these problems, it is necessary to perform a relatively simple operation—namely, to liberate the peasants, to sell to the peasants that portion of land now in the peasants' use and outside seigneurial control, and to apply the capital proceeds [from the land sale] to estate improvements and to the hiring of free laborers, whose labor is much more productive than serfs' labor and whose labor will save the lord from all these superfluous problems and expenses. This can be accomplished by emancipating the peasants with land, for the fair value of which they must compensate the lord. The lord will not only not be ruined by this operation, but will receive a significant increase in income as a result of better organization on his estate, and also he will benefit from an increase in the price of land. Already now in the central provinces, those estates with no serfs attached sell for the same price as those with serfs, despite the difficulty of finding free laborers. What will happen after the peasant emancipation, when the labor market and the number of free laborers will multiply, and land will be sold free of all the encumbrances of serfdom?

The same considerations apply to estates where the peasants are paying annual monetary dues, but here the transition to emancipation will be even simpler. Today the lord on such estates already has [borrowed] capital against his land, the interest on which is in most cases paid unfailingly by the peasants. After the abolition of serfdom these payments will cease and the capital will be returned to the landlord to spend as he may wish. Where is the economic loss and impoverishment here?

Thus the case that the landlords will be harmed by the emancipation is groundless. A much more important objection is that peasants will be unable to redeem the land with their own resources. This obstacle would even be insuperable if it had to be overcome at once. But there is no reason to demand that the peasants immediately pay off the redemption sum. The first step is to make a fair estimate of the land's value and then to permit the peasants to pay this sum as they are able; the peasants' emancipation would not occur until they had compensated the seigneur in full. In the meantime, the peasants would be governed by rules of the inventory system, which govern the transition to complete liberty. Without doubt, both peasants and their lords will try to hasten the final payment, the peasants because they will receive their liberty and title to landed property, the lords because they will prefer to sell peasant lands and to hire free laborers rather than to deal with workers who are half-free and half-serfs. For its part the government can render significant assistance to the peasants without incurring a great loss for itself. The government should: 1.) establish a peasant depository bank, in which peasants may deposit annual collections from the commune toward paying the redemption costs. Interest would accrue on these deposits, and therefore the balance of funds would grow until it reached the desired figure. At that point the money would be transferred to the lord, and the peasants would receive full liberty along with the right of ownership of the land. Because this financial operation is intended solely for the public good, the government should renounce any use of the funds for its own purposes. Instead of the 4 percent interest usually paid to state creditors, the government should pay 5 percent—that is, the amount it usually takes from its borrowers. 2.) The government should create a peasant credit bank to assist the poorest peasants, who without loans would have to wait too long to secure their liberty. 3.) The government should transfer onto the peasants a part of the debt owed [by landowners] to the Trust Council, and, if necessary, the entire debt, and should credit this amount toward payment of the redemption sum. A large number of noble estates are mortgaged to the Trust Council, and mortgage debt is a great burden to the lords. By transferring this debt to the peasants as a credit against the redemption payment, the government will make it possible for the peasants to emancipate themselves quite easily, and the peasants for their part, since they no longer will have to perform duties for anyone else, will be able to pay the Trust Council the annual interest [on the mortgage principal]; the need to pay this interest will also force them for a longer term during their free time to seek work from the noble landlords. It is very likely that the peasants will occasionally default on these payments, but what will be the significance of even significant defaults compared to the enormous and obvious benefits accruing to the state? The state has for so long and in so many respects taken advantage of peasant resources and peasant labor that perhaps it will now make a certain sacrifice in their behalf.

Against this arrangement there is only one argument: that if the government today makes an estimate of land value and permits the peasants to pay off this amount over ten or twenty years, then the lord will lose the entire profit accruing from increasing land value over this period. But legislation cannot take into account this hypothetical future profit. A statute must be based on the existing circumstances and should only take care not to treat inequitably either party. Otherwise, there is no hope of reconciling antagonistic interests. If the lords start to demand compensation for hypothetical future profit, then why can't the peasants demand monetary compensation for past inequity? Simply because they were forced to be silent in the past? But past silence is no evidence before the law. In order to put an end to all pretensions, the law has but one recourse: to take as a norm the existing situation and to make its directives accordingly. If a future rise in the price of land may benefit the peasants, it is also true that a decline of land prices will benefit the lord. Even assuming a rise in land prices, on estates where peasants now perform labor obligations the lord will profit, for as prices rise, both on peasant lands and seigneurial lands, the total gain in assets will be divided between the two parties. And the very elimination of serfdom will, as pointed out earlier, facilitate an increase in the price of seigneurial land, and so it will also compensate [the lords] for the loss of land to the peasants. Finally, legislation might take the following perspective: from the time inventories are imposed, the law may consider peasant parcels already alienated from the lord, but the peasants will continue to work for the lord until such time as the debt [accrued from the land transfer] is retired.

In any event, the landlords' position will be no worse as a result, and the peasants will be emancipated little by little, without conflict and turmoil. Some will purchase their liberty and their land more quickly, others more slowly, depending on their resources and their circumstances. The necessity of paying off their debt through labor and the prospects of future rewards for their exertions will awaken in them activity and energy, and the intermediate condition between freedom and slavery will make this transition imperceptible. The legislation will have done its deed by permitting the peasant to move at his own pace. Whether the emancipation is accomplished over a more or less extended period is unimportant, so long as it has an equitable and solid foundation and so long as the government and the people move consistently and deliberately toward their well-defined, shared goal.

However, some people will be dissatisfied with this outcome. Such people may be found even among those holding high political office, among the state's leading officials. Blinded by the spirit of the most absurd conservatism, they claim that dividing the land among a vast number of small proprietors will serve to institutionalize democracy and will lead inevitably to turmoil and to popular government. Although the superficiality of this objection is apparent from the the first glance, that neither hinders its spread nor refutes it.

The real question is whether to free the peasants or not. If not, then their patience will ultimately be exhausted and the existing order will lead us to one of the most terrible revolutions in human history. The lower classes who have suffered for centuries under the yoke of slavery will rise up, and, instead of avoiding popular government, we will have to confront an uprising and perhaps even the triumph of democracy, but a democracy of the most savage and ungovernable kind. This is the unavoidable consequence of living under a conservative system, [for conservatism] always leads to consequences that are the opposite of what it desires. If [we] emancipate the peasants, then the question is: what is more advantageous for the state? To have within itself two Estates whose interests may be different but who are not constantly in conflict, or two Estates in constant antagonism as a result of legal constraints which they cannot escape? And if the latter cannot be permitted, then again, which is more advantageous: to have several million property owners or several million [propertyless] laborers? The answer is obvious. Laborers are the main supporters of all rebellions. As a mobile mass, which has neither stable connections nor associations and which has nothing to lose, the propertyless comprise the most democratic element [in society]. On the contrary, a property holder, always anxious about his property, fears disturbances most of all. This is especially true of landed property owners, who are tied to the land and who love stable, unchanging circumstances. They are the most conservative element that one can imagine, and so the state, which also seeks stability in institutions, must inextricably link its own interests with the interests of the greatest number of landed property owners.

If this proposition is true in general, it is especially true with respect to Russia. It would be hard to find someone less capable of democratic government than the Russian peasant. Democracy requires constant initiative, activity, and commitment from each member, and all these qualities the Russian lacks. The Russian peasant is the most submissive person in the world; only when driven to extremes will he come out of his meekness, and then he may well act like a wild beast. But leave him in peace, give him his own little corner, his own parcel of land which he loves more than anything in the world, and you can do with the Russian peasant anything you wish. For this reason a government that gives the peasant his due—that emancipates him and guarantees his well-being—will find in him a solid and reliable support of its authority. The contrary can be affirmed only by advocates of a distorted conservatism, which proceeds from a false interpretation of contemporary western European history. Through this dark prism they gaze at the situation in Russia, and, not surprisingly, they spy God knows what spectres. In the present circumstances, however, one must point out that this conservatism originates not so much from obtuseness as from selfish calculations. So the government must not take it to heart. It should bear in mind a single goal—the public good. If the peasant is unjustly oppressed, he must be emancipated; if he is happy and tranquil only when he has his own piece of land, then the government should give him landed property. Moral sensibility, political utility, and the popular welfare all require such an action.

Having presented the principles that should inform the peasant emancipation and having outlined the main provisions of such a law, we now turn to the other category of serfs—to the household serfs and to those peasants who pay annual dues from their industrial activity. Here our task is much simpler because we do not have to deal with the element of land that complicates the whole question.

The status of household serf was not created by a legislative act of the government. Household serfs came into being from the ancient Estate of slaves, most of whom entered into voluntary servitude as a result of debts. Hence they were subordinated to persons rather than to the land, and so we should view them as personal servants of the seigneur. True, among them many were transferred by the lords from the ranks of the serfs, but it is impossible to distinguish the two groups, and it really is unnecessary to do so. Time and various laws caused them to merge together, and we should examine them in their present guise—that is, as members of a single Estate.

Here there can be no question of various methods of emancipation. Those in personal dependence may redeem their own persons only by compensating their masters for lost seigneurial authority and for work obligations. For its part the government should involve itself in the emancipation by fixing a sum of money, whose payment will serve the lord as a sufficient compensation and should therefore entitle the servant to freedom. For to permit this sum to be set by the lord himself would mean never to emancipate the household serfs and to create an avenue for the greatest arbitrariness and oppression. Naturally, the sum should not be too great and should be identical for all household serfs. Whatever may be the skills of the household serf, his talent is his inalienable property, and the lord has no right to demand compensation for this talent as is done in cases of voluntary redemption.

But regardless of how modest the sum may be, if the lord does not wish to free a household servant, and if he attempts to retain the serf in his personal service, then the serf will never be in a position to acquire enough money to pay this sum and therefore will remain eternally a servant. To avoid this outcome it will be essential to limit the lord's authority. The law should give the household serf the right to leave his master and to look for other work. And to guarantee that the lord will not be gratuitously deprived of serf labor, the government should fix the amount of an annual payment that the serf will be required to make until such time as he has discharged his total obligation. In case this annual fee is not paid, the lord should have the right to take the debtor back into his personal service, but only if the debtor cannot prove that the failure to pay was the result of extraneous circumstances. If the failure to pay was in fact the result of circumstances beyond the serf's personal control, then the debt should be rescheduled over several years; if the failure to pay was the result [not of penury] but of deliberate calculation, then the serf should be returned to the lord for a year or two, or for whatever term legislators consider fair. At the expiration of this period, the household serf would again have the right to leave the master, but not unless he can prove that he has found work that will enable him to pay the annual fee.

This measure will greatly facilitate the emancipation of the household serfs. It will also serve as a guarantee against cruel treatment, for a serf discontented with his master may always leave the master's service. However, here again the law should specify certain limitations on the lord's authority. It may even fix a yearly salary that the master will be obliged to pay a servant remaining in his service due to failure to pay the annual redemption fee. But these are all details, and there is no point in discussing them here; such details will be addressed in any piece of legislation that seriously attempts to deal with the problem.

Much more important is the assistance that the government may render to those household serfs who want to be emancipated. As in the case of the field peasants, this assistance should consist of the following: 1.) in the establishment of a credit bank from which the household serfs may receive money to finance their redemption. Security for the loans can be in the form of a declaration that the household servants have work that will enable them to pay the annual 4 percent interest on the capital borrowed. The treasury may compel those who default on these payments to enter its own service, and then may subtract loan payments from annual salaries, if this is feasible. 2.) For safekeeping and to facilitate an increase in the capital being accumulated each year by the household serfs, the government should establish savings banks in all cities.

These measures will secure the gradual emancipation of the household serfs. What of the peasants who now pay money dues earned from handicrafts? In essence, they suffer from one of the most unjust forms of serfdom. Here the lord gives absolutely nothing to his subject—neither the land that he offers the field serf, nor the room and board that he offers the household serf. The lord stands to the side and merely collects from the peasant a fee, fixed according to the peasant's capacity for labor and skill. The more intelligent and resourceful the peasant, the greater the fee he will pay. The larger part of the peasant's annual labor goes to pay this irritating tribute, in which the last kopeck is taken from the poor peasant in order to satisfy the caprices of the rich lord. When a peasant defaults on these payments, nobody takes into account mitigating circumstances and the guilty party is immediately sent off to the army as a common soldier. Yet this Estate [originally] consisted not of personal slaves but of peasant farmers. Over time rational relationships disappeared and gave way to purely arbitrary ones.

Unfortunately, the law cannot take as its point of departure the original historical circumstances [of this Estate] and treat its members as tillers of the soil, emancipating them personally without giving any compensation to the lord. If a historical perspective helps us to make better sense of [past] relationships that still basically obtain even today, it does nothing to advance the abolition of an institution hallowed by centuries. History never moves backward in order to correct an anomaly created by the slow march of events. Peasant industrialists underwent a gradual legal evolution from one status to another, so current legislation cannot pay attention only to the original status but must take into account the existing situation. To emancipate these peasants without redemption payments would be tantamount to gratuitously depriving the lord of legally acquired property consisting of the annual dues payment, and this cannot be permitted. The government must content itself with fixing the [annual] amount of dues payments and the total sum required for emancipation; as it did for household serfs, the government may establish loan and credit institutions for the industrial peasants. The only difference in regulations should be that, in case of default on a payment, an industrial peasant should not be compelled to do personal service to the lord, but at the lord's request should be forced to do corvée labor with the proviso that the corvée be governed by the same rules applying to obligated peasants.

With this we conclude our presentation of those measures that should be undertaken to abolish serfdom. In addition to the enumerated three categories of serfs, however, there are others. Industrial peasants may also farm small parcels of land, a situation that is encountered rather often. Sometimes use of the land may be the basis for the peasants' market activity, as, for example, in truck gardening and horticulture. There may be other circumstances, such as newly settled lands, that required special provisions. But analysis of these special and widely varied circumstances would lead us too far from our main subject. We may content ourselves with presenting the main principles on which the peasant emancipation should rest and the basic steps that should follow from them. Details and special cases should be left to the government's legislative process or to the lords' discretion, should they decide on their own volition to liberate the serfs. General regulations covering such special cases can be drafted only after gathering statistical data establishing the number of people falling into particular categories and also describing their exact circumstances. Only after having arrived at general rules can the law easily treat all the complexities that may arise.

We are now in a position to repeat the measures that a rational and enlightened government ought to adopt to purge Russia of the burden of serfdom.

1.) Publication of comprehensive laws limiting the power of the lord. Under this category are: a) prohibition of transferring field serfs into any other status—that is, settling them on other lands, transforming them into household serfs, forcing them to do work other than fieldwork, and compelling them to work in factories; b) prohibition of arbitrary requisitions from peasants; c) prohibition of seigneurial interference with peasant tax payments and with collection of money owed the treasury; d) banning seigneurial interference in civil disputes between peasants; e) elimination of the right of punishment except in well-defined cases, within well-defined limits, and according to established legal procedures.
2.) Granting the peasants those rights of which they were deprived as a result of serfdom, such as: a) the right to enter into marriage without the lord's consent; b) the right personally to bring suit and to defend themselves in

courts of law; c) the right to bring suit against the lord himself, if the [local] noble marshal fails to satisfy a grievance; d) the right to leave an estate, provided the peasant supplies another workhand during the period of his absence.

3.) The introduction of inventories defining the amount of land in the peasants' use and the duties which they must perform for the lord, or the annual fee which they must pay him, as well as determining methods of emancipating superfluous households.
4.) Fixing the normal value of peasant land in each province and district, so that, once the peasants have paid that sum, they may be considered completely emancipated.
5.) Establishment of credit and loan banks that will assist in the peasants' emancipation and transferring to these banks the debt of the Trustee Council.
6.) Permitting household serfs to leave their masters in accordance with the rules set above, and fixing for them and for industrial peasants an annual fee to be paid to the lord.
7.) Fixing for household serfs and for industrial peasants a normal redemption value.
8.) Establishing for their use credit and savings banks.

If such measures are taken by the government, then within twenty years Russia will rid itself of serfdom, while rendering the proper measure of justice to the affected parties without violating their interests. To introduce one measure, then another in a leisurely and timid fashion will not solve the problem. This will only irritate everyone and put the various Estates in a false position vis-à-vis one another. Here, as always, it makes sense to act decisively and energetically, moving toward a clearly enunciated objective. Of course, caution is essential, but caution should not consist of hiding the ultimate goal and of leaving everything in uncertainty; instead, it should consist in mature discussion of both parties' interests and of reconciling these interests as equity and the public good require. A government worthy of the title must not shrink from expressing its firm intention to accomplish a good deed. It must publicly declare that the peasants should be emancipated, and it should act in accordance with this conviction. The first step toward the emancipation should be the general introduction of inventories; this should be done after initially establishing provincial committees of lords and peasants in order to hear their demands and in order to understand clearly the existing situation. As soon as the inventories have been introduced, then other measures may be implemented, for these other measures will not significantly affect economic life, since final redemption will occur by itself, slowly and gradually.

Some people may object that if this course is followed, there will surely be turmoil and disturbances, that the peasants will refuse to obey the lord, and that even worse may occur. But who has ever witnessed a case where people are consumed by dissatisfaction when their plight is being improved and when an end to their sufferings has been promised? If peasants sometimes manifest their anger today, that is because their lot is too burdensome and their relationship to the lord too ill-defined. They seize on any convenient pretext to somehow break loose from their servitude. But as soon as they have rights and responsibilities clearly defined by law, as soon as they see their freedom ahead as the ultimate result of their labors and exertions, they will calm down, for they will have received the chance to achieve their goal through peaceful labor and economic activity.

The emancipation of the peasants has occurred in all the European states—and nowhere did this process generate uprisings except in France, where it occurred during the time of the revolution. If we also put off a necessary reform until a revolution occurs, if we also wish to drag our feet until even more antagonism and hatred have accumulated, then we surely will not avoid disturbances. Today the peaceful introduction of inventories in the western provinces shows that in Russia such a step can be taken without coercion and without uprisings. One should not be overly afraid of the peasants, and, in particular, one should not oppress them out of fear of a future uprising, for the peasants do not want to believe that the central government's real intention is to oppress them, which is why they now direct their hostility toward local authorities.

Let us add that seigneurs themselves have the power easily to avoid violent changes, for they may voluntarily emancipate their own peasants. Who is stopping them from voluntarily introducing inventories on their own estates and from adhering to the rules outlined above on the basis of mutual agreement with their peasants? We have striven to demonstrate that their own advantage should inspire them to do so. Only the prodigality of our seigneurs, their inability to keep accounts and the existence of ancient entrenched privileges prompt them to prefer the continuation of serfdom. Any change strikes them as a dangerous proposition, and they prefer to accept long-established routine and to take advantage of manifest injustice rather than to make the slightest effort to improve things. However, we hope that this apathy is finally disappearing. The recent war has shaken the Russian people, has awakened its long-somnolent spirit and has turned its attention to public affairs. At last our nobility may come to understand what justice and the palpable interests of the realm require of them. They will see that that their responsibility is to act in the common interest, to help create a realm that is strong and prosperous, that is founded on the just and free relations of the citizenry.

Or will we remain deaf and dumb?

Contemporary Tasks of Russian Life

In the lives of individuals and of peoples there are moments when, shaken by unexpected events, they seem to awaken from a long slumber, look around themselves and arrive at a clear understanding of their situation.[1] Such a moment has arrived for Russia. For a long time we assured ourselves that our fatherland is great and powerful, and we carelessly followed the course which the government set for us. A few thoughtful individuals realized with sorrow where we were headed. They saw how, under the influence of a faulty system of administration, the state itself was becoming corrupt; how all the foundations of civic life were gradually being undermined and destroyed; how all the forces [of our national vitality] were collapsing; and how the people were condemned to stagnate and grow dull in mute bondage. These individuals saw that we were imperceptibly drawing near an abyss, and suddenly the abyss opened before our very eyes. Unexpectedly, like a flash of lightning, a crisis burst upon us [in the Crimea], and in that moment, animated by the danger to our fatherland, we surveyed the scene and we began to see that a faulty system of government had undermined the might of Russia, that we had neither the personnel nor the technical means to defeat our foreign enemies, and that all our efforts would remain futile, given the corruption that had spread throughout the social organism.

The hour of reckoning has come. The voices of preachers, poets, and journalists call us to repentance. We all have become aware of our internal blemishes and shortcomings, although perhaps not everyone understands clearly whence they originated and how they contributed to our general misfortune. The time has come to explain these matters to ourselves, and, having devoted ourselves to introspection and having gathered our strength, to cleanse ourselves of corruption and set out anew with a rejuvenated spirit and a rational self-consciousness.

Our plight is difficult and dismal to contemplate: from abroad we face a terrible threat, the *levée en masse* which we are in no condition to match, while at home there is universal disorder and disintegration. Everywhere there is lawlessness, everywhere oppression, everywhere complaints and dissatisfaction. Nowhere in the public realm is there a gratifying development that one might survey with satisfaction and from it derive reassurance. There was but a single city on the periphery of the realm [Sevastopol] where all the heroism of the Russian people was concentrated, and which, by its courageous defense, redeemed the disasters of a difficult era. But even this city fell at last in its unequal struggle. Despondency spread everywhere and the future came to seem, if that was possible, darker than ever before.

How did we come to this humiliating pass? How could young and powerful Russia fall into such desperate straits?

Let us turn to the past and try to find in it the key to comprehending the present. Let us examine the natural conditions under which the Russian people have developed, what are their traits, what is their history, and then we will perhaps better understand what kind of turning point the people have reached and what may extricate them from their current, sorry plight.

The territory of Russia extends over the immeasurable distance from the Black Sea to the White and Baltic Seas in a monotonous steppe interrupted only by large rivers and, in the North, by broad lakes. On the steppe there are no mountains, only insignificant, hardly noticeable eminences that are lost in the vast flatland. The sparse population is sprinkled over the plains; villages and cities lie enormous distances apart, the roads are often barely passable, and there is no link between the various towns. Yet on the other hand, there are no natural barriers to divide the population and facilitate their coalescence in separate, closed alliances. Everything is dispersed across a vast space, nowhere finding a natural concentration. Rich soil easily yields food: a man does not have to work hard and contend against nature. There is nothing demanding exceptional activity and the straining of mental and physical energies, there are no striking vistas or natural phenomena arousing the imagination, no variety for developing different aspects of the human spirit. Man seems lost in the vast steppe; he lives under the influence of monotonous nature and a limitless terrain that awakens in him an urge to wander like a nomad and a boldness that has no direction.

In such a milieu the national character took shape. The Russian nation is not composed of discrete elements, each living its own life and bearing its own peculiar stamp; it consists of a more or less homogeneous mass, dispersed across a vast area. Only Ukraine, separated from Russia as a result of historical circumstances, seems to be a discrete entity with its own characteristics. Furthermore, this homogeneous mass, dispersed over limitless territory, is nowhere concentrated. In it there are no central points that draw together scattered interests and facilitate the people's development and progress. Natural conditions led to the formation of a vast realm, but there are no tight social connections between the whole and its parts, no vital and closely woven relationships promoting human activity and constituting the life of society. The populace, scattered over the plains, lives under the influence more of natural determinants than of social ones. In Europe there is therefore no people in whom the civic spirit is so little developed as among the Russians; everyone lives aloof from everyone else, and no one troubles about common needs and interests. A Russian does not gladly leave that private sphere into which birth and environment have thrust him. He loves the nomadic life but not concerted activity. Being naturally talented, he may outdo and outperform others, but these moments are rare, evanescent flashes. In general, a Russian does not move untiringly forward, but does everything haphazardly, by chance, accidentally and lazily. He does not know how to create from his own resources an intellectually multifaceted world, and he does not tear himself away from the influence of his surroundings. In him the force of custom and tradition is astonishing; it is amazing how he uncomplainingly and humbly submits himself to the sovereign authority he recognized centuries ago.

These traits clearly suggest that the Russian character is more passive than active. But this passivity makes a Russian quite capable of accepting foreign influences, and when he is once forced to step out of his usual rut, he may easily, and with the same extreme devotion, submit to the new, just as earlier he clung stubbornly to the old. It is no wonder that under such circumstances he did not develop a multifaceted culture, he did not develop fully his talents in the fields of science, art, industry, and elegance of manners. Another factor in the development of the Russian character was Russia's distance from Rome, which passed on to Western nations the age-old achievements of the ancient world. The Russian people took from Rome the Christian religion, but accepted it, so to speak, in a pagan fashion. The Russian man did not assimilate Christianity's abstract spiritual content, its separation of the spiritual from the mundane, nor did high philosophical questions occupy him; Christianity did not prompt him to engage in indefatigable activity for the sake of his neighbor. No, he accepted mainly the external, ritualistic side of Christianity, which became for him just as strong a tradition, just as sacrosanct as other centuries-old customs. Trivial rituals became for him more important than substantive truths; from smokers of tobacco he turned with revulsion as from apostates; the change of a letter in a book became the basis of the most important schisms. And to this day among the people pagan rituals survive, so mixed up with the Christian as to be indistinguishable. It is sufficient to point to marriage and other rites, still practiced today as the fresh, eternal flowers of popular life.

Of course, given such natural circumstances, given such a national character and the estrangement of Russia from the ancient world, Russian history could not be as rich in great phenomena as the history of the West. But the Russian people are capable of developing; they belong to the family of European peoples, and, despite all their peculiarities and the utter modesty of their historical achievement, the Russian people have developed parallel with the Europeans. Patriarchal life, based on blood relations, prevailed originally in both the East and the West. But no tribe submitted so profoundly as the Slavic tribe to this natural form of organization. Its residual effects are still felt among us. On the other hand, no tribe was less able to move beyond the patriarchal life by means of internal differentiation and to create from its own resources new forms of social organization. Whereas in the West loyalty to the feudal prince [*druzinnoe nachalo*], along with the related concepts of personal freedom [*lichnost'*] and voluntary associations, developed organically, for us it was an alien notion. Patriarchal society was shaken by an influx of foreign influences, and when its internal insolvency finally showed, the Slavic tribes proved incapable of creating new forms of civic organization. To do this they needed to rely on an external authority, so they were forced to summon the Varangians, their old enemies. They left it to the Varangians to rule over them and to establish order.

This remarkable event, which has merited the attention of all historians, clearly demonstrates the passive qualities of the Slavic tribe and the inability of patriarchal leaders to unite themselves in an alliance based on their own forces and activity.

The Varangian princely retinue finally destroyed society based on the clan, and little by little replaced blood ties with voluntary alliances based on the will of individuals. But as we have noted, the principle of individuality [lichnost'] was unable to generate a rich culture or [to serve as a foundation for] significant social agglomerations. Torn from their natural social moorings, individuals plunged themselves into the nomadic life, and it was then that began the chaotic popular nomadism that characterized the so-called appanage period. Everyone—princes and boyars, servants, merchants, and peasants—surrendered to nomadic impulses; they all moved about the entire expanse of broad Russia, nowhere stopping to settle, nowhere shaping solid and durable forms of social organization. Even the free cities of Pskov and Novgorod, where social life was more developed, were examples of such disorder as could rarely be found elsewhere [in Europe].

Princes were the first to settle down, and, by so doing, they became the true founders and builders of the Russian land. Chaotic nomadism could not continue; order was needed, and so there appeared sovereign princes [*gosudari*] who arrogated to themselves political power, gradually reduced the scope of nomadism, and finally compelled the nomads to submit to the state's authority. There was no protracted, spirited resistance [from below], but it was hard to force the wandering masses to settle down and assume permanent obligations. Everyone fled from his place: the boyars fled to Lithuania, urban tradespeople [*posadskie*] and peasants fled from the lands to which they had been bound. It was no easy matter to establish a [modern] state in the Russian land. Ivan IV had to arm himself with all the fury of a dread king, Boris Godunov had to employ all the guile of a clever politician in order to put an end to nomadism. But the sovereign princes had barely managed to introduce a certain order when all the downtrodden elements again rebelled and broke out of it. The Time of Troubles arrived. Pretenders, boyars, Cossacks, slaves, peasants, Polish and Russian hordes—all wandered across Russia, roaming everywhere without a goal, without a plan, without rational design of any kind. But this was already the last festival of the old way of life; the people had grown sufficiently mature to prefer living in a modern state to chaotic wandering. Moreover, the Time of Troubles threatened the very foundations of national identity—the Russian nationality and the Orthodox faith. Invasion by foreigners was a bitter experience for Russians. The people rose up, this time of their own accord, without compulsion from above and, after a desperate effort, expelled the Poles and selected their own tsar. Afterward, the people again sank back into their lazy and submissive state, trusting their future fate to the government they had established.

The first Romanovs reintroduced order, but it soon became apparent that to rule in the old way was impossible, that a strong state cannot survive without thought and enlightenment. Before Peter the Great, Russia succeeded in elaborating a rudimentary form of social organization; now was the time to add rationality and proportion to this system—to enliven it by thought. So Peter the Great turned, as a pupil, to the Western peoples, the guardians of thought and enlightenment. The Russian tsar donned a sailor's jacket in order to serve the cause of [secular Western] education, which he wished to transplant into his fatherland. This great and noble enterprise demarcated a new direction in Russian history; since that time, secular education has spread and become ever more important in Russia. The Russian people are now part of the European family and are one of the peoples governing the course of historical events. Russia's external power has grown remarkably; domestically, the realm has developed and become stronger—a army and navy have appeared as if by miracle, the resources of the treasury have multiplied, education has spread, and there has appeared a literature in which talented individuals display their gifts, glorifying the Russian name. Whereas earlier the government was the source of all social institutions, of all measures for order and improvement, so [under Peter the Great] it now again led the new movement and fostered education. The government compelled Russians to study grammar and forcibly implanted on virgin soil science, art, industry, new manners, and customs. But it was also evident that the Russian man easily submitted to foreign influence; once having been forcibly divorced from ancient prejudices, having set off on a new course, he completely enslaved himself to the new way; he disavowed his old identity, borrowed a new language and customs, Frenchified himself, and, with a frenzy, now persecuted everything native, everything that earlier had been thought sacred. On one hand, the lower classes, which the reform did not affect, remained a stubborn negation of the foreign; on the other hand, the higher Estate transformed itself into a senseless negation of everything Russian, and, of course, in its still childish stage of development, it at first adopted only the superficial trappings of Western life and only later, little by little, did it investigate their rational content.

This quick glance at Russian history is enough to demonstrate that the government has always been a driving force in our development and progress. The Russian people, given their passivity, were not so constituted as to develop on their own initiative, without the state's interference, a multifaceted culture. The government led the people by the hand, and the people blindly followed its guide. For this reason there is no nation in Europe where the government is more powerful than ours. At no time in Russian history have the people posed a real threat to our government. The government should have fought harder against ignorance, stupidity, centuries-old and deeply rooted customs than it did against [the prospect of] serious, energetic opposition [from below]. The government's actual enemies were the seditious boyars, the wandering Cossacks, the ignorant defenders of the past. But the boyars had no roots in the people and could oppose the tsars only by secret intrigues and regionally based cabals; it was easy to deal with the Cossacks by instituting a standing army, while the devotees of the old ways [the Old Believers] could act only by silent and dull opposition and not by open force. There were only a few free cities; with one of them [Novgorod] there was a short struggle, but another [Pskov] surrendered without murmur. It was not so much independent centers and alliances that interfered with governmental activity as it was the absence of social connections, the universal disorder, and the enormous distances that made difficult the extension of the central government's power. But as these obstacles were overcome, the government's importance increased. With the growth of the population, with the establishment of stable social relationships, with the development of the state apparatus, with the growth of the government's resources, obstacles collapsed and the government grew stronger and stronger. Today it is stronger than ever before: an enormous army submitting to the state's desires alone, an enormous bureaucracy spreading across the Russian land and everywhere carrying out the center's decisions and orders, a universal uncomplaining submissiveness taught to us by centuries of Russian history—all these factors make the government's power limitless and unconditional. Any criticism is immediately silenced, any complaint crushed, any whim [of the sovereign] may be carried out in the most distant parts of the empire.

The government's great power is also the source of its vulnerability. There is no surer axiom in politics than that the state must never act with too much persistence. Statecraft is nothing but a series of uninterrupted compromises. Its secret consists in knowing how to reconcile various demands and interests of society, in satisfying each as far as others will permit and thus establishing universal unity, in integrating these demands and interests into an overall plan based on the entire society's welfare. Only by such activity can the government attain real strength, for through it the government will generate support everywhere. Once having received its legitimate due, every social interest becomes a defender of the established legal order and of the government. But if the government, proceeding selfishly, stubbornly supports one social interest and ignores all others, it will inevitably go to extremes, alienate its popular support, and arouse dissatisfaction. Precisely by seeking to make its social foundation unassailably strong and durable, it will undermine this very foundation. Superficially it may look ever more formidable, but in fact it will grow weaker, for in the process of acquiring the external trappings of greater authority, it will lose its base of support.

This is an inescapable axiom which must be borne in mind in governing any polity. But if, as a general proposition, each social interest, each substantive demand deserves an appropriate hearing, it is all the more crucial never to ignore the totality of needs and interests constituting popular life. The government and the people—these are the two basic elements of which any polity is composed. Each has its place and each must have the freedom of activity requisite to it. The people compose the body politic, but the government is the head and master. The former live and act, give birth to various designs, demands, interests; the latter makes coherent this varied activity, fosters harmony in society, prevents one set of private goals from interfering one with another, facilitates their development, and ultimately makes the people aware of what is good for the whole. But political unity does not have to develop at the expense of diversity. Governmental activity must not preclude the autonomy of the people, for popular autonomy is a basic precondition of public life. Of course, the government cannot permit a particular interest group to take up arms against another and to compel it to behave in a certain way, for this would be to legalize anarchy; yet to harbor and express views and demands different from the government's views and demands should be a people's legal right, for without it the people will lose all autonomy and forfeit all political significance. Every social interest around which individuals coalesce must live and develop in its own way, according to the laws of its own nature and not according to standards imposed from without. To develop properly it needs freely to express its grievances and its attitude toward the existing governmental system. Only then will it be able to assume its appropriate place in popular life. For the government to establish norms of behavior and opinion and to bend everything to these norms, to render the people voiceless and silent before the government, is to kill in the people any life and to destroy one of the fundaments of society. The suppression of popular activity by the government is the suppression of diversity for the sake of unity, the substitution of a dead machine for a living organism, the substitution of external forms for the inner development of social forces. For, once having suppressed the people's autonomy, the government itself will inevitably become a mere external form and a dead machine. Only from the people can it draw spirit and strength and life. The people live as autonomous subjects, and it is for their sake that the government itself is established, having no other purpose than to promote the common welfare. The people are that very society for whose sake all governmental institutions exist. Why deprive the people of [the opportunity to] participate in their own affairs?

To do so would obviously contradict good political sense. Both elements [the government and the people] should function side by side; they should help one another and should collaborate in working for the common public purpose. For this reason the dominance of either the government or the people always has deleterious consequences. As soon as one begins to outweigh the other, society experiences discord; a reaction sets in and there commences a historical process tending to restore the requisite equilibrium. The entire political life of states consists in the interaction of these two elements, in the eternal search for balance between them. History presents us with an edifying spectacle that all those governing the fates of peoples must study, for a short-sighted, thoughtless concern for the present alone will lead rulers to ruinous delusions. Within such a narrow perspective, transient concerns may appear to be vitally important, while great historical forces that have developed continually over centuries may seem to be matters of relative insignificance. Only study of the past can provide us the key to understanding the present or can afford us the possibility of divining the future. Let us see what that greater teacher reveals to those attentive to her voice.

If we turn to the origin of the history of contemporary societies, to that period when, having abandoned their original patriarchal structure, they began their historical lives, we see the almost total dominance of the popular element. In the Middle Ages the state as such did not exist, governmental authority was almost nonexistent, social ties were to the highest degree unstable and capricious. But this extreme circumstance engendered a powerful countervailing force. Lacking government, the people were but a chaotic mass subject to the reign of unbridled arbitrariness. Instead of relationships based on mutual benefit and justice, there prevailed the right of the strong; the majority was trampled under the feet of mighty personalities. Endless civil strife was ignited and anarchy ruled, universal and unbearable. [Strife and anarchy] generated a historical reaction, a movement to establish government that would introduce order and peace. The desire to avert endless troubles created a reaction against fractiousness and anarchy. The modern state arose, and history's main agenda became the gradual development and strengthening of the heretofore missing element in society—namely, the government. Anarchy diminished, order was established, the state apparatus was constructed, the government's resources were augmented, the authority of political agencies increased. The popular element became more and more secondary, and the government became ever more powerful.

Yet this dispensation also went to an extreme. Accustomed to following its own plan, the government began to consider itself a surrogate for the rest of society and to lose sight of society's other constituent element. The people became completely estranged from participation in public affairs. Every popular murmur was suppressed, and the government's voice alone filled the general void. At that point discord became evident in society; again it became apparent that there was some kind of important shortcoming, that the fullness of life had disappeared, that something essential was lacking in society. Everything became unstuck. No matter what measures were taken, they proved useless, for between legislation and its implementation there was a vast gap. The government became essentially powerless, and among the people dissatisfaction was reborn.

This is the situation in which we find ourselves today. Since the fifteenth century our state has evolved and the government's authority has grown; but only in our time has it reached an unbearable extreme. In Muscovite Russia popular life was not so restricted as it is now. At that time there was such disorder in both society and in government that the government was shackled hand and foot. With every movement it felt its own impotence. It could neither learn of social problems nor undertake any successful action [to remedy them] without the people's cooperation, and it was constantly forced to summon land councils [*zemskie dumy*] for advice on the management of public affairs. Individuals found it easy to avoid not only oppressive authority but also their legal obligations. They simply resettled themselves in other places, and, given the existing chaos, it was impossible to pursue or to find them. Entire communes not infrequently made use of this freedom. If cities or villages found too onerous the authority of an appointed governor, they simply sent money to Moscow and obtained for themselves favorable charters that freed them from the burdensome administrator. It even happened that junior officials, without authorization [from the central government], changed superiors, and this was thought to be nothing unusual. Government was so distant and so weak that it could not resolve justified complaints and had to allow all kinds of license and disorders.

Peter the Great's reforms put an end to all this. The state had built itself up and now ceased to tolerate the unauthorized actions of junior officials as well as exceptions in the general rules of administration. But the government had not yet acquired the kind of dominance [over national life] that would have made it oppressive to the people. The government's attention was directed toward general public concerns; it was building the army and navy, stimulating industry, implanting education. Citizens carried heavy responsibilities for the sake of Russia's greatness, but the government did not intrude into everyday life. Citizens did not ceaselessly confront some administrative body set up to supervise their every action. Authority gradually concentrated itself in the center, but in the provinces people still lived freely and easily, worrying little about the authorities. The government was thought something distant and glorious, something raising Russia's might and lifting high the fatherland's banner. On the throne Russians saw the genius of Peter, the liberal wisdom of Catherine II, and they embraced the throne as the source of the fatherland's glory and prosperity.

In the nineteenth century everything changed. The age-old process of state building finally completed itself: the administrative apparatus, gradually extending itself from its trunk like a tree, pushed its branches into every region of the country, while centralization crowned the whole edifice and made administration the obedient tool of a single will. The new bureaucratic machine enabled government power to flow unhindered like a stream from center to peripheries and to return from the peripheries to the center. Now humble citizens saw the government close up, face to face. The administrative apparatus grasped us from all sides, and the more it expanded itself and branched out, the more restricted was popular activity. The government was all-encompassing, dominating everywhere, penetrating everywhere, and the people grew ever weaker and finally shrank before it. Today it is impossible to take a single step without bumping into some official, without seeing in front of oneself a manager, a director, a supervisor. On every street one meets a policeman or gendarme; on village roads, where formerly one never saw official uniforms, now rings the bell of the district police officer. And this does not occur without harm. For the humble citizen is powerless and voiceless before the most petty official, who to us is not a defender and protector but a person completely foreign and, in addition, most vile. We find ourselves narrowly and tightly bound in administrative swaddling clothes covering us from all sides, and with every new day we sense ever more acutely that something important has gone out of life.

Meanwhile, the government's frightful dominance over national life grew ever greater as a result of its adoption of a faulty theory of administration. The inner logic of Russian history, the uncomplaining obedience of the people, bred in the government habits of despotism and arrogance; meanwhile, the conservative system borrowed from the Austrian court lent legitimacy to these habits and transformed them into theoretical conviction. Conservatism inculcated in government the notion that, besides itself, no other social element should exist in the realm, that every independent manifestation of life is lawless, something leading to troubles and revolutions, that a government desiring to preserve itself must suppress in the people every movement and all autonomous activity.

It was not difficult to create such a system in Russia. There were no obstacles; it was only necessary for the government to keep moving, oblivious to everything else, upon the same course. [The new ideology] demanded only that the government avoid distractions of the sort that may naturally issue from excessive solicitude for the popular welfare. Previously the government had been concerned about stimulating intellectual activity among the people, about spreading education; but now it was explained to the government that education engenders liberalism and atheism, that an educated people will inevitably want to participate in public affairs, and that revolution occurs when the government prohibits such harmful doctrines. The lesson was reinforced, of course, by obvious examples, and the government, giving in to such convincing proofs, renounced its former deeds. Public welfare, thought, intellectual development are compatible only with a certain degree of governmental power. These enterprises derive their vitality from the people and therefore require [that the people possess] a certain autonomy vis-à-vis the state; as soon as this autonomy is eliminated, they become estranged from and opposed to the government. It is only necessary [for the government] to cross a certain line, to move further away from the people, and these interests take on a completely different light; whereas formerly they were [the government's] allies, now they are inimical to it. Our government bravely crossed this line, and the consequence was the general decay of the state apparatus. From this came those social problems from which we now suffer. Let us try to enumerate them.

Once impregnated by the conservative spirit, the government's first concern was to find obedient servants [to staff the bureaucracy]. This was not difficult; it was only necessary to turn to the habitual slaves and cringing lackeys who, even without it being demanded, are always ready to satisfy the authorities. The government sought obedient tools and found them: it staffed itself with officials personally devoted to the tsar. Statesmen were replaced by courtiers. But the state did not benefit from this. Do courtiers care about the popular welfare and keep the government safe from delusions? They expect nothing from the people, but for them the tsar is the source of all favors, and personal advantage prompts them to indulge the tsars and to uphold the tsars' delusions. Only by such means do the courtiers become powerful in the state; only in an atmosphere of universal silence does their voice have a certain significance. They substitute themselves for public opinion. The government inquires of them when it wishes to seek support, and their judgments pass for the voice of Russia. Through them the government receives information about the nation's condition; they decide what to tell the government and what to conceal. In other words, given the suppression of popular autonomy, they are the only mediators between tsar and people.

It cannot be said, however, that these mediators are very conscientious. They were summoned to serve the crown because of their loyalty and obedience, and they do not go beyond that. Their only goal is to please the tsar personally, to keep away from him every unpleasant sight, and by servile bows to win favors for themselves. Standing at the summit of society, they pay attention only to the sun shining above them, and they care little about what goes on below. If you plunge yourself into the middle of an ocean wave, you see below monsters moving about and eating the small denizens of the deep; yet on the surface of the water everything is placid and calm! And in fact everything in Russia is improbably placid and calm. The most scandalous abuses are carefully concealed; crying grievances are kept from the tsar's hearing; everything is arranged, smoothed over and presented in such a favorable light that it looks beautiful. The truth is inexorably persecuted because it exposes both tsars and courtiers. A triple barrier of high courtiers keeps the truth from the throne, and the government remains completely ignorant about what Russia is actually thinking and doing. Sealed off from the people by servile courtiers, the throne stands isolated, and the people have ceased to regard the throne as a sacred thing to be trusted and loved.

The government itself senses its estrangement from the people, or, rather, it considers this estrangement to be a necessary rule of politics. The conservative system proclaims that the people are dangerous, that they harbor revolutionary ideas, and that the government must find support not in the people's affection but in an enormous army powerful enough to defeat any movement. Naturally, in accordance with these principles, the government has increased the size of its army to the outer limits and has devoted to the army its greatest attentions. The army has become the model for the entire state apparatus; everything must run on a military basis. Military discipline has become the fundamental principle of government; it has been introduced everywhere—in the civil service, in private relationships and in the public sphere. Ignorant generals have been appointed trustees of universities; military discipline and instruction have been introduced in educational institutions.

Yet this enormous army was not really necessary. No one seriously contemplated a foreign war, and, domestically, everyone obeyed without reference to the army. Hence the army became a toy. Instead of worrying about improving the army's fighting capacity, its material basis, the soldiers' morale, or officers' education, the government devoted its attention to superficial matters. Inspections, parades, maneuvers served the tsar as amusements; his concern was with decorous uniforms and elegant maneuvers. When finally, as a result of rashness [in Russian foreign policy], war burst upon us unexpectedly [in the Crimea], when there was a real challenge for the army, then its inadequacy became apparent at every step. The adversary encroached upon Russia's borders, and yet the Russian government could not oppose it with equal forces. The government had at its disposal neither sufficient material means for effectively waging war nor able generals. Constant levying of recruits had exhausted the people, while the badly equipped recruits themselves have died by the thousands without advantage to the state. The elite guards have been held far from the war theater, while hastily recruited levies have been sent to the Crimea—levies that have proved worthless in the actual fighting.

Similar shortcomings are felt in civil administration. The government's goal has been to transform the bureaucracy into a machine that will always operate reliably as an obedient tool of central authority. The rank system has functioned in such a way as to reinforce obedience; the failure to follow established bureaucratic routine, the systematic transmission of orders from the top to the bottom of the apparatus, has led to the replacement of otherwise capable officials whose independence and convictions did not harmonize with the government's will. The government actually has achieved its goal. A bureaucratic machine now exists; its methods of operation, its protocols governing written communications, have been refined to express the most precise nuances; bureaucratic discipline is observed as never before. Yet the bureaucratic machine lacks a soul, and from the perspective of public affairs it is practically worthless. Respect for rank leads officials to cultivate the favor of their superiors rather than to think about the public welfare or systematically improving matters under their jurisdiction. State service now means serving one's superiors. Instead of applying their talents and zeal for the nation's benefit, officials give priority to personal relations, for, beginning with the highest officials in the government and descending to the most petty ones, each may profit more from sycophancy than from actual performance of particular service obligations. Meanwhile, the bureaucratic routine has led to an appalling multiplication of paperwork, which has now replaced real business. To take care of a matter means to make a formal written reply to a request, to write something on a piece of paper; it means to copy down and pass along data. The upper bureaucracy must make do with such documents and take for granted that the reported data are accurate, for it has no other means of gathering information. So on the one hand, the circle of high officials obscures and replaces public opinion, while on the other hand, bureaucratic paperwork obscures and replaces an understanding of the real situation.

From this issues one of Russia's greatest problems—the omnipresent official lie. One can say without exaggeration that every official statement is nothing other than a lie. All reports and communiqués of high state officials are essentially lies; all reports and communiqués of governors and other provincial authorities are lies; all statistical data are lies; all assurances of loyalty to and affection for the throne are lies; all public ceremonies honoring higher officials, such as, for example, government-authorized presentations of awards, are lies; finally, even most patriotic declarations are nothing but lies. After all, we have watched private individuals give money to the government for patriotic causes, but nine-tenths of these gifts have been given under duress. We have read certain statements by members of the nobility in which nobles have assured the government of their readiness to sacrifice everything for the tsar and the fatherland, but when it was time to select levies for army duty, every noble strove to decline this honor. Under a faulty system of government the most sacred of human sentiments are perverted into disgraceful flattery and servile fear. And how could it be otherwise? When everyone must bow silently before the government, who will dare speak the truth? Only free public opinion can serve as a check on the public utterances of officials whose personal advantage always forces them to flatter the government. When public opinion is suppressed by all available means, when all who would dare to disagree with the servile choir of official praises and assurances are forced to be silent, then the lie necessarily insinuates itself into every aspect of public life. The government deprives itself of the possibility to learn of the people's real condition and to exercise restraint over the actions of its own agents, while the people lose all trust in the government.

Another no less serious problem in the existing order is the pandemic corruption of officials, both civilian and military. Abuses are the rule rather than the exception in our administrative system. As we noted earlier, it is enough [from the official perspective] to implement a law on paper; as far as the government is concerned, how the law is implemented in fact remains a mystery. Taking advantage of this state of affairs, the authorities permit themselves to do anything that strikes their fancy. They know that the cry of the oppressed will never reach the throne, and that at the very foot of the throne they will find themselves powerful protectors. Thus the power entrusted to them becomes an instrument of oppression; the law, which should be the people's defense, serves only as a means for enriching officials. Every government measure, every encounter with citizens becomes a pretext for officials to extract more money [to line their own pockets]. And subordinates remain defenseless and without recourse before their superiors because they are in no way protected against administrative arbitrariness, and complaints are themselves considered a violation of discipline. It is the duty of the highest state officials both to supervise those junior officials who actually execute the law and to prosecute those who abuse the law, yet wherever possible, these higher officials try to cover up abuses. On one hand, a desire to please the sovereign compels them to present everything in the rosiest light; on the other hand, flattery prompts them to look leniently upon their subordinates and to conceal lawlessness. Finally, many of these same high officials are themselves no strangers to bribes. For convenience they take money from their subordinates, selling positions and extracting from the takers an annual fee [obrok]; in turn, their subordinates take money from their juniors and so on until finally citizens pay out of their own pockets the salaries not allocated by law to high as well as low government officials.

A priori one might assume that government is established for the benefit of the governed, but in reality it turns out to exist solely for the benefit of the rulers who constitute a bureaucratically organized corporation based on the principle of mutual assistance in the robbery and oppression of their subjects.

It is, of course, difficult for a genuinely noble and capable person to submit to a system that transforms him either into a machine for sending letters or into the wheel of a hydraulic press designed to squeeze all life and resources out of the people. Moreover, noble and capable persons are not given a chance [to affect policy], except in very unusual cases when they enjoy the personal protection of an important high official. Consequently, there is a third serious problem—the widespread incompetence of those in government. The present crisis has demonstrated how few people there are in our government with expertise and talent. The few who have these qualities have been found either in the lower ranks or far from the central sphere that ruins everyone who enters its charmed circle. It is as if incompetence has become a prerequisite for receiving a responsible office. For the most part, the incompetent person has neither an independent character that would be unpleasant to the authorities, nor convictions in disharmony with prevailing views. He agrees with everything and serves as the most uncomplaining and obedient tool for implementing imperial orders on paper. One could entrust to him an entire ministry and everything would go on as before. It is only necessary that under his command there be someone initiated in the secrets of bureaucratic routine and knowing how cleverly to arrange matters so that the interests of high officials will not clash. People of this last type constitute the business section of administration, just as the policy and executive sections consist of those whose courtier's tact replaces statecraft.

After this is it surprising that our legislation has failed to advance and that the most crucial political and social problems remain unresolved? We have a Senate, a remnant from an earlier institutional structure, which does not fit at all with the most recently created agencies. Its multitudinous and utterly superfluous areas of jurisdiction should have been abolished long ago, while its genuinely important role as Russia's final court of appeals should have been emphasized. Yet the Senate has become a refuge for those high officials who are judged as incompetents even in our administration, and thus Russia's supreme court has become a place of exile for old men and idiots. We have a trial system that protects no one and that delays cases for decades by requiring submission of endless documentation. We have a financial system that rests all its weight on the lower classes and is a model of injustice and inefficiency in taxing the nation's resources. Finally, we have the serf system, an ulcerous wound, an institution swallowing an entire third of the nation's populace. Both equity and the interests of the state demand the abolition of serfdom. The illegality and harm generated by serfdom are so apparent as to be obvious even to a conservative government.

The government senses the incongruity of maintaining serfdom and would like to ameliorate this problem but does not know how to go about it. In general, recent legislation has been confused and contradictory. Every minute new laws are published, so that a decade's addendum to the *Code of Laws* almost exceeds the original code in length; yet among all these laws there is not one that can bring real benefit to the state, not one that can cure any of the terrible wounds of contemporary life. Individual decrees and half-measures often contradict one another; they are published today and are repealed or ignored tomorrow. Timid, venal, and incompetent hands have transformed our body of laws into chaos. There is no one in the government who can point to true principles, to the essential needs of the people; and if someone can do so, he keeps silent, so that by servile and mute obedience he may purchase for himself the tsar's favor.

Such are the political consequences of the hypertrophied development of governmental authority. Obviously, such a system could not help but have a deleterious impact on the people. The main goal of the conservative doctrine was, as I indicated above, to suppress popular initiatives of any kind and to thwart popular independence. In a sense the goal was commendable: by destroying opposition the government hoped to avoid internal dissension and to preserve its unity with the people. Unfortunately, the means were inappropriate to attainment of the ends. If the people could have been completely stricken from public life or transformed into a mute machine, then the conservative system would have been irreproachably correct. But fortunately, that could not be done. One cannot shake the people off the face of the earth; yet, if one forbids the people to speak, if one strives to create harmony by force, the people quietly become alienated from the government and refuse to cooperate with it.

That is what happened in Russia. What could have been easier for government than to uphold an alliance with the people, an alliance fortified by centuries? And yet the foolishness of the conservative system managed to weaken even this centuries-old loyalty. Having become conservative, the government began mercilessly to persecute every independent initiative; meanwhile, the idea of the people fostered by the government itself grew ever stronger and bolder and demanded for itself greater latitude. The very growth of governmental power generated a popular demand for greater freedom. When the government was but a distant authority, it was possible not to get entangled in its grasp, it was possible to overlook rare cases of arbitrariness. But when the government's presence was felt in every aspect of daily life, it inevitably provoked a political response; legal protection from administrative arbitrariness became a necessity. Indeed, how can one not criticize the actions of an authority that one sees everywhere around oneself! How can one tolerate restrictions and abuses that one encounters at every step? For us freedom of speech which exposes the shortcomings of our body of laws and reveals the abuses of our rulers has now become essential, a necessity, yet the exercise of this freedom has been more and more circumscribed. The consequence is discord between the government's aims and the people's demands, discord that has led to the destruction of the ancient alliance [between crown and people].

Popular alienation from the government has had an impact in every sphere of public life. All thinking and enlightened persons have concluded that between themselves and the government there is nothing in common. They hunger for freedom of thought, for the enlightened and free activity of the mind, but this freedom is suppressed by all available means. They involuntarily recoil from a government which has trampled on all their fundamental beliefs and convictions. The lower classes view the government as an oppressive agency gripping them from all sides and resting upon them with all its weight. There is no hut, no corner in the Russian nation where the government's unclean hand has not reached; and wherever it has been, it has never come away empty; wherever it has intruded itself, there invariably is heard the moan of the oppressed. For the lower classes the government may be characterized in a single word: the treasury—a word ominous and frightening to the people. It is, in the eyes of the people, a monster swallowing the money and sucking the blood of poor citizens. The treasury is the people's natural enemy. Ignoring just demands and complaints, the treasury's sole ambition is to squeeze out of the humble as much money as possible, and, for their part, the humble do not consider it a crime to steal from and deceive the treasury when this can be done without fear of punishment. It never occurs to the people that the treasury exists for their benefit. The interests of treasury and people are so different that they resemble two opposing parties that, despite formal assurances of mutual love and respect, secretly try to play on each other as many dirty tricks as possible.

Yet how touching are official expressions of loyalty and submission! How the people crowd all official ceremonies! How movingly the bribe-taking and servile writers describe the Russian people's love for the established authorities and the felicity which they enjoy under the blessed rule of autocratic monarchs! Officially everyone is improbably happy, yet if one could but lift this false curtain, how much different would be the spectacle unfolding before our eyes! It is rare for a private citizen to meet anyone contented with the actual state of affairs in Russia. Everywhere you hear endless complaints about oppression and bribery. Such is the theme of all conversations about public affairs; such are the innumerable stories which circulate everywhere, in the capitals and in the provinces, both in public meetings and around the domestic hearth. Such stories have educated the younger generation, who from their early childhood have learned to fear the government and to distrust the legal order. Under this influence a new civic life develops, a civic life full of bitterness and mistrust. It has replaced the former patriarchal ways, so carefree and tranquil, the former life on the plough so characteristic of the Russian people. How frightfully Russian society has changed in recent times! Everything that our fathers loved and to which they bowed has become foreign to us. Love for the throne and trust in the government have been beaten violently out of us. We have no memories like those that formerly delighted our grandfathers. Even the fatherland has lost its charm for us, for our public life is full of things that vex the soul and insult all noble human aspirations. No one dares say the word aloud, but secretly everyone grumbles and grows indignant.

Everyone understands, however, that grumbling and indignation lead nowhere. Active opposition, much less revolutionary opposition, is not at all in our character. For that we are too soft, compliant, and submissive. Our entire history has facilitated the growth of governmental authority, and before that power we are reduced to nothing. We know that the government is everything and we are nothing, and we see no way out of this predicament. Everyone is dissatisfied, but everyone understands that this dissatisfaction cannot be assuaged and so everyone resignedly views the situation as hopeless. Consequently, indifference to public affairs is universal. Everyone sees that he can do nothing for the fatherland's benefit, and therefore he concentrates on his private life and cares only about his personal affairs. If an individual runs into a problem with the law, he tries, where possible, to get around the law; if he has to make a monetary sacrifice for the nation, he tries to give as little as possible, and even this he gives reluctantly and under duress. There is no public spirit, no public interest, and this imparts to all public life the stamp of triviality and boredom. Not being drawn into nobler activity, most people surrender themselves to trivial calculations and vulgar passions, which are poor substitutes for intellectual passion and political engagement; those rare individuals with a more elevated vision are bored and succumb to despondency amid a monotonous, colorless, and petty life that offers no spiritual nourishment.

In general, intellectual life suffers much under the existing governmental system. Enlightenment cannot spread without a greater or lesser degree of liberty. Science and art are disciplines that do not bend to the government's prescriptions; they have their own methods and sources of inspiration over which no one has power. Science cannot change at the government's insistence the logical coherence of its concepts or the incontrovertible meaning of certain facts. Art seeks inspiration in life; it depicts the surrounding good and evil as they appear to the artist's eyes, not as the government understands them. The government is no judge of art at all. It cannot order an artist to think this way or that, to study a phenomenon in such a way but not in another way, to depict this rather than that side of life. Science and art do not subordinate themselves to such demands, for they are by their very nature free. You can destroy them, but you cannot direct them in an arbitrary fashion.

The government itself seems finally to have arrived at this realization. Having no tolerance for freedom itself, the government cannot tolerate those things that are even indirectly connected with freedom. But cowed by the opinion of the educated world, the government has not dared completely to eradicate science and literature; rather, it has simply pressured them whenever possible, so that they have come to a very sorry pass. The censorship regulations are so strict that one cannot write anything having a humane content. Every thought is hunted like contraband, and even facts are expunged from publications that might throw a not-altogether-favorable light on the existing political order or on those political, religious, and moral principles that are now accepted as the official norms. In educational institutions military instruction and military discipline have been introduced; ignorant generals have taken charge of our national system of education; universities have lost their former prerogatives and even the number of students has been reduced. One wonders what could be better for the state than the largest possible number of educated people? One wonders what to inculcate in the younger generation if not a desire to study? And yet this most exalted human aspiration is the object of prohibitions; the government regards education as dangerous to itself, and it limits the number of students.

Consequently, is it really surprising that intellectual interests in society have diminished, that zeal for science and art has diminished? Instead of the several hundred students who formerly entered our major universities each year, the universities now field hardly enough students to fill even the limited quotas. And the cause of this is not the war, for [restrictions on university enrollment] predated the war. The cause is governmental measures that impede intellectual activity. Educationally, Russia is going backward and the government will gain nothing by this, for [its hostility to education] has produced more dissatisfied youths than could have been produced by all the journal articles in the world. Everyone who has the least respect for education must involuntarily lose respect for a government that suppresses education. Only the most patent vulgarity can enable one to describe the government as enlightened or as a protector of science and art. Such a claim is a lie, refuted by facts at hand.

Education is also connected with Russia's material welfare. Industry cannot get along without science, but science in Russia is in disfavor. It is futile for the government to funnel personnel into those branches of science that have practical benefits. Science does not submit itself to such a disingenuous approach. Scientific advancement accrues from concentrated attention to basic science, not from [superficial attention to] its practical applications. It is necessary that there be a lively public participation in science, but this participation must spring from forces other than the government's dictates. One must first grant freedom to science, and then science will yield practical benefits.

In Russia, however, even the practical application of science suffers the same disregard as theory, and this disregard naturally is reflected in the primitive condition of industry. The ignorance of our managers and manufacturers is vast; there is only a handful of exceptions to the general rule. In most cases, when knowledge or a special skill is required, a foreigner is quickly sent for, and the administration of the firm in question is entrusted to him. This habit is very expensive; moreover, a foreigner, especially one not knowing the Russian language, usually finds it hard to deal with our workers. Those factory owners who do not have the means to hire a foreigner usually follow an age-old routine, make the most elementary mistakes, and needlessly waste time, money, and labor. Obviously, our industry is bound to suffer from this lack of enlightenment.

Other factors also contribute [to the primitive condition of our industry], factors that also ultimately arise from the same source. For the successful development of industry the first prerequisite is civil liberty, which provides the opportunity to use one's energies and talents in the most profitable fashion. Moreover, industrial growth presumes an active, energetic populace, for otherwise there will be no entrepreneurial spirit; it presumes the existence of legal safeguards against governmental interference and, in general, a system of government that will not hamper commercial exchanges. Finally, it presumes the development of society's material resources such as credit, communications, and so on. And we lack all these prerequisites for industrial growth. Serfdom diverts from work a significant portion of the people's energies and constitutes an obstacle to any improvement in agriculture; the financial system rests all its weight on the lower classes; the suppression of popular initiative and independence undermines popular industriousness; the faulty ideology adopted by the government generates ruinous restrictions for industry and trade, and it destroys private credit without which commercial exchanges are impossible; finally, the absence of good roads hinders market activity and depresses productivity everywhere. The government does not permit private entrepreneurs to build a communications network because it wants to do everything itself, and it does everything slowly and badly. It has at its disposal insufficient capital [for building a proper road network], and of those funds which are earmarked for the communications network, two-thirds goes into the pockets of officials and contractors.

Thus both the intellectual and material interests of the state suffer from the government's short-sightedness. Indeed, this short-sightedness has become so pronounced as to affect all aspects of life. The passive qualities of the Russian people and the nature of the historical development to which these qualities have contributed have led us to a situation in which the government is all-powerful. But instead of cautiously taking advantage of this omnipotence and, in consciousness of its strength, permitting the people to exercise their autonomy, instead of stimulating in Russian society the initiative that is wanting in it and which, given the national character, cannot be dangerous to the central government, the government has concentrated all its efforts on increasing the state's power and has ignored the other elements of public life. Little by little, the government has completely separated itself from the people. In the army it has created for itself a base of support separate from the citizenry; in the bureaucracy it has an obedient instrument; the tsar is surrounded by officials who are personally loyal to him but who have nothing in common with the people. From all sides the government has fenced itself off and shielded itself from the light. It lives and moves in a separate sphere, a sphere into which nothing penetrates from the lowlands where there is not audible even a whimper of civic life. Inside the government's charmed circle everything is unique, utterly distinctive, bearing no resemblance to things on the outside. There is official loyalty, official flattery, official falsehood, official satisfaction, official welfare, official information, official articles, official discipline, official routine. All of this is created and maintained with great effort for the tsar's amusement, but, unfortunately, all is illusion. It is a soap bubble which has taken shape around the omnipotent lord; it blinds him by its rainbow colors. Meanwhile, the people live their lives, mute and submissive, but not at all happy and contented. But who cares? Courtiers treat the people with arrogant contempt. The people are duty-bound to be satisfied with their lot. Dissatisfaction is something pernicious and seditious, something that cannot be tolerated, and, if anyone dares to say that Russia is unhappy, then he is classified as a Jacobin who ought to be thrown into prison or exiled to a distant province of the empire. If not for this purpose, then why does the [political police, the] Third Section of His Majesty's Chancellery exist?

Under such circumstances one cannot be surprised that Russia finds it difficult to wage war against foreign invaders. What good is all the great valor of the Russian people when their energies are sapped by the general corruption of the state apparatus, by the virtually universal corruption they see on all sides?

Russia has reached a critical moment in its historical life. The course that it has pursued for several centuries turns out to be incorrect; Russia has pursued that course to its logical limits and now suffers from the most ruinous consequences. Such is the law of history. The people (and along with them the government) have long been walking down one road, obsessed by a single ideal embodying their deepest desires. But as they reached the end of the road, as they grasped all the implications of their ideal, they suddenly realized that the road was perhaps not the correct one, that the idea did not make full use of all the nation's resources. Extremism inevitably entails absurd consequences. The very process of achieving an extremist program reveals the bankruptcy of that program and suggests the need to alter one's course, to pursue another, more rational objective. Then comes the turning point. Everywhere discord and frustration make themselves felt; today it is apparent that the very constituent elements of the body politic that have heretofore been held in contempt by the government are precisely those elements needed to bring about improvements in the common welfare. Happy is the nation whose government is sufficiently prudent to recognize its shortcomings, to sense its mistakes, and to lead the people onto a new course. How much misfortune and civil strife this will save the people!

For Russia such a turning point has now arrived. Heretofore in Russia the body politic has existed in name only; now the spirit of public life must be suffused into this body. Heretofore the only actor on stage has been the government; now the people must be allowed to play their role as well. Centuries of obedience have atoned for the people's anarchistic impulses. The people have submitted to the state order; they have been educated for political life. Now they must be treated not as a child wrapped in swaddling clothes but as an adult who thinks and acts independently. We will remain grateful to our mentor and prepared to love him as before, if only he will understand our needs and satisfy our just desires. We do not demand rights peculiar to our social station, nor the limitation of tsarist authority—a limitation about which no one in Russia even thinks. We need freedom! We want the opportunity freely to express and develop our thoughts, so the tsar will know what Russia is thinking and doing and can govern us with a clear understanding of social conditions and with a rational love for his people.

Liberalism! This is the slogan of every educated and sensible person in Russia. This is the banner which can unite individuals from all spheres, all social Estates, all convictions. This is the word that can shape a powerful public opinion, if only we will shake off our self-destructive laziness and indifference to the common cause. This is the word that can heal our profoundest wounds, that can heal our inner corruption, that can give us the opportunity to stand next to other peoples and, with renewed strength, to set off on a great course a harbinger of which lies in the great achievements of the Russian nation. In liberalism is the whole future of Russia. May both the government and the people rally around this banner with trust in each other and with the firm intention of reaching the avowed goal.

But what should be understood by the term *liberalism? Freedom* is a vague word. It may be either unlimited or limited, and, if unlimited freedom cannot be permitted, then in what should limited freedom consist? In short, what measures should a liberal government adopt and what should the liberal party in society desire?

Let us attempt to enumerate the chief principles connoted by the term *liberalism* and those measures which, in our view, are essential for Russia's prosperity.

1. *Freedom of conscience.* This is the first and most sacred right of a citizen, for if the government begins to concern itself with matters of conscience, then what will remain safe from it? A person's religious convictions are a sanctuary into which no one has the right to intrude. They constitute the inner world of his soul and do not fall under the jurisdiction of civil law, for law is public prescription applying only to citizens' public activities. Law defines citizens' rights and duties toward one another and toward the government, but a citizen's attitude toward God remains a matter of conscience. The means a person considers best for the salvation of his soul is no concern of the state. In this sphere one can act only by persuasion, not by force; persuasion is a matter for the church, to which must be left the right of counseling souls for salvation's sake. The law has no authority whatsoever here. It cannot compel a person to believe in one thing but not in another; coercion fosters only hypocrisy, not sincere worship. Legal coercion can have but one result: peaceful citizens, who heretofore have strictly discharged their public duties, will be insulted by interference in these most intimate matters and will become enemies of the law.

Such a result would doubtless harm the state just as it would harm religious belief.

The legal code itself recognizes this principle, and it proclaims freedom of conscience as the fundamental right of all citizens in the Russian empire. Unfortunately, this freedom is limited in practice. Several millions of schismatics, [the Old Believers], constituting perhaps the most industrious and developed part of the Russian peasantry, not only do not have freedom of religion but are subjected to every kind of persecution and oppression. While pagans are allowed to bow to their idols without interference, those sects closest to Russian Orthodoxy are persecuted in every way. Such an unjust contradiction in our institutions must be eliminated. Moreover, it is also necessary to abolish legal sanctions meted out both for failure to carry out religious duties and for conversion from Orthodoxy to other confessions. This is again a matter of conscience in which the civil law has no right to meddle. Finally, justice demands that oppressive restrictions be lifted from the Jews, for freedom of conscience is a right that must not be taken from any citizen of the Russian empire. No one should suffer for his religious convictions.

2. *Emancipation from servile status,* from one of the greatest evils now afflicting Russia. Serfdom reflects not on a lesser but on a grander scale the ideology that dominates the whole nation. The seigneur wields almost the same kind of omnipotent and irresponsible mastery over his peasants that the sovereign wields over his subjects. The seigneur has more than the power over life and death: neither the person nor the property of the serf is in any way immune from the lord's arbitrariness.

The position of the two authorities [with respect to their subordinates] is similar, their abuses similar, and the very arguments that they employ to justify themselves the same. The government speaks in favor of the autocrat's prerogatives, landlords speak in favor of the right of property. The government says that to permit freedom and opposition in the state would violate the patriarchal union based on mutual love for the sake of artificial relations based on political calculations; landlords say that destruction of their authority is tantamount to replacing patriarchal care (!) [of the peasantry] with a commercial system of free wages. The government asserts that the people to whom freedom is being granted are disposed to anarchy; the landlords assert that the liberated peasant goes to seed through drink and becomes a ne'er-do-well. The government says that every concession leads to revolution; the landlords say that peasant emancipation will be a signal for the general slaughter of the lords. The government wants to act by palliative measures, by eliminating abuses, but it wants to preserve the system that generated the abuses. Likewise, the landlords do not want to hear about the eradication of the problem itself; instead, they support sanctions for violating legal statutes that actually protect no one. The government eloquently describes the bliss being savored by subjects under its power; the landlords just as eloquently prove that their peasants are better and more fortunate than all free peoples in the world. The government points to Western peoples as an example of the unhappy effects of alternate forms of political administration; the landlords depict the lot of state peasants as a misfortune that their serfs have avoided. But neither the one nor the other authority wishes to take into account what their very own subjects consider the greatest happiness. If their subjects' circumstances should even begin to resemble the people's vision of happiness, it would serve the authorities as a lesson and a warning against ruinous schemes. Both the government and the landlords claim that the liberal projects amount to nothing more than imitations of Western models that cannot be adapted to Russia. Russia, in their opinion, is a country completely unlike any other, a country having such peculiarities as to make the existing order the only conceivable one. But nobody has taken the trouble to enumerate these strange peculiarities. Apparently, they are generally ones most convenient for the authorities.

Consequently, the arguments are uncannily similar; indeed, these are the arguments of all oppressors. But there is an important difference—namely, the government is the representative of society, a representative possessing necessary and legitimate authority which it now uses in a one-sided fashion. The landlord is but a private person invested with power, power that has no just and legal foundations. Authority over a person can belong only to the state, and private authority over other citizens is a violation of the state's prerogatives. It is repugnant to ethical sense, to justice and to the public good. It is a reward to one social Estate at the expense of another, because all citizens should equally enjoy the blessings of civic life. Therefore, there is nothing stranger than to hear a landlord speaking about his prerogatives, about government oppression affecting him, when he himself is a perpetrator and defender of the greatest oppression. The landlord has no justification whatsoever to complain about the existing order, for the abuses of seigneurial authority are much more serious than the abuses of the conservative government, and the harm done by the government is nothing in comparison with the harm done by serfdom, which ties the hands of all social Estates, perverts all social relations, hinders all institutional improvements, removes from the law's jurisdiction an entire third of the population, spoils the national character, destroys in the people a sense of human dignity, and fosters in the state apparatus immorality, illegality, and corruption. If the government is primarily responsible for the nation's sorry plight, then doubtless the burden of guilt also falls on the nobility, the primary supporters of the throne, for the nobility could have helped improve the sorry situation but did not do so. Given the prevailing moral laxity, if there is one social Estate that might still render true service to the fatherland, that Estate is the nobility. By emancipating their peasants, nobles can render a far more useful service to Russia than they render by the futile complaints and pointless lamentations now heard on all sides.

How one might accomplish the emancipation is not a matter to be examined here; that would digress too far from the issue at hand. It is enough to insist on the need for this step to be taken.

3. *Freedom of speech.* Our entire discussion suggests that freedom of speech is essential in Russia. Therefore, one should bring it to the forefront as the cornerstone of liberal politics. Let each Russian regard himself as a citizen of his fatherland who is called to assist the common cause. The government not only should not suppress political life among the people but is obliged by all means to arrange matters so that each individual may understand as clearly as possible the laws of Russia, its domestic condition, and its system of government. But this cannot be achieved by any other means than by granting to all the right freely to express their opinions and convictions. A person who for each oppositional word, for each bravely expressed thought, can be seized and subjected to arbitrary punishment is not a citizen but a slave. He cannot use his strengths and talents according to his convictions but can only silently obey another's will. But we have seen where silent obedience has led us. It is time to put it aside, and in its place to raise freedom of speech, which can be the best and most reliable aid to a government that has in mind the popular good. Free speech alone can uncover the truth, search out capable people, rouse the public to action, and finally impel the government itself to adopt necessary reforms. Free speech is the expression of the people's aspirations. Allow it at first to be shaky, immature, uncoordinated; it cannot be otherwise after centuries of silence. But freedom will educate and strengthen public opinion, and ultimately the government will find in the public its best ally.

4. *Freedom of the press,* a necessary consequence of the freedom of speech. It is not enough to have the possibility to express one's ideas in conversations; conversations are private exchanges. If popular opinion is to have a public impact, then it should be publicly accessible and widely known, and that is only possible through the press. Until censorship which subjects every expression of

ideas to governmental approval is abolished, only the government's opinion will be known and the people will remain silent. The abolition of censorship is the foundation of every liberal system desiring to rely on free speech and to give the people a certain autonomy. Only by abolishing censorship can the government prove that it does not intend to escape from trouble by ringing phrases alone, but that it wants to adopt genuine reforms. It has nothing to fear from the political tricks of the opposition. Opposition not only cannot weaken but will actually strengthen the government, provided the government knows how to behave prudently. The existence of an opposition will mobilize the government's defenders, who are today held in low esteem, for no one dares to contradict them; in the future these defenders will become more powerful and more important. Opposition will provide a legal channel for expressing the now-suppressed aspirations of the people; dissatisfaction once expressed loses half its force. Instead of a secret and widespread irritation extending to every aspect of life, whether justifiably or not, opposition will develop among the people a genuine understanding of things; it will educate their political instincts; and to the government it will reveal truth, it will indicate the government's shortcomings, it will proclaim the various desires of the people. Opposition consists precisely in expression of these heterogeneous aspirations; the nation's political life consists of debate and struggle between advocates of such [conflicting] perspectives. It is only necessary that this struggle be peaceful and legal, and that can be assured only by granting to it free channels for development. Let even absurd opinions be expressed; they will expose themselves as absurdities. The less rational the opposition, the less support it will find in public opinion and the stronger will be the government. For the government's moral strength does not consist in a populace that is outwardly silent but inwardly resentful; rather, the government finds strength as the majority joins it with trust and affection, under conditions where the possibility of opposition exists. Only by this means can government be certain that truth is on its side; today the government has only the power of physical coercion on its side. The government should not fear prudently expressed criticism; only a call to violate the law, only an attempt to overthrow public institutions cannot be permitted. But in such a case the government may rely on law for punishing the guilty party. It can always bring a writer to court or prohibit a journal that is engaged in destructive propaganda. The law must punish actual crimes but should not prohibit every activity that presents an opportunity for abuse. There will always be abuses, but from this it does not follow that everything must be prohibited.

5. *Academic freedom.* Scholarship must develop independently, and the gov-

ernment should not intrude its own views into scholarship. The government must limit itself to making certain that academic departments do not become centers of political and religious propaganda rather than vehicles for promoting scholarly instruction. Meanwhile, all measures should be repealed that now hinder public education, and public education ought to be based on liberal principles and not on military discipline.

6. *Publication of all governmental activities* whose disclosure would not be injurious to the state, and especially publication of the budget, state income, and expenditures. The people should know what is happening in the central government: public business is the people's own business, and a government that genuinely cares about the people's welfare cannot fear publishing a record of its actions.

7. *Public legal proceedings.* In order to guarantee fair verdicts and speedy trials, to eliminate the innumerable abuses now hidden under the cover of darkness, this measure is vital. Plaintiffs and defendants will find in it protection against oppression; judges will find in it an encouragement to render just verdicts; the government and the people will find in it the recognition of the judiciary's rightful place as one of the most important branches of government. In addition, the daily spectacle of trial and punishment will nurture in the citizenry a respect for rights and legality that is the ultimate basis of rational public life but which is unfortunately moribund among us today. How to implement this reform is a matter about which we do not now have space to speak.

These are the chief measures which should be the objects of an enlightened government's solicitous protection and which are the desire of the liberal party in Russia. In liberalism, as we said earlier, is Russia's future; it alone can awake Russia to new life and provide the opportunity to develop the nation's slumbering potential. Therefore, everyone who genuinely loves Russia, every enlightened citizen must rally around this banner. Having cast off our ruinous indifference toward the common cause, we must, by every means permitted under the law, strive to support the great and salutary principle of freedom. Let us proclaim loudly our desire for liberty, for our conviction is not the result of an intellectually empty, hyperemotional impulse toward license, but of genuine love for Russia and of a desire to extricate it from the sorry condition into which it has fallen. Perhaps certain people will be forced to suffer for their candor, but to suffer in a just cause is no hardship. It is time for us to dispense with our habitual servility and humiliating fear of authority and to recognize that a noble firmness of conviction is alone worthy of a great people. Civic courage is a virtue that has almost disappeared among us, but it is essential for everyone who wishes to accomplish something useful. We must act on our own, not expecting anything from the government and not blaming it for all our misfortunes. We ourselves are to blame for much in the current state of affairs in Russia. Only our own inactivity, our silent indifference to the public welfare, our unpardonable timidity could have permitted the government such a degree of blindness. Seeing no obstacles around it, having no admonitions to guide it, the government imagined that it was pursuing the proper course and it assumed that the people were satisfied with its rule. We must finally raise our voices and make evident our desire for improvements. Only when we begin boldly to tell the truth without fear of being exiled or punished, only when we ourselves act without waiting to be prompted by the government, only then will we have the right to say that we are a people that has within us the makings of a great future. And who among us does not want that for Russia?

In conclusion, let me say one more word. This exposure of our inner corruption, this public confession should serve as an answer to the call for repentance that is now heard on all sides. If it is the duty of each citizen who truly feels the shortcomings of his fatherland to speak about them for the benefit of his fellow citizens and to suggest ways to correct these shortcomings, then this duty is now doubly sacred. The call of our spiritual elders has not been made in vain. More than once from among the people the voice of true confession has been heard. We repent of our sins and we repent from the depths of our souls, with heartfelt grief, with the desire that all be well in our fatherland. But now it is the government's turn to confess. Why do our preachers, who speak so eloquently about the sins of the people, not call upon the government to repent? Do not the same transgressions that weigh down so heavily upon us also press upon the government's conscience as well? Until now we have depended on the government for everything; for centuries it has been our ruler and guide. It has now led its lost sheep to such a pass that it has called down upon itself God's punishment. Let it now make its public confession; let it show us an example of atonement. And this the government may do so by abolishing the ruinous system of administration now in place, by renouncing egoistic attempts to strengthen its authority, and by granting to the people that political life without which no enlightened state can survive.

"Indictment": An Open Letter to Alexander Herzen

Gracious Sir,

In the last issue of *The Bell* you answered, with your usual energy, the reproach of vacillation, of flippancy which you hear from various quarters.[1]

This reproach, along with several others, is repeated, I dare say, by a *significant portion* of the thinking people of Russia. I confess that I am also guilty of repeating it, and I do not retract my opinion after your answer; it even seems to me that you have not quite understood with what you have been reproached or, perhaps, the reproach came to you in a distorted form. Permit me to explain this rather more precisely. Here the question concerns various tendencies of thought in Russian society, differences in political *temperaments* that perhaps, more profoundly than anything else, divide people. Therefore, I hope that you will not refuse to place this letter in your journal. I appeal to you, because *we have no other free outlet;* otherwise, I would not argue with you.

I warn you beforehand that I shall approach you with rather heavy demands. I know that it will not be easy to satisfy them, but I also know how great are the responsibilities which lie upon you. In fact, your position is exceptional, one may say virtually unique in the world. Remember the vital importance, the character of the epoch in which we live in Russia; after the Sevastopol debacle, after the hardships of the recent war, the old system of administration has collapsed of its own weight. It has become obvious that we cannot continue in the old ways, that military order and bureaucratic formalism alone cannot ensure the national welfare, that the realm cannot survive without the government enlisting the cooperation of society as a whole. Meanwhile, the government has not finally and unequivocally committed itself to a new course; neither within the ranks of its own officials nor within society does it find sufficient support for the new course; it moves as if by touch, hesitating, making a step forward and a step backward, but it is listening to various voices and is ready at any moment to accept a sensibly expressed opinion. Such at any rate is the picture at which one arrives after assessing the current situation. Meanwhile, the common people contemplate with horror their own sorry plight; they beg for light, for medicine to heal their painful wounds. Such is the situation confronting the political writer: the government seeking support, the people hungry for free expression! Pondering these demands, you stand alone, far outside the censor's reach, at one remove from the contending parties, from the passions of the moment, from scandalous gossip and the unpleasantry of everyday life. You can weigh every word, calmly and dispassionately tell the truth to everyone and anyone, expose abuses, influence the government, give direction to society, develop a mature political program, and finally, you can show the world for what principles the free Russian press stands. In your position everything you say has meaning; *you are a force, you are a power in the Russian realm.*

How do you carry out your role? What of substance do you offer us? What do we hear from you?

We hear from you not words of reason, but words of passion. You yourself admit this; moreover, you even take a certain pride in parading your passion for show, and contemptuously you criticize thoughtful, precise people who, not being carried away with passion themselves, do not carry away others. You are a man thrown into battle, you proceed from passionate belief and passionate doubt, you exhaust yourself in anger and indignation, you repeatedly stumble over yourself. These are your own words. But is such a temperament appropriate in the political arena? I would have thought that in politics, thoughtfulness, caution, a clear and exact understanding of things, a calm discussion of means and ends are precisely what is necessary; I would have thought that a political figure who exhausts himself in anger, who stumbles at every step, who is carried this way and that by the prevailing wind, would thereby undermine trust in himself; I would have thought that by adopting an extreme view, he would only injure his own cause. Unbridled outbursts may have their political charm, but in public affairs what is necessary above all else is political sense, a political tact which knows the means and divines the moment to act; here not passion, which is easily distracted, but insightful and creative reason is what is necessary.

And do you really think that Russia now needs people with ardent passions, who burn out quickly from an excess of emotion and who expire halfway to the goal? Recall again in what epoch we live. In Russia great civic reforms are being planned, relationships formed over centuries are about to be undone. The reforms will affect the most vital interests of society, shaking it in the most profound way. What a skillful hand is needed to reconcile the contradictory aspirations [of various social groups], to harmonize inimical interests, to right ancient wrongs so as, by legislation, to transform an existing civil order into another! Here there is also a struggle, but a struggle of a different kind, one without theatrical effects, without angry outbursts, a struggle that is calculated, careful, guided by a master plan that makes clear how to traverse the chosen course. At a time like this one should neither fan the flames of passion nor rub salt in old wounds; instead one should calm irritated minds in order the more surely to reach one's goal. Or do you think that a new civic order can be brought into existence by mere passion, by the boiling of anger alone?

I forget, however, that you are rather indifferent toward reform of the civic order. For you civic spirit, enlightenment, is not a valuable plant which must be carefully set in the soil and nurtured, as the noblest expression of political life. Let it be lost in a fatal battle, let the habit of relying on the ax be introduced instead of respect for rights and the law—you are little concerned about that. You wish to reach a goal no matter what the cost, and by what means it is reached—insane and bloody or peaceful and nonviolent—this for you is a secondary question. You do not care by what means an issue may be resolved, whether it be by an unimaginable act of the most savage despotism or by the ferocity of an enraged mob; you will subscribe to anything, you will give your blessing to anything. You will not only subscribe to anything [including bloodshed], you even consider it inappropriate to try to avert such an outcome. In your eyes, such an outcome is the poetic caprice of history! Tell me please, when you wrote these words, how did you look upon yourself: as a statesman directing society along a rational path, or as an artiste, observing the accidental play of events?

A statesman must bear in mind not only the end but also the means. A mature discussion of the latter, a precise calculation of circumstances, a choice of the best path given the known situation—this is his task, and through it he distinguishes himself from the thinker, who only studies the general course of history, and from the artiste, who merely observes the play of human passions. That which you call the poetic caprice of history, the movement of nature itself, is in fact the product of human volition. "Nature" in this case is you, I, a third person, everyone who contributes his mite to the common cause. And each of us, no matter how obscure we may be, bears a sacred responsibility to uphold civic virtue, to calm rebellious passions, to avert violence. Do you act in such a manner, you whose position gives you a broader and freer field of activity than others enjoy? We have the right to ask you, and what answer will you give? You are opening the pages of your journal to insane appeals to savage force; you yourself, standing on the other shore, with calm and contemptuous irony, point us toward the rod [*palka*] and the ax, as toward poetic caprices with which it would be impolitic to interfere. The rod from above and the ax from below—these are the usual consequences of political preaching inspired by passion! O, from the party of violence you will encounter much sympathy in Russia. Ask the most dull and incorrigible enemy of enlightenment, military or civilian, but particularly a military man who, following orders, screams against bribes and abuses, ask him: what is the cure for our problems? He has one simple answer: the rod! The ax is not yet so popular; we are not so accustomed to it, but, judging by the letter that you recently published in *The Bell,* even this means is beginning to acquire popularity. No, he who holds dear civic life, who desires peace and happiness for his fatherland, will fight with all his powers against such [incitements to violence], and as long as we have breath in our body, while there is a voice in our breast, we will condemn both these tools and these appeals.

And why all this alarm? On what pretext does indignation flare up? Truly, when you ponder this question, the answer is both sad and amusing. Not a year has passed since the sovereign expressed the firm intent to reform the old serf system, and at that time you exclaimed: "Thou hast conquered, Galilean!" The business has now gotten under way; committees called by the government have assembled; and new measures are being discussed. It would seem that before the committees have finished their work, before the government has rendered its conclusions, one ought to refrain from making definitive statements about the reforms. You, I hope, do not imagine that the emancipation of the peasants is just as easy a matter as to write an article for *The Bell.* Ancient intricate institutions and relationships encompassing life to its very depths cannot be overturned in two or three months. Here people get in the way, here prejudices are involved, here the most contradictory and also most vital interests collide. Time is needed to study, to deliberate, to reconcile, and to build; patience is needed to impart to the reform a peaceful and legal beginning. But patience, the ability to bide one's time, the first political virtue of mature peoples, evidently has no appeal to those who are accustomed to exhaust themselves in anger and indignation. Before anything has been successfully completed, your anxiety has gotten the better of you. You have leapt from delight to despair; everything is lost; the government has retreated; Alexander has not justified the hopes placed upon him; peasants, sharpen your axes! But what really has happened in this interval? Have the committees stopped working? Have the principal assumptions of the reform been altered? Nothing of the sort. Muraviev sent out a circular, which is quite irrelevant to the question; Rostovtsev, they say, has prepared a faulty project; certain landlords continue to abuse their authority, which is inevitable as long as their authority is unlimited, and so on. Evidently, these are the things that provoked such a sudden change [in your attitude]. Well, tell me, isn't this something of a farce? In the last issue of *The Bell* you wrote to the empress a letter full of fine thoughts and feelings. I fear that she, too, will not justify the hopes which you have placed upon her. Your hopes are aroused so easily and are disappointed so swiftly!

In the heat of passion you forget not only time, people, circumstances, you forget even your own position. A journalist who lives in the midst of society may well follow its momentary fashions, he may well be carried along by the wind which changes directions. But when his printing press is on the other side of Europe, when his word only reaches his fatherland two or three months after it is written, then what will be the result? Against his will his criticisms will be dissipated into thin air. Let us suppose, for example, that the articles in which you say everything is lost, that Alexander II did not justify the hopes placed upon him, let us suppose that these articles arrived in Moscow just when the sovereign was delivering his recent speech to the nobility. What impression would these articles leave on their readers? They call for the tocsin, but the reason for pealing the bells is not only long ago forgotten, but it turns out that it is simply a hoax, based on your credulity. Do you think, being carried away yourself, that you are in a position to carry others away?

Unfortunately, even such blunders do have sad consequences. Moderation, caution and rational discussion of social questions might prompt you to place your trust in the government; instead, you only appear to be frightened of it. Everyone in Russia who is ignorant, backward, incorrigible in his prejudices, submerged in trivial interests, everyone of this sort points to you and says: there are the consequences of the liberal current; this is what the word, freed from fetters, produces. It is sad to say that the first free Russian journal serves as the strongest proof of censorship's advantages, if indeed there can be strong proofs of censorship's advantages.

In fact, imagine that you, who are yourself carried away and who carry away others, would carry away Russian society and that Russia would be filled by people who throw themselves to extremes, who exhaust themselves in anger and indignation, who burn out quickly and expire halfway to the goal. Imagine that in the depths of our fatherland were established several *Bells* which would all, in various tones, start to ring after your example, which would vie with each other in fanning the fire, inflaming passions, inciting to the rod and the ax in order to realize their desires. What will the government do with such a society? To what end will this fury of social passions lead? Will it not be to the most cruel despotism? Almost every revolution is an example of a like process. Indeed, if a sick person, instead of calmly and patiently submitting to treatment, engages in wild outbursts, reopens his wounds, and snatches up a knife, there is nothing that can be done with him except to tie him up, hand and foot.

In a young society, which is still not accustomed to enduring domestic turmoil and has not managed to acquire the steadfast virtues of civic life, passionate political propaganda is more harmful than anywhere else. Our society must purchase its right to freedom by exhibiting rational self-control, and in what do you train it? In shortness of temper, in impatience, in nonnegotiable demands, in unscrupulousness. By your peevish tantrums, by your jokes that know no limits and your sarcasm that wears the alluring guise of independence of judgment, you indulge that flippant attitude toward political questions that is already too fashionable among us. We need an independent public opinion—this is virtually our first requirement—but a public opinion that is moderate, stable, serious-minded, with a strong backbone of political thought, a public opinion that can serve the government both as a support for its good intentions and as a prudent restraint against false policy. This is what we lack, this is what we must strive to create. My God, I am scolding! Even without this letter the Russian land is full of criticism. Russians excoriate everything: from the lowest to the highest spheres, at every level of society, everywhere you hear the same thing—criticism purposeless, fruitless, and witless. One becomes nauseated from hearing such a chorus. Therefore, do not be surprised that some people find you still too moderate, do not rejoice that your jokes and mockery get a reaction and win approval. We are always ready to enjoy such good humor, it is produced and consumed so easily, and cleverness is so honored in Russia! It replaces all statecraft, education, ideas won by hard labor, knowledge of affairs. On cleverness brilliant careers, colossal reputations have been built: by it people have entered the ranks of ministers, generals, and diplomats. We have no surer way to win ourselves a universal tribute of gratitude and approbation than to resolve all national and philosophical questions by clever remarks. This saves the reader from work, from intellectual exertion. Easy and pleasant is the ready and yet delightful riposte that serves as an answer to all objections. An inexhaustible supply of witticisms—that is the most reliable guarantee of success for the journalist. Invite Alexander II to collaborate with you, sing the acathistus to Norov or Viazemskii, print farces based on Panin—this will all be received with enthusiasm, all will travel from mouth to mouth. Only remember that witticisms can scarcely win the sympathy of truly enlightened individuals in Russia. They look at matters a bit more seriously. To them it seems that the habit of replacing action by theatrical inaction is deleterious to the political education of a people, that a society tutored in clever remarks may become incapable of the rational resolution of questions confronting it; finally, they would like the free Russian word to satisfy the deeply felt need for real political thought, not the frivolous need for scolding and witticism.

Here, gracious Sir, is the explanation for those reproaches which made it necessary for you to justify yourself before the public. The basic idea behind the reproaches is that, in a political journal, the bent for passion should give way to maturity of thought and rational self-control. If such a demand be doctrine, then I am a doctrinaire: it is not worth fighting over a word. You do not fancy a rational approach to politics, you prefer quickly to burn out, to exhaust yourself in anger and indignation. Go ahead: exhaust yourself! Such is your temperament; you won't change it. But please realize that this will neither benefit Russia nor enhance the merit of your journal, and that, in any case, it is nothing to be proud of.

Otherwise, everyone gladly acknowledges your real contribution—the uncovering of abuses. The extortionist, the oppressor in the most distant provinces of Russia now has to take into account your testimony. He may not fear government control, for he is accustomed from his youth to circumventing that. But he cannot escape the control of free expression, which, unseen, stands sentry over him in the person of all his associates and denounces his crime at the other end of Europe, on an island which unfailingly upholds the sacred banner of liberty. From this perspective, I repeat, you have the right to the gratitude of all and everyone, regardless of his political beliefs.

Part Two **Excerpts from *On Popular Representation***

Representation and Sovereignty

When the ancient peoples were working to establish political freedom in their homelands, they called each citizen to participate directly in political affairs.[1]

The people gathered in the town square, a debate occurred in the presence of everyone, a vote was taken and a common decision was reached. Modern peoples rarely resort to this type of assembly. It is encountered in the earliest recorded meetings of German military retinues, in medieval cities, and most recently in those small states which have retained their former, more or less patriarchal character—for example, the Swiss cantons. Village meetings do occur and do play a role in communal administration. But in general, modern peoples have rejected the resolution of political problems through collective meetings of all citizens. The right to vote in a popular assembly has been replaced by the elective principle; the town assembly has yielded to representation.

This transformation represents an enormous step in the development of civic life. Political freedom acquires here a form much better suited to the requirements of modern statehood. By virtue of representative institutions the state can extend its jurisdiction across vast regions, over numerous peoples; it need not confine itself to a small territory, which it must necessarily do if it is to govern through a town assembly. Citizens need not constantly gather in an assembly for common deliberations, as they must do in a small polity; instead, elected delegates travel from the far corners of the earth. Moreover, political freedom permeates national life; representation makes it possible to spread political rights to a much greater number of people whose interests are thereby safeguarded. Participation in decision making requires genuine ability and intimate acquaintance with political issues; it distracts citizens from their private occupations, forcing them to dedicate themselves to civic activity. For this reason the ancient peoples limited the right of citizenship to a comparatively small number of individuals who devoted themselves almost entirely to the state, leaving economically productive labor to slaves and foreigners. Rousseau, an advocate of direct voting rights for every citizen, concluded that it is not easy to establish such a governmental system in the absence of slavery. Representation ameliorates such difficulties. The overwhelming majority of citizens do not have to interrupt their labors. They limit themselves to participating in elections, delegating daily responsibility for civic affairs to those few individuals who, by virtue of their social and economic status, are able to dedicate themselves to political activity. By this means economically productive labor can be combined with political rights. Representation also raises the level of ability among members of the assembly. [Participation in] the election of representatives does not demand the elevated vision, the sure grasp of political issues that is essential in the discussion and resolution of these questions. [The business of the assembly] may be left to people who have managed to win the trust of the many, to people who have distinguished themselves from the rank-and-file by their talents. For this reason Aristotle considered election to be an aristocratic principle. There is no doubt that the process of election will promote from the masses if not the best people in the land, then at least people who are above average in ability.

Therefore, in modern societies the mass of citizens enjoying political freedom and having the right to vote confine themselves to electing representatives to whom they entrust the conduct of affairs as well as the responsibility of guarding the rights and interests of the electors. Representation, however, is not a simple commission such as a private warrant or a proxy; its political nature lends it a quite different character.

When a private individual entrusts his affairs to another, he intends for that person to carry out his personal will, which either for his own advantage or convenience he is conveying to the trustee who acts in his stead. The trustee is an agent or instrument of the first party. The trustee is obliged to act solely in the interests of the principal, according to the principal's instructions and within the limits the principal has established. If the trustee deviates from the set goal, if he acts against the will of the principal, the latter may always demand an accounting, may revoke the proxy power, and may even bring suit against the trustee.

Under a system of popular representation very different arrangements obtain. The responsibility of the trustee is not to carry out the private will of a principal but to discuss and decide civic business. The trustee must consider not the advantages of the electors but the good of the state. Once summoned to take part in political affairs, he acquires a certain measure of authority, and this places him above the electors who, as loyal subjects, are obliged to obey his decisions. For this reason a representative acts quite independently of the electors. Sometimes he is even obliged to act against their will and against their interests, for their private desires and advantages may be at odds with the common welfare. If the representative has taken upon himself the moral obligation of pursuing a certain objective, circumstances may alter his convictions. During general discussions of national affairs new points of view may appear; on almost all occasions mutual concessions and deals are necessary; rapidly changing events may alter political objectives being pursued by the representative. No matter how a representative acts, no matter what positions he may adopt, he can be held neither strictly accountable nor legally responsible for changing his political opinions. In a political community, accountability and responsibility are concepts applying only to subordinate officials charged with executing the will of their superiors, and an elected representative [is not subordinate to voters] but enjoys a certain authority relative to them.

Thus the will of citizens is transferred in its entirety to their representatives; citizens retain nothing except the unadorned right to vote. Moreover, an elected delegate represents not only his own electors but those electors who did not vote for him, the mass of citizens who lack the electoral right as well as the minority who cast ballots against him. In the houses of the legislature deputies are considered to be representatives not of the districts that elected them but of the entire country, of the entire nation. A member of the lower house in England represents neither a county nor a city but the entire English people. Broadly speaking, the concept of representation is a legal fiction, but a fiction inspired by necessity, by the principle of the state, by the relationship of government to citizens, by the ascendancy of the common welfare over private ends.

But this does not completely explain the nature of representation. If in one respect, in the independence of the representative with respect to electors, in his acquisition of authority, representation may be coincident with election to a public office, representation nevertheless has another side that distinguishes it from the first. A representative is not only an individual serving the state, but in this service he takes the place of the citizens themselves to the extent that they are called upon to participate in political affairs. In him is expressed the citizens' right; through him their opinions are conveyed to the government. While serving as a representative of the entire people, while acting in the name of common national objectives, he is also an agent of the majority which elected him. When electing someone, the voters are guided not so much by that person's abilities as by the correspondence of his way of thinking and political ideology to their own opinions and interests, and although he is juridically independent of them, he must constantly share his thoughts with the voters; there remains a moral dependence [upon them]. If this connection disappears, if the representative or the voters themselves deviate from earlier convictions, then new elections will give the citizens the chance to reestablish agreement by replacing their former representative with another. Frequent elections are intended constantly to reestablish this moral connection between representative and voters, while the intention of infrequent elections is to protect common national interests by giving representatives greater independence from the accidental changes and fluctuations of public opinion.

This intimate link between a representative and the electors is essential if the representative assembly is to be a true expression of the country's sentiment. Different strands of public opinion, various interests of the people must make themselves felt in the assembly in roughly the same way that they make themselves felt in society. This objective can be achieved by giving districts the power to elect their own representatives. Although an elected delegate may be a representative of the entire country, he is, nevertheless, sent to the assembly from a certain area and therefore reflects the political tendencies dominant in that area; all these tendencies taken together form public opinion, whose highest expression and focal point is the representative assembly. The chief task of the electoral laws is to make sure that the relation between sentiment in the country at large and in the legislature is a proper one, to ensure that in the legislature the real voice of the nation will be heard and not the opinion of a minority that has somehow acquired an artificial preponderance. The representative principle is the reign of public opinion expressed by conveyance of citizens' will to their elected representatives.

But the relation between representation and society should not be construed to imply that the opinion of each citizen who enjoys the electoral right must find its representative in the assembly, as certain radical thinkers suggest. John Stuart Mill, in his work *Considerations on Representative Government,* recommends a plan that would replace electoral districts by a completely new system of elections: a candidate who has received a certain number of votes, however these votes may be distributed across the realm, must be considered as elected since not only the majority, but every significant minority should receive access to the assembly, and every person, every opinion should be represented in it. It is impossible to think of this plan as being in accord with the true principles of popular representation. The demand that each citizen should be represented in Parliament by the very individual for whom the citizen has voted is an exaggeration of the individual element in politics. In effect, this system confers a proxy upon the representative. In reality, a citizen's personal right is confined to participating in elections; it does not entail the success of his candidate. An elected delegate is a representative not only of those who have voted for him but of the entire people and their essential interests. Representative government has the purpose of raising public opinion to a higher level, of stripping from it everything merely personal and accidental until what remains is its essence. Parliament does not express the infinite number of political views current among the people; it must not be a motley collection of dissonant opinions, as society necessarily is, but a center bringing together the main political ideologies that have succeeded in winning popular support and that by virtue of this support have become important for the realm as a whole. Otherwise, it will not be possible for delegates to constitute themselves into a stable majority and to govern. A private opinion may be very meritorious and well founded, but before it can be expressed in Parliament, it must acquire influence in the country at large. The right of a minority consists solely in the free dissemination of its convictions. In a representative assembly, where political issues are decided, the minority may enter only when it has managed to win a majority in some electoral district. By winning an election in a district it demonstrates its strength. If it is not able to acquire local influence anywhere in the country, then it will remain for the time being no more than an anomaly. Basing electoral representation on particular geographical districts is an excellent way of determining the public resonance of a given view. Every locality is a combination of various interests and social elements; it is a state on a small scale. To find several thousand supporters [in a large country] is not difficult; there is no sect so absurd as to lack numerous adherents. But the political power of an opinion is demonstrated by its influence on others, on people outside the sect, on various classes of society, and here local opinion serves as the touchstone. The common sense of legislators has always held to these principles, which are simpler and more practical than the artificial designs that one finds in theory.

Thus at the very heart of representation there lies a dual character, which must be borne in mind during discussion of all issues that concern it. Representation is both a manifestation of liberty and an instrument of government. Here liberty rises to the level of governmental authority. We must therefore examine the interrelation between these two crucial elements of political life.

Political Liberty and Its Development

The duality of principles at the heart of popular representation is also to be found in its very source—in political liberty. Freedom beckons citizens to take part in political affairs. In a representative form of government this participation mainly takes the form of the electoral right. What exactly is the electoral right upon which representation is based? What is its essence? On this question the opinions of publicists are divided.

The democratic school usually views the electoral principle as the right of each free person to participate in public affairs. Interpreting society as the product of the free will of the individual, this school sees free will as the basis of any government, and therefore it asserts that the right of participation in elections cannot be taken away from a citizen without violating the ideal of justice. On the contrary, writers who hold more conservative views understand the electoral principle not so much as a right but as a duty placed upon citizens for society's benefit. The rights of individuals, they contend, are limited [to the enjoyment of] liberty and do not extend to domination of others. Any public authority therefore necessarily has the character of an obligation. The electoral right gives to one person power over others; consequently, here too we can see only an obligation discharged by a citizen for the public good. This opinion is defended even by certain radical writers—for example, by Mill, who falls into a strange contradiction with himself when he argues elsewhere that it is unjust to deprive anyone at all of the customary right to vote on public issues that affect him in any way whatsoever. What has escaped Mill is the necessary consequence of this view for the electoral right conceived as duty—namely, that this right can belong only to those capable of assuming it. The basis of this right is not *freedom* but *competence*—a fact that has a crucial influence on the form which elections actually take.

The divergence of opinions [between democrats and more conservative thinkers] arises from the fact that the electoral right has two aspects. Like representation, it is simultaneously an expression of liberty and an instrument of government. Yet here liberty is the dominant consideration; in this respect the democratic school is closer to the truth than are the conservatives. The electoral right is first of all a right; it is given to a citizen not as an officeholder with duties to discharge but as a member of society in order that he might propagate his opinions and defend his interests. And the source of any such right is liberty. A right is liberty as defined by law or the possibility to act. Therefore, the electoral right is synonymous with political liberty, or with the freedom of citizens as members of the body politic.

By what means can liberty, understood as a concept applying to the individual, justify giving one person authority over another? How can liberty sanction the participation [of certain individuals] in government?

The answer is that free individuals share membership in a community, and therefore they inevitably exert influence upon one another. As soon as people enter into certain kinds of relationships, the freedom of one individual must affect the freedom of the other. Hence there arises the need for mutual limitations on the exercise of individual liberty. Each member of society must know what he can and cannot do. Liberty must be defined and limited by the law—that is, it must be translated into a set of statutory rights. In the state of nature, an individual may enjoy unlimited freedom without the need for legal definitions; in a more sophisticated society, liberty can be preserved only if statutory rights are clearly spelled out. Where conceptions of liberty are inconsistent or poorly developed, there liberty disappears. But by being encoded as statutory rights, liberty's writ is entended to the entire community. It is defined and preserved by the public authority which issues the law and to which each individual must subordinate himself, for no one can be a judge of his own right. On the other hand, any right must be safeguarded against governmental arbitrariness. Where individual liberty is subordinated to public authority, arbitrariness can be avoided only by allowing the citizen to participate in the very government that defines and preserves rights. As long as the government is independent of the citizens, their rights are not guaranteed against its arbitrariness; with respect to such a government, an individual is rightless. The communal dimension assumed by liberty in human societies entails that individual freedom under law can find a sure guarantee of its existence only in the exercise of the political right, by virtue of which each person participating in public affairs will acquire the same influence over others that they possess over him. Given the reciprocity of rights and duties, political liberty is both a consequence of individual liberty and the ultimate guarantor of the latter's survival. On this basis, citizens are allowed more or less participation in the courts, in the executive branch, and, finally, in the legislature. Furthermore, political liberty flows from individual liberty not only in the form of a guarantee of right but as a consequence of the fact that citizens, as members of an association, take part in affairs that concern them all. The polity is a community of free individuals, and its interests are essentially wed to the interests of citizens, understood not as private individuals but as members of the whole. The activity of a citizen occurs here not in the private but in the public sphere; his liberty and rights express not the principle of individualism alone but the relationship of the individual to the community. Political liberty consists in the fact that the citizen, as a member of the body politic, participates in public affairs, and this makes him a participant in the government that oversees these affairs. The citizen acquires influence over others because he is a participant in public business that is of concern to himself.

Political liberty is thus the culmination of individual liberty. Liberty is the source of political right, just as it is the source of every other right. On the other hand, there is no doubt that, having reached such a stage of development, liberty acquires a completely different character than it has in private life. It is transformed from something personal into something public and social, it decides the fate of all, it becomes an instrument of the entire community. Therefore, in the body politic the concept of duty is joined to the concept of right. A citizen who has a share in authority must act not on behalf of his personal advantages but for the sake of the common good; he must be conscious not only of his private goals but of the common purposes that take precedence in civic life. To do so demands an unusual competence. A person who does not understand the public interest must not be permitted to take part in government. Were he to do so, this would sacrifice the higher principle, the common good, to individual liberty, when in fact all civic life depends on the subordination of the individual to the public good. Those lacking in competence must therefore be prevented from participating in political rights. This rule is recognized by every state in the world, even the most democratic ones, where freedom lies at the basis of the entire system of government. Everywhere women and children, as incompetents, are deprived of political rights, although as free individuals they enjoy civil rights. While certain democrats, even serious ones such as Mill, demand for women the right to vote, this strange misunderstanding of the difference between the two sexes remains an isolated error. The common sense of the human race has never permitted this theory to be applied to legislative practice. However, even these writers demand political rights for women not in the name of liberty as such, but in the name of competence, for they consider woman to be just as competent in political life as is the male.

Thus, if liberty serves as the source of political right, competence is a necessary precondition [for its exercise]. The principle of competence applies not to individual persons who disappear into a mass and who have no significance for public administration but to those social classes who are licensed to participate in public affairs. The usual indicator of political competence is thus ownership of property, although other prerequisites may also be attached, such as proof of a certain level of education. With respect to certain individuals, the proprietary indicator may occasionally prove mistaken: a poor person may be more competent than a rich one. But when applied to entire classes, this indicator is very accurate.

One may be easily convinced of this if one looks at those qualities of which political competence is an amalgam.

These qualities are of various orders—intellectual, ethical, and material. Among the first type is a consciousness of the needs of the realm, and the preconditions of this consciousness are education and familiarity with public affairs. In those places where blind instinct rather than rational consciousness dominates public life, political liberty acts as a destructive force, to the clear detriment of national interests, which interests require a lucid grasp of means and ends. Government must always be in the hands of the rational portion of the people. But political consciousness must be joined with an ethical quality: the constant readiness to support the common cause with all one's resources. Political liberty demands from citizens indefatigable activity, energetic pursuit of common objectives; otherwise, it rests on an unstable foundation. Political liberty also presupposes in citizens both a lively interest in politics and an attachment to order—that is to the foundations of political life, to the imperatives of government, to the rule of law, to those things benefiting the fatherland, to the family, to property—in a word, to those principles on which a given society is constructed and the violation of which will lead to ethical and physical upheaval. Finally, in addition to all this, political activity presupposes a greater or lesser degree of social independence, which makes it possible for an individual not to be a tool in others' hands but to possess his own voice.

All these qualities, as noted, may not characterize every individual who enjoys the political right. To demonstrate their presence in each separate case would be both impossible and pointless. It is only necessary that these qualities be present in those classes entrusted with a share of political authority. By and large, property is the most important factor in facilitating the development of these qualities. It provides an individual the chance for an education, the leisure to consider political questions, a high stake in public administration, an attachment to order, and, finally, independence of position. Only abstract radicalism can deny this self-evident truth. In and of itself, property does not provide political competence, but it conveys all the preconditions necessary for acquiring such competence. Property distinguishes those classes which dedicate themselves to intellectual work from those which are devoted to physical labor, and the difference in occupations obviously affects the political competence of the various classes. Of course, one can imagine a situation in which education is equally distributed in society, where political interests and attachment to order permeate the lowest strata of society, where the ease of finding employment and high wages provide even the day laborer a certain independence of position. Under such conditions, there is no reason to deny political rights to the working classes. But here as well, relative to the other necessary qualities, the propertied classes have an evident advantage over the workers. Therefore, property generally serves as the best indicator of political competence. In this respect it is far better than proof of a certain level of education. Going through school provides neither an independent position nor a practical view of the world, nor does it provide an attachment to order. On the contrary, education without property too often makes a person dependent on those able to promote him, or it arouses in him a dissatisfaction with an existing social order in which it may not be easy to make his way. Education makes one demand more in life without necessarily providing the means to satisfy these demands; it may therefore be the most favorable soil for radical ideas. An educated person must first of all demonstrate his competence by arranging his own affairs, by acquiring the material means to guarantee his independence in the world. That is the lot of humanity in general, for whom the acquisition of material goods serves as a precondition for obtaining spiritual goods. There is therefore nothing ethically troubling in denying political rights to the poor. The labor and attention of the poor are focused on the material world; as they subjugate nature, the poor acquire the possibility of rising to political activity which presupposes economic self-sufficiency, leisure, and higher education.

Yet political competence limited to the elite or to one class, one social Estate, is alone insufficient to sustain free institutions. For free institutions are based upon the collective activity of the various elements composing the nation. Popular representation must express the concerns of society as a whole, and not merely of a certain portion of society, for the state's business is the liberty common to all, the public authority and decisions affecting everyone. If the lower classes, due to a lack of competence and sophistication, are excluded from political rights, then the upper classes must themselves speak for the panoply of substantive interests and elements that make up popular life. Therefore, in order to establish political liberty it is necessary for political competence profoundly to permeate society, to spread among the various social strata who are summoned collectively to take part in common business. Among them must be developed not only a degree of political sophistication but also the habit of working together, for otherwise consensus will never be established, and the wise conduct of public business will become impossible. In those countries where the various classes have contradictory interests that inspire in them a mutual hostility, freedom will breed dissension. One can say that the political competence of citizens consists chiefly of the ability to encourage the pluralistic pursuits of a free society while meeting the paramount needs of the realm. But to accomplish this task it is essential that competence be the possession of entire classes, so that various elements of the people are bound together by a consciousness of the general needs of the realm.

Given these imperatives, political liberty obviously may be more or less developed in a certain realm. The different branches of the state apparatus do not require an identical level of competence among those called to participate in public business. The degree of competence that will suffice for the lower spheres of government may be quite insufficient for the higher spheres; for it is easier to comprehend more immediate interests than the more general and distant ones, it is easier to operate in a sphere one knows than it is to act on a broader stage. As a consequence, the political right of citizens may be confined to participation in the courts or in local administration, or may extend to participation in the central government. By the same token, the representative principle implied by political rights may operate in the capital city as well as in the provinces, it may take as its jurisdiction national affairs and/or local and

Estate matters—in a word, its place is anywhere where a citizen's own voice is replaced by the voice of an elected delegate. Everywhere representation serves as an expression of citizens' rights to participate in deciding public business, and therefore it entrusts them with a share of public authority; but in different spheres this right has different meanings. The main forms of representation are provincial and central.

Local assemblies—for example, our zemstvo institutions—are based on the representative principle. The law bids these institutions to play a role in the administration of local affairs. They not only give advice but issue regulations that are binding on citizens. Consequently, they enjoy a certain measure of power, limiting the authority of the provincial governors appointed by the central administration. The governors, acting in the name of general interests, link provincial administration with the central administration into which the provinces fit as so many parts. Local assemblies represent local needs [to the central government]. Power is divided and shared between [local assemblies and the governors], for together they constitute the general system of provincial administration.

All this concerns only the purely administrative sphere; political matters in the narrow sense of the term—that is, matters affecting the interests of the realm as a whole—are absent here. The zemstvo assemblies are bidden to discuss local interests, not general national problems. Above the provincial administration there rises the central government, which controls the activity of the provincial administration, acts as a judge of it, gives it rights and takes them away. Sometimes, in exceptional cases, local assemblies may assume a partially political character. Without referring to institutions still extant in several countries, institutions that are vestiges of the medieval order and of former national fragmentation, one can still cite examples in modern states. Thus in Prussia in 1823, provincial assemblies were established to discuss laws affecting the provinces. But such broadening of the jurisdiction of provincial assemblies is not in accord with their essence. In Prussia [the grant of broader authority to provincial assemblies] proceeded from the desire to avoid instituting a promised representative assembly at the national level, to grant in its stead incomparably lesser rights. In general, the discussion of political matters, including legislative ones, is a prerogative of central institutions, regardless of the form of government. Local representation, by its very character, must limit itself to local interests with respect to which it may be granted a share of authority. If by the term *political right,* as opposed to *personal liberty,* one understands any sort of participation in government, then local representation will be an expression of political right; but this right is confined to the purely administrative sphere.

Much more important are national representative assemblies. They are bidden to discuss and decide general public business. In them is expressed political right in the true sense—that is, the participation of citizens in national government, in the central government of the realm. Here too, however, political right may have greater or lesser scope. There may be assemblies of representatives that have a purely advisory character. They may discuss issues put on the agenda by the executive, but decisions as such do not depend upon them. They offer advice, which may be either accepted or rejected by the central administration. Here the minority's voice has the same weight as the majority's. Both serve only as mechanisms to elucidate an issue from all sides and to indicate the view most widespread in society. [Advisory assemblies] are one of many elements that guide the central government in its decisions. But decisions are left entirely to the central government; the assembly may express a certain idea, but it has neither will nor the right [to impose the decision].

We shall return later to advisory assemblies and we shall analyze in greater detail their strengths and weaknesses. Here we shall limit ourselves to several observations. First, it must be noted that history presents no examples of such assemblies as permanent institutions. One encounters advisory assemblies that are convoked rarely, in cases of need, at the whim of the sovereign. Since they do not constitute permanent, necessary agencies in the system of public institutions, they are not granted any rights; they only respond to questions submitted by the government for their consideration. In this form, advisory assemblies do not even possess a representative character. Elections convey no right upon them; they do not represent the citizens' will. Delegates are nothing but experts, knowledgeable people who are elected to serve the government's ends; and for the same reason, and with the same benefit, they may be appointed by the government. Indeed, the electoral principle is superfluous here. But as soon as an assembly of elected delegates becomes a permanent state institution, an indispensable agency for the discussion and resolution of public issues, then such rightlessness becomes unthinkable. In such a case, it is essential to define by law the assembly's jurisdiction, to outline its operational authority, to specify its rights. It stands at the summit of the state, and it does so not as the government's pliant instrument but as a manifestation of the popular will which it attempts to represent. An elected assembly, by its very nature, must be independent of the executive, and if it is granted certain statutory prerogatives, then by this fact it becomes a partner sharing sovereign authority. Questions that come under its jurisdiction cannot be decided without its consent; consequently, its will is no longer subordinate but sovereign.

It should be clear what an enormous gap lies between local representation and popular representation [at the national level]. Obviously, these two forms of representation are intimately connected. A national assembly may be considered the logical consequence, the culmination or crown of local representation, the focal point toward which the people's otherwise disparate thoughts and desires may be directed. Even the structure, the membership, and jurisdiction of the assemblies in both cases may be the same or quite similar. Within the sphere of provincial administration local representation occupies an analogous position to that which the central representative assembly occupies at the national level. Therefore, the national assembly is the natural completion of the edifice whose foundation is local representation. Yet behind this similarity there lurks a profound difference: the difference has to do not only with the scope of interests under the assemblies' jurisdictions, but with the very quality of representation which, by becoming broader and more extensive, acquires a completely different character and significance. Local representation deals with administrative matters, while national representation deals with political matters; the former provides citizens a contingent right to participate in local administration, while the latter makes citizens full partners in shaping the sovereign will of the entire community; the former leaves unaffected the unity and independence of the central government, while the latter divides central power among various agencies, if that power is not entrusted in its entirety to the assembly. The introduction of local representation, with all its implications, can occur without altering the basic foundations of the state system; the institution of a national representative assembly changes the very root, the very foundation of a nation's political life—sovereign authority itself. It can be said that such a change is the most important, the most significant step in the history of a state. A form of government is the consequence of the entire evolution of national life; it is determined by the character of a people, its makeup, position, level of education. The central government is the people's guide, the highest judge of their needs and interests, their agent in the international arena. Therefore, to adopt the representative form of government is not analogous to giving local inhabitants the right to build a road or to erect a charitable institution. Local representation is not the logical culmination of national representation; national representation is the result of much more sophisticated processes and considerations. National representation requires quite different conditions, another level of competence.

The Doctrine of Popular Sovereignty

In the preceding chapter we tried to demonstrate that popular representation constitutes the highest stage of liberty's evolution, that its indispensable precondition is political competence. Yet not infrequently the people's participation in sovereign authority is treated as an absolute imperative of a just social order, and this opinion is buttressed by arguments that at first glance may seem quite convincing. National affairs affect everyone; they are the collective business of all citizens, of every member of the realm. "The national interest of England is the private concern of every Englishman," says an English dictum. Evidently, nothing can be more just than participation in government by those individuals who are affected by public affairs. The self-government of a nation or people is a dictate of natural law, and since the purpose of sovereign authority is to conduct the public's business, then sovereign authority ought to belong to the people. Self-government is equated with the sovereignty of the people. Having accepted this premise, we quickly arrive at the conclusion that citizens may always demand popular representation as an innate, inalienable right. This conclusion follows directly from the premise.

The doctrine of popular sovereignty is very widely disseminated. Not only is it embraced by many writers, it constitutes the heart of every form of government based on the popular will. This notion, however, takes two different forms. Some advocates understand popular sovereignty to mean a nation's right to determine its own destiny, to establish whatever form of government suits it. Others understand popular sovereignty to mean democratic government in which sovereign authority belongs to the people whose inalienable right is to govern either directly or through deputies. These two different conceptions are even designated by different names. The former is sometimes referred to as national sovereignty *(souveraineté nationale);* the latter is called popular sovereignty *(souveraineté du peuple).*

Before we turn to discussion of this question, we must observe that the word *people [narod]* or *nation [natsiia]* is used in two different senses, the confusion of which provides ground for fundamental misunderstandings. *The people* sometimes connotes the collectivity of citizens forming a single body politic inclusive of the government, which constitutes an essential part of the political arrangement; sometimes *the people* connotes the collectivity of citizens as opposed to the government. In the first case, the sovereignty of the people is synonymous with the sovereignty of the nation-state, for the people, organized in a single body with the government as its head, is the nation-state. To govern this body there exists within it a sovereign authority, which belongs to an agency defined by law: to a popular assembly, an aristocratic collegium, to a monarch, or to several agencies together. All these are forms of government which one encounters in history and which exist today; each of them has its own legitimacy and is recognized by the people. But in this sense one cannot speak about the self-government of a people, for that would imply popular control of public affairs through legally established agents of sovereign authority.

The word *people* takes another meaning when used in the phrase *the doctrine of popular sovereignty.* This term connotes the collectivity of citizens in opposition to the government. The government is made dependent on the citizenry, to which is attributed sovereign authority within the state. The difference between the two variant forms of the doctrine is that one considers as the inherent property of the people only constituent authority or the right to establish within the realm a certain form of government; the other sees the people as possessing the plenitude of sovereign authority, the right to control all the branches of government: legislative, executive, and judicial.

In political science, theorists argued long ago that when individuals first unite themselves in a state, the people have the right to establish one or another form of government, transferring to selected persons the sovereign authority belonging to them. This theory disappeared along with the concepts of the state of nature and an original compact between individuals. But today some theorists claim that a people has the right to establish whatever form of government may suit its needs. In this interpretation there is an attempt to reconcile democratic principles with the possibility and legitimacy of various forms of government, which otherwise, from the democratic perspective, lack any legal justification. This theory has even been embodied in certain legislation. Thus the current French constitution, which is based on the will of the people, makes the emperor legally responsible to the people. This is quite logical, for whoever determines the form of government also has the right to hold rulers responsible, to remove them from power and replace them with others. But the question arises: By what means can the French people express their sovereign will? Where is the agent of their executive authority? The constitution gives no answer. This authority does not reside in the legislature, which has a clearly defined purpose: to discuss the laws proposed by the government. Of the emperor's responsibility to the legislature there can be no question. The legislature does not even have the right to criticize him. Therefore, even if the people wished to make use of the authority attributed to them, they could do so only by means of revolution. But revolution is not a right but a violation of right. It can sometimes be justified by circumstances, by oppression, but it never can be an activity sanctioned by law. In a properly functioning political order, revolution is inconceivable. The right to make an uprising, a right proclaimed by the French constitution of 1793, is the legitimation of anarchy. Obviously, then, the current French constitution contains an inconsistency. It gives the people a right and deprives the people of the possibility of implementing that right; it establishes a prerogative and creates no agency to make use of that prerogative. But a prerogative without an agency to make use of it is a pure fiction. Without legal agency, a government cannot issue binding decrees; nor without such an agency can there be that unity of will that is an essential earmark of government. Power may belong to the people as a collectivity of individuals, as an organized body, but it cannot belong to isolated individuals who, lacking the legal means to enforce their will, can exercise no power.

The inconsistency is not a simple oversight or a ploy of the constitution's author. The contradiction lies deeper: it has to do with the incompatibility of hereditary monarchy with the right of the people to exercise sovereign authority. A monarch is not the president of a republic: by nature, he is independent of the people. Originally, the people may have entrusted sovereign authority to him, but subsequently that authority is transmitted by hereditary succession, as a statutory right, and it no longer proceeds from the will of the citizenry. The same thing can be said of any other form of government in which there exist agents independent of the people. Only in countries where the plenitude of power is concentrated in the people does the right belong to the people to establish this or that form of government; the authority to constitute a form of government is the most substantive element of sovereign authority. A people may even introduce a hereditary monarchy. But as soon as that act has been completed, as soon as sovereign authority has been transferred to another person, as soon as a new and independent agency for the possessing of that power has been created, then the constituent authority of the people ceases to exist. Its will is no longer sovereign. It loses the right to change the form of government as it wishes, just as a limited monarch, once having granted a constitution, loses the right to change or abolish that constitution arbitrarily.

Thus the doctrine of national sovereignty leads to inconsistencies that arise inevitably from the desire to reconcile two irreconcilable principles: the inalienable sovereign right of the people and the existence of forms of government legitimated by history and by circumstance, which forms of government do not recognize the people's sovereign authority. Hoping to avoid extremes and the contradictions arising, as we shall see below, from another more logical theory, this doctrine is a kind of compromise and is itself tangled in contradictions. It suggests that the people have the right at any time to constitute a government and that various branches of government directly depend upon the people. While granting the people the unadorned right to make a revolution if they wish to alter a governmental institution, this doctrine provides no legal mechanism for the people to make use of their sovereign authority. Given the logic of this doctrine it could not be otherwise, for as soon as the people acquire a permanent legally sanctioned agent with the right to dismiss officials and appoint others, then the authorities become dependent on the people. The authorities cease to be sovereign; political sovereignty is then concentrated entirely in the people. Such an arrangement exists in democratic republics, where not infrequently special mechanisms and regulations [make it possible for the people to exercise] constituent authority—for example, special assemblies or requirements that any changes in the constitution be approved by a unanimous vote. In such cases, the plenitude of sovereign authority belongs to the people, who, on the one hand, establish the fundamental law of the state and, on the other hand, govern through elected representatives. In mixed systems of government, the people possess a portion of constituent authority;

but history knows no examples of a governmental system where sovereign authority belonged to a certain individual or individuals while the people reserved for themselves the right to dismiss officials and to establish a new form of government. Everywhere the right to alter the structure of the government belongs to the agent to whom the right to govern is entrusted, regardless of whether the system is monarchical, aristocratic, democratic, or mixed. This rule is violated only by revolutions; but a revolution, as noted earlier, is not a right but an event that overturns rights.

Much more consistent are those writers who attribute to the people not an imaginary, theoretical right to alter the form of government, but sovereign authority in its entirety; these writers regard popular self-government as a natural, inalienable prerogative of the people. This doctrine has a rich literature, is based on very powerful arguments, and is the theory informing certain existing political arrangements.

What are the theoretical bases of this doctrine?

The cornerstone of the entire system of thought lies in the concept of innate human freedom. By nature, human beings are free beings and, as such, are equal to one another, for human freedom is identical for all. The only justifiable limit on one person's freedom is the freedom of others. Positive law consists entirely in the mutual limitation of freedom. This concept of freedom was enunciated in the famous "Declaration of the Rights of Man and Citizen," which was worked out by the French Constituent Assembly in 1789; the same concept was defended by Kant in his teaching on natural law. But because the implementation of statutory law is inconceivable in the absence of coercive authority, individuals who enter into society create a government in order to safeguard the liberty of each individual from violations by others. Free individuals enter into society by their own volition, by mutual consent, on the basis of an agreement for the mutual preservation of rights. They establish public authority to safeguard liberty, not to violate it. An individual thus remains free in society as well; subordinating himself to a set of universally binding rules, he is obeying his own will and is acting in his own personal interests. The government that executes the laws is the instrument and expression of the general will of citizens, and therefore it is in constant dependence on the citizenry. If it oversteps its bounds, if it violates liberty and the rights of citizens, the people may dismiss it and appoint another. The logical consequence of the doctrine is the establishment of a republican form of government as the only legitimate form of government.

But defenders of this doctrine disagree among themselves over the amount of liberty that should be accorded citizens in society or the state. The various and contradictory views on this issue reveal the bankruptcy of the entire theory. It is obvious that an individual cannot retain in society the same degree of liberty that he might enjoy in solitude, in the desert where he is not surrounded by other people, where his will does not collide with the will of others. In social life, limitations on liberty are unavoidable, collisions of will are inevitable. But where is the proper limit of an individual's right, and who is the judge of this? Natural law, which is deduced from reason [in the abstract], is an inadequate guide here; specific legal definitions are needed. An individual, by virtue of the rights ascribed to him, lays hands on the external, objective world, subjects it to his needs and desires, makes it his property. But natural law, which has placed nature at our feet, does not define what should belong to one individual and what to another. Concerning property, its limits, its characteristics and its transfer from one person to another, there must exist positive statutory regulations binding on everyone. Even under the aegis of positive law, constant disputes between individuals are unavoidable, for the rights and interests of individuals overlap at every step. Who will be the legislator and the judge in such a case?

If in the definition of rights and the disposition of disputes sovereign authority is entrusted to a public authority, to government [*obshchestvennaia vlast'*], then there is no guarantee whatsoever of the liberty of the individual. In a given society there may be unjust statutory laws, a court may issue a wrong judgment, the government may act in support of certain individuals to the detriment of others. History and life present innumerable examples [of such abuses]. Even where public authority belongs to citizens themselves, the majority may act improperly, may oppress the minority. If, for example, property holders should have the political ascendancy, then nothing will prevent them from promulgating laws and regulations disadvantageous to the have-nots, from making it difficult for the have-nots to acquire property, from placing them in a dependent position. Conversely, a majority of have-nots will attempt to despoil property owners, to turn property holders' possessions to the majority's use by means of taxes, excise charges, and expropriations. As a consequence, an individual who has entered society for his own good, in order to safeguard his liberty, may find it to be not the guarantor of his rights but a source of oppression. No system of government, so long as it is faithful to this doctrine, can circumvent this problem. Moreover, nothing except a person's own will can compel him to obey the government. As soon as we take individual liberty to be the basis of public life, then the subordination of the minority to the majority is no longer justifiable under natural law. If an individual, upon entering society, has agreed to abide by decisions of the whole community, then he has given free consent to this limitation; he has limited his innate liberty for the sake of his own perceived interests. If these interests turn out to be illusory, or if the ends for which he entered society are not attained, or if his freedom and his rights are violated, what prevents him from taking back his consent, from refusing to obey the government? Removal of consent is all the easier because, under the principles of the theory, public authority is not considered to have unlimited rights over individuals. According to Locke, government has only those rights which have been transferred to it by the consent of free individuals. But no one can transfer to another rights that one did not possess in the first place. According to natural law, no one has the right arbitrarily to take control over another individual or over his property; consequently, the government's rights extend only to the preservation of the natural rights of the individual. Paine goes still further when he asserts that individuals entrust to the government only those rights which they cannot defend on their own. These are the principles underlying the doctrine on the innate rights of the individual, which rights should remain inalienable and inviolable even in a political community. But if each member of society retains innate rights upon which the government may not infringe, then who will be the judge if the government should violate these rights? Obviously, the individual himself who considers his rights to have been violated will be judge, and on this basis he may at any time refuse to obey a governmental decree. This consequence has been explicitly recognized by eighteenth-century publicists, who, following this train of reason to its logical conclusion, have claimed that at any moment the individual has the right to weigh the advantages and disadvantages of living in the social compact, and if the disadvantages should outweigh the advantages, the individual may refuse to obey the government and may leave the social compact.

It is obvious, however, that such a social arrangement is utterly impractical. If an individual, by virtue of his innate liberty, remains judge with respect to the decisions of the public authority and if he can refuse to obey these decisions as soon as he finds these decisions unjust or disadvantageous to himself, then social order will break down. Instead of a single will prevailing in society, private arbitrariness will be the dominant principle; disputes [between individuals] will generate anarchy. A genuine community can exist only where the individual has renounced his natural liberty, where he ceases to be judge with respect to his own rights and interests and accepts decisions of the publicly constituted authority, however disadvantageous or unjust he may consider these decisions to be. This was understood by Rousseau, who replaced the theory of innate human rights with a new theory—the theory of sovereignty of the people [*narodovlastie*].

Rousseau is a leading spokesman of the democratic school; his work *The Social Contract* is the culmination of the theory of popular sovereignty. It not only became the handbook of the democratic party in France but had an enormous influence upon the first-class German thinkers of the late eighteenth century, upon Kant and Fichte, who took a significant portion of their political theories from it. And no one before or since has defended so forcefully and so elegantly the principles of human liberty and popular self-government, no one has imagined with such logical rigor the consequences of these principles. But the very logical rigor of Rousseau's conclusions exposes the inadequacy of his initial premise.

"Man is born free, but is everywhere in chains." Thus Rousseau begins his treatise. What is the cause of this enslavement? Man cannot voluntarily alienate his own liberty; he has no right to do so, for he cannot renounce his own nature. Considered in the abstract, any act based on such alienation is null and void. Consequently, a government that subordinates liberty to its own interests is illegitimate. Indeed, all governments of present, past, and future which do not rest on the free will of citizens lack legal foundation. They are the fruit of violence against which the people always have the right to rise up.

But how can man retain his innate liberty in the state? To transfer to the public authority a certain portion of his rights while holding another in reserve is impossible, for in this case each person will be judge of his own rights, and the result will be not order but anarchy. The complete alienation of natural liberty for the state's use is unavoidable; but an individual may receive this liberty back in altered form. Compensation consists in the fact that he becomes a member of a sovereign entity, he shares in the sovereign authority of the state. He has renounced his own liberty for the sake of all, but has acquired in return a share of power over everyone. He has exchanged his natural liberty for political liberty. He has subordinated his natural liberty to decisions of the general will, but, participating in these decisions, he is submitting only to his own will. This is the essence of the original social compact which constitutes, according to Rousseau, the sole proper foundation of government. The only legitimate form of government is one based on the inalienable and inviolable right of popular sovereignty, on the direct participation of each citizen in the decisions of government. Rousseau thus rejects the principle of representation, for here a citizen transfers his will to another individual. In representative government,

Rousseau claims, a citizen is free only at the moment when he casts his ballot in elections; thereafter he lacks rights in a meaningful sense, he ceases to be a citizen and becomes a nullity.

The train of logic should have led Rousseau to recognize the political rights of women and children. Like men, women are also free beings; on what basis can women be excluded from a share in political rights if the only source of this right is liberty and if the principle of competence is not taken into account? By the same token, if a man is born free, then freedom belongs to him from infancy; no one has the right to subject a child to public authority if the child has not announced his consent, and if he has not participated in making general decisions. But Rousseau does not touch upon these questions; this is the only logical inconsistency with which one can reproach him. All the other difficulties inherent in the social order he has invented he faces directly and refutes boldly, no matter how incongruous the results may be. And the difficulties of his system are numerous.

It is easy enough to say that, by taking part in making general regulations binding on everyone, I am merely submitting to my own will and that by this means I am preserving my liberty. In practice the matter comes out rather differently. In an assembly various opinions are expressed, a majority and a minority take shape. If I remain in the minority, then the [assembly's] decision was made against my will; I am compelled to submit to another's will, and my freedom disappears.

Rousseau foresaw this objection; how does he refute it? He claims that while voting in the assembly, no one desires his own opinion to triumph but wishes the general opinion—that is, the view of the majority—to triumph. As soon as the numerical advantage appears on the other side, then each citizen sees that he was mistaken to regard his own opinion as the general one, and therefore he immediately changes his will and adheres to the other side.

This obvious sophism flies in the face of the existence of political parties in every free state. Parties, both in society and in legislative assemblies, engage in constant competition with one another and do not desire the triumph of their opponents. If an assembly makes a decision not in harmony with one or another party's opinion, then the defeated party not only does not renounce its former views and desires but, on the contrary, redoubles its efforts to win the majority to its side and to vanquish its opponents. Therefore, instead of a general will which must be expressed in the law, what prevails is the particular will of one or another political party. Rousseau understood this as well, but he tried to obviate the problem by completely prohibiting parties in his state. Each citizen must vote by himself, on the basis of a view that he has arrived at himself. Any preliminary meetings, any caucuses, any actions undertaken alone [outside the assembly] are strictly prosecuted by the laws. In place of liberty is established despotism.

Still, even the prohibition of parties does not eliminate the possibility of decisions unfair or disadvantageous to the minority. Again, this difficulty did not escape Rousseau, who, to resolve it, thought up a remedy just as impractical as the first. The remedy derives from his postulate that every decree issued by the sovereign authority should apply to all citizens; each citizen, therefore, when casting a ballot, knows that the decision will affect him. This postulate rules out narrowly framed special legislation, defining the rights or prerogatives of a certain stratum of persons in the realm—for example, laws applying only to farmers or only to merchants. Such legislation might be justified if everyone had the same occupation, the same amount of property, even the same gender. Otherwise, the law could not conceivably establish the same rights for all and offer the same benefits to everyone. Another consequence of this rule is that the popular assembly is deprived of executive and judicial authority, for these powers always concern individuals. Even the right to hold elections cannot be granted to the people in its capacity as sovereign authority, because elections affect not everyone but only certain individuals. On this ground Rousseau explicitly denies the people the right to hold elections. Meanwhile, because the government must originate from the people, because it must be an obedient tool for executing the sovereign's will, still another difficulty arises. Rousseau circumvents it by arguing that once the popular assembly, acting in its capacity as sovereign authority, has established a certain form of government, it then suddenly changes into a democratic government, which may hold elections and accomplish other tasks of government. The utter childishness of this argument is patent.

Thus the government can promulgate only laws applying to all citizens identically. In theory, this proviso guarantees proper decisions, for no one desires to do evil to himself, and therefore universally applicable legislation must in every instance be advantageous to everyone. Yet Rousseau understood that the people do not always see where their real advantage lies. He says that legislation is a very complex business. The positive effects of a law or an institution may rarely be grasped by individuals who have not experienced these effects in practice. Good legislation presupposes a rare combination of conditions and qualities in the nation, a combination so unusual that it is almost never encountered in the real world. Rousseau claims that it is essential for society to be educated by good legislation; only then will it be able to understand the benefits [of this legislation]. But what follows from this argument is that the people are incapable of making laws for themselves. The sovereignty of the people turns out to be inadequate here; what is needed is a legislator.

But a legislator cannot act against the will of the people; that would violate the fundamental social compact. He has the right only to offer a set of laws for the people's approval. Meanwhile, the people, not yet educated by legislation, are in no condition to understand the advantages of the proposed laws. How to break out of this vicious circle? In order to do so, Rousseau says, there is only one remedy: religious deception. The legislator must pass himself off as a prophet of the will of God and by this means compel the people voluntarily to accept the laws he proposes.

A religious deception! That is where Rousseau's logic ultimately leads, just as, at another point, he finally admits that slavery is essential after having asserted earlier that slavery is morally wrong. This is very odd indeed. Rousseau's absurd notions, his shocking conclusions usually escape people who, taking on faith the principle of innate human freedom and popular sovereignty, never carefully examine the underlying premises of his argument or the implications of it. Meanwhile, Rousseau sinned only by force of logic. Having accepted innate liberty as the only basis on which a society can be constructed, he wanted to preserve this liberty in the state: even here, each citizen must submit only to his own will. But because that is impossible, since a fundamental precondition of political life is the subordination of individual will to higher entities, then contradictions are unavoidable, and Rousseau can extricate himself from them only by means of new inconsistencies and contradictions.

It is not difficult to rebut Rousseau's doctrine through simple comparison of it with reality. In practice, man is never born free; on the contrary, he is always dependent. From the cradle he is a member of a certain family, society, political community; he is subordinate to familial and public authority; he is bound by the assumptions and rules of the milieu into which he is born. In a word, he is born not as an abstract being who enjoys unlimited freedom and knows no obligations, but as a member of a certain social organism that encompasses in an integral whole not only the present generation, but past and future generations as well. The original state of nature, about which writers of the seventeenth and eighteenth centuries dreamed, is nothing but a fiction. It never existed and could not have existed; it violates human nature. Another fiction is the social contract by virtue of which individuals make themselves into a political community. History knows no such contracts. Really-existing states have been founded in other ways, most often by force of arms, by conquest, by voluntary or compulsory subordination of inchoate societies to unified, already existing governments; sometimes, although this is extremely rare, states are based on the popular will, but on a will already educated by political life, a will taking as its basis not innate human liberty but the subordination of individual will to the community for the sake of the public and private benefits that the community may offer. These are the foundations on which existing democratic states are based, states in which the sovereignty of the people designates not the right of each citizen to submit only to his own will, but the duty to submit to another will—that is, to the decision of the majority or of the majority's representatives. On this basic public obligation, on the obligation to submit to duly constituted public authority, the other forms of government—monarchical, aristocratic, and mixed—also rest. History and life recognize the legitimacy of each of these systems; each is suitable for the pursuit of certain political goals, certain human objectives, and certain developments, and therefore each has the same right to exist as the others.

The fundamental error of the doctrine on sovereignty of the people is that it places individual liberty, the individual will, at the basis of the entire public edifice. The doctrine is one-sided. Liberty is one of the elements of public life, a crucial element to be sure, but not the only or even the most important one. Man by nature is a free being and therefore has rights. These rights must be respected in the state, which consists of free individuals, not slaves. Slavery is a denigration of human dignity, the diminution of man to the level of a tool or of an animal. But a man is not only a free being; he is also a sentient moral being. He not only lives and acts for his own ends, for personal benefits and satisfactions, but he is conscious of principles and laws that are more elevated and take precedence over personal ambitions; he is aware of common interests that link people together and create the spiritual world in which human life takes place. This spiritual link not only binds together individuals living in a given time but also binds different, successive generations. Each receives from its predecessors an intellectual and ethical heritage which it reworks, augments by its own activity, then conveys to its successors. This process constitutes the organic development of peoples and of humanity. An individual person is a member of an organic entity, which introduces the individual into a community of shared values. The individual's ultimate task as a sentient moral being is not to satisfy personal needs but to act for the common good, to serve those ideas and interests that are most important in the world. This elevated moral life is what makes man the possessor of rights. The rights of man must be respected precisely because he is a sentient moral being who is conscious of universal principles and who serves the highest goals of humanity. Otherwise, he descends to the level of an animal who has no rights, because he does not live a rational life but seeks only to satisfy his own needs. Human liberty is the liberty of a sentient moral being. A man has rights because he has responsibilities. Conversely, he has responsibilities because he has rights: if he were not a free being possessing rights, then one could not demand that he discharge his duties. Rights and responsibilities are inextricably linked.

Membership of the individual in society is consequently not only a right but a responsibility. Man enters into society not only to satisfy his needs but out of ethical and rational necessity. He comes into the world not only as a free being but with innate responsibilities that he acquires along with the spiritual legacy of his ancestors and that alone make it possible for him to enjoy his liberty and fully to exercise his rights. Of those human associations in which rights and responsibilities are recognized and play a role, the most important is the state. In it, popular life acquires a general framework which links together isolated individuals and succeeding generations. It establishes in society a higher order, it introduces justice, it governs common interests, it fulfills the historical mission of a people. Born in a certain country that becomes his fatherland, an individual comes into the world as a member of a particular polity with all the responsibilities of a citizen. He submits to the law that establishes public order, he obeys the government that issues and enforces the law; he is obliged to serve the end pursued by the polity—the common good. In this service a man satisfies not only his sentient moral nature but his personal ambitions, for in the common good is also private good; the common good entails the well-being of all. Here he finds the realization of his liberty, for liberty is one of the most important blessings a man can enjoy, one of the fundamental principles of society; without liberty a rational life is impossible. The development of liberty, since it is one of the demands of society, is also one of the goals of the state. But it is not the state's only goal; while liberty is part of the political organism, it is subordinated to higher principles. For this reason the greater or lesser degree of liberty extant in a particular polity depends on the other elements of political life: on the government's needs, on order, on the law, on various material interests over which the government presides, and on the conditions under which the government operates.

The ideal purpose of the state, the ultimate demand of the community, consists, of course, in the full and harmonious development of all elements of public life; but peoples approach the realization of this ideal gradually and by various means. Each people has its peculiarities; in one a certain element predominates, in another a different element, in one the element of rights, in the other responsibility; one establishes a democracy based on the personal participation of citizens in governmental administration; another submits to the dictates of a government animated by faith, by the law, by history; a third, finally, tries to combine the two opposed principles in common institutions. Even one and the same people, at various times in history, may embrace one goal, then another, depending upon its needs. The intellectual and ethical condition of society, the interrelationships among its various elements—Estates, parties, regions—and, finally, the external environment of the polity and the circumstances in which it must operate, all these factors affect society's needs and influence its political arrangements.

It follows that the degree to which liberty develops, its role in the polity, its primary or its secondary importance, are determined not by the abstract dictates of reason but by the contingencies of life. Political liberty is not the inalienable right of a people; it is not an indispensable precondition of every political order. Popular representation is established in countries where it is required by the good of the community, where it answers the needs of the polity, where it is able to operate in harmony with other elements of public life, where it can contribute to the attainment of certain objectives. Therefore, the basic question is what advantage popular representation brings [to a given society] and what preconditions are necessary to sustain it.

Properties of Popular Representation

If representation is not the eternal, inalienable right of every people, if it is established or disestablished in the name of the public good, then the question arises: What advantage does it carry? To the attainment of what political objectives can it contribute and with what objectives can it interfere? What are its benefits and shortcomings? In a word, what are its properties?

The benefits of political liberty and of representative institutions are so obvious, the liberal ideas based upon them are so well known in the literature and in society, that it is almost strange to discuss them. One cannot even address the question without falling into clichés. Yet the disadvantages quite frequently escape the attention not only of the public but also of progressive thinkers, and unless the disadvantages are taken into account, many phenomena in history and contemporary life will remain incomprehensible. Nothing is easier or more trite than to explain the absence of political liberty by referring to the people's ignorance and especially to governmental coercion. Yet such interpretations fall short of explaining the true course of history, just as long-ago discredited theories [fail to explain the nature of] mythology in terms of priestly deceptions. A society which governs itself by the concepts [of liberty and representation], which sees political liberty as an absolute requirement and its rejection as oppression, can neither lucidly understand its own situation nor properly develop its political system. Indeed, political liberty and the representative institutions upon which it is based do not always correspond to the public good, nor are they an inherent requirement of justice. They consolidate themselves when their attendant benefits outweigh their shortcomings, but often they collapse as a result of their inner bankruptcy, since, under certain conditions, they are more obstacles to civic development than they are its prime movers. To understand clearly the political realities, we must therefore pay attention to both sides of the ledger.

In our time almost nobody will deny the enormous and positive effects of representative institutions upon those peoples who are prepared for them, in countries where the desired harmony between political freedom and authority, between order and the public good, has been attained. Above all, in these countries, citizens' rights and materials interests find their ultimate guarantee. The classes that are invested with political rights have the possibility to stand on their own, to defend both their own privileges and the common good. As a participant in government, the elected representative acts as the legal tribune not only for his own electors, but for the entire citizenry. The law, which rests upon common consent, safeguards the rights of all and is subject neither to arbitrary changes nor to violations. The [various branches of government], which hold each other in check, eliminate arbitrariness, prosecute abuses, contribute to the stability of the legal order. There is no doubt that a representative system is not the sole guarantee of justice and of liberty. On the contrary, it can be effective only if there exist other institutions that are close to the people and that affect popular life. An independent, incorruptible, well-organized court system, an appropriate amount of local self-government much more effectively safeguard the individual, property, and the citizens' interests than does citizen participation in the central government. This last is the apex of the edifice, not its cornerstone. But without political liberty, none of the underlying guarantees is safe from violation. An unrestrained government is easily inclined to arbitrariness. The lower agencies of government, the ones that are in closest contact with the citizens, receive their life, their strength and their direction from the central government, and therefore the ultimate guarantee of rights and of the people's interests can only be popular representation that takes part in the actions and decisions of the central government itself. According to Burke, the entire constitutional system of England exists in order to seat twelve impartial individuals on the jury bench. Even in England, however, an unconditional guarantee of popular rights is impossible to find, for in human societies an unconditional guarantee is inconceivable; nevertheless, this is the highest possible guarantee.

Protection of rights, the safeguarding of liberty against governmental arbitrariness, stimulates popular energies and contributes to the general prosperity. Concerted activity by an individual requires a certain latitude and security. Confidence in the future, in the stability of order, in safeguards against arbitrariness is the precondition for any enterprise. Only in a free society can the energy of the individual exert itself fully; liberty is the mainspring of individual advancement. Wherever we may turn, this rule makes itself felt. Industry attains a high degree of development only in those countries where freedom is secure and rights are safeguarded. Freedom is even more crucial to intellectual and spiritual activity, which flows from free thought; for such activity freedom is as necessary as is air for the physical organism. Free peoples are therefore the richest and most enlightened. The ancient republics, the medieval free communes, the new representative governments variously serve as illustrations of this point.

Yet one must not exaggerate the importance of free institutions. On the one hand, as we have noted, the lower, more immediate guarantees of liberty can exist without the higher guarantees. Assuming a certain stage of civic development, assuming prudence on the part of the central government, the lower guarantees may completely satisfy popular needs. Government arbitrariness is restrained by the public's moral sensibility, by the fear of arousing dissension, by the rulers' desire to promote the common welfare, for rulers are generally prepared to grant to their subjects any institutions that will safeguard the individual and property, providing these institutions do not infringe upon the government's prerogatives. On the other hand, the storms that accompany political liberty may subject the lives and property of citizens to far greater danger, may introduce into civic relations far greater instability than the most potent despotism. Private interests therefore usually seek tranquility from revolutionary storms in the safe haven of autocratic government, which offers each citizen the possibility peacefully to go about his business and to achieve his personal objectives. Enlightened absolutism, which offers citizens all the guarantees needed in private life, contributes much more to the development of popular welfare than do republics torn apart by factionalism. In this connection it is worthwhile to compare revolutionary France with Prussia after 1815. While the abuses of unrestrained government sometimes lead to general stagnation, to the exhaustion of popular resources, it is also true that peoples may grow stronger and more prosperous under autocratic rule. To prove the point it is enough to refer to Russia. The argument of liberal writers that absolutism inevitably leads to the collapse of societies is not always historically warranted. While these writers draw our attention to the example of nations that have declined under the power of monarchs, it is important to ask about the cause: is the cause of the decline to be found in the form of government, or rather in the disintegration of society, a disintegration that makes despotism the only conceivable form of public authority? Corruption obviously played a role in the collapse of the Roman Empire, a case that liberals often cite to prove the devastating impact of autocracy. Yet the ancient republics began to disintegrate and to decline despite the existence in them of free institutions. In this instance, absolutism did not accelerate, rather it slowed the inevitable decline. Senescent societies as well as nascent ones need a unified, strong government, which alone is capable of preserving peace and security. Political liberty is useful for peoples only in their maturity, in the prime of life. Therefore, the argument mentioned above that representative government, by safeguarding the liberty and the rights of citizens, facilitates the development of civic energies, cannot be accepted as a universal truth, applicable to any period of history and to any society. Representative government plays a positive role only under certain conditions.

The preservation of liberty, the guarantee of rights, and the attendant stimulus to popular energies are not the only, and not even the most important, objectives of a political community. In a polity individual liberty and private advantages are subordinated to higher principles; pride of place belongs to the welfare of the entire community. In discussing the utility of representative institutions, one must therefore examine their impact upon the political objectives of the community as a whole—that is, whether representative institutions are a help or hindrance.

Here, too, in many respects their beneficial consequences are undeniable. Political liberty makes possible all the contributions that social thought may make in the political sphere. Popular representation serves as a permanent forum of public opinion. True, representation is not the only way that public opinion makes itself felt; there exist other mechanisms, such as provincial and Estate assemblies. But in popular representative assemblies isolated, private judgments acquire a focal point, public opinion receives an appropriate forum for expression. When a thought is expressed by individuals or by corporations, it is hard to judge to what extent the thought is widely shared in society; but when it is expressed in a representative assembly, then one may assume that the opinion is generally held or at least widely disseminated. When an opinion becomes entrenched in a central assembly, it also acquires a gravity that isolated, individual judgments lack; it becomes a force to be reckoned with in the eyes of the government and the people.

Nobody would claim that public opinion always sees things accurately and judges them correctly. In theoretical questions the judgment of the masses has no weight whatsoever; often a single individual is closer to the truth than is an entire people. Moreover, in practice, it is not infrequently necessary to resort to theory. The need is especially apparent [when the legislature considers] new, untried legislation; but even in the disposition of normal business theory is often essential. Take, for example, financial questions which, despite their purely practical character, require a sound knowledge of economic science and, therefore, can be sensibly discussed only by a very small number of individuals. In other practical matters public opinion is not infrequently mistaken, and even more often it is carried away by some transitory emotion or by the prevailing, one-sided ideology. It identifies a problem, but knows no means of ameliorating the problem, or it rushes to embrace a cure that is worse than the disease. It rarely sees distant objectives and obstacles, and therefore it does not always grasp the full complexity of an issue. The government, standing above private interests and the momentary passions so common in politics and having the resources to know each issue in its full context and to solicit the views of the best informed individuals, not infrequently judges political necessities better than does society.

Yet while public opinion cannot be regarded as an impeccable judge of political questions, if it will not do to follow public opinion in every instance, nevertheless the free expression of public opinion always has incontestable benefits. Above all, it reveals the true condition of society and the administration. Problems are not hidden but are brought into the light of day. Popular needs become known to everyone, and therefore the means of correcting shortcomings will be discovered more swiftly and more easily. In states where political liberty does not exist, where the revelation of social problems is regarded as disrespect toward authority, the government and especially the monarch may not always find it easy to learn about the true state of affairs. Abuses are carefully hidden because the only people who can expose them are those who are either guilty of them or who must answer for them. It is to the advantage of the rulers to depict the results of their administration in a favorable light and to suppress any criticism. The absence of criticism makes it possible for them to reassure themselves that everything is going well, until an unexpected event awakens them from the pleasant dream. Thus, behind the brilliant facade poverty, disorder, and lawlessness are not infrequently hidden; the government lacks genuine support and a firm foundation for action, problems secretly accumulate, dissatisfaction grows, the material and ethical resources of the people decline. The result of such a system is either the weakening of the entire political organism or a social revolution which at one blow changes the entire regime.

Such dangers are obviated by popular representation, which stands constantly on guard, speaking on behalf of society's needs and revealing the true situation. In a representative system one might sooner expect an excess of criticism than a lack of it, at least in countries where representatives enjoy the requisite independence. But superabundant criticism, whatever its inconveniences, is a much lesser evil than reassuring illusions. Criticism always contains a spur to action. One may probe wounds before they fester; treatments are accomplished gradually and it is not necessary for all neglected steps to be taken at once, with the danger of producing a general convulsion in the realm. In a representative assembly public criticism acquires a peculiar gravity and significance. As long as complaints are confined to petitions, to private meetings, to the press, it is difficult to know what in them is true and what false; not infrequently, the critics' thoughtlessness or desire to play a political role leads to exaggeration. The government cannot investigate every complaint nor can it respond to all criticisms, and the answers themselves do not always become known to everyone. In a representative assembly criticisms pertain only to what is genuinely important, an answer immediately follows the criticism, all elements necessary for judgment are at hand, and therefore it is easier to uncover the truth.

Popular representation not only serves as forum for addressing society's needs, but it also renders the government a signal service during discussions of ways to ameliorate problems. If the assembly does not always judge soundly, it at least offers for consideration new arguments, new perspectives, especially concerning the application of the laws in practice. The government, which stands at the apex of society, often does not know what is going on below. Laws drafted in chancelleries and discussed by various bureaucrats often smack of bureaucratic formalism and utter impracticality. To submit these laws to the judgment of society is always useful, and the best vehicle for this purpose is the representative assembly, in which the flower of public opinion is concentrated. Even unsound judgment has its benefits. The applicability of a law, the benefit that a certain measure can bring about, depends not only on its intrinsic virtue but on the condition of society in which the law is enacted, on the opinion which the people may harbor about it. A law that has garnered universal support as a result of a thorough public debate acquires incomparably greater authority and enjoys more trust than a law discussed secretly and introduced in an unprepared society.

Thus, in assimilating into itself a popular assembly, a government acquires new resources and new support. It sees more clearly society's condition, it understands more profoundly society's needs, it has at its disposal new elements of judgment and can act more decisively, because it can count on the people's trust and on a general predisposition to support measures approved by elected representatives.

But the advantage to the state from representative government is not confined to the free expression of public opinion. In any case, public opinion has other channels of expression. Much more important is that, in an assembly, words may be transformed directly into deeds, that public opinion becomes an expression of the popular will, of citizens' participation in national affairs. The government must not only listen to public opinion when this suits its purpose, it also must come to terms with that opinion. The only way to accomplish this objective is if society has a genuine control over political administration, and this control is most useful. Personal views, ambitions and passions are inherent aspects of human nature that affect the conduct of public business the more easily when the government is less restrained. An assembly which serves to check the executive and to represent everyone's interests, an assembly in which private views are forced to give way to the public good and in which each member operates under society's scrutiny—this is the best way to counteract bias in public administration. A system of checks and balances among the branches of government is the most reliable guarantee of good administration. Those individuals entrusted with public authority must answer not only to the monarch upon whom personal factors may have a strong impact, as innumerable cases demonstrate, but they must answer to an independent assembly representing the entire people, who directly experience the benefits and shortcomings of administration.

The representative assembly's power of control also obviates the danger of arbitrary and poorly thought-out decisions which not infrequently bring disasters in their wake. A government invested with unlimited power is easily enticed into wars that exhaust the treasury and have a deleterious impact on the people. This may occur when a representative assembly's rights are insufficiently broad in definition; one need only recall the Mexican expedition undertaken by the current French government as a case in point. Such an expedition is more likely to occur when public control over the government is altogether absent, where there is no representative assembly with power over money and personnel. The wars of conquest undertaken by Louis XIV and Napoléon demonstrate the dangers of a government unrestrained by the rights of the people. The same point is valid for domestic politics as well. The history of states where popular rights are insecure offers many proofs of this. In a society without rights, where restraints on the executive are altogether lacking, an energetic regime devoted to the suppression of civil liberty will meet no opposition whatsoever. In the midst of universal silence, it may pursue its objectives without hindrance. No matter how much citizens may complain in secret, they have no recourse against the problem; many years [of such a regime] may do the greatest injury both to private and to public life in that nation. If abuses finally become unbearable and if universal discontent finds an outlet in a successful revolution, the situation may not improve, for revolution is an evil in itself and always brings great misfortunes in its wake.

Public control is especially useful in finances. It would be unjust to claim that in representative states finances are always in a better order than in autocracies; one can cite more than one example of an unlimited government that knows how to manage its financial affairs, and of a representative government that has ruined its finances. The French republic fell into bankruptcy despite the sale of church properties, and only Napoléon restored the fallen treasury. Contemporary Italy has been compelled to resort to constant loans to cover its deficits. Austria does the same. Representative assemblies even have certain disadvantages in comparison with autocratic governments; they find it easier to raise taxes and to contract loans because they have less fear of popular dissatisfaction. On the other hand, public control certainly contributes to the soundness of the national economy. Guarding the purse strings, representatives restrain arbitrary expenditures whenever possible and avoid the thoughtless liberality which so often shatters finances in autocratic states. Generally speaking, constitutional states enjoy better credit than autocratic ones, though this is far from a universal rule. Credit is acquired through faith in the stability of the existing order and in the government's ability to manage its affairs. Therefore, popular representation has a beneficial effect upon finances only when it manages to consolidate itself and to demonstrate its competence, and this is a matter of time. To regard representative institutions as an immediate remedy for financial ruin is unfounded both theoretically and practically.

While representative assemblies sometimes act as a restraint [upon the executive], they may occasionally stimulate it to take action. In fact, this is one of the substantive benefits of political liberty. It is hard to remain inert when there is an agency constantly observing the rulers and reminding them of the public's needs. In every assembly with any degree of independence there exists a more or less powerful opposition, which by bold criticism, by incessant attacks, by raising new questions, by identifying public needs, presses the government forward, forces it to pay attention to what it has overlooked and to adopt measures to correct things. The government is compelled to maintain its vigilance so as not to permit its opponents too easy a victory, and because it is engaged in a constant struggle requiring the expenditure of enormous energies, it must find competent individuals to serve in its ranks. In representative regimes, more is expected of statesmen than in autocratic ones. In an autocracy a statesman can maintain himself by routine, by knowing how to be on good terms with others, by personal obsequiousness, and sometimes by patronage; in a representative system his inadequacy becomes evident at once, for he must defend his actions against watchful enemies who use every device to bring him down. A minister who by his incompetence brings discredit upon the government cannot defend himself before the legislature. To maintain its standing, a government must possess not only physical resources but an immense moral influence upon society. Directly confronting the power of organized opinion, the government itself must be a genuine force, and so must summon the assistance of the most capable individuals in the nation.

Representative institutions themselves furnish many of the elements necessary for good government. This is one of the most important services they render the state. Here people stand out, develop their talents, and show their abilities. One of the crucial shortcomings of unlimited government is that high official posts can be attained only by the bureaucratic route. But bureaucracy is far from the best milieu for the development of political abilities. In it the qualities that advance a career are experience at high rank and knowledge of procedure—not sophisticated views on national affairs. On the contrary, dealing less with living forces than with dead forms, operating in the narrow sphere of the chancellery, bureaucracy naturally falls into routine and formalism. Only unusually gifted people are able to diverge from the beaten track, to adopt a broader approach; mediocre talents not only fail to develop but become narrower and weaker the longer they stay in this milieu, the higher they climb up the service ladder. To overcome this shortcoming, a monarch must have an ingenious ability to handle people, to attract them to himself, to promote them before they have lost their freshness and have stagnated in formalism. Otherwise the consequence is the virtual disappearance of political thought and of political talents, and when the government, aroused by circumstances, finally seeks talented people to correct things, it confronts a wasteland that drives it to despair. It finds a countless number of bureaucrats, but no statesmen.

Representative institutions ameliorate this problem. In order to act on this stage, one must escape the bureaucratic channel. In a representative system one must deal with real social forces, apprehend questions from various angles, exercise all one's faculties in a constant struggle. Here society and government are joined in a common activity, and there is no better milieu for acquiring an intimate and well-rounded familiarity with national problems. Experience and the knowledge of affairs acquired here, breadth of vision and the ability to get along with people, are the best qualities of genuine statesmen. Parliament provides a state with its ablest servants. In this connection, one may cite the example of England, where statesmen distinguish themselves by their unusual practical sense and where statesmen are usually drawn not from ministerial departments but from the representative bodies. Parliamentary experience may even be a substitute for an expert knowledge of a subject. Not infrequently an experienced politician becomes war minister without ever having served in the army, or navy minister without having served in the navy, and turns out to be more able than the specialists. Of course, this cannot be taken for a general rule; such phenomena are only possible in a society which by centuries of practice has acquired experience in dealing with political problems. But there is no doubt that tenure in Parliament compensates for want of government experience and for the shortcomings of bureaucratic service, and may significantly increase the political talent [at the nation's disposal].

Representative institutions also serve as a people's best school in politics. Once having attained a share of influence in national affairs, electors naturally play a lively role on the political stage. The public discussion of national problems develops in the people the habit of political thought, while the need for collective action refines their practical capabilities. It may be said that only with the help of representative institutions can public opinion achieve the requisite maturity. Even where there is complete freedom of the press, the discussion of political issues in journals is always subject to bias, and some important questions may be ignored entirely. The rare reader undertakes the effort to read journals of different ideological perspectives; the overwhelming majority holds to one journal and therefore has no possibility of seeing questions from various angles, of distinguishing truth from falsehood. By virtue of habit and the daily repetition of stories, the journals confirm their readers in a single ideology. On the other hand, a writer is not subject to the same restraints that exist in a representative assembly. For him there is no need to make deals and concessions for the sake of collective action; he expresses only his personal opinion. He assumes no responsibility because he has not been charged with the duty of making a decision. Because his ideas do not have to be applied in practice, they necessarily assume a theoretical character; the journalist discusses questions, imagines solutions, directs the fate of the world inside the walls of his study. His opinions are not the fruit of mature reflection over a lifetime; they arise from the need to say something every day, to fill up a newspaper's columns, to catch the interest of the readers. Journalism is a profitable trade, which can fall into the same sort of routine as chancellery activity, with the difference that the latter is in firmer contact with reality. Public opinion, fed by journalism, naturally reflects the shortcomings of journalism: it is superficial, one-sided, impractical. Only a representative assembly can counteract this deficiency. In an assembly, political issues are discussed from all sides by people who enjoy the nation's trust, who are authorized by the nation to undertake practical activity, and who have assumed that responsibility. They are the focus of the people's attention and they become the people's guides; journalism takes a back seat to them. In the absence of a representative assembly, freedom of the press itself lacks guarantees and firm soil; it fosters a continual ferment of ideas, the play of accidental, superficial, and divergent opinions, without providing any resolution, any corrective, any guidance. Only in a representative assembly do the people acquire the perspective necessary to confine the chaos of opinion within its appropriate sphere. Thought that is not carried into practice always remains abstract and impractical; reality serves as its measure and guide. A society can try out its political judgments only if it is licensed to participate in national affairs, and, if public opinion turns out to be mistaken, then society will bear the responsibility for its own actions; from its mistakes it can derive lessons for the future. Without experience neither an individual nor a people can acquire the sublime qualities necessary for rational activity: self-possession, steadfastness, a clear and calm view of things. The opportunity to gain practical experience is the more essential because political thought is rarely dispassionate; the struggle of political parties can lead to bitter rivalry. Therefore, before extremism triumphs, political thinking should be confined to a legitimate channel in which its movement will make it less dangerous for the state. A people to whom free institutions open no opportunities to realize its ambitions not infrequently resorts to revolutions. And here experience teaches the people most severe lessons; but this kind of experience is much less fruitful than that which can be acquired by legal activity in a properly functioning political order. Representative rule does not always prevent revolutions, but it does make them less likely to occur, for it provides a mechanism to achieve objectives by peaceful means, through the struggle of ideas and words.

Finally, representative institutions inculcate in the people a greater attachment to the existing order. These institutions satisfy the innate human desire for liberty. Just as every adult wants to have control over his own actions, so every people that has attained political maturity naturally strives for self-government. Participating in government, a citizen feels himself to be not a dependent but a free individual; he is satisfied by the consciousness of his own dignity, of his rights and his power, by a consciousness that lends value and beauty to life itself. As an individual, he is subordinate to a higher order, but as a rational being, he internalizes this order, supports it, regards it as part of himself rather than as a yoke imposed from the outside. He therefore becomes the more deeply attached to those institutions which protect him and offer him an enhanced role. Regarding himself as a living member of the body politic, he is vitally concerned about its preservation. The state acquires new support in the minds and hearts of its citizens.

These are the significant benefits that popular representation may bring to a state. Firm guarantees of liberty, a stimulus to public initiative, new thoughts, new energy—representation may provide all these things once it enters political life as an constituent element. Society as a whole comes to the aid of the government, and this must elevate the state to a higher stage of development. If the entire question [of representative government] were exhausted by the enumeration of these benefits, if liberty always yielded similar fruits, then there would scarcely be any other kind of state besides ones with representative assemblies. The suppression of liberty would be a matter not of internal necessity but of external coercion that might hold a temporary preponderance but upon which no state could rely for long. History would not be a spectacle of heated struggles for liberty, of its slow development, of its violent inauguration, of bitter disappointments and frequent collapses. Everything would be done peacefully and amicably. But like any other human institution, political liberty has, in additional to its positive aspects, negative ones which sometimes equal or outweigh the former. Too often it turns out to be incapable of instituting a stable political order and of serving national objectives; not infrequently, it collides with other principles at the root of political life, principles without which no society could function, the principles of power and order, and in such cases the people naturally holds to those vital principles which it regards as the bases of society and sacrifices other, lesser benefits. Liberty within a given polity must be subordinate to social order as a whole and the good of the entire community; liberty can attain its full development only in countries where it is able to act in harmony with other principles. But achieving this harmony is one of the most difficult tasks of political life, an ideal whose attainment is often impossible.

To govern a nation requires of the executive two essential qualities: higher consciousness and unity of will. Neither quality is necessarily provided by political liberty.

Liberal writers not infrequently claim that each individual's own affairs are closer to him than anything else and that consequently these affairs may be managed more successfully by the individual whom they concern than by someone else. From this premise the liberals conclude that the people themselves should manage their own affairs, rather than entrusting them to their rulers. This conclusion represents a strange confusion between matters pertaining to the individual and matters pertaining to society. Undoubtedly, each person is the best master of his private affairs, for in these affairs the mainspring is individual interest. Usually a person knows his own affairs better than does someone else, and he cares more about them. Even if, as it sometimes happens, a particular individual is incapable of managing his own affairs, if he ignores them or makes a muddle of them, then the responsibility is his alone; it is a matter that does not concern others. But public affairs are an entirely different matter. Here, too, private interests are involved, but not to the extent that they are in private enterprises. Here individual interest is not the mainspring of activity; on the contrary, participation in public affairs not infrequently demands self-sacrifice. It entails fulfillment of a higher duty, work for the general welfare. An individual must tear himself away from his private concerns, from personal advantage. Private interest may be presumed in any man; but disinterested activity for the general welfare is a rare trait. Of course, when the matter at stake is the preservation of society, each citizen feels more keenly his link with the whole and forgets about himself. In moments of danger, a people in whom patriotism has not dried up is prepared to sacrifice everything for the fatherland's sake. Yet in peacetime the overwhelming majority of citizens is concerned mostly about private affairs; public affairs are a secondary concern. Most people find it more convenient to turn public matters over to their rulers and not to trouble themselves with superfluous worries. That is why private interest, which in private activity is the driving force, is, on the contrary, an obstacle to political liberty, which demands from the citizen uninterrupted attention to public affairs, readiness to sacrifice private advantages and privileges for the general welfare. Free institutions, which do not have the continual support of the people, are always unstable. Moreover, a vigilant pursuit of the common good presumes either a weakly developed private life of the sort typical of the ancient states, or a politically sophisticated citizenry of the kind not everywhere encountered.

A lack of initiative in matters affecting the general welfare becomes more evident in individuals the less they are acquainted with public issues. Everyone knows well his private interests, because they are constant preoccupations. They constitute the immediate sphere of everyday activity. But by no means is everyone familiar with public affairs. Understanding of them requires talents of a high order: a broad vision, attention not only to one's own but to others' interests are essential here; so are broad considerations quite beyond the individual's circle of daily activity. The more sophisticated the community to which the individual belongs, the more complex and far-reaching become the issues, and the further from the common understanding of most people. Political questions encompass the most daunting problems that the human mind can imagine; therefore, they demand for their resolution the highest degree of intellectual development. A nation-state is an institution that may exist for a millennium, a community that encompasses countless generations. On the earth, sovereign authority belongs to it; all human interests depend upon it. Therefore, in statecraft practical experience alone is insufficient for correct judgment. It is also necessary to take into account historical data, the general laws of human societies, the experience of other states, international relations, the historical mission of a people on the earth; one must rise to an understanding of the ultimate ethical and philosophical principles—the essence and significance of liberty, the origins of authority, the relation between religion and the state, between justice and politics. Political judgment is not the same thing as calculating the profit of a certain product or of concluding a commercial deal. It would be insane to claim that all these questions must be accessible to everyone because they concern everyone. Everyone is affected by them, but only a few people will understand them—the few who have the talent and opportunity to study them. The overwhelming mass of individuals is as little able to judge about the forms of government and administration as it is to judge about the laws of physics or chemistry, although these same individuals are also subject to the effects of such scientific laws.

Moreover, political liberty presumes that this knowledge is generally accessible or at least very widely diffused among the people. It is required not only of members of the legislature but of the electors themselves, who must judge the thoughts and ideologies of their deputies. If the electoral right must be given a broad basis so that all crucial interests and elements of society may be represented in the assembly, then the resolution of political questions inevitably must depend upon a mass of uninformed individuals, and the more profoundly representative government penetrates a people, the more powerfully this disadvantage will make itself felt. The attendant harm to the state cannot be likened to the losses which a private individual sustains from the failure to manage his own affairs. The citizen's incompetence affects not him alone but everyone; to prematurely entrust political rights to one generation determines the fate of subsequent generations and may bring upon them innumerable misfortunes.

To those disadvantages resulting from a low level of political knowledge must be added the difficulty of uniting many dissenting wills. This is again a fundamental, unavoidable shortcoming of political liberty. National government demands a single will and a single authority; meanwhile, in popular assemblies are gathered various, often contradictory opinions, ideologies, interests, and all of them must be reduced to a common denominator, all must be united in a single decision. This objective is achieved through the rule of the majority, whose will is considered the will of all. But the very process of forming a majority involves major difficulties. The majority is also composed of countless shades of opinion brought together by mutual concessions, by a common sentiment, or by an accidental coincidence of material interests. And when this difficult process has been completed, the result does not always correspond to the nation's true advantage. Majority rule does not automatically entail pursuit of the wisest policy; passion plays an all too important role; and one can rarely count on the constancy of a majority. Therefore, even a well-ordered representative system will always suffer from the inevitable shortcomings that are inherent to it.

Anyone who has paid attention to the activity of legislative houses knows with what dilatoriness, or, on some occasions, with what unnecessary celerity they go about their business. Preliminary meetings, the work of commissions that prepare reports, repetitive debates in the assembly itself involve a substantial expenditure of time. Each member wants to take part in judgments, to place himself on view, to reveal his activity to the electors. The result is an infinite number of useless speeches, which are the bane of assemblies. Even worse are the numerous amendments which are introduced into the bills considered by the legislature. Usually these alterations are proposed by people who are little acquainted with the technical substance of a bill or even with jurisprudential language; the changes are often hastily drafted and are therefore unclear and unsatisfactory. Sometimes, after long debate during which the most contradictory opinions are expressed, an assembly randomly seizes on a version of a bill so as to put some kind of end to the debate. The history of the English Parliament shows more than one example of carefully drafted bills, completely distorted by numerous and random amendments, which forced ministers to withdraw their proposals. To this must be added the contests between political parties, which usually take more of the legislature's attention than does the matter at issue itself. How much time is wasted on endless interpolations, on systematic criticism, on fruitless answers! As soon as a question touches the relationship between parties, it arouses universal and burning interest, speaker after speaker demands to be heard, and there is no end to the speeches. When the matter to be discussed is a purely practical matter of vital interests—but one that presents no pretext for partisan dispute or for political oratory—it passes unnoticed, amid universal inattention, and it is decided quickly in a haphazard fashion. In the English Parliament, toward the end of a session there are usually many very serious matters that [the legislators are eager] simply to get off their hands in any way they can.

It may be said that the last thing a legislative assembly is capable of producing is carefully planned, far-sighted, orderly legislation. The vast majority of representatives consists of people who are acquainted with practice but who have not studied the theory of laws and who have had little involvement in national politics. Farmers, merchants, factory owners who have influence in their own neighborhood are bidden to decide questions of civil or criminal law, judicial procedure, civil administration. It is obvious that in many cases they must cast their vote blindly, trusting in their party leaders or being carried away by the brilliance of some lawyer who knows how to speak on behalf of any cause and who knows how to touch the hearts of his auditors. Composed as it is of such a multitude of elements who have no firsthand acquaintance with the matter in question, the majority not infrequently constitutes itself of random elements. Perhaps it is too much to demand of such a majority an intelligent, far-sighted decision, a logical extension of existing principles, a careful weighing of details, and, finally, a well-drafted law. Far-reaching and complicated legislation is best entrusted to a group of statesmen and experts acquainted with the issues who stand above parties and emotions of the moment, who are not tempted by the passion for political oratory, who do not wish to place themselves on display before their constituents or to acquire popularity. Such was the

State Council of Napoléon I, to which France owes legislation exemplary in its simplicity, clarity, organization, and utility. Conversely, the laws of England which have been developed under Parliament's influence are a chaotic heap of the most heterogeneous regulations into which it is most difficult to introduce light and order. This fact is admitted by even the most fervent defenders of representative principles. "The incongruity of such a mode of legislating would strike all minds, were it not that our laws are already, as to form and construction, such a chaos, that the confusion and contradiction seem incapable of being made greater by any addition to the mass." For this reason Mill suggests that the legislature be given the right to approve or reject laws in toto, as is now done in France.

A representative assembly has little talent for drafting innovative legislation. Knowing something about how the laws work in practice, representatives can point to their deficiencies in one or another respect and to ways to remedy these deficiencies suggested by practice. Therefore, their advice can be useful for making particular improvements. But in cases where radical reform is needed, practice ceases to be a reliable guide; practice reveals the existence of a problem, but does not indicate how the problem might be ameliorated. In such cases a broader perspective is demanded; by necessity, legislation must rely on theory for guidance; it requires profound and careful study both of general principles and of the institutions and practices of other peoples. The majority of a representative assembly upon which a decision depends does not possess sufficient knowledge for such work, for it consists primarily of practical people.

Another circumstance is also relevant: any radical reform inevitably affects very considerable material interests, and therefore it will engender strong opposition. Since these interests have their representatives in the assembly, they must be taken into account. The party holding the majority will not agree to violate the interests of one or another part of its membership, for it might lose their support. It even exercises care concerning the minority's interests out of fear of strengthening the opposition and of producing a tumult. Or, if there exists no such restraint, if the assembly is dominated by revolutionary passions bent on destroying the opposition by any means, then the reform will be informed by a one-sided ideology that clearly disregards the just demands of the minority. That, in turn, not infrequently leads to turmoil and to the collapse of popular representation. In touching upon the vital interests of a certain, often very powerful class, the assembly turns members of that class against itself and thus undermines its own foundations, for its power depends on the people's univocal determination to uphold its actions and its legitimacy. In this connection, instructive examples are presented by the assemblies of the French revolution and by representative assemblies on the Iberian Peninsula in the 1820s. In countries where various strata of the populace diverge in their objectives, where in particular it is necessary to impinge on the material interests of the upper classes, reform can be successfully accomplished only by a government independent of the people, capable of dispassionately weighing the demands of contending sides, and having the right and the strength to enforce its decisions against the will and despite the opposition of interested parties. A measure such as peasant emancipation can be carried out most efficiently by an unlimited monarchy; otherwise, it almost inevitably results in turmoil and civil strife. As proof, one can cite the current course of events in Russia and in North America. In Russia emancipation was accomplished peacefully and through legal channels, by the will of the autocratic government; in North America, where political liberty dominates, the abolition of slavery has cost torrents of blood.

As a result of such factors, in a representative system genuine reform is very difficult to carry out. An idea must come slowly to maturity in public opinion, powerful obstacles must be gradually overcome, there must be slow movement forward by half-measures and partial concessions. Usually change comes only in an emergency, in a crisis, on the brink of impending disaster, when powerful interests are finally compelled to yield a position which they are no longer able to defend. The history of England can serve as an example. One can see with what difficulty Parliament moved to adopt the most useful reforms. Legislation moves slowly, by small improvements, long retaining numerous abuses connected with the interests of the ruling classes. This gradual process has its definite advantages: interests and customs are not swept away at one blow and may accommodate themselves to the new order; social relations retain a greater stability; legislation goes hand in hand with life and is not carried away by theories that are often impractical. But all this is possible only where a particular political order has acquired stability over time and has gained popular acceptance. In any case, precisely due to this stability, useful reforms will encounter delays and difficulties. A people for whom swift action is crucial, who must rise quickly to the level of other peoples in order to preserve its political position, cannot be content with such incrementalism. Not infrequently, historical circumstances themselves, long-term stagnation or bad administration, lead to the necessity of radical changes. As an example one might cite the position of France before the revolution, Prussia after the Jena debacle, or finally Russia at present. In France legislative authority was entrusted to a representative assembly; the result was general ruin and disaster. In Prussia and

Russia reforms were accomplished or are being accomplished without tumult, by the will of unlimited monarchs.

Concerning legislation it is generally the case that, under normal circumstances, a representative assembly strives to avoid extremes. The assembly tends to block patently bad legislation and not to facilitate passage of good legislation; thus it gravitates toward the mediocre. It does not permit complete stagnation, but it also hinders passage of reforms; it contents itself with making the kind of slow and gradual improvements to which its talents are best suited.

Elective assemblies are much less suited to administration than to legislation, for administration requires unity of will above all else. One may again cite the testimony of Mill, whose impartiality in this case cannot be doubted: "At its best, it is inexperience sitting in judgment on experience, ignorance on knowledge: ignorance which never suspecting the existence of what it does not know, is equally careless and supercilious, making light of, if not resenting, all pretensions to have a judgment better worth attending to than its own. Thus it is when no interested motives intervene: but when they do, the result is jobbery more unblushing and audacious than the worst corruption which can well take place in a public office under a government of publicity." The subject being described in this passage is the English Parliament.

Instead of participating in administration, a task for which, in Mill's just view, a representative assembly is radically unfit, he proposes to place upon it [the responsibility for] control over the government—the only business which, by its essence, ought to be the prerogative of the houses of the legislature. There is no doubt that this task is more appropriate to popular representation; however, assemblies do not always execute the task satisfactorily. The question is: "Where is the guarantee of national interests if ignorance must sit in judgment over knowledge?" Judgment presumes both complete familiarity with the business at hand and also competence. If both should be missing in the assembly, then no task may safely be entrusted to it. Mill cites the example of the military commander who cannot conveniently direct his army's movements, if he himself must fight in the ranks or must lead his troops in an assault. But no one denies the military commander's ability to do the one or the other; he could hardly command an army if he did not know how to fight or how to lead an assault. He is a commander precisely because he possesses superior talents. But an assembly which is in no position to govern can scarcely be expected successfully to exercise control over the government's actions. In this respect the best representative assembly will always have serious shortcomings; furthermore, the right of control inevitably entails direction of affairs, and hence their ultimate disposition. Let us take, for example, foreign policy. Questions of war and peace almost always fall under the executive's jurisdiction, but since control over the purse strings and over personnel belongs to the legislature, which also not infrequently has influence over the appointment of ministers, then the resolution of these issues usually depends upon the legislature. Meanwhile, it cannot be argued that in such matters the legislature is the best judge. If autocratic monarchs sometimes get carried away by their ambitions for conquest, if they undertake ill-thought-out enterprises, this is usually because they have at their disposal an excess of power. Representative assemblies, on the other hand, often act under the influence of emotions or passion, without considering their resources or their international position. A striking example is contemporary Denmark, where the party dominating the legislature has lost, through an irrational policy, half the territory of the state. It is virtually certain that an autocratic monarch would not have been carried away to such an extent by nationalism, that he would have been more careful in his actions and would have managed better to weigh means and ends. Concerning the legislature's policy oversight, which surely entails exercising influence over administration, one might draw the same conclusion as we did earlier in referring to the framing of legislation: representative assemblies certainly diminish abuses and hinder arbitrariness, but they do not always make the best decisions. Here, too, they tend toward a middle position that corresponds to the public mood.

The preceding discussion assumes that the legislature's membership is of good quality. It is a different matter when an assembly comes from a society unprepared for political activity, possessing an insignificant number of educated individuals, or divided by parties. In this case, the best that can be hoped is that the legislature will be a nonentity; although it may discredit the reputation of free institutions, at least it will do no serious harm to the national interest. Much worse is an assembly having real pretensions but being incompetent to conduct public business, an assembly which considers itself the representative of the people and therefore tries to control everything, an assembly which uses all its energies to undermine trust in the executive and yet itself is in no condition to do anything positive. The result of its activity may be only the weakening of the state or a profound social dislocation.

Whether the membership of the legislature is of high quality or not, even under the most favorable circumstances it moves and acts as a result of partisan struggles. Here again is one of the basic shortcomings of a representative system. In the struggle among and domination by political parties—a system that, incidentally, has its positive side—lies the gravest danger to political liberty. Parties are a natural and inherent consequence of political liberty. One may dream about an ideal order in which everyone works amicably for the common good, in which public interests do not divide the people into factions and do not present a cause for struggle, intrigues and passions; in reality, all these things are unavoidable where freedom of opinion and of action exists. The opposition between interests as well as different perspectives on the common cause generate a variety of political ideologies; people with similar convictions and interests naturally unite to achieve common objectives, and when they are compelled to overcome opposing views, to struggle with their adversaries, then, as a result of human nature, passions flare, justice sometimes disappears, and means are employed that cannot be ethically justified.

The origin of political parties is rooted in the very nature of the body politic, in the composition of society, and finally in the dynamic of human progress. A political community is a complex organism: it is composed not only of different elements, but of contradictory ones which can coexist only in a climate of mutual toleration and self-limitation. Freedom must be subject to authority, to the law, to order; conversely, authority must restrain itself for the sake of liberty, granting liberty its proper scope and even influence on the general business. It is natural that each element finds its own advocates; people incline to one side or the other, depending upon their personal traits, their position, their material interests, and even their age; youth, endowed with an excess of energy, having faith in itself, having no experience of the requirements for authority and order, tends to support liberty, while age and experience drive people to respect the higher principles of public life. Given the shifting boundaries [between freedom and order], boundaries determined by place, time, and circumstances, a conflict of opinions and a struggle for ascendancy are inevitable. The struggle stops only where liberty itself is disappearing. On the other hand, society is divided into classes differentiated by wealth, position, occupations, and interests. Given universal participation in government, each of them tries to tip the scales in its direction, to exercise the predominant influence over government. Hence aristocratic, democratic, and middle-class ambitions, colliding with one another, enter into struggle. Finally, to these factors must be added the preconditions for social progress which are determined by the peculiar form taken by the struggle between old and new. Every existing order has its roots in national life and is linked with a multitude of interests which have arisen from it, which have grown dependent upon it, and which lend it support. A demand for change naturally arouses opposition; the result is new parties, a new struggle.

Until a multitude of forces extant in a given polity have the possibility to participate in political activity, inchoate political groups may exist but will lack organization; they will tend to represent the various ideological currents present in the society, in all their complexity, without becoming actual political parties. But as soon as they gain access to the forum provided by a popular assembly, in which opposing interests are bidden to arrive at a common decision, then the need will arise for a closer cooperation between these like-minded individuals. In an assembly a contest of opinions inevitably breaks out; each group tries to attain the advantage, to constitute the majority not only on a single question but permanently. But the formation of a stable majority is inconceivable without disciplined political parties. Absent such parties, the multiplicity of opinions present in the assembly can give rise only to accidental combinations, and therefore to random results. Where each individual follows only his own opinion, the assembly's activity displays neither consistency nor logic, yet such qualities are necessary not only to the survival of the parties but for the polity itself, for it requires steadfastness of direction and of will. When the government convokes an assembly, it seeks cooperation and support; consequently, it must count upon a certain majority that is ready to support it. A majority that is formed accidentally on each issue cannot meet this requirement. What is needed is the ingredient central to the existence of a governing majority party: consistency of vision, a willingness to support the government, and the ability to make constructive compromises. Thus parties are an inevitable feature of any system of government that gives scope to political liberty and requires the cooperation of the popular representative assembly. Agreement on the common purpose not only cannot be achieved when the possibility of prior arrangements between members of the assembly has been ruled out, as Rousseau demanded they be, but on the contrary, success in promoting the common cause unavoidably depends upon such prior arrangements. Political liberty can operate only through partisanship, for it is entirely based upon the majority's domination of the minority.

Nevertheless, many very unfortunate consequences flow from majority rule. An individual belonging to a political party systematically holds to a one-sided view. He refuses to engage in impartial discussion of public questions, he loses sight of the common objective and concentrates his attention on that which may contribute to his party's victory. Therefore, the liveliest debates are aroused by precisely those issues which serve as apples of discord; the contest of opinion which, in essence, is only a necessary evil, a means to a higher end, now becomes the end itself, passionately pursued and enlisting party members' best efforts. In this contentious climate, people are naturally carried away by their emotions. Mutual irritation drowns out the voice of justice and conscience. Each side depicts its adversaries in the darkest colors and stops at nothing to justify its own actions. Hence the terrible prevalence of the lie, which penetrates the very nucleus of society and becomes an omnipresent, incurable public ailment. It is sometimes argued that the public discussion of national issues will always allow the truth to prevail, or that the truth is always revealed in the clash of opinions. The history of partisan struggle in free institutions often demonstrates the opposite. It is impossible to persuade people who systematically do not wish to know the truth and would prefer to stand upon their own views. There is no cause so mistaken that it cannot be defended by brilliant sophisms; there is no fact so self-evident that it cannot be subjected to deliberate distortion. The bulk of the public usually does not take upon itself the labor of analyzing a question in detail, of penetrating to the bottom of an issue; it is content with the claims of party leaders and especially journalists. This is what makes possible such a development as, for example, the systematic dissemination of the most absurd views and the most unconscionable slanders in the Polish question. And this is not an accidental case but an inherent problem of partisanship. "It will be curious to observe," Lord Melbourne once said to the general approval of the House of Lords, "whether the English people will long tolerate a press, which, as a rule, never tells the truth and showers the public with nothing but lies." In democratic countries, in America, in Switzerland, unconscionable behavior is even more widespread. Well-known are Washington's complaints about the scurrilous attacks to which he was subjected near the end of his term in office. Furthermore, parties do not neglect other tactics that may increase their influence and undermine their adversaries. Machinations, conspiracies, and not infrequently even sabotage [of rivals] are common phenomena in representative states. A government which must have a majority in the legislature can hardly attain one if it relies solely on morally unobjectionable tactics. In order to win a solid majority, it is forced not only to try to influence elections with all the resources it possesses, but in the legislature it must win over members, especially more or less influential ones, by private deals and enticements of every sort. Otherwise, all the dissatisfied members, the ones whose requests have been ignored, whose pride has not been satisfied, will go over to the opposition and will try to shake the government's position. In England this fact has lead to a vast system of patronage in the distribution of government offices. For its part, the opposition resorts to no less reprehensible tactics: to the manipulation of elections, which in England is an art form, and sometimes to arousing the lower instincts of the populace; in order to shake faith in the government, the opposition circulates systematic slanders and tries to throw dirt upon every government official, regardless of whether the official in question is deserving of respect. Sometimes the opposition makes league with extremists in order to defeat a government standing in the middle [of the political spectrum], a position which is therefore doubly difficult to maintain. If the two major parties are more or less equally represented in the legislature, then an insignificant third party, by supporting first one, then the other major party, can actually control the course of affairs and can win for itself significant concessions in exchange for proffered support. What trust can there be in the decisions of a majority thus composed, as a result of coalitions, intrigues, private deals, and concessions which are not always in accord with the public good?

The flaring of passions that accompanies partisan struggle is not confined to the elites, to those few individuals who are conducting their struggle in the representative assembly, in elections, and in the press. The divisiveness, the enmity, the mutual hatred of partisan adversaries penetrate to the depths of society, which, in observing its representatives, comes to accept their ideological orientation, to share their hopes and indignation, and therefore tries to support them with all its resources. A people may be sundered into hostile camps, whereas national unity and the strength of the body politic must be based on the common sensibilities, interests, and objectives shared by all citizens. When the adversarial spirit is confined to the peaceful struggle of ideas and words, when it stays within its legal boundaries, when it is accompanied by respect for partisan opponents, when, finally, it focuses on secondary questions rather than on the very foundations of a state or a society, then these disputes, these collisions, stopping short of undermining the community's unity, may be said to constitute only a natural manifestation of pluralism in politics, even if this manifestation is attended by inevitable difficulties. But when the very foundations of the social order and of the political system become the subject of dispute, when the importance of the issues and the attendant interests arouse powerful emotions, particularly in periods of social instability, if parties are unaccustomed to self-restraint and to legitimate activity, if the government is weak, then the adversarial spirit can assume dimensions inconsistent with order, tranquility, and the security of the community. Such antagonism may lead either to civil strife or disruption of the entire social organism. A quite normal consequence of such struggle is the collapse of political liberty. If unrest is moderate in intensity, then representative institutions diminish the problem by providing a legal outlet for intellectual ferment; it is better to concentrate the partisan struggle in the capital city than to permit it randomly to spread to all corners of the nation. But when inflamed passions become a widespread phenomenon, then representation is quite inadequate to ameliorate the problem. On the contrary, it will only make things worse. On one hand, the right of assembly and the opposition between parties will prevent the government from suppressing the unrest and introducing order; on the other hand, discontented individuals will act with greater energy, with more hope of success, when they are attempting to win a majority in an assembly that shares in the prerogatives of sovereign authority. The stronger the measures adopted against anarchistic unrest, the more inflamed hatred will become, and the sooner pretexts for civil strife will arise. Once passions become so aroused, the only way out is to inaugurate a government that will suppress the parties. Hence come forth revolutions which either lead to the absolute domination of one of the factions, or which establish a government that will dominate them both. The execution of the Girondins, the terror of 1793, the revolutions of 18 Brumaire and of 2 December are recent examples of these two outcomes.

Yet even the most peaceable and legal struggle has its dark sides. The government is put face to face with systematic opposition—a phenomenon that is absolutely inevitable as soon as political parties take shape in the nation at large. The hope of universal cooperation is nothing but a dream. If the government holds to a certain ideology, if it is consistent in its actions, then it will find itself engaged in struggle against another, opposing ideology which, elaborated during legislative debates, ultimately crystallizes into an opposition. If the government tries to satisfy everyone, if it makes concessions on all sides, it risks losing the support of both and becoming an object of general contempt. Only an autocratic government can stand above parties, for in countries where there is no political freedom, organized parties do not exist, either. Because the government has no representative assembly to deal with, it is not compelled to seek support from a majority. But as soon as the representative element is introduced into the body politic, then political parties become a necessary instrument of action. The government is formed from people of a certain ideological bent, and therefore it becomes the head of a party that must struggle against an opposition.

One cannot deny the benefits which come from such a political order. Being subject to constant criticism, the government always stands on guard and tries to remove pretexts for justifiable censure. It can succeed in its struggle against the opposition only if it attracts to its side the most gifted individuals. Abuses diminish in number, while bureaucratic formalism, incompetence, and mediocrity become rarer. On the other hand, rulers are forced to spend a significant portion of their resources and their energy in the struggle against their opponents [in the legislature]. They direct their activity toward one-sided objectives, toward shoring up the support of their party, toward the preservation of their own power. The calm management of national affairs, dedication solely to the common good, the impartial resolution of questions facing the nation become impossible. Common national interests, and in particular the objectives of the minority, suffer from systematically one-sided ideology. Finally, there is no doubt that continual criticisms in the assembly and in the press—attacks in large part composed of unjustified claims and lies—weaken the government and may even lead to its undeserved fall. Criticism aimed at the government always has great resonance in society; a peccadillo may have a stronger emotional impact upon the public than do the advantages of the existing order, which are taken for granted; scandal offers grist for idle minds, who clamor more loudly than anyone else; condemnation of the government serves as a badge of independence; the opposition cloaks itself in the alluring guise of liberty, while support for the government is easily confused with intellectual stagnation, with cringing servility, with pursuit of selfish ends. For this reason the formation of a moderate governmental party is always more difficult than the unification of various dissatisfied groups into an opposition. But as soon as the government, shaken by the attacks, tries to deal with its energetic opponents, it discovers that it does not enjoy sufficiently strong support from its own partisans, its influence [in the country at large] is shaken, and it forfeits a large portion of the citizens' trust and respect. In order to save itself, it not infrequently is forced to curry the favor of extremist groups, to make concessions that cannot be reconciled with the general welfare. The interests of the nation inevitably suffer under such circumstances.

On the other hand, the opposition devotes all its resources to continual criticism. The capable individuals who are its leaders waste substantial parts of their lives in fruitless activity instead of dedicating their lives to the common good, to the direction of national affairs. Long tenure in the opposition is deleterious to the gifts and the very character of statesmen. Systematic criticism makes the mind negative and petty. The opposition, in its one-sidedness, not infrequently embraces principles that are inconsistent with the exigencies of good government, principles that the opposition itself will disavow as soon as it assumes the responsibility for governing. Desiring to win over the people, to attract supporters, it makes promises to the people that cannot be fulfilled. To attain its objectives, it tries to stir up open dissent, to mobilize the pressure of public opinion against the government; and this tactic may lead to a reliance upon anarchistic forces rather than the organized elements of society. In general, long-term opposition is the most harmful school for statesmen and for parties. The only means of counteracting this problem is parliamentary government, in which parties take turns in office, depending upon which party acquires a majority in the assembly. Taught by experience, each party knows the requirements of government and of public order. But the opposition does not always have what it takes to form a government, and the very change of parties in power carries with it substantial disadvantages. Consistency in governmental action disappears, one ideology is suddenly supplanted by its complete opposite; a large number of capable individuals is dismissed from the government and is replaced by others, who often are quite unprepared to hold office; junior officials who remain in office are placed in a very difficult and false position; finally, the competition between parties is transformed into a struggle over the spoils of office. We shall return to this problem later, when the establishment of constitutional monarchy is discussed.

All the enumerated disadvantages are natural consequences of political liberty and of the representative system. Every human institution has its dark sides; evil is always and everywhere mixed with good. Under a given set of circumstances, and taking into account the political sophistication of a people, one must decide whether the advantages [of political liberty and representation] outweigh the disadvantages. The conclusion will not always be the same, and, for this reason representative government is not always appropriate. Consequently, the problem is to specify those conditions which are necessary for popular representation to sustain itself and to contribute to the welfare of the people and the realm.

But comparison of the various sides of representative government does not exhaust the question. Making a proper judgment also requires consideration of the form of sovereign authority itself. Popular representation is the dominant element of government in republics, but it only shares authority in representative monarchies. Each of these forms of government has its own properties and consequences. Therefore, we must examine the forms of representative government, for form reveals the character of each.

Part Three **Studies in European Thought**

Plato and Aristotle

1. PLATO

Plato placed reason at the foundation of his system, but his ideas are not the static, abstract, and otherworldly postulates we find in the thought of the Megarian philosophers; rather Plato's ideas bear directly on the external world.[1] All material things are connected through them; the entire physical world is constructed on their model. They live in individual objects, as the universal in the particular, as unity in difference. Their relation to the external world is implicit in their very definition, for reason itself can be understood as a synthesis of dialectical opposites: unity existing in the midst of plurality, and plurality constituting itself as unity. Plato develops his conception of the dialectic in his well-known dialogue *Parmenides.* Plato's entire philosophical system is based on the fusion of dialectical opposites, the universal and the particular, idea and matter, the finite and the infinite. The highest idea, the one in which all the remaining ideas culminate and the one that fosters universal harmony, is the Good, the final goal of all existence. The Good is God, ruling in the world and ordering the world according to rational criteria.

The Good also exists in nature, but its primary manifestation may be found in human beings, who have access to reason and who may consciously recognize eternal ideas. In the arena of human affairs the highest realization of the Good is the state, for the state represents a perfected organism into which individuals may enter as members. Politics is therefore the crown of philosophy. Plato summarized his political teaching in two dialogues: *The Republic* or *The Public Order,* and *The Laws.* He wrote another dialogue under the title *Politics* and began a political novel, *Crito* or *Atlantis;* but these last are of secondary importance.

In *The Republic* Plato sketches an image of an ideal political community embodying the eternal ideas of justice and the Good. *The Republic* is the first so-called utopia, a description of a political arrangement that is not only unattainable but inherently unworkable. Idealism is found here in all its exclusivity, denying the autonomy of all other components of life. Any social arrangement based exclusively on Idealism must necessarily remain unrealizable.

The dialogue begins with the question: what is justice? Having rejected the then-fashionable teaching of the Sophists, Plato commences to analyze the concept of justice itself. In order to define the term, one might expect him to proceed analytically, first by distinguishing the various human virtues and then by identifying justice among them. But Socrates, the main character in the dialogue, finds it more convenient to shift the focus of attention from the individual human being to the state, for the state, he says, is a structure like the individual, only on a larger scale. He therefore proceeds to outline an ideal model of a well-ordered state in which one may find justice; from this outline he expects the definition of justice to emerge by itself.

Of what parts is the political community composed?

First of all, people join together in a society for the satisfaction of their needs. An individual is not capable of providing for himself or herself all the necessities of life; the individual must rely on others' assistance. Therefore, the first thing that is required for a political community is a quantity of people sufficient to satisfy its physical needs: that is, a sufficient number of tillers of the soil, artisans, merchants, and so on. Among them there must be a division of labor, for each individual is born with a certain gift, and each does best that work which he or she is regularly accustomed to doing. Consequently, it is necessary that each worker be confined to the appropriate occupation.

In modern European societies the laboring class comprises the majority of the populace; this class is now being granted access to political rights. But in the Greeks' eyes, this group is nothing more than the lowest Estate, one scarcely deserving the title of citizens; it is mired in manual labor and charged with satisfying men and women's base needs. Once having mentioned laborers, Plato dismisses the subject and turns to another class, the defenders of the state, or the warriors. Warriors are citizens of the state; on them the philosopher concentrates all his attention.

Warriors should possess contradictory qualities: they must combine bravery against enemies with gentleness toward their fellow citizens. This combination can be achieved only through painstaking moral education and through adherence to a carefully prescribed lifestyle. Recognizing that the community's welfare depends above all on the customs of the populace, Plato offers a detailed summary of the system of education, based—according to Greek custom—on music and gymnastics. Each of these arts develops one of the opposed traits of the human soul. By exercising the body, by imparting to it strength and agility, gymnastics inculcates bravery in the student. Music should be taught through songs that reinforce certain moral values in youth. The system of moral education is precisely defined by law, and any innovation is strictly forbidden. Poets, who write under the inspiration of the Muses and who often construct images that correspond neither to moral imperatives nor to true conceptions of God, are banned by Plato from his ideal community.

Warriors educated in this fashion live in complete communism. They possess no private property, no wives, no children. Everything must be held in common so that among citizens there will be no private interests to arouse mutual animosity. The polis, being a single entity, must live a unitary life, so that each citizen must think and feel the same as others. Women must receive the same education as men; they must have the same occupations; they must lead an identical style of life. In order to justify such complete equality of the sexes, Plato cites the example of animals, among whom females of a species cannot be distinguished in lifestyle from males of the species. The destruction of all private life, of all personal interests, will naturally deprive men and women of many satisfactions; but well-educated warriors, Plato says, must bear in mind not the good of individuals but the good of the whole community, upon which the happiness of the individual members depends.

From among the warriors will finally emerge rulers or guardians, those senior in years and possessing the greatest ability. They must necessarily be few in number, because wisdom is the attainment of the minority. From childhood they must undergo a whole series of ordeals and must show themselves to be models of all virtues. To them is entrusted unlimited authority in the polis, which they rule by upholding the laws and keeping watch over citizens from birth to death. First and foremost, their attention is directed to the new generations. In spite of the sharing of wives, intercourse between the sexes is not left to chance but is placed under the supervision of the guardians. They take care that there will always be children in the appropriate number and that a pattern of breeding be preserved that will facilitate the maintenance of the state. To this end, sexual unions are arranged primarily between men and women of outstanding qualities, while children with defects are either sent away or destroyed. The guardians direct the education of citizens; they assign each to his or her appropriate place and occupation in the community by determining the aptitudes of children and dividing them among the various Estates. For although within a polis that comprises a single entity each person must be treated fraternally, each person nevertheless has his or her aptitudes and vocation. The gods infuse gold in the souls of those destined to be guardians, silver in the souls of the warriors, brass and iron in the souls of artisans and laborers. For this reason they constitute separate Estates, each carrying out a prescribed task for the sake of the entire community; all together are members of a single organism.

A community so organized represents a model of all virtues, which, according to the ancient teaching, are four in number: wisdom dwells in the guardians; bravery in the warriors; moderation in the lower Estate, which is subordinated to the leadership of the upper Estates; finally, above all reigns justice, the source of and link among the individual virtues. Justice consists in each individual carrying out his or her own assignment—that is, that community is just where, in the distribution of responsibilities, assigned tasks correspond to the capacities of each individual. This formula also defines the just life for the individual, who, like the polis, also consists of three parts, each with its prescribed function and virtue. In the head resides wisdom; in the heart bravery; in the lower parts of the body, from which the sensations emanate and which are the source of satisfactions and of suffering, there must rule moderation, which may be achieved by the subordination of the passions to reason; finally, justice orders the relationship among these three parts and thus establishes an wholeness of soul and inner harmony.

If we compare these four virtues to the above-mentioned elements of any social order, then we will see that wisdom corresponds to reason and to law; bravery corresponds to strength and power; moderation, which restrains the personal appetites, corresponds to rational liberty; and justice is the concept that orders these elements so as to constitute a single whole.

Thus, according to Plato's teaching, the polis, like any individual, forms a complete organism composed of various parts, each having its function and all being bound together in a single body, under the aegis of justice. The establishment of such harmony constitutes the goal and the welfare of the entire community. Each element is animated by a common ideal, which is also the greatest good for each individual.

But how can such an order be established in the polis? By what means can such an ideal structure be achieved? The means of achieving the objective is this: philosophers should be made guardians. Only the philosopher can keep in view not the accidental, the transient interests, but the unalterable laws, the eternal truths that lend firm foundation to any political order. Contemplating the Good in absolute terms, the philosopher draws legislation according to this ideal, and frames the law so that it will be suited to human nature. For this method of legislation to work, it is essential that the souls of future citizens be transformed in advance into empty slates, upon which the outlines of the perfected ideal may be written. Such a system could be implemented if in one of the Greek cities there should appear a tyrant, possessing unlimited authority but also loving wisdom. He might select out all the children under ten years of age and give them an education that will make them capable of being citizens of the ideal community.

The ideal form of government, in which wisdom rules, can therefore be either an aristocracy or a monarchy, depending upon whether consciousness of the advanced ideas belongs to the few or to the one. But reality presents many cases deviating from this ideal; hence, the various forms assumed by existing political institutions. Plato counts four such deviations from the ideal and describes them in order of precedence, thus naming the stages of the polis's gradual decline. The first form, which is the closest to the ideal type, is a *timocracy*, where not wisdom but ambition or love of honor [*chestoliubie*] predominates. This form of government has much in common with the Spartan state. It devolves from an aristocracy or from a perfect republic when, due to the inattention of the guardians and as a consequence of that corruption which inevitably affects everything human, the distribution of citizens into Estates is not done in a manner that corresponds to natural aptitude—in other words, when gold and silver are mixed with brass and iron. Then the harmony of the community is violated, and enmity among Estates is inflamed. After prolonged internal wars, the strongest and bravest subjugate the rest; they assign ownership of the land to themselves and turn their countrymen into laborers and slaves. In such a state strength and bravery dominate; here the martial qualities predominate over others; ambition develops; ambition for power fosters ambition for wealth. But this last development leads timocracy to ruin. The accumulation of wealth in the hands of the few generates superfluous wealth among a few isolated individuals along with the impoverishment of all the others. Money becomes the measure of worthiness and influence on public affairs; the poor are excluded from participation in political rights; a property qualification for voting is introduced; and thus from timocracy the form of government changes into an *oligarchy,* where the rich dominate. Here the base appetites predominate; greed runs wild. A certain moderation still exists, however, for the rulers take care to preserve their acquisitions and they restrain their inferiors from license. But government is entrusted to people not according to their merit but according to their wealth; therefore, it is always deficient. Given the universal lust for monetary gain, each person receives the right to dispose of personal property according to his or her wishes; a consequence of this is the development of a proletariat, along with an entire swarm of idlers and profiteers, who wish to survive at others' expense. The state is divided into two opposed camps, into the rich and the poor, each hostile toward the other. Finally, the struggle between the parties leads oligarchy to collapse. The poor, being more numerous than their rivals, overcome them, and, in place of oligarchy, there is established a *democracy.* Here unlimited liberty predominates. Each citizen considers himself or herself entitled to anything; total disorder is introduced into the polis. Passions and desires that had been restrained previously now assert themselves in unbridled form; insolence, anarchy, dissolution, shamelessness reign in society. Into government are introduced people who flatter the crowd; respect for the government's authority and for the law disappears; children equate themselves with their parents, pupils with their tutors, slaves with their masters. Finally, the very excess of liberty undermines its own foundations, for one extreme leads to another. The people persecute anyone who stands above the crowd, in wealth, in celebrity, or in talent. This situation gives rise to new and ceaseless discords. The rich enter into conspiracies to defend their properties; meanwhile, the people search for a leader. The leader little by little takes power into his own hands; he surrounds himself with hired bodyguards and finally suppresses all the people's rights and becomes a tyrant. *Tyranny* is the worst of all forms of government. Here predominates an insane and immoderate passion for power, a passion resorting to any and all means to satisfy itself. The tyrant must commit an endless series of evil deeds in order to sate his desires and to save himself from everyone who might harm him. He seeks support among the slaves and among people of the worst quality, because only among those who resemble him can he find loyalty.

Meanwhile, he must foster endless confrontations and wars so that the people might always feel the need for a martial leader.

Such is the gradual deviation of forms of government from the ideal. So far as we know, Plato was the first thinker to outline the order of transition from one political form to another. Of course, we should not ascribe to this political law a mechanical regularity. Aristotle rightly notes that, not infrequently, the transitions occur in different fashion. If we glance at the course of Greek history, we will see that in most cases aristocracy was transformed into democracy through the intermediary stage of tyranny. But it did happen in Greece, and even more often in Rome, that the transitional form was government based on property qualification, that which Plato calls oligarchy and which essentially is a mixture of aristocratic and democratic features. The origin of tyranny from unbridled democracy is a phenomenon that occurs rather frequently in all periods of history. In any case, we find in Plato a masterly description of various forms of government as embodied in his own time. Breadth of historical vision is combined here with profound psychological analysis of society.

Plato adopts a completely different perspective in his *Dialogue on the Laws*, a composition written in his old age and evidently never revised. In *The Republic* he tried to describe the ideal of a perfected state; here, on the contrary, he describes a government better adapted to reality. In *The Republic* total unity was imposed on the community; in *The Laws* we have opposed elements combined in a harmonious whole.

Plato regards this structure as the second [in his hierarchy], after the perfected state. But this political structure is not a timocracy, which in *The Republic* was held to be the deviant form of government nearest to the ideal state. The *Dialogue on the Laws* begins, on the contrary, with a critique of the political institutions of Crete and Sparta. The main goal of these communities is the development of military power and bravery; yet, Plato argues, a legislator ought to concentrate attention not on one virtue in isolation but on all virtues in their totality. The state's goal should consist of happiness in all aspects of human life, in which the first place is occupied by spiritual and intellectual goods, the second by bodily goods, and the third by external goods or wealth. In *The Laws* Plato, departing from his previous system, places bravery in the last place among virtues. Plato also declares here that the optimal combination of all the virtues may best be fostered by that political structure wherein all goods, including wives, children and property, are held in common among citizens, and wherein the very term *property* is unknown, because a body politic represents total unity among its members. But in reality, he admits, society can only approximate this ideal. Therefore, it is best of all to adopt a form of government combining the two opposing elements from which all others are constituted—namely, monarchy and democracy. Each of these political forms, taken in isolation, tends to take its one-sided principle to an extreme, the former to an excess of state authority, the latter to an excess of liberty. For a political community nothing can be more harmful than a surfeit of government power, no matter what form government may assume. Expanding uncontrollably, governmental power undermines its own foundations and leads the community to ruin. As an example, Plato cites the Persian monarchy, which collapsed from its own despotism. On the other hand, he cites the Athenian democracy, which remained strong so long as it was restrained and which fell into complete disorder as soon as liberty was transformed into complete license. Political wisdom, Plato asserts, consists in the capacity of self-restraint; therefore, a monarchy should be limited by the freedom of citizens, and a democracy by the exertion of governmental authority. Only then will moderation, comity, and wisdom rule within the political community.

These profound thoughts remain valid in our time; upon them the entire theory of constitutional monarchy has been built. But for Plato the significance of the monarchist element in the state remained obscure. All Greek life had developed under the impress of the republican form. Therefore, in spite of the principles he had just enunciated, the political structure that he describes in *The Laws* represents a combination of democracy not with monarchy, but with an oligarchy or aristocracy. The scope of liberty is moderated here by the establishment of a property qualification for voting and a complex system of elections.

Although this new community cannot pretend to the total unity [of the Platonic republic], still everything here is directed toward and made to contribute to a common objective, which informs all aspects of political life. A citizen belongs not so much to himself or herself as to the political community. The same principle can be applied to children and to property. The law intrudes into every detail of life, regulating the most trivial circumstances. In home life, Plato says, apparently insignificant changes occur not infrequently; but when they depart from the goals of the legislator, they lead to a violation of public order and thence to the gradual decline of the polis, for a political order is sustained primarily by mores. Plato understood, however, the impossibility of determining everything by legal prescription; therefore, the law, in his opinion, should act as a moral guide. With this end in mind, he claims that every law should be preceded by a preamble that contains exhortations to citizens on a life virtuous and in accordance with the needs of the political community. Thus should the power of the law be united with moral conviction. Plato also understood that not everything that he advised could be universally implemented in practice; but in theory, he says, one should bear in mind the optimal case and then in practice leave to the side that which turns out to be infeasible.

Any political community to which it is proposed to give the best laws should be removed from the sea, for maritime commerce leads to wealth and luxury, and intercourse with foreigners corrupts morals. The populace should be sufficiently numerous for defense but not so numerous as to hinder the preservation of order. Plato fixes this quantity as 5,040 families, a number convenient for purposes of efficiency. The rulers should take measures to assure that this quantity might never increase or decrease—that is, they should alternately stimulate or restrain the rate of procreation; in case a population surplus should arise, the excess may be sent away to the colonies. By lot, each family receives a certain plot of land divided into two parts: one closer to the city, the other to the periphery; the land on the periphery is meant to give each citizen a stake in defending the borders of the state. Similarly, each family receives two homes, one in the city center and the other on the periphery. In this community there is no complete communism of the sort described in *The Republic;* nevertheless, private property is subjected to every sort of restriction. Land allotments are considered to belong not so much to citizens as to the entire community; their alienation is not permitted. In order that the number of family hearths remain unchanged, the right of succession will pass to one of the sons designated by the father; the remaining male children may be adopted by the childless. Daughters are not to receive a dowry, and if they be the sole heirs of their father's land, they are to be given in marriage to poor males. Having thus restricted citizens' immovable property, the law also limits the excessive growth of movable property. Gold and silver are banned from the community in order to remove the temptation to greed and inequitable consumption. Because in general, extremes of wealth and of poverty lead to disturbances of the public order, the amount of legally permissible property is to be bounded by upper and lower limits. The lower norm is equivalent to the allotment of land given to every citizen, even the poorest one. The upper norm is defined as four times the value of this allotment; anything in excess is to be confiscated for the use of the community. In accordance with this rule, citizens are divided into four classes, which serve as the bases for allocating tax burdens and subsidies. Plato demands that the one and the other be made proportional to a citizen's total wealth; for equity among unequals, he says, is determined by mathematical proportion, and deviation from this rule leads to strife. In general, equality is of two types: the first is numerical equality, which can easily be enforced by casting lots; the other is truly proportional equality, which constitutes the essence of justice. Here Plato offers another definition of justice than the one he gave in *The Republic.* In *The Laws* justice is defined as fair compensation to unequals, in accordance with their nature. We shall see in Aristotle an elaboration of these notions.

The right to vote for the leaders of the community is not determined by property qualification alone; here the principle of liberty must also be taken into account, because government should represent a combination of opposed elements. The methods of election will differ according to the office in question. The foremost authority in the community belongs to those who preserve the laws. They are to be elected by all who bear arms, according to a complex formula: in the first stage, 300 will be elected; then from them 100; and finally from these 37. The second office is that of military commanders, who are also to be selected by soldiers: the senior commanders from those recommended by the guardians; the junior commanders on the recommendation of the senior command. Then there will be a Senate consisting of 360 members, 90 from each class. Here again everyone votes, but for the higher classes there will be a penalty for failing to vote, so as to ensure their participation in public affairs; meanwhile, the poorer classes, with certain exceptions, will be exempted from this penalty. The first stage of elections will involve selection of candidates to Senate membership; the second stage will consist of selection of 780 potential members; the actual members will be half of this group, to be determined by lot. This complex system of election has the function of combining opposing elements. In like manner, other high officials are selected: those who supervise the city; those who supervise the market; those who act as police in the villages; and finally, the priests. But the instructor of youths and the judges of the highest court are to be elected by the officials as a whole, because these offices demand greater talents. Judges in the lower or district courts are appointed by lots so that no one should be excluded from participating in the courts. These "judges" are the equivalent of our jurors. Finally, in cases of crime against the state, the entire people shall sit in judgment; the investigation of such crimes will be done by three officials who are to be selected by the accuser and the accused.

After describing the government, Plato turns to a very detailed presentation of the laws. They encompass the entire life of citizens from cradle to grave. First, the laws must regulate everything having to do with religion, for this is of greatest interest in the political community. Then marriage regulations, and laws concerning slaves and children are outlined; a law defining the system of education, which must be universal in scope, is outlined. Even children's games are established once and for all by the law. Innovations are forbidden, so as not to inculcate into children the passion for change. The law determines what songs and dances are permissible; poets are subjected to censorship. Women are prescribed the same physical exercises as are men. The law dictates to adults the entire order of life from dawn until dusk. Midday meals are to be taken in common, as in Sparta, not only by men but also by women and children. Agriculture is regulated in detail, and here it is obvious to what extent Plato is concerned to limit private property in his political community. In each district, constituting one twelfth of the entire territory of the state, everything produced is divided into three portions: one for free people, another for slaves, and the third for foreigners and craftsmen. Each citizen receives two portions to be divided among family members and slaves; the third portion he or she may sell at market. As far as the crafts are concerned, they are strictly forbidden to citizens and even to their servants. Citizens should completely dedicate themselves to service of the political community. Craftsmen constitute a special stratum of people, each of them being dedicated solely to his or her craft, according to the principle of the distribution of labor. Private individuals are forbidden to engage in foreign commerce; only the guardians are permitted to import from abroad items essential to the community. After describing the laws regulating the building of houses and commercial establishments, the judiciary system, crimes and punishments, and taxation, Plato leads his citizens to their death and prescribes the method of their burial. In conclusion, he indicates how the political order may be preserved. His method consists of a council of the best people, who gather every day at dawn. The council is composed of ten guardians of the laws, who summon in addition the most virtuous men, travelers who have seen other lands, and the best youths. These last are to observe everything happening around them and make reports about it to the elders, who then take all necessary measures to preserve the community.

From the above, it is clear that Plato remains a pure Idealist in *The Laws.* Although he had promised to present a political arrangement adapted to human nature, even here he sacrificed liberty to public utility. Greek life, of course, gave him a pretext to do so; after all, the ancient citizen was supposed to live for the sake of the political community. But even in Greek city-states the regulation of private life did not attain the scope granted it by Plato. The disorder that the great thinker observed with his own eyes prompted him to demand an even greater subordination of private interests to public interests. Taking as his point of departure the ultimate aim of any political association—namely, the common good—he lost sight of all other legitimate public aspirations. Plato's indelible achievement is that he made the eternal ideals of justice and the Good the central aspirations of the political community; but in the name of these ideals he constructed a uniformity that contradicts human nature. Objecting to the political arrangements proposed by Plato, Aristotle rightly noted that too much uniformity destroys the very essence of the political community, which ought to be less uniform in nature than a family, and should by no means resemble a single individual. To build a political community on a model of homogeneity is to pervert its nature, to destroy the distinction and variety within it, a distinction and variety that are vital in a genuine community. Aristotle objects particularly to the communism defended by Plato. Holding wives and children in common, Aristotle claims, will not produce uniformity of thought, for if each man may say of a wife or child, "This one is mine," then endless quarrels will result. If wives and children belong not to a particular individual but to the community as a whole, then they will belong to nobody at all. If so, then this arrangement will destroy the sweetness of familial ties and will make likely bitter arguments and confrontations between children and parents who will not know one another. Communal property carries another disadvantage as well: each individual will devote less care to common property than to his or her own property. For the individual the two main incentives to diligence and love are property and emotional attachment; both these incentives are eliminated by Plato's system. Communal property can lead only to endless quarrels because of the unequal distribution of consumption and labor. Those who work much and receive little will rebel against those who, for less labor, receive greater benefits. The owners of property held in common will quarrel among themselves more frequently than will independent property owners. In general, the sense of proprietorship is a source of the greatest satisfactions. Love for oneself is not a base emotion so long as it does not exceed the proper measure, and property also affords one the possibility of doing good to others.

One can only agree with this critique, a critique authored by a student of Plato himself, a student who is one of the very greatest thinkers of all times and all peoples. Moreover, Aristotle's teaching serves as the point of departure for the subsequent evolution of political doctrines.

2. ARISTOTLE

With Aristotle, thought moves from the realm of the Ideal to external reality. He studies not the eternal models according to which things ought to be arranged but the essence of those things themselves. Therefore, in his views there is greater sobriety than in Plato's. But the foundations of Plato's and Aristotle's political doctrines are the same. Aristotle is no empiricist, as some critics claim; he remains an Idealist. But he seeks the idea inherent in things, the idea that constitutes the inner purpose of a thing, that lends direction to its life and development.

In Aristotle, as in Plato, the world is defined as a synthesis of opposites, but Aristotle gives these opposing principles a different name. Instead of ideas and matter, he adopts the categories of matter and form, or, what amounts to the same thing, of potential and actuality. In Plato ideas are unique, intellectually apprehensible models or patterns of things, models rooted in divine reason; Aristotle rejects this hypothesis. The essence of things, he says, cannot be separated from the things themselves. An intellectually apprehensible model cannot be the source of a thing's motion; one must assume the existence of another motive force. To claim baldly that things are connected to eternal ideas is nothing but empty rhetoric and a poetic metaphor, for the means by which things and ideas are allegedly connected remains a mystery.[2] In order to discover the true essence of things, one must seek it in the things themselves, by dividing them into their constituent parts. Aristotle assumes four fundamental elements of being: essence or form; matter; the element of motion; and ultimate purpose.[3] As I have argued above, these elements in somewhat different guise comprise the points of departure of all the main philosophical systems. But Aristotle reduces the four elements to two main ones, because the end or purpose, the highest element, consists in the realization of the rational essence or form, or in the translation of matter into form, while the element of motion is nothing other than the process of striving to realize the end or purpose. The entire world is composed of matter and form. The first is a undifferentiated element that contains the potential of infinitely varied and contradictory concrete definitions; the second is the reality of things, that concrete definition of them that contains their true essence. In receiving form, matter moves from its undifferentiated condition, from potential to actuality. Thus, for example, brass, as matter, contains within itself the potential of a statue, but also any other form; when matter receives the form of a statue, then it moves from potential statue to actual statue. But in this example form is something external to matter; it first exists autonomously in the artist's mind as the goal of his or her creativity, and only subsequently is it communicated by the artist to matter. In works of nature, as distinguished from the work of the artist, and with greatest clarity in organic bodies, form is inherent to matter itself. Form is also an idea, an inner purpose, which by its own activity causes things to emerge from their hidden potentiality, lends them life, binding together their parts into a single entity. Thus matter and form are opposing categories of a single essence: an essence which, in matter, is a potentiality, an essence which, in form, is actuality. The essence of form is actuality, and the goal of its activity consists in the realization of the form itself, that is in the gradual elevation of matter into form, or in the translation of the potential into the actual. There follows the whole series of products constituting syntheses of opposing principles, the world of nature and the world of the spirit. In human beings the dominance of form is manifested in thought, which is consciousness of form or consciousness of the rational essence of things. But the most elevated manifestation of form is thought entirely divorced from matter, pure thought or pure actuality, thought about thought. This is the Divinity, the ultimate goal of all being, that toward which everything strives, the unmoved mover of the universe.

Thus, in Aristotle's system, thought is conceived as a living, acting principle, flowing everywhere, lending animation to matter, giving to things determinate being, and finally raising all toward ultimate unity, toward the ultimate purpose of creation, to the pure self-consciousness of spirit.

Among those forms which manifest the actuality of thought, the political community, for Aristotle as for Plato, occupies the highest place in the realm of human relations, because it constitutes the ultimate embodiment of human aspirations. But whereas Plato had demanded of the political community the most complete uniformity, considering other structures to be deviations from the ideal, Aristotle immediately assumes the perspective that his teacher had adopted in the *Dialogue on the Laws.* Instead of the greatest possible uniformity, Aristotle seeks the best practical synthesis of opposing principles. And here he is not distracted by dreams of an ideal social arrangement; rather, he contends with reality, trying to define more precisely the various existing forms of political life, to discern their essence, and to show what conditions may lead them to flourish or to decay.

Aristotle's *The Politics* is the most remarkable of all the political treatises ever published. It is the only one that combines philosophical views with profound and multifaceted practical understanding. On the one hand, the book explores the philosophical nature of the political community and elucidates the principles upon which it rests; on the other hand, it delves into the purely pragmatic dimensions of politics. The treatise is not confined merely to one political form; instead, it deals with all forms, both the good and the bad, at equal length. In a word, this is the only treatise that is simultaneously philosophical, juridical, and political.

For Aristotle, as for Plato, the polis is the highest form of human community. Its overriding principle is the goal toward which it leads the individual. This point of view makes itself known from Aristotle's first sentences. A city or political community, he says, consists of individuals; but every community exists for some purpose, for the sake of a certain good. The most important, the highest good to which a human being can aspire, will be the purpose of the highest form of community, the community that encompasses all others. That community is the political community or state. Therefore, political authority substantially distinguishes itself from private authority, from the authority of the father within the family or of the master vis-à-vis slaves. It is easy to convince oneself that this is so by analyzing the origins of the body politic. The polis arises from and encompasses other communities. First, from the union of a man with a woman, from the association of a master with slaves, there forms a household; then individual households join together in villages; from a certain quantity of villages that collectively possess everything needed for an autonomous existence there springs the polis, which is the ultimate community designed to facilitate a virtuous and autonomous life. Thus all private goals contribute to the common goal, but the goal of the polis is not a private but rather a public one. The polis is not a local community like the village; it is not a community fashioned for the mutual pursuit of material advantages; nor is its purpose limited to establishing the right of mutual self-defense; but all these things must preexist in order for the state to come into being. The polis itself may be defined as an all-encompassing community; it claims an individual's highest allegiance.[4] For this reason, the polis is not the artificial contrivance of certain individuals, as the Sophists claimed. It exists in nature, for an end is nothing other than the fully expressed nature of an object, the realization of which also constitutes its mission. And since the polis's end is the one toward which everyone is striving, then the polis must be the highest or most significant institution in human life. A human being by nature is therefore a political animal. Outside the state there can live only the beast, who is unsuited to community life, or God, who is self-sufficient. A human being outside the state is the least among animals. Therefore, in human beings there is a natural affinity for public or political life. And although by order of physical origin the individual human being may have preceded the polis, still by nature or by essence, the polis is prior to the individual, since the whole precedes its parts; for the nature of the whole determines the nature of the parts, and not vice versa. Only in the whole do the parts find their function and attain their true purpose. Only in the polis, under the aegis of justice and law, does an individual truly become a human being.

Thus, according to Aristotle, the highest end, the common good, determines all human life. The polis encompasses everything; a human being cannot be understood other than as its member. This notion is a consequence of the classical world picture, in which individual citizens had not yet received autonomous status. In the modern world, the individual always retains a greater significance, even among those thinkers who assign priority to the community.

Having elaborated in these profound passages the nature of the polis, Aristotle turns to its constituent parts. The lowest social unit is the household, which consists of the union of husband and wife, father and children, master and slaves. He looks first at this last relationship. Here we find a famous justification of the slavery upon which the classical state was based. The ancients did not recognize the absolute significance of the human being; that notion developed later, particularly under the influence of Christianity. But even in Aristotle's times there were people, belonging to the school of Sophists and of Socrates, who claimed that slavery is contrary to nature and had arisen out of violence. The subjective principle led them to this view; but Aristotle, who had in mind primarily an objective goal, rejects this argument and tries to justify slavery not only as a social necessity but as a consequence of human nature itself. Every activity, he says, including domestic activity, requires tools; the slave is a living tool serving for a lifetime, and therefore comprising the master's property. It is only necessary to know whether there exist people who are predetermined by nature to be slaves. That there are indeed such people it is easy to convince oneself. In every human being there are two aspects, body and soul, of which one is destined to exercise power and the other to manifest submission. In the soul itself, reason governs the appetites. The same law is repeated everywhere: where many are united in one, there must a be ruling principle and subordinate parts. Therefore, if there are people who distinguish themselves from others, as the body from the soul, or the beast from human beings, then it is obvious that they by their very nature ought to submit to others and become slaves. This is the character of all those whose vocation in life is manual labor and who therefore serve as the tools of others. Such people have no dominating faculty of the soul, no reason; or, rather, they have it only to the degree necessary to comprehend others' commands, but not to the degree necessary to issue command themselves. Therefore, their vocation is to be slaves. Nature itself has shown this by endowing them, at least most of them, with a physique different from that of free men, whose vocation is political life and not physical labor. Being based on nature, slavery is just and useful, both for the master and for the slaves, who through it are able to practice their natural vocation. Then Aristotle turns to the righteousness of that form of slavery imposed by violence. Unlike other commentators, Aristotle does not regard as just every type of slavery based on war, for wars themselves may be unjust; [in his opinion], that subjugation is just which is based on natural superiority. Aristotle regards barbarians as people by nature destined to slavery. In their souls there is no element created for mastery. By nature, the slave and the barbarian are one and the same.

In this teaching we see, on the one hand, the purely secondary significance assigned to manual labor and, on the other hand, the total absorption of the individual by the polity. As everywhere in this world picture, people are divided into two elements, each with its function: one element called to exercise mastery, the other to subordination. This doctrine naturally emerged from the very structure of ancient life, where slavery was omnipresent. Slavery was considered contrary to nature only by those who regarded the polis itself as an artificial contrivance. Those who regarded the political organism as the realization of the highest good justified slavery. Indeed, where the common purpose permeates one's entire life, there one must be totally dedicated to the polis in which one finds the possibility of living out one's natural vocation. Yet such total dedication is incompatible with the development of private life and especially with physical labor. [In the ancient world] the political calling and the vocation of labor were strictly demarcated. On the one hand, slaves were thought essential to satisfy the material needs of citizens, while citizens dedicated all their efforts to the polis; on the other hand, laborers were excluded from political life on the grounds that private pursuits of any sort were considered entirely incompatible with the business of politics. In antiquity politics was the preserve of a tiny circle of citizens, and within this tiny circle it dominated everything. By contrast, in modern times, with the development of private life, an individual may simultaneously be a private actor and a citizen. A member of a modern political community has no need for slaves; furthermore, since no individual need be wholly absorbed by the state, nobody need be devoted exclusively to political life. The laboring population may therefore be admitted to political rights. In our time politics no longer has the importance that it assumed in antiquity;

instead of the all-consuming place it once had for the citizen elite in the polis, political life today encompasses a greater portion of society; it involves citizens from various strata of society and affords an identical degree of protection to all.

In connection with slavery, Aristotle discusses economic relations. He divides the means of acquisition into natural and artificial or commercial, the former connoting what is necessary for domestic life, the latter connoting efforts to achieve the infinite multiplication of wealth. Only the first sort of activity can be approved; the second is condemned because its purpose is self-gratification, not virtue. Aristotle especially rejects interest payments, by means of which money is attained from money itself; this means of acquisition he considers most contrary to nature. His judgments here reflect the the ancient world, in which private enterprises had no autonomous significance.

Besides slaves, the group of social inferiors living in the household included women and children, but women and children are sharply distinguished from slaves. Their vocation is not physical labor but living in community with the paterfamilias. Therefore, women and children are free people, although they possess different aptitudes from adult males. Women possess reason, but theirs is an of inferior sort; among children reason is still imperfect. Both women and children are created to obey, just as the vocation of the males is to command. The head of the family's authority over his wife ought to be aristocratic, in recognition of her liberty; authority over children should be monarchical, based on seniority and affection.[5]

But Aristotle does not dwell on familial relationships. The education of women and children, he says, is to be determined mainly by the political culture, for a household is a part of the polis, and the disposition of the parts ought to be in accord with the arrangement of the whole. Therefore, he turns his attention directly to the body politic. Having analyzed the theories of his predecessors, especially Plato, and also the most noteworthy political institutions that have existed, such as the Spartan, Cretan, and Carthaginian, he commences at last to present his own teaching.

Here again he begins with the constituent parts of the state, yet always he bears in mind the common good. By Aristotle's definition, a citizen is he who participates either in the courts or in legislative councils; consequently, political rights are an inherent characteristic of the citizen. To possess political rights is to be a citizen in the full sense of the term; others—children, for example—are not full-fledged citizens. They are not citizens who have no political rights. But because in different states various classes are permitted to participate in governance, the definition of citizen is not everywhere the same.

A citizen lives for the sake of the polis; thus his distinguishing characteristic is virtue. By this term Aristotle means in general those qualities that lead to the attainment of the Good; in the given case, therefore, he means those qualities that make a person capable of participating in the courts or legislative councils of the polis. What is the virtue of a citizen? Is it identical with the virtue of a human being as such? The answer to this question, Aristotle says, is "no." The virtue of a citizen pertains to the polis, but the polis may vary in form and purpose. Therefore, the polis demands from citizens the virtue appropriate to its peculiar circumstances, whereas the virtue of the individual human being always remains the same. Moreover, citizens in one and the same state have different missions, which demand different virtues. But is there not a stratum of citizens whose virtue corresponds to human virtue in general? According to Aristotle, there is such a stratum—that of the rulers, who must possess the highest ability. Because in an ideal polis each citizen should be able both to obey and to command, here the virtue of the citizen will correspond to the virtue of a human being.

By these considerations Aristotle answers the question of whether [manual laborers or mechanics] should be numbered among citizens. He says that if mechanics are granted access to political rights, then one should not demand of citizens any virtue, for virtue belongs solely to those who do not work physically to acquire their food. He who labors for another person is a slave; he who does wage labor for the polis is a hireling. It is enough to indicate such a fact, Aristotle says, to answer the question. There are, of course, constitutions that permit manual laborers to exercise political rights; but in the well-organized polis this cannot occur.

Having thus defined the nature and characteristics of citizens, Aristotle turns to the structure of the polis itself. The structure may vary; in what does the variability consist?

The structure of the polis is determined, first of all, by differences in its purpose. The true purpose of the polis is the common good; therefore, those political forms in which the common good predominates must be considered *true* or *proper;* those which govern with a view to the interests of the rulers alone, not the people, are *corruptions.* In the latter the polis resembles the relationship between master and slaves, which is established mainly for the master's advantage. Both the true and the corrupted forms of government in their turn are divided into several types, depending upon the composition of sovereign authority, for the political structure is defined mainly by the distribution of authority among its parts; and above all by the [location of] sovereignty.

Power may belong to one person, to many, or to the majority of citizens. Hence, there are three forms of government: *monarchy* or *kingship; aristocracy,* or the dominance of the best people; and *rule by the polis [politiia],* or a *republic.* In *Nicomachaean Ethics* Aristotle calls this last form *timocracy,* because here political rights are distributed according to the criterion of property ownership. We have seen that Plato described timocracy as the form of government where love of honor predominates. Aristotle's term has another meaning, as a result of another derivation; his meaning is the one that has remained in usage. For each of these three forms of government there is a corresponding corrupt type: for monarchy there is *tyranny,* where only the ruler's good is borne in mind; for aristocracy there is *oligarchy,* where the rich rule for their own good; for a republic there is *democracy,* where the poor rule in their own self-interest.

In reality, all these forms of government may exist and, indeed, do exist. One may yet ask: to whom, by the nature of things, according to a true understanding of the state, should the sovereign authority belong? This question, Aristotle says, presents great difficulties. If one entrusts power to the best people, then all the rest will be dishonored; if one concentrates power in one person, then this will be even more oligarchic [than oligarchy]. It would seem that one ought to entrust power to the entire people; for although in the crowd each individual may be worse than selected individuals, the people as a whole not infrequently exceed the upper classes in reason and wealth. What is dispersed in small quantity [among individuals] is here gathered together, so that in the mass one may find the highest quality. But sometimes the crowd is no better than a herd of beasts. Sovereignty theoretically should be vested in the law, which is based on reason. Everybody recognizes that, in an ideal political community, justice ought to prevail, for justice is its highest good, since in justice is to be found the common good. But how then should power be distributed on the basis of justice? All seek justice; in its name each demands power, but usually people err in applying this principle.

Following Plato, Aristotle in the *Nicomachaean Ethics*[6] divides justice into two sorts, in accordance with the dual meaning of equality that constitutes its essence. Equality may be numerical and proportional; therefore, there are two kinds of justice. One Aristotle calls *rectificatory* justice, the other he calls *distributive* justice. The former operates according to arithmetic proportion; it obtains in commodity exchanges between citizens and in payment of debts, so sometimes it is also called *commercial* or *commutative justice.* It assumes that individuals are equal to each other in every respect and that therefore they must be treated equally. The latter operates according to the principle of geometric proportion, through the award to each of a value corresponding to his or her nature or merit: to the greater a greater value, to the lesser a lesser value is given. Distributive justice is what ought to govern political relations; but how can it be defined in practice? What index should serve as the basis for the proper distribution of power? Each stratum of the people has its own yardstick: the elites in an oligarchy claim that wealth should be the basis of authority; the crowd in a democracy asserts that liberty should be the basis of authority. The wealthy claim that citizens who are unequal in property should be unequal in other respects; the poor, on the contrary, say that people who are equal in liberty should also be equal in their political rights. Both parties err, for the mainstay of the state is neither wealth nor freedom but virtue. But if, on the basis of their greater virtue, the best people claim power for themselves, then one may object that the mass of the people, although it may be inferior when taken individually, is, when taken collectively, superior to the virtuous minority. Thus, Aristotle concludes, there is no superiority that fully corresponds to the imperatives of justice and that may serve as the foundation for a unilateral usurpation of power by any one person or group. Only if one person or several should so exceed others in political virtue that no comparison between them would be possible, only then should government become their exclusive domain. In such a case, they would appear not as equals among their peers but as gods among men.

In these notions of Aristotle one sees the beginning of the doctrine of constitutional monarchy, which, developing from the assumption of the preeminence of reason and justice in human societies, rejects the idea that these traits belong exclusively to one person or to a single assembly, and therefore demands joint participation of all social elements in collective decisions. In modern times we find this teaching in the work of Guizot.

Having thus resolved the basic question of political life, Aristotle turns to the examination of the individual forms of government and, in the first instance, to monarchy. He divides it into several types, which are reducible to two main types: the first is the kind that existed in Sparta, where the king was nothing but a hereditary military commander; the second is an autocracy where sovereign power is concentrated in the person of the king. The first type of monarchy is not really a peculiar form of government, because one or another military command structure can accompany any governmental system. As far as the second is concerned, Aristotle considers it useful only in rare circumstances. In general, he thinks it is better to be ruled by law than by any individual; it is better that the state be controlled by several virtuous people than by one man who will not be able to supervise everything. Kings, after all, are inevitably forced to depend upon their close associates. Finally, here it is always unknown on whom governmental power will devolve. Therefore, an autocracy may be suitable only where one individual is so obviously superior to others that they ought naturally to obey him. This is the right of genius. From such explanations one may judge in what sense Aristotle, writing in the *Nicomachaean Ethics,*[7] says in passing that a kingship [*tsarstvo*] is the best form of government. The true significance of monarchy was beyond the Greeks' comprehension. In a place where the overwhelming mass of the populace is not taken into account at all and where government is the monopoly of a select few whose entire lives are dedicated to political activity, there is is no reason why, from the midst of this tiny minority, one individual should be singled out to be elevated above the others. Here a republican structure is much more suitable.

In *The Politics* Aristotle calls the best form of government that in which the best people rule, regardless of whether the highest virtue belongs to one individual, or to a clan, or to a certain quantity of people. But because the first case can be nothing more than an accident, the description of the most perfect form of government amounts to a sketch of a well-organized aristocracy. Following Plato's example, Aristotle gives himself this very task, but unfortunately, this section of *The Politics* remained incomplete or descended to us only as a fragment.[8]

Turning to a sketch of the ideal political structure, Aristotle, like Plato, begins by summarizing the necessary preconditions for such political community. It should be neither too large nor too small, for in the first case it will be difficult to establish order, and in the second case there will be insufficient resources for the community to survive. The quantity of citizens ought to be sufficient to supply all necessities, yet still small enough to permit effective supervision. The land should supply all the alimentary needs of the inhabitants. Unlike Plato, Aristotle prefers his capital city to be located in a maritime region, which offers the conveniences of commercial ties and affords better defense. Finally, it is vital that the community consist of Greeks, for the northern peoples are brave but lacking in reason, while the Asiatic peoples are rational but lacking in bravery. The Greeks, however, possess both qualities. Citizens in the ideal community must be completely dedicated to the political life and to virtue. The right of citizenship is not to be given to simple tillers of the soil, to artisans, and to merchants, for a vulgar style of life leads to a vulgar way of thinking. The lower classes are to be excluded from property ownership. Land will belong only to citizens; it will be tilled by slaves and paid laborers, for the occupation of farming is forbidden to citizens. Their sole vocation is service to the polis. But because service to the polis will entail various duties—namely, defense of the fatherland and the administration of it—the question arises as to whether both these tasks should be carried out by the same individuals or by different ones? Plato had demanded that the government of his ideal community be entrusted to the wisest individuals, those predestined to the task by nature or by Providence; Aristotle, who did not assume that any innate superiority could serve as a basis for holding power, tries to combine the possession of a certain talent with the freedom of all. To this end he divides citizens by age; because to the young belongs physical strength and to the mature belongs wisdom, he says that the young should bear arms and their elders should govern. In this way nobody will be excluded from government, and everyone will take a turn in administration. Moreover, since the community also needs priests, this office ought to be entrusted to old men approaching the end of their lives. Thus a right common to all citizens can take into account differences in the ability and in the vocations of individuals. That is how Aristotle satisfies the requirement that each individual be both ruler and ruled.

But in order that each citizen might in time be a member of the government, it is essential that he be educated in virtue. Education is the primary pillar upon which the ideal state rests. Aristotle therefore gives a detailed description of [the method of education]. But here, in the very midst of the description, the discussion breaks off; the remainder of Aristotle's description of the ideal state remains unknown to us.

From the best state Aristotle turns to that which is most suited to human life at present. This is a republic [*politiia*]. It consists of a synthesis of opposing elements. This is the same notion that Plato developed in the *Dialogue on the Laws.* But Plato's dialogue had sought the ideal synthesis in a union of monarchy and democracy, although in practice he had recognized the need to deviate from this ideal; Aristotle, who is more concerned about actual practice, takes up immediately not the various forms of government but the elements making up society. The constituent parts of every populace are the rich and the poor. Hence the two opposing types of government, oligarchy and democracy, base themselves on these two segments of the populace. In oligarchy the minority rules, in democracy the majority rules; but this occurs mainly because wealth is usually the attainment of the few, whereas the majority consists of the poor. Each of these forms of government may be subdivided in turn into several types, according to the degree of development of its principal constituency. In fact, it is generally desirable to combine the two forms. Such a union may be of two sorts: when in the distribution of power, virtue is taken into account along with wealth, then the consequence is some kind of aristocracy that more or less approximates oligarchy; when, on the other hand, the democratic element dominates the polis, then a so-called politiia or republic may come into existence. Aristotle considers this the best of the actual forms of government, and because it combines the rich and poor, then a middle class must necessarily predominate. In general, Aristotle says, the upper classes, made proud by their wealth, are unjust toward the common people and are not easily subordinated to governmental authority; the lower classes, for their part, tend to govern poorly. Only the middle class combines a sense of equity with the ability to submit to the dictates of reason. Again at this point it is impossible not to recall the most up-to-date theory of constitutional monarchy, whose distinguishing traits consist of a synthesis between order and liberty and of the domination of the middle classes. Ancient thinkers saw such a synthesis occurring within the republican form of government [rather than in a monarchy], but the idea is comparable to that of modern constitutional theory. Idealism everywhere leads to one and the same conclusions.

Considering mixed government the best in practice, Aristotle does not reject others. Political institutions should be in conformity with a people's actual condition and with the actual social makeup of the populace. Basing his argument on this assumption, Aristotle offers advice concerning the proper structure of each form of government, explaining the reasons for their corruption and the means of their maintenance. The basic rule for every state is that the portion of the populace wishing to uphold existing institutions must be stronger than the portion wishing to change it. Here one must distinguish two elements: the quantity and quality of citizens. Where the quantity exceeds the quality, a democracy is established; where, contrariwise, quality predominates over quantity, an oligarchy is inaugurated. Yet regardless of the form of government, whenever a legislator is summoned to draft a fundamental code of laws, he must always bear in mind the middle class, which alone can impart stability to the state.

What institutional arrangement should exist in each form of state? Here it is necessary to distinguish the separate branches of government. Every sovereign authority consists of three agencies: an assembly that deals with current business, administrators, and judges. We see here the origin of the theory of the division of powers into the legislative, executive, and judicial branches. Each of these agencies has its own structure corresponding to the character of the general form of government.

In a democracy, sovereign decisions are left in the hands of the popular assembly to which all citizens have access, though the actual assembly may vary in composition and jurisdiction. These variations depend on the degree of development of the democratic government; indeed, such variations are the defining characteristics of the different types of democratic state. A state in which the popular assembly usurps all authority and leaves none for the executive is an extreme case, where demagogy prevails. In more moderate forms a different combination of powers can be observed. In oligarchy, decisions are left to the minority, a system that also admits of various nuances. The extreme case is a hereditary oligarchy or one where the oligarchy rules solely in its own interests and places itself above the laws. Finally, there can be a division of powers in an aristocracy and a republic such that certain issues are left to the popular assembly and others are left to administrators, who may be elected or chosen by lot.

Political authority may also assume a still more heterogeneous institutional structure. They may be considered rulers who have the right to command; exercise of this prerogative is their defining trait. Rulers exist everywhere, of course, but each form of government has its own unique institutional typology. Thus in order to prepare legislation for submission to the general assembly, oligarchical governments may set up commissions consisting of several members; in democracies such matters may be the province of a large senate. In aristocracies there may be appointed special officials with the duty of exercising supervision over women and children; in democracies such officials are inappropriate. The means by which government officials are chosen may vary, depending upon the form of government. If they are elected, then the elective right may be granted either to everyone, as in democracies; or to a few individuals, as in oligarchies; or to the common people and the upper class together, in various combinations and degrees, as in the mixed forms of government. The same is true of the right to stand for election. Besides elections, officeholders may be chosen by lot. The last method is peculiar to democracies, for it is the logical consequence of complete equality among citizens; election is more common in aristocracies and oligarchies, for these systems are intended to choose the best people. Finally, elements of all these systems may be combined so as to produce new forms of government. The same can also be said of the courts.

One may ask how, in a given circumstance, one ought to distribute authority so as to lend institutions the greatest stability. To answer this question, one must know what are the causes leading to corruption of governments and by what means governments are maintained. This chapter is one of the most noteworthy parts of *The Politics* of Aristotle, who in this respect is a forerunner of Machiavelli. He made use of the rich treasury of political experience provided by the heterogeneity of Greek life. His clear and profound vision enabled him to penetrate to the core of these phenomena, while supporting his general observations with examples from reality.

Aristotle sees the main cause of political revolutions as [the impulse to strive] toward one form or another of equality, either arithmetic or proportional. They resort to uprisings who consider themselves treated unjustly and who think that they have not received what they deserve. Therefore, a system of government that bases itself exclusively on one type of equality is inherently unstable. It is best to combine equality of both types, arithmetical and proportional; this is the best way to avoid revolution. But in general, democracy is more stable than oligarchy, because the people have ranged against themselves only a minority, whereas the wealthy in oligarchies are threatened with danger from two fronts, from the common people and from members of their own Estate.

Along with the demand for a certain kind of equality, a demand that lies at the basis of all revolutionary movements, there may be other more immediate causes of upheavals. Among these are human passions, ambition, envy, indignation aroused by insults, the fear of punishment, intrigues, contempt toward the rulers, and also an exaggerated sense of superiority of one person or one segment of society toward others. The pretexts for revolutions may even be trivial issues, although the consequence of raising them—a revolution—is always very serious indeed. We see that Aristotle knew how to distinguish in revolutions the essential from the accidental; he did not rest content with superficialities but looked beneath the surface play of events to find the more profound causes of these phenomena.

All these causes act differently in different forms of government. Each form of government confronts a danger peculiar to it. In democracies, revolutions proceed mainly from the fury of demagogues, who force the upper classes to unite and make a conspiracy to overthrow the democracy. Sometimes the demagogue himself becomes a tyrant. In oligarchies, there are two main causes of collapse: first, the oppression of the lower classes, who in response to oppression make a rebellion; and second, dissension among the oligarchs themselves, when authority is concentrated in too narrow a group, and the rest, being excluded from power, make a revolution, or when from within the ranks of the oligarchs themselves, there appears a demagogue to lead the people. Almost the same set of causes may effect the collapse of aristocracies, which resemble oligarchies so closely. In mixed systems of government, the cause of collapse may inhere in an inappropriate combination of opposing elements—that is, a certain class may not receive the status appropriate to its excellence. This cause sometimes makes itself evident insensibly: small alterations lead to larger changes until ultimately the entire political order is corrupted.

From this explanation of revolutions it is obvious what ought to be done in this or that case to uphold existing institutions. In a well-organized state, the first concern should be the strict enforcement of the law. The introduction of new mores and customs should not be permitted. To this end governments may find it useful to establish an agency of specially appointed officials charged with supervising those citizens who may lead lives not conforming to the established order. It is essential also to prevent the appearance in private hands of armed force that might challenge the government. But the most important thing of all is the prudent use of governmental authority. Therefore, to the extent possible, oligarchies ought to assume democratic forms, particularly in matters affecting the relationships of members of the upper classes among themselves, for only complete equality among the privileged can prevent mutual dissatisfaction and machinations from occurring. On the other hand, for the same reason oligarchies should devote themselves primarily to securing the welfare of the common people, while democracies should refrain from infringing on the property of the rich. Public offices in general, in whatever form of government, should not become means of private enrichment; this is particularly true in oligarchies, for when honors are combined with wealth, the resentment felt by those excluded from power is doubled. For the same reason, in whatever form of government, it makes sense to offer the secondary offices to those classes that have a lesser share in making policy, for these offices will satisfy their vanity. In a word, in any system of government the main rule is to adopt a policy of moderation in everything. Sometimes people assume that consistent support of the dominant element in society is most conducive to the government's survival; in practice, however, the exaggerated development of one element of the political structure leads to its fall.

Aristotle applies the same assumptions to monarchy. It is divided into kingship and tyranny. The first is established primarily for the benefit of the upper classes, who seek in royal authority a defense against the common people; the second is supported by the masses against the upper classes. The causes of their collapse are the same as for republics. Tyrannies fall for the same reasons as do exaggerated forms of oligarchy and extreme forms of democracy. A kingship is least susceptible to external dangers and is therefore more stable than other systems; the internal causes of revolutions against monarchies are two: conspiracies of commoners and the tendency of rulers toward despotism when kings attempt to expand their powers at the expense of the law. Furthermore, hereditary monarchies not infrequently fall into undeserving hands.

The causes of monarchy's destruction indicate the means by which a monarchy may be maintained. A kingship is preserved only by moderation; the more limited is sovereign authority, the more stable it will be. Aristotle cites here the remark of the Spartan king Theopompus, who himself proposed a limitation of royal power. His wife reproached him for passing to his sons in diminished form the authority he had inherited from his ancestors; Theopompus had answered: "No, [I am not ashamed], for the power which I leave to them will be more lasting." As far as tyranny is concerned, it is maintained by two opposing means. The first consists in the moral degradation of subjects, in arousing among them mutual mistrust and in attempting to hold them in poverty. The tyrant uses these means to divide his subjects among themselves, to set the lower classes against the upper classes, and to circumvent any assembly where people might meet and arrive at an agreement among themselves. He establishes a vigilant watch over all actions of his subjects; throughout the polity is inaugurated an extensive system of spying, so that even relatives and friends should fear one another. Women and slaves are granted liberty so that it will be easier to find spies among them. The tyrant himself associates only with base and corrupted people; everyone who rises above the crowd must be ruthlessly destroyed. Nobility of soul is hateful to the tyrant; virtuous people are his greatest enemies. All these measures, Aristotle says, are not infrequently adopted to maintain tyranny, but they are profoundly immoral. The other system consists in modeling tyranny after monarchy. The tyrant ought to hold to moderation in everything, and not take after extremes. In spite of all these precautions, however, tyranny and oligarchy remain the most unstable forms of government.

Having thus shown that moderation is the best means of maintaining any government, Aristotle outlines those institutions that may be conducive to this moderation in governments based on homogeneous social foundations, namely, in democracies and oligarchies. These steps amount to adjusting each element by incorporating its opposite. Governments with homogeneous social foundations can count on some degree of stability only when they approach the golden mean.

This is Aristotle's general conclusion. Indeed, this is the basic idea of his work, an idea that permeates every detail. Seeking, as Plato did, to combine opposing elements in a harmonious whole, Aristotle does not limit himself to outlining the best form of government; he does not wish to remake people after his own fashion and to impose upon them laws conforming to the pure dictates of reason. Instead, by encompassing with his multifaceted intelligence the entire variety of political phenomena, he points out what corresponds to or contradicts the true goal of a political community and what leads to the maintenance or the destruction of an existing political order. Both thinkers hold to a common assumption: they regard the polis as the highest embodiment of the ideal of justice and of the Good, an ideal which constitutes the *telos* of human life. But for Plato the main thing is the unity of the idea as comprehended by reason, whereas for Aristotle the main thing is the multifaceted instantiation of that idea in reality. Their systems are the finest examples of ancient thought, and these two thinkers remain immortal teachers of humanity in politics and philosophy.

More and Machiavelli

At the threshold of the sixteenth century stand two thinkers of contrasting character, although both were educated through the study of antiquity and drew the essence of their worldviews from it: Thomas More and Machiavelli.[1] One is a dreamy Idealist on the model of Plato, who served him as an exemplar; the other adheres to the practical wisdom of Aristotle, but unlike Aristotle he makes no pretense of being a philosopher and he sacrifices morality to the good of the state. Therefore, the contrast between More and Machiavelli is much sharper than that between Plato and Aristotle.

In 1513 the English chancellor Thomas More published a work under the title *Utopia,* that is, imaginary place. *Utopia* is a representation of an ideal order of things in which, as in Plato's state, there is no private property. But this is no mere imitation of the Platonic republic. Both in the critique of the contemporary order with which the author begins and in the arrangement of his ideal society are perceptible opinions and principles issuing from the imperatives of the modern age.

The work is written in the form of a dialogue between the author and his friend and fellow traveler Raphael, who reports on what he has seen during his journeys. The first book is devoted to a critique of the existing order in European nations. Raphael relates a conversation with the Archbishop of Canterbury concerning cruel punishments applied to thieves in England. Objecting to such punishments, Raphael says that one must first turn one's attention to the underlying causes that motivate people to engage in thievery: the main causes are that wealth is concentrated in the hands of gentlemen who, on the one hand, retain an enormous number of idle servants that wind up, after the death of their master, without a morsel of bread; and who, on the other hand, substitute sheepraising for farming and thereby force small landowners and farmers off their lands, depriving them of all means of subsistence. Raphael also regards capital punishment for property theft as inhumane: thieves should be directed to do public work, which would serve to benefit society and to rehabilitate the thieves themselves. The same logic applies to treatment of vagabonds; the infirm and the old should be quartered in monasteries in order that they might be cared for, and monks should be made to care for them as a contribution to the public good.

Being surprised at his insight and knowledge of people, Raphael's collocutors ask him why he does not occupy himself with political affairs and does not visit courts in order to give advice to princes. He answers that if once he began to say what he thinks, no one would listen. Usually, the advisers of princes devote all their attention to questions of foreign policy: they think about how to conquer more lands, with whom to conclude alliances, and against whom to make war; he would counsel the princes to reject entirely the idea of conquests and to apply themselves to improving the domestic welfare of the realm. Present-day advisers seek by means of guile and coercion to enrich the treasury; they attempt to corrupt judges in order to render the judges obedient to the prince; they declare that everything belongs to the sovereign, and if subjects possess anything, it is only by the sovereign's favor. He, on the contrary, would argue that the prince's strength is not in the treasury but in the welfare of citizens; that the prince exists not for his own sake but for the people's sake; that to rule over oppressed subjects means to be not a king [tsar] but a guard over a dungeon. Given the current climate of opinion, his advice would have little prospect of success. The collocutors object that a rational man should adapt himself to circumstances and try to improve the existing order without going directly against it. Raphael answers that by this means you will not correct others but will yourself become mad, [for you will be] forced constantly to agree with decisions that lead only to the harm of society. The present order is based on false principles. Everywhere, where private property exists, injustice and misfortune of all types are inevitable. Wealth is concentrated in the hands of the few, and consequently, honors and power do not fall to the best people but rather to the worst—the idle, the arrogant, and the incompetent. The only path to general happiness is the one indicated by Plato. It consists in the communal holding of property, for an equal distribution of goods is impossible to achieve where private property exists. The collocutors object that under such circumstances the incentive to work will disappear; everyone will hold back from working and there will not be enough common property for everyone. Raphael answers that they say this because they cannot imagine any other order of things than the one they see before their eyes; yet during his travels he has been in a state where complete communism is established and where people lead a most blessed life. This state is Utopia; the second book is devoted to its description.

Utopia is an island located near the shores of America. It has the form of a half-moon whose ends come near to each other, forming a large harbor convenient for trade but inaccessible to foreign enemies. Other parts of the shoreline are also inaccessible. On the island there are fifty-four cities; to each of them is apportioned a certain amount of land. The fields are distributed among families; everywhere are houses which the inhabitants occupy by turns. Every family consists at a minimum of forty persons and two slaves assigned to it. Of them twenty persons move each year to the city, leaving their places in the countryside to the others; so every two years there is a complete resettlement of the populace. The family brings everything necessary for farming from the city, whence rulers distribute goods for free. In the cities inhabitants also change domiciles, but only every two years and then by casting lots; gardens are everyone's common property. Raphael describes these gardens and municipal buildings in captivating colors. City administration is based on the elective principle. At the head stands a prince-for-life from the senate; important matters are presented for discussion to an assembly of all the deputies, and sometimes even to an assembly of the people. Each city sends three deputies to the capital to discuss issues of general import. Outside of the senate and the assemblies all discussions of political affairs are forbidden on pain of death. This is done to prevent disturbances and conspiracies.

All the island's inhabitants labor in agriculture. In addition, each person has a particular craft, usually one transmitted from generation to generation. If in childhood a youngster shows an aptitude for a craft not practiced by his family, then he is adopted by another family which practices that craft. But nobody is forbidden to practice other crafts besides his or her own. No one is permitted to remain idle; supervisors watch to see that each person carries out his or her assigned task. Only scholars and writers, having a special vocation, are freed from physical labor in order to have the opportunity to dedicate themselves exclusively to intellectual labor. In general, the Utopians are not dispirited by labor. They work a total of six hours a day; the remaining time they spend in repose, in assemblies, and most often in literary studies that develop the mind. Six hours of physical labor are quite enough to satisfy all their needs, for 1.) here there are no idlers, as there are in other states where there is an enormous number of monks and clerics, of soldiers, rich men, unemployed, poor people, and finally of women, who in Utopia work just as the men do; 2.) here needs are fewer, for no one works to satisfy empty whims. Everyone wears the same clothes made of coarse fabric; houses are not constantly rebuilt according to the fantasies of their owners; gold and silver are reserved for use only in case of foreign wars, while in peacetime they are made into chains for slaves and into the lowest vessels in order to show contempt for their value; precious gems serve as toys for children. Thus there is always a surplus of things necessary to sustain life. But in order that the population should not exceed the means of subsistence, the surplus population in one city is transferred to others less populated, and the surplus population of the whole island is sent out into colonies.

Families carry all their produce to common storage houses, where each takes what he wants; for is there any reason to deny a person's request when everything is in abundance and no one has any cause to take more than is needed, everyone being certain that no one will never want? Cupidity springs either from the fear of scarcity or from vanity; but neither exists in Utopia. Foodstuffs are taken to a common market where they are accepted by supervisors in charge of preparing common meals according to the number of guests. It is not forbidden to eat at home, although no one does so. Only in the countryside does everyone eat at home. The principle of communal ownership of property also applies among cities: if one city suffers a shortage, it takes from another, without payment. The surplus that remains above the necessary stock of food supplies is sold by the government abroad at a fair price. These sales bring in gold and silver that are held in case of war.

Although they have established among themselves common ownership of property, the Utopians do not permit communality of wives. Instead, marriages are strictly observed, and a violation of fidelity to one's spouse is punishable. Divorce is allowed by mutual consent, but only with the state's permission.

In Utopia slavery is legally sanctioned because it is unavoidable under the communal property regime. There are unpleasant jobs that no one wants to do;

slaves are used to do them. The ranks of slaves are filled not by prisoners of war but by criminals from among the Utopians themselves and by slaves bought from other peoples. In addition, foreigners who voluntarily hire themselves out become part of the service labor contingent.

During wartime the Utopians seek out foreign assistance. Yet in general, they attempt to live in peace without concluding any alliances, which they take to be superfluous and to provide pretexts for deception. They wage wars for their self-defense, or to avenge insults, or to save other peoples from tyranny. Their objective is not conquest but the restoration of justice. Citizens who wish to do so may join the infantry; but because citizens should be safeguarded, the Utopians usually employ mercenaries who are put forward in all dangerous situations. The Utopians try to wage war more by cleverness than by use of force, for force is a characteristic of all animals, but reason belongs only to humans. For that purpose they send assassins to kill their adversary's generals, and they boast not only of bloody victories but of the success of intrigues.

Finally, Raphael speaks of the Utopians' philosophy and religion. Their philosophy affirms the attainment of happiness as the highest goal of human life—not just any happiness, but one honorable and consonant with virtue. Virtue consists of living according to nature—that is, following one's reason. Therefore, it is impermissible to seek happiness for oneself while violating someone else's. Humaneness demands, on the contrary, that one should instead sacrifice one's self for others. By this means one attains a much higher blessing. In Utopia there are various religions, but all are united in the worship of one Supreme Deity. While there is complete religious toleration, those citizens who recognize neither the immortality of the soul nor Providence are forbidden to hold public office. Utopians believe that such people seek only their own enjoyment and try to evade the law as soon as they find it unpleasant. Atheists are forbidden even to discuss their opinions among private persons so that they will not lead others astray. In Utopia there are also people who dedicate themselves to work and a temperate life for the sake of attaining eternal bliss. They enjoy special respect. Priests also are treated with special respect, thought there are few priests and they are elected [by the people, as are the magistrates].

Such a republic, says Raphael, alone truly deserves the title of republic, for in others, when people speak of the common good, they really have in view only their personal advantage. Here, because private interests do not exist, the public welfare is genuinely taken into account. In Utopia there is no unjust distribution of wealth, no needy and no poor people; everyone is rich, although no one has anything of his or her own. Who, continues Raphael, would dare to compare this egalitarian system with the order that exists in other states, where there are scarcely even traces of justice? For can one call it just when a nobleman or a rich man or those who do nothing and render no service to the state live in peace and opulence, while the farmer, or worker without whose labor the state could not be maintained for a single year, must drag through a life so miserable that one would prefer over it the life of animals whose labor is not so onerous, whose food is no worse and who have no worries about the future? These unhappy souls are literally dispirited by fruitless labor, and they are ground down by the thought of a helpless old age; for daily wages scarcely provide them a meager subsistence, and so allow them to save nothing for the future. Should one not label as unjust and ungrateful the state which squanders all its funds on so-called nobles and on idlers of every sort who seek empty pleasures, and which does nothing for the workers without whom it could not get along? Such a state can be called nothing else but a conspiracy of the rich who seek their own advantages under the guise of public welfare and use all means to rob the poor, turning the labor of the poor to their selfish benefit. And all these machinations are sanctioned by the laws issued in the name of the sovereign authority, which authority the rich take into their own hands. Thus, as a result of the insatiable greed of people who grab everything for themselves, the goods that might otherwise suffice to support everyone benefit only the few. Only the elimination of private property can remedy this evil. Deception, theft, robbery, uprisings, and murders, against which existing laws are impotent, and also poverty, cares, and onerous labor—all will disappear along with money, the source of all evils. Only when property is held in common will the blessed life be inaugurated in Utopia.

These sharp attacks on the [sixteenth-century] social order remind one unmistakably of the views of our present-day socialists. Although More was inspired by Plato, a new order of things is nevertheless reflected in him, both in its positive and its negative aspects. More is a son of modern times, not only in his critique of existing institutions but in the cures which he prescribes and in the goal which he has in mind. Plato was chiefly concerned about the good of the whole community; to secure it, he insisted that individuals sacrifice their narrow personal advantage. For More, the good of the entire community consists in the welfare of all its members. In Plato, therefore, communism is extended only to citizens who totally dedicate themselves to the state; the mass of the working populace remains outside the communal property regime, for laborers constitute a lower class about whom it is not worth even talking. In More it is exactly this group that becomes most important. This group is the basis of the state; its welfare constitutes the purpose of all institutions. In Utopia the social structure is built on two principles that were unknown to the ancient world: the equality of people and the sacred nature of work. The recognition of these principles signifies the enormous step taken by humanity during the Middle Ages, when people were educated under the influence of Christianity.

In spite of its broader application by More, however, the communist principle has become no more workable in practice. Aristotle's critique is still quite relevant to Utopia. The impracticality of such an order of things is even more palpable here, for one can perhaps imagine a social elite renouncing selfish ambitions and dedicating itself totally to the polis, thereby finding rewards in its high vocation and its privileged position; but can one realistically expect the masses who are engaged in manual labor to renounce personal gratifications? One would have to destroy human nature itself to efface the uniqueness of each individual, along with all his or her peculiar inclinations and affections, passions, and vices. Utopia presupposes only virtuous citizens; it is based entirely on the false idea that the individual's ambitions and passions are rooted not in the individual psyche but in social circumstances. If the renunciation of personal ambitions led demonstrably to universal prosperity, then there might be some basis for believing that self interest would prompt people to choose communal ownership of property; but such an outcome can never occur in practice. Here again everything is based on the false assumption that poverty and the misfortunes accompanying it originate solely from the unequal distribution of wealth, and that easy and pleasant labor will suffice to satisfy all human needs. But labor is above all labor; the human fate is to earn one's bread by the sweat of one's own brow. Only by heavy and dogged labor can we subdue nature and transform it into an instrument of our purposes. And as soon as labor becomes labor, and not a light and pleasant occupation, then it is essential that there be the strongest of all incentives to work—personal interest. One works first of all for oneself, not for others. Selflessness is the exception, not the rule; it can only be a consequence of free choice and can never be the result of coercion by society. Under communism, therefore, the overwhelming majority of people will avoid work that does not provide them direct benefit. Concerning unpleasant tasks, More himself can find no other answer except slavery. Over everyone else there must be careful supervision; officials are obliged to see that each person does his or her duty. But is such public supervision of private labor possible, and how does one determine the relation between labor and demand under conditions where everyone is inclined to do as little as possible and take as much as possible? More claims that no one will take extra, because everyone has all necessary things in abundance; but again, this is a quite arbitrary assumption. Even granted the most modest needs, light and pleasant labor cannot produce an abundance of goods. This is even less feasible because industry demands enormous capital, and in Utopia the very accumulation of capital is unthinkable because who will save anything? It is unlikely that anything will be left when everyone takes what he or she wants. As soon as there is no abundance of everything, then each person will hoard as much as possible, and then inevitably there will be quarrels, personal intrigues, mutual recriminations, and finally the distribution of produce on the basis of labor—that is, the beginning of private property. The communization of property is intended to avoid the unjust distribution of wealth following the establishment of universal equality, but in substance it contradicts the basic rule of equity—to each his or her own. According to the principle of equity, everyone should own that which he or she has earned. Each person is free to dispose of the fruits of his or her labor as he or she sees fit; he or she can invest them to his or her advantage, consume them, give them to another, or transfer them to children as a legacy. Therefore, private property, not communism, is the basic requirement of justice. If the unequal distribution of wealth generates many misfortunes, then the cure prescribed by dreamy idealists is worse than the disease, for it contradicts human nature, the laws of industry, and the highest principles of social life. Therefore, Utopia has become a nickname for an unworkable social structure. It represents an ideal way of life that has never existed in reality and can never exist, for it ignores fundamental rules of human behavior.

We see in Machiavelli quite different ambitions than in More. Whereas More is a pure Idealist, Machiavelli is above all a politician. And Machiavelli has in mind not ideal political ends but practical ones. He seeks to discover not the perfect structure for human societies but the means by which a given order is created and maintained. These means should be compatible with human nature. Whereas More saw the source of all vices exclusively in the social structure which violates justice, and whereas his ideal institutions assume all people to be virtuous, Machiavelli looks not so indulgently at human nature. According to him, people in general are evil and likely to surrender to base inclinations any time the chance presents itself. Every ruler must begin with the assumption that humans are ungrateful, inconstant, secretive, cowardly in the face of danger, and greedy for profit. He who counts on the good qualities of the people will always be deceived. By moral means alone one can achieve nothing. The ruler, without doubt, must keep in mind a moral end: the common good. He who acts for the benefit of society will acquire eternal glory;

on the contrary, the tyrant who has in mind only his personal advantages will be covered with shame. But a worthy end justifies all possible means. If it is impossible to act virtuously, then one must be ready to commit any evil act, for the middle way is always the most disastrous. Machiavelli does not recognize the duty to conduct oneself in politics according to moral precepts; the practical end is his sole concern.

From this perspective, constantly drawing lessons from history and contemporary life, Machiavelli teaches rulers how to act in one circumstance or another, and especially how to govern human inclinations and passions. In uncovering this side of political life he is an inimitable master. Clarity and force of thought, profound knowledge of human relations, many kinds of information, and a broad practical experience—all are united in him and make him one of the greatest political writers ever to have lived. He simultaneously offered his advice to princes and to peoples, for he understood that not every form of government is applicable everywhere. The state's structure depends both on the social milieu in which it is established and on the purpose for which it is intended. One government is necessary to create a state, another to preserve institutions; one for a strong and moral people, another for a weak and dissolute people.

But Machiavelli also has his ideal. Educated by studying antiquity, he seeks the ideal in the classical world. But whereas More was inspired by Plato's republic, Machiavelli's practical perspective demands a grounding in reality. For him the ideal is ancient Rome, which conquered the whole world and for centuries wisely administered its domestic affairs. He exhibits Rome as the model and exemplar for his contemporaries. "The virtue which prevailed at that time and the vice which reigns now are clearer than the light of the sun," says Machiavelli, "and therefore I shall say candidly what I think so that the young who read my works may turn away from the latter and imitate the former each time they are forced to act. Now even a fragment of an antique statue is valued highly and everyone attempts to make something similar; but the models of virtue and wisdom which the ancients presented in their own lives remain without imitators." In order to remedy this shortcoming and to show through the examples of the Romans how one ought to act in politics, Machiavelli wrote his most noteworthy political work: *The Discourses on the First Ten Chapters of Titus Livius (Discorsi sopra la prima deca di Tito Livio).*

The work begins with an explanation of different forms of government and their transformation into one another. Here Machiavelli follows Polybius almost verbatim, and, like the latter, concludes that the best government is that which combines all three elements: monarchy, aristocracy, and democracy. Among the pure forms he prefers democracy. In several places in the book the citizen of free Florence expresses his sympathy for the people. Many claim, he says, that nothing can be more superficial and inconstant than the crowd, and that in this respect princely authority is incomparably superior. But such traits belong not only to the crowd unrestrained by laws; they are encountered to a still greater degree in princes who know no restraints. All individuals become crazed when they can act with impunity. But the people, well-managed and bound by law, are more rational, more consistent, and gifted with better judgment than is a prince. The voice of the people is the voice of God. Moreover, a willful people can easily be made rational and led into a proper channel, but against a bad prince there is no other medicine except iron. However, Machiavelli does not pronounce this verdict unconditionally. As a profound politician he understood that every form of government has its relative merits and serves to attain certain ends. He admits, therefore, that a prince is superior to the people in establishing the structure of a state or in introducing new laws and institutions; but popular government is better when the task is the preservation of an established order. Besides, a necessary condition of democracy is the valor of citizens. A corrupted people cannot maintain its liberty; for it there is no salvation outside a monarchy. Only regal authority can correct a corrupted people. Also incapable of democracy are people accustomed to slavery. Freedom can maintain itself only where it is acquired by a people still vigorous and unspoiled by despotism.

Machiavelli prefers popular government to aristocratic. He asks: to whom would one sooner entrust the preservation of liberty—to the people, or to the aristocracy? Machiavelli considers nobles in particular to be enemies of freedom. In a country where there is a nobility, he says, especially one having castles and ruling over lower classes, no other form of government is possible except a monarchy. Laws are impotent to restrain such nobles; they need a strong ruler. To establish a republic where there are many nobles is impossible unless they are all destroyed. Conversely, one cannot establish princely authority in a country where equality exists unless one first creates a nobility. Equality leads to a republic, just as inequality leads to monarchy. Even aristocratic government similar to the Venetian is impossible when there exists a nobility with large tracts of land, castles, and the power over justice. Only a purely political aristocracy, based on the exclusive possession of honors and high offices, can establish a stable order. Such a government Machiavelli admits to be sometimes useful. In a small self-contained state, aristocratic government can be introduced, as it was in Sparta and Venice. The strict observance of law by the upper Estate gives such institutions unusual stability. But a pure aristocracy is unthinkable in a state that is forced into constant confrontations with other states and is compelled to make war. Here it is necessary to depend on popular force and, therefore, to allow the people to take part in government; otherwise, the people themselves will demand the right to participate in politics. For a republic that wants to grow and make conquests, the best political structure is the Roman one—that is, a mixed system.

Against Roman institutions it is objected that they provided a pretext for endless quarrels between the patricians and the plebeians; but these domestic troubles, says Machiavelli, did not diminish in the least the greatness of the republic. Before the times of the Gracchi, they rarely led to exiles and even more rarely to the shedding of blood. Struggle led only to the establishment of laws and institutions beneficial to society; by these laws and institutions freedom was safeguarded and the arrogance of the nobles was restrained. An example of these beneficial institutions was the office of the plebeian tribunes, who were the most zealous guardians of popular freedom.

Machiavelli describes in detail the ways the Romans preserved their system of government. First, he points to religion as one of the most reliable methods of influencing the people and fostering virtue among them. For Machiavelli, religion's sole significance is as a political tool, and he, without a moment's hesitation, advises the use of religious deception to achieve political goals. This demonstrates how far people of the Renaissance epoch had diverged from those of the Middle Ages. Furthermore, says Machiavelli, one must pay special attention to restraining strong men. Usually their ambition knows no boundaries, and they constitute the greatest danger to a republic. It is necessary to watch them vigilantly and to block all paths to their elevation, particularly the elevation of those who try to flatter the people and to stand out above others. For this purpose it is useful to grant citizens the right of making public criticisms [accusations]; this right also serves as a pressure valve through which accumulated discontent can escape. Where there are no such channels of expression sanctioned by law, people will resort to illegal means of expression and may destroy a republic. It is also dangerous to concentrate power in the hands of one man, for he may easily abuse it. In Rome, dictatorship was beneficial in emergencies; it was established for a short period and did not destroy other offices. But the prolonged concentration of all powers in the hands of the decemvirs subjected the state to danger. Finally, in a republic, strict morals are necessary. Machiavelli praises the institution of the censors, who, overseeing citizens and preventing the corruption of morals, served as one of the best mechanisms for the preservation of liberty. The general rule which Machiavelli draws concerning domestic administration is that institutions should often be returned to their original principle, for, by the force of events, every agency changes little by little and is gradually corrupted. Achievement of this goal may be facilitated by the laws and by the examples of virtuous men who often influence their fellow citizens more than the laws. Machiavelli obviously had no inkling of the historical progress of humanity, of the law of human perfectibility. To a son of the sixteenth century who saw his ideal in the ancient republics, any deviation from the original form of a state could only be interpreted as a corruption.

After treating the domestic politics of Rome, Machiavelli turns to foreign policy. He considers the republican form of government more capable of expanding the state's domain than is monarchy, because the main thing that increases the state's power is constant attention to the common good, and such attention manifests itself more in republics than in monarchies. There are three ways open to peoples who wish to increase their external might: an alliance with states of equal strength; leadership of an alliance; complete subjugation of other peoples. The last way is the most unreliable, because it is impossible continuously to subdue peoples who do not wish to be subjugated. Conquests are fatal for states which acquire new territories without acquiring new power. The first system is good, but only for defense because in it there is no unity of will; there may always be a disagreement [between allies], and even conquests for the alliance's benefit are not so tempting. Therefore, the best way [to increase a state's external might] is the second way; and this is the one which the Romans constantly pursued in their wars. They attracted allies, leaving them their rights and self-government and giving them part of the spoils of victory, but always retaining leadership in the alliance. Thus they subjugated the entire world. Machiavelli advises, after the example of the Romans, to conduct short wars but with all one's forces, to enrich with booty the treasury and not individuals, to establish colonies to guard conquered lands, never to end military exercises, and above all to maintain one's own army instead of mercenaries, who are always unreliable. To these political reflections are added a multitude of comments on the art of war, an art Machiavelli studied in detail. All this taken together, presented not in a systematic fashion but in the form of judgments on individual cases, is one of the most instructive political tracts ever published. Aristotle was the founder of politics as a science; Machiavelli was its restorer in modern times. And if one cannot always agree with his conclusions—if, reading him, one is sometimes perturbed by the absence of moral sensibility—one is always amazed by the force of his mind and the breadth of his vision.

The Discourses on the First Ten Chapters of Titus Livius had the purpose of indicating the means to preserve a republic. Machiavelli poses for himself a quite different task in another book which has acquired much greater notoriety—that is, in *The Prince (Il Principe).* Here are presented the methods by which a prince may acquire a new state and consolidate his dominion over it. Many scholars have seen this book as contradicting the contents of Machiavelli's first work. There [in *The Discourses*] Machiavelli is a republican ardently loving liberty; here [in *The Prince*] he writes for the benefit of the most shameless despotism. This retreat from his convictions many ascribe to a desire to win the favor of Lorenzo di Medici, to whom the book is dedicated: banished from his home [in Florence], Machiavelli wanted to return and again to take part in political affairs, and for this it was necessary to cater to the then-head of the Florentine government. Others, on the contrary, have seen in this work an irony: a republican by conviction, Machiavelli ostensibly wanted to warn the people against those intrigues to which princes resort in establishing their dominions. Such was the opinion of Rousseau. Careful study of both works of the great politician should, however, convince one that there is no contradiction between the two works. In *The Discourses* Machiavelli explicitly states that for the creation and consolidation of new states a monarchy is better than a republic; for corrupted peoples he considers monarchy to be the only practical means of government. And both these conditions were extant in contemporaneous Italy, where the people, according to Machiavelli, were the most corrupted of all and where, moreover, there was a need for a united and strong state to be created. No nation can enjoy domestic harmony and happiness, he claims in *The Discourses,* unless it is entirely subordinated to a united republic or to a single prince, as in France and Spain. In Italy this condition did not obtain because of the interference of the Roman Church, which was not strong enough to unite Italy under its dominion and meanwhile divided the country, calling to its assistance first one prince then another. Machiavelli recognized clearly that only a prince could unify Italy, free it from foreign enemies, and put an end to civil strife; therefore, he appealed to Lorenzo di Medici, suggesting to him the means to achieve that goal. And in relation to the use of various political methods, *The Prince* distinguishes itself but little from *The Discourses.* There, too, Machiavelli justified Romulus's murder of Remus by appealing to the need for unified authority, and he censured Baglioni, who resolved not to kill Pope Julius II and the entire Papal party when Julius unwisely surrendered himself to Baglioni's control. In *The Prince* this policy is presented in still cruder form, for here the problem is to establish authority by crushing all one's opponents, and, for that purpose, more forceful and less selective means are available than may be employed for the preservation of liberty. But the essence of the views is the same in both books.

Machiavelli begins with a general division of principalities according to their origin: there are hereditary and new principalities; the latter may be either united to old dominions or may acquire independent status. On the other hand, the people among whom authority is being established may be either accustomed to a prince or attached to liberty. Finally, the means by which authority is acquired may be armed force, fortune, or virtue. All these different cases require different tactics for the establishment of princely authority.

Hereditary authority is the easiest of all to preserve. A prince must only avoid violating the existing order. If he has no unusual vices that make him an object of hatred, he will always be loved. Difficulties manifest themselves only where authority is newly acquired. When a prince unites to his old territories a new region, the essential question is: does the new populace belong to the same nationality as the other subjects or not? If the nationality is the same, then the fusion will occur easily; in the contrary case, real skill is necessary to accomplish it. It is good if the prince himself moves to the new territory; it is also useful to place military colonies in the area. But above all, it is essential to adhere to the rule: weaken the strong and strengthen the weak. This rule must be observed in relation to neighbors, so as not to foster dangerous competitors, and in relation to nobles of the subjugated territory. On the latter one must never rely: they are always ready to offer allegiance to a foreign prince in order to free themselves from their own, but just as easily they defect from a conqueror. From this one can see the importance for a conqueror of the political structure of a subjugated country. Where there is no powerful aristocracy, where all authority is concentrated in the hands of a monarch, subjugation is difficult because a foreigner finds no allies; but afterward it is easier to hold the area in bondage, for with the monarch's fall there will be no further resistance. On the contrary, where there are strong nobles, it is easy to subjugate a country with their help, but to maintain oneself thereafter is more difficult. As far as peoples who are accustomed to free institutions are concerned, they cannot be managed in any fashion except by destroying them altogether; for they are always ready to rebel in the name of liberty and their former rights, whose memory cannot be effaced by the passage of time or by the good deeds of the prince.

Sometimes new authority is acquired by virtue, when a valiant man introduces new institutions and thus becomes the leader of a state. To acquire such authority is difficult but to maintain it is easy, for here there are few domestic enemies. The difficulty of acquisition consists mainly in people's reluctance to subject themselves to new systems of government. The people generally are inconstant: one may convince them of a certain idea, but it is not easy to hold them to this conviction. Therefore, an innovator must always keep in reserve other means of acting and the force of arms; when people cease to trust him, he must compel himself to trust in force.

Those who become princes by accident or by means of foreign help are in a quite different position. Power comes easily to them, but as soon as they have attained the height of power, endless difficulties begin. Usually these people do not know how to maintain themselves in their positions because they are not prepared for such posts and they have neither friends nor support. But a sensible man can achieve great results even in such a case. Machiavelli holds up the famous Cesare Borgia as a model of such a wise and courageous man, noting that one cannot give such a prince better advice than to follow the example of the duke. Then he relates how Borgia pretended to be a friend of his enemies in order the more surely to crush them, how he deceived his rivals under the pretext of negotiations and then murdered them, how he, out of caution, destroyed even the posterity of those persons from whom he had taken territories. "Analyzing all these actions of the duke," Machiavelli states, "I cannot condemn him, for, having a noble soul and grand purposes, he could not have governed otherwise." Apparently, Machiavelli does not consider even these acts immoral, for he treats under a special rubric those persons who have acquired power by crimes. "One cannot call it virtue," he says, "when a man murders his fellow citizens, betrays his friends, has neither truth, nor honor, nor religion; by these means one may acquire power, but not glory." He adds, however, that even such a rule may be established; all depends on the successful or unsuccessful use of cruelty. Whosoever must commit crimes should do so in one swift stroke, in order not to leave the people in constant fear. If cruelties continue or even intensify, the prince will have no chance to maintain himself; everyone fears for himself or herself, and all will unite against a tyrant.

As far as winning power by the will of one's fellow citizens, this is done in two ways: either with the help of the nobles or with the help of the people; for each state is divided into two parts. In the first case, it is more difficult to maintain power, for a prince has many rivals. Nobles always want to rule, while the people want only not to be oppressed. Every ruler should therefore rely on the masses, not only he who has obtained power with the help of the people, but he who has won it with the nobles' support. A prince whom the people do not love has no refuge in misfortune.

Machiavelli mentions religious principalities, but states that because they are maintained by God's help, it would be too audacious for a man to judge them.

Having investigated the rules peculiar to each type of principality, Machiavelli turns to the rules common to them all. The main bases of all states, both old and new, are good laws and a good army; but because laws are powerless without an army, and because where there is a good army there must be good laws, one should speak first about the army. Machiavelli says there are three sorts of army: a militia, mercenaries, and allied forces. He expresses a decided preference for the first. A mercenary army serves only for money and therefore cannot possess love for the fatherland nor loyalty to the prince. One can never count on a mercenary army. Even more dangerous are allies, who, in case of victory, will themselves become potentates. A wise prince should always rely on his own army; therefore, his main effort should be devoted to military affairs. Whoever ignores the military craft always risks losing power. He is not respected by soldiers and therefore he can never trust them.

After treating the army, Machiavelli deals with civil institutions. Here, says Machiavelli, one must bear in mind not imaginary states but the real status quo, not that which should be but what is; otherwise, a prince will inevitably fall from power. Whoever wishes to act virtuously must perish among so many people who adhere to other rules of conduct. From this perspective Machiavelli comments on the qualities becoming a ruler. A prince should be thrifty rather than generous, for by generosity one will not satisfy everyone, and ultimately it will become a burden for the people from whom money is collected, whereas thriftiness enriches the treasury, not burdening the subjects. A prince should rather be feared than loved, for one cannot rely on love due to the inconstancy of the human race. People are always inclined to insult him whom they love rather than him whom they fear, for fear is a constant emotion which never leaves a person, whereas love surrenders to other feelings. It is most important of all, however, that a prince not be hated and that he not acquire domestic enemies. He must therefore avoid taking both the property and wives of his subjects. Such temptations are most likely of all to arouse dissatisfaction and to arm people against his rule. A prince should keep his word only when it is to his advantage; otherwise, he will always be deceived by perfidious people. In general, the person of the prince must unite the qualities of man and beast. He must have the lion's strength and the fox's cunning. It must be taken as a rule, especially in the case of a new prince, that to preserve power he will often be compelled to act against all justice, all charity, all love of humanity, and all religion. For appearance's sake, a prince should always seem to be adorned by all virtues, but he must always be prepared to act quite differently.

Machiavelli also gives counsel concerning the selection of advisers, for that is the first sign by which the ruler's mind is recognized. A wise prince also has wise advisers. In particular he must avoid flatterers, the scum of court life, and surround himself with men who will openly tell him the truth when he asks them. In conclusion, Machiavelli makes a grand appeal to Lorenzo di Medici, exhorting him to liberate Italy, which languishes under the barbarians' yoke.

Machiavelli's works became the reference manual for rulers in the sixteenth and seventeenth centuries. The contradictory opinions about him and interpretations of him constitute a vast literature. On the one hand, all are struck by his enormous intelligence and talent, and on the other hand, by the absence of moral precepts, which he discards so brazenly. His name has become a symbol of political perfidy. In fact, one cannot defend him from this reproach, but an excuse lies partly in the general requirements of politics and partly in the character of that milieu in which Machiavelli lived and acted.

It is impossible to conduct politics in a absolutely moral fashion, just as it is impossible to judge the state by principles of absolute justice. The highest goal of political life, the common good, supersedes them both. This goal is, in and of itself, a moral principle; but it cannot always be achieved by impeccable means. One can demand of a private individual that his or her actions be irreproachable, for the private person's goal, personal happiness, is neither absolutely indispensable nor necessary; indeed, it should always be subordinated to higher considerations. A private individual is obliged to sacrifice his or her happiness for the sake of moral rectitude. But the people's prosperity cannot be sacrificed to the absolute discipline of moral precepts. In politics the supreme law is the common good (salus populi suprema lex); for the salvation of the people one must sometimes sacrifice everything. The ruler can never turn away from reality; he is obliged to govern the state, to choose practical methods of governance. But because the goal must be attained without fail, it is excusable, in case of emergency, to use those means which are not justified morally. Here is a confrontation of two principles in which moral law can have no pretension to unconditional dominion.

But on the other hand, it is impossible to remain completely indifferent toward what Machiavelli has advocated. Moral principle must be observed in politics where possible. It is the more necessary that such principle play a role in politics, for people trust and respect it. Moral acts win people's affection, immoral ones alienate it. But this moral force has by no means the same impact in all cases. In a vulgar, corrupt, or unstable society, moral precepts little affect the masses. Here it is too often necessary to resort to guile and to force in order to achieve a political goal. Unscrupulous methods are not infrequently a precondition of success. In this regard, Machiavelli was a son of his century. In all European states, the struggle of royal authority with the medieval order was accompanied by outrages. It was necessary to pacify individuals who had acquired too much might and to suppress the private rights and interests that prevailed in a divided society. The first requirement was to put an end to anarchy and to establish a stable system of government, regardless of the means [required to do so]. Moreover, not one of the European countries presented such an appalling spectacle as did Italy at the beginning of the sixteenth century. Dotted by petty tyrannies and exhausted republics, having become a battleground for the ambition of foreigners, Italy sought an escape from its cheerless plight and did not find one. Machiavelli lived in this milieu, and he reflected its tendencies and shortcomings. Accustomed to seeing around himself violence, deceptions, and crimes, he ceased to be troubled by them and wished at least to employ them to good end, and this end was shown him by his fiery patriotism, which elevated him above his contemporaries and which is his most edifying trait. Future events imparted to moral principle an even greater import than it had in the sixteenth century. Today if one may not yet expect from statesmen absolute morality in the pursuit of political goals, one still finds it impossible to remain completely indifferent toward the terrible crimes we see described in Machiavelli's work. Social conscience cries out against such outrages. In our day in Italy a great statesman [Cavour] has set himself the same goal as did Machiavelli, but his means of achieving it are very different. Among a mature people he has appealed to the principle of liberty and to public opinion, and he has accomplished his task without resorting to crimes and without losing the respect of his contemporaries.

Even in the sixteenth century, however, Machiavelli's ideas aroused strong protest. The moral faculty, because it is humanity's most sublime guide, is inherent to all human societies. Christian peoples, in particular, can never afford to lose sight of its dictates. Eclipsed for a time, it soon reemerged and reclaimed its rightful place in society's consciousness. The main impetus for its reemergence was provided by the Reformation.

Montesquieu

Locke wrote about government, Montesquieu about laws.[1] His famous work *The Spirit of the Laws (De l'esprit des loix),* published in 1742, was intended to analyze the laws governing human societies, especially those laws which safeguard liberty. This book served as the basis for the constitutional doctrine in Europe. The English constitution, which developed from practice, required a theorist who could identify the general principles contained in it, thereby making it into a model for other peoples. Locke could not be such a theorist: devoting his attention elusively to the revolution that transformed his fatherland before his very eyes, he dedicated himself to analyzing the origin of government and its subordination to the sovereign will of the people. But a constitution already firmly rooted and able to maintain the legal order needed another interpreter. He appeared in the person of Montesquieu. The French publicist, the finest in the modern period, showed that the relationships between branches of government, its checks and balances, were the most essential guarantee of liberty. In antiquity Polybius had presented the same teaching in his Roman history; but Montesquieu fully developed the theory in all its complexity and linked it with general principles governing the life of nations. [Montesquieu's theory of checks and balances], of course, did not exhaust modern teaching on constitutional monarchy. Standing on the ground of individualism, Montesquieu chiefly directed his attention to guarantees of liberty while ignoring all other requirements of the state. But it was easy to correct this oversight subsequently; indeed, [later theory] has been nothing more than an elaboration of the theory of this famous eighteenth-century French writer. He laid the foundation for subsequent theory, and the foundation is a solid one.

The English constitution, which Montesquieu saw as his ideal, was not the starting point of his investigations. Like his predecessors, the French publicist did not commence by collecting data. "I have laid down the first principles," he writes, "and have found that the particular cases follow naturally from them. . . . But when I once discovered my first principles, everything I sought for appeared."[2] We see here, as with Locke, a system constructed from pure theory, in which particular cases and the relationships among them serve as a justification. This perspective is evident in the very definition of law, with which Montesquieu begins his study.

Montesquieu defines laws in the broadest sense as *necessary relations arising from the nature of things.*[3] In this sense, all beings have their laws: the Deity, the material world, intelligent creations, animals, and human beings. Because it is absurd to propose that rational beings came from blind chance, one must recognize a prime reason [behind the creation of rational beings]. The laws are the relations subsisting between prime reason and various beings and the relations of these beings to each other. These relations are constant: everywhere in diversity there is uniformity, and in change is constancy. In this respect, the difference between the physical universe and rational beings is that the former is subject to invariable laws, while the latter, being endowed with freedom and also being liable to error as a result of their limitations, may refuse to conform to their laws. Therefore, men and women, who as physical beings are governed by the invariable laws of nature, may, as intelligent beings, continually transgress the laws imposed by God and established by society. In order to restrain us from errors, God gave us religious law, philosophers provide us with laws of morality, legislators remind us of our duties through public laws.[4]

We see here a completely different conception of law than that which was adopted by Locke. Law is not something externally imposed by an official, but an inherent feature of nature itself, something to which all beings without exception are subject. This new notion, however, is rooted in the theory of

Locke, who, as we saw, attributed to reason the ability to compare concepts derived from experience and to observe their necessary relations. Locke himself sought the bases of morality in the necessary relation between God's will and human will. But the principle of God's will, which lent to the law a purely external character, was inappropriate here [for Montesquieu]. It had already been rejected by [Samuel] Clarke, who in his *Treatise on the Existence of God,* which began with Lockean assumptions, derived the moral law from the necessary relations of things to each other.[5] The argument was that, if there are things with various natures, then the relations among them must be of various kinds necessarily determined by their nature. Certain traits and properties may belong to given subjects, others do not belong to them. These eternal and necessary relations are observed by rational beings, who, by virtue of their consciousness, make them guidelines for their own actions. Therefore, God, as Supreme Reason, cannot act otherwise than on the basis of eternal and necessary relations originating in the very nature of things. Rational human beings must be guided by the same rules. Hence it is clear that human actions possess inherent goodness or injustice; it is also clear that moral concepts flow from the very nature of things and not from the arbitrary prescription of a supreme legislator.

Montesquieu's definition is obviously borrowed from Clarke. We see here a repetition of the same sort of intellectual process that we noted in the moral school: a definition moves from a purely external conception of law and then is transformed into a conception of law that is immanent, that is based on the necessary relations of things. Between the definitions of the moral and individualist schools, despite their general similarity, there is, however, a basic distinction that differentiates the one from the other. As noted earlier, Leibniz saw in the laws of the universe "the determinant cause and organizing principle of things" (la raison déterminante et le principe régulatif des existences mêmes). This is something more than a simple relation; here law is not a consequence but a cause. This distinction arises from the completely contradictory points of departure of the two schools. Both thinkers see in law that which it is in fact—a link between things; but in Montesquieu the initial point of departure lies in the heterogeneity of subjects, and therefore the law is defined as the relationship between them, that is, as a consequence of the nature of things. In Leibniz, conversely, the point of departure is a universal principle—unitary reason, which initially creates from itself the general, ideal system of the universe; and later, in accordance with this system, gives birth to things, determines their logical development, and defines for each an appropriate place in the general chain of subjects. These are two facets of the same concept, but one approach moves from particular to general and the other from general to particular. If we penetrate to the essence of both definitions, we find that Leibniz's view is more profound and better grounded. Question: What is it in the nature of individual, changeable things that can establish between them a constant and necessary connection? And how from particular relations can an integrated, unitary system, such as the universe, come into existence? It is obvious that at the basis of particular elements there must lie a common nature conforming to general laws. For this reason Montesquieu himself recognizes possible laws as preceding actually adopted ones—a point of considerable import in its application to human beings. Before intelligent beings existed, he says, they were possible; consequently, among them were possible relations and possible laws. Before any positive laws there existed possible relations of justice, even as the law of equality of all radii in a circle existed before the first circle was drawn.[6] But if this be true, the law is first of all a relation between ideas, and later a relation between things; reason, consequently, imposes its laws on things whose actual connection is a consequence of a prior ideational link. And it is true that a universal connection between things is conceivable only if it originates from a universal, supreme principle that orders the universe—that is, from Reason. Accordingly, Montesquieu in another place, speaking about human laws, defines them as follows: "Law in general is human reason, inasmuch as it governs all the inhabitants of the earth: the political and civil laws of each nation ought to be only particular instances of the application of human reason."[7] Thus, by force of things, he was inclined toward Leibniz's notions, although the latter went completely against Locke's views. However, these purely philosophical conclusions remain for Montesquieu a sort of unnecessary appendage. He did not advance the theory of natural law but was interested in the role of law in public life. Here his perspective, limited to the analysis of relations between individual elements, turns out to be fully applicable.

Montesquieu devotes several lines to the general principles of natural law. Recognizing that natural laws precede positive law, he, like other interpreters, investigates their manifestation in the state of nature that preceded the appearance of community life. The first man, he claims, could not have had speculative ideas; therefore, he could not have had a conception of God. His first concern was survival. But sensing his weakness, he feared everything and tried to avoid any confrontation with others. For this reason peace, not war, is the first law of nature. The desire to subordinate oneself to others, which Hobbes attributes to the first people, does not apply here, because the notion of authority is very complex and consequently could have appeared only later. The sense of weakness is also associated with physical wants; the second natural law, therefore, is the need to seek nourishment. The third law is the attraction of the sexes for each other. Finally, when the sense of instinct is supplemented by acquired knowledge, there appears among human beings a new link, which prompts them to live in society. The desire to live in society is, therefore, the fourth law of nature.[8]

We see that Montesquieu applies to natural law the same perspective that Locke developed in his work on epistemology, but which he completely banished from his work on politics. Rational laws are the fruit of advanced development; they are preceded by laws of instinct, which alone prevail in the state of nature. This view refutes Locke's entire doctrine, which grounds civil societies on legal rights that apply to human beings in the state of nature. Although Montesquieu spent little effort developing his positions, one cannot but recognize his enlightened vision. In this respect, Locke is far inferior to him.

As soon as human beings join together in societies, Montesquieu continues, individuals begin to sense their own strength and try to convert to their own advantage the advantages of society. The result is a state of war between individuals. The same process occurs between individual societies. The disadvantages of war, in turn, lead to the need to establish positive laws and to define relations among societies as well as among individuals living within a single society. Laws of the first sort shape international law, whose basic principle is that different nations ought in time of peace to do one another all the good they can, and in war as little injury as they can, without prejudicing their real interests. The domestic laws of each society are again of two types: political laws, which define relations of rulers to the ruled; and civil laws, which define the relations of citizens to each other. Since both political and civil laws must be adapted to the people for whom they are framed, the institutions of one people rarely fit another. Laws must take account of the form of government, the physical characteristics of a country, its climate, territorial expanse, the way of life of a people, its religion, mores, wealth, commerce, and so on. Laws also have relations to one another, as well as to the intent of a legislator and to the order of things upon which they are established. Analysis of all these relations captures the *spirit of the laws*.[9]

Montesquieu first examines various forms of government. He divides them into three types: republican, monarchical, and despotic. The first type, in turn, he subdivides into two sorts: aristocratic and democratic. The distinction between monarchy and despotism is that the former is governed by fixed laws, while the latter is governed arbitrarily. Moreover, in many passages of the book all three forms of government—monarchical, aristocratic, and democratic—are treated under a single rubric: these are moderate governments, which are juxtaposed to despotism. The contrast between government based upon law and lawless government is the main point of Montesquieu's thought.

Each of these forms of government has its own nature, determined by its composition. From this source flows the basic laws upon which its political structure is grounded.

The nature of democracy is that sovereign authority belongs to the body of the people. Consequently, the people appear here as rulers in some respects and as subjects in others. The people become rulers by voting, which is the means of expressing their will. The laws must therefore define who has the right to vote, how votes are to be cast, and under what circumstances; that is, the first order of business is to determine the composition and means of operation of the popular assembly, to which sovereign authority belongs. Other institutions also are necessary: to execute the laws, ministers are needed; to offer advice and guidance, a senate. The people have a remarkable sense for determining the merit of individuals, but they are unable to manage affairs themselves. They are either too remiss or too violent in their actions. In a democracy both ministers and the senate should consist of elected representatives. This makes the rules for and method of elections important. Electors and those they elect not infrequently are divided into classes, in order to provide a greater or lesser advantage to the more prosperous. Such divisions were made by Solon in Athens and by Servius Tullius in Rome. Here the wisdom of the legislator becomes apparent, for the stability and well-being of the republic depend upon an appropriate division. The means of selecting representatives also constitutes a fundamental law of a democracy. Usually aristocracies elect representatives, while in democracies lots are cast; but the latter demands moderation and correctives, and this task also falls to the legislator. The basic laws also determine how ballots are cast: whether secretly or publicly. In democracies, voting should be done in public, for the people need guidance from the educated classes; [yet] in public voting, there is something to be feared from the machinations of political parties, which are an inevitable part of democratic government. Conversely, parties are dangerous in an aristocracy or in a senate; therefore, in those cases voting should be done secretly.

The nature of aristocracy consists in sovereign authority belonging to a portion of the people. If those sharing authority are numerous, then here too a senate will be needed to manage affairs. However, senators should not have the right to name their own colleagues: this practice leads to great abuses. It is even more dangerous to entrust significant authority to a single person; if this becomes necessary, then at least the duration of this authority should be limited to a short period. Short-term authority, however, is useful only in cases where it is to be turned against the people; a case in point is the dictatorship in ancient Rome, where the people acted through passion, not design. Conversely, dictatorial power which an aristocracy establishes against its own members must be of long duration. An example is the state inquisitors in Venice. In an aristocracy, institutions that permit the people to participate in government are also useful. Generally speaking, the fewer the citizens excluded from government, the less insecure and more stable will be the aristocracy. The best aristocracy is that which most closely resembles a democracy; the most imperfect is that in which the people are subordinate to the lords not only in political but also in civil relations, such as in Poland, where peasants are mired in serfdom.

The nature of monarchy, where a single individual governs by fundamental laws, consists in the existence of intermediate, subordinate, and dependent powers. The last trait is essential, because in a monarchy a prince is the source of all political and civil authority. But his activity must proceed through legal agencies; otherwise, there will be nothing stable, and there will be no fundamental laws. The most natural intermediate power is the nobility, which is essential to a monarchy. In countries where Estate privileges disappear, monarchical government is inevitably transformed either into popular government or into despotism. In monarchies, therefore, another essential element is ecclesiastical power, which is harmful in republics. Finally, monarchies require a special political agency to safeguard the laws. The nobility are incapable of this; the prince's council is too dependent; therefore, an independent institution, whose existence is fixed in law and whose membership is sufficiently numerous, is essential.

In a despotism, where the arbitrary will of a single individual reigns, administration is also entrusted to a single person. The despot himself, who considers himself to be everything and others as nothing, usually gives himself over to amusements and cares little about affairs of state. But if administration were to be given over to several individuals, they would quarrel among themselves. Consequently, it is simpler and more convenient to entrust administration to one person. The appointment of a vizier is, therefore, a fundamental law of despotism.[10]

This last proposition of Montesquieu is too one-sided. He had in mind the customary practice in Eastern states, but that practice is not the general rule.

Many writers also reject the distinction he drew between a monarchy and a despotism. Voltaire, in his reactions to Montesquieu's book, says that a monarch and a despot are two brothers who so resemble one another that they are often confused. Some interpreters still regard despotism as an independent type of government; but it is difficult to agree with this view. The difference between forms of government is determined first of all by who holds sovereign authority, and in both cases authority is held by a single individual. The most that can be said is that a despotism is a corruption of pure monarchy, as Aristotle taught. The difference between them is not generic but specific. With this caveat, Montesquieu's ideas remain profound and true. The essential difference between monarchy and despotism is that in the one there are checks [upon personal authority], at least in subordinate spheres, while in the other case there are no checks. The significance of these checks, which are less juridical than moral, is far from trivial. In a well-ordered monarchy, where the rights of Estates have been hallowed by time and have become rooted in customs, the monarch cannot infringe upon them without arousing against himself the hatred of the upper classes and without causing a profound shock to the state, whereas there are no rights which a despot will leave intact. Under certain historical circumstances, a pure monarchy may preside over even a very educated people, whereas a despotism is possible only among tribes which stand at a low stage of development. There is no doubt that between these two forms there may be imperceptible gradations, such that it is sometimes difficult to determine to which category one or another government belongs; but gradations exist even between polar opposites, and this does nothing to diminish the distinction between these opposites. The whole point of Montesquieu's thought is to indicate the need for checks in any form of government; as soon as these disappear, that government is transformed into a despotism. That idea is subtle and right on the mark.

Montesquieu distinguishes between the nature of various political forms and their principle *(principe).* By this term he means the moral force active within the state mechanism. In a democracy, the basic principle is virtue *(la vertu)*—that is, love for the commonweal. Virtue also exists in other forms of government, but only in democracy does it constitute the mainspring of the entire political organism, a precondition for its existence. As soon as it disappears, authority falls into the hands of the ambitious and avaricious, and then democracy falls into decline. The principle of aristocracy is also virtue, but of another sort; this virtue is not characteristic of the entire people, who do not require it for obedience's sake, but it is a trait of the governing Estate alone. In an aristocracy it is vital, on the one hand, that one individual not try to elevate himself at others' expense, and, on the other hand, that abuses of power not exhaust the people's patience. In this type of government moderation of personal ambitions is therefore more important than anything else. Thus moderation constitutes the basic principle of this form of government. In monarchy, which depends upon intermediate political bodies, the motive principle also attaches to social Estates, but it is of a different sort: it is rooted in relations of subordinate Estates to the authority at the apex of society. It is that sense which prompts citizens to strive for honors, but only while preserving their autonomy. Honor is the principle of monarchy. Finally, despotism perpetuates itself by fear alone. Here nothing is demanded of subjects except unconditional obedience. Thus in a despotism there is nothing of that which belongs to the essence of any moderate form of government—no tractability, no caution, no reconciliation of differences, no negotiations, no remonstrations [by society], no conditions [exacted by society]—in a word, there is nothing of that which flows from respect for autonomous individuals.[11]

These arguments of Montesquieu's have been repeatedly criticized. Many writers dismiss them as arbitrary. Yet nowhere perhaps is his genius so profound as in these propositions. That civic virtue is the very soul of democracy, the first and necessary precondition of universal political liberty, can scarcely be doubted. As soon as civic virtue disappears, the people must find themselves a lord. It is also beyond doubt that aristocratic rule demands of its members both restraint of their personal ambition and moderation in their use of authority. From the same source come respect for laws and customs, firmness and composure in decision-making, a desire to preserve the old while making appropriate concessions to new demands—qualities that are the essence of a good aristocracy. Apparently less convincing is the view that honor is the basic principle of monarchy; this thought strikes one as more brilliant than well-founded. But if we look into the essence of the situation, we see the profundity of the idea. Montesquieu distinguishes monarchy from despotism by noting that in the former there exist checks, while no such checks exist in the latter. In a state where sovereign authority is concentrated in a single person, legal checks alone cannot be effective: they must be combined with moral restraints. But where can these moral restraints be found? They may be found in the upper Estates that constitute the core and essential element of political life, Estates that remain loyal to the monarch but also defend their own rights and preserve their moral independence. And the key here is a sense of honor, which prompts individuals, on the one hand, to discharge the social obligations attending their position in society while, on the other hand, demanding respect for the moral dignity of their persons. Therefore, one may wholeheartedly agree with Montesquieu that monarchy is more likely to descend into despotism when the sense of honor disappears in society.

The nature of each form of government and its motive principle also determines the character of laws by which a community is ruled. Thus laws on education have the intention, in a monarchy, of developing a sense of honor and obedience to the will of the sovereign and also a sense of personal dignity and independence; in a republic, of inculcating love for the fatherland and for the laws; in a despotism, of debasing the human soul and transforming it into slavishness.

In a democracy, where equality prevails, the laws must enforce egalitarian tendencies and moderation in standards of living. For this reason there are rules that preserve family plots and prohibit the accumulation of legacies by a single individual. In commercial republics, it is useful to prevent the accumulation of wealth by establishing a law dividing inheritances equally among children. To the same end, the rich may be taxed so as to ease the lot of the poor. But because, in general, equal distribution of property is almost impossible to accomplish, one must resort here to other means as well. The most important of these is to uphold morals and respect for the laws. For this purpose it is useful to create a senate, as guardian of morals; one must also strictly subordinate citizens to rulers; finally, it is vital to develop the authority of the state in order to make up for the insufficiently developed civic authority.

In an aristocracy the law must be designed, on the one hand, so that the people will not feel the burden of being governed by a single Estate, and, on the other hand, so the members of the ruling Estate should retain a sense of equality among themselves. For the two main dangers that threaten aristocracy are too great an inequality between rulers and ruled, and inequality among the rulers themselves. In order to avoid the former, it is wise if leading citizens not be distinguished from the lower classes by symbols that arouse envy, and if these citizens not assume privileges that are too onerous for the people. They must not live well at the people's account; on the contrary, they are obliged to allot part of their income to the common good; in financial matters great economy should be observed; very strict justice must be applied to the common people. In order to achieve the second end, it is essential to eliminate any distinction between members of the noble Estate. Therefore, the right of primogeniture and of substitution, both of which serve monarchy, are inappropriate in an aristocracy. To preserve unity among members of the ruling Estate it is also crucial quickly to resolve any disputes that may arise among them. Finally, in order to suppress personal [political] ambitions, there must be a tribunal invested with tyrannical authority.

In a monarchy, the law must be designed to support the nobility, the guardian of honor. This end may be attained by establishing entailed Estates, substitutions, and privileges. In this form of government it is useful to sell offices, something that is unthinkable in other regimes, for this sale lends more constancy and independence to social corporations, and also eliminates the machinations of courtiers. The advantage of monarchy over a republic lies in expeditious action; but in order that efficiency not give rise to ill-considered initiatives, the laws should establish some contrivance to reduce its celerity.

The emblem of despotic government is as follows: the savages of Louisiana desire fruit, so they cut the tree at its root and then gather the fruit. In a despotism, it is unnecessary to have many laws, for here arbitrariness prevails. Administration is very simple, for the application of civil authority is nothing but the application of the rules of a single household. Succession to the throne is determined not by law but by the will of the ruler; but this fact opens up the door to every sort of intrigue. For this reason Eastern rulers, once on the throne, try to avoid death at the hands of their relatives. In order to hold the people in fear, the despot is forced to depend upon the army, but due to this dependence, the army becomes a danger to the government because the ruler must take measures against his very own armed forces. Sometimes in despotisms, the ruler declares himself the owner of all land and and the legatee of all citizens' property; but such a step leads to the impoverishment of the land and of the people. In general, under despotic government, insecurity of property destroys government and commerce, and leads to usury. Under despotism one sees bureaucratic corruption, for unjust government requires officials to carry out injustice, and these officials naturally do not forget about themselves. For this reason, in despotisms it is useful to confiscate property, something that is unthinkable in moderate forms of government where confiscations are an infringement upon property. On the other hand, in order to bind his servants to himself, a despot must offer them monetary rewards—a practice that in republics and monarchies is a sure sign of decline; for it suggests that all sense of honor and of love for the fatherland have disappeared in a people. In general, Montesquieu says, despotism is so repugnant to human nature that it is surprising that peoples have been subjected to it. The problem is that to establish moderate government, where various forces exist and balance each other, requires considerable political acumen, whereas nothing is easier than to institute a despotism.[12]

The principles of various forms of government affect their civil and criminal laws and also the judicial system in each state. In moderate governments more complicated laws are needed; [the system] is more formalized than in despotic governments. In moderate governments the rights of citizens cannot be left to the arbitrary will of magistrates but must be clearly and firmly defined by law and by jurisprudence. Everything having to do with the life, the liberty, and property of individuals must be surrounded with all possible guarantees, so that each person may be afforded a means of defense [against the state] and so that magistrates may not impose verdicts except with the greatest care and with full knowledge of a situation. In a despotism, these guarantees are superfluous: here the magistrate's will dominates and can be imposed with greatest rapidity, as happens in Turkey. Therefore, simplification of the laws is the first sign of despotism. Moreover, in despotic governments, the prince himself may render decisions; in monarchies, this is inconceivable: if it does occur, intermediate bodies are destroyed, formal procedures abolished, and arbitrariness takes the place of the law. A prince acting as magistrate is the source of endless abuses, for courtiers are always able to wheedle out of the prince judgments in accordance with their personal desires. Even ministers must not act as judges in a monarchy; between a prince's council and courts of judicature there is a fundamental incompatibility. Finally, in moderate governments punishments themselves must be moderate and must be proportionate to crimes. Conversely, in a despotism punishments are harsh and are calculated only to deter criminals. But cruel punishments dull the people's sensibility and for the most part are not carried out. Even when they achieve their purpose, they remain an incorrigible evil. The corruption of the people is a natural result of despotism.[13]

The attitude of the laws toward luxury also depends upon the variety of forms of government. In a democracy there must exist sumptuary laws, for luxury is incompatible with equality of fortunes; moreover, it leads to the predominance of private interests over public ones, and this violates the essence of democracy. In aristocracy, the principle of moderation also demands limitations upon luxury in private life; but because the ruling Estate must be wealthy, it must devote excess wealth to civic expenditures. In a monarchy, conversely, inequality of fortunes makes luxury essential. Therefore, laws against luxury are inappropriate here: each individual should enjoy complete liberty in this respect. Finally, in a despotism luxury also exists, but for another reason: uncertainty about the future impels people to the greatest possible enjoyment of the present.[14]

Another issue is the freedom of women, which may be subject to the least restraint in a monarchy. Conversely, in a republic, where strictness of morals is essential, women's liberty may be subject to tight constraints. As far as despotism is concerned, here women are nothing but slaves. Accordingly, dowries should be large in monarchies, modest in republics, and insignificant in despotisms.[15]

The corruption of every government generally begins with that of its principles.

Democracy is corrupted not only by deviation from its principle but by exaggeration of that principle—that is, by excessive love for liberty and equality. When no one wants to accept the command of another, society loses all respect for seniority. The people tolerate no authorities except their own; they take rights from the senate, from magistrates, from government officials; they assume control over all business and themselves become despots. But such a state of affairs, becoming more and more intolerable, inevitably leads to the appearance of tyranny. In a moderate democracy, individuals are equal to each other only as citizens; in an unconstrained democracy, a superior is equal to his subordinates, a father to his son, a master to his servant. Virtue may easily coexist with liberty, but it is as far from excessive liberty as it is from slavery.

An aristocracy is corrupted when the authority of nobles becomes arbitrary. Moderation disappears along with respect for the law, and then the people are ruled despotically: only instead of one despot, there are many. Corruption occurs especially when an aristocracy becomes hereditary: the assurance of acquiring power eliminates the need for restraint.

Monarchy is corrupted when its intermediary bodies are destroyed and when the privileges of Estates are taken away: then the government ineluctably becomes a despotism. It is also corrupted when the monarch desires to govern everything directly, when he gathers control over all affairs at court, when he arbitrarily alters the laws, when he reduces the power of the lords by making them tools of his personal will, and finally, when he destroys the sense of honor among the people, showering awards upon undeserving individuals whose only boast is the depth of their servility and who suppose that they owe everything to the monarch and nothing to their country.

As far as despotism is concerned, it is, by its very nature, already a corrupted government and it corrupts everything more and more.[16]

Incidentally, the corruption of governments may occur from purely external causes, from territorial expansion or contraction. In general, the republican form is capable of sustaining itself only in small states. In large states an excessive inequality of property is engendered. Furthermore, the accumulation of wealth in a few hands leads to extremism in ideologies. The interests of social classes diverge, and the common good is sacrificed for the sake of private gain. An individual senses that he may be important even without a fatherland, and therefore he tries to advance himself at his country's expense. Conversely, in a small territory, the common interest is immediately apparent to everyone; abuses fall under constant scrutiny. In a small independent community it is hard to set up any other form of government besides a republican one. In this context a prince would be an oppressor, because his means would not be proportionate to his authority, and he would always live in fear of internal and external enemies. Monarchy, by its very nature, should control a moderate amount of territory. If it is too small, it turns into a republic; if too large, then nobles, being distant from the center and hoping to escape punishment, may refuse their obedience and thus lead the state to ruin. The only medicine against this evil consists in establishing unlimited authority, a medicine which itself is the greatest evil. Large states naturally incline toward despotism. Swiftness of decision must make up for the distance [from the center to periphery]; the recalcitrant will be restrained by fear; finally, the law must take account of differences in local conditions and circumstances that are inevitable in a large region. It follows that in order to preserve the existing order of government, a state must remain within its existing borders. Otherwise, with expansion or contraction, the very spirit of the people will change.[17]

These rationale lead Montesquieu to an analysis of the defensive and aggressive policies pursued by states.[18] A dual danger threatens a republic: if the republic is small, it may be destroyed by a foreign power; if it is large, it may be destroyed by an internal flaw. There is only one way to avoid this double threat: by a confederate structure, which combines the advantages of large and small states. Confederation is more suited to republics than to monarchies; besides, member states must have similar political institutions: otherwise, the link between them will be unstable. It is important that individual members not have the right to enter into alliances without the consent of other members; it is also important that members' voting power and responsibilities be proportionate to their significance; finally, it is desirable that magistrates and officials of the confederation be elected by a general assembly, not by each member state separately. It is obvious that Montesquieu is arguing the case for a confederate state over an alliance between states. He sees the ideal form of confederate state in ancient Lycia. His view is surprisingly shrewd, appearing as it did at a time when the United States had not yet declared its independence and when the various features of a federated order were not so apparent as they are today.

In contrast to republics, which are sustained by uniting forces, despotisms defend themselves by dividing, by keeping themselves separate from their neighbors. They turn their borders into deserts and thus save themselves from their enemies. Sometimes they place vassal princes on their borders to serve as a means of defense, and, in case of need, these vassals become expendable.

Finally, monarchy, which cannot afford to lay waste to itself after the fashion of a despotism, must have at the ready all necessary means of defense. It needs fortresses and an army. A modest territory is more easily defended, for it is easier for the army to move in any direction in order quickly to engage an adversary. Conversely, in a large state, where part of the army is defeated, it is difficult for the remaining part to come to its aid, and then it is easy for the adversary to penetrate to the capital itself. Therefore, monarchs must be careful in expanding their realms. Trying to avoid troubles of one sort, they may fall prey to other, even more serious troubles. Self-restraint is all the more essential when the weakness of neighboring states tempts [the monarch to consider] conquest, for such weakness is a great convenience in political relations. By subjugating a weak state one rarely increases one's power; rather, one usually diminishes it.

Among the various forms of government, a republic is most endangered by aggressive policy. Because it is based upon popular authority, it must necessarily extend civil rights to conquered peoples; it must therefore limit its conquests to that quantity of people that democracy may bear. If a republic transforms conquered peoples into subjects, then it undermines its own liberty, for the power of officials in charge of the subjugated regions will be excessive. There is another disadvantage as well: republican government is always more harsh than is a monarchy; thus it is more hated by conquered peoples, who enjoy neither the blessings of liberty nor the advantages of sovereignty.

Monarchy also may make conquests so long as it does not go beyond the natural limits of its powers. Here conquered nations must retain the same laws, institutions, and customs by which they lived previously; there should be no other alteration than that of the army and the name of the sovereign. Treatment of such peoples should be very lenient. Otherwise, peripheral regions, ruined and dissatisfied, will always prove unreliable. In any case, aggressive policy has unfortunate consequences for a monarchy: the effort that is demanded in warfare leads to the exhaustion of provincial areas within the monarchy, while in the capital there is a great concentration of acquired wealth. Therefore, an aggressive monarchy usually presents shocking luxury in the center, misery in the provinces, and abundance in the conquered regions.

Conquests on a large scale presume a despotism. In order to retain such extensive territories, a despotic prince must have a loyal army, one ready to crush any dissent. Here as well, however, the governors of distant regions have difficulty in restraining subject peoples; on the other hand, the prince himself may find it hard to deal with his own appointed officials who want to act autonomously. It is therefore most useful for a despotism to allow conquered countries to retain their former governments, while placing them in a condition of feudal dependence upon itself.

Montesquieu's general conclusion concerning the corruption of various forms of government is that the corruption of any government is, in essence, tantamount to a movement toward despotism. This is what determines the attitude of various forms of government to liberty. Liberty in general, says Montesquieu, is not the possibility to do anything that one desires. In a state, that is, in a society which is governed by laws, liberty means the possibility of doing what one ought to will, and of not being forced to do that which one ought not to will. In order words, liberty is the right to do that which is permitted by the law. If a citizen had the right to do that which is forbidden by the law, then his liberty would be destroyed, for that would give everyone else the right to do the same.[19] In this sense, liberty is not one of the advantages of a republic over a monarchy; liberty may not exist at all in a corrupted republic, even though power may belong to the people. Liberty exists only in moderate governments, where citizens are more or less immune to abuses by the government. In general, liberty can be divided into two types: political liberty, which has to do with the state mechanism, and personal liberty, which applies to individual citizens. The former exists where one authority is restrained by another. The eternal experience of the human species shows that any individual, once invested with authority, will attempt to abuse it unless he is aware of its limits. Thus checks are essential. It is therefore clear that political liberty is guaranteed only by institutions which establish a division and mutual balance between the branches of government.[20] As an example of this type of governmental structure Montesquieu cites England, which alone among nations declared its intention to realize political liberty.[21] Montesquieu's famous chapter on the English constitution served as the basis for the constitutional doctrine in Western Europe.

Power, Montesquieu says, is divided into the legislative, executive, and judicial. Anytime two of them are united in the same hands, liberty is in peril.

Uniting legislative and executive authority gives the person or political body to which they are entrusted the possibility to publish tyrannical laws and tyrannically to enforce them. Uniting judicial authority with legislative leads to judicial arbitrariness; for the judge here is a legislator and so does what he wishes. Finally, uniting judicial authority with executive gives a judge the possibility to be an oppressor. In moderate monarchies, judicial authority is entrusted to independent bodies or persons, and for this reason there is more liberty than in despotisms and republics where all three powers are concentrated in the same hands.

To achieve the best balance among the branches an organization of the following type is demanded: first, judicial power must not be the property of a fixed tribunal but must be entrusted to people elected from the people to serve a temporary term. Thus the judiciary will be almost invisible and will not arouse dangerous opposition. Judges should be peers of the accused, who should have the right in some measure to except against a large number of them so that the remaining part may be deemed his or her own choice. The right to imprison citizens should generally remain the province of the judiciary; otherwise liberty again disappears. Only in emergencies may the legislature temporarily grant this right to the executive. Such arrangements are useful because they eliminate the need for such constant defenders of order as the Spartan Ephori or the Venetian inquisitors. As far as the legislative authority is concerned, it must naturally belong to the people, for each free individual must govern himself. But because in large states an assembly of all citizens is impractical, and because the people, who do have the ability to elect good representatives, are unable to decide all matters by themselves, the making of laws and their supervision are entrusted to elected representatives. These two tasks may be discharged by a representative assembly, since it is incapable of taking real action itself. The right of voting in the election of representatives should belong to all citizens, excluding those whose low social position deprives them of autonomous will. But in the state there are always people superior to others by birth, in wealth, in honor. If they be swallowed up by the common mass, then liberty for them would become slavery and would cease to arouse in them any interest. Therefore, it is crucial to give them a role in the legislature appropriate to their position in society. This is accomplished by creating for them a special aristocratic chamber, which can restrain popular enthusiasms, just as the people, in their turn, restrain the personal ambitions of the nobles. This structure is the more essential because, of the three branches of government, the judiciary possesses the least power. There are therefore two branches [one of which must be subdivided to form a third], so as to moderate their confrontations. That is the justification of the aristocratic chamber. Membership must be hereditary: 1) by its very nature and; 2) because it needs a strong inducement to defend its rights, which otherwise, in a free state, will always be subject to danger. [To guarantee that the upper chamber] not sacrifice the common good to private advantages, it should have the prerogative to block the budgetary decisions of the other chamber, not the prerogative to issue its own regulations. Finally, executive power should be located in the hands of the monarch, 1) because execution of the laws is more efficient when entrusted to a single person than when entrusted to many; 2) because executive authority entrusted to persons elected from the legislature again leads to a combination of two branches of authority in the same hands.

What should be the relations among branches of government so divided? Popular representatives are not always in session; [year-round sessions] are superfluous and impractical both for citizens and for the executive. Representatives cannot, however, assemble at their own discretion, for an assembly possesses a will only when it is already in session. Furthermore, the tenure of a session depends upon the nature of business to be discussed, and the only judge of this is the executive. The latter, therefore, should have the right to convoke and dissolve a legislative session and also to veto its decisions; otherwise, the legislators might take all power into their own hands and act as despots. This is the executive's share of the legislative authority. But the legislature must not be granted the same sort of share in executive authority. If the legislature had the right to block actions of the executive, then it could halt conduct of all business. Instead it should be granted the right to exercise supervision over the executive's actions and to make sure that the laws are properly executed. However, the assembly cannot force the person invested with executive authority to answer to it. This would again place the executive in complete dependence upon the legislators, and that would lead to despotism. The person of the supreme executive should be sacred and inviolable. But because he cannot act except through ministers, the latter can be held accountable and may be subjected to punishment in case of abuses. The popular representatives themselves, however, may not judge the ministers, for they are the accusers and are generally too self-interested in the outcome of a trial [to act impartially]. The normal courts cannot act as judge, for their standing is too low and they are easily subject to influence by higher authority. Therefore, the right of judgment should be granted to that portion of the legislature that is more independent and impartial and that occupies an intermediary position between monarchy and people—that is, the aristocratic assembly. The danger emanating from the executive is especially great, because it controls the expenditure of money and use of armed force. Special guarantees are therefore in order here. One guarantee is that the legislature should appropriate money every year, not for indefinite periods. Moreover, the army should be merged with the people. This can be accomplished by levying recruits only from the well-to-do, or by a system of short-term enlistments; finally, if it is necessary to support a standing army levied from the lower classes, then the legislative assembly should have the right to dissolve it. But to place the army under the legislature's command is impractical, for the army's mission is action, not judgment. Furthermore, taking command of the army may exercise a deleterious impact upon the legislative power, which will either itself become part of the military or will become contemptuous toward soldiers. Therefore, the executive power should command the army.

Such are the relations of the three branches. Because they check each other, says Montesquieu, one might think that the result would be a lack of action; but since the force of events compels them to move, they will move harmoniously. This system, he adds, originated with the ancient Germans; it was invented in the forests. Montesquieu does not depict it, though, as the only structure in which liberty is possible. Moderation and the golden mean, he claims, generally suit human beings better than do extremes. But all moderate governments should more or less approach this ideal; otherwise, they fall into despotism.

In the eighteenth century this theory of constitutional monarchy, which Montesquieu was the first to elaborate in modern times, received the almost unconditional approbation of moderate liberals. Later it was subjected to criticism that not infrequently went too far. There is no doubt that Montesquieu's doctrine suffers from basic flaws. Its sole purpose is to safeguard liberty, which it does through division of powers. Yet statecraft requires unity in administration; how is that to be achieved? Montesquieu has no answer to this question. His statement that all three branches of government should move cooperatively because they cannot stand in place is more clever than serious. In reality, in constitutional states, unity of action is institutionalized through parliamentary rule—that is, by appointment of the ministers from the majority party among the popular representatives. But that method of administration was finally established only in the nineteenth century. In the eighteenth century, genuine parliamentary rule was replaced in England by the mutual connections of titled families that dominated the state—a fact that Montesquieu ignored. Judging by theoretical criteria rather than historical experience, he did not take into account the significance in the English political system of the tight aristocratic circle that dominated the legislative chambers and held executive authority in its hands. There is no doubt, however, that such oligarchical rule was compatible with liberty only because the aristocracy was held in check by other social elements. The guarantees of liberty were nevertheless found in a division of powers; in this Montesquieu was absolutely correct.

Another important shortcoming of this doctrine is the incorrect application of the notion of division of powers to the three branches of government. An independent judiciary undoubtedly provides the most essential guarantees of liberty, but more of personal than of political liberty. The judiciary occupies a subordinate position within the state, and its independence should not be confused with the division of sovereign authority itself. Montesquieu wanted to treat all political guarantees under a single rubric, and so he incorrectly conflated intermediary, but inferior agencies that restrain the actions of the government even in the most centralized systems, with those bodies that take shape when sovereign authority is divided among various agencies. Montesquieu subsequently compensated for this error in another aspect of his theory. Having laid out the structure of a constitutional monarchy, Montesquieu explicitly says that the judicial power should be quite insignificant; he deprives it of any political significance and places it so low, puts so little weight on its independence that he does not give it the right to judge ministers for abuse of their authority. The role of intermediary in confrontations between the higher authorities is entrusted to another social element that participates independently in the legislature and occupies an intermediate position between monarch and people. Thus, in essence, according to Montesquieu's doctrine, the three branches among which governmental authority is divided are not legislative, executive, and judicial but monarchical, aristocratic, and democratic. The most that can be said is that one of them is entrusted with the executive power and others primarily with the legislative. Hence it is clear that Montesquieu's perspective completely coincides with the teaching of Polybius. The basic idea is the same for both thinkers: the necessity of dividing political authority among independent bodies that check each other. In both thinkers the basic elements of this division are the monarchy, aristocracy, and democracy. Montesquieu's mistake is the not quite accurate application of these notions to the various branches of government; but he compensates for his own mistake. On the other hand, Montesquieu's great advantage over Polybius consists of his fuller development of both these notions. In ancient republics, the monarchical element, if it even existed, was of negligible importance; therefore, the theory of the division of powers could not be fully applied in them. In Rome, to which Polybius points as evidence for this theory, there were really only two elements eternally vying against each other. Consequently, Polybius's teaching was more the fruit of abstract speculation than of actual events. Among modern peoples, by virtue of historical circumstances, all three elements exist and have developed independently. Everywhere they have vied against each other. In England, under most fortunate circumstances, they ultimately came to cooperate and elaborated a general structure in which each found an appropriate place. In the English case Montesquieu possessed a model in which the theoretical notion of the ancients found its realization. He described this model, compared it to abstract theoretical constructs, indicated the significance of each of its parts, analyzed their necessary relations, and thus raised constitutional monarchy to the level of a universal ideal for the safeguarding of liberty. This is the French publicist's immortal achievement.

Much less satisfactory is his analysis concerning laws that protect the personal liberty of citizens.[22] Here, too, however, he makes numerous apt remarks. According to Montesquieu's definition, personal liberty consists in security or in the opinion that one has security. This definition is obviously too narrow; it encompasses only one aspect of personal liberty, not the totality of rights attending it. This view of liberty, Montesquieu continues, depends not on political laws alone but also on the means of their application, on civil laws, on morals, and legal precedents. A constitution may be liberal, yet personal liberty may not exist in the country, whereas, conversely, a citizen may feel himself to be free, but there may be no liberty in political institutions. Mostly, personal liberty depends on criminal laws, for security is most often violated by arbitrary accusations and punishments. In this sense, liberty's great triumph is when each punishment is proportionate to a criminal offense. Then arbitrariness disappears, and punishment depends not on the caprice of the government but on the nature of the offense. Thus religious crimes should be subject to religious punishments; crimes against morals should be punished by deprivation of those rights and privileges attached to the purity of morals, and so on. But thoughts alone that are not carried into action should not under any circumstance be liable to prosecution; otherwise, the liberty of the individual disappears. In general, one should be very careful in prosecuting crimes whose definition is arbitrary. Examples are witchcraft and heresy. Accusations of this sort are most destructive to liberty, for they create a pretext for endless oppression. Just as dangerous are vague laws concerning lèse-majesté; where such laws exist, government inevitably becomes despotic. Worst of all is when people are accused of lèse-majesté in their thoughts or in careless expressions. Even written works should fall under the law only when they explicitly call for criminal actions against the sovereign. Otherwise, arbitrary rule will prevail in the state, and arbitrariness is followed by despotism. In a monarchy in particular liberty is most endangered by arbitrary punishments. Thus nothing is worse than establishing special commissars as judges over private persons. This does not serve the interest of the prince; rather, it inaugurates judicial arbitrariness. In a well-organized monarchy there is no need to resort to spying [on citizens]. A citizen has discharged his obligation when he has remained faithful to the law; his home should remain inviolable. Spying is the more harmful in that its instruments can only be people of an inferior sort. Secret denunciations should also not be permitted; when an accusation is made in the name of public welfare, it must be presented not to the prince, upon whom it is easy to exert influence, but to the established courts. In general, good criminal laws can introduce a certain amount of liberty even in a despotic government.

Having analyzed the relations of the laws to political life, Montesquieu then treats their connection with natural conditions in the country. Here the first issue is the question of climate's influence upon institutions. Making reference to certain superficial and occasionally even perverse observations, Montesquieu constructs a theory of climates which essentially resembles the views of Aristotle and Bodin. Like his predecessors, Montesquieu claims that northern peoples possess more strength and bravery but less impressionability than southern ones; the latter, conversely, are distinguished by greater effeminacy, timidity, and indolence, but also by greater refinement of emotions and strength of passion. These various qualities influence conditions of life, morals, and therefore the laws. However, Montesquieu notes, a good legislator is not one who by his legal code favors the vices of climate, but he who opposes those vices.[23]

Montesquieu devotes special attention to the impact of climate on the development of slavery—civil, familial, and political.[24] He criticizes previous theories of slavery. All legal justifications of that institution cited by other writers he rejects unconditionally. He says that war cannot be a source of slavery, for to kill another is permitted only in case of necessity; if one allows a conquered adversary to live, then one may not impose slavery upon him. The victor's only right over his captives is to deprive them of the possibility of doing harm. It is also illegitimate for a person voluntarily to sell himself into bondage. Every sale presupposes a price received by the seller, but the slave receives nothing of worth in return for his or her sale. It is said that the slave receives food from the master; if that is so, then slavery ought logically to be restricted to those individuals who are unable to feed themselves, but no one would wish to hold such slaves. Moreover, the liberty of every citizen is a part of public liberty, and no one has the right to sell his citizenship. Along with voluntary sale a third source of slavery is also delegitimated—namely, birth—for if an individual has no right to sell himself, he has even less right to sell his children. Aristotle claims that slavery is in conformity with nature, but because all people are born equal, then it should be said on the contrary that slavery is repugnant to nature. However, there are countries where slavery is established due to natural conditions. In despotic states, where citizens are helpless against the government, they sell themselves to powerful men who hold the government itself in fear. This is the source of the mild servitude that one encounters in certain countries. Another source of slavery, of very cruel slavery, is in climate. In southern regions such indolence and effeminacy prevail that a person will not agree to perform hard labor except under fear of punishment. Moreover, here the lord finds himself in the same relation to the prince as does the slave to him—that is, civil slavery is accompanied by political slavery. In all other cases, slavery may be abolished through the efforts of free individuals. The defenders of slavery speak in the name of luxury and comfort, not of love for the common welfare. Whatever sort of slavery may exist, the laws should always prohibit abuses and strive to eliminate the dangers that can arise from this social arrangement.

Familial slavery also is correlated to climate. In southern regions, women attain beauty before their reason has developed. Therefore, they find themselves completely subordinated to men. On the other hand, they age quickly, and this leads to polygamy. Finally, the fervency of passions aroused by climate engenders the need to hold women under lock. Conversely, in temperate countries where women mature later and are better preserved, a certain equality develops between them and males. The passions here are not so ardent as in the south; therefore, women may enjoy liberty. But because the character of familial authority is also reflected in the form of government, this may be taken as one of the reasons why in Asia republics could never take root, and despotism always prevailed.

Finally, political slavery is also closely linked with climate. The effeminacy and lack of bravery of southern peoples make them the victims of despotism, whereas the courage of northerners preserves their liberty. In Asia there is no temperate zone to speak of, only the contrast between north and south: consequently, in Asia there are always victors and vanquished. In Europe, however, where the temperate zone is more extensive, peoples equal to each other live side by side, and, for this reason, each insists on its own independence. Moreover, Europe is geographically broken up by mountains and seas, a circumstance that favors states of moderate size, whereas the enormous plains of Asia constitute a natural stage for despotism.

After climate the next factor is soil.[25] Fertile soil, according to Montesquieu, favors servitude, poor soil favors liberty. The former attracts people to agriculture, but tillers of the soil, preoccupied by their own affairs, are easily subjugated by any government. Fertility of soil also gives rise to luxury, effeminacy, and attachment to material life, whereas less fertile lands make people industrious, hard-working, courageous and capable of conducting war; they must attain through their own efforts that which the soil denies them. Finally, fertile lands are usually plains, which are difficult to defend against conquerors. Conversely, in infertile mountainous regions it is easy to defend oneself; here liberty is the only thing upon which one sets value. On the other hand, liberty that develops on less fertile soil itself facilitates the tilling of that soil. According to Montesquieu, lands are tilled not in proportion to their fertility but in proportion to the freedom of their inhabitants. Another important factor is the maritime position of a country. The inhabitants of islands generally are more inclined toward liberty than are inhabitants of a continent. Islands present an obstacle to external invaders; internally, given the modest amount of territory, it is not easy for one part of the people to enslave another. Finally, liberty persists among savage peoples who do not till the land at all, and who therefore can always flee from oppression. Preservation of their liberty is facilitated by ignorance of money; individuals have few wants and nothing to take from others. Therefore, willy-nilly, equality is maintained here. However, unusual contingencies can alter these laws.

The laws must always take into account the manners and spirit of a people, which depend upon natural conditions; otherwise, the laws will not accomplish their purpose. For the best laws [to function], it is necessary that minds be prepared for them. Liberty itself, says Montesquieu, sometimes seems insupportable to peoples who are unaccustomed to it, just as fresh air is harmful to inhabitants of marshy countries. In general, a legislator should follow the spirit of the people, for people do better that which they do voluntarily. Nature itself corrects every shortcoming; even vices not infrequently engender their opposite. If it is necessary to alter manners, then it is better not to do so by laws, for that would have the air of tyranny; instead, change should be accomplished by introducing other manners. In despotisms it is especially dangerous to touch established customs. Here customs take the place of laws; citizens are more attached to them because, under despotic governments, they are least inclined to embrace changes in their ways of life. But on the other hand, manners themselves are elaborated under the influence of the laws. As an example, Montesquieu offers a most subtle portrait of the manners of Englishmen, deducing their manners from the political liberty that prevails among them.[26]

Then he examines the relation of the laws to commerce, to money, and to population. This is of little interest for [the understanding of] politics. There are curious observations in his treatment of the laws and religion. He notes that Christianity, which propagates meekness and respect for others, favors moderate government, just as Islam leads to despotism. Of the Christian confessions, Catholicism is more suited to unlimited monarchies, Protestantism to free states. Montesquieu is exceptionally vigorous in insisting upon religious toleration. He strictly condemns any punishment for religious opinions. It is better to grant privileges [to a given religion] than to use force [against another]. In order to avoid religious altercations, however, it is wise not to introduce new confessions, when the people are satisfied by an existing one. The general principle should be: not to receive a new religion if that is possible; if it is already received, then it must be tolerated. Throughout this discussion, Montesquieu's adopts a purely political perspective. He warns against confusing God's laws with human laws: that which should be under the jurisdiction of the one should fall outside the jurisdiction of the other.

Finally, having presented, in the form of anecdotes, the history of testamentary laws among the Romans and of civil laws among the Franks, Montesquieu summarizes his thought concerning the method of writing laws. He says that the spirit of the legislator should be the spirit of moderation. The political good, like the moral good, is to be found between two extremes. The laws should be precise and clear but not overly refined or unnecessarily detailed. They should not be altered, unless it is necessary to do so; finally, it is not wise to strive for too much uniformity in legislation. "There are certain ideas of uniformity," writes Montesquieu, "which may sometimes impress great minds, but which invariably will transport small souls into ecstasy. The latter discover therein a kind of perfection, which they recognize because it is impossible for them not to see it; the same authorized weights, the same measures in trade, the same laws in the state, the same religion in all its parts. But is uniformity right always and without exception? Is the evil of constantly changing less than that of suffering inertia? And does not one of the qualities of genius consist rather in distinguishing between those cases in which uniformity is requisite, and those in which there is a necessity for differences?"[27]

The last section of the work, which constitutes a kind of appendix, Montesquieu devotes to analyzing the historical development of feudal institutions, which, having established everywhere independent bodies, became a source of political liberty in Western Europe.

This is the content of that splendid book, which, together with the works of Aristotle and Machiavelli, occupies the highest niche in the political literature of all ages. Standing on the soil of individualism, writing mainly in order to safeguard liberty, Montesquieu did not succumb to the natural temptation to make liberty the alpha and omega of political life. He saw that too much liberty could be just as harmful as too little, and therefore he tried to connect it to those general laws and preconditions which, by confining it to the limits of moderation, are alone able to lend it durability and strength. He saw its preconditions in the existence of independent bodies that serve as checks upon one another. This notion, which in antiquity was applied only to the way sovereign authority itself was organized, Montesquieu developed in great detail and applied to various forms of government. Everywhere he pointed to the most important rule of politics—namely, that the excessive concentration of power, whether in the hands of an autocrat or of a majority, is always deleterious to the state and imperils its citizens. Therefore, in a monarchy, the foundation of wise government is respect for independent bodies and persons. Any government attempting excessively to strengthen itself and to suppress other elements is heading toward despotism. Thus the fundamental rule of political life should be to observe moderation, which flows from mutual respect among autonomous political elements. These profound views on politics should make Montesquieu's work the standard reference book of all rulers, whether they be autocrats or democrats. No one before or since has identified so subtly and distinctly the despotic tendencies to which governments so easily succumb when they lack restraint. Relying on theoretical assumptions, Montesquieu did not always adequately support his theory with facts, but his thought is always perceptive and profound. One cannot but notice, however, that having devoted so much attention to the need for independent branches of government, he lost sight of that which is necessary for their cooperation in pursuit of a common objective. A certain concentration of power is always necessary in a state, and there are moments and circumstances when it is simply an imperative. Montesquieu did not deny this: in preaching moderation, he did, however, reject extremes, both of one-man rule and of liberty. But preoccupied by a certain idea, he ignored everything else. Checks and the division of powers—that is the entire basis of his views. His theory unquestionably betrays the one-sidedness of the individualist perspective. Therefore, his work, despite its exceptional virtues, is far from the final word in analyzing politics.

Another shortcoming for which he may be reproached, this time from the perspective of individualism itself, lies in the rather weak development of the theoretical principles of legal right and of the state. These questions, as we have seen, he touched upon very lightly and unsatisfactorily. On the source and significance of liberty he says not a word, yet liberty is the grounding principle of his theory. He analyzed the laws governing liberty, but not the nature of liberty itself. It is not surprising that other branches of the individualist school, attempting to fill this lacuna, chose different approaches and arrived at different conclusions.

Montesquieu's theory found numerous followers in the eighteenth century. To Englishmen themselves it revealed for the first time the logic of their constitution. The famous jurist [William] Blackstone, who laid the foundation for the scholarly study of English law, was guided by Montesquieu's interpretations. Another adherent was the Genevan [Jean-Louis] De Lolme, in his work on the English constitution, a book which in its time enjoyed enormous notoriety. In the Scottish school, about which we shall speak below, Montesquieu found a follower in the person of [Adam] Ferguson. In France itself there arose an entire school, which played an important role in the Constituent Assembly of 1789. Finally, in Italy, Montesquieu's system had resonance in the works of [Cesare] Beccaria and Filangieri. The former dealt with the subject of criminal law; the latter treated all fields of legislation and composed what amounted to a general code incorporating all the reformist tendencies of the eighteenth century. In its time, it enjoyed quite remarkable popularity. For this reason it deserves the historian's attention.

The Science of Legislation (La Scienza della Legislatione) of the Neapolitan Gaetano Filangieri began to appear in 1780 and remained unfinished at the author's death in 1788. Filangieri recognizes that he owes a great deal to Montesquieu but claims that he also departs at many points from his predecessor. Montesquieu, according to the Neapolitan publicist, sought in the relations of things to find the causes of what actually has happened in the world; Filangieri takes upon himself the task of establishing the rules for that which ought to happen.[28] He wants not so much to explain existing phenomena as to provide a guide for the legislator. His objective, therefore, is more idealistic, and so it was easier for him to get carried away by pure speculation. On the other hand, Filangieri's task is not so much to elucidate the higher principles of political life as to apply legislation to administration and to the courts. He has in mind more civil reforms than political reforms, though he also touches upon the latter.

Filangieri regards the preservation of society and maintenance of its tranquility as the only subject of legislation. He deduces this from the justification for civic order itself. Rejecting the hypothesis of the individual's original, solitary condition, he nevertheless posits an original state of nature in which people lived in complete independence, without being subordinate to any authority. The individual was created for society and therefore can never remain in solitude; but in the first societies there was no link among individuals except for natural law and their common needs. Given the inequality of physical strength among individuals and the ungovernability of passions, this link could not be a stable one. Therefore, in order to achieve preserve themselves and secure their community, individuals found it necessary to subordinate themselves to civil authority. [According to Filangieri,] civil authority must function so as to preserve the community, that is, by extending and interpreting natural law, it must establish rules of community life, define legal rights and duties of citizens, and thus foster arrangements capable of balancing the limitations upon individual liberty with the advantages of life in the community. Such is the origin of states, and such is the sole and universal purpose of legislation.[29]

How should terms like the "preservation" of individuals and "security" of society be construed? Filangieri understands them very broadly. According to his theory, "preservation" connotes both the means of supporting life and its comforts—that is, the increase of wealth and its distribution. Therefore, this category encompasses all laws concerning the population and economic relations. "Security" or "social tranquility" consists of the assurance that the person and property of society's members are safeguarded against violence. This end is facilitated chiefly by criminal laws.[30] That is not all: it is not enough, says Filangieri, to punish crime; it is necessary to prevent crime by developing virtue. Virtue is attained primarily through education. But because legislation can lend direction only to public education, not domestic education, and because only public education can engender in society identical rules, sensibilities, and institutions, then domestic education should be permitted only as an exception. In addition, the state should generally provide the appropriate direction to the passions or morals of citizens. In particular, by acting upon the main human passion, upon that which is the source of all the others, on self-esteem, legislation can turn private ambitions to the advantage of the community. Finally, a legislator should exercise influence upon the inner world of the individual. But here public authority reaches its limit: domestic life must remain outside its domain; religion alone may fall under its sacred jurisdiction. Therefore, it is essential to have laws relating to religion.[31]

Obviously, such arrangements far exceed the limits of society's preservation and security. [The excess] is a result of the shakiness of Filangieri's philosophical convictions. Having assumed that legislation has a certain, very limited objective, he imperceptibly broadens that objective to the point that legislative activity ultimately encompasses citizens' entire lives, both public and private.

But Filangieri tries to limit the legislature's purview by elucidating the rules of the legislative art. Every art, he says, has its own rules, and the more perfect these rules, the more perfect the art. The science of legislation cannot be exempted from this general law. Only despotism affirms that the sole rule of legislation is the will of the legislator. However complex the political mechanism, however changeable its constituent parts, or however active the forces within it, there exist rules which explain the nature of these parts and forces, and indicate means to govern them.[32]

In order to determine these rules, Filangieri distinguishes between the absolute and relative good of laws. The former consists of their agreement with the eternal and fixed principles of morality. The natural law is the prescription of right reason or of that moral sensibility which is inculcated in the heart of the individual as a measure of justice and honesty, of that sensibility which speaks in the same language to all people and at all times prescribes identical codes of conduct. The savage as well as the educated man understands that the fruits of another's labor may not belong to him, and that only self-defense gives one the right to take another's life. Every legislative code must follow these rules. It must also take into account another principle, one just as exalted, Divine Revelation. God has the ultimate right to our obedience, and therefore human legislation must not contradict divine law. The latter, moreover, represents the most perfect ideal of morality. Therefore, Christian peoples far outstrip pagans in respect for the individual. Ancient legislators did not recognize the inalienable and inherent rights of human liberty. It must be admitted, however, Filangieri adds, that even Christian legislation does not everywhere apply these principles. America, to humanity's shame, is full of slaves.[33]

The relative good of laws consists in their relation to the condition of the people, for whose sake they are promulgated. One epoch does not resemble another, nor does one people resemble another. Legislation must take account of these differences. The very best laws may be harmful if applied under inappropriate circumstances. In general, the receptivity of a people to law is the first precondition of its conscientious observance. It is therefore very important that new laws be introduced only when the need for them is felt and when people's minds are properly prepared for them. A legislator must first convince a people of the necessity of changing the law. To win greater trust, it is useful to summon the best people from society to compose the laws. That was done by Catherine II in writing the *Ulozhenie*.[34]

Largely following Montesquieu, Filangieri analyzes one after another of the various elements which contribute to the welfare of a people and with which a legal code must deal. The first of these is the form of government. Laws that are suitable to one form may not suit another. Concerning the pure forms of government—democracy, aristocracy, and monarchy—Filangieri fully subscribes to Montesquieu's principles. Thus, like Montesquieu, he calls monarchy the rule of a single person who governs by means of fundamental laws. And therefore he recognizes the necessity of intermediate bodies, through which the monarch's will becomes operative: the nobility is needed to preserve the balance between king and people, and a magistracy is needed to safeguard the laws. Filangieri notes, however, that these rules are little observed by modern legislatures. He says that jurists, in defining rights, seek more historical entitlements than rational foundations. Meanwhile, neither history nor custom, neither historical concessions nor charters can give to kings, high officials, and nobles the right to act against popular liberty, the security of citizens, and the public good, which should always be the supreme law of the state.[35]

While adhering to Montesquieu's views on the pure forms of government, Filangieri completely departs from his view concerning mixed forms. Montesquieu was a zealous adherent of the English constitution; Filangieri, in contrast, subjects it to sharp criticism, noting that it provides a pretext for the introduction of tyranny even while preserving the external forms of liberty. The events that accompanied the secession of the United States led him to this conclusion. He sees in the English constitution three main flaws: 1.) The independence of the executive from the legislative branch, which ought to possess sovereign power in the state. In England, the monarch has control over all social forces, and therefore he is more powerful than the sovereign authority itself; if he abuses his rights, the Parliament cannot replace him, for his person remains in any case sacred and inviolable. Thus, against the usurpations of the executive power there is only one remedy: rebellion. 2.) The secret influence of the king upon Parliament: having control over all offices and state expenditures, the king may always bribe a majority of representatives and thus, [by manipulating] the representative body, he may do anything he wishes. The example of Henry VIII shows how dangerous is the sort of tyranny that, hiding under the guise of personal liberty, relieves its main perpetrator of responsibility. 3.) Finally, as an inevitable consequence of mixed government, the endless vacillation of authority among various agencies, and thence instability of the laws. In England the spirit of institutions utterly depends upon the king's character. Under a weak monarch, the houses of Parliament constantly usurp authority [from the crown]; under an energetic prince, conversely, royal authority achieves dominance.

Filangieri proposes various remedies against these evils. The first, which was adopted by the English constitution itself, consists of the complete independence of the judiciary. The second lies in restricting as much as possible the king's rights over the distribution of offices. In particular, the making of peers must be the prerogative of the chambers themselves, to which should also be granted the right to dismiss unworthy members. Finally, to avoid institutional instability, it is necessary to make a rule that any fundamental law may be changed only by unanimous consent of the chambers.[36] It is hardly worth saying that both these last measures are inadequate; these proposals reveal only Filangieri's complete lack of political sense. History shows that the English constitution itself contains the remedy against the aforementioned shortcomings. Not a change of the existing structure, but Parliamentary rule established the appropriate relations between political actors and eliminated the possibility of abuses by the royal authority.

What ideal does Filangieri hold up in place of the balance of power he has condemned? Living under an absolute monarchy, he does not speak out explicitly concerning the advantages of one or another form of government; but his sympathy obviously rests with America. Speaking of democracy, he exclaims: "Here is how heroes are born; here is how the famous and virtuous Penn, philosopher of morals, a man worthy to live in those times when people were poorer but more virtuous than they are today; a legislator whose glory would have outshone Lycurgus and Solon, if he had lived twenty centuries ago, this is how Penn extolled Pennsylvania, the home of heroes, the refuge of liberty, and the wonder of the entire world. He saw that the legislator's great task was to link private interests with public ones; he saw that the only means of achieving this objective in free states is for the people themselves to distribute offices; he accomplished this, attained the desired result, and laid the foundation of a republic which now draws the jealous attentions of the entire earth. And the annals of philosophy make immortal the memory of this man who first gave happiness to America at a time when, it seemed, all Europe had united to bring upon it destruction and misfortune."[37]

Deviating from Montesquieu in his evaluation of the English constitution, Filangieri deviated even further from the views of the French publicist on a second subject relevant to legislation—namely, the motive principle of various forms of government. Here he proves to be a follower of the egoistic school, to be analyzed below. He not only cites Helvetius's objections against Montesquieu but assimilates Helvetius's doctrine on the mainspring of political action. In all forms of government, the mainspring of action is love of power, which is always and everywhere the individual's overwhelming ambition. By nature, the individual seeks the greatest possible happiness and so strives to acquire power through which others may be compelled to satisfy his or her desires. This principle operates everywhere in a similar fashion, though its consequences are different in different forms of government. In a republic it makes a citizen virtuous, in a despotism it turns him or her into a monster. The legislator's whole task is to channel this passion, which is present in all people, toward the common good, and to do so in such a way that an individual cannot acquire power except by serving society. This objective is most easily accomplished by a free government.[38]

We shall see below that this love of power, which we have also encountered in Hobbes, is a logical result of Helvetius's philosophical teaching. But in the work of Filangieri, it is somehow torn from its roots and is without consequential link to the rest of his views. This is a symptom of the eclecticism into which the gifted Neapolitan often fell.

The third subject with which legislation must deal is the spirit and character of a people. Filangieri has two things in mind here: on the one hand, the spirit of an age that affects the greater part of peoples in a given epoch; and, on the other hand, the peculiarities of a given people. The former changes with the history of humanity, as circumstances change. So in antiquity, the increase of wealth was the main cause of the decline of peoples, and for that reason legislators tried to limit its accumulation. As far as the peculiarities of national character are concerned, the legislator should, on the one hand, take advantage of them for his own purposes, and, on the other hand, correct them when they are harmful. In this regard, Filangieri gives the legislator very wide discretion. "Do not cite against me," he says, "the common objection that this is impossible. For the wise legislator nothing is impossible." Here he refers to Peter the Great and Gustavus III.[39]

Filangieri criticizes Montesquieu's theory of climates—the fourth subject with which legislation must deal. He claims that Montesquieu's ideas are more clever than true and points out that despotism is also to be found in the north as well as in the south. His own theory consists of four points: 1.) Climate influences the physical and moral nature of the individual, but it does so in combination with other things, and its influence is not absolute. One may make the general rule that in primitive conditions physical influences predominate, while in educated society moral factors are more important. 2.) Climate's influence is noticeable only in very hot or very cold places; in the temperate zone its influence is almost negligible. 3.) Climate is not only determined by a country's position relative to the sun but by other circumstances as well, such as elevation above sea level. 4.) Whatever climate's influence on the individual may be, a legislator should not ignore it. He should take advantage of its beneficent effect, cancel its deleterious effects, and respect trivial peculiarities. In the last respect, Filangieri notes that it is irrational to build up branches of industry not favored by the climate.[40] These observations are all quite accurate.

After discussing climate, Filangieri turns to soil fertility. He does not enter into any political analysis here but confines himself to measures that a legislator should take in one or another circumstance to stimulate industry. If a land is very fertile, the legislator should not be afraid to take manpower away from agriculture and to protect manufacturing. Conversely, if the land requires many hands, excessive attempts to stimulate factory production may be harmful. Finally, if the soil is completely infertile, the only means of enriching the country is industry and trade.

Filangieri looks at the geographical location of a nation from a similar perspective. He cites the maritime position of Holland, which predisposes it to commercial activity, and condemns Peter the Great, who wanted to develop manufacturing and commerce in a country suitable for agriculture. The legislator's general rule should be to oppose nature as little as possible. Filangieri also objects to Montesquieu's notion that large states require despotic rule. He does not make any actual arguments but only says that such a view would be too dismal for humanity. He holds up Catherine II to prove the inadequacy of Montesquieu's view.

Concerning the relations of the laws to religion, Filangieri tries to distinguish between true faith and false ones. In the one case, the legislator must correct the shortcomings of religious laws by secular ones; in the other case, he must confine himself to protecting [religion]. By the term "protection" he means, however, the elimination of abuses. Thus, for example, Filangieri regards as useful laws that limit the quantity of clergy to the number required to meet the actual needs of a particular religion, and also laws that prevent the excessive enrichment of a portion of the clergy at the expense of another.

The last subject with which a legislator must deal is the degree of maturity of a people. In the period of infancy, legislation itself is in an infantile state. Then comes youth, when the people engage in feverish activity and undertake ambitious enterprises. This period is full of uninterrupted changes. The legislator must adapt to the new imperatives without permitting basic reforms for which society is not yet ripe. Wise administration must make up for the inadequacy of laws. The period of rational reforms begins when a people attains full maturity, and when it has begun calmly to move in a fixed channel. This is the time to repeal laws passed during infancy and to replace them with a new code based on reason. This period has commenced for the majority of the European peoples; unfortunately, Filangieri says, governments have not taken advantage of this, and the laws are still in a state of infancy. [Contemporary laws] present a motley mosaic, without any inherent connection. Over time their number has multiplied, and so has their disorder. Filangieri exhorts peoples not to despair over this phenomenon. At present, he says, philosophy has thrown new light on all subjects affecting popular welfare, and public opinion itself demands reforms. If governments manage to take advantage of the favorable combination of circumstances, the lost time will be returned a hundredfold, and peoples will acquire new strength and new youth.[41] These lines were written almost on the eve of the French Revolution.

These are the basic principles to which Filangieri adheres in his work. The remainder of the book consists of an application of these ideas to various fields of legislation, an application interesting in the eighteenth century but having little theoretical significance. From the preceding it is clear that if, in certain particulars, the Neapolitan writer corrects several of Montesquieu's mistakes, in his general views he is nevertheless far inferior to the latter. He possesses more talent and love of humanity than depth and subtlety of thought. Essentially elaborating upon Montesquieu's ideas, he mixes them with quite different points of view and falls into eclecticism, an eclecticism that makes apparent the faultiness of his conceptions. His interpretation of legislation reveals two opposing tendencies: on the one hand, he demands that a legislator take account of existing conditions; on the other hand, he attributes to the legislator the power to alter existing conditions at will, saying that for him nothing is impossible. However, the tensions [in Filangieri's thought] are a logical consequence of the perspective generally adopted by eighteenth-century thinkers. On the one hand, they began with particular principles and tried to analyze the interactions of these principles; on the other hand, because their initial assumptions were theoretical rather than empirical, they ultimately subordinated reality to the imperatives of abstract reason. This tendency manifested itself in all the reform programs of the eighteenth century, and ultimately, and most graphically, in the history of the French revolution.

Hegel

The development of German Idealism culminates with Hegel.[1] [Friedrich Wilhelm] Schelling had attempted to link opposites by identifying their source or productive cause. After Schelling, ethical and individualistic Idealism again adopted a one-sided perspective: [Johann Gottlieb] Fichte tried to derive dialectically opposed categories of being from a single foundation, from pure reason—that is, from formal cause; on the other hand, [Johann Friedrich] Herbart asserted that at the basis of all existence is particular being, or material cause. Finally, Hegel synthesized dialectical opposites by understanding their unity in terms of an ultimate cause. Indeed, this is Idealism's present perspective. Arising from an original unity, dialectical opposites are then recombined in a higher, or ultimate unity. In purely abstract terms, the ultimate unity or synthesis is *Idea,* an assertion of the inner purpose of existence, the mainspring of development; in more mundane terms, the synthesis of opposites, the liaison between reason and matter, can be apprehended as *Spirit* [*dukh*], the source of life, the ultimate good [*verkhovnoe blago*] or harmony of existence. Hegel's doctrine comprehends the Absolute as Spirit which, developing in accordance with an inner law, generates dialectical opposites and then combines these elements within itself, subordinating them to a higher unity. Therefore, the true essence of the Spirit is revealed only at the end of the evolutionary process. The first self-definitions [of the Spirit] are only philosophically crude and one-sided moments that the Spirit generates as steps in an ongoing process. These moments are points of departure for further development, and the more primitive they are, the more meager their philosophical content. However, these self-definitions are not obliterated in the final synthesis; they are preserved within it, not as autonomous principles but as logical moments of a single being—that is, as moments that possess relative autonomy but are subordinated to the whole.

Thus dialectically opposed elements of the universe, the universal and the particular, reason and matter, are combined in a single living entity, which is the ultimate unity of the Idea or the Spirit. Obviously, with Hegel's doctrine philosophical thought reaches its [historical] culmination. Inadequate and one-sided systems of thought are treated here as parts of a satisfying whole. Nevertheless, even Hegel's system has its flaws. When a doctrine advertises itself not as the pinnacle of preceding developments but as an exclusive system making all others outmoded and as a system wherein all things are deduced from a single original hypothesis, then this doctrine itself succumbs to one-sidedness. The ultimate unity or synthesis is the highest, but not the sole, element of being. A final synthesis presupposes both an initial ground of being and the independent existence of dialectical opposites which then join together in the ultimate synthesis and which lead to a greater harmony but do not themselves issue from this ultimate synthesis. Yet if the ultimate synthesis is seen not only as the end but as the beginning of all existence, then the initial ground of being loses its autonomous significance and the dialectical opposites are transformed into simple moments of the higher unity. And this is precisely Hegel's view. In his system there is nothing besides the Spirit. Reason and nature constitute only dialectical manifestations of the Spirit, manifestations generated by the Spirit, which then, by its own inner logic of development, reincorporates them into itself. In this fashion Hegel's entire doctrine takes on a one-sided character. While the doctrine is a great achievement, a pinnacle in the development of philosophical thought, it is nevertheless inadequate as an exclusive system. Therefore, it is quite mistaken to regard Hegel as representative of all German philosophy and to judge the rest of it by judging him. That would be to confuse the roof of a building with the rest of the edifice.

Both the strengths and weaknesses of Hegel's teaching are expressed in its characteristic peculiarity, one might say in the very soul of his system—namely, in the dialectic. The dialectic is the development of a system of categories of pure thought. The law of the dialectic consists in the deduction of dialectical opposites from an original unity and in the recombination of these opposites in a higher unity or synthesis. This law is the fundamental law of reason, which involves the negation and synthesis of concepts on the basis of certain characteristics inherent in and necessary to the concepts. Every category or concept, by its very nature, integrates two opposing principles: the universal and particular, identity and diversity. Being opposites, these principles negate each other and also negate the connection between themselves. In this sense they may be considered as autonomous. But because no identity can exist without diversity and no diversity without identity, then these principles, taken separately, are self-contradictory. In negating their opposite, they also negate themselves. By excluding from themselves any relationship to their opposite, they destroy a necessary condition of their own existence and thus are transformed into nothing. However, this new negation is essentially only a negation of their autonomy—that is, a negation of the negation. The result [of this double negation] is something positive—namely, the imperative to connect the opposed principles. This imperative leads to a new concept, to a synthesis that encompasses opposites not by direct fusion but in their full development, as moments of the whole that have gone through the process of negation and have transcended this negation.

The dialectic is the mainspring of the entire development of human thought. The history of philosophy serves as its most brilliant factual confirmation. The law of the dialectic alone explains all human history. Therefore, in every philosophical system we find a certain trace of it. Obviously, it could be elaborated fully only by Idealism. The ancients regarded Plato as the inventor of the dialectic; in the modern period Hegel transformed it into an entire science. This is Hegel's immortal achievement, one that gives him a leading place in the history of human thought. One may even assert that without the dialectic there is no philosophy. Whoever rejects the dialectic cannot understand the first principles of philosophical inquiry. Nothing so clearly testifies to the complete collapse of philosophy as the disregard into which the dialectic has recently fallen.

Still, the dialectical edifice erected by Hegel certainly cannot be regarded as the last word in scholarship. In many respects this edifice requires corrective work. The exclusivity of Hegelian Idealism also left its mark on the dialectic. Exclusivity led to an erroneous understanding of the law of development itself and consequently to the Hegelian system's incorrect construction. From previous remarks it should be clear that the law of dialectical development actually entails the assertion of four categories in three stages. The first stage consists of the original unity, the second of two opposites, the third of a higher unity or synthesis. Hegel makes this point at many places in his work. Thus in describing the development of a concept through the successive stages of the universal, the particular, and the synthesis, he attributes to the particular two opposing categories: the purely particular and the abstractly universal. The abstractly universal, as the opposite of the particular, itself comprises a particular concept, while the truly general encompasses both the abstractly universal and the particular.[2] On these principles Hegel builds the entire skeleton of his logic. The first stage is composed of undifferentiated being, the second is composed of the contradiction between abstract essence and appearance, the third stage encompasses the concept as synthesis of the two opposites. In addition, there is a construct of another type, one issuing from the predominant importance attaching to the ultimate synthesis [in his system]. According to Hegel's theory, as we have seen above, the ultimate synthesis [Spirit] posits dialectically opposed self-definitions and then subsumes these self-definitions into itself in a higher synthesis. Consequently, the original ground [of development] disappears and only three self-definitions remain: the two dialectical opposites and the ultimate unity or synthesis; each of these self-definitions now constitutes a stage in the three-stage development. The first stage is composed of one of the opposites, the second of its antithesis, and the third of their synthesis. And because one may begin with either of the two dialectical opposites—for each is defined with reference to the other—it follows that Hegel defines the first stage now as abstractly universal, now as the particular, now as the subjective principle, now as objective. The outcome [of Hegel's logic] may be correct, for the dialectical development of opposites nevertheless surely leads to a synthesis; but in the logical movement of [Hegel's] thought, there are lacunae, artificial transitions and finally a confusion of the various stages—namely, of the original unity with one of the dialectical opposites, sometimes with the particular, sometimes with the abstractly universal principle. Given such errors, there is naturally nothing easier than to criticize the details of Hegel's logic. But demonstration of particular shortcomings in his system begs the question of the value of the system as a whole.

Hegel's not entirely correct understanding of the law of the dialectic affects the way that various parts of his system fit together. Hegel divides philosophy into logic, philosophy of nature, and philosophy of the Spirit. It is obvious that the logic, or, what amounts to the same thing, the dialectic, represents the abstractly universal principle, the development of the laws of pure thought; nature, on the contrary, expresses the form of particular being; finally, the Spirit constitutes the synthesis of these two principles. But in Hegel's thinking, as a result of the confusion of original unity with the abstractly universal moment, pure thought appears to be the original basis [of the entire system], which later passes into nature and finally returns to itself in the Spirit. Therefore, Hegel's logic begins not with immediate or determinate—that is, concrete being—but with the greatest possible abstraction—namely, with pure or simple being, which, as a pure abstraction, is nothing other than pure negation. Of course, the final result is the same: for Hegel the truth is found not in the primary, most philosophically primitive categories of thought which for him are only points of departure; in Hegel's system, truth is the Spirit. But according to the laws of logic, primitive or simple being cannot be equated with the Spirit, and vice-versa. It follows that the basis of the system must contain both dialectical opposites, and should not be equated with only one of them. Obviously, here is a pretext for misinterpretation of Hegel's entire system.

Erroneous formulation of the point of departure led Hegel to an erroneous construct at the end. Dialectical law entails a coincidence of end with beginning: the final synthesis is a combination of opposites, just as the original unity is. Hegel argues this point explicitly. Yet because his point of departure is not concrete but abstract unity, the latter must also constitute the culmination of development. Therefore, the highest manifestation of the Spirit he considers to be not history but philosophy, which represents a return to logic. Thus abstract thought is the alpha and omega of the entire dialectical process, although Spirit, being the final synthesis of everything existing, is by Hegel's reckoning not an abstraction at all but a living combination of opposites.

Finally, Hegel's logic is also the source of an erroneous depiction of the way that the spiritual world fits together. Hegel repeats the three stages of development: subjective Spirit, objective Spirit, Absolute Spirit. The first is the Spirit taken in and of itself, as the totality of its internal moments. Initially, it appears in undifferentiated form, as a natural product, as *soul.* Then, in the soul *consciousness* develops: the subject juxtaposes itself to the external world. Finally, fully developed consciousness posits itself as self-determining *reason;* this is the Spirit in the genuine sense of the term. Reason appears as *theoretical Spirit* in rational consciousness, as *practical Spirit,* governing the complex of impulses or appetites, as *free Spirit* in rational, self-determining will. Thus, free will is the highest category of subjective Spirit. Having reached this stage, Spirit passes into external activity and builds from itself the objective world, where the basic principle is *liberty.* The stages of the development of liberty or objective Spirit are *justice* or *right* [*pravo*], *morality* [*moral'*] and *ethics* [*nravstvennost'*]. By the term *ethics* Hegel means the social principle which represents a combination of right and morality and which manifests itself in the development of human associations. The highest of these associations is the *state.* But the state, as an expression of a certain nationality, itself constitutes only a particular manifestation of the world *Spirit.* Therefore, it undergoes a trial or contest with other, similar associations. This contest is *universal history,* the highest manifestation of objective Spirit, a manifestation which also constitutes a transition to the third and final stage, to consciousness of Absolute Spirit. The last develops in three stages: in *art,* in *religion,* and in *philosophy.* Philosophy culminates the entire development of thought and being; here the end coincides with the beginning.[3]

Such is the structure of Hegel's philosophy of Spirit. One cannot deny that it possesses a breadth of vision and a certain profundity of understanding. Nevertheless, it suffers from inconsistency. If we compare the internal moments of the Spirit with their subsequent elaboration, we see the lack of consistency. Self-determining Spirit develops, as noted above, in three stages: as theoretical Spirit in rational consciousness, as practical Spirit governing appetites or impulses, and as free Spirit in the will. This is the true relationship of these three elements. If we add to it sense [*chuvstvo*], which is relegated by Hegel to the undifferentiated form of the Spirit, to the soul, we will have a complete outline of mind's internal moments. Sense represents the primitive, immediate, determinate unity of mind; reason and the appetites constitute its two opposed aspects, of which one relates to the inner world and the other to the external world; finally, free will is the synthesis. The forms of mental life correspond to activities of these categories. The world of sense is the inner world of the soul; theoretical ideas make up the realm of reason; the subjugation of nature, or the system of economic relations, corresponds to appetites or impulses; finally, the ethical world forms the realm of the will. The last, obviously, ought to occupy the highest place in the mind's development, for it represents a living or concrete synthesis of opposites, of reason and nature, of universal and particular, of infinite and finite. Yet Hegel says nothing about the subjugation of nature; [for him] economic relationships constitute, as we shall see, only a secondary moment of juridical society. The practical side of Spirit is realized in the ethical world, while the theoretical side is elevated above the latter, as the consciousness of Absolute Spirit. The incongruity of this structure with the outline of mind's inner moments presented above is obvious. The reasons for this incongruity should also be obvious.

Let us now examine the inner structure of the objective Spirit, which comprises the real subject of our investigation. Despite the place incorrectly assigned to it in the general system of Hegel, this structure, following the dialectical law, generally speaking develops the true essence of ethical categories and correctly construes their mutual relations. Yet here, too, for reasons explained earlier, there are substantial lacunae and shortcomings.

Freedom of will is the fundamental category of objective Spirit. Will is practical reason—that is, reason acting upon the external world. Therefore, will encompasses two opposites: the universal and the particular. On one hand, as thought or as an abstract universal principle, will possesses the capacity for absolute abstraction or pure indeterminacy; will is not bound to a particular objective or to the satisfaction of particular appetites; will may renounce everything concrete. It need not be mired in finitude. On the other hand, will has a content, it desires something. From indeterminacy it passes into determinacy. This determinacy can take shape either from pure reason or from the complex of appetites. In either case will always recognizes a specific content as its own creation, as something posited by itself, for will is not bound to a particular objective and it may pass from determinacy to indeterminacy. As a principle, will is the synthesis of particular and universal. It encompasses opposed categories as ideal moments that are both dependent on it and posited by it: will itself is the absolute possibility of transition from the one category to the other. Even in taking determinant form, will nevertheless remains itself—that is, it preserves within itself an element of pure indeterminacy; therefore, will recognizes determinacy as a moment which it can always renounce, just as, conversely, it can pass from indeterminacy to the determinacy posited by itself. In this consists its freedom, the freedom which constitutes the essence of will, just as mass constitutes the essence of matter. Therefore, all beings endowed with will recognize themselves as free; but Idealism alone is able to reveal the true import of this principle.[4]

These passages of Hegel contain the most remarkable and profound reflections ever uttered about the freedom of the will. The instinctive sense of anyone approaching the subject of will straightforwardly and naively has always been and will always be to regard freedom as a fact upon which the entire ethical world is constructed. But explanation of this "fact" is a riddle for the enterprising mind, because explanation requires a sophisticated understanding of metaphysical principles. Therefore, the baser forms of epistemology, empiricism, and formal logic inevitably tend to reject freedom of the will. One-sided metaphysical systems are also incapable of grasping freedom of the will. Only the most sophisticated Idealism can penetrate the true essence of will, for Idealism alone comprehends the individual human being as a synthesis of opposites, of infinite and finite, possessing the absolute possibility of passing from one category to the other.

But according to Hegel's teaching, just as every other term [in the dialectic] reveals its true essence only at the end [of the dialectical process], so, too, will becomes fully free only when it reaches its highest stage of development. Will acquires its content from outside, from appetites and inclinations; will itself, remaining an abstract universal principle, appears here as the capacity of *choosing* between various appetites. This form of the will is *arbitrary choice* [*proizvol*]. Content does not correspond here to form, because content is for will something external and accidental; consequently, arbitrary choice involves an inner contradiction. This contradiction appears in the guise of struggle between various appetites, which engage each other in conflict. Choosing between them, arbitrary choice posits for itself a general goal—happiness; because the achievement of happiness nevertheless depends upon achieving some balance between random appetites, then the goal itself must be particular and accidental. And strictly speaking, there is nothing universal in the goal of happiness, for appetites are infinitely various and exclusive of one another. Therefore, happiness, defined as the satisfaction of the appetites, is something unattainable; the pursuit of happiness is a process infinite in duration. The rationale for the pursuit is hunger for precisely the sort of general principle that can subordinate to itself every particular. In order to accomplish this task, however, we must distinguish between will's essential appetites and its inessential ones. The essential appetites are those which have not only a content received from the outside, but which answer to the essence of will itself, to its own self-definitions. Such is the nature of a true universal, within which the abstractly universal and the particular are only moments. Self-determining will is free will in the true sense. Its purpose is to actualize its own freedom in the external world. This is free will which desires to be free will. The actualization of this freedom constitutes right [pravo] in its broad sense.[5]

In Hegel, right develops in three stages: 1.) abstract or formal right, expressing the self-actualization of will in the external world; 2.) morality or inner self-actualization of will; 3.) ethics, which represents a synthesis of right and morality. The universal imperatives of morality, once realized in the external world, become a system of juridical institutions defining the rights and responsibilities of people in social groups.[6]

Abstract right or right in the narrow sense is a manifestation of individual liberty. The sphere of right encompasses individuals and their mutual relations. An individual, as a free being, has the capacity to bear rights [*pravosposobnost'*]; this capacity makes him or her a [legally recognized] *person.* The law of right declares: "Be a person and respect others as persons." This law is purely formal; it is limited by one prohibition, the prohibition against infringing on the freedom of other persons. At this stage content is supplied by the natural inclinations of the individual, by his or her appetites. Therefore, content is accidental in character; the law of right determines nothing. It can only permit.

The essential element in permission is that the external world be subordinated to freedom, for the external world has no autonomous standing in relation to freedom. In the name of right, a free person lays hands on nature, and this right must be respected by others. [The right of appropriation] is the basis of *property,* the first manifestation of personal freedom. A thing is mine because I want to possess it; this is a right of my liberty. The content of this right is accidental; I may want to possess more or less; from the juridical perspective the amount of property possessed is all the same. Law prohibits one from touching things belonging to others. Things which belong to no one are appropriated by those who take possession of them. Legal appropriation requires, however, that will really be expressed in things; this expression is accomplished through physical possession, by taking care of a thing, or finally by simple designation [of a thing as property]. On the contrary, when will ceases to be expressed in a thing, the thing may be acquired by another person. As a result, the right of property may have an expiration date. An appropriated thing is at the complete disposal of its owner. The owner may arbitrarily use or even destroy the thing to satisfy his or her own needs. The owner is also free to offer the thing to another. Finally, he or she is even free to transfer the right of ownership to another, for things, by their nature, can pass from one person to another. External nature is the medium through which individual persons enter into legal relationships with one another. These relationships are expressed in agreements or *contracts.*[7]

A contract is a second manifestation of personal liberty. Here, too, content is still accidental; it depends on arbitrary choices. The essential moment is mutual consent [*ugovor*]—that is, an expression of wills; execution [of the contract] is only a consequence of consent, for through the consent an object ceases to be the property of one and becomes the property of the other. As a result, failure to fulfill the contract's conditions becomes an infringement on someone else's property. This kind of will is not yet *universal* (allgemein); rather, it is only the *collective* (gemeinsam) will of the parties. The signatories [to a contract] are not acting in unison for a common purpose; each remains an autonomous person, with his or her particular goals and interests. Thus, a universal principle, right, depends here on a particular element, on the accidental will of the parties, and because particular wills may diverge, the contract may be violated. Thence issues a third manifestation of individual liberty, *crime* or *injustice* [*nepravda*].[8]

Crime is also a manifestation of liberty, a manifestation which is also simultaneously a negation of liberty, for crime violates the freedom of another. Consequently, freedom contradicts itself and therefore, in turn, must be negated. A positive manifestation of right consists in the negation of this negation—that is, in the coercion exercised by the law-abiding [*pravomernom*], which overcomes the coercion employed by the law breaker. The consequence here is that legal agreements have a coercive character. The negation of the damages done to another involves compensation for the losses. But the source of crime lies in the violator's will, which negates right; therefore, the restoration of right must consist of the negation of that will, which, as a violator of right, is now subjected to coercion. The negation of the negation is *retribution* [*vozmezdie*]; it prescribes an equivalent punishment, not in the literal sense of an eye for an eye, but based on an evaluation of [the seriousness of] the criminal act. This principle amounts to the requirement that punishment be commensurate with the crime, an imperative of penal justice that is also the true basis of criminal law. Any other consideration here is merely secondary. But in the sphere of personal right, where there is not yet a judge standing over the individual parties, retribution is effected by the most injured party. Therefore, retribution is not an abstract expression of the law, but has a personal and accidental character; it takes the form of revenge. As a consequence, revenge in its turn, prompts retribution, and so on ad infinitum. This eternal cycle demonstrates the inadequacy of formal or abstract right: it leads to a demand that cannot be satisfied. Justice is not a matter of revenge only but also of punishment; punishment must take into account not the accidental relationship of external actions but the criminal's own will, within which the sway of universal legal norms must be restored. Through punishment external right passes into another sphere, the sphere of inner self-determination or morality.

In morality, will recognizes itself as something inherently self-determining, independent of external stimuli, as something operating exclusively on the basis of principles inherent in itself. But morality does not prescribe the content of these principles; even in this sphere the law remains formal. Therefore, law does not determine will in its concrete manifestations but relates to it in the manner of an abstract requirement or *obligation* [*dolzhnoe*]. This is will as an abstractly universal moment.[9]

The first definition of will in this sphere consists in the relation between internal self-determination and the act that results from it. Will recognizes as its own only that act to which it bears some conscious relation—that is, an act to which it has given conscious and free consent. [Consent] establishes moral responsibility or *culpability* [*pravo viny*]. Then, the content itself of the action, the purpose accompanying its execution—that is, its *intention*—must correspond to the inner imperatives of the actor. The actor has the right to find personal satisfaction in an act. In this satisfaction is to be found the *gain* [*blago*] [accruing to the individual]. But personal gain may have a random or accidental character. Will is more than a matter of personal gain; indeed, as a universal rational principle, will actualizes itself not through a personal but through a universal purpose, and by the latter it attains its satisfaction. The universal purpose is the idea of the *good* [*dobro*], which comprises the inner law of self-determining will. But because this idea opposes itself to personal gain, it appears in the form of an imperative; the subject regards it as a *duty.* Moreover, this imperative is purely abstract and formal. An individual ought to conform to the universal law; one ought to do one's duty for the sake of duty; but what exactly requires the individual to perform this duty is not determined by the universal law of morality. Filling this category with actual content is a matter left to the personal discretion of the individual, who decides what for him or her constitutes a duty and what does not. This element of subjective decision is *conscience,* the inner, inviolable sanctuary of personal liberty, the focus of the individual's ethical world. An individual has the right to define his or her attitude to the good solely on the basis of conscience. However, even conscience does not correspond completely to the idea of good. As the center of the individual's moral life, conscience encompasses two dialectically opposed definitions of will, one universal and the other particular—the written law and arbitrariness—and the possibility of passing from one to the other. Conscience may deviate from good and pass to the opposite principle—that is, to *evil.* The phenomenon of evil demonstrates the insufficiency of the various manifestations of morality, the insufficiency consisting precisely of the fact that the idea of good is here an abstractly universal, formal, and therefore a purely subjective principle, lacking as a consequence vital content. Overcoming this shortcoming requires passing from the subjective principle to the objective. Inner self-determination must be conjoined with the external world; the universal must inform the particular. The synthesis of right and morality is ethics.[10]

In ethics, individuals are bound by a universal ethical code. This code appears not as a subjective, formal idea, but as an objective system of laws and institutions in which the idea of good is realized. An individual obeys the laws; that is his or her duty. In this sense, the individual's duties are already determined. On the other hand, written laws express will in rational form, [they express] the content of ethical liberty; the laws embody the principles of right and of the common welfare. Therefore, obeying the written laws is also a right of the individual; in written laws the right of the individual finds its vindication. In the sphere of ethics, rights and duties are inextricably connected; an individual has as many rights as responsibilities and vice-versa. As a consequence, obeying the laws becomes for an individual a kind of second and higher nature, so [these laws] are called *mores* [*nravy*]. The correspondence between a person's character and ethical imperatives constitutes that individual's *virtue.* Because these mores are identical for many individuals [in a community], they shape the spirit of that community or people. Thus a universal ethical code is the living spirit of any ethical or legal community, which is animated by a common purpose. Individuals are members of this community and find their satisfaction in it. By this means, complete harmony of subjective and objective principles is achieved.[11]

The communities uniting individuals are: 1.) the family; 2.) civil society [*grazhdanskoe obshchestvo*]; and 3.) the state. They represent different stages of the development of the ethical principle.

The family is a community based on natural relationships. It is bound together by a natural sentiment, love. This sentiment is the basis of marriage. But it is the force of an ethical-legal principle that transforms the natural union of the sexes into a spiritual union constituting a single ethical person, and hence into a union that is elevated above the accidental play of the [sexual] appetites and is by its nature indissoluble. This spiritual union becomes visible or external in children, who constitute the purpose of the union. After the birth of children, after their education, the family disintegrates. Children become independent of their parents, and each forms his or her own family. Among families a new type of relationship is established. Family passes into civil society.[12]

Civil society is a community of individuals who retain their autonomy. Its basic element is the individual personality with its needs and interests. The broader entity [of civil society] serves here only as a means for satisfying individual objectives. Hence there arises a complex network of private relationships which constitute the essence of this community. First, by virtue of mutual needs, individuals enter into economic relations with one another. There takes shape a common *set of economic needs,* which leads to the systematization of the means of satisfying those needs—that is, to the division of labor. The division of labor, in turn, entails *differentiation of occupation.* This differentiation is the product of the principles underlying each status group. The first or *natural* occupational group, consisting of those who gather the fruits of nature, comprises farmers; the second occupational group, devoted to business or *industrial activity,* includes artisans, factory workers, and merchants; the third or *universal* occupational group devotes itself to pursuit of public purposes. The general principle dominating this entire system is *right,* which safeguards the labor and property of each member. In civil society, right appears in the form of positive law, establishing norms recognized by all. As a consequence, personhood and property receive legal recognition; a contract becomes something inviolable, and crime justifies the imposition of punishment by society. The law's application to individual cases becomes a matter to be adjudicated in a *court,* which comes into existence only in civil society. The security of individuals and of property requires the prevention of contingencies that might impinge upon them, while, on the other hand, the network of economic interests leads to the adoption of common measures designed to satisfy the needs of society as a whole. Thus arises the need for the *police,* who establish external order and supervise public institutions. However, external order is insufficient; an inner connection between right and interests is demanded. In civil society this connection is created by private associations or *corporations.* Each person enters a social Estate, a commune, a guild, and finds in it a way of achieving his or her private goals, of finding assistance in time of need and of locating himself or herself in a defined social position that provides a certain network of connections. Corporations constitute the ethical element of civil society; they are the second pillar of society after the family. But being limited to private goals, these small units have a tendency to hold themselves apart from others and to confine themselves within their own rigid and narrow frameworks. In order to maintain the links between these units, it is necessary to establish a supervisory agency mindful of the common civic purpose to which private goals must be subordinated. The task of supervision is the responsibility of a new community—the state, which, in distinction from civil society, embodies civic unity and pursues common civic purposes alone.[13]

The state is the fullest realization of the ethical idea, the actualization of ethical spirit or of objective reason. The state is not a means for attaining other ends; it itself is an absolute idea. Therefore, it has a sovereign right over the individual, who in it achieves his or her ultimate objective. The highest duty of the individual is to be a member of the state. But the converse is also true: in the state the individual finds the ultimate realization of his or her freedom and rights. The subjective and objective principle coincide. The objective principle itself flows from the subjective—that is, from will, but not from personal and accidental will, will as contract, but from the essential will of the members of the community. The basis of the state is the national spirit that lives within citizens and attains in the state its highest self-consciousness.[14]

The idea of the state manifests itself: 1.) as an organism; 2.) in external relations between various states; 3.) in the universal Spirit reigning over the entire process of the development of states—that is, in universal history.

The state, being the ultimate realization of the idea of liberty, rises above the family and civil society; it does not obliterate them but recognizes their rights and allows them their proper autonomy, subordinating them only to itself as sovereign authority and constituting for them an ultimate purpose. Thus private liberty retains its significance within the state, but to it is added political liberty based on recognition of the community's common purpose. This is particularly true in modern, as opposed to ancient, states. The ancient polities conflated private and public authority; consequently, the private sphere was not fully developed, and private freedom was swallowed up by public liberty. The modern state, on the contrary, represents the return of already fully developed private elements to the public sphere: it is their synthesis. Here private and public elements are in harmony.[15]

But the state does not confine itself to wielding authority over other, subordinate spheres. Being itself an autonomous community, it constitutes a unitary organism [whose various features] are expressed in the different elements of the polity. Of course, any organism can be said to represent the elaboration of a single idea in all its aspects. In the state, these aspects form a system of separate branches, which, in spite of their relative autonomy, neither fall into conflict nor limit each other as independent bodies might, but act together as parts of a single whole. These branches are: the legislature, which sets general norms for conduct; the executive, which applies these norms to individual cases; and, finally, the crown, which represents will's sovereign authority and binds together the other branches. These branches correspond to the three moments of the Idea's development: universal, particular, and their synthesis. Thus, of all political forms, the most complete embodiment of the idea of the state is constitutional monarchy. Other forms of government—pure monarchy, aristocracy, and democracy—are suitable to the more primitive stages of political development where the universal Idea has not yet reached full flower. The earlier stages are still characterized by a superficial division of authority, based upon the number of persons holding power.

What should be the structure of an ideal constitutional monarchy? The role of leader should belong to the prince. He is representative of the polity's sovereign authority, the goal of which consists in subordination of all parts of the body politic to the whole and of all private ambitions to common civic purposes. Sovereign authority properly understood belongs not to the people as a mass but to the political community, which acts as a unitary individual on behalf of all its members and constituent elements. This "unitary individual," in reality, can be represented only by one physical person to whom final decisions should therefore be entrusted. No assembly, whatever its type, can adequately represent the unity of the polity. For the same reason, monarchy should be hereditary; otherwise, the leadership of the state will be made dependent on the private wills of various individuals and on the struggle of factions and parties. The integral representation of the polity in the monarch's person need not, however, make the state a hostage to accidents of birth or to arbitrary rule. Accidents dominate political life only during the more primitive stages of the state's development when the different moments of the Idea have not yet acquired the requisite autonomy; in a mature state, decision-making authority vested in a single individual is only the culmination of many other arrangements. No special personal qualities are required of the constitutional monarch. He is neither compelled to meddle in every matter nor to direct all affairs. He must only say *yes* and dot the *i*. (Er muss nur *ja* sagen und den Punkt auf das *i* setzen.) Here the monarch's position makes it possible for him truly to speak for the entire polity.[16]

Hegel distinguishes between the executive branch and the crown; [for him] the executive includes both police and courts. The executive's task is to apply the law in individual cases. Consequently, it directly confronts citizens and those private communities into which civil society divides itself. These communities directly oversee local and corporate interests, but the state's task is to look after the common interests of society. Discharging this task is the responsibility of a special group of civil servants appointed by the crown and paid by the state. This group's main organizing principle is the division of labor; however, at the top of the apparatus various departments must be tied together by common institutions. The difficulty [for the state] is to work out a harmonious relationship between the highly compartmentalized bureaucracy and the many branches of corporate and local associations. Corporate associations must preserve their autonomy; otherwise, both the organic structure of civil society and the freedom of private life will disappear. The ruled should be safeguarded against the arbitrariness of their rulers. In part, a safeguard can be found in the hierarchical structure of the government itself and in the supervision exercised by high officials over their lower-ranking subordinates. But the insulation of high officials from direct contact with the people makes this guarantee inadequate. It must be augmented by another barrier [to official power], one in which officials' arbitrary will is juxtaposed to the independence of corporate rights.[17]

Three elements participate in the writing of legislation: the crown by granting sovereign consent; the executive by supplying material for the legislature to consider; and the people by discussing proposed legislation through their representatives. Popular representation is based not on the notion that the people somehow better understand society's common needs and interests than does the government; on the contrary, the people usually understand these factors less clearly than do officials. The true justification of popular representation is the necessity of combining subjective liberty with objective liberty. Through representation, the written law and the state enter popular consciousness and find in the people their most steadfast support. But what must be represented in the legislature is not the personal will of isolated individuals but the people as such through their vital organizations—corporative associations and Estates. By this means, each of the substantive interests [within civil society] will have a voice in the representative body. Of the three social groups into which civil society is divided, one—namely, the group exclusively dedicated to public affairs—already has its own separate sphere of activity within the official apparatus; consequently, the representative body should draw on the other two groups—agricultural and industrial. But the role of these two groups in the political structure is not identical: one of them must play the role of intermediary between the other two elements. In general, organic links among the various elements of the polity require intermediary bodies. There must exist intermediaries between the crown and the representative body if these two organs of the government are not to be in constant opposition but are to function harmoniously. From the crown's perspective, the intermediate element consists of officials who bear the responsibility for supervising the administration; from the representative body's perspective, the intermediary ought to be drawn from the group most conscious of society's common interests—

namely, the agriculturalists. But for representatives of this group to discharge their task, they must not only belong to the most advanced, educated portion of this group but must have independent, economically secure positions. Such a status can be attained through the institution of entailed [*maiorat*] estates, which make the elite's property inalienable. The creation of inalienable landed estates, however economically inefficient, is in the interests of the state as a whole. As intermediaries, [members of the landed elite] should make up the upper house of the legislature. The lower house should consist of representatives of the industrial group, as divided into corporations and communes or guilds. In the lower house the state may demand guarantees that laws will be discussed in a businesslike fashion. The main guarantee may be that elected deputies should prove their knowledge of public affairs by occupying certain social positions. The significance of subjective liberty in the state is not limited, however, to citizens' participation in the legislature. Public debate in the two houses spreads an acquaintance with political issues to the entire populace, which exercises influence on the outcome of the debates through free speech and the press. This is the domain of public opinion, which expresses subjective liberty not in an organic fashion [as though through a single voice] but haphazardly, though individual voices. In public opinion, therefore, two dialectically opposed principles are combined: the essential and even eternal element around which national identity has taken shape, and the arbitrary and accidental component that comprises the basis of personal opinions. The statesman's task is to make a distinction between these two elements and to seek out the truth hidden in the chaotic mass of personal judgments.[18]

Such are the components of the state. [Viewed from outside,] the state appears as an integrated organism, as a unitary individual, and as such it enters into relations with other similarly constituted entities. These relations are indicia of the state's sovereignty with respect to other states. The demands of external sovereignty outweigh in importance all private interests. All citizens are obliged to sacrifice their lives and property for the defense of the fatherland. The state is not only a vehicle existing to protect private interests, it is a higher principle for which private interests are only instrumentalities. But because external defense is only one function of the government, a special Estate is required to deal with it—the armed forces. Only at moments of peril when the very existence of the state is in question are all citizens summoned to arms.[19]

As a sovereign power, the state demands that other states recognize it. Diplomatic recognition establishes its rightful independence in the ranks of sovereign states. Subsequent relations between states are regulated by agreements between or among them. Observance of these pacts is the basis of international law. But because states are sovereign entities, they may always violate treaties. In the event that agreement between them becomes impossible, the result will be war. In war, the very existence of a state is exposed to danger and is called into question. As a manifestation of a certain national spirit, the state is limited and therefore finite. It may perish, but its place will be taken by others. The upheavals affecting states account for the course of world history, in which political life itself becomes the instrument of the Universal Spirit.[20]

The history of humanity represents the unfolding of the inner content of the Spirit, the evolution of its self-consciousness and freedom. In history, the Spirit is independent of all external factors; its self-actualizations are entirely internal to itself, and it makes of itself in "external reality" that which it already is in essence. All developments share these characteristics; but the Spirit, unlike nature, develops not organically—that is, by unfolding its inherent traits—but by means of consciousness and freedom, through the struggle of opposites. The instruments of this development are individuals with their passions and interests. Each person pursues his or her private goals, seeks personal satisfaction, but unconsciously fulfills common objectives and realizes that which the Spirit demands. Such is particularly the case with historical personages who are elevated above their contemporaries and play a historical role, precisely because they understand better than do others the demands of their time. The milieu in which the self-actualization of the Spirit occurs is the state, the highest expression of freedom on earth. Only those peoples play an historical role who constitute themselves in a body politic. But a particular state, having been constructed by a certain nationality, can only be a finite manifestation of the Universal Spirit. Historical peoples and states represent various stages of the Spirit's development. A nation or people which at a given period more than others epitomizes the logic of the Spirit's development is the dominant nation of that time; when it has executed its task, it recedes from the historical stage and concedes its place to another.

In history there are four different stages. Each represents a successive stage of freedom's evolution or of the Spirit's being. In the first stage general substance predominates, and individuality is completely submerged. Only one person is free—the head of the state; therefore, he is a despot. Such was the Oriental world. Then, little by little, consciousness of freedom awakens. It does not suddenly differentiate itself from the general substance but coexists with it in harmonious fashion. This is the aesthetic worldview that constitutes the basic trait of Greek life. But youthful harmony quickly disappears, for the Spirit has not yet overcome its own duality. This duality becomes clearer in history's passage to Rome. Here one finds an opposition between the abstract universal principle and the particular, at first in the struggle between aristocracy and democracy, and later in the development of an abstract universal state on the one hand, and in private law and personal interests on the other. In Rome humanity arrived at a profound state of inner disharmony; yet during the Roman era there was a reconciliation [*primirenie*] that provided a new point of departure for subsequent development. Individuality, attaining its most extreme form, identified itself with God's animating purpose. This identification reestablished the inner unity of the Spirit, making possible its reconciliation with itself. Such was Christianity's significance. But at first [the Christian] reconciliation remained purely internal: it formed an exalted spiritual world juxtaposed to the secular one. The subsequent development of history witnessed the penetration of spiritual values into secular life, the mingling of the mundane and sacred spheres. Completion of this process is the task of modern history, a task whose execution is the vocation of the German people and the German state.[21]

Such is the content of Hegel's philosophy of right. From the preceding one can judge its value and its shortcomings. The virtues of his approach far outweigh the shortcomings. Hegel's philosophy of right, like his system in general, is the culmination of the entire previous evolution of thought. Various schools of human thought meet here at a single focal point, and [Hegel treats them in such a way as to demonstrate their] ultimate harmony. Among his predecessors no one so penetratingly and accurately defined the places and mutual relations of various elements of the ethical world. At the basis [of this world] Hegel places the true source [of the other elements], freedom of the will, which he described with such profundity as to leave nothing to be desired. Freedom's dialectical self-actualizations—right and morality—which constitute its external and internal aspects, are juxtaposed to one another and are then brought into synthesis in the polity, where ethical ideas are made to satisfy the requirements of the human personality and where man, as individual and as a sentient moral being, can reach his destined potential. The elaboration of these principles is one of the most fruitful aspects of the philosophy of right, and it will remain Hegel's immortal achievement. The movement of the dialectic culminates in a vision of the state as an agent of Universal Spirit unfolding its content in history. The basic notions that make up the foundation of the edifice Hegel has constructed are undoubtedly sound. The reader will discover that the entire preceding history of political thought only serves to confirm these notions. Experience brilliantly vindicates the conclusions suggested by speculative thought. Criticism can be directed only at details. Careful study reveals that certain notions have been inadequately developed or unsystematically analyzed, but not that they are entirely wrongheaded. Hegel's general interpretation emerges from criticism strengthened and purified.

What are the shortcomings of Hegel's theory? Here again we must point to the faultiness in his dialectical structure. Instead of four categories we find only three. If we study all possible relationships among human wills, we will see that they are grounded initially and directly in community life, that community is what naturally defines the individual. Community life has four essential elements: authority, law, freedom, and purpose. From it develop, on the one hand, right as a particular and, on the other hand, morality as an abstract universal category. This is proven by the history of political thought itself. The school with which the modern philosophy of right commences is the communitarian school, whose basic principles were outlined by Hugo Grotius. Then thought diverged into two contrasting approaches, the moral and the individual, which again were synthesized in Idealism. Hegel's scheme, for reasons already outlined, ignores the fundamental contribution of Grotius. In its place, the first stage of development is one of the dialectical terms—on this occasion not the subjective, internal, abstract universal one, but the objective, external, particular one—namely, right. Hence the exaggerated importance of right in Hegel's thought, an exaggeration that leads to conceptual confusion. Because of this confusion, morality is interpreted as something that develops from the principles of right—an obvious error if right is taken in its strict sense. Hence, finally, the utterly artificial transition from the first stage to the second. In explaining principles of criminal law, [Hegel finds himself] combining right and morality in the state, instead of making a transition from the one concept to the other. Nevertheless, while Hegel is essentially correct in his analysis of the basic categories of right, his definitions of morality are insufficiently developed. The essence of morality as an abstract universal concept flowing from the pure or formal demands of reason is properly understood by Hegel, but his systematic elaboration of this principle is extremely crude. Hegel incorrectly treats virtue under the rubric of ethics instead of morality, and even then he hardly touches on it. The principle of law is scarcely developed at all; the idea of perfection which determines the ethical ideal is completely ignored. Indeed, Hegel's teaching about morality is the weakest aspect of his philosophy of right. It is a subject deserving a fuller treatment.

Hegel's treatment of ethics is incomparably better. The gradual development of social communities is correctly described and is confirmed much more by history than even Hegel himself might have suspected. But here we find the same error in dialectical logic. Instead of four communities, there are only three. The fourth community, the church, is omitted. Treating religion under the rubric of Absolute Spirit as something superior to the state, Hegel obviously could not include the church in his list of social communities [that constitute civil society]. Only in passing does he touch on the problem of religion's relations to the church and state, and, although the view which he develops is quite sensible, it does not fit the general structure of his system. Hegel claims that religion, expressing the consciousness of Absolute Spirit, undoubtedly constitutes the basis of all ethics, and therefore of political life. But it is only a basis, in relation to which the state is a higher stage of development, for here the Spirit constructs from itself the objective world. These two moments [of church and state] are divided by the enormous passage from internal to external, by the penetration of reason into life, a step over which all history has labored and through which humanity has acquired a consciousness of rational activity. Therefore, to the state belongs a historical right higher than than of the church. The church not only is subordinate to the state in the institutional sense, but, because it represents a subjective principle, the church cannot pretend to determine the objective foundations of the state. In opposition to subjective belief and convictions, the state possesses the higher right of objective knowledge. On the other hand, however, the subjective principle, consisting in the property of inner man and being defined by his conscience, must remain inviolable by the state. Therefore, [Hegel concludes,] these two communities should be separated. The state that interferes in the church's sphere and the church that meddles in politics are both tyrannical. The state fulfills its duty when it acts to defend and protect a religious community, meanwhile exercising secular oversight over that community. Caring for the ethical spirit of its citizens and seeing in religion the main support of ethical conduct, the state may demand of its citizens that each belong to some church; but it may not extend its jurisdiction beyond this point: it cannot prescribe a particular belief and must treat different confessions impartially.[22]

From these propositions of Hegel it follows 1.) that the objective Spirit, being the actualization of absolute principles in the material world, should be elevated above the subjective consciousness of the absolute; 2.) among the various communities [existing in society] the church is the one embodying principles of subjective morality—that is, it is the institution that guides the conscience of the individual. In this respect, the church may be contrasted to civil society, which is the result of the evolution of abstract right—that is, of the purely personal or private element of community life. Hegel apparently did understand the church in this way, although in certain passages he confused private ends with public ones. Here as elsewhere, therefore, we find Hegel's dialectic including three instead of four categories. [We ought instead to think] of the family as the primary social group, of a dialectical opposition between legal institutions (that is, civil society) and moral institutions (the church); and finally, of the synthesis of these categories in the state. Moreover, these four institutions correspond to the four basic principles of community life: the family to the inner purpose or Idea; civil society to freedom; the church to [moral] law; and the state to authority or power. They also correspond to the four basic aspects of the human soul: sense [chuvstvo], appetite, reason, and will, where, of course, each of these principles and aspects, which together form a comprehensive ethical universe, implies the others.

We note that, according to this scheme, the state is not the realization of the community's inner purpose; rather, it embodies authority or power; therefore, its unity is external rather than internal. If civil society and the church were synthesized in the state in the same fashion that right and morality are inextricably linked in the family, if the synthesis between church and civil society was such as to encompass the entire life of the individual, then the autonomy of private communities would surely disappear. But if we conceive of the state as representing the external principle of authority raised above civil society and the church, then [we can conceive of] civil society and the church as retaining relative autonomy. It does not follow, however, that the state is the foundation of community life, or that the family is an ideal association superior to it. The state, after all, is a synthesis of dialectical opposites. The apparent contradiction [in Hegel's logic] can be explained if we analyze the difference between the Spirit's development and the development of nature. In nature the evolutionary process moves from universal forces to the unique synthesis that constitutes a living organism. In fact, nature's purpose is to generate the individual living thing. The Spirit, however, moves from particular to universal. Its point of departure is the solitary soul, and its highest self-definition is the Universal Spirit, unfolding its content in history. Therefore, in the evolution of human communities, the logical point of origin is the family, an organic community representing the complete fusion of two individuals; the end of the evolutionary process is the state, which represents the idea of authority or power. Of course, because the state is the culmination of the evolutionary process, a synthesis of civil society and the church, it carries within itself the particular units that made up its point of departure. Therefore, the state can be conceived not only as an external authority but as a personality, as the unique manifestation of a particular national spirit. A people can exert will only in the state. We have seen how the definition of the role and significance of each human association and of the interaction between them depends upon the general philosophical perspective we adopt, on the interpretation of principles and laws that inform the development of the Spirit.

In Hegel's thought we do not find any indication of the way various institutions correspond to the basic principles of community life—authority, moral law, freedom, and inner purpose. In his system, the state as synthesis of opposites is the highest realization of the ethical Idea. Nonetheless, as we noted above, he knows that it is important for institutions subordinated to the state to retain a relative autonomy. Only certain imprecise formulations provide a basis for the accusation that Hegel's state engulfs everything else and allows no place to individual liberty. We have seen that, in recognizing the autonomy of the subjective principle, Hegel posits a substantial difference between the modern state and the ancient one. Guided by a profound and correct insight, he does not give in to the temptation inherent in pure Idealism, the temptation to resolve all problems in some final structure, the temptation that led Plato to sketch his outline of the ideal republic and which has animated modern socialists. In Plato, the systematic subjugation of the individual to the polis is explained by the weak development of personal liberty in the ancient world. But even Plato himself understood that it was impossible to implement his ideal, and so, in his book on *The Laws,* he described another way to order the polis. Aristotle subsequently rejected the very foundations of Plato's view. The extreme version of Idealism defended by modern-day socialists flies not only in the face of a correct understanding of politics but in the face of history itself. They reject all the fruits of modern development. The past and present are renounced for the sake of a purely theoretical vision of the future. Hegel's Idealism sharply distinguishes itself from these utopias. Yet not infrequently Hegel's Idealism, too, becomes exclusive; in his thought, too, historical moments are understood as transient phenomena and not as manifestations of persistent features of human life. Still, these moments do retain a relative autonomy within Hegel's synthesis. Hegel understood the process of development not as a negative but as a positive process, as the unfolding of the inner content of a subject. Therefore, he sought his ideals not in a fantastic representation of the future but in living reality, in an understanding of the rational imperatives of life and of the principles animating the evolution of that life.

In the political sphere, his ideal was not socialism but constitutional monarchy—that is, the form of government that is the fruit of the entire preceding evolution of European life and that was recognized as such by the best minds of the era.

In presenting this political ideal, Hegel, following the general logic of his system, adopts a purely speculative approach. He treats the legislature, the executive, and the crown respectively as universal, particular, and synthetic moments. Here, too, the general shortcoming of his system is revealed: instead of four categories there are only three. Hegel conflates the executive branch with the courts. In fact, to the courts belongs the responsibility of applying the law in individual cases; therefore, the courts should be regarded as the particular moment. The executive's task is to act as guardian of the community's common interests. According to the scheme adopted above, the executive is the universal moment, while the legislature is the abstract universal moment, and the prince or crown is the synthetic moment. If we attempt to correlate the branches of government to the basic principles of community life, we will find that the executive tries to realize the community's ambitions, the courts safeguard liberty and rights, the legislature establishes the law, and the crown represents the principle of authority. This scheme enables us to make a distinction between constitutional monarchy and other forms of government, a distinction that Hegel treated too superficially. For example, pure monarchy represents the principle of authority, aristocracy represents the law, democracy represents freedom, while mixed forms of government, and constitutional monarchy above all, represent a combination of the various principles and their synthesis in an ideal form. Thus everywhere the same dialectical logic repeats itself. This is only natural, for in all political systems the same elements express themselves, and these elements are at the basis of every human community.

We have seen that placing a monarch at the head of the ideal state is logically entailed by Hegel's views. The synthetic principle, the union of opposites, must constitute the apex of the political edifice; but as the representative of the community's pure will within the state, the crown should be free from any bias. What should matter is not the character of the monarch but his position. We find the same view among those French publicists who were contemporaries of Hegel; while adopting a completely different approach [to political philosophy], they also conceived of an ideal constitutional monarchy operating according to similar principles. In their view, above the various branches of legislature, executive, and judiciary there stood royal authority, the highest authority in the realm, the apex of the edifice of state, which unites the other opposed elements of the state in a single, harmonious whole. Hegel's remark that "the prince must only say *yes* and dot the *i*" is identical in meaning to another famous dictum: "The king should reign but not govern." Thus, by virtue of an inner law [of the Spirit], a similar process of thought, although traveling different paths, arrived at identical results.

We shall not analyze the details of Hegel's political theory. When assessing the implications of a philosophy, it is much more important to analyze general principles than to look at their practical application. Hegel never set himself the task [of investigating how his theories applied in practice]. As far as his philosophy of history is concerned, we cannot agree with those critics who see in it the destruction of liberty and the annihilation of the individual by general substance. The real issue is this: should history be seen as a product of arbitrary human choice and of accidents, or as a process governed by general laws? To say that an individual, in pursuing his personal ambitions, not infrequently accomplishes something he never intended and thus that he unconsciously becomes a tool of higher forces; that among historical agents the demands of the time, the spirit of the people and so on make themselves felt—this is to utter a simple and perhaps even a banal truth. Those who see human beings as tools of Providence say the same thing. But to recognize as much neither annihilates personal liberty nor obviates ethical responsibility, as Hegel himself explicitly notes. An individual, by virtue of his liberty, is free to do anything he wishes; but he is not empowered to violate the laws of the Spirit, just as he is not empowered to violate the laws of nature. Accidents remain accidents; an accident has meaningful consequences only when it coincides with the general tendencies of a historical period. This view alone can be reconciled with the imperatives of liberty. For a rational being there can be no higher satisfaction than to see oneself as an instrument of some general purpose. Not the accidental play of arbitrary choices but the unfolding of the basic categories of the Spirit constitutes history's content. Hegel had precisely this in mind when he asserted that everything real is rational and everything rational is real. He explicitly stated that by the term *reality* he did not mean accidental and arbitrary phenomena but those basic elements of life flowing out of the depths of the Universal Spirit. From this remark one cannot draw a justification for successful crimes, nor can one find legitimation for every political order that establishes itself. The law of the Spirit is not stagnation but development. Negation of the established order, if negation is based on the demands of reason, itself is an expression of the dialectic present in the Spirit. In general, the true sense of development, conceived as the inner self-actualization of the Spirit, has never been grasped so profoundly as Hegel grasped it. He also revealed the dialectical law governing this evolution. This is his great achievement, one that subsequent scholarship can only further elucidate. Study of history as a whole certainly convinces us that it is driven not by accident but by ideas unfolding in logical sequence. Any true historian will defend this proposition.

While Hegel profoundly understood the general principles of the philosophy of history, his efforts to apply this interpretation to historical facts were not always so profound. Here we encounter the boundaries separating speculative reason and empirical observation. It is one thing to state a general law a priori, and another thing to demonstrate the operation of this law in concrete phenomena. The latter demands empirical investigation of the phenomena themselves, as Hegel himself recognizes,[23] and this is a quite different sort of work than the former. [Analysis of concrete experience] requires knowledge of a vast range of data, critical evaluation of them, and precision in drawing factual conclusions; in a word, this is the proper place for employing the empirical method. Given the differences, however, the conclusions suggested by the one method do not always coincide with conclusions suggested by the other. A law may be properly formulated but, given inadequate experiential data, it may not seem to fit the facts. If sufficient data are collected but are not adequately analyzed and then are subsumed under a general law, then the interpretation will be forced. Hegel suffered precisely from this problem. He was a powerful speculative thinker but was weak on the empirical side. Having deduced the existence of certain general laws, he sought to find concrete phenomena that might fit his interpretive framework, but his efforts did not always succeed. Incidentally, this failure alone is clear proof that Hegel's formulations derived not from historical experience but from speculative reasoning. If historical experience were the sole guide of human knowledge, then wrong understanding of that experience could never enable one to make right deductions about general laws of history.

The first criticism that can be made of Hegel's philosophy of history concerns his overly narrow understanding of nationality as a stage in the development of the Spirit. There is absolutely no reason that a given historical epoch should be associated with a single dominant nationality which, having carried out its assigned mission, should then recede from the historical stage. Such an interpretation might be justified, though with caveats, in ancient history; modern history presents a phenomenon of another sort altogether. Here a more complex set of relations exists; at one and the same time, various aspects of the Spirit find their expression in different nationalities, and a general movement forward is produced by the interaction of these nationalities. Therefore, one cannot agree with Hegel when he interprets all modern history as a product of the Germanic spirit. In modern history, no one nation is the dominant nation in a given epoch; all are members of a common system. On the other hand, one and the same people passes through different stages of development, participating in the general movement as far as its nature permits. Hence the far broader impact of nationality in modern history and the dialectical development within the milieu of a given nationality. To a modern nationality, Hegel's dictum is least applicable that nationality, as a category of the Spirit, necessarily requires a certain form of government and, accompanying it, a certain religion, a certain philosophy and a certain art.[24] This argument is contradicted even by the history of the ancient polities. The national spirit, as a manifestation of the Spirit which is common to all humanity, cannot be confined to this or that form or direction; passing through various stages of development and experiencing interaction with others, the national spirit can change its content.

Another even more important shortcoming of Hegel's philosophy of history may be found in his erroneous interpretation of the general course of human development. He correctly understood the Orient as a milieu representing a primitive submergence of the individual in general substance, while Greece was the first harmonious manifestation of liberty; but in defining the subsequent stages of development, Hegel fell into serious errors. Having made up his mind that a reconciliation of opposites should be sought in Christianity, Hegel ascribed to Rome an absolute duality of consciousness, and this ascription cast a quite false light both on Roman history and on the medieval order. The historical movement of the Spirit actually proceeds from unity to duality and then from duality to unity; but duality was the distinguishing characteristic not of Rome but of the medieval period. Classical polities represent the process of gradual disintegration of the Spiritual substance under the influence, on the one hand, of abstract universal principles, and, on the other hand, of particular interests. The result of this process is the medieval order which represents two opposed worlds—the secular and the sacred, civil society and the church, the one encompassing the idea of personal rights, the other the moral-religious principle. Between these two worlds there arises a struggle which leads ultimately to the need for a reconciliation. The process of reconciliation constitutes the content of modern history. Above the opposed institutions there arises a higher institution, the state, which bears modern ideals and returns to certain principles that dominated the ancient world. The same course may be observed in art and philosophy.

Finally, we will formulate in greater detail and with more precision the law which explains the entire history of humanity. Here we must limit ourselves to certain elements already treated above, but the reader will find this law confirmed by the entire corpus of preceding political thought. Thus the empirical investigation of history, while serving as a corrective to Hegel's interpretation, still justifies his basic conclusions. It also confirms the argument of his philosophy of right. The disintegration of the ancient polis leads to the opposition of the principles of right and morality, of civil society and church, and, conversely, their unification leads to the reestablishment of the modern state. One may ask: what happened to the family which supposedly constitutes the first stage in the development of human communities? Here history provides us with an answer. Family or clan life actually constitutes the first stage of development for all peoples, whether ancient or modern. In antiquity, however, the transition from clan life to the polis occurred in the prehistorical epoch and was necessarily quite different in character from that which occurred later, in the Middle Ages. The original synthesis did not allow for a sharp conflict between extremes. Thus in antiquity, as clan life disintegrated, the theocratic principle merged with the political principle; the result was the theocratic state, which in its original form encompassed both clans and the polis. This development occurred in the Orient, but also in Greece and Rome. When the ancient states disintegrated, when church and civil society again came into opposition, the construction of the new system required modern peoples who, also ascending from clan life, passed through an era of conflict between moral and legal communities and finally arrived at the modern state, at a synthesis of the earlier institutions. The fundamental difference from antiquity was that modern peoples stepping upon the historical stage encountered an absolute duality already prepared by preceding history. They transcended this duality and attained a new synthesis. Therefore, today they do not need to fear a new disintegration; disintegration lies behind them. Modern peoples bear the seeds of a development capable of bringing the human historical process to its culmination and conclusion.

Thus history confirms the argument of Hegel's philosophy of right. We see here a more complicated law than the one formulated by Hegel, but the basic categories remain the same. Hegel himself did not suspect to what degree his speculative conclusions might be justified by phenomena; only empirical investigation of the subject could clarify the issue. At this point we reach the boundaries of philosophy and must necessarily adopt another approach. Hegel culminates the preceding development of thought; he is the pinnacle of all modern philosophy. But philosophy, being a speculative discipline, cannot move beyond general principles and laws. To investigate the form taken by these principles in historical actuality is a task of another kind altogether, a task that proceeds quite differently than the former, for here it is necessary to start with the particular and gradually work toward the universal. Such an approach can also serve to verify the conclusions of speculative thought. If a law is properly formulated, then it should be confirmed by empirical research. If not, then the mind remains dissatisfied and its trust in speculative conclusions declines. The more philosophy resorts to straining the evidence to support its conclusions, the more inadequate it will appear as a discipline. [The widespread tendency to stretch evidence to defend philosophical deductions] explains the distrust attaching to philosophy in the present day. Having reached the apogee of its development, philosophy suddenly loses all credit. The human mind turns from it and sets off on another course. From the preceding remarks it is clear that this turn of events is to be expected. Realism, like rationalism, is a necessary stage in the development of the Spirit: the study of facts serves not only as a supplement to, but also as a means of verifying, the conclusions of pure reason.

But as it happens, one extreme leads to another. Empiricism, in turn, takes a negative attitude toward philosophy and considers itself the sole source of knowledge. Meanwhile, one-sided empiricism still less than philosophy can pretend to uncontested primacy in scholarship. Pure empiricism is confined to the study of particulars. Its disagreement with philosophy cannot serve as proof against philosophy, for disagreement may result as much from inadequate study of concrete phenomena [as from philosophical bias]. Narrowly circumscribed empirical research yields narrowly circumscribed philosophy. Such is the case with today's exact sciences, which everywhere seek nothing but mechanical causes and laws. [The exact sciences] lead ineluctably to a mechanical worldview and to atomist philosophy—that is, to the lowest form of philosophy, to materialism. On the contrary, broader empirical research focused on the world of Spirit leads to broader philosophical conclusions. Here embracing materialism only proves one's ignorance. But whatever the nature of the empirical investigation, if it is to be more than a simple collection of data, it cannot get along without philosophy, for it cannot get along without a certain method of understanding things, and methods of understanding are provided by the laws of our reason that find their purest expression in philosophy. For us, reason is the only reliable means of knowing; therefore, in the external world we can know only what reason's rules [of observation, inference, and deduction] enable us to know. The remainder, if it indeed exists, must remain for us eternally unknowable. Therefore, it follows that the conflict between empirical observation and philosophy can occur only over the interpretation of particular matters; in general, however, empirical observation and philosophy must necessarily coincide in their insights, for both are elaborations of one and the same principles, the principles of rational knowledge. Narrow and one-sided empiricism is negatively disposed to philosophy; genuine and multifaceted empiricism serves to supplement and confirm it. Those who take the narrow perspective imagine that their narrow view is all-encompassing; but those who rise to an understanding of the general movement of human thought see narrow interpretations as separate links in a common intellectual chain. One may say that in this process, rationalism is the major premise, realism the minor premise, and the conclusion remains to be drawn.

On the basis of the preceding commentary, we can assert that principles elaborated by German Idealism should be regarded as genuine scholarly achievements. Indeed, many of Idealism's conclusions have already entered into the warp and woof of contemporary reality. The notion of historical development, the importance of nationalism, the essence of right and of the state—all have been assimilated by contemporary thought. But Idealism is destined to play an even greater role in the future, when, on the basis of both approaches, philosophy and empirical research, the ultimate conclusion will be drawn. Not realism but universalism is the future agenda of the human mind. Of course, in this pursuit Idealism alone cannot serve as guiding principle. When the question is posed so broadly, then one cannot hold to a single interpretive framework, much less adhere to this or that system. The future guide of human thought can only be a universal history of philosophy—that is, the record of the evolution of reason in all its phases. But in this overall movement German Idealism is the latest and highest link of the chain. It provides us the key to understanding everything else. In particular, it illuminates the sciences of humanity. Idealism is first and foremost the philosophy of Spirit; therefore, it more profoundly than all other interpretive schemes reveals to us the nature and activity of the Spirit.

Marx

Sharing common ground with [Friedrich] Lassalle is Karl Marx, the well-known chairman of the International Working Men's Association, and also, like Lassalle, of Jewish origin.[1] In intellectual power, in talent, in erudition, in philosophical sense, he cannot be compared with Lassalle; yet he did that which Lassalle had only dreamed of doing: he provided a theoretical formulation of a social utopia. His book, *Das Kapital,*[2] is the culmination of German scientific socialism. Although heretofore only the first part has been published, it fully expresses the bases of Marx's theory. Judging by this book, we can determine what scientific socialism is capable of offering. The importance of the subject impels us to analyze the book in detail and to follow the chain of deductions on which the entire doctrine depends.

Karl Marx's method of investigation is the same as we saw in Lassalle's work. This is the dialectical method, inherited from Hegel. Karl Marx explicitly avows himself to be a student of the great thinker and even says that in his basic conclusions, here and there, he has coquetted (!) with Hegelian terminology.[3] The Hegelian principle of contradiction he considers the "mainspring of any dialectic."[4] Yet he also announces that his own dialectical method is directly the opposite of Hegel's dialectic. In the latter's work the intellectual process is embodied in the so-called Idea and is the creator of material reality, which is merely the Idea's external expression.[5] In Marx's view, the truth is grounded in reality—that is, in the material world; everything ideal is nothing but the material world as reflected by the human mind and translated into thought. Therefore, he says, Hegel's dialectic is standing on its head. It must be turned right side up in order to discover the rational kernel within the mystical shell.[6]

After this, one might suppose Hegel's dialectic to be the negation of reality, and Marx's dialectic, on the contrary, to be the restoration of reality. But just the opposite is the case. It is the dialectic of Hegel, the one which allegedly inverts, or "stands on the head," the true relations of things, that uncovers the positive side of material existence and speaks as its defender, whereas it is the other dialectic, the one which purportedly takes material existence as its foundation, that in fact assumes toward reality a negative attitude and calls for destruction of "every mature form in the current of history." In a word, it is "by its essence, critical and revolutionary."[7]

Thus the Marxian dialectic must simultaneously serve as the expression of extreme materialism and extreme Idealism; on one hand, it must find its point of support in material reality, taking this reality as its basis; on the other hand, it must negate this very reality in the name of an ideal that is to be found only in the human mind.[8] Karl Marx evidently does not suspect that he is serving two different gods. In Lassalle's work we have already encountered the notion that every mature form is destroyed in the current of history; this notion is the result of a one-sided development of the principle of negation found in Hegelian dialectics. With his lucid philosophical mind, Lassalle could sometimes use materialist arguments for his own purposes, but he could never mix up two completely different schools of thought. For anyone acquainted with philosophy and able to think logically, it is indeed difficult to understand how materialism and socialism can be combined in a single thinker. Yet in fact this occurs rather frequently.

Given this conceptual confusion, it is not surprising that Karl Marx wants to depict his [version of the] dialectic as being grounded in concrete experience. He says that one needs to distinguish the method of presentation from the method of inquiry. "The latter has to appropriate the material in detail, to analyze its different forms of development, to trace out their inner connection. Only after this work has been done can the actual movement be adequately described. If this is done successfully, if the life of the subject matter is ideally reflected as in a mirror, then it may appear as if we have before us a mere a priori construction."[9]

Of course, given a genuinely scholarly mode of thinking, that could never happen. A basic proposition must be proven, and in the process of presenting the proof it becomes apparent whether the proof is grounded in abstract speculation or empirical observation. An author may assure us a thousand times that he, in ways not known to the reader, has derived his principle from the most detailed factual research; the reader who has some familiarity with scholarly standards nevertheless will not believe him: the reader knows that scholarly proof precisely depends upon elucidating the process by which a principle is derived. In the absence of such elucidation, the most detailed factual presentation consists of mere curiosities gathered in the service of a preconceived idea—that is, of data presented in a completely false light. Such is the factual material presented in Karl Marx's book. He has not even a scintilla of factual proof for his basic propositions; thus, after having formulated his theory, Marx erects upon it a factual edifice in the form which is most convenient for him. Consequently, when Karl Marx assures us that his principles only seem to have been derived a priori, he merely succeeds in making it clear that he has neither deductive nor empirical proof. He himself does not know whence his first principles come. There is neither a theoretical nor empirical justification [for Marx's initial position], only logical tricks played for the sake of a predetermined goal. The reader will be convinced of this if he follows the author's train of thought, step by step.

The book begins by analyzing the value of a commodity. A commodity, Marx says, is the original cell out of which a nation's wealth builds itself. It is the more difficult to observe because we have here neither a microscope [in which to visualize the cell] nor chemical reactions [to record its growth]. The one and the other are replaced by the *force of abstraction.* And so, instead of [beginning with an observation], we begin with an abstraction. What is a commodity?

First of all, a commodity is an object useful to man, or which serves his needs. Utility gives it a *use-value* [*Gebrachswerth*]. On the other hand, the essence of this object is that it is exchanged for other objects. In this lies its *exchange-value* [*Tauschwerth*]. The latter is the main subject of Marx's inquiry.

Exchange-value is expressed by the relation of equality between two commodities, for example: 1 *chetvert'* of wheat = x *poods* of iron. But this relation does not exhaust its essence. Wheat may be equated not only with iron but with a multitude of other commodities: therefore, there must be a common content independent of these individual modes of expression. In each equation there is necessarily something in common, a third thing "that is neither the one nor the other" but to which both members may be reduced. Commodities are distinguished one from the other by their use-value or utility; consequently, the exchange-value, in which they are supposedly equal, must be distinct from use-value. Exchange-value, Marx claims, does not contain within itself a single iota of use-value.

Here the reader stops and asks himself: why is this so? That between two objects which are being exchanged there must be something in common is undoubtedly true; but that this common property must be in *neither the one nor the other,* this contradicts common sense: a common property is precisely a property that resides *in the one and the other.* If we ask what is common to two commodities being exchanged, any rational person would probably answer: that they are both useful; that is why they are being exchanged. The first object is more useful to one person, the second object to another; but they are both useful. If we disregard their different uses, there remains the common element of utility, of *use-value* in general. We cannot make any other deduction here. Disregarding what is particular leaves us with the quality common to both, with their generic trait, but nothing else.

But can common utility serve as a basis for a quantitative comparison? That is another question, but one cannot answer it affirmatively either. In any exchange a person compares the use which he is giving with that he is receiving; this is what prompts him to make the exchange. The degree of utility of any object is also determined by what the buyer is willing to give for it; he will give more for something he needs more and less for something he needs less. According to the view of all economists, demand is one of the essential elements in determining value. Another element is the possibility of obtaining an object by another means. No one will give more money if he can pay less. This second element, supply, is determined by various circumstances which must be investigated in order to decide the question of a commodity's value. And this economists do. Simply disregarding utility not only leads us to no result but, on the contrary, destroys the very basis of decision. If we were to disregard utility *entirely,* then value would also disappear because there would be no exchange. No one exchanges objects that are not useful. Consequently, when Karl Marx asserts that exchange-value contains not a single iota of use-value, this is not only an unjustified logical jump but a direct contradiction of what occurs everyday in the exchange of commodities.

What do two commodities have in common, if we disregard their utility? [What they have in common], Marx says, is *one trait alone*—namely, that both objects are the product of labor.[10] Here the reader comes upon an even greater misunderstanding. He knows nothing about labor. Why is labor the only common trait? I, for example, am buying a forest and I pay gold for it. Can it really be so that, independently of the utility of these objects, their only [common] remaining trait is that they are products of labor? But they are also, and to a much greater degree, the products of nature. Perhaps in the forest that I am buying no labor has been done at all, and yet I pay for it, and, depending on the circumstances, I may pay quite dearly. Obviously, labor is regarded by Marx as the agent of production; but Marx himself admits that it is not the only agent: nature is also an agent.[11] So is capital. Objects being exchanged may themselves be capital—that is, they may be agents of production. This is also a trait that may lend value to the objects. Why is all of this disregarded and labor alone taken into account? Because it is so convenient for the author. There is no other answer that we can give. Let the reader look through all 822 pages of Karl Marx's book; he will find no other reason. Everywhere in the subsequent presentation, the proposition that the exchange-value of commodities is determined exclusively by labor is taken as a given; the only proof is that, having disregarded the utility of commodities, we are left with only one trait as a residue—that is, that they are the products of labor. And this pretends to be a rigorous scholarly conclusion![12] The reader sees that here there is not only no rigorous scholarship but no common sense, either. There is no factual analysis whatsoever of exchange-value; of empirical proofs there is not even a hint. The book is reduced to logical deduction, but in the deduction there is not one iota of logic. As we have already noted, [*Das Kapital*] is grounded in neither theory nor concrete experience, but is simply a magic show which throws dust in the reader's eyes.

Like Marx, certain English economists have tried to explain the value of commodities solely in terms of productive labor; but they conducted a serious analysis of the subject on this basis. The analysis was wrong, because income from land and interest on capital, which, independently of other changing circumstances, constantly determine the value of products, cannot be understood solely in terms of labor. But here at least one can argue, one can try to prove the proposition. But when an author simply asserts that something is so and considers the matter proven, then the real question is no longer the particular scholarly issue being debated but the intellectual competence of the author.

But let us move on. Let us assume that the value of commodities is, in fact, determined solely by labor. But what kind of labor? If we disregard the utility of commodities, Marx says, then obviously we must also disregard the utility of the labor that produced them; with the former disappears the latter. Useful labor is a particular kind of labor, one of its aspects; and what we need is the property common to all labor, labor in general. Homogeneous or abstract labor is labor understood as the expenditure of human labor-power. It is measured by time, by its duration. This is the measure of all values, the unit to which they may be reduced.[13]

On this occasion Marx's deduction is correct; having disregarded the various types of labor, we arrive at labor in general. But here is another difficulty. I can work for God knows how much time, but if I produce a thing that is not useful to anyone, then it will nevertheless have no value, and my labor will be wasted. Karl Marx even admits this. Consequently, labor, in order to have value, necessarily must be *useful.*[14] Thus, on the one hand, we disregard utility entirely and claim that value is determined by labor, by the expenditure of labor-power alone; on the other hand, we require that abstract labor must necessarily be useful—that is, we admit through the back door what we have driven out of the front door. The contradiction here is obvious, glaring, but the author is not embarrassed by it in the least and so, taking no notice, he continues his logical procession.

If the value of products is determined exclusively by the time used in their manufacture, then obviously all work should be recompensed at an identical rate. Whether the worker produces a greater quantity of use-value or a lesser quantity in a given time, the value must be the same. Marx also admits this. The productive force of labor, he says, affects its utility but not its value. The result of greater productivity is merely that one and the same value is spread over a larger quantity of commodities; consequently, each commodity is cheaper.[15] But if this is so, then work of different quality must have the same value. By this standard, a painting by Raphael would have less value than a painting by the most ungifted apprentice, provided that Raphael's canvas was completed more quickly. Here it does no good to point out that Raphael's painting is worth more because of that artist's previous work. The apprentice might very well have more prior experience than Raphael: yet a genius easily accomplishes what the apprentice can never achieve even by the most painstaking labor. Consequently, it must either be admitted that the value of products is determined not by the quantity of labor alone but also by its quality, or the most obvious and incontrovertible facts must be disregarded as lacking in validity. Marx does not select the latter solution. As is his custom, he introduces a contradiction into his argumentation without bothering to resolve it. He divides labor into simple and complicated: the latter he also calls *intensified* or *multiplied,* as if a qualitative difference could be explained away by a quantitative relationship! Simple labor, in his opinion, is the unit by which all values are measured: complex labor can be understood in terms of simple labor, because a lesser quantity of the former equals a greater quantity of the latter. The reader asks how is this possible, when what we are discussing is undifferentiated labor, labor in general understood as an expenditure of labor-power. One might call more productive labor intensified or multiplied, but the category of more productive labor has been disregarded as having no influence on value. True, at another point Marx says that "labor performed with especially efficient labor-power acts as intensified labor, for it produces in a given time more than does average social labor of the same sort."[16] This only magnifies the contradiction, and we still do not know by what means it is possible to reduce work of different quality to a single quantitative measure. The author himself ceases to discuss the matter and simply refers to experience. "That this reduction is constantly being made," he says, "is shown by experience. A commodity may be the product of the most complicated labor, but its value can be expressed in terms of simple labor, and, therefore, it represents only a definite quantity of simple labor. The different proportions in which different sorts of labor are reduced to simple labor as their quantitative unit are established by *a certain social process that occurs behind the backs of the producers,* and consequently seems to them to have been fixed by custom."[17] For this reason Karl Marx considers it quite pointless to discuss qualitatively superior labor, for it can always be understood in terms of simple labor.

Of course, this is a very easy way to avoid difficulty. But the question is: what sort of social process goes on behind the backs of the producers? If we refer to experience, it would seem that labor does not serve as a measure of value, but money serves as a measure of labor, and that the relation of one kind of labor to another is determined neither by the character nor by the duration of the labor itself but by exogenous circumstances. One and the same painting, requiring a month's work by a artist, may be 100 or 1,000 or 10,000 times more valuable than the same quantity of simple labor, depending on whether the artist is famous or not, whether the demand for his work is great or not, whether he is living or dead, and so on. If we, together with Marx, say that society, in establishing prices, does not itself understand by what mechanism it is guided, then it is necessary to explain the true character of this process, and then the question again arises: how is the value of labor having different qualities to be determined? According to Marx's theory, when we say that twenty *arshins* of linen equals one frock coat, then that means that in both values is contained an equal quantity of work days; but when we say that a greater quantity of simple labor equals a lesser quantity of complex labor—that is, of superior labor—what is the basis of this equation? In order to make up for the missing quantity, we must introduce another element, quality, an element incommensurable with quantity. We will say nothing about the absurd proposition that a greater quantity [of simple labor] serves [in Marx's system] as a unit of measure for a lesser quantity [of complex labor]. Obviously, one can reduce all values to the unit of the working day by one means only: by completely disregarding the quality of the labor performed in that day. Karl Marx does precisely this when he says that value is determined by labor in general understood as the expenditure of labor-power, regardless of its quality. But then [the concept of] quality should not be introduced again by the back door; instead, it ought to be bravely argued that Raphael's picture is less valuable than the product of an ungifted apprentice who has worked longer on his painting.

But even this assertion will not save us from contradictions. Even the simple labor of a day laborer can be of various quality. Karl Marx himself notes that superficially it might seem that the lazier and more untalented a person is, the more valuable are the commodities he produces, for making these commodities requires him to spend a greater amount of time. In order to avoid this difficulty, it is necessary once again to reduce labor of different qualities to a common unit of measure. "The labor that constitutes the substance of values," says Marx, "is homogeneous human labor, the expenditure of one and the same human labor-power. The total labor-power of society, which expresses itself in the values of the commodity world, counts here as one homogeneous mass of human labor-power, composed though it be of innumerable individual units of labor-power. Each of these units is the same as any other, so far as it has the character of the average labor-power of society and acts as such; that is, so far as it requires for producing a commodity no more time than is needed on an average, no more than is socially necessary."

Thus in order to find a unit of labor we are compelled to make a new abstraction. Initially, we disregarded quality and took into account only quantity; now we disregard the infinite variation of individual labor-power and take into account only average labor-power. But this new abstraction has a different character than the first. There we took one aspect of a real object and disregarded the other; here we move from the realm of reality to the realm of fiction. For a unit of social labor-power is nothing but a fiction; in reality there exist only individual labor-powers. In speaking of social labor-power, we do not even know what society we are talking about, or, for that matter, whether we talking about a single nation at all. Indeed, the exchange of commodities occurs between nations. According to Marx's theory, we would have to argue that on the international market the value of commodities is determined by the average work time of the entire human species, taken as a unit of labor-power. But this is an utter absurdity. When we take as a unit of measure for real-world relationships a fictitious unit known to no one, this signifies only that we have gotten ourselves quite lost. In fact, the value of commodities is determined not by the calculation of the average working time for all of humanity but simply by a competition between particular labor forces. Cheaper commodities drive from the market more expensive ones. Competition occurs not because various forces are reducible to a single one but because the forces in question are different.

Another false notion is connected with the fictional unit of social labor-power. If the reader heretofore had assumed the measure of values to be labor actually performed, then he must be disabused of this notion. Not actual labor, but *required* or, as Karl Marx puts it, *socially necessary* labor determines the value of a commodity. But socially necessary labor is not a constant. As Marx himself admits, this is a unit of measure that is constantly changing. Today a certain quantity of labor is needed to produce a given commodity, but tomorrow, as a result of new techniques, only half the labor is needed. Despite the fact that the former work day has already been transformed into the cost of the commodity, if this commodity is not sold and is later returned to the market, its price, and consequently [the value of] the labor expended upon it, is cut in half. The excess labor expended in its production is wasted.[18] Therefore, when Marx asserts that the price of commodities reflects congealed labor time [*festgeronnene Arbeitszeit*], this contradicts his own conclusions: labor is not congealed in a price but, on the contrary, constantly changes along with it, even though the labor has already been performed and obviously cannot change. Furthermore, it should be noted that socially necessary labor time is not the time required to produce one or another commodity but the time required to produce the entire total of known goods necessary to society. The time needed to produce individual items may remain as before, but if the amount produced exceeds the necessary quantity, then only the time necessary to satisfy the general need is counted, and that time is distributed among the larger quantity of commodities. Both labor-power and the entire mass of commodities on the market are considered as a single entity whose total value is distributed among individual objects, in accordance with their total quantity.[19] Conversely, therefore, if the quantity of commodities is less than necessary, a commodity is still regarded as the product of socially necessary labor, although this labor has not even been performed; in this case, the price of a commodity is greater than the labor actually done in producing it.

From the perspective of this theory, it is clear that labor ceases to have independent significance. Actual labor is transformed into imaginary labor, the imaginary sum of labor is determined by the sum of objects essential to satisfy demand—that is, by the sum of useful objects. From the realm of fiction the unit of measure again crosses back into reality, but into a reality determined by use-value and not by labor. Hence the result at which we arrive is quite the opposite of what we had assumed at the beginning. The point of departure was to disregard use-value; as Marx puts it, from the sensory realm we then ascended into the supersensory, or even into the supernatural realm. Moving from abstraction to abstraction, we ultimately arrived at a pure phantasmagoria, one that eludes all definition; when at last we wanted to grasp hold of something concrete, we found nothing except the use-value that we had discarded in the beginning. Not without reason does Karl Marx assert that, under analysis, a commodity turns out to be a kind of "social hieroglyph," which has to be decoded. In Marx's analysis, one is not surprised to learn that this same commodity "evolves out of its wooden brain grotesque ideas far more wonderful than 'table-turning' ever was."[20] But Marx is mistaken when he ascribes the mystical fog and the contradictions emanating from it to that form of production that expresses itself in the commodity.[21] The contradictions exist only in the author's mind, and this same mind produces the theological niceties and all the ideas that are more wonderful than "table-turning." The actual process by which commodity values are generated is utterly absent here.

And this is not the most sublime example of the new form of dialectics. In our subsequent presentation we will encounter even more astonishing things.

Having based exchange-value on this metaphysical table-turning of a commodity, Karl Marx turns to the transformation of a commodity into money. This would seem to be a relatively simple issue. Money serves as a tool of exchange, an expression of exchange-value; consequently, according to the author's theory, money is the embodiment of abstract human labor. But Karl Marx is not satisfied with this claim; again, he wants to be profound and, as is his wont, he entangles himself in contradictions from which there is no escape.

According to Marx's theory, the price of commodities being exchanged can be expressed in an equation making clear that the quantity of work contained in each is the same. One might take the equation as indicating nothing more than the quantitative identity of the two terms. But being tutored in German philosophy, Marx sees here a polarity, a qualitative contradiction. One commodity, he says, expresses its value in the other; consequently, the first plays an active, the second a passive role. The first appears in the guise of a *relative value,* the second in the guise of an *equivalent.*[22] One may object that in any exchange this relation is reciprocal. True, says Marx; but in order to express the price of the second commodity in the first, one has to transpose the terms, and then the first term becomes the equivalent.[23] The reader understands that this transposition is being done on paper, yet in reality the relation between the two commodities remains the same. No matter how one transposes the terms of an equation, an equation nevertheless expresses the equality of the terms and nothing more.

But where, in Marx's opinion, is the qualitative contradiction between relative value and its equivalent to be found? According to him, it can be found in a certain opposition between money value and utility, or between exchange- and use-value. The latter was disregarded at the beginning of the book. Commodities themselves, in Karl Marx's words, tell us: "Our use-value may interest a person; but as things, use-value does not belong to us. . . . We relate to each other only as exchange-value."[24] Nevertheless, use-value again and again enters the relation between values. The polarity of the terms consists precisely in that the exchange-value of one commodity expresses itself in the use-value of the other commodity. And the contradiction is not limited to this. Not only is a previously discarded concept secretly reintroduced here, but the very terms that are supposedly contradictory are unexpectedly transformed one into the other. Explaining what he calls relative value, Karl Marx explicitly states that it expresses exchange-value, while the equivalent expresses use-value. "The exchange-value of commodity A, expressed in the use-value of commodity B, has the form of relative value."[25] The explanation is that for a seller, from whose perspective we view the comparison, the commodity being sold has no utility but has exchange-value; conversely, the commodity being acquired does have utility for him.[26] Toward the end of a long and tiresome argument that is mostly tautological, it suddenly turns out that utility is relative value and exchange-value is the equivalent. "The opposition or contrast existing internally in each commodity between use-value and value, is, therefore, made evident externally by two commodities being placed in such relation to each other, that the commodity whose value it is sought to express figures directly as a mere use-value, while the commodity in which that value is to be expressed figures directly as mere exchange-value."[27] How this metamorphosis was accomplished remains a secret to the reader. One may suppose that it has also occurred without the author's knowledge, for it yields him no advantage at all. [What we are witnessing] is just a logical shell game in which the unskillful player never knows where his idea will end up.

In any event, the result is that money, as the universal equivalent, serves as the pure expression of exchange-value—that is, as the embodiment of abstract human labor.[28] Karl Marx himself labels this expression as absurd [*verrückt*], but he asserts that commercial production cannot help but express itself in absurd forms.[29] [Marx goes on to say that] the value of gold is determined by the labor-time required for its production, and is expressed by the quantity of any other commodity that costs the same amount of labor-time.[30] A commodity's price is the money-name of the labor realized in the commodity. However, Marx notes, "Although the price, being the exponent of the magnitude of a commodity's value, is the exponent of its exchange-ratio with money, it does not follow that the exponent of this exchange-ratio is necessarily the exponent of the magnitude of the commodity's value." *Circumstances* may force a reduction in price or permit its increase, and then the market price of a commodity will cease to correspond to its true value. It may even happen that the market price of a commodity not only quantitatively but also qualitatively is distinguished from its actual value. A person sometimes receives payment for something that does not represent any work—for example, for acts contrary to honor and conscience. In such a case, the market price will be a false indicator [of the commodity's actual value]. Karl Marx attributes such deviations from the norm to the capitalist form of production, in which the general rule is merely a blind law stating the numerical mean of irregularly fluctuating price movements.[31] But we cannot help but see here an admission by Marx that the price of commodities is determined not by labor-time alone but also by other *circumstances.* Meanwhile, the determination of exchange-value exclusively by labor-time was enunciated as an absolute law, independent of the form of production. We were informed that the equation expressing an exchange of commodities signifies that an identical quantity of labor is contained in both terms of the equation. Having accepted this principle, we must necessarily recognize that in the monetary value of a commodity is expressed its exchange-value, or the quantity of labor-time contained in it, and nothing more. However many times we compare the quantities and from whatever end of the equation we begin, the relation of equality [between the terms] will nevertheless remain a relation of equality. To claim that the exchange-value is expressed in the monetary price of the commodity, but that the price of the commodity does not always express an exchange-value, is the same as saying, for example, about measurements of a table that, starting from one end it measures 2 *arshins*, but from the other perhaps 3 *arshins*. The contradiction here is not in the subject being discussed but in the author's theory alone.

Marx arrives at the same absurd position when he explains the disparity between a commodity's market price and its true value by saying that the *substance* of a price—that is, the labor embodied in it—can be increased or decreased when the commodity is exchanged.[32] This loss or depreciation of substance is a phenomenon unknown to economic science. It is a miraculous creation from nothing or transformation into nothing. Not without reason does Karl Marx relate the price of commodities to the supernatural world.

Having analyzed the transformation of exchange-value into money, Marx then investigates the transformation of money into capital. This is the cornerstone of his entire system, and here the author radically disagrees with all "bourgeois economists." These economists mean by the term *capital* any product that is an instrument in new production, but Marx, returning to notions of the classical world, depicts capital only as money earning interest or "begetting offspring," in Aristotle's expression.[33] Once placed in circulation, capital itself is transformed into a commodity, but only in order again to be transformed into money. For capital the commodity form is transitional; its monetary form is the beginning and the end of its movement. Thus the circulation of capital is essentially different from the circulation of commodities. In the latter case, a commodity is the beginning and the end of the process of circulation. A producer sells a commodity and with the money received from the sale he buys a new commodity for consumption. Consequently, the process involves the exchange of two equally valuable commodities through the agency of money. The formula for this circulation is Commodity—Money—Commodity. The goal is consumption, and with consumption the process comes to an end. Conversely, the circulation of capital is expressed by the formula: Money—Commodity—Money. The goal here is not merely to recover one's money, for that would be pointless. The goal is to make a *profit* on the money being circulated, to obtain a surplus of value [*Mehrwerth*]. By circulating, capital grows, and this growth has no limit, for each completed cycle of exchange gives rise to another.[34] Marx claims that this type of circulation is usually thought to be characteristic only of commercial capital, but [he says] that it also may be characteristic of industrial capital. Everywhere commodities are bought with money, then resold. In capital lent for interest, this type of circulation is manifested in its purest form. Indeed, here the true essence of capital expresses itself: it is money begetting money.[35]

The reader asks where may we find the simple commodity circulation that is being juxtaposed to the circulation of capital? Marx cites the example of a simple peasant producer who sells grain in order to buy clothing; yet in order to produce the grain for sale, that same peasant must first invest money in production. Let us assume that he already has land at his disposal; he still must buy his farming implements, draught animals, materials for farm buildings, and perhaps his seeds. [Furthermore,] not all the money he receives from selling commodities will be used to buy necessities; part of the proceeds will be reinvested in production. In fact, the merchant-capitalist does the same thing: he consumes part of his profit and reinvests the rest. The only difference between the two methods of circulation is that in the first case, Marx arbitrarily begins with the commodity, as if the commodity had fallen from the sky, and ends with consumption while ignoring that part of the earnings that is devoted to new production; in the second case, Marx does the opposite—he arbitrarily begins with money, as if money had fallen from the sky, and he pays attention only to that part of the profit that is returned into circulation. The real difference is not that we arbitrarily begin with one term or another, but that some expenditures are earmarked for consumption and others for production. The latter expenditures also constitute capital, capital without which no production could occur. To depict capital as money alone is to return to [a concept extant during] the primitive periods of political economy. The ancients could look with contempt on commercial profit and monetary interest payments, just as they could look with contempt at physical labor: they considered as worthy of a citizen only the administration of a household and preoccupation with politics. To be guided by such assumptions today, however, makes no sense.

This difficulty pales before another. Oddly enough, while Marx explains the increasing value of capital as a function of the circulation of money, he simultaneously asserts that it is impossible for capital to increase in value. If the value of commodities is determined by the labor expended in their production, then indeed, no matter how many times you transform a commodity into money and money into a commodity, the value will still be the same. This we see in a simple commodity transaction: a commodity purchased for consumption is equal in value to the commodity sold [in exchange for it]. There is no difference in the exchange-value of the commodities, only in their use-value: one person needs a certain product; someone else needs another product; that is why the exchange occurs. Only for the sake of greater convenience does the exchange occur through the agency of money. Therefore, even in a monetary transaction, the end term must equal the beginning term. However many intermediate equations may occur, we nevertheless will discover only relations of equality. Circulation, says Marx, does not generate value, and this entire intermediating process is nothing but a trick, for the buyer could purchase a commodity directly from the producer. The merchant places himself between buyer and seller as a parasite, and his gains are explicable as the result of his having cheated both of the other parties. By pure economic laws, there can be no profit here.

How so? the reader asks in amazement. Does it not cost the merchant much trouble and expense in order to bring a commodity, produced sometimes at the other end of the earth, to the buyer? Could just anyone who needs tea or cotton go after them to China or to America? Even a producer who lives right next door will not retail his own commodities. Retail sale again requires trouble and expenses. The producer hurries to sell his commodity to a wholesaler in order to reinvest the proceeds in production. Consequently, an intermediary between the producer and consumer is necessary, but this intermediary is beset by expenses, troubles, and risk. He needs buildings, ships, warehouses; the merchant must travel, make purchases, and estimate [future sales]. Can it really be true that for all this he will receive no compensation and that the commodity sold by him must, by economic laws, retain the same price as that for which he bought it? It is enough to ask such questions to have them answered. This is a matter about which scholarship, common sense, and everyday experience speak too loudly to ignore. But Karl Marx, flying in the face of scholarship, common sense, and everyday experience, bravely asserts that the merchant is nothing but a parasite and that the circulation of commodities can never generate new increments of value.

If we look at another form of profit, at interest on capital given out in loans, we shall see the same thing. Capital placed in a trunk and hoarded as a treasure does not earn interest. Why then does it accumulate when put into circulation? For the same reason that human labor receives a reward: because it becomes useful. According to Karl Marx's own admission, the only work of value is that which serves to benefit another; the same principle applies to money. A borrower needs capital; if he does not receive it, he may be forced to close his factory. He may even search far and wide for the necessary capital. In his need he turns to whoever has money. But the banking industry is not a charitable institution. If economic laws were to enjoin a lender to risk his money solely in order to receive back his principal, and this God knows when, then he would say to himself that it would be much better to leave the money in a trunk. Following Marx's so-called "economic laws" would thus guarantee that the borrower would not receive his money and would be ruined. But if it should occur to the potential borrower and the capitalist to violate "economic laws" and to agree on a fee for the use of the money, then both parties would benefit. The difference between the hoarder of money and the capitalist, Marx claims, is that the former acts stupidly and the second intelligently. That is so, but in what do the former's stupidity and the latter's intelligence consist? Why in one case does capital not accumulate and in the other accumulate? Simply because in the first case it remains without use, while in the second in becomes useful! Someone may object that a capitalist does not perform any work and, according to Marx's theory, work alone determines the value of products. But who is to blame if your theory turns out to be worthless? You have arbitrarily taken into account only the utility of labor and have disregarded the utility of capital!

Karl Marx understands, however, that cheating alone cannot explain such a universal phenomenon as interest payments on capital. One must deduce it from inherent laws governing the exchange of commodities. [Unfortunately,] neither commercial capital nor credit provides the necessary data for such deductions. Therefore, Marx turns to another form of capital, to factory production, which operates by means of the hiring of workers. Capitalist production begins, he states, where pure capitalists appear on the one hand, and where wage laborers appear on the other—that is, no earlier than the sixteenth century. Thus those forms [of capital] which Marx himself considers the original and most ancient ones—commercial capital and credit—remain unexplained.[36] Capital existed for thousands of years and carried interest payments, and all this happened contrary to economic laws! The author does not even bother to formulate an explanation that covers all forms. When he must prove that capital cannot accumulate by circulation, then he takes into account commercial capital alone; but when he must prove that accumulation occurs through the exploitation of the workers, he takes into account only industrial capital and pays no attention to the fact that what applies to the latter case is irrelevant to the former.

Factory production, in Marx's opinion, is peculiar in that it involves the purchase of a special sort of commodity, labor-power, which not only has a value itself but also is the source of new values.[37] Marx carefully tries to prove that a capitalist buys not labor but labor-power. When the contract is signed, labor itself does not yet exist and so cannot be sold, but when labor has begun, it has already been sold and so does not any longer belong to the worker. Labor is the substance of monetary value and the yardstick by which monetary value is measured, but it itself has no monetary value. Therefore, the common expression "cost of labor" is a misnomer. In fact, labor-power alone has monetary value, and it is the thing sold on the market.[38]

If the reader had imagined that labor-power is sold on the market only in countries where slavery exists, then he must now disabuse himself of that notion. In vain would we point out that labor-power, according to the author himself, remains in the continual possession of the laborer and that what is sold is only the temporary use of that labor-power—that is, work, for the author himself defines work as the *utilization* of labor-power.[39] Also in vain would we try to prove that the utilization of labor-power, in distinction from the renting of homes, machines and so on, is not something controlled exclusively by the capitalists, for the worker applies his own will and his own attention to manufacturing and controls his own appendages in the performance of his labor. In vain would we refute the childish objection that labor cannot be sold on the market if it does not yet exist, by pointing to contracts where not-yet-existing products are sold. In vain, finally, would we try to prove that it is pure nonsense to deny the value inherent in the effect of or the expenditure of labor-power, that is, to deny the value of something which is communicated to and made an integral part of the value of commodities, while recognizing the value of the source of that effect, labor-power itself, which tranquilly remains in the worker's body. Why the logic chopping here, when Karl Marx himself, in dozens of passages in his book, recognizes that a worker offers to a capitalist not labor-power but precisely a certain quantity of work measured in units of time? For example, on page 172 we read: "To the purchaser of a commodity belongs the use of the commodity, and the possessor of labor-power, in selling his labor, is selling in essence only the use-value [*Gebrachswerth*] thereof." On page 512: "Use-value, which a laborer sells to a capitalist, in actuality is not his labor-power but its function, a certain useful work." On page 564: "But it is clear that, depending on the length of the work day—that is, on the amount of time expended in labor, the very daily or weekly wage—can represent a quite different value of work—that is, quite different monetary sums for the same amount of work." On page 153, in a footnote, Marx even cites an extract from Hegel's *Philosophy of Right,* which says: "Single products of my particular physical and mental skill and of my power to act I can alienate to someone else and I can give him the use of my abilities for a restricted period, because, on the strength of this restriction, my abilities acquire an external relation to the totality and universality of my being. By alienating the whole of my time, as crystallized in my work, and everything I produced, I would be making into another's property the substance of my being, my universal activity and actuality, my personality."[40] And after all this Karl Marx nevertheless asserts that work is not being sold, but labor-power, that the former has no value, but the latter does!!

But why is this nonsense so important to the author? Because without it [his chain of reasoning will be broken]. If we say that work is sold and we ask about its value, then, according to the preceding theory, the answer cannot be in doubt. The value of labor is expressed in monetary terms, and we know that the price of money is a precise representation of labor time. Therefore, the question is answered very simply. If, for example, a quantity of gold equal to one ruble represents one working day, then it is clear that the value of a working day equals one ruble, and this would be true for the entire earth. Nothing further can be deduced from the theory. The formula is pure mathematics: if $A = B$, then $B = A$. But this result is what [Marx wants to avoid]. It has to be proven that if $A = B$, then B is not equal to A at all. To obtain the latter result, it is necessary to substitute the value of labor-power for the value of labor, and then one may reason in this fashion: labor-power is sold like a commodity; the value of any commodity is determined by the amount of labor required for its production; for production and for the maintenance of labor-power certain means of subsistence are required, and for the production of such means of subsistence labor is again necessary; therefore, the value of labor-power is determined by the amount of labor necessary for the production of the means of subsistence essential to the worker. Let us assume, for example, that the daily upkeep of a worker and his family requires six hours, or one-half a working day, which in money is expressed as one dollar. In that case, the value of one working day would equal one dollar or six hours of work.[41] But because a working day is equal to twelve hours, then one dollar represents both six hours and twelve hours of work. Half of a working day equals the whole of a working day.

The reader sees at once the implications of substituting the value of labor-power for the value of labor. Had it been explicitly claimed that "twelve hours of labor are exchanged for ten or for six hours of labor," then the resulting "equation of unequal quantities," as Marx recognizes, "would not only destroy any determination of value, but this self-refuting contradiction could not even be expressed or formulated as a law."[42] Our presentation has led us indirectly to this very conclusion. After all, Marx himself admits that "we reach from the first view the absurd result that labor that produces a value of six shillings itself has a value of only three shillings." But having introduced, by means of an intermediate term, another absurdity—namely, the substitution of the value of labor-power for the value of labor, Marx may in a certain fashion hide the first absurdity from the view of the naive reader. With the help of the reasoning presented above, Marx can pass off the first proposition as an immutable law of capitalist production.

Marx notes, however, that this "economic law" is subject to certain modifications. Having established the general principle that the value of labor-power is determined by the *average* amount of social labor necessary to produce the means of subsistence necessary to maintain that labor-power, he then says that this determination constitutes the *minimum limit* of the value of labor-power. At such a price, labor-power stands even *below* its actual value, for it cannot maintain itself at its normal quality. The normal quality is determined not by essential physical requirements alone, but also by local and temporary conditions, by the degree of a society's development, and chiefly by the *customs* and *expectations* of the free working class. Therefore, Karl Marx concludes, the determination of the value of labor-power, *unlike that of other commodities,* includes a historical and ethical element. It would seem that this [admission alone] would be enough to refute Marx's entire theory. The author himself recognizes that the value of labor-power is determined not by the amount of work necessary for its maintenance but by the customs and expectations of the working class. Yet in spite of this, Marx insists on the validity of his "economic law," and he bases all his conclusions on it.

A direct consequence of this "law" is that no matter how long work may continue, its value is always the same, for its value is determined by the quantity of labor needed to produce the essential means of subsistence—that is, by six or perhaps eight or ten hours of labor, depending upon the circumstances. If we ask: "What is the value of this latter work incorporated in the means of subsistence?" then we receive the answer that it again is determined by the amount of work necessary for the maintenance of these latter workers—that is, again six or perhaps eight or ten hours of labor. Thus, six, eight, ten, and twelve hours of labor have exactly the same value. If a worker has worked a total of three hours in a day, then in this case the value of his labor-power would be determined by the means of subsistence essential for his maintenance; but then the worker would be living at the expense of the capitalist. The duration of work by which the value of products is determined, according to this theory, is not a factor in determining the value of labor received by the capitalist.

The innocent worker is unaware of his labor's amazing property: however long he may work, the value of his work according to "economic laws" is the same. But the more discerning capitalist soon guesses this fact, and bases all his calculations upon it. Karl Marx describes in detail how this happens. A capitalist wants to produce, for example, cotton yarn. For this he needs, first of all, material. He goes to the market and buys, let us say, ten pounds of cotton, which costs ten shillings, representing the amount of labor necessary to produce the designated quantity of raw cotton. This sum must enter into the value of the future product. Then it is necessary to allot a sum for machines and other capital. This capital also represents a quantity of accumulated labor, which again must be included in the cost of the future commodity. Let us assume that to process ten pounds of raw cotton, an amount of labor accumulated in capital equal to two shillings must be expended. In all, twelve shillings represents the value of two working days or of twenty-four hours of labor. Finally, one has to add the cost of labor to process the cotton. The price of the working day purchased by the capitalist equals three shillings, representing the six hours of work necessary for the daily maintenance of the worker. If the production of ten pounds of cotton yarn requires only six hours of labor, then we have to add another three shillings to the cost of the product. The total cost is fifteen shillings. This is the actual exchange-value of ten pounds of yarn, the value representing the sum of all labor expended on its production.

In selling the yarn at this price, the capitalist receives compensation for all his expenses, but no profit.[43]

"Our capitalist is surprised," says Karl Marx. The reader is also. In fact, how can one not be surprised when, after all his trouble, risk, and expenses, the capitalist, according to the ledger presented above, should not receive any profit? In such a case, it would not be worthwhile to produce [the yarn at all]. Of course, against this accounting one may make numerous objections. But instead of a serious discussion of the objections, Karl Marx offers us only the most vulgar depiction of the capitalist, who having been deceived in his expectations, lashes out in every direction. He threatens that he will not produce anything more; he "catechizes" [the workers]; he "becomes importunate"; finally, he himself assumes the demeanor of a worker and demands payment for his labor. Although Karl Marx says in another place that the capitalist is forced to spend all his time supervising someone else's work and the sale of the products of that work,[44] here the capitalist's pretension to a monetary reward is dismissed simply by the observation that "his own overlooker and his own manager try to hide their smiles." But soon a smile dawns on the capitalist's face. As a practical man, he has guessed the answer to his problem. He has bought the entire working day for three shillings, that is, twelve hours of labor, and only six hours of labor have entered into the value of the ten pounds of yarn. Consequently, the worker will work the remaining six hours for the capitalist for free. The additional ten pounds of yarn processed in the second six hours will also be sold for fifteen shillings; but this time, the capitalist will have spent only twelve shillings on raw material and capital costs, and he will have paid nothing for the labor. Thus, strictly holding to "economic laws," the capitalist has duped the worker: the value produced by the worker winds up in the capitalist's pocket. "The trick has finally succeeded," exclaims Karl Marx. "Money has been transformed into capital."[45]

Indeed, a trick has been played here, only not by the capitalist but by the writer, who, moving from absurdity to absurdity, has finally arrived at the conclusion that one-half equals one whole. It would seem that if a half-day, or six hours of labor, equals three shillings or, say, five pounds of bread, then a whole day or twelve hours of labor would equal six shillings or ten pounds of bread; but here it turns out that both half the day and the entire day equal only five pounds of bread. If a mathematician made such a conclusion in his calculations, he would no doubt decide that there is a mistake in his figures. But the disciple of Hegel is not fettered by such restraints. He simply passes off a contradiction that was born in his own mind as a contradiction inherent in the subject. True, not a shadow of Hegel's logic remains here; but who will bother to analyze that, especially these days when all metaphysical fantasy, including logic, is considered the property of the archive?

But Karl Marx himself explains how the trick was done. He says: "But the past labor that is embodied in the labor-power, and the living labor that it can call into action; the daily cost of maintaining it, and its daily expenditure in work, are two totally different things. The former determines the exchange-value of the labor-power, the latter is its use-value." But [Marx has argued elsewhere that] "use-value and exchange-value are two incommensurable quantities." What is the use-value of labor-power? "In fact," says Karl Marx, "the use-value which the worker sells to the capitalist is not his labor-power but its effect, a certain useful work," but this work has the property that it creates value. This last property constitutes the special use-value of labor: it is a source not only of value but of more value than it has itself. In other words, the utility generated by labor not only compensates for the expenditure of labor-power—that is, for its exchange-value, but it also produces new values. Let us now recall what we were told at the beginning of the book. We heard that in the exchange-value of commodities was not a single iota of use-value; that the value of commodities is determined not by the utility of the work [involved in their production] but solely by the amount of work expended upon them; that the productivity of labor is not taken into economic account but is irrelevant to the economic equation. This is the theory to which the laborer adheres when he is selling his labor-power. He accepts payment for his labor-power, which he treats as a commodity, not as something productive. He realizes its exchange-value and parts with its use-value. But the capitalist, when he determines the price of his commodity, proceeds on an entirely different theory. He takes into account the significance of labor-power not as a commodity but as something productive, not as exchange-value but as use-value. Is it surprising after this that one and the same labor-power acquires two quite different values? The worker thinks that prices are determined by exchange-value, but the capitalist thinks that they are determined by use-value—by what Marx himself calls two incommensurable quantities.

The reader sees that the "trick," in essence, is rather simple. Its formula is the following: if we want to prove that ½ A = A, then, in the equation A = A, we must divide both members into two halves; then, talking of the first member, we will assert that one of the two halves is entirely unimportant in the equation and can therefore be disregarded, while the other half must be retained. The reader might not guess this if the formula is stretched out over 822 pages.

And this unfathomable rubbish is passed off on us as a strictly scholarly conclusion!!

One can only ask oneself whether [the deception] is conscious or unconscious. Apparently the author himself is hopelessly confused, for having said that the special use-value of labor is its capacity to produce new values, Marx concludes: "We now see that the difference between labor, considered on the one hand as producing utilities and on the other hand as creating value, a difference which we discovered by our analysis of a commodity, resolves itself into a distinction between two aspects of the process of production."[46] In fact, the opposite is the case: what was formerly distinct has again been conflated, so that Marx now arrives at the utterly "absurd result that labor which produces a value of six shillings itself has only the value of three shillings."[47] One of two things follows: either the value of labor-power is determined solely by its exchange-value, and not by its use-value, in which case the exchange-value enters into labor exerted [in making the product] and into products themselves, for they represent a certain sum of labor; or, if the value of commodities is determined by the use-value, that is, by their utility, which is actually the case in the real world, then the principle [of use-value] also applies to labor-power, for in a commodity, understood as a product of labor, there can be nothing that was not in labor, and in labor there can be nothing that was not in labor-power. "Out of nothing, nothing can be created," Karl Marx says. "The creation of value is the transformation of labor-power into labor."[48]

The same reasoning applies to capital, which, just like labor, is an agent of production. If only exchange-value and not use-value enters into the value of labor, then the same thing applies to capital. In that case, capital will yield no interest, just as labor does not produce any surplus of value; labor only supports itself. But if the value of commodities is determined by the use-value of labor—if labor, beyond its own maintenance, produces or can produce a surplus of value—then obviously the same is true of capital: besides the return of the principal amount invested, the capitalist receives an additional compensation for the use of his capital. But this is precisely what Karl Marx will not admit. The principle that he applies to labor, he refuses to apply to capital. In his opinion, "Capital is dead labor that, vampire-like, only lives by sucking the blood of living labor."[49] Only the latter is really productive: living labor not only produces new value but also *transfers* the exchange-value of capital to products. The first activity it accomplishes through its quantity, the second by means of its quality. But because the quality of labor is freely given, then the transfer of capital's exchange-value is nothing other than a gift which the worker gives to the capitalist. The worker is unaware that "living labor's capacity to preserve value at the same time it adds it is a gift of Nature." The whole process occurs behind the worker's back. But the capitalist takes advantage of it to cover his expenses. As proof, Marx notes that when the means of production are improved, the productive power of labor increases: during a given time more material is processed and greater value is transferred to it, yet the cost of labor remains the same, only now it is spread out over a greater quantity of commodities. Conversely, if the productive value of labor remains the same, but if the cost of raw material increases, then the same labor, processing the same quantity of material, nevertheless transfers greater value to its product.[50]

This last example could also have been cited as evidence against the author's theory. Greater value is transferred here not as a result of any improvement in labor but simply because, quite independently of labor, the cost of raw material has increased; consequently, labor is not relevant here. But the first example also proves very little. If with improved tools the same worker, in the same amount of time, does more than he formerly did, then this shows that greater productivity comes not from his hands but from his tools. A child with a machine can do more than the strongest and most skilled worker without a machine. Therefore, [in this case] the value of labor also stays the same, or perhaps even decreases. In reality, the transfer of the value of invested capital to a product is accomplished not by the worker but by the capitalist who demands for his commodity a price that will cover his expenses; otherwise, he would not be a manufacturer. Karl Marx sees in this transfer a kind of physical act akin to the "transmigration of souls";[51] but he is forced to confess that, strictly speaking, there is no reproduction of values here. The former use-value has disappeared; a new value has been produced in which the former exchange-value appears, but this reproduction is only *apparent*.[52] He forgets even his earlier theory according to which the value of commodities is determined not by actually accomplished personal labor but by the average social labor necessary for production. Consequently, the actual worker cannot transfer any actual values; yet even if he could, should the average socially necessary labor decrease, the value transferred would be virtually nothing, despite the natural gift of living labor to preserve value.

From all this Marx draws the conclusion that the materials and tools of production cannot impart to commodities more value than they themselves have. If partial depreciation [of a machine's value] occurs during the use of a machine, for example, then only that portion of the depreciation is transferred into the value of its products. According to Marx, a curious phenomenon arises during this process: during production the machine depreciates only *in part*, yet it is *wholly* at the service of the productive process. The former [the amount of depreciation] represents its exchange-value, which is transferred to the value of the products; the latter [the machine as a unit] is use-value, which operates for free. However useful a tool of production may be, its value is determined not by the process in which it is involved as an agent but by the process from which it comes as a product. In the productive process, the tool serves only as use-value, as a thing with useful properties; yet if it had no value before the beginning of the productive process, it could not very well impart any value to the product.[53] The greater is the productive value of the machine in comparison with simple tools, Marx contends, the greater the extent of its free service. Only in large industry has man learned how to force the products of his own expended labor to operate for free on a large scale, a scale resembling that on which natural forces operate.[54]

Why, however, does the use-value of labor enter into the price of commodities but the use-value of capital not enter into it? Why does the former not only compensate for its expenditure but also produce surplus value, while the latter only compensates for its value but surrenders its surplus for nothing? In a word, why of the two agents of production is labor valued both as product and as producer, while capital is valued as product alone? One cannot plausibly argue that labor is a genuine agent of production, whereas capital is only a dead tool. We have already seen that that which Marx calls the productive force of labor is, in essence, the productive force of capital. Marx himself recognizes that with the introduction of machines, roles change: the former tool now becomes the main agent, while labor-power is transformed into a tool of the machine.[55] He also recognizes the greater productivity of labor in a large factory to be a consequence of capital which gathers together scattered [productive] units and binds them into an integrated whole.[56] Why then should the capitalist do all this for free? Obviously, here too, Marx is using a double standard of measurement. In the one case [the discussion of capital] he rejects the very logic that he applies in the next case [the discussion of labor], solely because it is convenient for him as author.

Thus Marx concludes that profit in production can come only from labor, and if the capitalist receives it, then this is nothing but the illegitimate appropriation of the fruits of another's labor—that is, of another's property. The worker uses part of the working day for himself, to cover his living expenses; the remainder, which Marx calls the "surplus labor time," he offers as a gift to the capitalist, and this is the source of the capitalist's profit. Karl Marx calls it a hidden surplus.[57] There are, to be sure, phenomena that contradict this explanation. If one accepts the logic of Marx's theory, one would have to contend that it would be advantageous to the capitalist to use as many workers as possible in his factory and not to replace them by machines. Marx says that "it is impossible to squeeze out of two workers as great an excess of value as out of twenty-four. If each of twenty-four workers in the course of twelve hours gives only one hour of surplus labor, then together they give twenty-four hours of surplus labor, whereas the total labor of two workers equals only twenty-four hours."[58] In reality, however, the contrary is true: it is more advantageous to the capitalist to employ two workers rather than twenty-four. But this again is one of those "inherent contradictions" of capitalist production! The theory remains intact in spite of everything.

From such a perspective it is not difficult to depict all industry as a series of robberies and extortions. And that is what Karl Marx does. A free contract that determines wages is, in his eyes, a mere legal fiction that keeps up the appearance of the worker's independence. "The Roman slave was bound by chains, the wage laborer is bound to his owner by indivisible threads."[59] The "vampire" who has chained himself to the worker will not be detached while there remains a single muscle, a single vein, a single drop of blood for profit."[60] We shall not follow this narrative line. The reader can judge for himself the scholarly merit of a presentation highlighted by the theory we have analyzed.

In conclusion, Marx attempts to demonstrate, just as Lassalle did, that "capitalist production" has a purely [transient] historical significance. He ignores antiquity and the Middle Ages and begins directly with the sixteenth century, when the distinction between capitalists and free laborers first appeared. A precondition for this distinction was the formation of a class of proletarians. According to Marx, this class is formed as a result of the expropriation of agricultural laborers, who had formerly possessed land. The wholesale expulsion of peasants from the land is therefore the basis of the entire process. Marx briefly presents the history of this expropriation in England, where it had its "classic form."[61]

It is well known that in England peasants were emancipated earlier than in other countries, but were emancipated without land. It is also well known that landed property [in England] is concentrated in relatively few hands. But capitalist production is not to blame for this concentration; rather, the aristocratic structure of society is at fault. This is a sacrifice that England made for the sake of its political development. On the European continent there is nothing similar. In most cases on the Continent peasants were liberated with land. There the main problem was not the concentration of landed property in a few hands but the limitless fragmentation of land. All these facts are well attested. But Marx carefully moves around them. He limits himself to England alone because otherwise the so-called historical development of capitalist production would have turned out to be pure fantasy.

In England itself he ignores the economic reasons for the "agricultural revolution" and contents himself with a discussion of the coercion used to effect it.[62] Surprisingly, we learn that English landowners found sheep more advantageous than laborers, and they therefore restricted the latter in favor of the former. The landowners did not suspect that labor-power alone yields surplus value and that one cannot extract surplus work time from sheep. To our still greater surprise, Karl Marx relates that in the most recent times, being motivated by insatiable greed for profit, landowners have begun to turn sheep pasture into hunting wilds. It would seem that these vacant lands, which are not touched by human hands, can yield an income. Finally, instead of hiring laborers themselves and extorting surplus work time, the landowners prefer to lease their lands to farmers who do not work for their landlords but only pass them money. The farmers are genuine agrarian capitalists. But they have not resorted to any use of force for their own enrichment. If they have deprived anyone of landed property, it is only themselves. A farmer's capital in England yields higher interest than does land. Therefore, the petty landowner not infrequently prefers to sell his parcel, and so the petty landowner yields to the prosperous farmer. That is one reason for the disappearance of the class of petty landowners in England. But Marx is silent about this. Having no pretext to attribute the enrichment of farmers to compulsory "expropriation," he mentions another cause—namely, that in the sixteenth century, when the cost of gold fell and consequently inflation affected the prices of other commodities, long-term contracts for the renting of land continued to be paid at the former nominal price; therefore, the farmers earned windfall profits.[63] It turns out once again that one may become rich not by the exploitation of workers alone. Here the capitalists made fortunes at the landowners' expense.

Finally, factory production is also established through the "expropriation" of independent small producers who work with their own tools. Here the so-called expropriation consists in the inability of small producers to withstand competition from the more profitable factory production; therefore, the small producers go out of business. Small manufactories are brought together under the roof of larger factories.[64] But Marx admits that the first large-scale capitalists actually came from the ranks of small producers, ranks they were able to leave by gradually increasing their scale of production.[65] Here too, [Marx argues,] the source of enrichment is brute force, the culmination of which is the colonial system. "Force," Marx says, "is the midwife of every old society pregnant with a new one. Force itself is an economic power."[66]

Thus it turns out that the historical accumulation of capital "means only the expropriation of the immediate producers, i.e., the dissolution of private property based on the labor of its owner."[67] At a certain stage of economic development this scattered form of property becomes inadequate. Its profits are too meager; therefore, it also has to give way to the more concentrated form of capitalist production. But even this last, in its turn, is only a transitional stage of development; it must also yield to a higher form. The principle of exploitation, applied formerly to petty landowners, continues to operate; now it must be applied to the capitalists themselves. Capitalist production itself paves the way: as a result of competition, small firms are ruined by larger firms. The result, on the one hand, is a constant diminution of the number of capitalists directing industrial production for their own benefit; on the other hand, [the result is] an increase in poverty, oppression, and humiliation [of the workers]. Yet accompanying [the workers' impoverishment] is the growing revolt of the working class, now already united and organized by the effects of capitalist production. What was formerly scattered production has already become societal in scope. In this new system, the growing monopoly of capital becomes an unbearable fetter for the workers. The chain is ultimately broken. "The hour of capitalist private property has passed," exclaims Marx. "The expropriators are themselves expropriated."[68]

The new form now taken by production constitutes to a certain extent a return to the first stage. Workers again receive control of the tools of production, but this time the workers are no longer scattered but united. The tools of production are again made into their property—not personal property, but socialized property. The path to this destination has been paved by capitalist production itself, which united the scattered workers in masses and thus undermined itself. The completion of this last process is a "negation of the negation."[69]

We see that everything occurs here in accordance with Hegel's dialectic. Exploitation, playing the role of the principle of negation, is the mainspring of all economic development, and it also has three classical stages. We must believe that from the earliest times until the sixteenth century there are only independent workers, however disunited, who are also owners of land and of tools; then they are deprived of their property for the good of a few capitalists; finally, the capitalists in turn are deprived of property for the good of the united workers. This third and highest stage of development is the negation of the negation.

Karl Marx assures us that this "negation of capitalistic production occurs on its own accord, as the necessary outcome of a natural process,"[70] but he does not explain to us by virtue of what laws this is accomplished. In reality, we do not yet see any expropriation of capital. True, we are told that, as a consequence of competition and the concentration of capital in the same hands, the number of capitalists is constantly diminishing while, on the other hand, the number of proletarians is constantly increasing. Yet we also know that in modern Europe, also as a result of capitalist production, the middle class, which is the chief actor both in industrial production and in the political sphere, is growing all the time. In any case, if the competition provided by large capital can destroy small capital, then it is not known by what economic means large capital will pass into the control of the impoverished workers. Competition is not a factor here. The solution of the problem can be reached if we remember that "force is an economic power" that serves as the midwife of the new society. Then all is quite simple. "The transformation of scattered private property, arising from individual labor, into capitalist private property is, naturally, a process incomparably more protracted, violent, and difficult than the transformation of capitalistic private property, already practically resting on socialized production, into socialized property. In the former case, we had the expropriation of the mass of the people by a few usurpers; in the latter, we have the expropriation of a few usurpers by the mass of the people."[71]

This very same prescription was offered [at the end of the eighteenth century] by Marat in hopes of making humanity happy. Marat thought that it was worthwhile to cut off a few thousand heads so that humanity might flourish. But the most immediate result of the practical application of this ideology was that those who cut off others' heads soon lost their own heads as well; moreover, the republic collapsed, the very republic the revolutionaries had hoped to prop up [by their tactic of executing political adversaries]. Today the mere memory of this remedy serves as one of the most formidable obstacles to human freedom. Karl Marx's prescription, the honor for whose invention belongs not to him but to his predecessors, the French socialists, has not been applied on the vast scale [that Marx wishes]. But in 1848 revolutionaries proclaimed the principle of the expropriation of the rich for the benefit of the poor. There was even an unsuccessful attempt to implement this principle. The result, as is well known, was just as lamentable as in the first instance. A frightened society threw itself into the arms of despotism. And heretofore the memory of these events is an evil spectre that inspires in the prosperous class distrust toward democratic institutions. The social question has always been and will always be the stumbling block of democracy. When state power is found in the hands of the have-nots, they need considerable moral virtue and a high level of education to recognize that they must not turn that power into a tool for their own enrichment. Yet that is just what utopians, who, like Karl Marx, take themselves to be the workers' leaders, urge the working class to do. The utopians take advantage of the workers' ignorance in order to propagate under the name of science teachings that are destructive to human societies.

This does not mean, however, that socialism is only an accidental delusion of the human mind. As we have already noted on more than one occasion and as the preceding text has made clear, socialism is a necessary moment in the development of thought, but a moment that is nevertheless radically false in its content. It is an extreme version of one-sided Idealism; it calls for the negation of the particular in the name of the universal, the absorption of the individual by the state, and, finally, for the negation of history itself in the name of a fantastic future. Later we shall study socialism in its genuine fatherland, in France. Traveling by another route, the French arrived at the same results [as the

Germans]. In the French socialists, who were the real founders of this movement, the utopian character of the ideology is even more obvious. Yet in French thinking there are also certain redeeming features: a lively regard for reality, a sincere love of humanity, sometimes profound opinions and accurate criticisms [of existing society], and, finally, a genuine creativity, though with a preponderance of imagination over thought. With the move onto German soil, these positive traits disappear. The Germans, or one ought to say the radical German Jews (for I treat only them here) have thrown out all the adornments [of French thought]. Their intention was to build a social utopia on purely scientific grounds. But because the task is impossible, the only result of their efforts is a brutal, drily pedantic, shameful lie. Karl Marx speaks of "the vulgar bourgeois view of the political-economist," of his "limited mind."[72] Yet when confronted by Marx's pseudoscientific criticism, the bourgeois political-economist can point triumphantly to his own scholarly achievement. Anyone who can think logically and understand what he is reading cannot fail to see that the purely scientific approaches [of the bourgeois political-economists] stand immeasurably higher than the arrogant and also pedantic sophistry of their adversaries. In Germany socialism, which has invested itself with scientific terminology, has managed to reveal its own imperfections. Only superficiality and ignorance can win it a following. That does not mean that the fate of the lower classes deserves no attention from theoreticians and statesmen. But the resolution of such questions must not be sought in a perverse interpretation of the economic laws governing human societies.

Part Four **Excerpts from *Property and State***

Liberty

We are social beings: this is the first, incontestable and universally recognized premise from which any investigation of social relationships must proceed.[1] In the animal kingdom many species live in isolation; but human beings live only in society, for only in society can specifically human capacities manifest themselves and develop.

Yet in the animal kingdom we also encounter societies, even ones with very complex structures, that have reached the point of dividing tasks among members. That is why comparison is necessary, for only by comparison can one make clear the peculiarities of human community.

The most obvious essential difference between animal societies and associations of human beings is that members of animal species live in identical structures and are governed by the same laws. These laws are established not by the animals themselves but by nature, which has inculcated in animals certain instincts that undeviatingly direct them toward a predetermined objective. By virtue of these innate instincts, which constitute for them an inherent, immutable law, animals behave in identical fashion. In societies [of a given species], therefore, there is no development. In fact, considering the entire animal kingdom as a whole, we may even observe a paradox. The most complicated and sophisticated societies are found among animals of the lower orders, among bees and ants; conversely, mammals, which stand closest to human beings, live either in herds without any organization whatsoever, or even in isolation. Animals that occupy if not the highest, then at least a very high niche in the animal kingdom—that is, lions, tigers, foxes—live alone. Apparently, the explanation for this phenomenon is that among the more sophisticated animals, the force of instinct diminishes. An animal frees itself from the power of instinct; it develops an individual identity and thus weakens its links with other individuals of the same species. To re-create this link with other individuals requires a degree of intellectual development which is unknown in the animal kingdom.

Intellectual development occurs in the human domain. Unlike animal societies, human societies are by their very nature subject to change. Not only does each individual society have its own identity and its own laws, but one and the same society over time will pass through quite different forms of community organization. The reason is that we create our own laws and change these laws at our discretion.

But that does not mean that the structure of human societies and their governing norms are matters of human caprice. Nature has not deprived us of principles to guide our life. In our soul there is also the natural law which should serve us as a guide to action; but this law does not bind us to an immutable course of action that we must necessarily follow; we may deviate from it. Obedience to the natural law is not a matter of blind instinct that always operates in the same way, but a matter of conscious deliberation and liberty. We obey the natural law to the extent that we consciously recognize it and to the extent that we wish to observe it. And because consciousness and will are subject to change and development, then the laws governing human societies also are subject to alteration and improvement.

Thus the fundamental mark of human community—the characteristic which profoundly divides the animal kingdom from the kingdom of the spirit—is liberty. We human beings fashion our own law and choose whether or not to observe this law. Hence it is clear that any treatise on human community must begin with the question of liberty. What is liberty? Whence does it spring into existence? Where are its limits? What are its consequences? These are the questions that confront us as soon as we embark upon an investigation of social relationships, questions which have decisive significance for our entire interpretation of human community.

These questions have a purely philosophical component. Empirical observation alone will not get us very far. By empirical observation alone we cannot evaluate freedom and slavery. In history we see examples of even highly enlightened peoples to whom humankind owes its greatest achievements, and whose entire social structure was nevertheless based on slavery. Which of these two principles harmonizes with human nature? Toward which principle should we strive? And if human nature demands liberty, then what is the origin of slavery and what is its justification?

To answer such questions we must turn from the historical record to human nature as such. By what notions should we be guided in this inquiry? Having been forsaken by external experience, which presents us a contradictory picture, can we rely on inner experience? Even partisans of the empirical method will tell us that, for purposes of such an inquiry, inner experience can be deceptive. If we make reference to the fact that each individual considers himself or herself free, then they will answer that the consciousness of liberty exists only because we often do not recognize the real causes of our actions, which causes lead us to behave in one way or another according to the laws of natural necessity. Inner experience, like external experience, only furnishes us with sensations; it does not disclose to us their causes; and the question of liberty requires comprehension of the real causes of an action. It is crucial to understand the very essence of liberty and its link with our hidden nature: otherwise we will be unable to determine its imperatives and its limits.

To resolve this question it is vital, therefore, to rise into the suprasensory world, to enter into the realm of metaphysics, which alone can elucidate our problem. If this world is closed to us, if metaphysics is nothing but the empty rumination of the human mind, then the question of liberty must remain for us eternally insoluble; if so, then our investigation of the human community will lack a guiding principle. The science of society will be transformed into a chaos of contradictory phenomena.

That is what we see in contemporary literature. With the decline of philosophy the question of the nature and source of liberty was dismissed. Some thinkers treat liberty as a fact, and upon that fact they base their entire teaching; but because this fact has not been the subject of a proper investigation and because it has not been grounded upon the appropriate foundations, it is apparent that all the deductions following from it lack solid foundation, and the result is an edifice of thought built upon a completely arbitrary assumption. Other thinkers treat only the external manifestations of liberty; but because its inner nature remains unplumbed, they cannot deduce any guiding principles from it: their results are confined to vague propositions that cannot withstand criticism. Still others, without even trying to penetrate to the core of the subject, simply reject inner liberty on purely logical grounds, all the while paradoxically clinging to external liberty, as if the latter did not draw its power and significance solely from the former. Finally, there are thinkers who, holding to pure empiricism, absolutely dismiss the question of liberty and yet imagine that they are still able to say something of value about the human community. One may come across huge sociological and even legal treatises in which the question of liberty is not even raised or in which it is mentioned only in passing, as an unimportant subject. The reader, upon opening such a book, can be certain not to find in it a single word of genuine scientific value.

Therefore, in investigating the laws of the human community we cannot get along without philosophy. At the very threshold of inquiry we are confronted by the question of liberty, which must be resolved on the basis of philosophical proofs. How shall we approach this question? The first step is to define the term itself.

Liberty is to be understood in two senses: as external and inner liberty, as freedom of actions and as freedom of will. The former consists of the independence of one's actions from another's will, or in the determination of actions by a person's own will—in short, in the possibility to do what one wishes. The latter consists of the independence of the will from external forces, or in the will's capacity to define itself in its own fashion.

Certain philosophers reject the very notion of inner liberty, and recognize only external liberty. In this category is the leading representative of sensationalism in the modern period, [John] Locke. He claims that liberty is the ability to do or not to do what one wishes—that is, to harmonize one's acts with the dictates of reason—but it is absurd to speak about the freedom to want or not to want as if one will could be defined only in terms of another will. Locke even asserts that to raise the question of the freedom of the will is tantamount to asking whether a dream is swift or a virtue is square. In his view, liberty resides not in a capacity but in an agent, that is, in a rational being who is free to the degree that his or her actions are in harmony with his or her wants and unfree to the degree that these actions are imposed by an external force.[2]

In elaborating this theory, Locke himself shows that a person's will, in its most rudimentary manifestations—that is, in its blind impulses—may be restrained or directed by a higher will—that is, by a rational principle. Here he falls into self-contradiction. Let us examine his arguments; they offer us the key to analyzing these phenomena.

Locke bases his opinion on an analysis of volition. Volition is the movement of a will directed toward a certain action. Volition is distinguished from desire because a person may voluntarily do something contrary to what he desires. What determines volition? The agent himself or herself—that is, mind. And what determines the mind in its decisions? The sense of ease or of uneasiness: the former prompts a person to remain in the same condition as before, the latter prompts that person to change his or her condition. The latter Locke also calls desire, and he shows that it is the sole motive for action, for desire is nothing other than striving for happiness, and happiness is the ultimate goal of every living being. Thus, having distinguished desire from will, Locke again conflates the two terms. But he makes another error here which gives the issue an entirely new twist. A powerful desire may move the will, but it does not always do so. For reason, as is evident from experience, has the capacity to restrain desire and to weigh various desired objectives. "But yet," Locke says, "there is a case wherein a man is at liberty in respect of willing, and that is, the choosing of a remote good, as an end to be pursued. Here a man may suspend the act of his choice from being determined for or against the thing proposed, till he has examined whether it be really of a nature in itself and consequences to make him happy or no." According to Locke, the mind's judgment based upon an evaluation of good and evil is the source of all liberty; it is this that is improperly called freedom of will. We are free because we may determine ourselves by the actions of our own mind, for the end of liberty consists in the attainment of that good which we choose for ourselves.[3]

It turns out, then, that there exists a will above will. Actions are directed by desires, but above desires there is a higher faculty to which the prerogative of final decision belongs. Thus freedom consists not only in the direction of actions in accordance with desires but in the direction of desires in accordance with the mind's informed dictates. A man may not only restrain his desires but even alter them. Locke asks "'whether it be in a man's power to change the pleasantness and unpleasantness that accompanies any sort of action?' And as to that," he answers, "it is plain, in many cases he can. . . . It is a mistake to think, that men cannot change the displeasingness or indifferency that is in actions into pleasure and desire, if they will do but what is in their power. A due consideration will do it in some cases; and practice, application, and custom in most."[4]

Thus the most obvious facts of consciousness show us that whereas, like other animals, we possess the ability to control our actions, we also, being rational beings, have the ability to control ourselves. The first capacity constitutes our external liberty; the second our inner liberty. And only the latter makes the former truly significant: it transforms external liberty into a principle or an imperative. As fact, external liberty exists for animals as well as for human beings. There are some animals living in freedom and others of the same species living in cages, in stalls, in harness. But here there is no issue of principle. We do not consider such a difference to be an injustice toward animals in captivity any more than we consider it an injustice that certain animals are killed for food while others continue to enjoy life. It cannot be said that long life is the only condition appropriate to the nature of living beings, because if the purpose of nature was for each living being to live and enjoy life, then it would not have created certain animals to prey upon others and would not have made this carnivorous activity a precondition for the survival not only of the predators but also of the species preyed upon, for without predators they would reproduce without limit.

Among humans, however, external liberty is not merely a given but an inner imperative. The actual situation may contradict liberty; from the beginning of history to our time we see millions of people living in slavery. Had we been guided solely by empirical data, we might have said that liberty and servitude are equally rooted in human nature. But despite the empirical evidence, we claim that human beings should be free, and we make this imperative the goal of the development of human societies.

What is the justification of this imperative? In arguing the case for the natural freedom of human beings, Locke says that "there is nothing more evident, than that Creatures of the same species and rank promiscuously born to all the same advantages of Nature, and the use of the same faculties, should also be equal one among another without Subordination or Subjection."[5] But such reasoning also applies equally well to animals, and we do not demand universal liberty for animals. Locke himself subsequently admits that this principle does not apply to children, who live in natural subordination to their parents. The justification he offers for this exception is that children do not yet possess reason, which alone can guide them in the proper exercise of liberty. He then concludes that "the Freedom of Man and Liberty of acting according to his own Will, is grounded on his having Reason, which is able to instruct him in that Law he is to govern himself by, and make him know how far he is left to the freedom of his own Will."[6]

Consequently, the imperative of external liberty is based upon inner liberty. The source of the latter is reason, which restrains blind impulses and indicates to an individual the law by which he or she must be governed and the goals which he or she must bear in mind. Only about human beings can it be said that they are by nature free, for we alone, in contrast to animals, are rational beings capable of self-determination on the basis of inner, rational decisions.

What is the content of this law and what is a rational exercise of the will in contrast to [blind] impulses? The law is that which makes our actions independent from private goals and desires but subordinates them to a higher principle originating in pure reason, and therefore has the character of absolute truth: consciousness of duty, an ethical law which for Locke and in general for the empirical school, despite all attempts to grasp it, has proven an eternal enigma, but which was revealed in all its profundity by the father of modern metaphysics, [Immanuel] Kant. Reason is capable of controlling impulses only because it constitutes an independent force possessing its own law, one that is supreme, absolutely prescriptive, and absolutely prohibitive. This law is inextricably linked with liberty. It presupposes the capacity to renounce all particular impulses and to determine oneself on the basis of a rational recognition of one's duty. Only under this condition can it be understood as an absolute imperative for every rational being. Actions possess moral dignity only to the degree that they are freely undertaken: a coerced action is not a moral action. This is the basis for conceptions like responsibility for one's actions, liability, merit, and guilt—conceptions upon which all our moral judgments are based and upon which all legal codes depend. The consciousness of inner liberty revealed by metaphysics is also a phenomenon observable in the world. All human societies depend upon it and without it they would disintegrate.

But does inner liberty really exist? Perhaps its apparent existence is illusory?

Many claim that is the case; but in rejecting inner liberty as a phantom, its adversaries refer not to lessons drawn from experience, which [lessons], as noted earlier, do not go beyond phenomena and cannot reveal to us the inner foundations of the will's activity, but they refer to the law of necessity, to which all phenomena of the world are subject. Meanwhile, the law of necessity, which itself is a construct based upon philosophical speculation,[7] deals with [physical] phenomena, not with the inner essence of things. This law declares that every phenomenon has its cause—that is, is the effect of a certain force; but what determines the action of that force? Why does it behave in one way and not another? About this the law of causation says nothing; empirical science contents itself with the proposition that [producing a particular behavior] is the property of a force. Thus everything comes down to the nature of a motive force. This nature can be of various types: there are blind forces and rational forces. Blind forces, by virtue of their blindness, cannot operate except according to the laws of necessity, inherent and external; rational forces, however, operate according to the law of rational consciousness, and the law of reason is the law of liberty. For this reason we say that human beings, by nature, are free beings. The law of necessity that reigns supreme in the physical world does not extend to us. The analogies drawn from this view do not stand up to criticism.

Defenders of necessity argue that mind and will always operate under the influence of certain impulses, of which the most powerful inevitably proves dominant. But the most potent impulse is that to which mind and will lend their preference. Even the adversaries of inner liberty admit that the impact of motives depends not so much on external forces as upon receptiveness to those forces. They do not claim that this receptivity is determined by the peculiar character of each person, a character which also behaves in each case according the the laws of necessity: for the character of a rational being is not something fixed and unalterable and which always manifests itself in the same way. As we have seen, we have the capacity to restrain our desires, inclinations, passions; we can even change them by force of will or by adopting a new habit. If our character draws us toward evil, then, universal human experience tells us, the moral law will demand that we change our character. This demand is logical only because it is directed to free beings able to control our actions and impulses. Otherwise, it would be an absurdity.

All objections against freedom of the will are based on the attribution to rational beings of characteristics belonging to irrational nature, whereas in fact a rational being is part of the world of the Spirit and has its own peculiar nature and its own laws to guide it. A rational being relates to irrational nature as a universal to the particular, or as infinite to finite. Everything particular, every fragment, has well-defined characteristics and a defined sphere of action, from which it cannot escape. Thus it is also subject to the law of necessity. Reason is the conscious recognition of absolute universal principles and laws, and as such it contains the infinite. It is not bound, therefore, by any particular appetite; to any appetite it can juxtapose not only an infinite number of other appetites but also the general moral law that governs them. In the same way, [a rational being] is not bound by any particular characteristic of finite being; as an infinite principle, [a rational being] rises above all particular determinations and is capable of renouncing absolutely any of them. But because on the other hand, human beings are not only rational beings but also sensual ones, because in us the infinite is combined with the finite, then the second, irrational side of our nature is governed by laws of natural necessity and not infrequently enters into conflict with the first side. Therefore, the rational-moral law does not necessarily control our every action but manifests itself to us only as an eternally present imperative, which always to one degree or another must be reckoned with but which may never be entirely fulfilled. Here is the essence of our moral nature, and here also is the supreme manifestation of our liberty. We may not only choose to obey the moral law but may also choose to deviate from that law, and in deviating we nevertheless retain the capacity to return to its observance. [Observance and violation of the moral law] are the actions through which inner self-determination is achieved. From the infinite we freely turn to the finite, and from the finite we again return to the infinite. Our entire moral worth depends on the outcome of this process; in this process our merit and guilt develop.[8]

But if inner self-determination of the will manifests itself not only in obedience to law but also in the violation of it, in the capacity to surrender oneself to an opposing principle, then obviously one must regard as one-sided the view of those who equate liberty with obedience to moral law on the grounds that submission to natural inclinations and passions is not liberty but moral servitude. This view, which represents a position directly contradictory to the one outlined above, is shared by a significant number of thinkers, thinkers who otherwise hold quite different perspectives. For example, we find such a view in the work of Spinoza, who explicitly rejected the freedom of the will. He regards as free a person guided by the promptings of reason, for such a person follows the dictates of his or her own nature; the inability to restrain one's appetites Spinoza calls slavery, for appetites come from external causes.[9] Kant himself, having placed his doctrine of liberty on unshakeable foundations connected with the moral law, falls into the same one-sidedness as a result of his distinction between inner nature and external nature. In the negative sense, he calls freedom of the will independence from sensory impulses, and positively he calls it the self-determination of pure reason, while nevertheless recognizing as liberty purely external activity defined as the formal statutory law.[10] Subsequently, other philosophers have accentuated this one-sidedness. So, for example, [Heinrich] Ahrens, following Kant, defines liberty as the self-determination of the Spirit on the basis of rational concepts. He therefore sees liberty only where activity is guided by an ideal recognition of duty; sensory impulses, in his view, destroy liberty. According to Ahrens, liberty is the sole integral authority rooted in our inner nature; this kind of liberty is inner, moral liberty, which, making itself manifest in the external world, thereby becomes external. But external liberty that is cut off from inner liberty is purely negative, nihilistic liberty, or rather license. Ahrens calls it the *ugly tail* of true liberty, which because of it is subjected to dangers and restrictions.

Most recently [Felix] Dahn has adopted a similar view. "To be free," he claims, "means to obey reason alone."[11] We find a similar point in [Albert] Schäffle: "Freedom," he says, "is self-determination—that is, determination based not on external impulses foreign to my nature, but on the imperatives of my moral-social nature." Subsequently, Schäffle claims that coercion not only of the inner sort, springing from the moral law, but also of the external sort, coming from legal right, is liberating, because it frees us from the obstacles imposed upon us by our own and others' caprice, by stupidity, by malice, by passion, and so on.[12]

In nobody's work is this one-sided conception so sharply expressed as in that of one of the most noted partisans of liberty, [Johann Gottlieb] Fichte, when in his later work he adopted an exclusively moral perspective. The goal of all human activity and of all human development he takes to be the realization of the moral law on earth; the means for accomplishing this objective is liberty. But here a contradiction becomes apparent: on the one hand, as rational beings we must be the sole source of our own actions, we must not be coerced; on the other hand, the moral law must be observed unfailingly, even if coercion is necessary. How is this contradiction resolved? According to Fichte, we may be subjected to coercion only as physical beings, not as moral beings or as members of a moral community; meanwhile, only in this latter capacity do we enjoy freedom and rights, only in this respect are we not subject to coercion; in other respects, our errors cannot be tolerated but, on the contrary, we must be suppressed as one might suppress a destructive flame or a wild beast. "Without mercy or quarter, and whether it understands it or not," Fichte says, "humankind must be compelled to submit to the rightful authority of sublime reason. This compulsory submission constitutes not only the right but also the most sacred obligation of anyone who possesses such understanding."[13] When we recall that by the term "legal order" Fichte meant not only the determination of all external relationships among individuals but also everything demanded for the rigorous observance of the moral law, then we will see that no place remains in his system for liberty. On these principles Fichte based his entire theory of the socialist state, in which, by his own admission, all liberty disappears and we become mere tools for the realization of universal objectives. In order to save our inner liberty, we are afforded only a few hours of leisure, which we may devote to our moral self-improvement. If in external respects we become slaves of the state, the spirit in which we endure our servitude remains a matter of our own discretion. According to Fichte, the whole purpose of the political order is to supplant servile submissiveness by voluntary obedience.[14]

The logic of Fichte's presentation provides an instructive example of those confusions into which a principle, understood in a one-sided fashion, draws a thinker, and it provides an example of the inherent contradictions to which any one-sided perspective inevitably leads. Fichte is dealing with what superficially seems to be a very innocent thing—that is, with the metaphysical definition of liberty; but from his definition, with mathematical precision, flow consequences which lead to the complete destruction of liberty. In the works of other, less rigorous thinkers, these conclusions do not present themselves so clearly, but the basic problem remains the same: a given conception inevitably entails certain consequences.

The error lies in the understanding of liberty exclusively as a moral principle, as freedom to do good, when in fact it also encompasses freedom to do evil. If I must unfailingly observe a law, if I cannot deviate from it, then my freedom disappears, and along with it my moral dignity also disappears: I observe the law because I am coerced. For a perfect being, the possibility of deviating from the law is never realized, because such a being, by virtue of its perfection, never makes use of the freedom to deviate from the law, and a perfect being cannot be impelled by external coercion to deviate from the law, because otherwise freedom itself would disappear and so would personal responsibility for actions. Yet by its very nature the moral law is not a coercive law.

For rational and sensual beings, like us, the impulse to deviate from the law lies in our own nature. We violate the moral law when, instead of choosing to be guided by moral dictates, we yield to the appetites that contradict moral imperatives. But because we, by virtue of our liberty, are free to assign one or another motive to our actions, then only conviction, not coercion, can account for our actions. And because inner freedom manifests itself in the external world, then in the external world as well, coercion in the name of the moral law also contradicts human freedom. We are free to act morally or immorally; no one has the right to prohibit this choice.

It does not follow, however, that external liberty is unlimited. In the sphere of external actions another type of law reigns, a coercive law arising from the free mutual relationships of various rational beings. In this sphere conflicts are possible, and there must therefore be limits which are enforced by a coercive order. Each individual, as a rational free being, exercises his or her liberty in the external sphere. Each individual creates a certain realm of activity which belongs exclusively to him or her; there the individual may freely act as he or she pleases. But as soon as we enter the realm belonging to another individual, then we must accommodate ourselves to the imperatives of the second individual's liberty; for the law of liberty is the same for everyone. Deviation from it is an act of coercion that is negated by a similar coercion justified in the name of the law. This is the law of right, which has a purely external character and defines the mutual relations arising from the external liberty of individuals.

In this sphere as well terms must be precisely defined, for otherwise the principle of external liberty can lead to quite false consequences. In this regard the most recent literature is quite instructive. For example, Adolph Wagner, in his works on the economic and legal foundations of human societies, published for some unknown reason in the Rau handbook, completely ignores the basic issue upon which everything else depends—namely, the question of the nature of liberty; but in passing, in footnotes, he makes assertions which he considers incontrovertible, but which in fact constitute an utter distortion of [basic] conceptions. Wagner argues that from the recently proclaimed principles of freedom and equality for all members of society flows the rule that no one can be granted the right to acquire luxury goods until the minimal needs of every other part of the populace have been satisfied. As proof he notes: "The most important premise, which needs no further demonstration here, is that in our contemporary society, in which we do not recognize slavery, every living person has an equal right to perpetuate his existence, and therefore he may demand, insofar as the totality of economic goods of a given people of a given period will permit, in other words, insofar as the national income [will permit], that he, like every other person, be furnished with conditions to perpetuate his existence—in other words, that his minimal subsistence needs be satisfied."[15]

It would be difficult to contrive a falser conception of liberty. External liberty consists in the possibility of doing what one wishes, that is, of having discretion over the use of one's energies and means; because this possibility is granted to everyone in society, all members of society are, in this respect, equal. But freedom and equality do not entail the right to demand from others anything except respect for one's own liberty. Any positive requirement must be based on other principles. The right to perpetuate one's own existence does not belong to anyone, whether free or a slave, whether rich or poor. From liberty of the individual flows only the right to do what one can in order to perpetuate one's existence. A person with greater means will obviously be able to do more; a person with lesser means will be able to do less. A rich man who has contracted tuberculosis may travel to a warm climate in order to improve his health; a poor man will not have that option. A poor man may meet a benefactor willing to subsidize a cure; but the poor man, by virtue of his liberty, has no right to demand of others that they send him to Italy to cure his disease. Conversely, it may occur that the rich man in this respect is in a worse position than the poor man. A rich man suddenly stricken down by disease in a remote provincial area may be forced to content himself with poor medical services, while a poor man sick in a hospital in Petersburg may enjoy the advantage of access to the best doctors. Of course, a rich man in the provinces might summon a well-known doctor; but in order to do this, he would have to have sufficient means and the doctor would have to consent to make the journey: the rich man here again has no right to demand anything.

This example graphically demonstrates how important it is in works on the human community precisely to define one's philosophical terms, and to what radically false conclusions one may be led by a lack of philosophical education. Wagner was led into error because he adopted the theory of [Karl Christian Friedrich] Krause and his followers who see in legal right a means to achieve every human objective. But in order critically to analyze Krause's theory, one needs sound philosophical training, which in our time is available to very few individuals who have avoided the general temptation. [Rudolf von] Ihering's remarks, cited in the introduction, serve as proof of this proposition.

From what has been said above it is clear that freedom is not a single, unitary principle governed by a single law, as Ahrens asserts. Even in the purely moral sphere this principle has two components, for it includes the freedom to do good as well as to do evil. With respect to beings consisting of a combination of opposing elements, rationality and sensuality, the concept of liberty falls into two opposing categories, inner liberty and external liberty. Each has its own separate sphere and is governed by its own laws. In the sphere of inner liberty the moral law reigns supreme, a law which unconditionally demands that the individual be guided by recognition of duty; but observance of this law is a matter of free choice: here coercion is completely absent. In the sphere of external liberty coercive law reigns supreme; but this law is concerned exclusively with the external manifestations of liberty; each individual within his or her own sphere can act as he or she wills: the law cannot require the individual to act in a particular fashion. Both these spheres, complementing one another, are constituent elements of human freedom. Without inner liberty, external liberty loses its foundation and its significance. Taken in isolation, the right to choose has no claim to respect; it is respected and preserved by coercive law, solely because it is a manifestation of inner liberty. If inner liberty did not exist, then the entire legal code and the whole of human society based on it would be senseless. On the other hand, inner liberty without external liberty would lack actuality. Our vocation is to act in the external world, and in fulfilling that vocation we behave as free beings. If our external liberty is denied, then our vocation will be in vain. A Stoic can be spiritually free while in chains; a Christian can be spiritually free even in slavery. But both cases presume alienation from the external world and striving for another, purely spiritual end. The fulfillment of an earthly vocation worthy of human dignity requires external liberty. Otherwise, we cease to be human; we are diminished to the status of mere tools.

But freedom's manifestations cannot be confined to these two spheres; there remains the higher connection between them. Because inner liberty and external liberty flow from the same principle, which constitutes an inalienable property of our spiritual nature, they naturally affect one another and enter into various combinations. In addition to the opposing principles and spheres they also fit together [in dialectical unity]. This unity is expressed in those organic communities of which we are members. In the name of the moral law we submit to the political community or polity as the highest expression of the spiritual connection between individuals, and in this community or polity we have obligations; on the other hand, as free individuals, we enjoy rights. Here liberty acquires another character: it appears as public or political liberty defining the relationship of its members to the whole to which they belong, the degree of their legal submission and their share of participation in decision making. But this new sphere of liberty does not destroy its predecessors; it only complements them, bringing them into unity at a higher level.

Thus the principle of liberty, moving through various categories, forms separate, autonomous spheres of human relations, which all flow from a common source and are bound together. Freedom of will, which consists of self-determination on the basis of one's own decisions, may be divided into inner, moral liberty, consisting of the possibility of defining oneself on the basis of rational-moral impulses, and external, juridical liberty, governed by the coercive law of right; finally, it attains its ultimate objective in public or political freedom, which determines the relationship of the individual to the whole of which he or she is a member. Human life has various aspects and various spheres of activity, in each of which liberty takes different forms. But regardless of the sphere in which we may move or the kind of law to which we may be subordinate, everywhere we are free beings, for liberty constitutes an inalienable characteristic of our spiritual nature.

Yet if this be so, how can one explain the denial of liberty that one so often encounters in history? Why from humanity's inception to the present day have millions of people been sunken in slavery? Apparently, historical facts utterly contradict theory, for one cannot regard as an inalienable characteristic of human nature a trait that has not belonged to it always and everywhere.

This contradiction is resolved by the law of historical development. The essence of development is the gradual realization of the inner nature of the developing being. At first this nature shows itself in embryonic form, or as potentiality; later it moves through various stages, in which the heterogeneity of its aspects is manifested, and only at the end does it reveal itself in its entirety. Thus, for example, in the sphere of physical development, a flower and a fruit undoubtedly express the nature of a plant, but they also constitute the culmination of its growth, even if at some earlier moments [in the plant's gestation] they may not appear at all. Similarly, in the sphere of the Spirit, we find at the first stages only the germs of what later will be revealed in full flower. Therefore, the true nature of the Spirit is knowable only at the higher stages of development. But because the principles dominating the higher stages of development manifest themselves gradually and can be found in rudimentary form already in the original forms of human community, then the historical process is a logical development of principles inherent in human nature.

This is certainly true for liberty. There is no form of community where free individuals have been entirely lacking. Where there are slaves, there are also lords. But from here to a consciousness of liberty as the inalienable property of every individual, and to the realization of that principle in life, is a very long path. This consciousness demands the sort of self-knowledge and the kind of understanding of the inherent unity of human nature which are possible only at a very high stage of enlightenment. The greatest minds of antiquity did not yet comprehend that unity. Aristotle asserted that certain people, by their very nature, are destined to be lords, and others are destined to be slaves. The notion that all individuals are free by nature was developed mainly by Stoic philosophy; this notion was borrowed from Stoicism by Roman jurists, in whose work it remained a purely abstract principle without any concrete application. Then Christianity, summoning to salvation all people whether they be free or slave, affirmed the notion of the unity of human nature. Christianity thus revealed the inner, moral liberty of human beings, and the moral dignity connected with this liberty. Yet even as it directed the individual toward an objective beyond the grave, Christianity remained indifferent to external liberty. While holding out to slaves the promise of eternal happiness, it demanded their submission to the lords. Inner liberty itself, as a consequence of this one-sided development, fell into contradiction with itself and became coercive. The principle of external liberty, not as an abstract concept but as a living element of history, was developed primarily by the Germans; but this principle, too, in its one-sidedness, sundered from inner liberty and unfettered by a higher law, was an unbridled force that led to the enslavement of certain individuals by others. The contradiction between inner liberty and external liberty, like the inner contradiction of each of them, taken in isolation, was the characteristic trait of the medieval order. The synthesis of both principles is the fruit of the modern period. This synthesis is the mission of modern history, which has finally led to an unprecedented phenomenon, the recognition of the freedom of all.

Such is the process of development of human liberty. Hegel formulated this law not entirely accurately when he said that in the East one is free, in the classical world a few are free, and in the German world all are free.[16] The imprecision is that, in fact, history is not simply the quantitative extension of the principle of liberty. Without mentioning the qualitative development of its various aspects, or the juxtaposition of inner liberty and external liberty, or their subsequent synthesis, the qualitative process itself does not move with smooth regularity. In certain epochs liberty is temporarily suppressed, in others it rises with new force. This is so because liberty is not the sole element of human development. It constantly assumes a relation to other important principles, and from these relations, depending upon the demands of time and place, one element predominates over another. These relations explain, moreover, the contribution of slavery to the history of humanity. The development of consciousness shows us only the negative side of this phenomenon: where the consciousness of our true nature is insufficiently developed, there full and genuine liberty obviously cannot exist. But slavery plays in history a very positive role which should not be forgotten.

We are not only spiritual but also material beings. The arena in which the Spirit operates is the material world, and therefore higher development demands material means. For lordship over nature tools are necessary; preoccupation with intellectual/spiritual issues requires guaranteed leisure. The lower the stage of social development, the fewer the resources an individual will likely possess. An individual is forced to compensate for this insufficiency of resources by subordinating to himself other individuals, who are thereby transformed into mere tools. Even at higher stages of development the work of certain individuals serves to support the welfare of others; but here these relationships are freely established, by virtue of mutual consent. At lower stages of development this [mutual consent] is impossible. The free organization of economic life requires a degree of perfection in the civic order which is inconceivable here. Therefore, here the only resort is violent subordination, and it is accomplished the more easily because there do not yet exist concepts that would serve as an obstacle to it. It is even regarded as a charitable action to transform one's military adversary into a slave instead of exercising the right of war to kill him, and there is no doubt that, compared to annihilating an enemy, the enslavement of the conquered is indeed an important step forward. In ancient times, even a free man gladly surrendered himself into slavery. The paucity of material means and the endless dangers surrounding him forced him to seek aid and protection from a richer and stronger neighbor. To an insecure life at liberty he preferred tranquil servitude. Until quite recently, surrender into bondage was a common phenomenon. Finally, modern legal codes, in the name of the highest principles, have put an end to this practice. Yet mutual interest led to the establishment of slavery, and slavery even benefited humanity, for only by means of enslavement of some individuals did the higher development of others become possible. On the shoulders of slaves there arose the civilization of the classical world that still dazzles us. The citizen of the ancient republic lived for the polis; he occupied himself with politics, philosophy and art; but that was possible only because slaves saved him from material cares and guaranteed his welfare. The law of development, as history clearly shows, consists not in uniformly raising everyone to the same level, but in certain individuals being raised to the heights while standing upon the shoulders of others. And this process has served the common good, for, having reached the [summit of development], these individuals have brought others behind them. Liberty, formerly the preserve of the few, with time is becoming the property of all.

Political development also follows a similar process of enslavement [*zakreposhchenie*] and emancipation. A polity always requires a certain order and obedience to authority in society; otherwise it could not exist. But free obedience is possible again only at a very advanced state of development of civic consciousness and civic spirit [*grazhdanstvennost'*]. The lower the level of a society, the greater the need for coerced obedience. Therefore, almost all polities are founded by conquest. A strong tribe subjugates its neighbors and creates a stable body politic in which there is a distinction between victors and vanquished, lords and slaves. We see this process in the East—for example, in India, where the Aryan conquerors, after subjugating the indigenous tribes, transformed them into a lower caste. The same process with certain differences of detail was repeated in Greece, quite graphically among the Spartans, in Rome, and finally in modern Europe during the barbarian invasion.

Even where polities arise not by external conquest but by virtue of the inner imperatives of a given society, the new political order comes into being only through liberty's violent suppression. This is why absolutism appeared everywhere in Europe at the end of the Middle Ages. In place of medieval anarchy social stability had to be established, and that could not occur unless contentious elements of society were brought forcibly to heel. In the West it was mainly the upper classes' liberty that was destroyed, because the other classes were already enserfed [and had no liberty to lose]. The Russian case clearly shows how a developing state entails universal bondage. Here, during the Middle Ages, though slaves did exist, the bulk of the populace remained free. And this freedom was unlimited. Boyars, servitors, and peasants moved from place to place, from one principality to another, entering into long-term obligations only on the basis of free contracts. This was a time of general nomadism on the Russian land. But this nomadism was incompatible with the emergent state. As soon as the Muscovite tsars had begun to gather the far-flung community in order to fashion a single edifice, they imposed upon all social Estates a tax burden. Free movement was prohibited; freedom disappeared; all groups were compelled to bear the heavy burden of state service. The first to be bound were the boyars and servitors: they were transformed from free men into slaves of the sovereign, obliged to serve him for their entire lives. Later merchants [*posadskie*] were bound to state service; finally, the peasants' turn came. In order that the service elite might bear the cost of their service, they needed an income, and the empty lands given them by the government provided none; the peasant populace had therefore to be enserfed to that land. Thus the bondage of one group led to the enserfment of other groups. This onerous universal servitude persisted until the state grew sufficiently strong, until its institutions no longer needed to rely on coerced service but could survive with voluntary service. Then the process began to reverse itself: the first to be liberated from compulsory service were the nobility, then the urban Estate, and finally the peasants. In place of universal servitude, universal liberty prevailed, but now quite different conditions existed. Medieval anarchy had given way to a well-organized state, in which the best ambitions of educated society might be accommodated. Universal serfdom undoubtedly facilitated social development; thanks to it, Russia became a great and well-ordered state. But in accomplishing its historical purpose, servitude prepared the way for its own abolition.

The abolition of bondage is a response to economic, political, and moral factors.

The economic cause is the higher productivity of free labor. If the lower categories of work can be performed by slaves, sometimes as well as by free men, and sometimes better because the former are inspired by fear, it is nevertheless the case that skilled labor, requiring energy, persistence, and know-how, can be successfully performed only by free individuals, acting on their own initiative, not under fear of punishment. Therefore, advanced industrial development inevitably presupposes liberty.[17]

The same logic applies to political relations. A polity where forced labor dominates cannot attain the degree of might that a free polity can attain. By enlisting all the energies of an individual, liberty mobilizes inner resources that otherwise would remain unutilized. Neither economic prosperity nor rapid intellectual progress can occur without liberty. Therefore, any state that wishes to maintain parity with its free competitors must sooner or latter adopt free institutions. Otherwise, it will fall into decline.

All these factors, however, are of secondary importance. Of course, under conditions of universal servitude advanced industrial development is out of the question; but if only a certain portion of the populace is held in bondage, and especially if it is an alien tribe being held in subjection and if slave labor is confined to certain types of work, then a high degree of material prosperity is still quite conceivable. American planters felt no economic imperative whatsoever to abolish slavery; on the contrary, they understood quite well that slavery's abolition would deprive them of a significant portion of their income. They were forcibly compelled to give up slavery not for economic reasons, over which they were the only judges, but for other reasons altogether. Similarly, in the political sphere the example of Russia demonstrates that a state may attain great power status even while the lower classes are held in universal bondage. Serf-holding Russia alone on the European continent was strong enough to overcome the regiments of liberated France, led by the greatest military genius in the world. For an extended period Russia had the decisive voice over the fate of Europe, and if it suffered a defeat in the Crimean campaign, it still demonstrated the degree to which it was capable of fighting on its own. On the other hand, if we look at North America, we will see that its outstanding statesmen came from slaveholding states. Involuntary servitude inculcated in the slaveholders a habit of command that facilitated the development of statecraft.

These economic and political factors could not have brought about the abolition of slavery had they not been accompanied by an ideological and moral factor—namely, the conviction that liberty alone is compatible with human dignity and that the return of liberty to the slaves is an imperative of human justice. History shows that this principle was the mainspring of liberation movements among modern peoples. Already during the Middle Ages, in the name of moral principle, dying Christians and Christians departing to fight in the Crusades freed their slaves. French kings also cited moral principles in their decrees of manumission: "Since under natural law each man should be born free," said Louis X, "and meanwhile, by virtue of certain customs introduced long ago and heretofore observed in our realm and also due to certain crimes of our predecessors, many individuals from our inferior people have fallen into the bonds of slavery, which we do not approve, We . . . etc." The ideal of universal human liberty also inspired the philosophy of the eighteenth century, which has exercised such a powerful influence on the cause of emancipation, and whose most remarkable expression is the *Declaration of the Rights of Man and Citizen.* In the name of an ideal, slaves were liberated in the English colonies and in our own day were liberated in the United States. And if we turn to our own experience, we will see that the Sevastopol campaign only provided the final impetus for a step long ago recognized by both government and the best minds in society as the highest imperative of justice. Those who dismiss metaphysics as unimportant, who regard it as empty gibberish, forget that metaphysics is the driving force behind human progress. In the case at hand, that point is quite striking. Modern peoples owe their liberty to metaphysics. It could not be otherwise, for the existence of an ideal that constitutes the goal of development originates not in what already exists but in that which we recognize as the highest imperative of reason. In the name of a conviction arrived at by means of philosophical deduction, we alter material reality.

Has the process of emancipation among modern peoples now reached its culmination? One would have thought that this was beyond doubt. In Europe there are no longer serfs; everyone, from great to humble, is free; all possess control over their person and property. The few transient exceptions that one encounters, among peoples who have recently emerged from serfdom, do not affect the general picture. Yet many thinkers deny this and see the emancipation of the lower classes as a task of the future. Socialists constantly assert that the working class is still in bondage, just as before: for the sake of bread the impoverished working class is forced to work for a miserly wage and is completely under the control of the owners. Socialists claim that only the form of slavery has changed, not its substance, for the private ownership of industry inevitably leads to the de facto enslavement of the proletariat, who will be emancipated only when all industrial production has been concentrated in the hands of the community.[18]

These criticisms are based on conceptual confusion. Liberty and economic welfare are two different things. One may possess absolute freedom and not have a piece of bread. A solitary figure wandering in the desert is an excellent example of this, and liberty not infrequently impoverishes those who do not know how to make use of it. A free individual may find himself or herself in penury worse than that of a slave; but this penury has nothing to do with the one being free and the other being a slave. Only by deliberately twisting the meaning of words can one equate private employment with involuntary servitude. A worker enters with an employer into mutual contractual relations and is always able to terminate the contract. That workers do make use of their freedom is demonstrated by constantly repeated strikes, in which the employers do not always emerge victors. The socialists' slogans are nothing but empty wordplay. The emancipation of the fourth Estate, the proletariat, about which we have heard so much, cannot occur in the future because it has already been accomplished. [Improving] the welfare of the lower classes is a different matter: it is a real and pressing issue. Yet those who are most vocal in advocating the improvement of workers' living standards are demanding not the extension but the destruction of liberty. This phenomenon will be treated below.

Thus we ought to recognize that today the ideal of human society, universal liberty, has already been introduced [in various institutions]. But the next question is: Has this ideal been fully implemented? Has liberty attained the degree of development required to satisfy moral imperatives? Finally, what can we expect in the future: the extension or the limitation of liberty?

These questions are tightly connected with the issue of the ideal bounds of liberty, of external liberty, for inner liberty by its very nature is absolute, as all authorities agree. Legal constraints upon freedom of conscience, once so common, are now rejected as violations of the most sacred rights of the individual, and if there still exist regulations that contravene this principle, they are nothing but holdovers from a past that must disappear as society progresses. By the same token, freedom of thought is beyond doubt so long as it is confined to the inner world of the individual; legal limits on its exercise apply only to its external manifestations. As was shown above, external liberty by its nature is subject to limitation. But what sort of limitations should these be? Is it possible theoretically to establish certain rules which can serve as guidelines in practice?

This issue has occupied many thinkers and has been resolved by them in various ways. The philosophy of the eighteenth century, which devoted itself chiefly to the principle of external liberty, expressed its view in the *Declaration of the Rights of Man and Citizen.* The fourth article of this legal monument states: "Liberty consists in the ability to do whatever does not harm another; hence the exercise of the natural rights of each man has no limits except those which assure to other members of society the enjoyment of the same rights. These limits can only be determined by law." But in his *Anarchistic Fallacies* [Jeremy] Bentham noted that, holding to this principle, no one can be sure whether he has the right to act in a certain fashion because any action may be harmful, if only to one other individual. Despite that objection, [John Stuart] Mill in his treatise *On Liberty* repeats the same rule: "The only purpose for which power can be rightfully exercised over any member of a civilized community, against his will, is to prevent harm to others. . . . The only part of the conduct of any one, for which he is amenable to society, is that which concerns others. In that part which merely concerns himself, his independence is, of right, absolute. Over himself, over his own body and mind, the individual is sovereign."[19] Against this, Ihering, repeating Bentham's objections, correctly notes that all actions about which it is worthwhile to speak and which are regulated by statute are actions affecting others. With this kind of rule one may utterly destroy individual liberty. "I pledge," Ihering says, "with this rule in hand to so limit and confine liberty that it will be unable to move at all."[20] It is surely true that, from the utilitarian perspective, the task [of defining the limits of liberty] is insoluble. Utility is a changeable principle that incorporates thousands of different rationales and offers no firm foundation for the determination of fixed rules of conduct.

But if utilitarianism offers no key to the resolution of this problem, that does not mean that the problem itself is insoluble, as Ihering suggests. The famous jurist sees in this question the columns of Hercules before which legal scholarship must terminate its voyage of discovery. If this view were accurate, then jurisprudence would be deprived of any guidelines; it would become merely a haphazard miscellany of regulations drawn from practice but having no rational foundation whatsoever. For the whole problem of legal right is to define the limits of liberty. If they cannot be rationally determined, if legal scholarship refuses to make the attempt [to fix liberty's appropriate limits], then what? Meanwhile, throughout history jurists have elaborated for themselves certain principles on the basis of which they have decided in a given period what was permissible and what was not. Undoubtedly, the jurists' outlooks have changed over time; every age or people has had its own ideal according to which it has devised its legal code. But in the totality of these ideals we can trace the evolution of juridical ideas in history. The scholars' task is to identify and to elucidate these ideas, to examine the logic of their development over time, and to suggest how they might evolve in the future. Even the most one-sided views provide material for our analysis. By linking one view with another, we arrive at that breadth of outlook which genuine scholarship demands.

Thus, if we look at the article of the *Declaration of the Rights of Man and Citizen* cited above, we will see that it contains a partial truth, although this truth is distorted by being combined with the principle of utility. The truth is that the rights belonging to one citizen are limited by the same rights granted to other citizens: in other words, the freedom of one individual is limited by the freedom of others. This is precisely the idea that Kant placed at the basis of his philosophy of right; it is also developed by Wilhelm Humboldt,[21] who is cited by Ihering. The one-sidedness of this doctrine, as Ihering properly notes, lies in its rejection of any positive activity of the state, which, according to this theory, is confined to the preservation of rights and of order in society. Meanwhile, both sensible theory and practice are demonstrating that the state has positive tasks, which, in their turn, place limits upon human liberty or even subordinate liberty to themselves. But it should not be concluded that just because a second constraint exists, that the first constraint should cease to exist. We must simply spell out how it operates by distinguishing between two spheres: the private and the public. In the private sphere—that is, in the relationships between individuals—the liberty of one individual is limited by the liberty of others; in the public sphere, the limits of liberty are fixed by the rights or prerogatives of the state which flow from needs of the community itself.

This last boundary is harder to define that the first, for the common good, upon which the prerogatives of the state are based, is again a changeable notion not given to precise definition. Nevertheless, it is not only possible but absolutely essential to establish general principles by which these relations should be governed.

The task of the state is not only to safeguard citizens' rights; it must also respond to the common interests of the people. Therefore, the legal constraint of liberty ought to be permitted only to the extent that it is required to satisfy these common interests. The entire sphere of private interests and relations must be left to liberty. There is no doubt that between private interests and general interests there exists a reciprocal connection, and that there are intermediate forms; there is also no doubt that over time the very nature of these interests and their imperatives can change; that which formerly constituted a private interest may ascend to the level of common interest, and conversely, something that once was done under coercion for the sake of the common good may at a higher level of development be left to the free decision of the individual. Therefore, by its very nature the boundary between private and general community interests is a shifting one; there is no norm that is unalterable and defined once and for all. Nevertheless, it is in the highest degree important to bear in mind the separation between private and public; otherwise liberty disappears. The inviolability of private life and private activity must be considered a fundamental law of every educated society. Governmental interference in this sphere can be justified only in emergencies, and then only as an exception, never as a rule. And if there are certain circumstances in countries where free activity has not attained the appropriate degree of development, circumstances in which intensive regulation of private relations in the name of the common good may be demanded, just as slavery was demanded at one time, there is no doubt that in the general course of historical development, advancing to a higher level of society means opening up to free choice areas that were once subject to coercion. Humanity's ideal must be the extension, not the limitation, of liberty.

We should therefore unequivocally reject the opinion of those who strive for the complete subordination of the individual to society and consequently to sacrifice individual liberty to that of the community. Such was the doctrine of Rousseau. He demanded that the individual surrender all liberty into the hands of the community in order to receive this liberty back in the form of participation in common decisions. The inadequacy of this outlook is too well known to need repeating, and this is not the place to discuss it.[22] Rousseau, having surrendered the individual entirely to the state, nevertheless wished to preserve the individual's liberty, and as a result he arrived at an impossible position. He demanded that the legislator set only those norms applying to everyone in identical fashion; in collective decisions he tried to distinguish the general will, expressing that upon which everyone agrees, from the will of all, which is nothing more than the sum of private wills; he understood that the people, as presently constituted, are incapable of acting as the unerringly just legislature that the system demands, and therefore he sought as legislator a wise man invested with supernatural authority. In a word, by trying to reconcile the irreconcilable—the preservation of liberty with its destruction—he fell into endless contradictions.

But at least Rousseau wanted to preserve liberty, which he saw as an inherent and necessary element of human nature. The socialists do not even go that far.

They simply obliterate human freedom for the sake of the community as a whole. And those who do so are not only the fanatics of socialism who see nothing else other than their noble yet poorly understood goal, but also the scholars who furnish their books with an entire scholarly apparatus. Take, for example, Schäffle. We have already noted above that he begins from a one-sided definition of liberty as the fulfillment of imperatives originating in the moral-social nature of man. Consequently, he sees liberty solely in the choice of vocation or occupation *(die Freiheit des Berufs);* and each occupation, according to him, should be recognized as a public post or as public service. An individual is obliged voluntarily to submit to a special form of service; he must reject license *(Eigenmacht);* he must permit himself to be defined *(sich bestimmen lassen)* by society, which provides him with the necessary training and tools, establishes a division of labor, and coordinates the productive process; according to statute, he must fulfill his obligations as a member of those associations to which he involuntarily belongs and as a member of public institutions. In a word, "each person, at his own post, for and through the collective—that is the ideal of just organization."[23] While Schäffle also claims that it is precisely inside such an organization that true liberty resides, this only proves how easy it is to rest content with words alone, after having emptied them of all sense. Liberty consists in the individual being the source of his or her actions; if he or she is transformed into a mere instrument of society, if he or she exists solely for and through the collective, then his or her autonomy as an individual disappears and there can be no more question of liberty. Schäffle compares the individual to a cell [in a multicellular organism]; and sure enough, in his system the individual is nothing but an organic cell, to which no one can ascribe liberty.

This outlook contradicts not only sound theory but the entire course of human development. Originally, the human personality was submerged in the general mass; only little by little did it differentiate itself from the latter and arrive at the consciousness of its own liberty. For that reason in the ancient world political liberty was of primary importance. However, neither the Greeks nor the Romans generally thought that a citizen should be a mere tool of the state: even in ancient times this outlook found refuge only in utopias. A citizen possessed his own private sphere, where he was sovereign lord. He disposed of his own home, his own estate, his own slaves, as he pleased; the polis did not enter into this sphere. But his chief activity was nevertheless directed toward political affairs; the private sphere served him only as a guarantee of material support, and as something that provided him the leisure for civic activity. We have seen that this was the real significance of slavery.

The incompatibility of this social arrangement with the imperatives of the human personality led to its collapse. The development of personal interests was the chief reason for the destruction of the ancient republics. This development led to the immortal monument of the Roman law, which set out norms and elaborated definitions for citizenship taking into account private relations; the fruits of Roman law served as a model for posterity. But progress did not stop here. In the Middle Ages relationships appeared that were completely contradictory to the ones that had prevailed in the ancient world. Here private liberty engulfed public liberty. A medieval freeman recognized no other authority besides the one to which he submitted when making a private, free contract. All public positions were transformed into private property.

If the social arrangement that had prevailed in the ancient world had proved to be incompatible with the development of individual freedom, the medieval order proved itself incompatible with public authority; indeed, the medieval order ultimately destroyed itself: for unlimited private liberty leads to the enslavement of some individuals to others. Hence the necessary reaction which led to the partial restoration of principles of the ancient world; but only the partial restoration, for liberty, won by the historical development of the individual, could no longer be entirely eliminated. The agenda of modern history is to achieve the synthesis of ancient principles with medieval ones. Private liberty remains the basic right of the individual, the source of the individual's autonomy; but above it rises another sphere, the public sphere, where political liberty is established. The former serves as the basis, the second as the guarantee. And this relation must be preserved inviolate, for it constitutes the most precious achievement of the human species, the fruit of its historical development. To reject it means to return to the past, [to a past] not only preceding the appearance of the classical world but preceding the appearance of educated life as such. Liberty, by its very nature, is bound up with the individual, for in it is expressed the autonomy of the individual. Therefore, the struggle against individualism is a struggle against liberty. This struggle may be justified in the sphere of politics, when it is directed against doctrines that attempt to base the state solely on the principles of personal will and free contract. In the state, private liberty should take second place to public prerogatives. But this struggle loses all justification when it leads to the entire private sphere being engulfed by the public sphere and to the sacrifice of individual liberty to the community's needs. Such a tendency is a great threat to liberty and to progress, for it destroys the source of both. And that is the very essence of socialism, which for this reason must be considered the great evil of our time.

Below we shall elaborate these ideas in detail and apply them in practice. Here it was only necessary to indicate what liberty is, what are its forms and manifestations, and what imperatives and consequences flow from it. The subsequent exposition will add new evidence to support our view.

Equality

Since ancient times equality has been considered a distinguishing characteristic of justice. Aristotle, whose teaching on this point can be regarded as the classic exposition of the question, says that justice in the proper sense is equality—that is, the mean between superfluity and the insufficiency; the latter two principles correspond to injustice.[1] But because equality may be of two types, numerical and proportional, the one being an arithmetic principle and the other a principle of geometrical proportion, so justice is divided into two forms, which Aristotle calls commutative and distributive. The first type applies to obligations imposed by commercial transactions as well as those resulting from violations of the law. In transactions things of equal value are exchanged, one for one; in the case of criminal acts, the harm done to one person is rectified by the penalty exacted from the other. Distributive justice is a rule governing the distribution of public goods like property, honor, authority, in accordance with services rendered or with the merit of each member of society. Thus the concept of justice encompasses four terms: two individuals and two objects, and the equivalence between objects should correspond to the equivalence between the individuals. From this it follows that equal distribution of objects is just only when the objects are distributed to equal individuals; an equal distribution of objects to unequal individuals is unjust. Moreover, it is apparent that an unequal distribution of objects may be just, if the unequal treatment is accorded to unequal individuals. Aristotle says that those who ignore this precept judge speciously, mainly because they are judging their own situation.

The same can be said of political parties, each of which defends a certain aspect of justice but remains silent about its most essential one. Thus oligarchs, being unequal to others in property, imagine that they ought to be unequal in every respect. For their part, democrats, being equal to others in their liberty, assert that they should be equal in all other respects. Neither the one nor the other is correct, for equality or inequality of a certain kind determines only the distribution of those objects to which it relates, not the distribution of all objects in general. In democracy the basic principles are liberty and numerical equality. Consequently, poor people have the same right to vote as rich people. And because there are more poor people than rich, decision making depends on the [votes of the] poor. But this inevitably leads to injustice, for the rich are driven from the government and the poor may divide among themselves the property of the rich. For its part, oligarchy leads to tyranny. A well-designed polity, Aristotle concludes, combines the two elements, democracy and oligarchy. In those countries where the two elements exist, justice demands that each play a role in government.[2]

Such is Aristotle's teaching, a teaching which lucidly, accurately, and profoundly presents fundamental definitions of equality and justice. From these definitions it is obvious that the principle of equality has different implications, depending upon the sphere in which it is applied. In civil society numerical equality predominates; here people are treated simply as free individuals, and with respect to their freedom they are equals. In the political sphere, on the contrary, the basic principle should be proportional equality. Democracy alone, although not always consistently, adheres to the notion of numerical equality [in the political sphere].

Democracy's characteristic mixture of civil equality and political equality dominates to a large extent the political movements of the modern period. The individualist philosophy of the eighteenth century treated people as abstract, equal units. From this perspective the French revolution, in which the ideas of the eighteenth century found their culmination, proclaimed liberty and equality to be fundamental and inalienable rights of man. Since then, these two principles have become the slogan not only of the democratic, but to a significant degree even of the liberal party in Europe.

Let us look into the teaching of the democratic school. Analyzing it, we shall see more clearly the true nature of equality and what role it should play in the human community. To study these issues we must first turn to those legislative monuments in which the French revolution expressed its view.

Article 1 of the *Declaration of the Rights of Man and Citizen* declares: "Men are born and remain free and equal in rights; social distinctions may be based only upon general usefulness." In article 6 we read: "Law is the expression of the general will; all citizens have the right to concur personally, or through their representatives, in its formation; it must be the same for all, whether it protects or punishes. All citizens, being equal before it, are equally admissible to all public offices, positions, and employments, according to their capacity, and without other distinction than that of virtues and talents."

These principles were applied to the constitution of 1791. In the preamble it says that "The National Assembly, wishing to establish the French Constitution upon the principles it has previously recognized and proclaimed, abolishes irrevocably the institutions which were injurious to liberty and equality of rights. Neither nobility, nor peerage, nor hereditary distinctions, nor distinctions of orders, nor feudal regime, nor patrimonial courts, nor any titles, denominations, or prerogatives derived therefrom, nor any order of knighthood, nor any corporations or decorations requiring proofs of nobility or implying distinctions of birth, nor any superiority other than that of public functionaries in the performance of their duties any longer exists. Neither venality nor inheritance of any public office any longer exists. Neither privilege nor exception to the law common to all Frenchmen any longer exists for any part of the nation or for any individual. Neither *jurandes* nor corporations of professions, arts and crafts any longer exist. The law no longer recognizes religious vows or any other obligation contrary to natural rights or the Constitution."

Then, in the first article, it says that "The Constitution guarantees as natural and civil rights: 1) That all citizens are admissible to offices and employments, without other distinctions than virtues and talents; 2) That all taxes shall be assessed equally upon all citizens, in proportion to their means; 3) That similar offenses shall be punished with similar penalties, without any distinction of persons."

Thus the entire medieval order, based on inequality, on Estate prerogatives, on privileges was abolished in one stroke and replaced by the complete equality of citizens, not only in the civil but also in the political sphere. But this was equality of rights, not of material possessions. Property, along with liberty and equality, was declared "a sacred and inviolable right, of which no one may be deprived unless a legally established public necessity obviously requires it, and upon condition of a just and previous indemnity" (article 17 of the *Declaration of Rights*).

Subsequent revolutionary constitutions reaffirmed these principles. In the *Declaration of Rights* that was placed at the beginning of the constitution of 1793—the most radical of all [the revolutionary constitutions]—equality, even before liberty, was recognized as an innate and inalienable right of man and citizen (article 2). "All men," it then says, "are equal by nature and before the law" (article 3). "Law is the free and solemn expression of the general will; it is the same for all, whether it protects or punishes; it may order only what is just and useful to society; it may prohibit only what is injurious thereto" (article 4). "All citizens are equally admissible to public office. Free peoples recognize no grounds for preference in their elections other than virtues and talents" (article 5). Even here, however, there is no discussion of any kind of equality other than equality of rights. Just as before, property is declared inviolable. It is defined as "the right appertaining to every citizen to enjoy and dispose at will of his goods, his income, and the product of his labor and industry" (article 16). "No one may be deprived of the least portion of his property without his consent, unless a legally established public necessity requires it, and upon condition of a just and previous indemnity" (article 19). "No kind of labor, tillage, or commerce may be forbidden the industry of citizens" (article 17). "Every man may contract his services or his time" (article 18).

The constitution of 1795, which, following a logical progression, treats equality after liberty in its enumeration of rights, provides a definition of equality. It "is a circumstance in which the law is the same for all, whether it protects or punishes. Equality does not admit any distinctions of birth, or any inheritance of powers" (article 3).

Such are the declarations made in the constitutions elaborated by the French revolution. In compliance with democratic theory, equality is extended both to the political and the civil sphere. But in both spheres what is proclaimed is equality of rights, or equality before the law which flows from the equality of men as free individuals. The legislators did not have in mind equality of property.

These principles have been subjected to rigorous criticism by Bentham. In his *Anarchical Fallacies,* the famous jurist, analyzing the *Declaration of the Rights of Man,* comments apropos article 1: "*All men remain equal in rights.* All men, meaning doubtless all human creatures. The apprentice, then, is equal in rights to his master; he has as much liberty with relation to the master, as the master has with relation to him; he is as much owner and master of the master's house, as the master himself. The case is the same as between parents and children, guardians and wards, husband and wife, soldier and officer. The madman has as good a right to confine anybody else, as anybody else has to confine him. The idiot has as much right to govern his family, as his family has to govern him. If all of this is not incontestably included in the article, then it means nothing, absolutely nothing."[3] "I know very well," Bentham notes, "that the authors of the Declaration, being neither lunatics nor idiots, did not intend to admit such unconditional equality. But what did they intend? Did the ignorant crowd understand them better than they understood themselves?"[4]

This critique undoubtedly has a certain validity. Absolute equality of the sort being proclaimed here cannot exist. Human beings are more than abstractly free individuals; they have other qualities and characteristics that must be taken into account by the law and which, consequently, alter the equality of rights that flows from liberty. But after taking due notice of these modifications and exceptions, we should not proceed to ignore entirely the principle [of equality], as Bentham does. From his utilitarian perspective, he does not see the forest for the trees.

In order to evaluate the principles proclaimed by the French revolution, one must first distinguish political equality from civil equality. When the *Declaration of Rights* says that social distinctions can be based solely on common usefulness, it is recognizing that equality in the political sphere cannot be absolute. This very point is applied to [the question of] public offices: although all citizens have access to these offices, the offices are filled according to virtue and talents. Here, not numerical but proportional equality is being established. When the matter in question is civic responsibilities, however, virtue and talents are not taken into account: here, citizens are considered simply as free and equal individuals. In the same way, proportional equality is being applied to the payment of taxes: not everyone pays the same amount, but each pays according to his means. Finally, when the Constituent Assembly, having proclaimed that all citizens have the right to participate in the making of the law, and yet, having established in the same breath a property requirement for voting, however small, and having even taken away from certain individuals the right to vote, it once again recognized that equality, when applied to the political sphere, is not absolute but conditional. Legally speaking, all citizens have equal access to rights, but the enjoyment of them requires conditions to be met that not all citizens may fulfill. In the most recent versions of the French constitution, the property requirement for voting has been significantly raised, so that the electoral right has been held by a very small number of voters; but except for the pure democrats, none of the adherents of the principles of 1789 has considered [such restrictions] a violation of equality.

Even the abolition of hereditary privileges cannot be considered a prerequisite for achievement of equality in the political sphere. As soon as it is allowed that, for the sake of the common good, social distinctions may be established, then the propriety of hereditary privileges is also being admitted, so long as they are required by sound policy. On this basis, the Constituent Assembly itself retained the hereditary monarchy. If in society there exists a hereditary Estate possessing superior political capacity, then justice itself demands that that Estate have greater political rights. In France, during the Restoration, there was an hereditary upper chamber which, it was commonly recognized, performed important political services for the country; when in 1831 heredity of the peerage fell before the people's democratic ambitions, even such liberal adherents of the ideas of 1789 as Thiers defended the principle of an hereditary upper chamber. The explanation of such phenomena is that in political life, according to Aristotle's teaching, not numerical but proportional equality must dominate; political capacity can take many different forms. We shall return to this issue subsequently.

Equality in the civil sphere is another matter entirely. Yet here, too, there are situations in which the principle does not apply. Take familial relationships. The family, like the state, is an ethical and legal community in which each member has a particular place and a peculiar task to carry out. In the family people relate to one another not only as free individuals but as husband and wife, parents and children, ward and trustee. Although each family member is theoretically free, each has different concrete obligations, from which different legal relationships result. For this reason it is wrong to claim that the rights of each family member are the same, that the law is identical for all its members. One can argue about the extent of the rights given to this or that member of the family, but one cannot hold to the abstract principle of liberty and ignore the different responsibilities of the family members. Nobody would claim that the rights of children with respect to their parents should be the same as the rights of parents with respect to their children.

As regards civic duties as such, the position of members of society is again different. Here they relate to one another as free, and consequently as equal, individuals. The subordination of one individual to another in the civil sphere can only be voluntary. Involuntary subordination of the sort represented by serfdom contradicts our nature as rational beings. The restriction of one person's liberty in comparison with another's is unjust. Equality of rights is the norm toward which all educated societies have already approached or must approach in the future.

Even here, of course, exceptions are inevitable. Natural or civic conditions may affect the rights-bearing capacity [*pravosposobnost'*] of individuals. Minors and the insane cannot use their civil rights in the same way as others. But the exceptions confirm rather than negate the rule. The basic principle of the civil order is, nevertheless, equality before the law. In this respect, the French revolution was an enormous step forward in the development of public life; [equality before the law] became a lasting attainment of humanity. This fact is understood by all thinkers and publicists of any significance who accept the principles of the modern era. Even the leading light of the German feudal party, [Friedrich Julius] Stahl, recognizes that all inequalities stemming from natural and civic conditions "must retain the basic equality of rights as the foundation for law lying at the very core of human nature." This, he says, "is the truth amid the errors of revolutions. The universal capacity to bear rights and honor should constitute the heart of the legal order. Inequality should be only an accident."[5] The most modern legal codes also hold to these principles.

Yet already in the eighteenth century, alongside the doctrine of citizens' equality of rights, another concept of equality developed. Not equality of rights but equality of material possessions was held out as the ideal of the human community.

[Jean-Jacques] Rousseau laid the foundation for this school of thought in his *Discourse on the Origin and Foundations of Inequality Among Men.* True to the spirit of eighteenth-century philosophy, which sought human nature in the individual torn from all external conditions and which regarded those individual traits originating in social relations as perversions of human nature, Rousseau turns to the circumstances preceding the foundation of society in order to discover nature's dictates [concerning our character]. According to his thinking, people [in the state of nature] enjoyed complete liberty and also absolute equality, for they had almost no needs; here, given a way of life identical for all, physical endowments received identical development, while intellectual capacities, which constitute the source of all human misfortunes, were not yet developed. In the state of nature people enjoyed inner peace and bodily health, so this period should be considered the time of greatest felicity for the human species. This felicity even continued while individuals banded together but were still at the level of savages. The first step out of this condition, in Rousseau's view, was the transition to agriculture, a stage that brought with it the establishment of property. "The first man who, having enclosed a piece of ground, bethought himself of saying 'This is mine,' and found people simple enough to believe him, was the real founder of civil society." With the establishment of property came the distinction between rich and poor—the primary source of human inequality. Property was the seed of further discord, which, in its turn, generated new inequality. For the preservation of peace governments were established, and with them came the distinction between rulers and subjects. But this new inequality, instead of fostering peace, became the source of new discords. Their consequence, instead of the original popular self-government, was despotism; and despotism brought a third source of distinction among men, the distinction between lords and slaves. Thus the first step led to all the others. The ineluctable march of events gradually corrupted natural man. The order established by nature gave way to associations of men with artificial inclinations, emotions, and traits.[6]

It is hardly necessary to point out that in this fantastic portrayal of history's course, human nature is quite wrongly understood. As we noted earlier, the true nature of a developing being is revealed not at the origin but at the culmination of its development. Rousseau himself considered it impossible to return to the original condition of humankind. In his *Social Contract* he explicitly recognizes that equality, which must be the legislator's goal, does not entail [that every citizen possess] an identical degree of authority or wealth. It is only necessary that authority never descend to violence and that the extent of wealth be such that no one should be able to purchase someone else and no one should find it necessary to sell himself. The goal here is purely political. Rousseau's whole intention was to replace individual liberty with political liberty, and therefore for him equality had mainly political importance.

[Gabriel Bonnet de] Mably went further. Inverting the true relationship of liberty and equality, he took the latter as the fundamental human trait, and he saw in liberty only a means for preserving equality. According to his teaching, nature has predestined people to be equals. Mably's proof was that community is essential for the individual and that, in entering society, the individual must sacrifice his liberty, whereas he may retain his equality throughout. Moreover, only in equality can the individual attain harmony and happiness, whereas inequality, by corrupting our natural emotions, elicits in us destructive appetites and vices. To those who claim that inequality lies in the very nature of things, for individuals are born with different inclinations, strengths, and talents, Mably objected that we cannot judge true human nature from our present condition. The difference in our talents comes chiefly from artificial education; given an identical education, all individuals would have almost identical talents, and outstanding individuals would find sufficient compensation in the respect with which they were regarded by others. The difference in strength also cannot lead to inequality, for the strengths of one individual are far outweighed by the combined strength of others. The difference in inclinations can lead only to a closer association among individuals, who are compelled to seek others' assistance. Even the establishment of governments, so long as they are based on the electoral right, cannot introduce persistent inequality among individuals, because each citizen, under such an arrangement, has identical rights and an identical share in sovereign authority, and in turn may occupy any public office. Property alone inevitably leads to inequality; but was the establishment of property essential to the community? Mably says it was not. In antiquity community of possessions could and did exist, so what prevented it from continuing? Some thinkers claim that community ownership takes away the incentive to work; but again, Mably says, one should not attribute to unspoiled humanity those emotions which develop only in corrupted societies. Those who most love to work can be rewarded by honors. Unfortunately, Mably argues, instead of resorting to this device, people dissatisfied with the lazy have made a rule that each individual should live by the fruits of his or her own labor. This irrational step brought others in its wake. As soon as property was established, inequality irresistibly extended itself to all social relationships.

Like Rousseau, however, Mably grasped the impossibility of attaining his ideal. Therefore, he proposed only palliative measures. Where feasible, the legislator should strive to hold individuals' appetites in check and should more or less equalize property holdings by means of regulations affecting every aspect of citizens' lives. This goal is to be attained by strict laws on luxuries, limitations on inheritance, restrictions on commerce, and finally, by agrarian laws restricting the dimensions of landed estates. Mably also understood that material equality is inconceivable without intellectual and moral equality. He therefore demanded that education should be universal and equal for all. He demanded the establishment of a civic religion which the legislator should make harmonious with philosophy. In Mably's view, intolerance should be the basic rule of the legislative code; tolerance, like the right of property, is nothing but a concession to corrupted humanity.

In this sort of civil order, obviously, there can be no question of liberty. From here only one step remains to complete community ownership of possessions. While eighteenth-century thinkers, living amid institutions that had evolved over many centuries, thought it impossible to return to humankind's original condition, to veterans of the French revolution difficulties of that sort seemed trivial. Why indeed not destroy at one blow the entire existing economic edifice, just as the old political order had been destroyed? If equality of material possessions was the ideal of the human community, then why not realize it on earth even at present? Such was the goal of [Gracchus] Babeuf's conspiracy, which marked the final period of the movement of 1789.

The conspirators began from the premise that nature gave each individual an identical right to enjoy all life's blessings. Hence the need for equality. But in order that equality not remain an empty word, simple equality of rights was not enough: all privileges of one individual over another would have to be eliminated. Therefore, not only should everyone have the same material resources, which could be guaranteed by communal ownership of possessions, but everyone should have the same intellectual level as well. Otherwise, the spirit of inequality would lead to the collapse of society. To this end everyone would receive the same education, which would be limited to the most necessary points. To read, write, and count, to know a little history and the laws of society—that is all a citizen needs. Everything else is luxury, which leads to the development of artificial appetites and to the perversion of the natural qualities of the individual. Freedom of thought, of course, is not permitted; all useless pursuits are banished from the state. Human needs are reduced to the bare minimum. Therefore, economic activity is limited to agriculture and to a few trades. Work is obligatory for all. In a word, [Babeuf wanted to set] a universal, obligatory norm, calculated to meet the modest requirements of the masses; anything rising above this norm would be cut off, as an evil thing.[7]

A more rigorous application of the principle of equality is impossible to imagine. But it turns out that to achieve such rigor, it is necessary completely to suppress liberty. The contradiction between these two principles is glaringly revealed. It surely is the case that while formal equality, or equality of rights, is the logical consequence of liberty identical for all, then material equality is the direct negation of liberty. Liberty consists of the possibility to control the disposition of one's own talents and resources. But because people's talents and resources are unequal, then the fruits of human activity will be different. A strong person will acquire more than a weak one, an intelligent person more than a stupid one, an industrious person more than a lazy one; and if they have children, and if we do not wish to violate natural human sentiments, then they will pass the unequal material wealth to their children.

It will not do to claim, as Mably does, that from corrupted humanity we should draw no inferences about humanity in the state of nature. Of course, if we disregard all life's diversity and, by abstraction, imagine a condition of complete homogeneity, then we shall have imagined an individual quite different from the ones we know today; but this individual will be nothing but an empty entity who is equal to other individual entities by virtue of the fact that he or she is utterly lacking in content. As soon as this individual begins to live and to acquire content, then inevitably inequality will appear, and at that point it will become necessary to take artificial measures to eradicate the inequality. Mably, who had no hope of achieving his objective, proposes palliative measures; Babeuf applies his principle rigorously to the end; but both thinkers agree on one point—namely, that material equality is inconceivable if liberty is granted to the individual. In order to achieve material equality, it is necessary not only to equalize possessions and to limit the right of the individual to dispose of what he or she has acquired, or even to take away from the individual all property and to transform his or her labor into a set of mandatory tasks, but it is essential to suppress in the individual any needs and ambitions that rise above the norm; it is necessary, by means of education, to treat the individual like soft wax, to mold him or her so that he or she can accommodate only the most common content and thus will become incapable of rising above the crowd. The Greeks portrayed this kind of education in an elaborate myth about the brigand Procrustes, who placed his victims on an iron bed and then either amputated their limbs or stretched them to conform to the bed's length. For this invention the Greeks condemned Procrustes to eternal sufferings in Tartary; yet modern socialists hold out this hellish torture as the ideal for the human community.

But why should this unprecedented tyranny be introduced? Mably claims that not liberty but equality is the natural law for humankind; liberty is only a means to preserve equality. We have already noted that this inverts the true relation between these two principles. Individuals are not equal one to another physically or intellectually or spiritually. Their concrete traits are infinitely various. They are equal only as human beings, taken in the abstract—that is, as morally sentient and therefore free beings. Consequently, equality issues from liberty, not vice-versa. But the equality inherent to liberty is equality of rights and nothing other, for the actual manifestations of liberty are again infinitely various. Liberty inheres in the right of each individual to act at his or her own discretion, not on someone else's command. Consequently, each individual will achieve his or her own end, and there can be no equating one person to another. To demand that the result of liberty be the same for everyone means to destroy liberty at its root and to subordinate the individual to a universal, externally imposed norm.

Still less can one argue, as do Babeuf and many other socialists, that all people have an identical right to the enjoyment of the good things in life. Health, intelligence, beauty—these are undoubtedly good things. Shall we say that every individual must enjoy good health? That everyone should have identical intelligence? That every woman must be just as beautiful as another? Shall we assert that no one has the right to enjoy more familial happiness than his neighbor? That everyone must have the same number of children? Or, finally, that everyone should enjoy the same climate and identical natural beauty? To make such claims is obviously absurd, yet this absurdity is implied in the basic premise. If it makes no sense to demand equality of those good things that are individual traits or that constitute the individual's environment, then it makes even less sense to demand equality of material goods which depend upon the former. Can it be said, without violating the most elementary principles of justice, that a lazy person should enjoy the same benefits as someone who has worked; that someone who has squandered a fortune should enjoy the same benefits as one who has saved it; that someone who did not manage to acquire property should enjoy the same benefits as one who had that skill? From whatever perspective we approach the question, equal enjoyment of the good things in life turns out to be a pure chimera that contradicts both human nature and the nature of human relationships. The inherent right of the individual is not to enjoy the good things in life but to be permitted freely to pursue the attainment of these good things; in other words, the individual has a right to legal equality but not material equality. The actual result of this right, given the liberty to operate, will be as various as the traits, inclinations, emotions, thoughts, and positions of individuals.

Socialism of the nineteenth century has moved the discussion concerning the distribution of goods from the personal sphere to the public sphere. It has sought a yardstick by means of which society can determine the distribution of goods among its members. The approaches to this question taken by various schools are correlated to different interpretations of the very idea of equality. The Saint-Simonians base their social order not on numerical but on proportional equality in accordance with the formula: "to each according to his or her ability." This principle is certainly of a higher order than numerical equality;

but when applied to the economic sphere, it also leads to the destruction of liberty, for the authority to measure ability is left to the government, which has unlimited control over the distribution of goods. [Charles] Fourier deviated even further from the principle of numerical equality; he replaced the Saint-Simonians' formula with another: "to each according to his or her labor, capital, and talent." Conversely, communism raised equality to an absolute dogma, which it derived from the universal human brotherhood. Nature, says [Etienne] Cabet, is the mother of the human race: all human beings are her children and so all are brothers. And because brothers are equal, then they must share equally nature's gifts. The differences that exist among them do not prevent them from having identical rights and duties or from enjoying the same prosperity, just as the distinctions among children do not prevent them from enjoying parental love that is identical for each.[8]

Here equality is derived from the ethical principle of fraternity; but what is the basis for the conclusion? The basis is that the human race consists of a single family and that all individuals are children of some indeterminate thing called nature, whose essence, Cabet says, it is useless and dangerous to investigate, for, as a result of the imperfection of human reason, such an investigation would only lead to endless arguments. And it is on this foundation that the communists think it possible to build their entire social edifice! Obviously, this doctrine follows the logic of Christian teaching,[9] which treats all human beings as sons of God and brothers in the same family. But the communists reject the religious foundation of this teaching which alone lends it meaning; they borrow only the conclusion, which loses its justification and has implications quite different than it had before. It is indeed the case that Christianity proclaims universal brotherhood; but it proclaims brotherhood as an ethical-religious precept, binding upon conscience but not to be enforced by coercion, for love cannot be subject to compulsion. Therefore, no Christian state has ever dreamt of transforming love into a right and of making it the basis of the civil order. Compulsory love is a monstrous notion, an infringement upon the most sacred elements of human nature. Moreover, it is upon this perverted notion that [Cabet] builds his entire theory of communism. The inevitable result of such an order is again the complete suppression of liberty. Personal property of any kind is prohibited. Members of society must be equal, not only in rights and responsibilities but in their work and enjoyments. Society, by a majority vote, decides all questions concerning food, clothing, housing, marriage, family, education, work, and so on, and it is claimed, as a dogma, that no one will experience even the slightest unpleasantness in obeying a law published in everyone's interest. It is also claimed that in society there will be no drunks, no thieves, no indolents, although it is by no means clear why such people would not inhabit such a society, for in it they could enjoy without hindrance the fruits of others' labor. [Pierre Joseph] Proudhon rightly notes that, under the name of equality, communism establishes a very great inequality: it licenses the exploitation of the strong by the weak. Here, he says, "the strong must perform labor for the sake of the weak, although this obligation is voluntary rather than compulsory, something advised rather than prescribed; the industrious must work for the sake of the lazy, although this is unjust; the intelligent must work for the idiot, although that is absurd; finally, a man, renouncing his ego, his spontaneity, his genius, his own affections, must deferentially efface himself before the majesty and the inexorable power of the community. . . . " "Communism," he continues, "is oppression and slavery. A man agrees to submit to duties imposed by law, to serve his country, to render services to his friends; but he wants to work at an occupation of his choice, when it pleases him and to the degree that it pleases him; he wants to be the master of his time, to discharge only essential obligations, to choose his own friends, his own forms of leisure, his own form of discipline, to render services to others at his own discretion and not on command, to sacrifice himself because he wishes to and not because it is his duty as a slave. Community ownership impedes the free use of our talents, contradicts our most noble inclinations, our most cherished emotions. . . . It violates the autonomy of our conscience and the principle of equality: the former by suppressing the spontaneity of mind and heart, by suppressing freedom in our thoughts and deeds, the latter by offering equal material rewards to work and indolence, to talent and stupidity, to virtue and vice."[10] Here as well the contradiction between liberty and equality is graphically revealed.

Proudhon himself tried to combine the two elements but was just as unsuccessful as his predecessors. Although in his criticism of communism he is lucid, in supporting his own system he is forced to resort to murky phrases which hide the poverty of his thought. Unlike the communists, he rejects equality in the enjoyment of goods, for such enjoyment depends on the individual's will, but he accepts equality in the means for acquiring these goods. This equality he deduces from the nature of community. He argues that voluntarily or involuntarily, due to the force of things, all human beings are comrades. They are bound together by common needs, by the laws of production, finally, by the mathematical principle of exchange. "No association," Proudhon says, "commercial, industrial, agricultural, is conceivable without equality; equality is a necessary condition of its existence." In equality is the essence of justice, which

Proudhon defines as "recognition in another of an individual who is equal to us." According to the ancient dictum, the just is equal, the unjust is unequal. Consequently, to act justly means to offer each person an equal share of goods in return for equal work.[11]

One needs only a moment's reflection to see how arbitrary are these conclusions. First, one cannot agree that all individuals, as a result of economic needs and the exchange of commodities, are part of a comradely association, comparable to a commercial partnership. If on occasion I exchange products with an inhabitant of South America, it does not follow that I am connected with that person in every other respect. Proudhon extends this principle so far that, according to his theory, if in a shipwreck I see a drowning man and fail to offer him assistance, I am violating my obligation to him as a comrade. But [Proudhon's theory] confuses the ethical bond among individuals with their economic connection. If I do not render assistance to a drowning man, I violate my ethical duty to love my fellow man, but this duty is entirely unrelated to the laws of production and exchange. [If it were the case that the laws of production and exchange applied to drowning men then] I should find myself negotiating with the drowning man over the fee [for my assistance].

By the same token, recognition of another equal person flows from respect for the individual as a rational, free being, not from membership in the same corporation or from economic intercourse. Yet recognition of another equal individual no more entails equality in the means of acquiring goods than it does equality of gender, of age, of physical strength, of size, of beauty, of intellectual capacities or anything else. Among human beings the only thing equal is the abstract quality of being human, not any concrete component of the individual personality, much less any external appurtenances. It may well be that equality is the essence of justice, but one must know what sort of equality and in what sphere. We have seen that equality may be numerical and proportional, and that assigning equal rewards to unequal individuals is not an imperative of justice but quite the opposite. Proudhon admits as much when he says that it is unjust to give the same wage to a laborer and to an indolent man. One ought not to refer to the classical dictum without having understood its implications. That leads only to complete conceptual confusion.

Much less can it be said that equality for workers must follow from the equality of rights enjoyed by individuals. It is a mystery how Proudhon arrived at the conclusion that no industrial or other enterprise can function properly without complete equality among their members. The importance of each person in any kind of business enterprise is determined formally by the relationships between members of the corporation, and materially by what each member invests in the corporation. A person who invests more ought to earn more. The director of an enterprise cannot stand on the same level as a simple employee, such as an architect or a mason. The same rule applies to joint-stock companies: the person having the most stock shares will have the greatest number of votes. In light of this, Proudhon excludes the property owner from his generalization about corporations, for he thinks that the property owner is no one's comrade: the property owner takes the surplus [profit] for himself, to the detriment of others' interests. But if we eliminate property, then there would be no commercial firms whatsoever: business enterprises could exist only on paper. Fictional corporations, aloof from real-life contingencies, might consist of completely equal members, for such members would be nothing but abstractions; real corporations, however, combine the most heterogeneous elements.

Finally, it cannot be said that Proudhon has succeeded in reconciling equality with liberty. What he calls liberty is a social arrangement combining the principles of communism and property. This arrangement admits the "mutual independence of individuals, or the autonomy of the individual, resulting from differences in talents and abilities." But of what do the rights of talent proclaimed by Proudhon consist? We have already seen the answer. Talent, he thinks, is the community's property; it is created by society and belongs not to the individual but to society, which, by virtue of this ownership, appropriates what talent has produced. Moreover, Proudhon claims, to society belongs not just that which talent produces but the product of all labor. A worker lives and dies as an insolvent debtor of society. How, one asks, is this liberty to be distinguished from slavery? We shall not be surprised at the contradiction if we look at what Proudhon means by the word "liberty." He derives the word *libertas* [liberty] from *libra* [scales]. "Liberty," he says, "is the balance between rights and responsibilities: to make a man free means to make him equal to others—that is, to place him on the same level."[12] It would appear that Proudhon's notion of liberty is a Procrustean bed—that is, a brigand's torture.

In the final analysis, it is nevertheless clear that material equality is tantamount to slavery; material equality is possible only with the complete suppression of human liberty and of all personal peculiarities. And because the only foundation for equality is liberty, then it is apparent that material equality is a self-contradictory principle, for it destroys its own foundation. Such is the obvious conclusion one reaches after analyzing socialist teachings, a conclusion that is endorsed by everyone capable of thinking logically.

In spite of this, modern socialists-of-the-chair and members of the Association for Social Policy boldly assert that socialists are logically correct when they derive equality of material conditions from the principle of equality proclaimed by contemporary societies. "The acquisition of legal and political equality," says Adolph Wagner, "has very little value for much of the populace without the achievement of the next consequence of the principle of equality—namely, equality of economic condition or, at the very least, equality in the conditions of production. Yet political economy, like the philosophy of law and politics, has resisted this conclusion. Conversely, the theories of communism and of socialism have accepted the conclusion, a conclusion that follows logically once one grants the premises upon which the requirement for equality is based. For their part the lower classes understandably have raised equality to a practical demand. Hence the struggle against historically outmoded forms of property relations, against private landed property, against private capital, against the right of inheritance. Hence, in other words, the origins of the 'social question,' which, at least from this perspective, can be formulated as the consciously recognized contradiction between existing economic development and the principle of social development, a principle which is both an ideal and something being realized in political life, freedom and equality."[13]

Of course, no one would make such a bold assertion if the true foundations of equality in the civic and political spheres had been clearly exposited. For it would become apparent at once that between the premises of the argument and the conclusion there is not only no connection but a contradiction. [That is why] Wagner has stated these fundamental propositions in an utterly perverse fashion. According to Wagner, the principle of individual equality comprises equal rights in the personal and the economic domain; equality of rights consists of establishing equal conditions for economic competition. Wagner believes such equality to be an imperative of justice; consequently, he rejects in principle any inequality which cannot be attributed to varying results of individual economic activity.[14] By [Wagner's] logic, equality of material resources for engaging in economic competition must be accepted as a precondition of any just economic order: this equality is already implied in the very premise of the argument, and it is quite unnecessary for us to deduce it. The problem is that the entire premise is arbitrary. In reality, equality of rights entails neither the establishment of equal conditions for economic competition nor the establishment of equality in the material or intellectual sense. Equality of rights means the establishment of equal rights for all—that is, the subordination of everyone to the same code of laws, rather than the bequest to everyone of identical material resources or identical intellectual capacities and educations, which would be necessary for equality in competition. That is the way that the people who originally advocated equality of rights understood that notion, and that is how it is understood today by those who are acquainted with the theory and practice of civic life. Equality of rights consists in the preservation of everyone's individual liberty and of their property, in the fulfillment of their duties, in respect for the right of inheritance—that is, in all of the things rejected by socialism. Consequently, socialist doctrine is not the systematic application to society of principles developed in the modern age, rather it is the systematic rejection of those principles. Wagner himself correctly notes that equality, a child of eighteenth-century philosophy, is a component of the individualist perspective; socialism is a radical protest against individualism. Equality is based upon the individual; socialism is based on society swallowing up the individual. Hence it is clear that, when advocating equality, socialism is theoretically dependent upon the very set of ideas that it in fact rejects.

Having portrayed equality of material resources as a logical consequence of modern principles, Wagner does not try to defend it without reservation. In his eclectic fashion, he rejects as abstract theory the systematic logical application of any principle, and contents himself with isolated observations, which amount to a compromise between opposed points of view. But because these observations lack the necessary logical foundation and consistency, they lose all theoretical and practical importance. Hence Wagner takes positions that are striking only because they are so odd. We have already seen above that Wagner accepts as indisputable truth the notion that everyone, by virtue of liberty and equality, has equal rights to the means of subsistence and to the instruments that make subsistence possible. From this he deduces, as a necessary consequence, something quite monstrous—namely that no one has the right to the least surplus so long as even one member of society lacks what is necessary.[15] We shall not repeat that such a right is nothing but pure fiction. In reality, granting assistance to the needy is always and everywhere a philanthropic duty, not something dictated by the principles of freedom and equality. We cannot deduce from equality of individual rights that charity should become compulsory under law.[16]

And so we arrive at the conclusion that although formal equality, or equality under the law, is an imperative of liberty, material equality, or equality of material status, contradicts liberty. As a free being every person is an independent source of activity; but because the material and intellectual resources and capacities of individuals, their inclinations, their status, the environment and conditions within which they act, are unequal, then the results of their actions cannot be identical. Liberty inevitably leads to material inequality. It clearly follows that to eliminate material inequality one must suppress the very liberty from which it originates, eradicate in individuals the autonomous center of their life and activity, transform individuals into tools of the government, a government which, by imposing a universal norm upon all individuals, may establish equality, but an equality not of liberty but of slavery.

The inequality inherent in human nature reflects a general law of the physical universe. Nature has everywhere established inequality of physical strength, of traits and positions, for only by this means can the infinite variety of life be manifested.

Human beings are not exempt from this universal law. They, too, are placed by nature in infinitely various conditions that determine their entire existence. Some are born in icy polar regions, others under the burning sun of the equator, still others in blessed climes where there is eternal spring. Some live off nature's largesse almost effortlessly; others must constantly work over every inch of ground in order to survive. Some are surrounded by deserts where they are seemingly isolated from the rest of humanity; others enjoy all the advantages of natural communications, which provide both the comforts of life and the possibility of intellectual development. These factors are accompanied by the distinction of race. Certain races [*rasy*] are apparently privileged and predestined to lead humanity, while others are evidently incapable of raising themselves to a high level of education. Whether these differences can be overcome, whether humanity will ever arrive at a condition in which all races stand at the same high level of intellectual development, we do not know. But throughout the course of previous history, this distinction has constituted a basic feature of human life, and entire tribes have perished in their encounters with higher civilization. Finally, there are distinctions between individuals' innate strengths and capacities. One person is born strong and healthy, another sickly and weak. The same point can be made about intellectual abilities. Only by averting one's eyes from reality can one claim that all people, by nature, have identical abilities and that distinctions among them arise solely from differences in upbringing and education. We know that some individuals are born geniuses and others are born idiots. Between these two extremes there is an entire spectrum with an infinite variety of subtle differences. Nature's gifts are not showered in identical measure upon everyone, they are not equally distributed, but, in accordance with nature's own law, these gifts are manifested in an infinite number of gradations. They endow life with all the variety and all the extremes that one might expect, given human nature.

Linked with these innate differences are others which flow from the peculiarities of human nature. In reality, an individual does not rely solely upon himself or herself; the individual does not begin from nothing. All human development is based on the fact that each generation continues the work of its predecessors. Its point of departure is determined by its legacy from the preceding generations, a legacy which, in its turn, it augments by its own labor so as to pass a new legacy to its successors. This point of departure is not the same for all. He who has achieved more can leave a greater legacy to his children. This is a new source of inequality, which sometimes accentuates and sometimes moderates the effect of innate inequality in talents. By virtue of this principle, people are born not only intelligent or stupid, strong or weak, healthy or sickly, but rich or poor, to distinguished families or in obscurity, with prospects for further education or with obstacles to higher development. And this difference in one's inherited legacy is important not only for individuals but for entire peoples, among which some enjoy all the advantages of civilization accumulated over centuries, while others ossify in a primitive state.

Can such an unequal distribution of the good things in life be reconciled with the imperatives of justice? Why does one person receive every privilege from birth and another person receive nothing? Simply because one person is born in the polar region, another near the equator, one black, another white, one intelligent, another stupid, one healthy, another sickly. A religious man sees in this the will of Providence, which fixes each person's place on the earth in accordance with his or her calling in the present and future world. This faith serves the individual as a source of support throughout life and as a consolation in adversity. True philosophy confirms this outlook, for it, too, by virtue of reason's dictates, leads the individual to recognition of an omnipotent, omniscient, beneficent Being, who governs the world and controls human destiny. Those who accept neither religion nor philosophy must content themselves with the knowledge that inequality of status is a universal law, from which human beings are as little exempt as are other creatures. It is absurd to rebel against this law and pointless to deny it, for in the name of what principle would we resist it? In the name of justice, which supposedly demands that no one have innate privileges? But in that case we must declare it unjust that one person is born stronger, healthier, handsomer, smarter than another. And because to do so would be absurd, then, obviously, our demand is inappropriate. Pure empiricists may attempt to explain one generation's innate inequalities in strengths and abilities as traits acquired from parents who brought them into the world. But if we should accept this explanation, then how shall we rid ourselves of other inherited privileges? If parents can pass on to their children better health, greater strength, more beauty or intellectual abilities than that possessed by others, then why can they not pass on to their children greater wealth or a better education? Not justice, but envy rebels against this kind of privilege. Justice requires that each person dispose of his or her own goods. In fact, justice would be violated if unequal individuals were to be subject to the same norm, if, in the name of abstract equality, we should take away from one person in order to give to another. It would be violated if we should maim the healthy because others are crippled, if we should deform the beautiful because others are hideous, if we should deprive the intelligent of an education because the stupid are unable to learn, if we should confiscate the legacy of the wealthy individual because someone else's father left nothing. Human laws, deriving from human nature itself, demand no less respect than nature's laws. Infringement of the one or the other is a violation of justice. Of course, we have more recourse against those laws which have come into existence by means of our own conscious efforts. But if we are free to confiscate the legacy of the rich, we shall also be free to cut off the legs of the healthy, to pour acid on the faces of the beautiful, or to bind the crania of the newborn so as to reduce them to the same degree of intellectual stupefaction. Are such actions compatible with the dictates of justice?

The law of unequal distribution of strength, of talents and goods, however, does not place upon an individual an irrevocable and ineffaceable stamp, which would bind him or her to one and the same place in the natural order or in the civic hierarchy. Inequality of privileges acquired at birth is not a life sentence from which one cannot be released. That which an individual receives at birth constitutes a point of departure; subsequent progress depends on his or her own initiative. As a free being, one can tear oneself away from one's native soil, create for oneself new living conditions, raise oneself to a higher level. In this respect, one is to a significant extent the maker of one's own destiny. Yet no matter how free one may be, one is nevertheless dependent in large measure on one's point of departure, on one's environment, and even more on the eternal laws governing human life and human development. Liberty does not consist of the opportunity arbitrarily to frame one's own life plans and to carry them out at own's own pace. One is as unlikely to act successfully while simultaneously violating the laws of the human community as one is to build a machine without consulting the laws of mechanics. Of course, one might theoretically construct such a machine, but it would not function. Analogously, one may also invent whatever society one wishes, but it will fall apart.

Furthermore, the liberty that provides an individual with the opportunity to escape from his or her original circumstances and to improve upon his or her unequal position also leads to a new inequality. In addition to the natural variation that arises from differences in the circumstances attending birth, there is the variation arising from the free activity of individuals, and the latter is much more significant a factor than the former. We see that animals of a given species are all more or less similar to each other; but among humans no individual is really identical to another: each has his or her own physiognomy and character. The source of this variety is liberty: liberty makes each person a unique being, a being who reflects the universal order in a peculiar fashion and who brings his or her own peculiar consciousness to life.

Finally, we must take into account the laws governing the development of human societies. The history of humanity illustrates how the variety of elements in the depths of the human soul generates an infinite variation in the positions of individuals. In their primitive state, all people are more or less alike. Under such circumstances what matters most is natural distinctions alone, such as whether one is husband or wife, father or child; among social classes there are not yet any sharp contrasts. Yet as soon as historical progress begins, social inequality inevitably is introduced. The upper classes are set apart from the general mass; the opposition of upper and lower classes appears. It cannot be otherwise, for education is at first the prerogative of the few, and only little by little, by means of a slow historical process and by an infinite number of small steps, education spreads to the remainder of society. As a result, higher consciousness is always the prerogative of the minority, which by virtue of this consciousness sets itself apart from the crowd. The beginning of development fosters a kind of fermentation within the homogeneous mass; the different elements contained within the mass separate themselves from it and stand apart; some rise to the top, others sink below. At the top of the social pyramid a new life is introduced, while the lower strata remain submerged in an undifferentiated condition.

This law, which is obvious to anyone acquainted with history, is recognized even by those who largely share the socialists' worldview. "Cultural imperatives," Adolph Wagner says, "arise and develop first among those individuals who are at least partly exempt from care about their material existence. [Because they do not have to worry about their survival] they have time to devote to other activity and the leisure to develop their intellects—preconditions essential if cultural imperatives are to make themselves felt. And these preconditions, in turn, are connected with another prerequisite for cultural life—

namely, that there exist other individuals and classes who save the elite from being concerned about their material existence. Thus social and economic inequality is the preliminary condition for the original appearance of any higher culture. . . . And later, inasmuch as, to a certain degree, cultural imperatives arise and develop first among individuals or in a small circle, one may, indeed one must, recognize as necessary the existence of a significant lower stratum that creates the material preconditions for the existence of the entire nation and which itself has only a modest share in the highly refined and advanced cultural life."[17]

The inequality attendant upon human development, however, plays different roles in the various stages of the historical process. If the first step forward is the appearance of opposing elements from within [a previously] homogeneous mass, then subsequent progress leads to the synthesis of these opposing elements. Such is the general law of human development. But this synthesis does not proceed through the destruction of the opposing elements and not through a return to primitive homogeneity, but by the insertion between them of intermediate strata that, by linking the extremes, transform the various strata of society into a harmonious whole. Thus the fruits of historical development do not perish; the variety developed by history is preserved, but the distinctions imperceptibly merge one into the other so that the intermediate strata of society gradually outweigh the opposing extremes. That is the normal impact of inequality, the law that rules both nature and the natural order of human relations. Statisticians, relying upon empirical data, have outlined this law in their theory of the average man, while philosophers and writers, both ancient and modern, who have examined carefully the nature and properties of social relationships, see this law as one of the foundations of a normal community. Thus Aristotle teaches about the predominance of middle classes in the ideal society, a teaching that has been rejuvenated in modern theories of constitutional monarchy. The laws of human development alter to some degree the natural distribution of inequality, for here, in the intermediate stages of history, one witnesses the appearance and struggle of opposing elements. But the predominance of the extremes is only a transitional phenomenon, one that, after subsequent development, gives way to the dominance of the middle elements. Thus if a developing society temporarily diverges from the normal order, it will return, but it will return only after the appearance and crystallization of whatever variation that is latent in human nature. Subsequent progress occurs as the middle stratum becomes more and more powerful; but this progress is driven not by an artificial leveling process which, destroying naturally developed variations, leads to primitive savagery, but by a free movement of civic forces that gradually and incrementally spreads improvements to the mass of society.

Conscious recognition and institutionalization of true civil rights can facilitate the process of civic improvement. We have seen that the law's essential role is the preservation of human liberty. [Initially,] the development of material inequality leads to a struggle between opposing elements of society, and thus to the subjugation of the weak by the strong. In the most rudimentary stages of its development the law reinforces this subjugation; it protects the liberty of the strong, not the liberty of the weak. Thus during the ascendancy of the clan order there exists the unlimited authority of husband over wife, of father over children. Subsequently slavery is introduced, serfdom is legalized, one Estate is granted civil and political privileges that others lack. Natural inequality becomes more pronounced as a result of legal inequality. Yet the higher development of consciousness and of institutions lead to another perspective. Men and women begin to understand that, in spite of the infinite inequality of strength, talents, and material conditions, everyone shares the same human nature, from which identical rights flow. Each and every individual is a rational, free being and therefore may demand liberty identical to that of others. Hence comes the legal precept that the law must be the same for all. Above the infinite gradations of the economic scale stands a formal principle asserting what is common to all human beings. This principle does not obliterate diversity but holds it within certain limits; it prevents natural inequality from becoming legal inequality—that is, it prevents the liberty of one individual from infringing upon that of another. Natural, material, and intellectual forces are permitted a full range of expression; but each individual must be sure his or her actions do not exceed legal limits, thereby violating another's rights; for everyone has the same rights; each person is recognized to be a rational, free being. This is the normal order of the human community, the highest achievement of theoretical legal consciousness and of human historical development. Law goes no further, and it is incapable of doing more for society. As soon as law passes beyond these boundaries, it infringes upon individual freedom—that is, it destroys its own foundation and falls into contradiction with itself.

There is no doubt that [the institutionalization of equal rights under the law] does not exhaust the task of human societies. While the normal distribution of inequality fosters the predominance of society's middle strata, the extremes nevertheless remain. It is pointless to be concerned about those who, at least in material terms, stand above the middle stratum: they are able to stand upon their own. But those who stand below the middle stratum may need assistance. This imperative can be satisfied not by law but by another principle—charity. The solution here lies not in the abolition of liberty but in finding ways to compensate for the inadequacy of [material] means. This can be accomplished first of all by private charitable activity; in those cases where charity turns out to be insufficient, the state can provide assistance through its bureaucracy. In either case philanthropy is not a violation but a fulfillment of rights under the law. Legal rights are one and the same for all; philanthropy is directed toward a particular portion of society needing assistance. If the state should take it into its head to alter legal rights in the name of philanthropy—that is, if, instead of establishing the same freedom for all, it should begin to despoil the rich for the sake of the poor, as the socialists demand—then this would be not only a violation of justice but a perversion of the basic laws of the human community. Applying Proudhon's critique of communism cited above, one may say that, if slavery is the exploitation of the weak by the strong, then socialism is the exploitation of the strong by the weak. And the latter, even more than the former, contradicts the nature of things. The enslavement of the weak by the strong, although it also violates justice, is at least compatible with the natural disposition of forces. Such enslavement, as we have seen, constitutes, at certain historical stages, a necessary precondition of social progress; the enslavement of the strong by the weak is the negation of development, for it does violence to the very elements of society upon which future progress depends. Such a system is nothing other than a irrational attempt to destroy the fruits of humanity's entire preceding history and, under the pretext of equality, to return us to a condition of primitive homogeneity—that is, to a condition of savagery.

As long as man remains a free being—that is, as long as he remains a man—the principles of legal right must remain inviolable. That is why one must preserve property in its full measure, freedom of contracts, and the right of inheritance, which is an integral part of the very notion of family; alongside equality before the law, material inequality must also be preserved, for it is the inevitable consequence of free activity, and it alone provides an opportunity for the infinite variety of life fully to manifest itself. To infringe upon these principles is to infringe upon the foundations of human nature, upon the imperatives of liberty, upon the dignity of the individual as a rational being. And because every rational polity and every enlightened community is based upon these principles, their violation would also destroy the true foundations of public life.

Such is the conclusion to which we are led by examining the principles that should govern the legal relationships [among citizens], a conclusion which is confirmed both by theoretical speculation and by the historical record. From the preceding it is clear that the law of right, springing forth from human nature itself, from the central characteristics of the human spirit, constitutes a well-ordered, integral system, in which all parts are mutually dependent and connected in a rational fashion. But this system is not only the fruit of abstract speculation; for it is a system developed throughout history and now realized in human institutions. Theoretical speculation is confirmed by experience, and in turn experience finds confirmation in theory. If, in view of contemporary institutions, we should not regard the existing system of law which is expressed in property, in contracts, in inheritance, as the abstract fruit of legal philosophizing, then neither, by the same token, in view of theoretical imperatives, should we understand the law as nothing but a transient historical phenomenon that, with time, must yield its place to another order. It is precisely the agreement between theory and practice that raises our theory of law to the status of an irrefutable truth, of an unalterable law of the human spirit and of human development. This conclusion is further reinforced by the obvious inadequacy of the opposing views, by the endless conceptual confusion and by the crying contradictions that characterize socialism of all types and also the social prescriptions so closely associated with it. The future imagined by socialists and their allies among political economists is nothing other than an idle fantasy, lacking both theoretical and practical foundation and having support neither in the realm of logic nor that of experience. The future belongs to that which is rooted in the eternal and ineffaceable qualities of the human spirit and which, for this very reason, is rooted in the entire preceding history of humanity. Hence it is our firm conviction that the edifice of the human community that has been created by millennia, whatever ills may beset it, will not perish. Only those doctrines that are rooted in our contemporary intellectual anarchy and that depend upon an appeal to the passions of the ignorant masses will disappear before the light of reason. Much misfortune and many sufferings have befallen humanity in its age-old quest; but humanity will find a remedy against such adversities neither in the idle dreams of utopians nor in the destructive designs of fanatics, much less in pitiful practical compromises between contradictory ideologies, but only in clear thinking, which, taking the infinite variety of life as one of the deepest foundations of the human spirit, is alone able to link the past with the future.

Capitalism and Socialism

We have examined the nature and characteristics of various factors of production.[1] Now let us investigate the impact upon them exerted by the fundamental economic principle, liberty.

The effect of liberty upon natural resources is to subordinate them to human will, to permit their acquisition by an individual. This is the primary economic imperative, an imperative which, when sanctioned by law, gives rise to [the existence of] property. The elements of entrepreneurship and labor are both involved [in this process]. Both these elements arise from the economic activity of the individual and acquire their content from that activity.

We have seen that there are resources and products of nature which exist in limited quantity and may be acquired by human beings in order to serve their needs. Who acquires them under the law of economic liberty? Obviously, they are acquired by those individuals who first make them objects of economic activity—that is, who use them to satisfy personal needs. A wild fruit belongs to the person who has picked it, an animal to the person who has killed it, a fish to the person who has caught it, the land to that person who has occupied it in order to cultivate it. Others may acquire these objects only from the original owners, either by voluntary agreement, as liberty and right demand, or through force, by enslaving the owners, or by crime. An economic objective can be achieved only by acquiring the resources necessary to achieve it, and these resources belong to the person who has transformed them into instruments for achieving the objective. If there should arise a new objective that requires use of resources already being employed to satisfy another person's objective, then according to the law of economic liberty, one must enter into a transaction with the first owner and must exchange something of equal value.

This principle applies all the more to those forces and products of nature which could not serve human needs unless someone adapted their form to suit this objective. In such cases, the economic significance of the object depends wholly on its form; the form, being a byproduct of economic activity, belongs to its inventor. And again, only in this way can economic growth occur. Nobody will work if the fruits of labor are to satisfy not one's personal needs but someone else's needs. In a free economic system, the utilization of labor to satisfy someone else's needs may occur only by means of a voluntary transaction or a voluntary concession.

Thus property and contracts inevitably result from the application of economic liberty to natural resources. But we have seen that liberty develops gradually among human beings. Liberty is the consequence of a slow historical process that raises us above the pressure of our environment and reveals our true nature. This is true of economic liberty as well as formal statutory liberty. Therefore, [the principle of] private property that is engendered by economic liberty is not immediately institutionalized in human societies, though in a rudimentary form it is found even at the most primitive stages of human existence. To the savage hunter belongs both the weapon used to kill a beast and the beast itself, once killed. Yet land usually is the common possession of those natural communities that occupy and protect it by their collective forces.

In agrarian communities, the land itself is transformed little by little into private property. From the economic perspective, this is an inevitable result of combining land with labor, capital, and enterprise. In order to make land produce that which is necessary to sustain human life, labor must be applied to it. A goodly portion of this labor may be of long-term significance: to farm one must clear forests, remove stones from the soil, or perhaps irrigate a parcel or drain the soil. Labor thus performed may permanently enhance the value of the land. And we have seen that the fruits of labor, according to the law of liberty, must belong to the person who has performed the labor, or to that person to whom the worker has sold his or her toil.

At more advanced stages of economic development, capital is combined with land. In intensive farming, an individual continually returns to nature everything that he or she has taken from it, and also adds to it various improvements. Thus modern production is to a large extent the fruit of human ingenuity. Finally, even a resource that may be easily exploited by virtue of its favorable location and a propitious environment belongs, according to the law of economic liberty, to the person who can make use of it, for a natural resource becomes an economic resource only when someone utilizes it. Herein lies the main incentive to turn natural resources to human use. Once acquired as property, a natural resource becomes a thing of value, something to be transferred from one individual to another, something which can no longer be acquired free of charge. When purchasing land, a person invests his or her capital in it. For an advantageous location and for more fertile soil he or she will pay more dearly than for land which lacks these characteristics. Consequently, here as well what was once a gift of nature is transformed into an acquisition. In the more advanced stages of industrial development, due to the commodification of the forces of nature, nothing free remains. Everything has been produced or acquired through the activity of the free individual, and therefore everything, according to the basic law of economic production, has become a possession of the free individual.

As to that which has been acquired through labor, this proposition is patently clear. The economic liberty of an individual consists in control over the use of his or her own energies and activities. Here the individual is master, no one else. Therefore, the individual exercises discretion over the disposition of his or her own labor; the individual may use it to satisfy personal needs or may assign it to someone else, either free of charge or for some specified reward. For this reason that which is acquired by labor belongs to the laborer and to no one else. This is an imperative of justice and it is an imperative of economic life as well, for, as we have seen above, acquisition is the objective of and incentive for productive labor; productive labor would be unthinkable in the absence of compensation. Each person works bearing in mind personal advantage, and, as a free individual, the laborer is the sole judge of his or her advantage. On the other hand, an individual who depends upon another's labor also seeks personal economic gain; and because he or she is also a free individual, and consequently judge of his or her own advantage, the condition upon which labor is performed can be determined only on the basis of mutual consent. In a free labor market, a contract is a necessary form under which any collaborative activity is performed.

There is no doubt that, given the struggle between interests that is finally to be resolved by mutual consent, the greater leverage may on one occasion lie with one party and on the second occasion with the other party to the contract. But this is an inevitable consequence of liberty; we have seen that liberty inevitably entails material inequality. Industrial transactions occur under the influence of an infinite number of circumstances which may give the upper hand to one or the other party. Achieving material equality is the more problematic because the very notion of advantage is to a large degree a subjective one. In essence, that party which needs the other less will always have the upper hand. But this party is not always the entrepreneur, as the socialists claim. Of course, the entrepreneur has leverage by virtue of possessing capital, and so may wait [to conclude a contract], whereas a laborer must eat. But the worker also has leverage in that, without his or her labor, the entrepreneur may be bankrupted; if the worker has savings he or she may wait [to conclude a contract] even longer than the entrepreneur. Where there is a shortage of laborers, the upper hand will always be held by the workers. Moreover, an entrepreneur always acts for the future, and the profits for the sake of which workers are hired may never materialize at all, whereas the worker in any case receives his or her wage. Which of these circumstances is of more importance in the negotiation of a contract depends partly on the parties' disposition, but also upon general conditions in which they operate, particularly on the relations between capital and the populace. Below we shall examine this question in greater detail; here we shall note that the very laws governing these relations operate only in free economic systems, and therefore the form in which they manifest themselves is also that of a free contract. Any deviation from this principle must be regarded as a limitation upon liberty and as a violation of the economic laws that operate by virtue of liberty.

It is equally obvious that these principles also apply to capital. Here as well, private property and contracts are the inevitable consequences of economic liberty. Capital, as we have seen, is a result of savings; consequently, it belongs to the person who saves it. For if I have the right to spend money and I do not spend it, if I may use it to satisfy my immediate desires but instead keep it to satisfy my future needs, then it surely belongs to me and to no one else. From a legal standpoint, this is an imperative of justice; from an economic standpoint, it is a basic precondition for the accumulation of wealth. Nobody will save if he or she will be unable to enjoy the fruits of saving. As soon as a thing is mine, then I, as the sole judge of my own interests, have the right to make whatever economic use of it that I wish: I may use it in my own productive enterprise, I may convey it to someone else to be used on the basis of a mutual agreement, or I may give it outright to someone else. But because saving is future-oriented, it is inextricably linked with the transmission of property by inheritance. Taking care of one's children is one of the main incentives for saving; if this incentive were taken away from the individual, then the process of capital accumulation would come to an end and the economic development of society would also cease.

We see here a new confirmation of the general rule that liberty inevitably leads to inequality. One person saves more, another less, a third nothing; one individual invests his capital in a profitable enterprise, another uses it unproductively. With the transfer of capital from hand to hand, and particularly in the case of inheritance, this inequality increases. The greater the capital, the greater the possibilities for savings. In free economic systems, capital accumulation is the chief source of the unequal distribution of wealth among individuals.

Finally, insofar as freedom of choice is concerned, a free economic system means that each individual is free to begin whatever enterprise that he or she may think fit, for each individual is the sole judge of his or her own energies and resources. Any limitation in this respect is an infringement upon the freedom of the individual. Because the individual undertakes an enterprise at his or her own risk, in the expectation of some future profit, then the profit received belongs to him or her and to no one else—not to the landowner who rents land to the entrepreneur, not to the capitalist who charges interest, not to the worker who receives a salary [from the entrepreneur], and still less to society which has the right to demand compensation for protection rendered but which has no interest in an enterprise as such. Here everything depends on the individual's will and on the entrepreneur's individual activity, and therefore the results of this activity accrue to the entrepreneur not to society. Again, these results may be infinitely varied; the success of an enterprise depends on the personal traits of the entrepreneur and on innumerable external circumstances. There may be a windfall profit, but a huge loss is also conceivable. Enrichment and impoverishment fall upon the entrepreneur alone, for the entrepreneur began the enterprise at his or her own risk. Others may share in gains or losses to the extent that they voluntarily have associated themselves with the entrepreneur's interests.

Thus a free economy, in its manifold guises, is necessarily based on private property and free contracts. This is not some arbitrarily designed legal order, with which, willy-nilly, the progress of industry has become accidentally bound up, as the *Kathedersozialisten* claim; it is an arrangement fostered by the free flow of property and contracts and finding its justification in their peculiar imperatives. The legal order takes these imperatives under its protection because they are also the imperatives of justice. Justice prescribes that one should render to each his or her own, and what belongs to an individual, by the ineradicable law of human nature, is that which is acquired through the exercise of liberty.

The consequence of this free flow of economic forces is that in society there appear individuals with different economic missions: landowners, capitalists, entrepreneurs, and workers. The different occupations of individuals, which are all equally necessary in economic life, have sometimes been compared to the various functions of an organism. As in a physical organism, the distribution of economic functions occurs on its own, according to natural processes, without any external regulation. In a newly discovered country where there are no preexisting social obstacles, occupational groups spring up without any external coercion, simply because they are demanded by economic life. Unlike physical organisms, however, occupational groups do not bind their active members for life. An artificial organization of social Estates or caste system is required if an individual is to be bound to a specific status group. In a free economy an individual may, by choice, move from one occupational category to another. A free individual has the right to occupy in society that niche to which his or her own activity may elevate him or her, and this again is a precondition for an advanced modern economy, for only in a free economy can each person's talent find a fitting place. In a free economy an individual is not even bound by a specific type of occupation; for the individual may engage in several activities at once and may participate in various facets of production. There is no need for a landowner to be exclusively a landowner, for a capitalist to be merely a capitalist. If a landowner cultivates his or her land and does not lease it out, then he or she may also be an agrarian entrepreneur. A small landowner will perform most physical labor himself. By the same token, an entrepreneur almost always possesses a certain amount of capital to invest in his or her enterprise. A small entrepreneur, a craftsman, a renter, is also a worker. Finally, even a worker is not limited to living off his or her labor: as soon as the worker manages to save some money, he or she becomes a small-scale capitalist; if he or she has a parcel of land, he or she may also be a landowner. The possible permutations are infinite, according to the various conditions and exigencies of life.

As to what distribution of productive forces is optimal for economic growth, here there is and can be no general rule. Everything depends on the character of the existing economic forces and on the natural or historical circumstances in which they operate; and because natural and historical circumstances may vary infinitely, it is impossible to classify them under a single rubric. Life itself must serve as the best indicator; but again, for this to occur, at least at the most advanced stages of development, there is a single ineluctable precondition—liberty. It is vital that the innumerable centers of activity upon which economic growth depends have the unfettered possibility to unleash their latent energies. Only then will there be established among them the relations that are demanded by the nature and character of these productive forces; only then will the economic development of society be able to attain its optimal level. Conversely, any artificial arrangement designed to foster among productive forces other relations than those which might arise from their unfettered activity is both a violation of economic laws and a diminution of productive capacity, which is rooted in the principle of liberty.

Such is the consequence of socialism. Socialists want to replace what Rodbertus calls "industry taken in isolation" with a general organization that receives its direction from above. In order to accomplish this objective, of the four factors of production mentioned above, three of them will be concentrated in the hands of public authority. Society is to be landowner, capitalist, and entrepreneur. At least this is the general direction in which socialist doctrine leads. "A truly logical and well-conceived system of socialism," Schäffle writes, "is to be found only where private capital is replaced by the capital of public institutions established for production and exchange."[2]

But not all socialists agree on what they mean by the term *society,* in whose hands all economic activity must be concentrated. The school of anarchists confines itself to calling for the overthrow of the state and for the replacement of private ownership by group or communal ownership, where collectives will deal with each other on the basis of free, contractual relations. Against this theory Schäffle properly objects that the organization of groups and distribution among them of members cannot occur except with the government's assistance; consequently, even here there can be no complete anarchy. Moreover, there is no guarantee that contractual relations between groups will lead to better results than contractual relations among individuals. In any case, the community's general interests, which are held to be the most important, lack an advocate in the anarchist system. The result of this system, Schäffle claims, will be that "in place of the existing anarchy among private individuals there will arise perhaps a much worse anarchy among groups."[3] It is obvious that the whole theory is based on utter conceptual confusion. [Anarchistic] socialists denounce the existing order because unsupervised production leads to anarchy, yet their solution proclaims anarchy as a basic principle of the economy. The contradiction is clear.

Schäffle himself prefers a system of self-government to anarchistic reciprocity. According to his theory, each separate branch of industry should constitute an independent whole, governed by individuals elected from society at large.[4] But this doctrine commits the same error as the first. On the one hand, society is proclaimed to be a unitary organism in which the parts stand in strict subordination to the whole; it is asserted that "only the organization and direction of social exchange of material goods by the united agents of the will of society can foster a truly national economy";[5] on the other hand, this unitary organism is divided into separate units administered by "independent central directorates of the separate branches of industry."[6] It is clear that these independent directorates, each bearing in mind the particular interests of its branch of industry, will seek their own advantages. The only way to avoid such an outcome is to subordinate the directorates to a single central agency representing the interests of the whole and directing production as a whole. Consequently, Schäffle himself, having proclaimed the directorates independent of each other, admits that to make the most important decisions "one may organize a general, central directorate from representatives of the special directorates."[7] But in that case, the supreme, general, central directorate will act as the controlling agent of production, and the autonomy of the individual directors will disappear. Schäffle sought a way to reconcile the socialist ideal with the principle of liberty, but could do so only at the expense of logic. The anarchy of groups that he rejected [in criticizing the anarchists] is transferred [under his system] to separate branches of production where freedom will be even less in evidence, for at least the anarchists' groups comprise integrated local centers, whereas separate branches of production that may exist in a given nation have no autonomous significance whatsoever and are economically interdependent upon all other branches. Each branch of industry produces not for itself alone but for all others, and, in its turn, receives from them everything it needs [to continue producing]. A separate branch of industry is not an economic community; the latter consists only of the totality of enterprises. A society constituting an integrated whole is that which is called a state. Therefore, the only logically consistent socialist system consists of acquisition by the state of all the instruments of production and of its appointment as the general director of all economic activities of a people.

Such was the system proposed by Louis Blanc, the forefather of this entire theory. Rodbertus demands the same thing. When Adolph Wagner speaks about the genuinely socialist organization of the national economy, he has in mind precisely the direction of all industrial production by the central state authority.[8]

Thus, according to this theory, all industry must be directed by the state. To the state belong all the instruments of production. The state is landowner, capitalist, and entrepreneur. An individual's task is simply to work; the products of this labor, at least according to the teaching of the moderate socialists, will be available to the worker—but only for consumption, not for capital accumulation. The worker has the right to consume what he or she has earned, but has no right to use his or her wages to found a productive enterprise.

If someone proposed a plan according to which all initiative in scholarship or in art would be removed from private individuals, and all scholars and artists would become agents and tools of the state, which would take upon itself the direction of all scholarly investigations and of all artistic works, then without doubt such a proposal would be taken for the fantasy of a madman. But this is precisely what socialists are demanding in the sphere of economic activity, which, like scholarship and art, is a manifestation of human liberty and an enterprise grounded on individual initiative. As a free being, an individual has the same right of free activity in the material world as in the world of ideas, and this free activity is the foundation of all economic development. Here personal and social utility coincide. An individual, applying his or her thought and labor to the subjugation of material nature, strives to maximize personal gain; the individual wants to be master of his or her own destiny and he has an inalienable right to be so. In this stimulus to personal energy and autonomy, society finds the source of all those material benefits it requires. Where there is no initiative, there can be no economic progress and no wealth.

The introduction of a socialist order would merely replace a natural agent of production with an artificial one, an effective one with a defective one. We have already noted that the state least of all possesses the qualities necessary to be an entrepreneur. In socialism the state operates under conditions most unfavorable to economic productivity. It is insulated from all competition, consequently from any stimulus to activity; it has no need to take into account the needs of consumers, for the consumer has no choice: he or she must be content with what he or she is given and with the prices that are demanded. Perhaps the consumer may raise a protest; but this will only transform the economy into an arena for endless altercations that will complicate the task of administration but will never bolster production. Industry is not driven by newspaper polemics or by parliamentary debates but by individual energy and initiative. If, by the introduction of socialism, energy and initiative are destroyed among citizens, how will they be resurrected in the government? To imagine that in the government will be found characteristics lacking in society is to fantasize to no purpose, to think that something can come from nothing.

The only result of a socialist system will be to replace the mainspring of economic productivity, individual self-interest, with bureaucratic routine and formalism. These are, to a greater or lesser degree, characteristics of any bureaucracy, and especially of a bureaucracy that possesses a monopoly. This problem cannot be overcome by any system of artificial mechanisms designed to replace the existing system of economic competition. Economic competence is not something that can be tested by a [civil service] examination; it can be demonstrated only by practical deeds. Nor can the problem be solved through the awards and prizes with which socialists intend to replace the factor of individual self-interest. We know that in a bureaucratic system awards themselves become a ritual, or, what is worse, they become an object of private machinations and protection. Socialists themselves admit this: "The public organization of competition," says Schäffle, "is open to the greatest corruption. It is particularly dangerous to grant a decisive voice to a far from perspicacious public authority, which will select not the most capable competitors but those in favor with the government."[9] No form of government can avert this woe. If in an autocracy personal intrigues predominate, in a representative government the domination of parties leads to the same result. The United States offers a striking example of such a phenomenon. But here, at least, the shamelessness of political parties is confined by the narrow parameters within which the government is permitted to operate. If individual self-interest, having been suppressed in the private sphere, has no other channel in which to operate except in the government, and if the government has open access to the pockets of every citizen, then there will be no end to official corruption. One can scarcely imagine anything more terrible than the exploitation of the entire material wealth of a nation and of the resources of private individuals for the sake of the ruling party. But that is precisely where socialism leads.

The inevitable diminution of productivity under a socialist order will be intensified because the desire to save will be suppressed along with personal initiative. Indeed, why should one save when the state is not only the sole entrepreneur but also the sole capitalist? All the instruments of production are located in its hands; the tailor cannot acquire for himself or herself a needle, the carpenter an ax, the farmer a plough. The socialists do not say whether an author will have the right to write with his or her own pens or whether he or she will be obliged to use those supplied by the treasury. We already indicated that the negation of property rights will entail such a limitation, and also will undermine the family, which is inextricably connected with the hereditary transmission of acquired wealth. From an economic standpoint, socialism leads to the destruction of the chief incentives to work and to accumulate capital; consequently, it will necessarily undermine economic activity as a whole. The individual will cease to be future-oriented, to turn his or her gaze afar, to take care to guarantee his or her children's future; that individual will be concerned with the present alone. Concern for the future will be the province of that universal overseer and entrepreneur, the state. It will save for everyone but will save in its own peculiar fashion. When a private individual saves money, that individual limits personal consumption and sets aside a portion of personal income for future use; this act has a moral significance. The state, in saving money, does not limit its own consumption but rather consumption by its citizens. According to the formula invented by the socialists, the state, by a simple discretionary act or by a bookkeeping manipulation, first takes from the total national income that which is needed to satisfy public needs, for the renewal and increase of capital, and then distributes what remains among its citizens.[10] The question is: will much remain?

The amount remaining for citizens will decrease as expenditures to renovate depreciated capital increase above that which might be spent by a private enterprise. A worker using someone's else's tools has no interest in their preservation; what is needed is the sharp eye of the owner, but under socialism it is replaced by the supervision of bureaucrats who have as little stake in preserving capital stock as does the worker. In private firms supervision of workers brings a certain benefit, but even then it is no substitute for the owner's own eye; under the domination of officialdom the supervisory function easily becomes a formalistic bureaucratic routine. In any case, the absence of the owner, of that essential element in any enterprise, inevitably must be reflected in a more rapid depreciation of capital stock.

On the other hand, the increase of capital that is such a natural process in a progressive society is bound to slow down under socialism, for a socialist order undermines not only labor but also inventiveness. Justice dictates that a new tool should belong to that person who has invented it, and this is one of the most powerful incentives for invention. Under socialism an inventor is forbidden to possess personal tools; the inventor cannot rely on the private investment that currently subsidizes experimentation and supports the production of new inventions so as to acquire a competitive advantage in the market. Under a socialist order, the inventor is given the right to present an invention to the government in the hope of winning an award. The inventor must submit to the judgment of bureaucrats who, on the one hand, have no right to risk treasury property, and, on the other hand, have no personal stake in whether a new product is introduced and quite often are self-interested in seeing that a new product will not be introduced, for that would violate the prevailing routine and would entail new arrangements. Under such circumstances it is evident that inventiveness will be limited; rather than being stimulated, it will be constrained.

Finally, as far as the land is concerned, the owner's absence cannot but be reflected negatively in production. Everyone knows that private property is a strong incentive to work. A small landowner tries especially hard to extract everything possible from the parcel of land belonging to him or her. Under socialism, there will be no ownership, and therefore productivity inevitably must diminish.

Thus the destruction of personal initiative and of personal property, which is inevitably associated with the introduction of a socialist system, cannot help but have a deleterious impact on production. Where the mainspring of progress disappears, there one cannot expect for progress to occur at the same rate as before. One can dream all one wishes about replacing this mainspring with some other motive force; but this will remain an idle dream, one lacking foundation both in theory and in practice.

Socialists of the chair who have not entirely lost their sense of justice and have not completely closed their eyes to reality do not even bother to deny this. They are ready to admit that with the introduction of socialism, productivity may decrease; but they assert that this decrease in productivity will be compensated for by [a more equitable] distribution of wealth—something [they regard as] more important, for equity in wealth constitutes [for them] the goal of production.[11]

Below we shall see which laws govern the distribution of wealth; we shall demonstrate that the leveling sought by socialists is nothing other than the equality of rightlessness and of penury. Here it is sufficient to say that one can regard as economically viable only that distribution of wealth that does not decrease productivity, for everything ultimately depends on productivity. Productivity is the primary factor and distribution of wealth the secondary one. One must first produce a sufficient quantity of goods, then one may attend to their distribution. To diminish production in order to secure better distribution of wealth is tantamount to chopping down a tree in order to pick its fruit. It is the sort of action typical of savage peoples. This perversion of the true tasks of the national economy is the less justified, for, according to the socialists themselves, even current levels of production are utterly inadequate to satisfy all human needs. "It is now surely apparent," writes [Friedrich Albert] Lange "that nobody would be happy if the existing mass of current goods were divided among the needy millions."[12] What would happen if production were decreased?

Under socialism the government's main concern would be to make sure that the growth of population does not outstrip the means of subsistence; otherwise, there will not be enough to go around. This concern is the government's, not the citizenry's, for with the introduction of socialism the state will assume the task of supervising the economy and of satisfying everyone's needs. But [socialism's introduction] will have destroyed initiative among the citizenry; it will have forbidden them to concern themselves with the future, to care for the future of their own children. By so doing, it will have undermined the family. The individual will have remained a producer of children, but the fate of these children will depend not upon the individual, not upon what he or she does for them, but upon what the children may receive from society. Under such circumstances, the moral restraints upon procreation, restraints imposed by the necessity of guaranteeing the future of one's children, will disappear. And because it will be essential in any case to restrain procreation in view of reduced productivity, then this concern will fall upon the government, which, as the universal producer, alone can calculate what quantity of people it can support on its existing income. Having destroyed the family, having removed from the individual the responsibility of caring for his or her children, the state is forced to intrude itself into family matters, to limit marriages, to regulate cohabitation of the sexes. Here again, the only arena of production left to individual initiative will be supplanted by government control.

It is apparent what sort of unendurable tyranny must be institutionalized under such a social system. Ostensibly, socialism's goal is to raise the dignity of the individual: all dependence on private persons will cease, and service to society alone will remain.[13] In fact, this transformation will consist only in the replacement of free private relationships by government regulation and bureaucratic arbitrariness. In a private contract, a worker is one of the contracting parties and is equal to the other party. The worker announces what terms he or she will accept, and not infrequently the worker can insist on them; if a worker is dissatisfied, he or she can leave the enterprise and seek work from another boss. Under socialism there is no other entrepreneur besides the state; therefore, the worker has no choice: he or she must work for a state-run enterprise, under terms that are dictated. A private entrepreneur is to a large degree dependent upon workers, for without the workers, he or she will be ruined; the state, of course, will not be ruined and can calmly wait for the starving workers to accept its terms. The magnitude of wage rates depends here not on mutual bargaining but on what remains after the satisfaction of all public imperatives. A private entrepreneur first satisfies the workers and then, after deducting expenses, receives his net income; the state, conversely, first takes what it needs to meet expenses and to cover capital investment, and only then distributes what is left among workers. And this distribution proceeds entirely according to the state's discretion. The evaluation of labor according to its quality depends either on a decision by bureaucrats who have no personal stake in the success of an enterprise, or, even worse, on the voice of the workers who have a stake in seeing that nobody receives a higher wage at their expense. All avenues of protest are closed to the dissatisfied worker. The worker cannot seek another master, for there is no other master, nor can the worker become an entrepreneur, for that is forbidden. The sole resort for the worker, the only possibility of escaping from a subordinate position, is to enter the ranks of officialdom. Therefore, in contrast to what occurs in a private industrial system, the interest of the working class will always consist in the disproportionate multiplication of officialdom. [The growth of bureaucracy] will be favored by everyone who considers himself or herself in any way talented, and only those who think themselves absolutely untalented will oppose it. Here again, this can only have a deleterious impact on productivity, the more so because the bureaucracy will be the arena in which all human passions play themselves out.

Under socialism what significance can freedom to choose one's occupation have, a freedom that is supposedly granted to each individual, and what significance can wages have, when they are attached to the individual as inalienable property? An individual may choose whatever occupation he or she wishes, but it is the prerogative of a single master, the state, whether to hire that individual or not. The state determines the quantity of workers necessary in each branch of industry, and because workers are completely under state control, their work assignment depends completely on the state. If in a certain branch of industry there are too many workers, then the state will simply reassign them to another branch where workers are in short supply. Under a system valuing private initiative, workers themselves would move to industries short of labor-power, for there they could attain more advantageous terms; but in a socialist economy, the terms of labor are everywhere identical, and mobility depends not on the will of workers themselves but upon the discretion of the state. A worker, like it or not, will be subordinated, for the individual has no choice; the state, for its part, has not only the right but the obligation to assign work at its own discretion, for having become the sole entrepreneur, it assumed the responsibility to give work to everyone and to organize this work so as to satisfy all needs. Thus everything rests in its hands. Under a state monopoly, the free choice of occupation becomes a fiction. The worker has the right to demand that he or she be given work, and that this work be on the same terms as that of other workers; but the actual job assigned him is left up to the state.

When the free labor market is destroyed, so is the very method of determining wage rates. In a socialist economy, a salary is determined not by a private negotiation between a businessperson and a worker but by each individual's degree of participation in collective production. From the national income is subtracted what is necessary for general needs, and what remains is distributed among workers. Consequently, each person's share depends on the labor of all the others. And so each has the right to demand that all others work in such a fashion as to may satisfy his or her needs. But as soon as such a demand arises, work inevitably becomes compulsory. Socialist production entails universal solidarity, and universal solidarity entails universal coercion, for under socialism there arise universal demands of all upon each and of each upon all. Liberty of the individual completely disappears. And because free labor is more productive than involuntary labor, the disappearance of free labor inevitably leads to decreased productivity.

Not all socialists are willing to admit these consequences of their theory. Schäffle, for example, rails against the omnipotence of the state and declares socialism suppressing liberty to be "insanity and a murderous attack upon civilization itself."[14] From the efforts to reconcile liberty with socialism arise the aforementioned doctrines of the anarchists and of the proponents of socialist self-government. But the very inadequacy of these efforts points to the irreconcilability of the principles in question. The more logically rigorous socialists do not deceive themselves on this account. Instead of depicting imaginary idylls of liberty, they candidly equate their ideal form of life with despotism. Thus, for example, Rodbertus, in trying to describe the character of socialist production, begins with the description of an Eastern despot, "an owner of land and of men," who disposes of each as he wishes. In place "of the property monopoly of a personal despot," Rodbertus says, imagine land and products belonging to the entire nation which will control production just as the Eastern despot controls it through his servants, and which will have complete control over all means of production, just as the agents of the ancient Persian monarchy exercised control by virtue of his right of ownership.[15] It is obvious that under such a system liberty cannot exist. Individuals and the land belong to a new despot, the nation. According to this theory, the narrower the scope for individual choice, the better. "The more centralized the organism," writes Rodbertus, "the more it approaches perfection."[16]

What is the purpose of wages under socialism? Their only purpose is to satisfy subsistence needs, for there is no point in saving, capital accumulation having been prohibited. A wage earner becomes a mere consumer. But what is the status of a consumer in a socialist order? In a private enterprise system, the consumer is the judge of the producer: the consumer makes known his or her demands and offers a price. The producer's entire task is to satisfy the consumer; if the producer cannot do so, he or she is ruined. The competition between producers and the predominance of certain producers over others are based on the fact that certain producers satisfy the consumer better than their competitors do. In a socialist economy, however, the consumer remains in utter dependence on the producer. The state will not be ruined for failing to satisfy the consumer. Consumption itself, like production, is under state control. The state determines what is necessary for consumers, and it sets the price at which they may purchase commodities. Consumers have no choice; they have before them a monopolist who forces them to make of their wages that use which suits not them but the monopolist. Let us recall the words of Schäffle, cited above: "The issue is not simply to take the sum of personal demands, many of which are irrational and deleterious to society, and to meet these needs, irrespective of the public's interests. Certain demands should be rejected entirely, others partially. Other demands should be introduced and satisfied. The personal liberty to set demands should be limited, restricted, or [in certain cases] enhanced in the interests of preserving the whole of society.[17] Schäffle explicitly calls consumption a public policy issue. "The purpose of consumption," he says, "is the acquisition of a socially useful resource and the extraction of social utility from the individual and from property."[18]

But if an individual, relative to the satisfaction of his or her needs, is completely dependent on society, then by virtue of this dependency the individual may demand of society that it satisfy these needs. Under conditions of universal solidarity, as we have seen, wage rates depend not on the labor of the individual but upon the labor of all. An individual is paid out of the total income generated by collective production controlled by the state. A wage represents not only the participation of each individual in this collective labor but also a demand addressed to the state that the labor of all should be sufficient for the satisfaction of needs. Moreover, the individual's demands go even further. In addition to paying the individual worker for his or her labor, the state is obliged to render the worker assistance; upon the state falls responsibility for performance of all services that under a free economic system might be accomplished by charitable institutions, by philanthropy, by private welfare agencies, by friendship. Having become the sole entrepreneur, having lifted from citizens the burdens of planning for the future, the state has assumed the obligation of satisfying all their needs, and therefore they have the right to demand that it fulfill this obligation in its entirety. Consequently, the treasury becomes a source for satisfying every conceivable variety of need, and a wage ceases to be the measure of this satisfaction. Each individual works for the state, according to the state's instructions, and in return receives from the state everything that he or she requires. Socialist production therefore entails socialist consumption. Socialism becomes communism.

Many socialists renounce communism. They intend to reconcile liberty and property with socialist production. Certain socialists even regard it as slander to accuse them of negating these principles. But we have already seen that in a socialist economy, liberty and property are transformed into figments of the imagination. The state controls everything—land, capital, and the productive enterprise, leaving to the individual his or her labor alone, and it makes whatever use it wishes of that. Consumption itself and even procreation are limited by the state. Under such circumstances, the individual's only resort is to demand of the state that it take upon itself the satisfaction of all personal needs. The individual has become a slave of society; society is obliged to feed him or her. This is the essence of communism, which is an extreme but logically consistent application of socialist principles.

There is no doubt, however, that communism is nothing other than the supreme expression of the inherent contradiction which lies at the basis of all socialist aspirations. Communism sets itself the goal of exalting the individual, but it transforms that individual into a slave; it proclaims the supreme moral principle, brotherhood, but it imposes this principle by coercion—that is, it drains the principle of its moral character; it aspires to satisfy all human needs but destroys every incentive to work and consequently makes impossible the broad satisfaction of these needs. Any one-sided principle contains an inherent contradiction, for it attempts to supplant the whole by one of its parts, to preserve the plenitude of life after having rejected half of it. But the one-sided development of a principle that is already false per se leads to a glaring contradiction. Communism is the denial of the entire individualistic half of human nature—that is, of that which makes human beings unique. But because it is impossible to destroy human nature, then the violently repressed individual personality will assert itself in another form: it will make itself felt in the aspiration of each person to take as much gain as possible from the public domain and to contribute as little as possible to it. The more unconscionable an individual, the more easily this will be accomplished. The loser under communism will be not the worst but the best elements. Communism, according to Proudhon's apt expression, is the exploitation of the strong by the weak, and not only in the material sense but also in the moral sense: it is the exploitation of the conscientious by the unscrupulous. Only the kind of exalted religious sensibility that leads the individual to total self-denial can counter this unfortunate tendency. Therefore, communistic societies are found only among individuals who have renounced all mundane aspirations for the sake of another world beyond the grave. But an absolute condition for the existence of such societies is that they be voluntary. Communism cannot be instantiated by state institutions. As soon as the [communist principle is] incorporated into law, communism is transformed into slavery.

Proudhon recognized very clearly the inherent inadequacy of communistic theories. "The inadequacies of communism," he wrote, "are so obvious that critics have not had to use much eloquence to turn people against it. The incorrigibility of its injustices, the violence committed by it against human sympathies and antipathies, the iron yoke which it imposes on liberty, the moral ordeal to which it subjects conscience, the apathy in which it mires society—in a word, the sanctimonious and stupefying monotony by which it enchains the free, energetic, morally sensitive, and recalcitrant personality of the individual has affronted universal common sense and has irretrievably doomed community ownership of property."[19]

After this one can only be amazed when [John Stuart] Mill, referring to the possibility of strengthening the moral character of humanity, claims that at present it is impossible to resolve the issue of whether communism or individualism is preferable, and for that reason it cannot yet be asserted that communism will not be the ultimate and most advanced form of human community.[20] Such a judgment, coming from a well-known writer, only serves as proof that the simplest and most obvious truths have ceased to be understood by contemporary thinkers.

It can be said with assurance today, just as it could have been said long ago, that communism is incapable of becoming not only the ultimate but even a transitional stage in the development of human society for the simple reason that the individual cannot cease to be a free individual—that is, an autonomous center of life and activity. The enslavement of the individual to society is just as contrary to human nature as is the enslavement of one individual to another. And while the latter was conceivable at the lowest stages of human development, the former is inconceivable at any stage, for society itself consists of individuals; consequently, this order must collapse from its own internal contradictions. For anyone who is capable of thinking clearly, communism is a theoretical absurdity and a practical impossibility. It belongs to the ranks of pure utopias.

There is no better way to conclude this critique than with the words of Proudhon, who mercilessly routed all socialists, except of course himself: "You spoke the truth," he exclaimed. "Communism is the fatal issue of socialism! But precisely for this reason socialism is nothing, never was anything, and can never be anything; for communism is the negation of nature and spirit, the negation of the past, of the present and of the future."[21]

Notes

FOREWORD. WHY READ CHICHERIN?

1. L. Tolstoy, *Anna Karenina,* trans. C. Garnett, rev. L. J. Kent and N. Berberova (New York, 1965), 489.
2. On this concept of opinion and its relation to "sideshadowing" and the philosophy of time and history, see G. S. Morson, *Narrative and Freedom: The Shadows of Time* (New Haven, 1994).
3. On prosaics, see G. S. Morson and C. Emerson, *Mikhail Bakhtin: Creation of a Prosaics* (Stanford, 1990), and G. S. Morson, "Prosaic Bakhtin: *Landmarks,* Anti-Intelligentsialism, and the Russian Counter-Tradition," *Common Knowledge* 2, no. 1 (Spring 1993), 35–54.
4. As cited in G. M. Hamburg, *Boris Chicherin and Early Russian Liberalism, 1828–1866* (Stanford, 1992), 196–97. For a detailed account of the Herzen-Chicherin quarrel, see pages 194–201.
5. T. Todorov, untitled reply to the Paul de Man controversy, *TLS,* June 17–23, 1988, pp. 676, 684.
6. F. Dostoevsky, *The Possessed,* trans. C. Garnett (New York, 1963), 424–25.

TRANSLATOR'S PREFACE

1. "On Serfdom," "Contemporary Tasks of Russian Life," and "Indictment."

These essays were published by Soviet historians and have appeared in facsimile editions devoted to the activities of the socialist Alexander Herzen. For bibliographic citations see below.

2. For further biographical data and interpretive arguments see G. M. Hamburg, *Boris Chicherin and Early Russian Liberalism* 1828–1866 (Stanford, 1992).

INTRODUCTION. AN ECCENTRIC VISION

1. Permit me to offer two anecdotes in support of this proposition. In 1986 I applied to the director of the Pushkinskii dom [Pushkin House], one of Russia's most important literary archives, for permission to read various correspondence from, to, and about B. N. Chicherin. My application clearly explained that the purpose of my research was to write an intellectual biography of this important figure. The director refused permission on the grounds that a foreigner should not be granted access to sensitive papers of a Soviet foreign minister. I assumed that the director was using a convenient pretext to deny my application: I could not imagine that a specialist on nineteenth-century Russian literature and culture was unaware of Boris Nikolaevich's reputation, let alone existence. I asked two friends, the Petersburg historian B. V. Anan'ich and the Moscow historian L. G. Zakharova, to intervene on my behalf. Both reported that the institute's director had glanced at my letter of application, seen the name Chicherin, and decided without reading further to reject the application for the stated reason. The director really had no idea that the liberal Boris Nikolaevich existed or could be a worthy subject for study.

   During the same research trip I spoke about my subject to a distinguished Moscow scholar, poet, and translator, who prided himself on a profound knowledge of nineteenth-century Russian intellectual life. Before our encounter he had never heard of B. N. Chicherin, yet his own (privately "dissident") political outlook uncannily resembled Chicherin's conservative liberalism. To a remarkable degree, then, Soviet culture had succeeded in effacing the memory of Chicherin's achievements. I discovered that, with a few exceptions, knowledge of his career and thought was limited to Soviet historians of the "late feudal" and "early capitalist" periods—that is, political historians of the mid-nineteenth century.
2. B. N. Chicherin, *Oblastnye uchrezhdeniia Rossii v XVII-m veke* (Moscow, 1856).
3. *Vospominaniia Borisa Nikolaevicha Chicherina: Moskva sorokovykh godov* (Moscow, 1929), hereafter cited as MSG; *Vospominaniia Borisa Nikolaevicha Chicherina: Puteshestvie za granitsu* (Moscow, 1932), hereafter cited as PZG; *Vospominaniia Borisa Nikolaevicha Chicherina: Moskovskii universitet* (Moscow, 1929), hereafter cited as MU; *Vospominaniia Borisa Nikolaevicha Chicherina: Zemstvo i Moskovskaia Duma* (Moscow, 1934), hereafter cited as ZMD.
4. For a harsh Soviet assessment from the 1950s see B. E. Babitskii, "B. N. Chicherin kak burzhuazno-liberal'nyi istorik russkogo gosudarstva i prava," in Belorusskii gosudarstvennyi universitet, ed. *Uchenye zapiski: Vypusk* 34, *Seriia iuridicheskaia* (Minsk, 1957), 163–196. The only extended Soviet attempt at political biography was that of G. B. Kizel'shtein, "Politicheskie vzgliady B. N. Chicherina v 1848–1867 godakh," candidate's dissertation, Moscow University (Moscow, 1966); this thesis was written under the direc-

tion of M. V. Nechkina, so it reflected Nechkina's powerful ideological bias against liberalism. A less hostile view of Russian liberalism, with extensive reference to Chicherin as well as his allies, can be found in V. A. Kitaev, *Ot frondy k okhranitel'stvu: Iz istorii russkoi liberal'noi mysli 50-kh-60-kh godov XIX v.* (Moscow, 1972). Kitaev's argument suggests that until 1861 the liberals were generally "progressive" but that they ceased to be so after the peasant emancipation. For a subtle treatment of Chicherin as Right Hegelian, see the short essay by the distinguished Soviet philosopher V. F. Asmus, "Konservativnoe gegelianstvo vtoroi poloviny XIX veka," in AN SSSR, ed. *Gegel' i filosofiia v Rossii 30-e gody XIX v. 20-e gody XX v.* (Moscow, 1974), 176–189.

Retrospectively, the most interesting Soviet publication on Chicherin was written by a specialist in the theory of law, V. D. Zor'kin, *Iz istorii burzhuazno-liberal'noi politicheskoi mysli Rossii vtoroi poloviny XIX–XX v. (B. N. Chicherin)* (Moscow, 1975). Although he criticized Chicherin for supporting the Russian government against its democratic critics, Zor'kin considered Chicherin's philosophy of law an important contribution to Russian jurisprudence. Indeed, Zor'kin was a pioneer of sorts, because he provided the first systematic treatment of Chicherin as a political thinker. It is worth noting that subsequently Zor'kin became the chief justice of the Soviet constitutional court during Gorbachev's time. After the dissolution of the Soviet Union, he presided over the celebrated case in which Yeltsin's government argued that the Communist Party of the Soviet Union had never been a true political party at all under the definition of the Russian constitution, and hence the Yeltsin government's decision to outlaw it was justified. Many observers praised Zor'kin and his colleagues for upholding decorum in the court, for their dispassionate demeanor, and for their obvious commitment to the rule of law; others felt that, in this case and subsequently, Zor'kin was too sympathetic to the Communist Party. It is an open question whether and to what degree Chicherin exerted an impact on Zor'kin's judicial approach. Zor'kin's scholarly interest in Chicherin had the effect of legitimating the study of Chicherin in the post-Soviet period. In summer 1992 Moscow pundits began to speak of "liberal measures and strong government," Chicherin's motto from the late 1850s. At a press conference reporters startled President Yeltsin by referring to Chicherin's attitudes toward government.

5. For Leontowitsch's idiosyncratic but still influential view equating liberalism with reformist thought and statecraft, see his *Geschichte des Liberalismus in Russland* (Frankfurt-am-Main, 1957). See also Schapiro's review of Leontowitsch, reprinted in Leonard Schapiro, *Russian Studies,* ed. Ellen Dahrendorf with an introduction by Harry Willetts (New York, 1987), 45–52. For Schapiro's highly sympathetic and moving assessment of Chicherin, see especially his essay, "The Pre-Revolutionary Intelligentsia and the Legal Order," in *Russian Studies,* 53–67. For Benson's analysis of Chicherin as Hegelian and reformer, see his very good essay, "The Conservative Liberalism of Boris Chicherin," *Forschungen zur osteuropäischen Geschichte* 21 (1975): 17–111.
6. See Walicki's handbook on Russian intellectual history, *A History of Russian Thought from the Enlightenment to Marxism* (Stanford, 1979), 150–151, 397–403; later Walicki wrote a model monograph that included a profound analysis of Chicherin's thought after 1881; see Walicki, *Legal Philosophies of Russian Liberalism* (Oxford, 1987), 105–164.
7. For a survey of post-Soviet efforts to recover Russia's partially lost philosophical (and

national) identity, see James P. Scanlan, ed., *Russian Thought After Communism: The Recovery of a Philosophical Heritage* (Armonk, N.Y., 1994). Among the post-Soviet efforts to understand Chicherin as a philosopher and political thinker, see I. D. Osipov, *Filosofiia russkogo liberalizma XIX–nachalo XX v.* (St. Petersburg, 1996), 62–86; and Rossiiskaia Akademiia Nauk, Institut Filosofii, *Liberalizm v Rossii,* ed. V. T. Pustarnakov (Moscow, 1996), 163–274.

8. The best intellectual history of the seventeenth-century debate over Parliamentary rights is J. G. A. Pocock, *The Ancient Constitution and the Feudal Law: English Historical Thought in the Seventeenth Century* (Cambridge, 1957).
9. For a brilliant and persuasive attempt to link Montesquieu and Tocqueville, see Raymond Aron, *Les Étapes de la pensée sociologique* (Paris, 1967), 25–66, 221–262.
10. It is worth noting that in the past two decades, American liberals have consistently looked to Kant for inspiration. Kant's impact on the two chief theorists of American liberalism, Ronald Dworkin and John Rawls, is an intriguing chapter in recent intellectual history. Americans have tended to be rather more skeptical of Hegel, a thinker frequently identified with Prussian reaction and an overweening state. Here and in Britain, however, revisionist scholarship on Hegel in the past thirty years has identified his liberal, progressive side. See, among others, Schlomo Avineri, *Hegel's Theory of the Modern State* (Cambridge, 1972); George Armstrong Kelly, *Hegel's Retreat from Eleusis: Studies in Political Thought* (Princeton, 1978); Judith Sklar, *Freedom and Independence: A Study of the Political Ideals of Hegel's "Phenomenology of Mind"* (Cambridge, 1976); and, above all, Charles Taylor, *Hegel* (Cambridge, 1975).
11. This is my argument in G. M. Hamburg, *Boris Chicherin and Early Russian Liberalism,* 1828–1866 (Stanford, 1992). Other historians have maintained that programmatic liberalism appeared earlier, in the generation of the Decembrists, or even in the late eighteenth century with N. I. Panin, S. E. Desnitskii, and A. A. Radishchev. For an overview of historiography on Russian liberalism see my brief essay "Russian Liberalism," *The Routledge Encyclopedia of Philosophy,* ed. E. Craig (London, forthcoming).
12. For details on the family's economic circumstances see TSGAOR/GARF fond 1154 [fond Chicherinykh], op. 1. ed. khr. 18, "Vospominaniia 1803–1846 gg.," ll. 1–45; and TSGAOR/GARF fond 1154, op. 1, ed. khr. 923, "Dukhovnoe zaveshchanie N. V. Chicherina," ll. 1–11 verso.
13. TSGAOR/GARF fond 1154, op. 1, ed. khr. 18, l. 18.
14. See N. K. Bestuzhev-Riumin, "Vospominaniia N. K. Bestuzhev-Riumina do 1860 goda)," *Sbornik Otdeleniia russkogo iazyka i slovesnosti Imperatorskoi Akademii Nauk* 67, Appendix 5 (Mar. 1900): 1–60.
15. On Krivtsov's project see V. I. Semevskii, *Krest'ianskii vopros v Rossii v XVIII i pervoi polvine XIX veka* (St. Petersburg, 1888), 2: 450–451.
16. See his letter to his wife, Ekaterina Borisovna, in ROBL/RO RGB, fond 334 [fond Chicherinykh], k. 12, ed. khr. 1, "Pis'ma Nikolaia Vasilievicha Chicherina k Ekaterine Borisovne Chicherinoi," ll. 64–64 verso. Letter of 26 December 1844.
17. The best portrait of Kavelin in English can be found in Derek Offord, *Portraits of Russian Liberals: A Study of the Thought of T. N. Granovsky, V. P. Botkin, P. V. Annenkov, A. V. Druzhinin, and K. D. Kavelin* (Cambridge, 1985), 175–213.

18. For a fine summary of Solov'ev's interpretation of Russian history see L. V. Cherepnin, S. M. Solov'ev kak istorik," in S. M. Solov'ev, *Istoriia Rossii s drevneishikh vremen* (Moscow, 1962), 1: 5–51; see also the more recent essay by S. S. Dmitriev and I. D. Koval'chenko, "Istorik Sergei Mikhailovich Solov'ev: Ego zhizn', trudy, nauchnoe nasledstvo," in S. M. Solov'ev, *Sochineniia v vosemnadtsati knigakh* (Moscow, 1988), 1–2: 6–48.
19. On Granovskii in the 1840s see the splendid biography by Priscilla R. Roosevelt, *Apostle of Russian Liberalism: Timofei Granovsky* (Newtonville, Mass., 1986), especially 72–146; and Priscilla Roosevelt, "Granovsky at the Lectern: A Conservative Liberal's Vision of History," *Forschungen zur osteuropäischen Geschichte,* Band 29 (Berlin, 1981), 61–192.
20. On the "classical" Slavophiles of the 1840s, see Andrzej Walicki, *The Slavophile Controversy: History of a Conservative Utopia in Nineteenth-Century Russian Thought* (Oxford, 1975), 121–286.
21. The Westernizers were too divided to construct a single "program," but Walicki has juxtaposed their various postures to the Slavophiles' retrospective utopia under nine headings; see *The Slavophile Controversy,* 446–450.
22. For Chicherin's assessment of his teacher, see B. N. Chicherin, "Neskol'ko slov o filosofsko-istoricheskikh vozzreniiakh Granovskogo (retsenziia), *Voprosy filosofii i psikhologii,* Jan.–Feb. 1897, 1–13.
23. An overview of the "dark seven years" of Nicholas I's reign can be found in the relevant chapters of W. Bruce Lincoln, *Nicholas I: Emperor and Autocrat of All the Russias* (Bloomington, Ind., 1978).
24. On official anti-Semitism see Simon M. Dubnow, *History of the Jews in Russia and Poland* (Philadelphia, 1916), 2: 1–64; and Michael Stanislawski, *Tsar Nicholas I and the Jews: The Transformation of Jewish Society in Russia,* 1825–1855 (Philadelphia, 1983).
25. The comparison of Nicholas to an emperor of the Praetorian guard was suggested by Alexander Herzen. See A. I. Gertsen, *Byloe i dumy, Sobranie sochinenii v tridtsati tomakh* (Moscow, 1956), 8: 62–63.
26. [B. N. Chicherin], "O krepostnom sostoianii," *Golosa iz Rossii.* (London, 1856), 2: 127–154.
27. "O krepostnom sostoianii," 131.
28. "O krepostnom sostoianii," 176–180.
29. "O krepostnom sostoianii," 186–187.
30. "O krepostnom sostoianii," 213.
31. "O krepostnom sostoianii," 188.
32. [B. N. Chicherin], "Sovremennye zadachi russkoi zhizni," *Golosa iz Rossii* (London, 1857), 4: 55–67.
33. "Sovremennye zadachi russkoi zhizni," 77.
34. "Sovremennye zadachi russkoi zhizni," 70.
35. "Sovremennye zadachi russkoi zhizni," 112–125.
36. "Sovremennye zadachi russkoi zhizni," 111.
37. For an earlier Slavophile reaction to Chicherin's emancipatory plan, see ROBL/RO RGB fond 327 [fond Cherkasskikh], razdel 1, k. 15, ed. khr. 17. This document is a longhand manuscript of "On Serfdom" with marginal annotations by A. I. Koshelev. At the end of

the document, in unknown hand, is a complaint that Chicherin's desire to abolish the peasant commune would "throw out the very thing in which may be found the main advantage of our form of life over the European order."

38. For a convenient summary of the Slavophiles' critique of European law, see Walicki, *Legal Philosophies of Russian Liberalism,* 34–44. Most extreme in his rejection of European-style legal guarantees of freedom was Konstantin Aksakov. See his memorandum on Russian internal affairs in L. N. Brodskii, *Rannie slavianofily* (Moscow, 1910), 69–97.
39. Certain Slavophiles tried to reconcile the convening of a national assembly with Russia's indigenous political traditions by calling for the revival of the medieval land assembly [zemskii sobor]. According to such theorists, the land assembly was not in any way analogous to a constitutional convention or western European–style representative assembly. See, for example, A. I. Koshelev, *Konstitutsiia, samoderzhavie i zemskaia duma* (Leipzig, 1862).
40. Herzen had developed his critique of the European bourgeoisie soon after his arrival in France in 1847. See especially the second and third of his *Letters from France and Italy* in A. I. Gertsen, *Pis'ma iz Frantsii i Italii, Sobranie sochinenii v tridtsati tomakh* (Moscow, 1955), vol. 5, especially 33–35.
41. In the third book of *Voices from Russia* Herzen criticized the liberals' moderation and the government's deliberate pace in writing the emancipation statute. He asked sarcastically: "Does the government want emancipation or not? Yes or no? *Liebt mich? Liebt mich nicht?*" *Golosa iz Rossii,* 3: iii–iv.
42. Hegel's remark "What is rational is actual and what is actual is rational," Herzen complained in a famous passage in his memoirs *Byloe i dumy,* "led straight to the recognition of the sovereign authorities, led to a man's sitting with folded arms, and that was just what the Berlin Buddhists [Hegel's followers] wanted." A. I. Gertsen, *Sobranie sochinenii v tridtsati tomakh* (Moscow, 1956), 9: 22–23.
43. Chicherin explained the decision to delete references to constitutional monarchy as follows: "Fully understanding the impossibility of changing the form of government at present, I recognized such a change as a goal to be achieved in the future. In my eyes, it would be the ultimate result of the reforms being demanded. Summarizing my views in a manuscript not subject to censorship, I expressed them with absolute candor. But when I gave the article to Kavelin, he observed that about distant goals it made sense to keep quiet for the time being. . . . I agreed with this and rewrote the article." MSG, 163.
44. For Chicherin's account of the meeting see PZG, 49–52; for Herzen's account see *Byloe i dumy* in Gertsen, *Sobranie sochinenii v tridstati tomakh,* 9: 248–249.
45. These remarks are excerpts from a long, devastating letter that Herzen sent to Chicherin, a letter that Herzen proposed to publish in *Kolokol.* For the text of the letter see Gertsen, *Byloe i dumy* in *Sobranie sochinenii v tridtsati tomakh,* 9: 250–253. For an English version see the Constance Garnett translation, *My Past and Thoughts: The Memoirs of Alexander Herzen* (London, 1953), 2: 398–402.
46. PZG, 52.
47. The phrase "Sharpen the axes [zaostrite topory]," occurred in a long letter printed under the title, "Pis'mo k redaktoru," in *Kolokol* 1, no. 25 (1 October 1858): 201–207, here 205,

column 2. Herzen printed the letter with no disavowal; he thanked the [anonymous] author "sincerely and cordially for his warm words."

48. A. I. Gertsen, "Nas uprekaiut." *Kolokol* 1, no. 27 (1 November 1858): 219–220.
49. [B. N. Chicherin], "Obvinitel'nyi akt," *Kolokol* 1, no. 29, (1 December 1858): 236–239.
50. "Obvinitel'nyi akt," 237, column 2.
51. For Kavelin's letter of reproach to Chicherin see PZG, 57–62.
52. For example, see I. V. Porokh, "Polemika Gertsena s Chicherinym i otklik na nee 'Sovremennika,'" in Saratovskii gosudarstvennyi universitet, *Istoriograficheskii sbornik* 2 (1965): 51. M. G. Platonova, "Nekotorye voprosy sotsiologii v trudakh B. N. Chicherina," in AN SSSR, *Aktual'nye problemy istorii filosofii narodov SSSR, Vypusk* 6 (1979), 42.
53. See Chicherin's inaugural lecture in public law at Moscow University, "Vstupitel'naia lektsiia po gosudarstvennomu pravu," in B. N. Chicherin, *Neskol'ko sovremennykh voprosov* (Moscow, 1862), 24–27.
54. For incisive remarks on the political landscape of this period see Terence Emmons, *The Russian Landed Gentry and the Peasant Emancipation of* 1861 (Cambridge, 1968), 381–385; see also G. M. Hamburg, *Politics of the Russian Nobility* 1881–1905 (New Brunswick, N.J., 1984), 60–64.
55. Emmons, *The Russian Landed Gentry and the Peasant Emancipation,* 410–411.
56. ONP, 1–6.
57. ONP, 8.
58. ONP, 11.
59. ONP, 13.
60. ONP, 11–12.
61. ONP, 23–26.
62. ONP, 30.
63. ONP, 30–31.
64. ONP, 28–30.
65. ONP, 33–34.
66. ONP, 35–47.
67. ONP, 50.
68. ONP, 57–62.
69. ONP, 393–400.
70. ONP, 408–409.
71. ONP, 418–419.
72. ONP, 509.
73. ONP, 519–520.
74. ONP, 412–415.
75. For a very critical assessment by a young Russian liberal, see A. D. Gradovskii, "Russkaia uchenaia literatura," *Russkii vestnik* 70 (1867): 717–748; 71 (1867): 287–315.
76. MU, 195–229.
77. For a brief statement of the initial plan see B. N. Chicherin, *Istoriia politicheskikh uchenii. Chast' I. Drevnost' i srednie veka* (Moscow, 1869), hereafter cited as IPU 1: ix.
78. The subsequent volumes of *Istoriia politicheskikh uchenii* included *Chast' II. Novoe vremia*

(Moscow, 1872); *Chast' III. Novoe vremia. (Prodolzhenie)* (Moscow, 1874); *Chast' IV. XIX vek* (Moscow, 1877); *Chast' V. XIX vek. (Prodolzhenie)* (Moscow, 1902). Various portions of IPU appeared as independent articles. See, for example, "An'silon i Krug," *Sbornik gosudarstvennykh znanii* 3 (1877): 171–221; "Nemetskie sotsialisty: I. Lassal'," *Sbornik gosudarstvennykh znanii* 5 (1878): 1–71; "Nemetskie sotsialisty: II. Karl Marks," *Sbornik gosudarstvennykh znanii* 6 (1878): 1–39. A long essay, intended for the never-completed sixth volume, appeared after the turn of the century. See B. N. Chicherin, "Sen-Simon i ego shkola," *Voprosy filosofii i psikhologii* 60 (1902): 615–698.

79. IPU 1: 1–8.
80. IPU 1: 12–15.
81. IPU 1: 2.
82. IPU 1: 43.
83. IPU 1: 52.
84. IPU 1: 53–54.
85. IPU 1: 57.
86. IPU 1: 59–60.
87. IPU 1: 63–64.
88. IPU 1: 67.
89. IPU 1: 300–301.
90. IPU 1: 302.
91. IPU 1: 303.
92. IPU 1: 313.
93. IPU 1: 314.
94. F. M. Dostoevskii, *Polnoe sobranie sochinenii v tridtsati tomakh* (Leningrad, 1973), 5: 112.
95. IPU 2: 385.
96. IPU 2: 365.
97. IPU 2: 363–364.
98. IPU 2: 386.
99. IPU 4: 575.
100. IPU 4: 576–577.
101. IPU 4: 580–581.
102. IPU 4: 597.
103. IPU 4: 604–605.
104. IPU 4: 597–599.
105. IPU 4: 602.
106. IPU 4: 602–603.
107. RO RGB fond 334, k. 8, ed. khr. 1, "Pis'ma B. N. Chicherina k Aleksandru Vladimirovichu Stankevichu, 1869–1876 gg.," l. 78. Letter of 14 September 1876.
108. ROBL/RO RGB fond 334, k. 8, ed. khr. 1, ll. 81–81 verso. Letter of 29 October 1876.
109. ROBL/RO RGB fond 334, k. 8, ed. khr. 1, l. 83 verso. Letter of 22 November 1876.
110. ROBL/RO RGB fond 334, k. 8, ed. khr. 1, l. 83 verso. Letter of 22 November 1876.
111. "Nemetskie sotsialisty. 2. Karl Marks," 2; IPU 5: 156.
112. "Nemetskie sotsialisty. 2. Karl Marks," 3; IPU 5: 157.
113. "Nemetskie sotsialisty. 2. Karl Marks," 4–12, here 7; IPU 5: 157–165, here 161.

114. "Nemetskie sotsialisty. 2. Karl Marks," 25–33; IPU 5: 178–185.
115. "Nemetskie sotsialisty. 2. Karl Marks," 33–37; IPU 5: 186–192.
116. IPU 5: 189–191.
117. IPU 5: 224.
118. IPU 5: 225.
119. TSGIA/RGIA fond 777 [St. Peterburgskii komitet po delam pechati], op. 2-1865, ed. khr. 60, "Delo St. Peterburgskogo tsenzurnogo komiteta po izdaniiu zhurnala "Otechestvennye zapiski,"" ll. 292–292 verso.
120. See V. L. Ger'e and B. N. Chicherin, *Russkii diletantizm i obshchinnoe vladenie. Razbor knigi kniazia A. Vasil'chikova "Zemlevladenie i zemledelie"* (Moscow, 1878).
121. N. K. Mikhailovskii, "Pis'ma k uchenym liudiam," *Polnoe sobranie sochinenii N. K. Mikhailovskogo* 4 (1909): 597–616.
122. "Pis'ma k uchenym liudiam," 617.
123. Mikhailovskii's reference to the *Kathedersozialisten* is expressed in Aesopian language. He speaks of "professorskaia ekonomicheskaia shkola," "Pis'ma k uchenym liudiam," 617–618.
124. The article was reprinted in N. I. Ziber, *Izbrannye ekonomicheskie proizvedeniia v dvukh tomakh* (Moscow, 1959) 1: 683–722.
125. On Ziber's polemic against Chicherin and his peculiar views as a political economist see the very interesting book by A. L. Reuel', *Russkaia ekonomicheskaia mysl' 60–70-kh godov XIX veka i marksizm* (Moscow, 1956), 272–371. I owe this reference to my colleague, Andrzej Walicki.
126. Ziber, *Izbrannye ekonomicheskie proizvedeniia* 1: 686–688.
127. Ziber, *Izbrannye ekonomicheskie proizvedeniia* 1: 691.
128. Ziber, *Izbrannye ekonomicheskie proizvedeniia* 1: 694–695.
129. For Ziber's long-term fascination with consumer societies, see Reuel', *Russkaia ekonomicheskaia mysl',* 328–330.
130. Ziber, *Izbrannye ekonomicheskie proizvedeniia,* 1: 714–716.
131. TSGIA/RGIA fond 776 [Glavnoe Upravlenie po delam pechati], op. 2, ed. khr. 19, god 1879, "Zhurnal zasedanii Soveta Glavnogo Upravleniia po delam pechati za 1879 god," "Sovet Glavnogo Upravleniia po delam pechati MVD, zasedanie 27 fevralia 1879 g., no. 15," ll. 110 verso–111.
132. TSGIA/RGIA fond 776, op. 2, ed. khr. 19, god 1879, ll. 107–107 verso. This was the second warning received by *Slovo* in a six-month period. Three warnings constituted grounds for closure of a publication.
133. Walicki, *The Controversy over Capitalism: Studies in the Social Philosophy of the Russian Populists* (Notre Dame, Ind., 1989), 27.
134. *The Controversy over Capitalism,* 45–80.
135. See the discussion in Walicki, *The Controversy over Capitalism,* 145–147. Later in the 1890s, Mikhailovskii renewed his attack on Marxian determinism in a polemic with Struve, a polemic in which Mikhailovskii cited V. G. Belinskii's famous letter to Botkin concerning the moral impulse to reject philosophical systems that overlook the fate of the individual. See Walicki, *The Controversy over Capitalism,* 161–163.
136. Perhaps it is relevant that Mikhailovskii's articles on "The Struggle for Individuality"

[1875–1876] praised Marx's "tolerance . . . toward some medieval forms of social life" and even classified Marx as a representative of "sociological romanticism." Walicki, *The Controversy over Capitalism,* 57. Mikhailovskii evidently seized on those (rare) moments in socialist texts that treated "old outlived forms of social life" as something to be "preserved at least in order to be studied and described." Such an impulse was to be expected in one such as Mikhailovskii who defended the Russian land commune.

137. Walicki, *The Controversy over Capitalism,* 166–167.

138. See Petr Andreevich Zaionchkovskii, *Krizis samoderzhaviia na rubezhe* 1870–1880-*kh godov* (Moscow, 1964); for an English translation see Peter A. Zaionchkovsky, *The Russian Autocracy in Crisis* 1878–1882 (Gulf Breeze, Fla., 1979).

139. In early April 1878 Chicherin wrote an essay on the Zasulich trial that he then circulated in lithograph. For the original see TSGAOR/GARF fond 1154, op. 1. ed. khr. 44, "Stat'ia Chicherina B. N. 'Delo Very Zasulich.' Litografiia [1878] (5 aprelia 1878)." This essay was later published as an appendix to the memoirs of the presiding judge, A. F. Koni. See A. F. Koni, *Vospominaniia o dele Very Zasulich* (Moscow, 1933), 376–384. For Chicherin's private reactions, see two letters to his wife, A. A. Chicherina: ROBL/RO RGB fond 334, k. 53, ed. khr. 4, "Pis'ma B. N. Chicherina k Aleksandre Alekseevne Chicherinoi, 1871–1882," ll. 135–136, letter of 1 April 1878; ll. 137–138 verso, letter of 3 April 1878.

140. See, for example, his letter of 23 January 1879: "My general impression is that no one here [in Petersburg] is looking seriously at our domestic situation. In the words of the Russian proverb, 'Until the temple collapses in ruins, the peasant will not cross himself.' Something disastrous will have to happen, before they [the authorities] will pay attention. Otherwise they will all content themselves with the thought that, even so, one can get along. And we shall sink deeper and deeper into the mire until we are awakened by an unexpected blow." ROBL/RO RGB fond 334, k. 53, ed. khr. 4, "Pis'ma B. N. Chicherina k Aleksandre Alekseevne Chicherinoi, 1871–1882," l. 159.

141. "I spent yesterday at Pobedonostsev's. I love him in intimate conversation. Besides intelligence, he possesses sincerity and a knowledge of people, but his view of the current situation is far from optimistic [daleko ne veselyi]. However, who is optimistic except for those, like Turgenev, who see flowers in the ruins, in the insanity of our literature and our society?" ROBL/RO RGB fond 334, k. 53, ed. khr. 4, "Pis'ma B. N. Chicherina k Aleksandre Alekseevne Chicherinoi, 1871–1882," ll. 243 verso–244. Letter of 30 March 1880.

142. See his letter to A. V. Stankevich on 15 September 1880: "If I wished to say something new, I could limit myself to the presentation of my own view. But to counter the arguments of the contemporary sophists, I must restate long-established truths, and therefore I am condemned to enter into a more or less detailed analysis of their [the socialists'] opinions." ROBL/RO RGB fond 334, k. 8, ed. khr. 2, "Pis'ma B. N. Chicherina k Aleksandru Vladimirovichu Stankevichu, 1879–1883 gg.," ll. 49–50.

143. B. N. Chicherin, *Sobstvennost' i gosudarstvo. Chast' pervaia* (Moscow, 1882), ii. Hereafter cited as SIG 1.

144. SIG 1: 14–17.

145. SIG 1: 18.

146. SIG 1: 18–25.
147. SIG 1: 17.
148. SIG 1: 29–30.
149. For Chicherin's remarks on Kant, see SIG 1: 8, 11–12, 28–29; for his debt to Humboldt, see SIG 1: 29.
150. Andrzej Walicki, *Legal Philosophies of Russian Liberalism* (Oxford, 1987), 136.
151. On Locke, see SIG 1: 5–8.
152. For Chicherin's view of Fichte, SIG 1: 12–14.
153. SIG 1: 25–26.
154. SIG 1: 249–250.
155. SIG 1: 259.
156. SIG 1: 251.
157. SIG 1: 253.
158. SIG 1: 267.
159. SIG 1: 260–261.
160. P. L. Lavrov, *Filosofiia i sotsiologiia* (Moscow, 1965) 2: 81; quoted in Walicki, *A History of Russian Thought from the Enlightenment to Marxism,* 237.
161. SIG 1: 251.
162. SIG 1: 267.
163. SIG 1: 274.
164. SIG 1: 275.
165. SIG 1: 276–277.
166. SIG 1: 278.
167. SIG 1: 279.
168. See the long quotation from Thiers, SIG 1: 287–288. For the original, see chapter 3 in Adolphe Thiers, *Du droit de propriété* (Paris, 1848).
169. SIG 1: 291–312.
170. For a trenchant summary of Mikhailovskii's theory of progress and his polemic with Spencer, see Walicki, *A History of Russian Thought from the Enlightenment to Marxism,* 252–257.
171. SIG 1: 394–400.
172. SIG 1: 403.
173. SIG 1: 404–405.
174. SIG 1: 409–412.
175. SIG 1: xix–xx.
176. *Vospominaniia E. M. Feoktistova. Za kulisami politiki i literatury* 1848–1896, ed. Iu. G. Oksman (Leningrad, 1929), 196.
177. On Baranov's frenetic activity and the disorientation in the government, see Zaionchkovsky, *The Russian Autocracy in Crisis,* 1878–1882, 192–198. For Baranov's tendency to spread groundless rumors, see A. F. Tiutcheva, *Pri dvore dvukh imperatorov. Dnevnik* 1855–1882 (Moscow, 1929), 220, entry of 20 March 1881.
178. The classic account of the showdown between reformist bureaucrats and conservatives remains Zaionchkovsky, *The Russian Autocracy in Crisis,* 1878–1882, 204–240.
179. Tiutcheva, *Pri dvore dvukh imperatorov,* 223, entry of 22 March 1881.

180. In the poem "Vozmezdie," Alexander Blok referred to the time when "Pobedonostsev's owl's wings" spread over the Russian land.
181. An unabridged copy of the essay, "Zadachi novogo tsarstvovaniia," may be found in *K. P. Pobedonostsev i ego korrespondenty. Pis'ma i zapiski. Tom* 1, *Chast'* 1 (Moscow, 1929), 104–120; excerpts were included in MU, 123–130.
182. For Chicherin's instructions to Pobedonostsev, see the cover letter of 11 March 1881 in *K. P. Pobedonostsev i ego korrespondenty. Tom* 1, *Chast'* 1, 104. MU, 123, 130.
183. Chicherin's letter of 25 March 1881 described in detail the mood of high officials in St. Petersburg and also summarized reactions to his own memorandum. See ROBL/RO RGB, fond 334, k. 53, ed. khr. 4, "Pis'ma B. N. Chicherina k A. A. Chicherinoi, 1871–1882 gg.," ll. 303–306 verso.
184. "Zadachi novogo tsarstvovaniia," 106.
185. "Zadachi novogo tsarstvovaniia," 113–114.
186. "Loris and Abaza were very happy with it [the memorandum], because it is support from the conservative side, and that works to their advantage." ROBL/RO RGB fond 334, k. 53, ed. khr. 4, ll. 304 verso–305.
187. Pobedonostsev approved the "first two-thirds of the memorandum, containing the critique" of [Loris-Melikov's] "liberalism" and of "socialism." But Pobedonostsev thought Chicherin's cure—adding new members to the State Council—"worse than the disease": "I don't believe that out of this will come the [governmental] unity that you desire; rather, I clearly foresee new disunity and new falsity. The problem is that the government has ceased to know what it wants and has lost the instincts of national self-preservation. You yourself write that your proposal assumes a *strong* government, yet you claimed that by means of this proposal the government will become strong. This is a logical flaw." MU, 130.
188. ROBL/RO RGB fond 334, k. 53, ed. khr. 4, l. 300.
189. ROBL/RO RGB fond 334, k. 53, ed. khr. 4, l. 305 verso.
190. *The Russian Autocracy in Crisis,* 1878–1882, 201.
191. Russkii patriot [B. N. Chicherin], *Rossiia nakanune dvadtsatogo stoletiia* 4-oe izdanie (1901): 153.
192. *Rossiia nakanune dvadtsatogo stoletiia,* 160.
193. For Chicherin's speech at the 1883 coronation banquet, see MU, 234–236. The outcry following the speech is described in MU, 236–259. For a scholarly account of the 1883 "Chicherin affair" and of similar confrontations between central administrators and city governments, see V. A. Nardova, "Gorodskoe samoupravelenie v Rossii v 60-kh—nachale 90-kh godov. Pravitel'stvennaia politika," Avtoreferat dissertatsii na soiskanie uchenoi stepeni doktora istoricheskikh nauk (Leningrad, 1985), 20–29; Nardova, *Gorodskoe samoupravelenie v Rossii v* 60-*kh—nachale* 90-*kh godov XIX v.* (Leningrad, 1984), especially chapters 4 and 5.
194. Boris Nikolaevich had been elected an honorary justice of the peace. His brother, Sergei Nikolaevich had served many terms as a justice of the peace; he had also served as chair of the Tambov justice court, and briefly as chair of the Tambov provincial zemstvo board. When the central government announced the creation of the land captaincy, Boris Nikolaevich resigned his honorific title of justice of the peace. Sergei Nikolaevich

resigned his (now honorific) status as justice of the peace and also resigned from the Tambov zemstvo. See MU, 284–288.

195. Authorship was indicated only by the initials "F. G." In 1986 I searched, quietly and unsuccessfully, in Soviet archives for a manuscript copy of this book and for information about the mysterious "F. G." At a dinner party, graciously arranged by the historian L. G. Zakharova to facilitate my inquiry, I asked the eminent historian Natan Iakovlevich Eidel'man for assistance. Eidel'man advised me that the best way to locate the document and information was to "follow Tolstoi's footprints." I did so, with success. I am only sorry that I did not manage to publish the material, with appropriate thanks, before Eidel'man's death.

196. See F. G[ets]., "'Slovo podsudimomu!' s pis'mami Grafa L. N. Tolstogo, B. N. Chicherina, Vladimira Solov'eva i V. G. Korolenko" (St. Petersburg, 1891), xx–xxi.

197. TSGIA/RGIA fond 777 [St. Peterburgskii komitet po delam pechati], op. 4, ed. khr. 52, "O beztsenzurnoi knige: 'Slovo podsudimomu!,'" l. 6.

198. See B. N. Chicherin, *Pol'skii i evreiskii voprosy. Otvet na otkrytye pis'ma N. K. Rennenkampfa* (Berlin, 1899); 2-oe izdanie (Berlin, 1901). Excerpts from the open letter appeared under the title "Iz pis'ma k N. K. Rennenkampfu. (V otvet na otkrytye pis'ma o pol'skom i evreiskom voprosakh, pomeshchennye v 'Kievlianine' v 1897," *Pomoshch' evreiam, postradavshim ot neurozhaia. Literaturno-khudozhestvennyi sbornik* (St. Petersburg, 1901), 56–62.

199. In a letter to A. V. Stankevich, Chicherin reported the affair as follows: "Another unpleasantry is that the authorities have placed one of my renters in prison on the charge of belonging to the *khlyst* sect. In our area here the khlysty are rather numerous; but they live peacefully and nobody has been complaining about them. If this [the khlyst belief system] is [religious] dissimulation, then it is by no means dangerous fanaticism. I was an eyewitness. It seems that the case arose from a preposterous accusation [po nagovoru] by a thirteen-year-old girl, who, on the instruction of an old woman from Inzhavinskoe, uttered God knows what. I offered [the court] to take the renter under my personal supervision, but to my great surprise, even the Tambov provincial procurator and the provincial judicial chamber refused me. Our existing judicial authorities, instead of defending citizens, are instruments of their persecution." ROBL/RO RGB fond 334, k. 8, ed. khr. 6, "Pis'ma B. N. Chicherina k A. V. Stankevichu, 1896–1899 gg.," l. 86. Letter of 19 November 1898.

200. Chicherin had offered to testify in defense of the khlyst but was refused permission. He wrote Stankevich: "This is incredible. Obviously, they wanted to keep away a person who by his moral authority might have had an influence on the jurors. Instead, they called from the Kazan' Seminary some bigoted professor [professora-izuvera], who categorized the *khlysty* as a pernicious sect which much be destroyed at all costs. . . . This is what our court has come to, a court in which justice and mercy ought to prevail." ROBL/RO RGB fond 334, k. 8, ed. khr. 6, ll. 89 verso–90. Letter of 17 December 1898.

201. TSGAOR/GARF fond 1154, op. 1, ed. khr. 66, "Pis'ma B. N. Chicherina k A. A. Chicherinoi, A. N. Naryshkine, i A. V. Stankevichu [1883–1900 gg.]," l. 305. Letter to A. A. Chicherina on 18 January 1899.

202. See the typescript, "Iz vospominanii B. N. Chicherina. N. I. Krivtsov," in the Andreevskii Collection, Rare Book and Manuscript Library, Butler Library, Columbia University, p. 31. A printed edition appeared in B. N. Chicherin, "Iz moikh vospominanii (Po povodu dnevnika N. I. Krivtsova)." *Russkii arkhiv* 28, no. 4 (1890): 524–525.
203. ROBL/RO RGB fond 334, k. 8, ed. khr. 7, "Pis'ma B. N. Chicherina k A. V. Stankevichu, 1899 g.," ll. 10–10 verso. Letter of 17 April 1899.
204. The phrase is from Isaiah Berlin's essay "Fathers and Children," in *Russian Thinkers,* ed. Henry Hardy and Aileen Kelly (New York, 1978), 297.
205. N. A. Berdiaev, "N. K. Mikhailovskii i B. N. Chicherin (O lichnosti, ratsionalizme, demokratizme i proch.)," *Sub specie aeternitatis. Opyty filosofskie, sotsial'nye i literaturnye* (St. Petersburg, 1907), 205.

ON SERFDOM

1. "On Serfdom" is a translation of an article first published in London in 1856. The article appeared, without attribution to Chicherin, as part of the second installment of the anthology *Voices from Russia* under the general editorship of Alexander Herzen. See "O krepostnom sostoianii," *Golosa iz Rossii* (London, 1856), 2: 127–229. Chicherin wrote "On Serfdom" at the request of K. D. Kavelin, his former teacher from Moscow University, who by 1855 had developed extensive ties with reform-minded St. Petersburg officials and progressive intellectuals. Shortly after Nicholas I's death, Kavelin laid plans for a "manuscript literature" campaign involving private circulation of anonymous manuscripts critical of the preceding Nikolaevan regime and offering liberal prescriptions for change. Kavelin hoped to rally educated society behind reforms that would eliminate serfdom and create the basis for free institutions under the new monarch's aegis. By fall 1856 Kavelin had received sixteen manuscripts from various sources. While circulating these materials through informal channels, Kavelin decided to risk sending the entire collection to London. Through an unidentified intermediary, probably N. A. Mel'gunov, Kavelin asked Herzen to print the material and to arrange for its clandestine dissemination in Russia.

   As the climate of opinion changed within Russia, Chicherin was able to publish on the history of serfdom in legally sanctioned journals. He considered the historical origins of bonded labor in Russia in a long article commissioned by the liberal journal *Russian Courier.* See "Nesvobodnye sostoianiia v drevnei Rusi," *Russkii vestnik* 3 (1856): 185–257. This article was reprinted with an addendum under the title, "Kholopy i krest'iane v Rossii do XVI veka," *Opyty po istorii russkogo prava* (Moscow, 1858). In 1858 he spelled out his proposals for postreform society in the short-lived étatist liberal journal *Athenean.* See "O nastoiashchem i budushchem polozhenii pomeshchichikh krest'ian," *Atenei,* part 1, no. 8 (1858): 486–526. None of the legally published essays offers the careful critique of alternative approaches to serfdom's abolition that one finds in "On Serfdom."

   For a comparison of Chicherin's abolitionist program to those recommended by others, see G. M. Hamburg, "The Abolition of Serfdom in Russian Social Thought:

The Case of B. N. Chicherin, 1856–1861," *Slavic Review* 50, no. 4 (Winter 1991): 890–904 [ed.].

CONTEMPORARY TASKS OF RUSSIAN LIFE

1. "Contemporary Tasks of Russian Life" was written in summer 1855 for K. D. Kavelin's liberal "manuscript literature" campaign. Because the essay was intended for limited private circulation, Chicherin expressed his political views "with absolute candor." The original draft of the essay even included a brief discussion of the possibility of constitutional rule in Russia. Chicherin understood the unlikelihood of a constitutional regime at present but foresaw that liberal reforms might facilitate the establishment of such a regime in the future. When Kavelin reviewed the manuscript in early 1856, he suggested that references to the liberals' "distant [constitutional] goal" be removed from Chicherin's essay because such references might prove politically counterproductive. Chicherin "agreed with this [assessment] and rewrote the article." See MSG, 163–172. Kavelin sent the second, rewritten variant of Chicherin's essay to London, where Alexander Herzen and Nikolai Ogarev published it in the *Voices from Russia* anthology. See "Sovremennye zadachi russkoi zhizni," *Golosa iz Rossii* (London, 1857), 4: 51–129. The English text is a translation of the published version of Chicherin's essay. Editors of the Soviet facsimile edition of *Golosa iz Rossii* described "Contemporary Tasks of Russian Life" as "the most precise formulation of the . . . theoretical foundations of the [Russian] liberal program." See "Kommentarii i ukazateli," *Golosa iz Rossii* (Moscow, 1975), 10: 177 [ed.].

"INDICTMENT"

1. "Indictment" was drafted as an open letter from Chicherin to Herzen in late fall 1858. The original had no title appended to it. When Herzen printed the letter in the first December number of his journal *Kolokol [The Bell]*, he added the title at the letter's beginning and provided a brief prefatory commentary. Herzen deleted Chicherin's name as author, so the letter appeared without attribution. This editorial practice was followed for much Russian correspondence printed in *The Bell.* Herzen himself published under the pseudonym Iskander, although the nom de plume was so well known that it fooled no one. For the original see "Obvinitel'nyi akt," *Kolokol* 29 (1 December 1858), 236–239. Excerpts from the letter were printed by Chicherin under the title "Pis'mo k izdateliu 'Kolokola,'" in B. N. Chicherin, *Neskol'ko sovremennykh voprosov* (Moscow, 1862), 11–19 [ed.].

ON POPULAR REPRESENTATION

1. On Popular Representation was written in the period from summer 1865 to the end of winter 1865–1866. It consisted of four books—*The Nature and Properties of Popular Representation, Types of Popular Representation, Historical Development of Representative Institutions in Europe,* and *Preconditions of Popular Representation.* The four chapters of *The Nature and Properties of Popular Representation* are translated here. See *Sushchestvo i svoistva narodnogo predstavitel'stva* in *O narodnom predstavitel'stve* (Moscow, 1866), 1–65. More

than thirty years later Chicherin prepared a second edition for the so-called Library for Self-Education [Biblioteka dlia samoobrazovaniia] under the editorship of A. S. Belkin, P. G. Vinogradov, N. D. Grot, M. I. Konovalov, P. N. Miliukov, and V. Ia. Sokolov. See *O narodonom predstavitel'stve,* 2-oe izdanie (Moscow, 1899), 1–93. The first edition was used for the present translation [ed.].

PLATO AND ARISTOTLE

1. During the period 1861–1867, Chicherin was professor of public law at Moscow University. As part of his responsibilities, he read a regular cycle of lectures on European political thought. In 1867 Chicherin resigned from the faculty in protest against violations of the university charter. Several colleagues—I. K. Babst, M. N. Kapustin, S. A. Rachinskii, F. M. Dmitriev, and S. M. Solov'ev—supported his protest. In 1869 Chicherin published the first volume of *History of Political Doctrines,* a volume based in large part on his university lectures. He dedicated the book to his supportive colleagues and to the students of Moscow University. The analysis of Plato and Aristotle appeared near the beginning of the volume in a discussion about classical Greek politics. See "Platon," in IPU 1: 42–55; "Aristotel'," in IPU 1: 55–73. Before his death Chicherin prepared a second edition of this volume: IPU 1, 2-oe izdanie (Moscow, 1903) [ed.].
2. *Metaphysics,* book 1, chapter 9.
3. *Metaphysics,* book 1, chapter 3.
4. Compare *The Politics,* book 1, chapter 1, and book 3, chapter 5.
5. Compare *Nicomachaean Ethics,* book 8, chapter 10 (Edition of Didot).
6. *Nicomachaean Ethics,* book 5, chapters 3 and 4 (Edition of Didot).
7. *Nicomachaean Ethics,* book 8, chapter 10.
8. The question of the completeness of and the order of chapters in *The Politics* is very controversial. It is discussed at length in the previously cited work of Hildebrand [*Die Geschichte und System der Staatswissenschaften*] and also in that of Barthelemy Saint-Hilaire, in his introduction to the translation of *The Politics.* I consider it superfluous to repeat the various conclusions and arguments here [BNCh].

   These citations by Chicherin are not entirely accurate. They should be: Karl Hildenbrand, *Die Geschichte und System der Rechts- und Staatsphilosophie. Erster Band. Das klassische Altertum* (Leipzig, 1860), and J. Jules Barthelemy Saint Hilaire, *La Politique d'Aristote,* 2d ed. (Paris, 1848) [ed.].

MORE AND MACHIAVELLI

1. Chicherin's treatment of More and Machiavelli was part of his regular essay cycle at Moscow University. In 1862–1863 he was invited to lecture the crown prince, Grand Duke Nikolai Aleksandrovich, on the history of political thought. Among the lectures Chicherin delivered was one on Machiavelli. This lecture was so successful that the grand duke read *The Prince* and *The Discourses* in the original Italian. See MU, 88–89. For the Russian version of Chicherin's essay, published in 1869, see "Tomas Mor i Makiavelli," in IPU 1: 294–315 [ed.].

MONTESQUIEU

1. The essay on Montesquieu was based on Chicherin's lecture cycle at Moscow University and his lectures to Grand Duke Nikolai Aleksandrovich in 1862–1863. The essay appeared in 1872, in IPU 2: 355–396. It was reprinted shortly before Chicherin's death in IPU 2, 2-oe izdanie, (Moscow, 1902) [ed.].
2. *Esprit des Loix,* Introduction.
3. *Esprit des Loix,* Livre I, chapitre 1: "Les lois, dans la signification la plus étendue, sont les rapports nécessaires, qui dérivent de la nature des choses."
4. *Esprit des Loix,* L. I, ch. 1.
5. So far as I know, Clarke never wrote a tract entitled *Treatise on the Existence of God.* Chicherin probably had in mind *Sixteen Sermons on the Being and Attributes of God,* published in Samuel Clarke, *The Works, in Four Volumes,* 2 (London, 1738). The *Sixteen Sermons* were translated into French and republished as *Traité de l'existence et des attributs de Dieu* in *Oeuvres philosophiques de Samuel Clarke,* Nouvelle édition (Paris, 1843), 1–132. The French edition was the most likely source for Chicherin [ed.].
6. *Esprit des Loix,* L. I, ch. 1.
7. *Esprit des Loix,* L. I, ch. 3.
8. *Esprit des Loix,* L. I, ch. 2.
9. *Esprit des Loix,* L. I, ch. 3.
10. *Esprit des Loix,* L. II.
11. *Esprit des Loix,* L. III.
12. *Esprit des Loix,* L. IV, V.
13. *Esprit des Loix,* L. VI.
14. *Esprit des Loix,* L. VII, ch. 1.
15. *Esprit des Loix,* L. VII, chs. 8–17.
16. *Esprit des Loix,* L. VIII.
17. *Esprit des Loix,* L. VIII, chs. 15–21.
18. *Esprit des Loix,* L. VIII, chs. 9–10.
19. *Esprit des Loix,* L. XI, ch. 3.
20. *Esprit des Loix,* L. XI, ch. 4.
21. *Esprit des Loix,* L. XI, ch. 6.
22. *Esprit des Loix,* L. XII.
23. *Esprit des Loix,* L. XIV.
24. *Esprit des Loix,* Livres XV–XVII.
25. *Esprit des Loix,* L. XVIII.
26. *Esprit des Loix,* L. XIX.
27. *Esprit des Loix,* L. XXIX, ch. 18, tome 2.
28. *La Scienza della Legislatione.* Piano ragionato dell'opera. Libro I.
29. [*La Scienza della Legislatione,*] Libro I, capitolo 1.
30. [*La Scienza della Legislatione,*] Libro I, capitolo 2, Piano ragionato. Libro II.
31. [*La Scienza della Legislatione,*] Piano ragionato, Libri IV, V.
32. [*La Scienza della Legislatione,*] Libro I, capitolo 3.

33. [*La Scienza della Legislatione,*] Libro I, capitolo 4.
34. [*La Scienza della Legislatione,*] Libro I, capitoli 6, 7.
35. [*La Scienza della Legislatione,*] Libro I, capitolo 10.
36. [*La Scienza della Legislatione,*] Libro I, capitolo 11.
37. [*La Scienza della Legislatione,*] Libro I, capitolo 12.
38. [*La Scienza della Legislatione,*] Libro I, capitolo 12.
39. [*La Scienza della Legislatione,*] Libro I, capitolo 13.
40. [*La Scienza della Legislatione,*] Libro I, capitolo 14.
41. [*La Scienza della Legislatione,*] Libro I, capitolo 18.

HEGEL

1. Chicherin's essay on Hegel was based on his regular cycle of lectures at Moscow University and his 1862–1863 lectures to Grand Duke Nikolai Aleksandrovich. Chicherin expanded on the lecture by adding many new materials. The published version may be found in IPU 4 (Moscow, 1877): 573–609 [ed.].
2. *Logik: Die Lehre von Begriff,* 1 Abschnitt, cap. B.
3. *Encyclopädie,* 3 *Theil. Philosophie des Geistes.*
4. *Philosophie des Rechts,* paragraphs 4–7.
5. *Philosophie des Rechts,* paragraphs 9–29.
6. *Philosophie des Rechts,* paragraph 33.
7. *Philosophie des Rechts,* paragraphs 34–71.
8. *Philosophie des Rechts,* paragraphs 72–81.
9. *Philosophie des Rechts,* paragraphs 105–108.
10. *Philosophie des Rechts,* paragraphs 115–141.
11. *Philosophie des Rechts,* paragraphs 142–151.
12. *Philosophie des Rechts,* paragraphs 158–181.
13. *Philosophie des Rechts,* paragraphs 182–256.
14. *Philosophie des Rechts,* paragraphs 257–258.
15. *Philosophie des Rechts,* paragraphs 260–262.
16. *Philosophie des Rechts,* paragraphs 275–286.
17. *Philosophie des Rechts,* paragraphs 287–295.
18. *Philosophie des Rechts,* paragraphs 298–319.
19. *Philosophie des Rechts,* paragraphs 321–329.
20. *Philosophie des Rechts,* paragraphs 330–340.
21. *Philosophie des Rechts,* paragraphs 341–360; compare *Philosophie der Geschichte. Einleitung.*
22. *Philosophie des Rechts,* paragraph 270.
23. *Philosophie der Geschichte. Einleitung,* 14.
24. *Philosophie der Geschichte. Einleitung,* 65–66.

MARX

1. This essay appeared as the second part of a two-part study of German socialism. The first part, devoted to Lassalle's *Das System der erworbenen Rechte* (The System of Acquired

Rights, 1861), appeared in the journal *Sbornik gosudarstvennykh znanii* 5 (1878): 1–71. The essay on Marx, entitled "Nemetskie sotsialisty. 2. Karl Marks," was also published later in the same journal. See *Sbornik gosudarstvennykh znanii* 6 (1878): 1–39. Chicherin republished the essay on Marx, with emendations, in IPU 5, (Moscow, 1902). I have used the 1878 version as the basis of this translation.

Chicherin wrote his analysis of Marx's *Das Kapital* during the period 1876–1878, when Russian socialism was on the ascendant and the public's attention was riveted by trials of young Populists. From Chicherin's unpublished correspondence with A. V. Stankevich, it is clear that the criticism of Marx was meant to serve as an antidote to the spread of socialism in Russia—whatever form socialism might take. It is equally clear that Chicherin had low regard for Marx, both as a person and as theoretician.

Ferdinand Lassalle (1825–1864), was architect of the German Social Democratic Party and Marx's chief rival as theoretician within the German socialist movement [ed.].

2. Karl Marx began to publish his composition in 1859, in separate installments, under the title *Zur Kritik der politischen Oekonomie.* This beginning, with certain changes, was incorporated into Marx's 1867 book *Das Kapital.* In 1873 this book was issued in a second edition, with editorial corrections. I am relying on the latter edition.
3. *Das Kapital,* 822.
4. *Das Kapital,* 619*n*11.
5. Hegel's central concept, *Geist,* is usually rendered in English as *Spirit, Mind,* or *Idea.* Chicherin used the word *ideia*—a direct cognate to the English *Idea* [ed.].
6. *Das Kapital,* 821–822.
7. *Das Kapital,* 822.
8. The "ideal found only in the human mind" of which Chicherin speaks is the ideal of communism—a notion that Chicherin regarded as purely utopian, rather than practical. See "Equality" below [ed.].
9. *Das Kapital,* 821.
10. *Das Kapital,* 12.
11. *Das Kapital,* 18.
12. *Das Kapital,* 813.
13. *Das Kapital,* 12–13.
14. *Das Kapital,* 15–16, 64.
15. *Das Kapital,* 15, 21.
16. *Das Kapital,* 325.
17. *Das Kapital,* 19.
18. *Das Kapital,* 86.
19. *Das Kapital,* 86.
20. *Das Kapital,* 47–48.
21. *Das Kapital,* 53, 82.
22. *Das Kapital,* 23.
23. *Das Kapital,* 24.
24. *Das Kapital,* 61.
25. *Das Kapital,* 28.
26. *Das Kapital,* 66.

27. *Das Kapital,* 37.
28. *Das Kapital,* 71–72.
29. *Das Kapital,* 53.
30. *Das Kapital,* 70.
31. *Das Kapital,* 80–81.
32. *Das Kapital,* 87.
33. *Das Kapital,* 135*n,* 137, 149.
34. *Das Kapital,* 129–136.
35. *Das Kapital,* 138.
36. *Das Kapital,* 128, 148.
37. *Das Kapital,* 151–152.
38. *Das Kapital,* 556–557.
39. *Das Kapital,* 163.
40. I have followed the English version of T. M. Knox in *Hegel's Philosophy of Right* (Oxford, 1952) paragraph 67, p. 54 [ed.].
41. *Das Kapital,* 155–158.
42. *Das Kapital,* 556.
43. *Das Kapital,* 174–178.
44. *Das Kapital,* 314.
45. *Das Kapital,* 179–183.
46. *Das Kapital,* 185–186.
47. *Das Kapital,* 560.
48. *Das Kapital,* 205*n*27.
49. *Das Kapital,* 224, 594.
50. *Das Kapital,* 187–190, 196.
51. *Das Kapital,* 196.
52. *Das Kapital,* 197–198.
53. *Das Kapital,* 193–195.
54. *Das Kapital,* 404.
55. *Das Kapital,* 444.
56. *Das Kapital,* 338.
57. *Das Kapital,* 554*n*20.
58. *Das Kapital,* 426.
59. *Das Kapital,* 597.
60. *Das Kapital,* 307.
61. *Das Kapital,* 745.
62. *Das Kapital,* 752.
63. *Das Kapital,* 774.
64. *Das Kapital,* 777.
65. *Das Kapital,* 781.
66. *Das Kapital,* 782.
67. *Das Kapital,* 791.
68. *Das Kapital,* 792–793.
69. *Das Kapital,* 793.

70. *Das Kapital,* 793.
71. *Das Kapital,* 793.
72. *Das Kapital,* 33, 591.

LIBERTY

1. Chicherin's *Sobstvennost' i gosudarstvo* [*Property and State*] consisted of three books: *Pravo* [Law], *Promyshlennost'* [Industry], and *Gosudarstvo* [State]. The publisher divided the work into two large volumes. Volume one comprised the first book on law and half the book on industry; it appeared in 1882. Volume two consisted of the remainder of the book on industry and the entire book on the state; it appeared in 1883.

   "Liberty" was the first chapter in Chicherin's discussion of law. See "Svoboda," *SIG* 1: 1–33 [ed.].
2. Locke, *An Essay Concerning Human Understanding,* book 2, ch. 21, paragraphs 8–25.
3. Locke, *An Essay Concerning Human Understanding,* book 2, ch. 21, paragraph 28 et seq.
4. Locke, *An Essay Concerning Human Understanding,* book 2, ch. 21, paragraph 69.
5. Locke, *A Treatise Concerning Government,* ch. 2, paragraph 4 [BNCh].

   [The document in question is, of course, Locke's *The Second Treatise of Government. An Essay Concerning the True Original Extent, and End of Civil Government*] [ed.].
6. *A Treatise Concerning Government,* ch. 6, paragraphs 55–63.
7. Proof of the speculative origins of the concept of causation and of the law of necessity based upon it can be found in my book *Nauka i religiia, 22 et seq.*
8. In summarizing the nature of liberty, I necessarily repeat points I have made more than once in other works; see *Istoriia politicheskikh uchenii,* 4: 149–154; *Nauka i religiia,* 144–146; *Mistitsizm v nauke,* 143 et seq.
9. Spinoza, *Ethices,* pars IV, proposit. 67, 68; Spinoza, *Tractatus Politicus,* cap. 2, paragraphs 7, 11.
10. Kant, *Rechtslehre. Einleitung in die Metaphysik der Sitten,* I.
11. Dahn, *Die Vernunft im Recht,* 60.
12. Schäffle, *Bau und Leben des socialen Körpers,* 1: 142, 188.
13. Fichte, *Die Staatslehre,* in *Werke* 4 (1845): 432–439.
14. Fichte, *System der Rechtslehre: Nachgelassene Werke* 2: 535–538, 543–544, 560.
15. *Lehrbuch der politischen Oekonomie von K. H. Rau. Vollständige Neubearbeitung von Ad. Wagner und E. Nasse.* 1 *Band Grundlegung,* 122*n*12.
16. Hegel, *Philosophie der Geschichte, Einleitung.*
17. See K. H. Roscher, *Grundlegen der Nationalökonomie,* paragraph 71.
18. See, for example, Schäffle, *Bau und Leben des socialen Körpers* 3: 95, 98, 99.
19. John Stuart Mill, *On Liberty,* ch. 1, p. 22 (1859 edition)
20. Ihering, *Der Zweck im Recht,* 530–531.
21. Wilhelm Humboldt, *Ideen zu einem Versuch, die Gränzen der Wirksamkeit des Staats zu bestimmen.* A summary of his theory may be found in my *Istoriia politicheskikh uchenii,* vol. 3. Recently this theory was revived by [Edouard] Laboulaye, in *L'Etat et ses limites.*
22. See the third part of my *Istoriia politicheskikh uchenii.*
23. Schäffle, *Bau und Leben des socialen Körpers* 1: 198, 199, 202, 2: 138.

EQUALITY

1. "Equality" was chapter six in book one [Law] of *Property and State.* See "Ravenstvo," in SIG 1: 238–269 [ed.].
2. See Aristotle, *Nichomachean Ethics,* book 5, chapters 3 and 4; and Aristotle, *Politics,* book 3, chapter 5; book 6, chapter 1 [BNCh].
3. Although Chicherin placed this passage in quotation marks, it is clearly a paraphrase of Bentham's text. For the original language, see *The Works of Jeremy Bentham,* vol. 2 (Edinburgh, 1843), 498–499 [ed.].
4. This quotation cannot be found in Bentham's text [ed.].
5. Stahl, *Philosophie des Rechts* 2, Buch 3, paragraph 14.
6. On this and the following points, see IPU 3, where the theories of Rousseau and Mably are presented in greater detail.
7. ". . . vse, chto vozvyshaetsia nad etim urovnem, otsekaetsia, kak zlo." Chicherin used the verb *otsekaetsia* to evoke the guillotine [ed.].
8. [Cabet,] *Credo Communiste.* It is cited in translation in Stein, *Der Socialismus und Communismus des heutigen Frankreichs.*
9. "eto uchenie nichto inoe kak skolok s khristianstva . . . " Literally, "this doctrine is nothing other than a copy of Christianity . . . " [ed.].
10. Proudhon, *Qu'est ce que la propriété?* ch. 5, seconde partie, paragraph 2.
11. Proudhon, *Qu'est ce que la propriete?* ch. 5, premiere partie, paragraph 2.
12. Proudhon, *Qu'est ce que la propriété?* ch. 5, seconde partie, paragraph 3.
13. *Lehrbuch der politischen Oekonomie von K. H. Rau. Vollständige Neubearbeitung von Ad. Wagner und E. Nasse. 1 Band. Grundlegung* (hereafter cited as Wagner, *Grundlegung*), 361.
14. Wagner, *Grundlegung,* 357.
15. Wagner, *Grundlegung,* 121–122.
16. "Iz ravnopravnosti liudei blagotvoritel'nosti vyvesti nel'zia" [ed.].
17. Wagner, *Grundlegung,* 129–130.

CAPITALISM AND SOCIALISM

1. "Capitalism and Socialism" appeared as chapter five in book two [Industry] of *Property and State.* See "Kapitalizm i sotsializm," SIG, 1: 394–416 [ed.].
2. Schäffle, *Bau und Leben den socialen Körpers* 3: 463; see also 458.
3. Schäffle, *Bau und Leben den socialen Körpers* 3: 396–398.
4. Schäffle, *Bau und Leben den socialen Körpers* 3: 482.
5. Schäffle, *Bau und Leben den socialen Körpers* 3: 381.
6. Schäffle, *Bau und Leben den socialen Körpers* 3: 470.
7. Schäffle, *Bau und Leben den socialen Körpers* 3: 483.
8. Rodbertus, *Zur Erklärung und Abhülfe der heutigen Creditnoth,* 271–277; Rodbertus, *Zur Beleuchtung der socialen Frage,* 28; Wagner, *Grundlegung,* 528.
9. Schäffle, *Bau und Leben den socialen Körpers* 2: 421.
10. Rodbertus, *Zur Beleuchtung,* 29; Wagner, *Zur Erklärung und Abhülfe,* 271 et seq.; Schäffle, *Bau und Leben den socialen Körpers* 4: 224, 229.
11. Wagner, *Grundlegung,* paragraph 108, p. 139; Samter, *Das Eigenthum,* 407, 415.

12. Lange, *Die Arbeiterfrage,* 289–290.
13. Schäffle, *Bau und Leben des socialen Körpers* 1: 197–198 et seq.
14. Schäffle, *Bau und Leben des socialen Körpers* 3: 541.
15. Rodbertus, *Zur Erklärung und Abhülfe des heutigen Creditnoth,* 271–277.
16. Rodbertus, *Zur Erklärung und Abhülfe der heutigen Creditnoth,* 279*n.*
17. Schäffle, *Bau und Leben des socialen Körpers* 3: 320.
18. Schäffle, *Bau und Leben des socialen Körpers* 2: 237.
19. Proudhon, *Qu'est ce que la propriété?* ch. 5, seconde partie, paragraph 2.
20. Mill, *Principles of Political Economy,* book 2, chapter 1.
21. Proudhon, *Contradictions économiques,* chapitre 12, paragraph 6.

Index

Russian Literature and Thought

Pushkin's Historical Imagination
Svetlana Evdokimova

Toward Another Shore: Russian Thinkers Between Necessity and Chance
Aileen Kelly

Dostoevsky and Soloviev: The Art of Integral Vision
Marina Kostalevsky

Abram Tertz and the Poetics of Crime
Catharine Theimer Nepomnyashchy

Untimely Thoughts: Essays on Revolution, Culture, and the Bolsheviks, 1917–1918
Maxim Gorky

A Voice from the Chorus
Abram Tertz (Andrei Sinyavsky)

Strolls with Pushkin
Abram Tertz (Andrei Sinyavsky)

1920 Diary
Isaac Babel